AMERICAN LABOR

FROM CONSPIRACY
TO
COLLECTIVE BARGAINING

HOW WOMEN CAN MAKE MONEY

Virginia Penny

Introduction by Leon Stein and Philip Taft

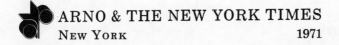

ARNO & THE NEW YORK TIMES
NEW YORK   1971

Reprint Edition 1971 by Arno Press Inc.
Introduction Copyright 1971 by Arno Press Inc.

LC# 75-156439
ISBN 0-405-02937-3

American Labor: From Conspiracy to Collective Bargaining—Series II
ISBN for complete set: 0-405-02910-1
See last pages for titles.

Manufactured in the United States of America

Introduction

"I have visited factories, workshops, offices and stores for the purpose of seeing men at work that I might learn the occupations into which women might enter. I have gone through wind and snow, cold and rain, nor stopped for midsummer heat."

So spoke Virginia Penny to an interviewer and, in the light of her dedicated life, it was an altogether modest statement. Endowed with a sense of justice and a gift for research, she undertook a crusade which has not yet ended. Her purpose was nothing less than to prove that in the world of work women were condemned to a secondary position solely because of sex, even though they were able to handle people, materials, and concepts and to learn skills and professions.

Virginia Penny was born in Louisville, Kentucky, on January 18, 1826. Even in the ante-bellum South, some women had to work. There, as elsewhere, the opportunities were few and with all of their charm many of the young ladies learned early in life that they were destined to become schoolmarms, seamstresses and—unless rescued by marriage—spinsters.

Miss Penny studied at the Female Seminary in Steubenville, Ohio, where she received her diploma in 1845. For a time she remained at the Seminary as a teacher. Then she moved on to other teaching jobs in Illinois and Missouri. When her health took a bad turn, she left teaching, living as best she could on a small patrimony.

But she had seen enough to realize that women were not welcomed in the world of work with the equality to which they were entitled. They could develop high skills; they could endure; they could do some work better than men. Yet ignorance of women's ability to work in the plant or in commercial enterprises or in arts and crafts kept them blocked out.

In the libraries of Louisville and St. Louis, Virginia Penny began to research the history of women as workers. With the doggedness of a hunter, she pursued the trail, eventually moving to New York in order to continue her work.

To gather more data, she wrote and broadcast a flood of circular letters asking for details on wage rates, conditions of work, hiring practices, living conditions, the nature of skills, the speed of work processes, the usual hours of work, and how to learn the trade.

She found friends. They perceived her dedication and helped. Dr. Cogswell of the Astor Library in New York helped her obtain information about women at work in Europe.

The result of her labors was an encyclopedic compendium of more than 500 articles on work for women. This was the volume that would open the doors. But no publisher would have it. She passed the manuscript among them, hope sinking in her heart, until at last one, Walker, Wise and Co. of Boston, agreed to publish it.

But first she had to condense it. Then she had to pay for having it set in type. After the printing, she had to pay for having it bound. Then and only then would the publisher buy copies from her—but only enough copies to meet the demand for the book. Thus it was published in 1863 under the title "Employment of Women."

There was no income from the book.

Virginia Penny opened a ladies' employment agency in the Bible House in New York. In six weeks some 150 applicants were helped. But, due to continued failing health, Virginia Penny closed the agency. By this time she had exhausted her patrimony of $6,000, sold her library and the family jeweled heirlooms. In desperation, she also sold the printing plates of her book for $100 to a Philadelphia printer.

He changed the title and reissued the volume seven years after it had first been published. It was an immediate success.

Meanwhile, Virginia Penny had returned to teaching in the public schools of Louisville. But the crusader within her would not be still. Her name and the name of her brother Alex appeared repeatedly in the Louisville papers. Against stern opposition by the authorities she once more raised a cry for human rights—this time for decent pay for teachers.

In everything she did, her boundless enthusiasm for detail and creativity made Virginia Penny's contribution to the world of work—and the dignity of women in and out of that world— timely, unique and profound.

New York
1971

Leon Stein
Philip Taft

AN AGENT,
CANVASSING FOR BOOKS. PUBLISHED BY
D.E.FISK & CO.SPRINGFIELD.MASS.

How Women

can

MAKE MONEY,

MARRIED OR SINGLE,

IN ALL BRANCHES OF THE ARTS AND SCIENCES, PROFESSIONS,
TRADES, AGRICULTURAL AND MECHANICAL PURSUITS.

BY

MISS VIRGINIA PENNY

AUTHOR OF "THINK AND ACT, MEN AND WOMEN, WORK AND WAGES," ETC.

SPRINGFIELD, MASS.:
D. E. FISK AND COMPANY.
PHILADELPHIA: McKINNEY & MARTIN,
1308 CHESTNUT STREET.

TO

WORTHY AND INDUSTRIOUS WOMEN

IN THE UNITED STATES,

STRIVING TO EARN A LIVELIHOOD,

This Book

IS RESPECTFULLY DEDICATED BY

THE AUTHOR.

Publisher's Note: This Preface is reprinted from the earlier edition (1863) of *How Women Can Make Money*, originally titled *Employment of Women: A Cyclopedia of Women's Work*.

PREFACE.

IT is very easy to obtain book after book on "The Sphere of Woman," "The Mission of Woman," and "The Influence of Woman." But to a practical mind it must be evident that good advice is not sufficient. That is very well, provided the reader is supplied with the comforts of life. But plans need to be devised, pursuits require to be opened, by which women can earn a respectable livelihood. It is the great want of the day. It is in order to meet that want that this work has been prepared. The few employments that have been open to women are more than full. To withdraw a number from the few markets of female labor already crowded to excess, by directing them to avenues where they are wanted, would thereby benefit both parties.

At no time in our country's history have so many women been thrown upon their own exertions. A million of men are on the battle field, and thousands of women, formerly dependent on them, have lost or may lose their only support. Some of the mothers, wives, sisters, and daughters of soldiers, may take the vacancies created in business by their absence—others must seek new channels of labor.

An exact estimate of woman as she has been, and now is, furnishes a problem difficult to solve. Biographies and histories merely furnish a clue to what she has been. Prejudice has exaggerated these portraitures. Woman as she now is, save in fiction and society, is scarcely known. The future position of woman is a matter of conjecture only. No mathematical nicety can be brought to bear upon the subject, for it is one not capable of data. More particularly is it difficult to define what her future condition in a business capacity will be. Man will have much to do with it, but woman more. I know of no work giving a true history of woman's condition in a business capacity. Socially, morally, mentally, and religiously, she is written about; but not as a working, every-day reality, in any other capacity than that pertaining to home life. It has been to me a matter of surprise that some one has not presented the subject in a practical way, that would serve as an index to the opening of new occupations, and present the feasibility of women engaging in many from which they are now debarred. It is strange there is no book on the subject, in any language, for it is a world-wide subject. Its roots are in the very basis of society—its ramifications as numerous as the nations of the earth—yes, as the individual members of the human family. The welfare of every man, woman, and child is involved in the subject. For who is entirely free from female influence—who is devoid of interest in the sex—who exists free from relationship, or any connection with woman? There is no man that is not involved in what affects woman, and the reverse is also true. It should therefore be a subject of paramount interest to all. Particularly does the subject appeal to the heart of woman. If she does not need to make a practical use of information on the subject, she will find its possession no disadvantage. It may assist her, from motives of friendship, or benevolent feelings, to advise and direct others. Is there any woman, not entirely devoid of all sensibility, but desires an amelioration in the condition of the working class of her sex—those who earn a mere pittance, scarce enough to keep body and soul together?

The work of single women has never been very clearly defined. Those that are without means are often without any to guide them; and the limited avenues of employment open to women, and the fear of becoming a burden on others, have poisoned some of their best hours, and paralyzed some of their strongest powers. There is a large amount of female talent in the United States lying dormant for the want of cultivation, and there has been a large amount cultivated that is not brought into exercise for the want of definite plans and opportunities of making it available. It exists like an icicle, and requires the warmth of energy, thought, and independence to render it useful. It shrinks from forcing itself into notice, like the sensitive plant, and may live and die unseen and unknown. Widen, then, the theatre of action and enterprise to woman. Throw open productive fields of labor, and let her enter.

Of those who speak so bitterly of women engaging in some pursuits now conducted by men, we would inquire, What would you have destitute single women and widows do, by which to earn their bread? You surely would not have women steal, that cannot obtain employment. What, then, can they do? Why may they not have free access to callings that will insure them a support? Those that oppose them, generally do so from selfish motives. Many men would banish women from the editor's and author's table, from the store, the manufactory, the workshop, the telegraph office, the printing case, and every other place, except the school room, sewing table, and kitchen. The false opinion that exists in regard to the occupations suitable for women must be changed ere women have free access to all those in which they may engage. Yet I would love to see thrown open to women the door of every trade and profession in which they are capable of working.

Women have not devoted their time and talents to mechanical arts, except to a very limited extent, and only within fifty years. How then could they be expected to equal men in proficiency, who have from the creation of the world been so employed, and who have had the advantage not only of their own exertions, but the experience of their fathers and forefathers to profit by? The superior mechanical talent of the United States is becoming known throughout the civilized world, and some of the work dictated by that talent is executed by women.

Some persons complain that women would become more material —less spiritual—if engaged in manual labor. We think not, if it is of a kind suited to their nature. Contact with the world does not always wear out the fineness and delicacy that we love in woman. She does not necessarily lose that softness and gentleness that render her so lovely.

A few women may by nature have a fondness for masculine pursuits; but the number of men that have from training and circumstances a partiality for feminine pursuits, is much greater. It has been estimated that there are 95,000 females earning a livelihood in New York city and its vicinity, by their labor, aside from those engaged in domestic pursuits; and I am confident there are at least 100,000 men in the same city engaged in pursuits well adapted to women.

As women become more generally educated, their energies will be increased—their limits of thought expanded. They will seek employments consistent with honor and delicacy. They will desire the elevation of their sex, and do what they can to bring it about, regardless of the shafts of ridicule sent by selfish men and heartless women.

"By elevating the standard and augmenting the compensation of woman's labor," a complete revolution would be wrought in the social and political standing of woman. Let woman once surmount the difficulties that now oppose her, and take her stand with dignified reserve, laboring and claiming what is her right as much as men—free labor and fair wages—and liberal men will applaud and admire her.

As a friend of my sex, I have made investigations, and obtained statistics that show the business position of woman at present in the United States. I present such employments as have been, are, or may be pursued by them, and give what information I can obtain of each one. I may have omitted a few, and there may be some that are not yet recognized as a distinct business. I have made the study a speciality for three years, and spent an almost incredible amount of labor and money in doing so. I have visited factories, workshops, offices, and stores, for the purpose of seeing women at their vocations. I have gone through wind and snow, cold and rain. If I could have had the time and opportunity, I would have endeavored to see, also, something of their home-life.

Much of the verbal information I give is impartial, as it has been given by those with whom I talked in a casual way, they not knowing I had any object in view; and frequently it was done in a respectful, yet off-hand way, when making purchases. I have often bought articles merely for an excuse to talk with people, and gain information on their occupations.

I desire to present to those interested a clear and succinct view of the condition of business in the United States, the openings for entering into business, the vacancies women may fill and the crowded marts they may avoid, the qualifications needed for a selected pursuit, and the pursuits to which they are best adapted; also the probable result pecuniarily of each calling honorably pursued: in short, it is intended as a business manual for women. I wish to make it a practical work—useful, not ornamental. It is more a bringing together of facts, than a presentation of ideas—more a book of research than reflection. Yet the statements given are important, not merely as facts, but as being suggestive of things essential to or connected with occupations. The limits of each subject must necessarily be short, as I wish to form a volume to come within the reach of every one that would desire a copy.

Any female who has in view the learning of any occupation mentioned in this book, would do well to go and see the process before making arrangements to that effect. And she should exercise her own judgment in making a practical use of that information. Many pursuits are now followed by women for which it was once thought they were incapable.

My book is not sectional in its feelings. It is intended to benefit women of the North, South, East, and West of this vast Republic. In the large cities of the North, most working women are acquainted with others engaged in different occupations, and so may learn of places to be filled in them. In the South, a smaller number of women have been dependent on their own exertions, owing to the existence of slave-labor, and the comparative smallness of immigration.

I strongly advocate the plan of every female having a practical knowledge of some occupation by which to earn a livelihood. How do men fare that are raised without being fitted for any trade or profession, particularly those in the humbler walks of life? They become our most common and ill-paid laborers. So it is with woman's work. If a female is not taught some regular occupation by which to earn a living, what can she do, when friends die, and she is without means? Even the labor that offers to men, situated as she is, is not at her disposal.

No reproach should be cast upon any honest employment. The dignity and value of labor in the most menial occupation is superior to idleness or dependence upon others for the requirements of life. What destitute but industrious woman would not be glad to earn for herself a snug little cottage, to which she may resort in her old age, from the cares and conflicts of life; to enjoy the independence of a competency, earned by remunerative and well-applied labor?

I will not be responsible for all the opinions advanced by those who have furnished me with information. The reader will often have to form her own deductions from the statements made. My work may not accomplish, by a great deal, the end proposed, but I hope it may be the means of securing, by honest industry, a livelihood to many now dependent and desponding. If it does not in itself accomplish any visible good, it may be the means of bringing forward some better method by which the desired end may be effected. It may perhaps impart information by which the philanthropic may best employ their time and means in advancing the welfare of others, by pointing out the wants of dependent women, and how best to meet those wants. It may open the way of usefulness to women of leisure and talents. If it saves any of my sex from an aimless and profitless life, I will feel that something has been done. In that way some may be kept from despair and sin. And it is certainly better to prevent evil than to cure it. Some have means, and if a plan were presented to them, they would engage in its execution.

Connected with this subject is a fervent desire on the part of the writer to see houses of protection and comfort provided in our cities for respectable and industrious women when out of employment.

Wealthy, benevolent people might build them, and appropriations be granted by the cities in which they are planted. Such a structure in each of our cities and towns would be a refuge to the weary, a home to the oppressed, a sanctuary to the stranger in a strange land.

When the place of gaining information is not mentioned in this work, it will be understood that New York city was the place. It will be remembered that most of the information was obtained from October, 1859, to February, 1861.

I hope much anxiety of mind, and uncertainty in the selection of a pursuit, will be prevented by my book, and many precious hours thereby saved for active, cheerful employment. If there should seem to be a want of practicability in any of the subjects I have treated upon, I think, after some reflection, it will disappear. Some of the employments presented may not find encouragement and proper compensation until our country becomes older, and calls for more variety in labor. I hope I may not hold out any unreasonable expectations of employment, or excite any hope that may not be realized. My ideas may appear vague and indefinite to some, but even such may perhaps pick out a few grains from the pile of chaff. But we must be doing, not saying—moving, not sitting—accomplishing something, not folding our hands in indolent ease. The active, restless spirit that pervades our people calls for action. It will not do to rest passive and let events take their own course. The progress of the age calls for earnest labor.

INTRODUCTION.

THE great, urgent, universal wants of mankind, in all classes of society, are food, clothing, shelter, and fuel. After these come the comforts and luxuries pertaining to the condition of those in easy circumstances. Above and beyond these animal wants, but of nearly equal importance, are those relating to the mind—written and printed matter, oral instructions, as lectures and sermons, and the handiwork of the fine ·arts. These, in addition to health, freedom, and friends, comprise the greatest blessings man enjoys. I would add that the means of transit are necessary to make him entirely independent. Nearly all honest occupations are founded on these wants; but they have been divided and subdivided until their name is legion.

The contents of this volume might be arranged in the same way that the articles exhibited in the Crystal Palace of London were, under the heads—Producer, Importer, Manufacturer, Designer, Inventor, and Proprietor. But we think the arrangement pursued, though rather irregular, may be quite as convenient. So great is the variety of subjects treated, that it is difficult to condense the contents in a smaller compass.

The general difference in character and habits of those engaged in various occupations—their comparative morality and intelligence, the effects of a decline in wages, the effects of trades-unions, are all, more or less, involved in this subject of employments; also the opinions of the working classes on machinery and its results. Employments that have for their object the health, comfort, and protection of mankind—those that produce the necessaries and the luxuries of life—those for amusement and capable of being dispensed with—are all treated of to some extent.

Numbers of women have been lost to society from the want of a systematic organization for their employment, and by a deficiency in the number of remunerative pursuits open to them. The destinies of thousands are daily perilled, mentally, morally, and physically, by the same cause. The disease has raised a great and turbulent cry; but, strange to say, few means, and they limited and inefficient, have been used as a cure. Indeed, a remedy has scarcely been devised. To open new and suitable occupations to women, and secure for them fair wages, would, I believe, be an effectual mode of relief. But to bring about a favorable change, not only must more occupations be opened to women, but, as Mr. Walker says, "employments of an equally indispensable character with those of the other sex." Many persons would be surprised to find the large number of people employed in such occupations as pertain only to civilized life—such as could be dispensed with in an emergency; and the small number employed in such occupations as really furnish us with the necessaries of life. In the first class, aside from those engaged in domestic duties and labors, the majority of women are employed.

In the selection of a pursuit, it would be well to take into consideration what occupations are most likely to increase in this country. Those absolutely necessary for the preservation of life are permanent. Those essential to the health and comfort of mankind must be pursued by some. The steadiness of employment the year round should also be considered. Another item is the danger attending a trade, and the effects of the occupation on the health of the individual. A better compensation should be given to those prosecuting either a dangerous or unhealthy pursuit. There is at present more danger of women suffering from either an excess of work, or the entire want of it, than from any peculiarity pertaining to an occupation. A matter of some importance is the ability of an individual to furnish herself with the implements of a trade, goods for merchandizing, or the appurtenances of a profession, if she intends to conduct business on her own responsibility and at her own expense. If she has friends to advance her the money, she might perhaps make an arrangement to refund as she advances in business.

It is a matter of doubt with us whether the labors of women are on an average less laborious than those of men. That they are generally performed indoors, is not saying anything in their favor as regards health. If we include domestic employments, we cannot say they are neater on an average. They may be better adapted to the constitution of the female sex, but the question arises, Are those in which women now engage, except domestic duties, more congenial to their taste, more acceptable to their feelings, more likely to develop their mental powers, and rightly direct their moral nature, than many others in which they might engage?

We find that the class of workers, both men and women, having the most steady employments, are the most steady and reliable people.

There are some employments in which it is well for a man and his wife to unite, as bankers, picture restorers, house painters, &c.

There is probably as much diversity in the abilities of individual men to acquire a trade, as in those of women. We doubt not but women, generally, are as capable of acquiring a knowledge of any vocation as men, if they spend as much time and application in doing so. Could not women learn those occupations quite as thoroughly that require of men an apprenticeship of three, five, or seven years, if they could give the same time? We are confident the majority of women could, particularly those who have had equal advantages in the way of education and society with men engaged in the same pursuit.

We think the time spent in acquiring a knowledge of different occupations is not at all proportioned to the variety of work and the skill required for proficiency in each. For instance, an occupation that could be learned in six months, must have three years' labor given; while an occupation that it requires twenty years to excel in, has the usual apprenticeship of three years. By the way, could not the most of those pursuits now requiring three years' time of serving be mastered in a shorter period?

Supply and demand must ever regulate, to a great extent, the wages of women as well as men. We think, in the different departments of woman's labor, both physical and mental, there exists a want of harmony of labor done and the compensation; also, between the time given and the occupation. For instance, a gilder in a bookbindery gets $6 a week, or $1 a day of ten hours, which is equal to ten cents an hour. A girl, at most mechanical employments, receives, for her sixty hours' labor, $3 a week, which is equal to five cents an hour. A cook, who requires as much preparation as either, for ninety hours' labor will receive her board and washing, say $2, and $2 a week as wages, $4, equal to four and a half cents an hour. Confectioners' girls, in some of the best establishments in New York, spend seventeen, and some even eighteen hours, attending to their duties, and receive only $2, and board and washing, $4.50, equal to two and a half cents an hour. Some seamstresses sew fifteen hours a day, and earn but thirty cents, equal to two cents an hour, without board.

Where there are discrepancies about the seasons for any particular kind of work, as given by different parties, it will usually be found to arise from some of the number being engaged in the wholesale business, selling to people from the South and West; others selling to city traders, or retail merchants selling to city customers.

When there is a repetition of statements on the same subject, it will be observed that it arises from the information being given by different individuals.

I have used the words girl and woman indiscriminately, except when mention is made of the age of the girls.

I would take this opportunity of returning my thanks to all who have been so kind as to furnish me with any information, or directed me how to obtain it.

Some errors will no doubt be observed by persons in their special branches of labor. By writing to the author, attention will hereafter be paid to the correction of such errors.

NATURE OF THE CONTENTS.

THIS work contains five hundred and thirty-three articles, more than five hundred of which are descriptions of the occupations in which women are, or may be engaged—the effect of each on the health—the rate of wages paid for those carried on in the United States—a comparison in the prices of male and female labor of the same kind—the length of time required to learn the business fully, and the time required to learn the part done by women—whether women are paid while learning—the qualifications needed—the prospect of future employment in each branch—the seasons best for work, and if in any season the women are thrown entirely out of work—the usual number of hours employed, and, if the working time exceeds ten hours, whether it could be shortened without serious loss of profit—and the comparative superiority or inferiority of women to men in each branch. Also, openings in the Southern States for certain branches of business—the prices of board for work-women, and the remarks of employers—with a list of the occupations suitable for the afflicted. In addition are articles on unusual employments in the United States, England, France, and other countries—minor employments in the United States, England, and France. Also, a notice of the occupations in which no women are engaged in any country—those in which none are engaged in this country—those in which very few are engaged.

HEADS OF SUBJECTS.

PROFESSIONAL Women. Artists. Those in Mercantile Pursuits. Employments pertaining to Grain, Birds, Flowers, Fruits, and Vegetables. Raisers, Makers, Preparers, and Disposers of Articles of Food. Textile Manufacturers—Cotton, Linen, Woollen, Silk, Lace. Metal Manufacturers—Iron, Brass, Steel, Copper, Tin, Britannia, Silver, Silver Plating, Bronze, Gold. Miscellaneous Workers on Indian Goods, Inkstands, Lithoconia, Marble, Mineral Door-Knobs, Paper Cutting, Papier Maché, Pipes, Porcelain, Pottery, Stucco Work, Terra Cotta, and Transferring on Wood. Glass Manufacturers. China Decorators. Leather Manufacturers. Whalebone Workers. Brush Manufacturers. Ivory Cutters. Pearl Workers. Tortoise-Shell Workers. Gum-Elastic Manufacturers. Gutta-Percha Manufacturers. Hair Workers. Willow Ware. Wood Work. Agents. Manufacturers, and Colorers of Ladies' Apparel. Fitters, Cutters, and Sewers of Ladies' and Children's Wear. Upholsterers. Manufacturers of Books, Ink, Paper, and Pencils. Chemicals. Those who serve as a Communicating Medium between Employers and others. Those that contribute to the Comfort or Amusement of others. Mistresses and Domestics. Miscellaneous Occupations. Employments for the Afflicted. Unusual Employments. Minor Employments. Occupations in which no Women are engaged, &c. Openings in the South for certain branches of business. Prices of Board for Workwomen, and Remarks of Employers. Number of Work Hours. Extracts from the Census Report of 1860. Industrial Statistics of Paris.

THE EMPLOYMENTS OF WOMEN.

PROFESSIONAL, LITERARY, AND SCIENTIFIC PURSUITS.

1. Amanuenses. Amanuenses are employed to write from dictation, generally by authors. Prescott, who was nearly blind for several years, employed one or more. Editors whose papers have an extensive circulation, sometimes require the services of an amanuensis. Female secretaries, or writers out of books, were not unusual in Rome. " Origen," says Eusebius, " had not only young men, but young women to transcribe his works, which they did with peculiar neatness." Some persons in London (whose employment, perhaps, scarcely brings them under this title, yet we know not where else to place them) make it a business to write letters for beggars, for which they are paid a small sum by each applicant. Amanuenses are usually employed by the week, month, or year. Some education is of course necessary, and will doubtless influence their pay. Experience increases their value still more; and those who have to exercise their brains, are of course best paid. I have been told by competent authority, that amanuenses are usually paid according to agreement; that authors of distinction can afford to pay a good price, and that the most common salary is $600.

2. Astronomers. Maria Cunitz is mentioned as an astronomer of the seventeenth century in Germany. Miss Caroline Herschel discovered two moons and several comets. Miss Maria Mitchell, of Nantucket, Mass., discovered a new planet, and received, in consequence, a medal from the King of Denmark. She formerly observed for the Coast Survey, but was not officially recognized. She computes for the *Nautical Almanac*. She

writes: "I know of no lady astronomers who are practical observers. Very good works have been written on the subject by
women. An observing room is never warmed by a fire; and as
a small part, at least, of the roof must be opened to the air, the
exposure is according to the weather, as the observations must be
made in clear evenings. I do not consider the danger to the
health great. I know of no way in which astronomical observations can be made to pay women. They could, without doubt,
make better observers than men, with the same amount of practice. The same delicacy of touch and of perception that makes
them good at the needle, would make them efficient in the delicate
manipulations of the micrometer. But I know of no man well
paid as an observer only. There are always volunteer candidates
in this department of an observatory. Women can make as good
computations as men, and do their work more neatly; but here,
also, the field is occupied by men, although, I think, never as
volunteers without pay. I have no doubt many of the computations professedly made by men, are really the work of women
employed as assistants. This has always been the case in the
long and tedious computations made for astronomical objects in
the early efforts of the science. My own observatory is wholly a
private affair, and supported entirely by my own means, which
are my daily earnings as computer to the *Nautical Almanac.*
I employ no assistant." I am happy to say Miss Mitchell receives the same salary for the observations and reckonings of the
Nautical Almanac that would be given to a man. In 1856, at the
Smithsonian Institute, a paper was read by Professor Foote, on
the heat of the sun's rays; after which a paper by Mrs. Foote
was read by Professor Henry, giving an account of experiments
made by herself on the same subject. Miss Harriet Bouvier
(now Mrs. Peterson) has written a very good work on astronomy
for schools. Mrs. Somerville, a distinguished astronomer of
England, has added much information to the science by her dis-
coveries. "Miss Anne Sheepshanks, sister to the late astronomer, has been elected a fellow of the Astronomical Society."

3. Authors. Many superior works of fiction have been
written by ladies of America, some of which have been translated
into the languages of Europe and introduced into those countries.
Many of our fair countrywomen have distinguished themselves
by their poetical effusions, and quite a number have published
their poems in book form. Mrs. Everett Green, author of the
"Lives of the Princesses of England," is now employed by the
English Government upon state papers. Research into historical
data, and the nice, careful arrangement of details, are well fitted
to the patience of woman. Several years ago, Queen Victoria

granted to Mrs. Gore and Mrs. Jamieson each $1,000 a year as pensions. These are not by any means the only instances of her liberality to literary women. During the year ending January, 1860, she granted pensions to thirteen ladies, either for literary merit of their own or that of some relative. The French Academy awarded to Madame Louisa Collet, in 1851, the prize of $1,000 for poetry; also one to Mlle. Ernestine Druet, a governess in a school at Paris. Mlle. Royer received the prize, a short time ago, from the University of Lausanne, for a philosophical essay. The labor of authors is not rewarded as well as other kinds of intellectual labor of the same extent : for instance, a physician or lawyer, with the same abilities, amount of learning, and application, would derive a greater reward pecuniarily. In the United States an author can retain the profits of his work a certain number of years, being at liberty to make any arrangement with his publisher he sees proper. In France and Russia he possesses the profits arising from the sale of his work during his life, and his heirs receive them during twenty years. The following is an extract from H. C. Carey's article on the Rewards of Authorship : " Mr. Irving stands, I imagine, at the head of living authors for the amount received for his books. The sums paid to the renowned Peter Parley must have been enormously great; but what has been their extent, I have no means of ascertaining. Mr. Mitchell, the geographer, has realized a handsome fortune from his school books. Professor Davies is understood to have received more than $50,000 from the series published by him. The Abbotts, Emerson, and numerous other authors engaged in the preparation of books for young persons and schools, are largely paid. Professor Anthon, we are informed, has received more than $60,000 for his series of classics. The French series of Mr. Bolmar has yielded him upward of $20,000. The school geography of Mr. Morse is stated to have yielded more than $20,000 to its author. A single medical book, of one octavo volume, is understood to have produced its authors $60,000, and a series of medical books has given its author probably $30,000. Mr. Downing's receipts from his books must have been very large. The two works of Miss Warner must have already yielded her from $12,000 to $15,000, and perhaps as much more. Mr. Headley is stated to have received about $40,000; and the few books of Ik Marvel have yielded him about $20,000. A single one, 'The Reveries of a Bachelor,' produced $4,000 in the first six months. Mrs. Stowe has been very largely paid. Miss Leslie's cookery and recipe books have paid her $12,000. Dr. Barnes is stated to have received more than $30,000 for the copyright of his religious works. Fanny Fern has probably received not less than $6,000 for the duodecimo volume published but six months since. Mr. Prescott was stated, several years since, to have received $90,000 from his books, and I have never seen it contradicted. According to the rate of compensation generally understood to be received by Mr. Bancroft, the present sale of each volume yields him more than $15,000, and he has the long period of forty-two years for future sale. Judge Story died, as has been stated, in the annual receipt of more than $8,000, and the amount has not, as it is understood, diminished. Mr. Webster's works in three years can scarcely have paid less than $25,000. Kent's 'Commentaries' are understood to have yielded to their author and his heirs more than $120,000; and if we add to this, for the remainder of the period, only one half of this sum, we shall obtain $180,000, or $45,000 as the compensation for a single octavo volume—a reward for literary labor unexampled in history." It is necessary that the reader, in considering the figures given, remember that the reputation of an author has much to do with the price paid by a publisher for manuscripts. The number of women authors is much greater than one unacquainted with the statistics in regard to the subject would suppose. "In 1847 Count Leopold Feni died at Padua, leaving a library entirely composed of works written by women in various languages, the number of volumes amounting to nearly thirty-two thousand. Whether the English and American lady writers were included in his list we do not know, but we wish some woman of taste and fortune, in our country, would make a similar collection." It is said that two thirds of the writers in *Chambers' Edinburgh Journal* are women. Some of the writers of our best periodicals are women. The success of women in works of fiction is unquestioned. This class of books requires less time, less study, and less money, and rewards the authors pecuniarily better than any other kind of work, considering, of course, the comparatively small amount of application required. As the females of our land become more generally educated, and have more leisure for the cultivation of their minds, no doubt more attention will be devoted to literary effort. The easy, natural manner of female authors is a marked feature. Different motives prompt to authorship—love of fame, wealth, influence, and a desire to do good. Persons are generally prompted to write by feeling that they know more of some particular subject than most people, or something entirely unknown or unthought of by any one save themselves. Some collect and arrange information obtained from books, observation, or experience, or all combined. E. Hazen says : "The indispensable qualifications to make a writer are—a talent for literary composition, an accurate knowledge of language, and an acquaintance with the subject to be treated." Good health and freedom from care are necessary for one who would give him or herself up to the severities of mental labor. Dr. Wynne says : " With him whose occupation is either intellectual or sedentary, or both, the nervous energy necessary to digest food is already abstracted by the operations of the mind ; and the meal taken under the circumstances is but partially digested and appropriated to the use of the body. The remainder acts as an irritant, and, if the practice be persevered in, terminates in dyspepsia, followed by that Protean train of nervous diseases which destroys the equanimity of mind, and finally terminates the life of so many of our most efficient and worthy business men, at the very time when their services are most valuable to their families and the community. The cares of business should be dismissed with the termination of the hours devoted to their pursuits, and their place supplied by those exercises or amusements which bring with them cheerfulness and exhilaration." Of all studies, the quiet and contemplative kind are most favorable to long life. Those of an exciting nature produce a reaction, sometimes, of the physical as well as intellectual powers.

5. Bible Readers. An incalculable amount of good has been accomplished by this class of persons. The originator is Mrs. Raynard, the L. N. R. of the " Missing Link," " The Book and its Story," &c., who lived in London. " One hundred ladies have joined her as managers and superintendents. The ladies each select from among the uneducated class the best women they can find, and send them out to read Bibles and sell them to their own class. They have now two hundred such Bible women in England, Ireland, Scotland, and France, and they are meeting with unheard-of success. Mrs. Raynard told me they made soup for the poor in winter, and sold it to them very low, and in such a way that the poorest could have his bowlful for some trifling service ; and while one is serving the soup, others serve them with portions of God's word. Then the lady superintendents have tea meetings without number, and sewing meetings, and clothing meetings. Beside, the ladies must first instruct their readers every week or day in the Scriptures, in teaching, in meekness, in manner, in helping the sick, and sympathizing with all suffering, and, above all, teach them to lean only on God. They must also pay the Bible women, who give up their time to this work, and keep an account with each one. These lady readers or superintendents in England publish a monthly of their own, conducted by dear Mrs. Raynard, so that they can all communicate with one another ; and God sends them funds to the amount of $35,000

2

the year." A lady of Baltimore writes me : " The Maryland Bible Society employs three paid Bible readers—all women—at eight dollars per month each. These are purposely selected from the poorest class of pious women, because it is thought that persons of that class have readier access to the homes and hearts of the poor, beside the aid it affords to honest poverty. Independently of this Bible effort, another has originated from the London charity, unfolded in the ' Missing Link.' " The lady of Baltimore (Miss W.) wrote from the Maryland Bible, &c., through the *Word Witness :* " Just one year ago, I engaged a pious poor woman, at two dollars per week, to labor among the destitute, vicious poor—a class that could not be reached by ordinary methods of voluntary effort, dwelling in localities that ladies might not safely visit. The work was to humanize these people; to wash and clothe the children, and put them in Sabbath and public schools; to read and pray, and teach their mothers; and to relieve personal suffering. She has done a good work. Another woman has been employed in South Baltimore, in the same calling. Recently, the ladies of the First Presbyterian Church have formed a union, and raised the salary of one of these female colportors, and thus the experiment promises to expand itself into a permanent benevolent organization. I may say that the plan adopted, if vigorously and efficiently carried out, would rid our crowded alleys of half the suffering and nearly all the vices and impositions that now render them intolerable to the refined. On Christmas, I assisted to serve up a supper, provided by a good lady for the poorest of the poor. It was given in the district, and at the house of a widow, and under the care of our colportors. There were forty-eight women and children present, not ragged and hopeless, as they were one year ago, but tidy and bright, looking hopefully to the future, as though they felt there is kindness in the world. It was a pleasant sight to witness." The New York Female Auxiliary Bible Society now employs thirteen Bible readers. A brief but interesting account is given of them in the last report of that society, from which we copy : " From the reports of the Bible readers for only a part of the year, we find that they have paid more than seven thousand visits, gathered more than two hundred children into the Sunday school, sold and distributed Bibles, induced many to attend church, ministered to the wants of the destitute, established sewing schools, and, in more ways than we can enumerate, have gone about doing good." A Bible reader is now employed in Philadelphia by the Pennsylvania Bible Society.

4. Bankers and Bankers' Clerks. Before the existence of savings banks, the poor had no safe place of deposit, where they could receive interest, and whence they could withdraw their deposits at pleasure. If they loaned their money, there was no certainty of recovering it. If they tried to accumulate by saving what they had, it was not always secure from depredation. Consequently they were tempted to spend any surplus money they had, and often no forethought of the future could save them from anxiety and misery. Now, by industry and perseverance, they are enabled to accumulate something for contingencies—to provide against want, sickness, old age, and slackness of employment. The idea of a savings bank was originated by a woman—Mrs. Priscilla Wakefield. It is a most worthy institution, and deserving of support and patronage. Holding office in a bank is a very responsible situation. The numerous men defaulters that have disgraced themselves in the last few years, are sufficient proof that the temptation to appropriate unjustly is very great. It requires men and women of fixed principle, whose honor is dearer to them than life itself. We think women could very well manage savings banks. They could at any rate attend in the female department, and in some parts of Europe do. We find in the census of Great Britain two female bankers reported. In the *Englishwoman's Journal* we read : " At St. Malo, a few years ago, the wife of a rich banker, during his absence, took her place at his desk amid the numerous clerks, received checks, and gave to the writer of this article French money in return. They are frequently found in offices, and often mainly conduct a husband's or a father's business." One of the Mrs. Rothschild, I have been told, even now spends two or three hours every day in her husband's banking house. Mrs. Mary Somerville says : " Three of the most beneficial systems of modern times are due to the benevolence of English ladies—the improvement of prison discipline, savings banks, and banks for lending small sums to the poor." Not many years ago a banking house was conducted by a lady in Nashville, Tenn. She was a widow, but had during her first husband's life attended to some of the duties of the bank, and accompanied her husband when he visited New York on business. She is now the wife of one of the late candidates for the highest office in this nation—that of chief magistrate. A lady was employed in a savings bank in Boston a few years back. A gentleman who has been cashier in a bank for many years writes me : " I have no doubt that women might be qualified for bank and brokers' clerks as well as men. In the offices of cashier and teller, they would have to come in contact with so many rough characters, I doubt whether it would do. I do not know the salaries paid in Europe, either in stores, shops, banks, or brokers' offices, but suppose it varies as it does in this country, according to the size of the city, the bank or broker's capital, the qualifications and character, and the situations the persons occupy. The cashier receives more than the teller; the teller often more than the clerk, and the clerks are graded.   In large banks in the city of New York, the cashiers get from $4,000 to $6,000 per annum, while in the country banks they scarcely get half that amount.   In the city their situations are very laborious, and very responsible, and many of them have been twenty-five or thirty years in the business before they got to be cashiers.   Tellers receive in large cities from $2,500 to $3,000, and in small places from $1,200 to $2,000.   Clerks get in New York banks from $600 to $3,000, taking the whole range from boys of seventeen to men of sixty with families and great experience.   In smaller towns they receive from $300 to $2,500, taking the same range, many of them getting not more than $1,500 at any time during their lives.   In stores and shops the salaries are much less, say not much over one half in very many instances; but persons in stores and shops have this advantage over bank clerks: when they learn the business, they are often taken into partnership with the proprietor, or they may set up in a similar business for themselves.   But bank clerks have no such prospects before them.   There may be salaries, in a few instances, over those mentioned, but very seldom; and on the other hand, some young men are placed in business sometimes without any remuneration for the first year.   I would also state that the situation of bank clerk, although very much sought for, is certainly not desirable, as $1,200 or $1,500 will not support a family in any city of the United States, without the most rigid economy; and then they have little or nothing to lay up for a rainy day.   Many bank clerks in this city are no better off now than they were twenty years ago, though they have lived poorly and economized all the time.   So, in some respects, the store clerk or salesman has the advantage.   One reason why young men prefer becoming bank clerks to mercantile clerks is, that they have more time for themselves.   Say, they commence by seven o'clock in a store, and nine at bank; they get through by two or three o'clock in bank, and they have to work until night in a store."

6. Brokers.   This is a business in which very few, if any, women engage without the aid of the other sex.   We are not aware that any women are stock brokers, exchange brokers, or insurance brokers.   We suppose women could not very well conduct the business without having to mix promiscuously with men on the street, and stop and talk with them in the most public places; and the delicacy of woman would forbid that. But the wife, the sister, or daughter of a broker might perhaps conduct the indoor business of the house, or keep the books at least. In Paris, where women are extensively employed in various departments of business, it would, perhaps, be more practicable for a woman to carry on the business than in this country. There are respects in which women of well-disciplined minds would be well suited for the vocation : they are their observance of order and method, and their close attention to details.

7. Colonizationists. This is a business that would never have entered our minds for women to engage in, had it not been for the course pursued by Caroline Chisholm. Says the author of " Women and Work : " " Ask the emigrants who went out to Australia year after year, under the careful and wise system of Caroline Chisholm's colonization, how women can organize, and what professions they should fill. I think they would answer : As organizers of colonies, promoters of emigration, secretaries to colonies, &c." Many a husband and wife may thank her for the comforts of home life. Some years ago, Mrs. Farnum proposed taking from New York a shipload of women to California. The matter was laughed at and passed by ; but if we may believe the reports that came from California of miners wanting wives, perhaps it would not have been a bad plan to have taken out a supply (in case they could have been had). In the early history of Virginia, women were brought over from England as wives for the men. " A society exists in England for the promotion of female emigration to Australia. Under the auspices of this society, about eleven hundred women, mostly distressed needle-women, of respectable character, have been sent to Australia, where they find employment, and, we presume, the most of them, husbands."

8. Colportors. " This is an important field of missionary labor in our own land, where women might be employed to great advantage—namely, as colportors, or distributors of tracts and books. The Boards of Publication now employ men only, whose services must be paid at a much higher rate than women would require. There are widows who need this employment for support, and single women who need employment for health, and many women would like this way of doing good. In every place, women would be found suitable and willing to undertake this profession. It is one exactly suited to them. It enters into their domestic circle of feelings and pursuits; and honorable women, not a few, would be found ready to engage in the work. A number of men would be needed to penetrate the wild places of our land; but throughout all the settled portions, women would be found the most effective agents. By this arrangement, a double gain would be secured. The talents of pious women, now allowed to be wasted on trifles, would be employed in the cause of moral improvement; and those men who now give up their time, often at a great pecuniary sacrifice, to the colportor's duty, would be at liberty to enter into other pursuits more beneficial to themselves and to society." Are there none among the gentler sex consecrated to the work of promoting the glory of God and the good of their fellow beings? Are none of those that owe all their privileges and blessings to the Bible, willing to make a sacrifice for its extension? Are all so selfish, that the desire of personal gratification is the ruling, the only object for which they live? a display in dress and style of living, the acquisition of property, or notoriety? Are these the only objects of woman's exertions? No: most women are too conscientious and unselfish to live for such a purpose. There are many that would gladly do what they could, but they have no definite plan in view. They know not exactly how to shape their course. If they were once started, they would neither lag nor faint in the race. Let such become colportors, deaconesses, physicians, painters, engravers, whatever best accords with their inclinations and abilities. Let them go forward. The mist will gradually disappear, the way be made clear, and they followed by others. It is best for one of strength and vigor to engage in the labors of a colportor. Walking from house to house all day is very fatiguing to persons not accustomed to being much on their feet. It requires a person that has at heart the good of her fellow beings, and is willing to converse with all classes and ages. It calls for a person of piety, and one of tact and judgment.

9. Copyists. Law copying is done by young women in charge of the society in London for promoting the employment of women. Miss Rye, who is superintendent of the class, says: " Of course it took the writers some weeks to unlearn the usual feminine spider-legged fashion of inditing; some weeks more to decipher the solicitors' signs, contractions, and technical terms. We dare not pretend, in defending the opening of this trade to women, that there is here, as in printing, a deficiency of workers, a cry among the masters for more; or that woman's work here, as in the telegraph offices, is intrinsically more valuable than that of the other sex." In France, lawyers often employ women to copy for them, and a number of women are employed by the French Government to write. At Washington, ladies have been employed to copy, not only for congressmen as individuals, but to copy government documents; and received the same salaries as men. A friend told me many ladies are thus employed at Wash-

THE COLPORTER.

10

ington. She knows two who each receive salaries of $1,200 per annum. Miss N. says some ladies in Washington make from $500 to $600 a winter, copying speeches and other documents for members of Congress. She knew a lady who wrote all the year at a salary of $1,200. "In Cincinnati, some lawyers employ women as copyists, when the work can be sent from the office." Ladies employed by lawyers must write a very clear, round, legible hand; if any mistake is made, the writer must copy the manuscript anew. A young lady told me she used to write for a lawyer, and received three cents for every hundred words. One day she earned two dollars and a half. She wrote in the office of the lawyer. Many ladies, she says, are so employed in New York. Mrs. N., copyist, charges twelve and a half cents a page of foolscap, for copying, estimating her time at nine cents an hour. She writes mostly letters in English for foreigners, and receives twenty-five cents a letter, usually of one page and a half. She is very careful, she says, never to divulge the business of the individual for whom she writes—a something very essential. Mrs. Blunt used to earn in Washington $700 or $800 a year for copying. One copyist charged $5 per week if she wrote at home, and $6 if away from home. I find that in the Western cities the prices for copying vary from eight cents to thirty-one cents a page. Ladies are occasionally employed at the Smithsonian Institute for copying, and are paid 5 cents per 100 words. I believe in New York a very common price for copying is 4 cents per 100 words. Miss W., an English lady, copied music about three years ago, and sent it to London to be sold. She often earned $12 a week.

10. Deaconesses. The order of deaconess was instituted at the same time as that of deacon, and corresponds in duty with that office. We read of deaconesses in the last chapter of Romans, Phœbe, Priscilla, Aquila, &c. The establishment of institutions for deaconesses affords a home to the unmarried women of our land, and widows without children, and furnishes them with such work as their health and previous employments fit them for. It carries out the principle, " Unity is strength." It is founded on that true spring of success—sympathy arising from similarity of circumstances and sameness of employment. Ministering to the sick and poor is so well adapted to women, that their time might be pleasantly as well as profitably spent. The desire in women to be employed is thus gratified, and the good of others as well as themselves thereby promoted. Those received as members would find it most harmonious to be of the same religion, and they should be willing to come under the regulations of the institution. Such an institution would have to be conducted by a person of discretion, piety, and wisdom. The members usually dress in uniform. Comfortable clothing is always furnished, boarding of course being provided in the establishment. The duties of deaconess in Protestant institutions are the same as those of sisters of charity in nunneries and convents. The institutions are usually commenced by public or private contributions, and some by both. When once firmly established, the members might receive a fair compensation for their services from the sick that are able and willing to pay. It might go to the support of the institution, and those who saw proper to devote themselves to teaching might throw their profits into the general fund. But such institutions should be secured on such a firm basis that those women who joined the order would ever be certain of a home, and of a kind and careful attendance in sickness and old age. If institutions are established in various parts of the United States, an inmate of one, if tired of remaining at that, might, by request, and after consideration by the principal, or a board of trustees, be permitted to remove to another. There are a number of institutions in Europe for preparing women for the duties of deaconess. The first intitution of modern times was established by Pastor Fliedner, at Kaiserwerth, Germany. "It has for its object the training of deaconesses—that is, female students to take charge of the sick and the poor, and superintend hospitals, infant and industrial schools, and, in short, to be the educators and preservers of humanity." An association has lately been formed in London of this order. Its object "is the diffusion of sanitary knowledge and promotion of physical training." "In Russia, the system for the practical training of deaconesses has spread in all directions. In Paris, Strasbourg, Echallens (in Switzerland), Utrecht, and England, the institution exists." Kings have not thought it beneath them to assist in the support of such institutions. Miss Bremer mentions several going to Jerusalem to take charge of a hospital, which the King of Prussia founded at an expense of $50,000. We find two or three such institutions exist in the United States—one in New York, another in Pittsburg, and one in an incipient state in Baltimore. The one in New York is conducted by Sisters of the Holy Communion (Episcopalians). Five of them make their home at St. Luke's Hospital. One or two of the number are engaged in a parochial school connected with Dr. Muhlenberg's church. Those of the hospital nurse the sick during the day. They employ nurses to do the night nursing, except in very serious cases that require especial attention. Their dress is simple, black, with white collars and undersleeves, and, when in full dress, a Swiss muslin cap. They do not take vows like the nuns of the Roman Catholic church, nor do they give up all their property, but make a quarterly payment, according to their means. One devotes herself to the measuring out and dispensing of medicine. There is a hospital in Pittsburg in charge of some deaconesses from Kaiserwerth. They belong to the Evangelical Lutheran church. The institution was commenced by the Rev. W. A. Passavant, but is now incorporated by the State, and the "members are empowered to engage in all works of mercy, such as the care of the poor, sick, fatherless, insane, and the education of the ignorant and the orphan. The sisters live in community—dress simply, and generally alike, so as to avoid any unnecessary distinction and useless expenses. Applicants for admission go first for a month merely as visitors, and pay their own expenses going and returning. If both parties approve, they then enter on probation for three months, and afterward for nine months, or longer, as the institution may deem best. Then, if their purpose is still the same, they are received by a vote, according to the charter, as members. It is distinctly understood, that if a change in their views and purposes, or nearer or family duties require them to leave after this, they are at perfect liberty to do so, but always, only, after giving the institution a due notice of three months, unless such a notification is impossible from the circumstances of the case. Those who are preparing for the work among the sick learn the duties of an apothecary. All the sisters know how to mix medicines." Miss E. Blackwell says : " In the Catholic church the wants and talents of all classes are met. Single wealthy women become nuns, and so devote their riches and talents and time to good works. They associate with the most refined and best educated of both sexes. Poor single women find a home and social pleasures. It requires practical business habits to become even a successful sister of charity. They should enter with an active interest and zest into the duties of every-day life. These orders can never succeed well among Protestants, particularly until female physicians are introduced." The Minister of the Interior, writing from Italy to Mrs. Jameson, says : " Not only have we experienced the advantage of employing the sisters of charity in the prisons, in the supervision of the details, in distributing food, preparing medicines, and nursing the sick in the infirmaries; but we find that the influence of these ladies on the minds of the prisoners, when recovering from sickness, has been productive of the greatest benefit, as leading to permanent reform in many cases, and a better frame of mind always : for this reason, among others, we have given them every encouragement." Many young ladies of education, wealth, and influence would, on becoming pious, or when disappointed in their hopes and aspirations, be likely to join such societies. At such times, many are willing to give themselves up entirely to works of active benevolence. Such a life, of course, involves some self-denials. Bishop Potter warmly advocated the introduction of such orders, and delivered an address in favor of it. The Bishop of Exeter recommended the establishment of such orders in England, and an institution for deaconesses has been opened in London.

11. Dentists. Some time ago, in New York, a few ladies prepared themselves for the practice of dentistry. We believe only one really practised, and she but a short time. We find her name in a New York directory as a dentist. It would be more agreeable to most ladies to have their teeth cleaned and plugged by a lady. They would not feel the same hesitancy in going alone at any time to a dentist of their own sex. Extracting teeth would require more nerve and strength than most ladies possess. Yet, if a woman has nerves sufficiently firm, and ability to control her sympathies, she may succeed. There are dental schools in Baltimore, Philadelphia, and Cincinnati. A professor in the dental school at Philadelphia writes : "I would suggest that if any ladies desire to become efficient practitioners in some branches of dentistry, it would be better for them to apply to a reputable practitioner, and with time and attention become thoroughly familiar with those branches. In doing so they will prove to the world their capability, and the rest in time will follow." Dentistry has been humorously called a 'woman's profession.' "There is nothing even in the surgical part of dentistry, to which she is not adapted. In this profession she will have a fair opportunity to foil her enemies and accusers; and her children's *teeth* would not be set on edge without the possibility of instant relief. There is no mystery in the dental structure, which the turnkey, in her magic hand, could not *unlock ;* and no terrible pain in tooth extraction, which her mystic power could not exceedingly mitigate." Most profit arising to dentists is from making and inserting artificial teeth. It is a lucrative business, when properly understood, and one which affords constant employment.

12. Editresses. The most powerful instrument for disseminating general knowledge in the United States is the newspaper press. It does a great deal for promoting a love of letters; and the cheapness of the papers is such as to render them accessible to almost every one. The literature of the day penetrates the most remote corner of our country. Obscure, indeed, is the place that knows not the printer's power. Even in California, more than a year ago, there were published 81 newspapers. In

New York city alone were published 154 newspapers, and 114 magazines. But this is not strange when we remember that no less than eighty languages are spoken there. A newspaper states that there are printed in Austria 10 newspapers, 14 in Africa, 24 in Spain, 20 in Portugal, 30 in Asia, 65 in Belgium, 85 in Denmark, 90 in Russia and Poland, 320 in other German States, 500 in Great Britain, and 1,800 in the United States. Taking merely newspaper and magazine literature into consideration, does not our republic offer inducements to intellectual culture? Does she not reward talent and encourage industry? Yes. Her general diffusion of knowledge and the learned men of her press give a positive reply. The dignity of man should be elevated, his affections purified, and his pursuits ennobled by the mighty influence of the press. Editors should live as ministers to the welfare of humanity. The aspiring character of our people and their thirst for knowledge will long make a heavy demand on the talent and taste of those who wield the editor's pen. There are several publications in the United States conducted exclusively by ladies; some in which the assistant editors are ladies; and a small number devoted to the interests of women alone. Several ladies have entered the editorial corps within the last few years. The Harpers, in their Magazine, state there are about six hundred literary and miscellaneous periodicals published in this country. If all the labor, as type setting, binding, &c., was done by women, what a fortunate thing it would be for many of the poor! I have been told that when an article is sent to a newspaper, and is known to have come from the brain and the pen of a woman, ten to one, her compensation will be smaller for it, and in many cases it will be rejected. There are a few exceptions. Fanny Fern, for instance, receives, we have seen it stated, at the rate of $100 a column from Mr. Bonner for a contribution to the *Ledger*. The sum total he will pay her for the amount he has engaged will be $6,000. Mrs. B. receives $600 for editing a monthly paper. Some time back contributors to the *Independent* were paid $3 a column, and to the New York *Observer* at the same rate. Mr. L. told me that a man is paid $20 a week for making out an index for the New York *Tribune*, which could be done by any lady with a cultivated and well disciplined mind. The man that was employed not long since had been a wood engraver, and had received no special training for his duties in the *Tribune* office. The papers to be sent away are directed by machinery, which a lady could attend. Some one writes me the qualifications for his business are strength of mind and body. We think there is generally a heavy draft on either one or the other in every occupation successfully pursued, and in some on both. Émile

Girardin was a French editress that died recently. Mrs. Johnson, of Edinburgh, was for years editress of the Inverness *Courier*, which was published in her husband's name. Miss Parkes conducts the *Englishwoman's Journal*. Mrs. Swisshelm edited the Pittsburg *Visitor* with much vigor and ability. Mrs. Virginia L. French has charge of the literary department of a paper issued in Nashville, Tenn. Miss McDowell might have succeeded with the *Woman's Advocate*, if her noble efforts had been appreciated as they deserved.

13. Government Officers. " Many Government offices could be creditably filled by intelligent and experienced women. Miss Wallace and Miss Thomas were employed as computers on the Coast Survey at Washington in 1854, with salaries each of $480, with perquisites making it $600. A man to do the same work would probably receive twice as much." " Mrs. Miller, at one time, was engaged in making observations of the weather— the thermometer, barometer, direction of winds, quantity of rain, &c., in which she was assisted by another person appointed by a society of which both sexes were members." Computations of this kind could be made at home. Mr. Blodgett, who had charge of the Smithsonian Institute in 1854, wrote : " The discussion of observations in physical science, meteorological observations particularly, has never been undertaken in a general manner until attempted in this department of the Smithsonian Institute, and I have found that accuracy and despatch require well-trained minds of great endurance. Only the best minds can successfully undertake scientific calculations and computations; and these must possess a sort of half masculine strength and endurance." Yet we would not offer this as a discouragement. If it has been done, it can be done again. " During Mr. Fillmore's administration, two women wrote for the Treasury Department at Washington, at salaries of twelve and fifteen hundred a year." Several ladies are employed in different parts of the United States for copying by registers of deeds; but the majority are relatives of the registers. In some towns of the East, however, other ladies than relatives are employed, who receive $1 per day for their services. Miss Olive Rose has performed the duties of the register of deeds, at Thomaston, Maine. She writes : " I was officially notified of the election, required to give bonds, &c. I am unable to state the exact amount of salary, as it is regulated by whatever business is done in the office. Perhaps it may average between $300 and $400 yearly." The Duchess of Leuchtenberg was elected to preside over the Imperial Academy of Science, in Russia, a few years ago. An acquaintance told me that in the warehouses at the London docks, silks, shawls, and such goods are exposed for sale, and many ladies go down in their carriages and purchase. If any female is suspected of concealing on her person goods that she has appropriated in the warehouse, the watchmen who guard the place remark they would like to detain her for a few minutes, and convey her to a room, where a woman is in attendance to search her. The present collector of customs at Philadelphia writes : " The only instance of employment of women in connection with the custom house here has been, while Liverpool steamers were coming to this port, some years ago, when one or two were employed to search female emigrants, to prevent smuggling on their persons. The employment was only for a day or two at a time, and is now discontinued." Some time ago it was feared that large quantities of precious stones and laces were concealed on the persons of some women, and so smuggled into New York. Consequently "two American female searchers were inaugurated in the revenue service as aids. They each receive $500 per annum, and are paid by the month. Men receive $1,095 (or $3 per day) for similar services. The qualifications needed are intelligence, tact, and integrity. They spend but one or two hours on the arrival of each steamer or passenger received from abroad." I think, in European countries, female police, who examine the persons and passports of women, receive the same salaries as men.

14. Lawyers. We cannot question the right of woman to plead at the bar, but we doubt whether it would be for her good. She might study law, to discipline her mind and to store it with useful information. She might profitably spend, in that way, time which would otherwise be devoted to music, painting, or the languages. But the noisy scenes now witnessed in a court room are scarcely compatible with the reserve, quietude, and gentleness that characterize a woman of refinement. Theodore Parker said : " As yet, I believe, no woman acts as a lawyer ; but I see no reason why the profession of law might not be followed by women as well as men. He must be rather an uncommon lawyer who thinks no feminine head could compete with him. Most lawyers that I have known are rather mechanics at law than attorneys or scholars at law ; and, in the mechanical part, woman could do as well as man—could be as good a conveyancer, could follow precedents as carefully, and copy forms as nicely. I think her presence would mend the manners of the court—of the bench, not less than of the bar." A lady lawyer would not be without a precedent, for we read from a note in " Women Artists :" " Jhristina Pisani wrote a work which was published in Paris, 1498. It gives an account of the learned and famous Novella, the daughter of a professor of the law in the university of Bologna. She devoted herself to the same studies, and was distinguished for her scholarship. She conducted her father's cases; and, having as much beauty as learning, was wont to appear in court veiled." We suppose this is the same young lady of whom we read elsewhere: " At twenty-six she took the degree of doctor of laws, and began publicly to expound the laws of Justinian. At thirty she was elevated to a professor's chair, and taught the law to a crowd of scholars from all nations. Others of her sex have since filled professors' chairs in Bologna." While we would not encourage women to act publicly as counsellors at law, we would claim for them the privilege of acting as attorneys. Writing out deeds, mortgages, wills, and indentures, would be a pleasant occupation for such women as are qualified and fond of sedentary life. We know that the hearts of most women would prompt them to relieve the poor and oppressed : but might they not do it in some other way as efficiently as by pleading at the bar? If the weak seek their aid, let them bestow the benefit of their legal lore. If the helpless seek their protection, let them bring their information and counsel to bear upon the case, but not by public speaking. By personal effort, or by applying to the good of the other sex, they may accomplish much. If a woman involve herself in the intricacies of law, may she not lose those tender traits that endear her to the other sex, and in time discard those graces that render her gentle and lovely at home ? The profession of the law is one suited to the inclinations, nature, and taste of but very few women. But if a lady will practise law, she will need great clearness of mind, a good insight into the motives of others, fearlessness in expressing her convictions of right, and ability in refraining from saying more than she should.

15. Lecturers. Lecturing is addressing people through the sense of hearing; writing is addressing them through the sense of sight. An individual can address a larger number by the latter plan than the former. Many people that would not devote the time, trouble, and expense to investigate books, will give their twenty-five cents to hear a lecture on a given subject. Rev. Mr. Higginson says : " We forget that wonderful people, the Spanish Arabs, among whom women were public lecturers and secretaries of kings, while Christian Europe was sunk in darkness." " In Italy, from the fifteenth to the nineteenth century, it was not esteemed unfeminine for women to give lectures in public to crowded and admiring audiences. They were freely admitted members of learned societies, and were consulted by men of preëminent scientific attainments, as their equals in scholarship." Theodore Parker felt the importance of public lecturing, and expressed gratification that women were occupying the field so successfully. In the Female Medical College of Philadelphia, great attention is given to the study of physiology ; and several graduates from that institution have lectured upon this subject, one or two of them with great success. It is thought best that a lecturer upon physiology should be a physician, all the branches of medical science being so intimately connected, that the separation of one from the whole is like the dismemberment of the human body, producing almost the same effect upon the severed member. " The field for competent female lecturers on physiological subjects is as broad as the nation, and promises a rich harvest for as many as can possibly be engaged in it, for the next half century." Dr. Gregory, of the New England Female Medical College, writes : " Some of the graduates of this college have lectured to ladies more or less on physiology, hygiene, &c., and with good success. One in particular has given courses of lectures, illustrated with the apparatus of the college, to the young ladies in our four State Normal Schools, with great satisfaction to the principals and pupils. One of our graduates is resident physician, and teacher and superintendent of health in the Mount Holyoke Female Seminary, where there are almost three hundred pupils." Other female seminaries throughout the country ought to be thus supplied. Among those who lecture on physiology are Mrs. Fowler, Mrs. Jones, and Mrs. Johnson. In cities, a number of ladies might deliver lectures in private schools, academies, and colleges, on physiology and hygiene. Quite a number of ladies have delivered temperance lectures, and some were employed at one time by the State Temperance Society of New York. Lecturers of note receive from $50 to $500 for a single lecture, beside having their travelling expenses paid. When lecturing on their own responsibility, the entire proceeds are theirs, save expenses for room, gas, and (in winter) fuel. Lectures are most generally given before societies, that pay the lecturer a specified sum. Lucy Stone was paid $263 for her lectures in Bangor, Maine. Miss Dwight lectured on art, a few years ago, charging at first ten dollars for a series of six lectures, but afterward she reduced the price to five dollars.

16. Librarians. There is a Woman's Library in New York. The object is to furnish women—particularly working women, who are not able to subscribe to other libraries—with a quiet and comfortable place to read in, during their leisure moments. A lady in Darby, Pennsylvania, attends a town library that was established in 1785. It has always been kept in the house of her family, and she has had no occasion to employ assistance outside of her family. In the Mercantile Library of New York, two ladies have charge of the reading room. One receives $200, and the other $250 a year. Lady librarians receive from one third to one half as much as men. The librarian says they are not physically so capable, and otherwise not so well qualified. They could always do the lighter work of a library. They are employed all the year, and spend about eight hours in the reading room. The secretary of the Apprentice's Library in Philadelphia writes: "Both our principal librarians are ladies, and we have two assistants of the same sex. The principals receive $308, and the assistants $90 each, per annum. The girls' library, in which one of the principals and the two assistants are employed, is open five afternoons in the week, from three to four hours each afternoon and evening. It is only lately we have employed a lady for a librarian for the boys' department, and we find the change to be a happy one. The boys are more respectful, more easily managed, and kept in better order than formerly, and the number of readers has increased." The gentleman who has charge of the public library in Boston writes: "We employ eleven American ladies, who do all the work of a library in its various branches, under the direction of the superintendent, and subject to revision by him or an able male assistant. Some cover and collate books, some go from place to place to get books, and some are occupied entirely with writing and copying catalogues, shelf lists, records, &c. The ladies are paid $7 per week. Some spend eight and some ten hours in the library. Much of the labor performed by males is the same as that performed by females; but in every instance, save one, paid for at higher rates. Why, I cannot say. The office of superintendent requires learning and experience. In Boston, the rate of wages for men is higher than for females. Ladies are paid pretty well here, in comparison with what they are paid for work elsewhere. Teachers are paid higher than in other places. A competent person soon learns the duties of a library, but experience adds to her value. Ladies are employed in preference to men because they are competent, because it is a good field for female labor, because they have a good influence on those who transact business with the library, and, I doubt not, because their work can be had at less rates than men's. Our schools are graded, and in schools of a given grade there are divisions. Of course a graduate from the highest division of the highest grade, other things being equal (that is talent, &c.), is the person for us. A qualified lady is as good for work as a qualified man. The work of a librarian cultivates the mind. All advantages, aside from education, depend upon the taste of the lady employed. If fond of reading and ambitious to excel, she can, by faithful application out of library hours, succeed. Three dollars is the lowest price for which a lady can be comfortably boarded in Boston." "In the Smithsonian Institute at Washington, a lady is permanently employed as librarian. She receives a salary of $500 per annum, and is employed six hours a day. The qualifications needed for the post are reading, writing, some knowledge of French, German, &c."

17. Magazine Contributors. Some of our periodical literature is futile and unsatisfying. It is light and trivial in its nature. It may delight a few hours, but then follows the reaction—a dull and heavy sinking of the heart—a sluggish dreariness—a neglect of duty—a disdain for the actual realities of life. The prose of most magazines is only love dreams—the poetry froth. Such light nutriment is unfit for the souls of women—such ethereal diet can never satisfy the cravings of an immortal mind. But some improvement has taken place in part of our magazine literature, and a few of our reviews equal those of any country. Subjects are as numerous as the objects around us, and suited to all moods and diversities of mind. To the contributor, I would say : Your writing will be likely to find readers—whether it be grave or gay—sad or sprightly—witty or jovial; whether one making a draught on the imagination or the judgment; whether one displaying your own attainments, or calling to aid the opinions and acquirements of others; in short, one of thought, fancy, or facts. Your friends may like your ideas draped in poetry, or the more substantial dress of prose. One is like gold, the other like iron. One serves for ornament, the other for use. The true poet is a gifted person; a heaven-born talent does he or she possess. If you have good descriptive talents, you can write stories, laying the scenes in far-away countries that are not much known, and yet eliciting some interest. And as to the subjects of a moral caste, their name is legion. Magazine writing furnishes a palatable way of drawing attention to individual foibles, or furnishing a satire on the inconsistencies and exactions of society in general. If you attempt to write natural stories, let your scenes and events be such as occur in every-day life. It has been suggested that a good publication, like the *Atlantic Monthly*, conducted entirely by women, would do great good, but we fear it would not be supported. I was told, however, by the gentleman who has charge of *Harper's Magazine*, that two thirds of the articles are contributed by women, and they receive better prices than men would. The *Saturday Press* says that *Harper's Magazine* pays its writers $7.50 to $10 per page; the *Atlantic Monthly*, from $6 to 10; the *Knickerbocker*, $3, which is equal to $5 for *Harper* and $6 for the *Atlantic;* the *North American Review*, $1.50 per page. The prices mentioned are said by one supposed to know, to be exaggerated, and made the exception, not the rule. Mr. H. C.

Carey, in an article styled "Rewards of Authorship," writes: "I have now before me a statement from a single publisher, in which he says that to Messrs. Willis, Longfellow, Bryant, and Allston, his price was uniformly $50 for a poetical article, long or short—and his readers know that they were generally very short; in one case only fourteen lines. To numerous others, it was from $25 to $40. In one case he has paid $25 per page for prose. To Mr. Cooper he paid $1,800 for a novel, and $1,000 for a series of naval biographies, the author retaining the copyright for separate publication; and in such cases, if the work be good, its appearance in the magazine acts as the best of advertisements. To Mr. James, he paid $1,200 for a novel, leaving him also the copyright. For a single number of his journal, he has paid to authors $1,500."

18. Missionaries. Miss Rice, a missionary in Constantinople, has a large school for girls. Some of her scholars live in Constantinople, but most of them are from abroad—different parts of Turkey and Western Asia. "In England, Scotland, Ireland, and Germany, females organize societies of their own, and send out teachers and readers of their own sex. Ladies in England have had a society there twenty-five years, expressly for sending out and sustaining single ladies to work for heathen women, and they have already themselves sent two hundred into the field, at a cost of many thousands of pounds. If any of the lady missionaries sent out by the ladies' society in England desire to leave the work within five years, they shall be at liberty to do so, but shall refund to that society the cost of sending them out." Mrs. Ellen B. Mason, a missionary of Burmah, is now in New York, endeavoring to obtain female missionaries to return with her. A lady (Mrs. Bigelow) was employed among the city missionaries in Boston, at a salary of $350. From the last reports of the American Board of Foreign Missions, the Old School Presbyterian, the Protestant Episcopal, the Methodist, and Dutch Reformed, we find 451 lady missionaries were supported by their Boards at the time of making out the reports. The American Board had in charge 185 among foreign nations, and among the Indians 41 = 226. Of those sent out by this Board, 26 are unmarried. The Old School Presbyterian has 78 among the Indians (33 unmarried), and among heathen 53 (3 of the number single) = 131. The Baptist Foreign Missions number 34 (none unmarried). The American Baptist Union require every lady and gentleman that go out as missionaries from their Board to marry before they go. The Dutch Reformed have 11 among foreign nations. The Protestant Episcopal have 26 foreign missionaries (all married). The Methodist 17 (2 unmarried). In a manual for the use of missionaries and missionary candidates in connection with the Board of Foreign Missions of the Presbyterian Church, we find the laborers needed for the foreign field are : 1st, ordained ministers of the gospel; 2d, physicians; 3d, school teachers; 4th, printers; 5th, farmers and mechanics; 6th, unmarried female teachers. In referring to all the other classes but the first mentioned, it reads : " Though not called to preach the gospel, their Christian profession requires from them the same devotedness to the cause of Christ, according to the circumstances in which the providence of God has placed them, that is required from the ministers of the gospel. The application should be in writing, and the candidate should state briefly his age, education, employment, the length of time he has been a professor of religion, his motive and reasons for desiring to be a missionary, the field he prefers, and the state of his health. For a female this information may be given through a third person. No person will be appointed to the service of the Board until the executive committee have obtained as thorough a knowledge as possible of his or her character. For this purpose a personal acquaintance is very desirable. In all cases, written testimonials, full and explicit, must be forwarded." The treasurer of the Presbyterian Board said the salary depends on place and qualifications. The Treasurer of the Dutch Reformed Missions said a single lady receives from $300 to $400, according to her qualifications. Piety and a good common education are all that is necessary. They learn the language after arriving at their place of destination. None go without a certificate from a physician, saying they are free from organic disease. If their health fails so that they cannot recover, their passage home is paid, and they are supported for one year after. The minister connected with the Methodist Board said the salary depends on the places, and no particular preparation is requisite. They have many more applicants than they have places for.

19. Medical Missionaries. An association in Philadelphia educates a limited number of ladies to go out as medical missionaries. Any information in regard to this association may be obtained from Mrs. Sarah J. Hale, 1418 Rittenhouse square, Philadelphia. The enterprise opens to such missionaries a wide field of usefulness, that cannot be reached in any other way. A number are now wanting in foreign countries. Rev. Mr. Dwight, writing from Constantinople in 1852, very highly commends the plan of giving to some female missionaries a medical education. He refers to the secluded lives of the females in oriental nations, to their ignorance, and the superstitious reverence felt by the people for those acquainted with diseases and their remedies. He thinks that in Constantinople, among all ranks of people, and even among the Mohammedans, a female physician would find constant practice, and gain an access to the female portion of the community that missionaries cannot. And, if pious, in the capacity of physician, she could do much to promote their spiritual welfare. A knowledge of the Turkish language would be indispensable; and some acquaintance with French and Italian, Dr. Dwight recommends. And it was thought by some of the missionaries in India, before the rebellion occurred, that medical missionary ladies could accomplish much good there, especially at Calcutta. Missionaries in various other countries have also given it as their opinion that a great deal of good might be done in heathen countries by medical ladies.

20. Physicians. It is only within the last few years that women have received any preparation for the practice of medicine in our country. But it is now advancing in a way that is very gratifying to the friends of the cause, and is beginning to be appreciated by the people. Many of the most learned and talented men in the profession approve of women devoting themselves to the practice of medicine on their own sex and children. The mildness and amiability of woman, her modesty, her delicacy and refinement, all tend to make her acceptable at the bedside. Her quick insight into the ailments of others and her promptness in offering a remedy enhance her value. Some think the modesty and delicacy that should characterize a physician are lost by a lady in acquiring a knowledge of the profession. We would think not any more than by a gentleman. Why should the result be different? And surely a woman wants in her physician, whether male or female, a person of pure thoughts and feelings. Some say women have not firmness and nerve enough to perform surgical operations—that if they have, it is only animal force. What is it but animal force that gives the superiority to men (if they are superior)? Some say that such a profession may call woman among an objectionable class of people. " The fact that the practice of medicine draws its support from the miseries and sufferings of the world is no objection to its respectability. What profession is there that does not draw its support from some suffering, necessity, or disability?—unless it be that of the mountebank." Another objection urged is, that women lose their delicacy by the study and practice of anatomy under a male physician. This offensive feature is removed in the Female Medical College of Philadelphia, where that post has been filled by a woman for six or seven years. It is filled, writes one of the professors, to the full satisfaction, I believe, alike of the class and the faculty. In 1758, Anna Manzolini was professor of anatomy in Bologna. We believe, if a lady acquires a knowledge of medicine, it should be a thorough one. Undoubtedly too much strong medicine has been used in the United States, and that will account to some extent for the bad health of American women. Night practice and the inclemencies of the weather are the greatest difficulties a woman must contend with in the practice of medicine. If a lady has means, she can command a conveyance of her own. As to practising at night, she can have some one to accompany her, if in the city. If in a town, village, or the country, she will be likely to know who the people are, and have a conveyance sent for her. If a woman acquires a thorough knowledge of medicine, she can better promote the well-being and preserve the health of herself and children. No lady should undertake the practice of medicine unless she feels competent in every way to do so. If she does, let her enter with her soul into it, and keep constantly in view her object to relieve the suffering and bring health to the diseased. The practice of medicine is more renumerative than teaching. Mrs. Hale, who strongly advocates the practice of medicine by ladies, says : " Teachers grow out of fashion as they grow old ; physicians, on the contrary, gain credit and reputation from length of practice." There is one department of medicine that we think belongs to women, and women alone. It is midwifery. In the feudal times many ladies of rank and wealth prescribed and measured out medicines for their tenants, and many women practised midwifery. It is proved by Dr. Saul Gregory, of Boston, founder of the New England Female Medical College, that the practice of male physicians in the department of midwifery is not only injurious, but destructive of human life. He writes: " I have within the past six months made an effort to ascertain the number of lady graduates, having written to the different schools where they have graduated. From the number certainly ascertained, with the addition of a probable number of others, I should say that there are at least two hundred graduated female physicians in the United States. The number from this (the New England Female Medical College) is thirty-four. The field is broad enough, of course, for many thousands ; and to women of good natural abilities and suitable acquirements there is a prospect of success in all of the cities and large villages of the country. They will more readily find professional employment now and henceforward than they have during the past ten years, inasmuch as the idea of female medical practice has become more familiar to the public mind, and the custom is becoming gradually established. The tuition in medical colleges generally is from $60 to $80 a term. Board is from $2 to $4, according to circumstances. About $30 worth of medical books are needed. This college has a scholarship fund, affording free tuition to a large number of students from any part of the world." Dr. Gregory expresses our views in regard to more unoccupied women entering the profession of medicine, so much better than we could do, that we will transcribe what he says on the subject: "Man, the lord of creation, has the world before him, and can choose his profession or pursuit— war, politics, agriculture, commerce, mechanic arts, mercantile affairs (not excepting ribbon and tape), and a thousand vocations and diversions. There are said to be 40,000 physicians in the United States. 20,000 of these ought to give place to this number of women, and turn their attention to pursuits better adapted to their strong muscles and strong minds. In addition to providing for the self support of 20,000 or more women, this change would relieve that number of men, and secure to the country the benefit of their mental and manual industry—quite an item in our political economy and national wealth. Of course, this very desirable change cannot be brought about so suddenly as to create any great disturbance in the established order of things, even if the enterprise is carried forward with all possible vigor; so that physicians now in the field need not be greatly alarmed in prospect of female competition." We think, all diseases peculiar to women, or surgical operations on women requiring any exposure of person, should be treated and performed by women alone. Many a woman suffers for months, or years, and often a lifetime, because of that instinctive delicacy that makes her rather suffer than be treated by a male physician. Those that prepare themselves as physicians should be ladies of honor, education, and refinement. In most families, after the minister of the gospel, the physician holds the next highest place in the esteem of the members. Other subjects than those of medicine are often discussed, and the advice of a physician sought on matters of vital importance to those interested. The free, unembarrassed entrance of a physician into the sanctum of home, gives an opportunity of learning much that should be sacredly preserved in their own hearts. A lady physician needs firmness and dignity in the maintenance of her rights and opinions. When a woman is weak both in body and mind, timid and fearful, how much better can one of her own sex soothe her! It may be the nurse has not time, in a charitable, or even in a pay institution. But if her physician is a woman, well acquainted with her profession, and possessing discernment, sympathy, and some knowledge of the human heart, how readily may she read the inner as well as the outer wants of her patient! She will treat her gently and tenderly; and if the patient be a mother, the physician will see her family now and then, to relieve her patient's anxiety. If she is poor, she will speak to some of her rich patients, or acquaintances, to see that she is furnished with suitable employment when she is well. And so she will interest herself about those matters most male physicians would never think of, or, if they did, would consider beneath their attention. " In Paris, for a long period, women have studied medicine with the best physicians, who used them as supplements, to attend the poor and do some of the hospital practice." Two lady physicians became quite distinguished in Paris, and a hospital was in the entire charge of one. The statistics and professional reports of these ladies are now accepted by the best physicians in all countries. Dr. Elizabeth Blackwell has lately established a hospital in New York city, where ladies studying medicine can have the benefits arising from the observation and experience acquired in a hospital. This has long been considered almost essential in the education of male students. In the same city is a preparatory school of medicine conducted by professors connected with the medical schools of the city. They give separate instruction to a class of ladies, who are admitted to the clinical teachings of two of the largest dispensaries in the city. These dispensaries furnish upwards of 60,000 cases of disease annually. In 1850, a charter was granted to the Female Medical College of Pennsylvania. A college was commenced in Boston about the same time. Both of these schools are for females exclusively, and each has graduated about fifty pupils. In the Pennsylvania Medical University both sexes are received. In some branches the presence of mixed classes is embarrassing to both professors and pupils, and that free communication desirable for acquiring and imparting information is partially checked. This difficulty is done away in some female colleges by employing competent lady professors. In Europe, women are not permitted to receive instruction with the male students, but in hospital practice they have excellent opportunities of gaining information as nurses and physicians. I know of no pursuit that offers a more inviting field for educated women than the practice of medicine. The ability of woman to study and practice medicine has been satisfactorily demonstrated. Some ladies have graduated at both the allopathic and homœopathic schools in Cleveland. The allopathic school in that place was the first to admit ladies. Different motives actuate ladies in the study of medicine. The wives of some manufacturers, planters, and others, who reside where medical advice is not easily obtained, study medicine that they may prescribe for their husbands' employées. Some study medicine that they may have something to rely upon in case other resources should fail them. Some teachers have studied that they may instruct their pupils in the laws of hygiene and remedies for disease. Quite a number of lady physicians are employed in female boarding schools. The benefit resulting from having the advice of a physician at any hour of the day or night is very great, and must relieve the superintendents of schools and absent parents from much anxiety. Some ladies prefer giving advice at their residences. A lady that devotes herself to a speciality should endeavor to keep posted in all the branches of her profession, so far as she can without neglecting to acquire all the information possible in her speciality. "In the United States there are 40,564 physicians, 191 surgeons, 5,132 apothecaries, 456 chemists, 923 dentists, 59 oculists, 59 patent medicine makers. There are 35 medical colleges, 230 professors, and about 5,000 students." Dr. Ann Preston, of the Pennsylvania Female Medical College, writes me : " Of those in practice who graduated with us, quite a number have found it very remunerative, and the prospect for others to secure practice is most encouraging, if they only possess the requisite qualifications. The desire to employ ladies as physicians is constantly extending, and my faith in the triumphant and extensive vindication of the movement deepens from year to year. There are openings in perhaps nearly all the cities and villages of our land—certainly in Eastern Pennsylvania; but in choosing a physician, people must have confidence in the sound judgment, good character, and professional ability of those they employ. A woman settling among strangers is more liable to suspicion than a man; and in such a case it takes *time*, and a long continuance in well doing, to become established in a lucrative practice. It also requires *means;* and unless these are abundant, it is much better for the lady physician to settle where she is already known and respected, and where, among her friends, she can live at small expense. Still, in one or two cases, our students have gone *successfully* among strangers, earning enough to bear their expenses during the first two years. The cost of fitting a lady of moderate abilities for the practice of medicine varies. The whole cost of two or more courses of lectures and graduation is $175. Board here is from $3 to $5 a week for students, everything included. The needful text books would cost from $20 to $25 ; then travelling expenses, clothes, &c. I have known ladies commence with only one or two hundred dollars in advance, teach school during the summers, and graduate in three or four years. Sometimes these have come as beneficiaries. Still it is much more comfortable to have six or seven hundred to depend upon during the course of study. The time also varies, but we think no person should graduate who has not studied two years and upward. A large proportion of our graduates have studied medicine three years, and several have spent the next year in the hospital in New York. We are about opening a hospital here, which, in case of some, will obviate this necessity. I believe ladies in practice here generally make the charges common among men physicians; and several of them realize a handsome competence, and are gladdened by seeing, year by year, that prejudice is passing away, and that medicine is proving a fitting and glorious sphere for the exercise of woman's best powers." There are several regularly educated female physicians engaged in the practice of medicine in Philadelphia, some in New York, and some in Boston, with a few in other cities of the North, South, and West, and here and there scattered through towns, villages, and the country. There is an opening for one or two well-qualified physicians in New Orleans that can speak the Italian and Spanish languages. Many physicians find it an advantage to have a knowledge of the French and German languages, on account of the large foreign population in our country. Dr. Elizabeth Blackwell writes: "It is very difficult by letter to answer your question about medical education. It is almost impossible for a lady to get a *good* medical education without going to Europe. Philadelphia or Boston would give a woman the *legal right* to practise medicine, and that is the chief value of what is given, for the exclusively theoretical instruction of those colleges could be as well obtained by reading and private tuition. New York can furnish much valuable practical instruction, but not the legal right. Between the two places, a student who will spend four years may become a respectable young physician, without going to Europe; but fully that period of time is necessary to pick up scattered knowledge, &c. A lady should be able to command $2,000 during the four years. She is otherwise very much crippled in her studies. There is a real necessity for women physicians; therefore, in course of time they will be created; but the imperfect efforts and most inadequate preparation of those who now study, rather retard the movement, and the creation of practice is a very slow thing." I called on Mrs. ——, M. D. She goes out at night when called—sometimes alone, sometimes takes her female student. She thinks there must be openings South and West, and that the prospect for lady physicians is very good. She supposes the cost of a medical education would be about $1,500. I called on Mrs. ——, M. D., who practises medicine, and often lectures on diseases and their remedies. She walks to see her patients, or rides in stages, but the majority come to her dwelling in office hours. She never goes out at night except where she is acquainted. She has a small number of students. She has a speciality, but does not confine herself to it. She attends several families by the year, charging, I think, $200 a year. She thinks many intelligent ladies might, if they would qualify themselves thoroughly, succeed in establishing themselves as physicians.

21. Preachers. A friend once said "the professions of ministers and lawyers ought to accord. One is the interpreter of the divine law, the other of human law. A preacher is a lawyer for heaven." The promptings and workings of the human heart must be well understood by a minister. One in this holy office should not connive at the faults of her congregation, or give herself up to the acquirement of popular applause. We think one half the good accomplished in a church is done by the ladies of the church, particularly single women. And we know well that ministers are aware of this, and readily enlist the ladies of their congregations in good works. In old times, Angela de Foligno was celebrated as a teacher of theology. " In Spain, Isabella of Rosena converted Jews by her eloquent preaching, and commented upon the learned Scotus before cardinals and archbishops." In modern times, two or three ladies have studied theology, and preached with success. Mrs. Blackwell and Mrs. Jenkins are both said to be ladies of literary merit and genuine piety. Their mild, amiable, and lady-like deportment make them beloved by all who are sufficiently acquainted with to appreciate them. Some one writes : " It seems to me that woman, by her peculiar constitution, is better qualified to teach religion than by any merely intellectual discipline." Women are more susceptible to religious impressions than men. Two thirds of the communicants of our churches are of that sex. The Quakers, Shakers, and Methodists, we think, are the only denominations in which women speak in religious meetings. The founder of the Shakers was a woman—Ann Lee—who established her faith in 1776.

22. Proof Readers. The reading of proof has become a regular branch of business. Many of the large houses in cities where publishing is done, employ persons expressly for this purpose. We think proof reading opens a charming prospect to the employment of cultivated women. Girls could just as well be trained to read manuscripts aloud, for proof readers to correct their first sheets by, as boys. A proprietor of one of the largest publishing houses in this country kindly furnished us a reply to the question, what are the duties of a proof reader, and are ladies ever so employed ? Hoping it will not be considered a breach of courtesy to use the reply, we give it in the words of the writer : " Proof reading consists in the reading of proofs, marking the errors, and making the work typographically correct. A good proof reader ought to be a practical printer, as there are a thousand minute details which one can hardly learn except by daily experience at the composing case and imposing stone. In addition to this he should have more or less knowledge of various languages, ancient and modern, and be well informed in history, art, and science. Proof reading is considered the best situation in a printing office; and the most intelligent printers usually gain and hold these situations. We know of no case in which this duty is performed by a woman; the cases must be rare indeed in which one has had an opportunity to qualify her for performing its duties. Moreover, it is a position the duties of which must be performed in the printing office." It is true that proof reading must be done in the printing establishment; but separate rooms, we believe, are always provided for proof readers. So ladies need not be frightened by supposing they must do their reading in the composition room. One of the firm of the Boston Stereotype Foundry writes: " We employ but three young ladies to read proof, and pay from $3 to $5 per week. They are Americans, and work nine hours. At one time we employed women in the type-setting department, who received two thirds of the price paid to men. Women are paid less than men because they are *women*, and because plenty can be found. Women possessing a good English education can learn in two months—if apt, become expert. They commence at $3, and finally get $5. The prospect of employment is good for a few. Occasionally there is a dull time, which affords opportunity for a little sewing, &c. Unless very dull, the occupant retains her position and wages. Good workmen consider women an innovation. To sum up the whole matter in a few words, women (barring the heavy work) can perform the labor appertaining to proof reading and type setting as well as men." A lady told me that one of her daughters assists her father with his newspaper. She reads the proof, looks up articles he wants, helps select matter for the paper, and translates French stories for his paper. Her services are worth to him from $500 to $600 a year. On visiting the Bible House, I learned that a lady is there employed as proof reader. She corrects both in English and German. Four or five male proof readers are employed, but she is the only lady. She gets $5 or $6 a week. The principal proof reader gets $12 a week. " Accuracy, quickness of eye, thorough knowledge of orthography, grammar, and punctuation, with a knowledge of languages, and a vast deal of learning and general intelligence, are necessary for a proof reader. An intuitive perception, arising from this cultivation, enables one to detect errors immediately, often without knowing how and why."

23. Publishers. We find in the census report of Great Britain, 923 women reported as booksellers and publishers. What the number of publishers alone is we cannot tell, nor do we know whether any of them conduct the business on their own responsibility, or whether they are widows, and have men to conduct the

business for them.   We know of two large publishing houses in
New York that pay 10 cents on the dollar to an author for the
manuscript of any book they see proper to publish; that is, for a
book they will sell at retail for $1, and at wholesale for 60 cents,
the author receives 10 cents, which gives the publisher 50 cents
for getting up the book and running the risk of selling it.   If the
author incurs the expenses of getting the book up, they may allow 15
cents.   They will pay no larger a percentage for any subsequent
edition than for the first.   But they will not undertake a book
unless they think they can make money out of it.   The same
book might be printed and stereotype plates cast at 85 cents a
volume.   The author could then sell it for 65 cents a copy to the
book merchants, and they would sell it at 90 cents a volume.
After the first edition of one thousand, the author could probably
get it printed at 40 cents on the volume less.   If the book takes,
the merchant may allow the author twelve to fifteen per cent.
Some publishers purchase the copyrights of books they think
may succeed, paying a specified sum, as agreed on with the author.
Publishers calculate to have two out of every three books fail that
are brought into market.   Some publishers sell for authors on commission.   The authors get up their own books, and the publisher
sells, receiving forty per cent. from the retail price.   He sells to
the trade at a discount of from twenty-five to thirty-three per
cent., according to amount and distance.   The average discount
would be thirty per cent.   This leaves the publisher ten per cent.
to transact all the business, advertise, &c.   From the first edition
the publisher will not be likely to derive any profit; but if the
book takes, the publisher will make a handsome profit from the
subsequent editions.

24. Readers to the Working Classes.   In China,
at almost every store where cups of tea are sold, a number of men
make it a business to read to those that come in to buy or drink
tea.   A gratuity is bestowed by such as feel disposed.   The working classes that are not able to read and buy books, are thereby
enabled to have the benefit of those that can.   Now we do not
see why the same principle may not be carried out in this country.   Shakspearian readings, it is true, have been popular and
fashionable for a few years.   We have seen it stated that " seven
of Fanny Kemble Butler's recent Shakspearian readings in New
York city netted the fine sum of $6,000."   Beside, lectures
have been delivered and poems recited, mostly of the readers'
composition.   Now might not competent ladies make it useful to
the working classes of their own sex, or even both sexes, to spend
an evening, occasionally, in reading to them?   Charging a small
entrance fee, if there is a good attendance, would support the

reader, and enlighten the audience. It would be better if the poor, hard-working classes had more elevating and refining amusements. We know of none better calculated to improve while it entertains than reading. Might it not be done in saloons ?—properly qualified men in the gentlemen's department, and properly qualified women in the ladies' department. In our large cities, where time is so precious, many a lady, we doubt not, would give an additional sixpence to have a book she carries with her or the papers of the day read aloud while she eats her lunch. The only difficulty is, the prices paid would scarcely justify one sufficiently qualified for the undertaking.

25. Reporters. This is rather a new arena for the exercise of female talent. A reporter must be a close observer of matters and things in general that pertain to individual or public affairs. A verbal or written account is furnished to the publication in which the reporter is interested. A reporter attends public assemblies of any kind, and writes down or stenographizes the proceedings of said assembly. In a city, places of amusement, lectures, political and church meetings, form subjects of interest to a newspaper reporter. Noting the proceedings of legislative and other legal assemblies forms the most regular and reliable employment. In London, there are seven publications that employ from ten to eighteen reporters each, during the meetings of Parliament. Two from each paper are always in attendance— one in the gallery of the House of Lords, and another in the gallery of the House of Commons. A reporter seldom remains more than two or three hours. His place is taken by another, while he writes out his notes and prepares them for the press. The reporters are well remunerated, and give very faithful reports. In the United States, the subscription price of even the very best papers, and their comparatively limited circulation, will not justify so great an expense for the reporter's department. Yet most good papers have one or two reporters. Not long since, a lady stenographer received $1,000 damages from a railroad company, for an accident that occurred on the car, which unfitted her for her calling, as it deprived her of the forefinger on her right hand. A lady reporter, in Boston, writes me : " The art of reporting needs constant drilling, like music, dancing, &c. Few women have the education and nerve for professional reporting." A lady teacher of phonography writes : " A person of common capacity could learn phonography in from four to six months, studying three hours per day ; but to practise for reporting is quite another thing : that depends upon the unremitting industry of a person. I know of but two ladies whose business is reporting. It is hard work, but pays well." This lady also states that her terms of tuition are seventy-five cents per lesson of one hour. "Phonographers generally receive from ten to twenty dollars an hour; and it takes about five or six hours to write out what may be spoken in an hour, if done by one person. With an amanuensis, it takes about four hours of writing to one of speaking." Several ladies are acting in Ohio and Michigan as phonographic reporters. Mr. James T. Brady, in a public speech in New York, said : "Without disparagement to his friends who were here engaged in catching the extemporized words of the speaker, he really would be happy to see the day when women, who had the capacity, should be engaged in making reports." "Among the American Indians, the women, being present at councils, preserve in their memories the report of what passes, and repeat it to their children. They have traditions of treaties a hundred years back, which, when compared with our writings, are always exact." A telegraphic reporter told me a first-class reporter can earn from twenty-five to thirty dollars for three or four hours' labor. It requires a knowledge of stenography, of which there are several teachers in New York, and which can be learned in a short time. Some reporters are paid by the week; and some by the page of foolscap, which is considered, I think, as counting eighty words. Mr. B., a reporter of New York, had a sister in Washington with him, ten years ago, who attended the sittings of Congress, and took notes, and wrote them out fully. Her brother then revised and sent them to the press. Another lady attempted it for the *Tribune*, but was ridiculed, and very foolishly gave it up. I was told that Mrs. W., wife of a reporter for the *Tribune*, took notes of Dr. Chapin's sermon on Thanksgiving day, and made a report for the *Tribune*, with which the readers of the paper were well satisfied. The reply of Mr. Webster to Mr. Hayne was saved by Mrs. Gales, the wife of one of the Congressional reporters, by writing out her husband's short-hand notes, which he for the lack of time found it impossible to do. Otherwise that remarkable speech of an eminent orator would have been lost. Mr. L. remarked to me: "A reporter in New York has to move and write with railroad speed. Everything needs to be done with a rush; and so dense are crowds, that a woman would have to lay aside hoops to make her way."

26. Reviewers. A reviewer of new books should be a rapid reader and of quick understanding. A reviewer should also be a person of judgment. The vast number of books now published might afford employment, and a good compensation, we suppose, to those so engaged. But too often publishers use a moneyed influence in giving a false reputation to their publications. Frequently the editors of magazines and newspapers are their own reviewers.

We heartily wish that reviewers would endeavor to check the circulation of some of the light literature of the day. We refer not so much to that which is vapid—unsubstantial—wanting stamina —as that which is impure—immoral. Much is of a kind to open the floodgates of vice and crime. Stories cast in the old-fashioned mould of hair-breadth escapes, marvellous incidents, and impossible events, are less popular than formerly. No doubt much reading is done as a recreation—to forget one's self—to banish care—to unbend from severe study : let such reading at least be pure and chaste. Books undoubtedly exercise a great influence over the disposition, taste, and character ; and reviewers have it much in their power to direct the general taste for books. They can do much toward forming a high and correct literary tone in society. The number of those who devote themselves to the review of new books in England is small—in the United States, still smaller. How they are paid I am unable to learn.

27. Teachers. Teaching, in its various branches, would form a large volume ; but we will endeavor to take as general, yet comprehensive, a view of the subject as our limits will permit. The instruction of youth has ever been an honorable and useful calling : in an enlightened and refined community an institution of the first class always stands high. The influence of a teacher over her pupils is almost unbounded. Pupils watch the looks and actions of their teachers with a closeness of observation surprising to those unaccustomed to children. A teacher should strive to be consistent, for any palpable inconsistency will greatly lessen the respect of scholars. There are many systems of teaching ; many plans ; many theories. Much may be learned from visiting schools, and selecting, for one's own use, such improvements as suggest themselves. But the most valuable assistant in teaching is a thorough and extensive knowledge of mental and moral philosophy. They bear directly on the subject. They will prove the best guides, if penetration and judgment, patience and perseverance are used in the application. There are laws governing mind just as there are laws governing matter. Learn the opinions and wishes of parents as far as possible, but always act independently. Never permit yourself to be trammelled by them. The European method of giving instruction is by lectures. The plan is used in the professional schools of our country, and to some extent in our colleges, but in our seminaries, academies, and high schools the method is seldom practised. The inability of a hearer to apply to a lecturer, in case the subject is not understood, or the meaning of the lecturer not rightly apprehended, renders the method as a general thing objectionable to the young and inexperienced. Where students are instructed by lectures, a thorough examination on the lectures should be made the day after, and an explanation given if any parts are not rightly understood. One difficulty with a lecturer to the young is likely to be in gaining their entire attention, and presenting ideas to them in a clear, forcible manner. In the majority of girls' schools no oral instruction is given. Recitations are heard from text books, and frequently the pupils are unable to understand what they, parrot-like, recite in class. We think a combination of the two plans mentioned is best; that is, for the teacher to deliver lectures on some subjects, and hear recitations from text books on others. The more oral instruction given by a competent instructor the better. A teacher needs ability to command order, to promote discipline, and work systematically. A teacher should endeavor to produce harmony and a proper balance among the mental faculties, while they are being expanded. No unnatural and undue prominence should be given to any one of the faculties. Too many exercise the memory only. Those studies that will be most serviceable to a pupil should be pursued. Religious principles, common sense, good health, and a uniformly cheerful disposition are necessary to make a good teacher. A teacher should well understand the springs of human action. Add to these, ability to discriminate, perfect command of temper, unwearied perseverance, patience that never flags, and tact for imparting knowledge, and you have the desiderata for a most excellent teacher. If there is any office in life that calls for the exercise of every virtue, it is that of a teacher. It is the most responsible office in life except that of parent. Teaching is a vocation peculiarly fitted to women, and will ever be open to women of superior talents and extensive attainments. In worth and dignity it is inferior to none of the professions of men. It is finally taking its place among the learned professions. Female education has been too superficial. A more thorough and extensive course is needed in most of our schools. Woman must be taught to think for herself, and to act for herself. She needs to depend more on her own abilities—requires more self-reliance. Miss Beecher maintains that there is no defect in temper, habits, manners, or in any intellectual and moral development, which cannot be remedied. There are said to be more than 2,000,000 of children in our land out of school, and requiring 100,000 teachers to supply them. We would not give the impression that if 100,000 ladies were to prepare themselves to teach, they would find 100,000 places awaiting them. No; we believe the supply now fully meets the demand; and we are sorry to see the impression being so often given by editors and others, that teachers are needed

THE TEACHERS.   36

and in demand; because we think many ladies of limited means
are thereby induced to spend what little they have in preparing
themselves to be teachers; and when they are qualified, ten
chances to one, if they get a school, it is only for three months out
of the twelve, and that not regularly.   A precarious subsistence
is obtained, and, to those without homes, certainly a most unrelia-
ble one.   We love to see ladies educated, and would gladly see
them all qualified to teach; but we do not like to see inducements
thrown out to qualify themselves, under the impression that there
are hundreds of places vacant only because they cannot obtain
teachers.   There is no employment more uncertain than that of a
teacher.   Many causes tend to produce this.   Among them are
dissatisfaction on the part of teacher or people, low wages, the
fluctuating condition of country schools at different seasons of the
year, a large mass of people not knowing the advantages of an
education, and the want of endowed institutions of learning.   If
a lady has sufficient capital to establish herself permanently as a
teacher, she will be far more likely to succeed.   As new places
are settled and population advances there will no doubt be openings, but they will require teachers willing to endure the hard-
ships and privations incident to a new country.   Some lady
teachers might get employment if they would go to the country,
but the variety and excitement of the city they are not willing to
relinquish.   An active life is happiest, and none, if well filled,
affords more constant employment than that of a teacher.   Evening schools are established in most of our large cities, for the accommodation of those that labor through the day.   In New York
these schools are in session two hours, and a teacher receives one
dollar an evening.   Some lady teachers are employed in schools
for the blind and for the deaf and dumb.   In Germany, teachers
are treated with a degree of respect and delicacy that should
serve as a model to other countries.   The acquisition of knowledge has long been too mechanical an operation.   Girls are expected to receive as undoubted truths all they meet with in their
school books.   They are not taught to pause and consider if
statements are grounded on certain or uncertain premises.   They
are not taught to exercise their own thoughts and judgment.
School agencies in the large cities of the North are establishing
branches in the South and West.   Where there is no established
organization of this kind, families and neighborhoods are often
at a loss how to obtain a governess or teacher, while a teacher
is equally at a loss to know of such situations as she desires.
There is considerable difference in the character and qualifications
of the teachers sent out by the different agencies of New York.
Connected with these agencies might be a means of communica-

tion for obtaining amanuenses, copyists, and translators. Few
parents are willing to intrust their children to those who are not
trained for their business. The establishment of schools for the
preparation of teachers is one of the great inventions of the age.
There is one in almost every State. There was, and probably still
is, an educational association, that centres in New York city,
which has for its object the *free* instruction of a limited number
of young ladies desirous of preparing themselves for teachers.
One of the institutions is in Dubuque, Iowa; the other in
Milwaukee, Wisconsin. The principal of the Normal School,
New York, receives $600 a year, and he does not hear a single
recitation. He spends five hours in the room every Saturday,
which, for all the year of 48 weeks, equals 240 hours—nearly $3
an hour, merely for the light of his countenance. The number
of governesses in England is very large. Their duties are more
severe and their remuneration less than in any other country.
In the United States, governesses receive higher salaries in the
Southern than the Northern States, and are treated more like
members of the family. The salaries of teachers are also higher,
but it costs more to live in the South. One way in which so
many men get situations as teachers to the exclusion of females,
" may be attributed, in a degree, to favoritism of Odd Fellows'
and other social and political bonds." As time advances, more
attention will be given by the ladies to special branches of education. There will be professors of mathematics, languages, &c.,
just as there are in male institutions. Each one will cultivate
most highly a knowledge of that science to which her talents and
wishes incline. In the public schools of New York, there are
thirty-nine gentlemen conducting the male departments, who
receive a salary of $1,500 per year; while, of the lady principals
of the female departments, there are only ten getting a salary of
$800, the highest salary paid a lady in the public schools of New
York. There are said to be 1,183 female teachers in New York
city. In Louisville, Ky., the gentleman principals of the gram-
mar schools receive a salary of $1,000 a year, the lady principals
$650. In the male and female high schools, the principals
receive $1,600 a year. The lady preceptress in the female high
school has a salary of $900. The lady who teaches mathematics
in the Female Presbyterian College of Louisville receives a salary
of $900. In Chicago, the maximum salary of female teachers is
$400 a year. In the Cleveland Female Seminary, in 1854, the
lady teacher of rhetoric and English literature received a salary
of $500 and board; of English branches, $500 and board; of
history, $500 and board; of mathematics, $500 and board. We
have seen it stated that female teachers are growing scarce in

Maine, because the wages are so low. " At the New York Central College for students of both sexes, there is one female professor in the faculty, and she receives the same salary as the other members, and has the same voice." It is a manual labor school, where the same justice is not exercised in regard to the pupils, as the " male students get eight cents per hour for labor, females but four cents an hour." In the twelfth ward of New York city, the subject of paying lady teachers the same salaries as those of the other sex was agitated last winter: the result I did not hear. Higher prices are paid to lady teachers in Boston than any other city of the United States, except the cities of California, where ladies conducting the same branches as gentlemen receive as good salaries. The majority of teachers in San Francisco are ladies. In the United States there are 150,000 teachers in the public schools, and 4,000,000 scholars. " There is one scholar for every five free persons ; in Great Britain there is one scholar to every eight persons; in France, one to every ten persons." According to an estimate made by Rev. T. W. Higginson, there are in fourteen of the United States, in all schools, both public and private, 152,339 male teachers, and 162,687 female teachers. In the New England States, according to his estimate, there are 45,619 male teachers, and 87,645 female teachers. In the Western States. settled mostly by New Englanders, we find the proportion of lady teachers greatest. We hope the number of lady teachers may increase in the different States in proportion to the increase of the population. In Brooklyn, L. I., there is a female seminary endowed by Mrs. Packer, which usually, we believe, has an attendance of between 300 and 400 pupils. " Matthew Vassar, Esq., of Poughkeepsie, it is said, has devoted a sum which will soon amount to $400,000 to the endowment of a college for girls in that city. He hopes to make it a rival of Yale, Brown, and Harvard. It is not to be free, but the tuition rates will be very low. In the plan provision is made for a library, cabinets, apparatus, galleries of art, botanical gardens, and the like. If well carried out, this institution may be a lasting monument to the wisdom and benevolence of Mr. Vassar."

28. Teachers of Bookkeeping. In the catalogue of Comer's Commercial College, Boston, we find the following statement : " As an inducement to ladies to prepare themselves for mercantile employments, a discount of twenty per cent. from the terms for gentlemen is made, although the course of instruction is precisely the same." Twelve free scholarships have been founded in the institution for deserving cases of either sex. With all

large commercial schools is now connected a separate department for ladies; and efforts are made by the principals to obtain
situations for their pupils as they leave school. A letter from
Misses McIntire and Kidder, Boston, states: "We have been
engaged in preparing ladies for bookkeepers, saleswomen, &c., for
the past ten years. It was at first difficult for ladies to obtain
such situations; but as those who did succeed gave entire satisfaction, others were induced to give them a trial; and now they
are very generally employed in our retail stores, at prices varying from four to eight dollars per week, and a few at a still
higher salary. The time required for a person who has received
a common English education, is from six weeks to three months.
The terms for the complete course in bookkeeping, which em-
braces improvement in writing, with rapid methods of calculat-
ing interest and averaging accounts, are $14; and for bookkeeping
only, $12; and three months' time is allowed. The chances
for obtaining employment are very favorable, as more situations
are opened to them every year. Each student is instructed
separately and assistance rendered in obtaining employment.
Bookkeepers are usually employed ten hours a day. The employment is not so unhealthy as needlework. Women are superior to men in faithfulness in the performance of duties." The
principal of a mercantile college in Brooklyn says he thinks
"many ladies might obtain employment as bookkeepers, if they
would only properly qualify themselves for the duties. He had
six or seven lady pupils that are now employed as bookkeepers
in New York. Their compensation depends on their abilities and
the amount of labor they have to perform. They are not so
well paid as male bookkeepers. Much depends on the kind of
friends a lady has to secure her a place. It is the same case
with a young man. If he acquires a reputation for integrity and
faithfulness, he may get even as much as $2,500; while one more
obscure and unknown may be as competent, but not able to command more than one third as much. So, one may have to work
but a few hours; another, from eight in the morning until twelve
at night. Some have a great deal to do in some seasons, and
but little in others; while some are kept nearly equally busy all
the year." This gentleman charges $10 for instruction. Mr.
D., who teaches writing, bookkeeping, and arithmetic, in New
York, gives private instruction to ladies at his rooms. They are
comfortably fitted up. He charges for bookkeeping, practical
course of twenty lessons, $15; unlimited course, $25;—arithmetic, commercial course of twenty lessons, $10; of sixty les-
sons, $20. His charges for all branches required to prepare
pupils practically for business are, for one month, two or three

hours per day, $15; three months, $30; for twenty lessons in writing, public room, $10; private room, $15. Mr. B., of the firm of B. S. & Co., says a person of good abilities could learn bookkeeping in one month, by spending most of the day at it. His price for ladies is $25. It entitles them to an attendance at one of their branch schools, of which there are eight in the Northern and Western cities. They endeavor to secure places for those who learn bookkeeping with them. They also assist their pupils to open books when they have obtained situations. Millinery establishments, trimming and fancy stores, &c., are the kind that mostly employ women as bookkeepers. Many wives of business men learn bookkeeping, that they may keep their husbands' books.

29. Teachers of Gymnastics and Dancing. Dancing, calisthenics, and gymnastics furnish excellent exercise for young people, and in many boarding and day schools for young ladies gymnastics are now taught. A lady teacher of calisthenics and gymnastics told me that in winter a fire is kept in the dressing room, and in very cold weather the practising room is warmed a little. Gymnastics are performed with apparatus. Calisthenics are arm exercises. The terms of this teacher are $6 for one month, $15 for three months, and $20 for six months' tuition. In New York and Philadelphia there are schools where instruction is given to girls as well as boys in gymnastic exercises. At one gymnasium in New York the terms are $16 a year for tuition, $10 for six months, and $7 for three months. At a ladies' gymnasium in Brooklyn, I was told by the instructress that her prices for tuition are $4 a quarter in summer, giving three lessons a week. A physician prescribes the kind and amount of exercise necessary.

30. Teachers of Drawing and Painting. There is scarcely any branch of mechanical labor in which a knowledge of drawing is not an advantage. Correct drawing is essential to the success of an artist; but coloring is something very difficult and desirable, particularly the coloring of the flesh. It is indispensable to the portrait painter. A lady artist of some note told me that artists do not ground themselves in drawing as they should; that drawing tells almost the whole story of a picture: coloring only gives beauty and adds strength. She thinks there are many openings in the South and West for first-class teachers of drawing and painting. Miss G. received a salary of $800, as teacher of painting in the School of Arts in Baltimore. It is folly for any one to devote herself to art as a career, unless she has some genius and a fondness for it. Mrs. H., of Boston, the wife of the sculptor, has supported her family by painting and giving instruction in the art. Teachers in oil painting are well compensated, if they have pupils enough to occupy all their time. Prices vary in cities from fifty cents a lesson of one hour to two dollars. Art classes have been formed, both in New York and Philadelphia. Some artists receive pupils, but the time required for instruction renders it objectionable to most. Miss G. charges $15 a quarter of twenty-four lessons, two hours each. In ordinary times, she gives but one hour's instruction at a lesson. Miss J. charges $10 dollars for instruction in oriental painting. Mrs. C. was profitably engaged, in Providence, in teaching drawing and taking crayon portraits. One lady, who taught for several years with success, charged fifty cents a lesson, the pupils attending at her room. Those working in crayon in the New York school draw almost entirely from casts; those in the Philadelphia school, from plates. There is now a life school in New York, where instruction is given at $20 per quarter of eleven weeks—two lessons a week. For instruction in drawing from plates, $12 per quarter of eleven weeks. In some of our public schools, drawing is taught free of expense to the scholars.

31. Teachers of Fancy Work. The accomplishments of women are useful in their times and places. Music and drawing are elegant accomplishments, the earliest as well as the most universal pastimes known. Those teachers of accomplishments that have acquired a reputation can command in a city a high price. At Madame D.'s, crochet work and embroidery are taught at 25 cents a lesson of one hour. Misses H., Philadelphia, give five lessons in leather work for $6, and charge, for giving instruction in wax fruit and flowers, paper and rice paper flowers, &c., $1 a lesson; in embroidery in silk, gold bullion, &c., $15 for twenty lessons—the same for hair flowers and bead work; for the arrangement of shells with mosses and grasses, $1 a lesson. Madame N., who teaches crochet work and fancy knitting, charges 50 cents an hour. One stitch can be learned by a quick person in an hour. She thinks there is plenty of that kind of work to supply all and even more hands than are so occupied. She employs a number, and pays by the piece. They work at home, and can earn from $3 to $4 a week.

32. Teachers of Horsemanship. The prices of the riding school, New York, attended by the most aristocratic classes, are: 16 lessons, $20; 10 lessons, $15; 5 lessons, $8; single lessons, $2; road lesson, one pupil, $5; two or more pupils, each $3. For exercise riding, single ride, one hour, $1.50; single ride, half hour, $1. After taking 16 or more lessons, the prices are somewhat reduced. At another riding school in New York, the terms are: 20 lessons for gentlemen, $25; 20 lessons for ladies,

$20; 10 lessons for gentlemen, $15; 10 lessons for ladies, $12; single lessons, $2. The rules are very good, and laid down in the circulars. At another riding school in New York the prices are: $20 for 20 lessons, $12 for 10 lessons, $7 for 5 lessons; single lessons, $1.50; road lessons, one person, $5; road lessons, three or more, each $3; 20 exercise rides for $15; evening rides for $1; road rides, 10 for $8; single, $1; road ride to a lady, $2.50. The regulations are very good. The expenses for keeping up a riding school are considerable; so it may not prove as profitable as the prices would seem to indicate.

33. Teachers of Infant Schools. Teaching is interesting to those that love children. But I would say, let not those without patience and tenderness, or those whose feelings can in an hour change from the boiling to the freezing point, attempt to teach young children. In ordinary schools, young children are liable to be either cramped or stunted. If children must be placed at school early, let it be where they can exercise their little bodies frequently, and not be confined in school long at a time. To accomplish this, we think the infant school the most efficient. Lord Brougham gives it as his opinion that a child learns more the first eighteen months of its life than at any other period; and that it settles, in fact, at this early age, its mental capacity and future well-being. Mr. Babbington fixes the period of the first nine years as the seedtime of life. Some object to infant schools, on the ground that they divert the mind, and unfit it for continued and concentrated thought in after life. But we cannot think so, unless the course is pursued an unreasonable length of time. The first two years of a child's schooling may be passed profitably in an infant school; at any rate, if the child enters as early as six years of age. Indeed, we think the variety embodied in the infant-school system is one of its most pleasing and useful features. The minds of children cannot rest long on any one subject, any more than their bodies can retain the same posture long at a time. It stagnates thought, prevents boldness of spirit, and stunts the growth of a young child to sit quiet hour after hour. Some mothers send their children early to school to have them out of their way. Such children could be more pleasantly and more efficiently taught in an infant school than in any other. Yet, we are rather inclined to the opinion that a child should be taught the alphabet at home. Gentle but firm treatment is necessary for children, who need much sympathy and affection; and it therefore requires the greatest patience on the part of a teacher, in order to conduct an infant school successfully. Infant schools are scarce in the United States; but still they exist in some parts of New England. There was an infant school in Troy, some time ago (and perhaps it is still in existence), in connection with one of the public schools. The infant-school system has been partially adopted in some of the public schools of our Western cities; and the same system applied to Sabbath schools has been extensively and happily carried into effect, both in the South and West. There are several infant Sabbath schools, of which we know, numbering considerably over one hundred children. These schools are usually conducted by ladies. The exercises are varied, as in day schools, and consist generally of chanting responses, catechism, memorizing from cards, telling Bible stories, lecturing, explaining pictures, singing, &c. This order of exercises, sustained in a lively manner, cannot fail to interest children, and make the school room for them a happy and longed-for place. Nature itself points out the course to be pursued in the education of a child : first, physical training; second, moral training; and third, mental training. Mind and body are so closely united that an injury to one is resented by the other. One is placed as a protector to the other, and will not permit injury to its companion with impunity.

34. Teachers of Languages. A knowledge of Latin is desirable for ladies that expect to devote much time to books. The study of it is fine discipline for the mind. The German and French are studied by many ladies : the French more for the purposes of light literature and conversation ; the German by those that wish to dive into metaphysics. These languages are, both, useful to ladies engaged in stores : the French mostly in New York city and in the South; the German more at the North and West. In Italy, at different times from the fifteenth to the nineteenth century, learned women occupied chairs in the universities, as professors of music, drawing, philosophy, mathematics, and the languages, both ancient and modern. The author of " Women and Work" says : " Women should teach languages and oratory. Aspasia taught rhetoric to Socrates. The voice of woman is more penetrating, distinct, delicate, and correct in delivering sounds than that of man, fitting her to teach both languages and oratory better." The prices paid for private instruction in the languages are higher than when received in a class, and run from 25 cents an hour to $1. A language is best taught by a native of the country in which said language is spoken.

35. Teachers of Music. Vocal music is taught in most of our schools, and is required to be taught in the public schools of Germany and Prussia. In Germany, instrumental music is also taught free of charge. It is not uncommon to see a German mechanic performing on the piano. Instrumental music is probably the most expensive accomplishment attending the education

THE MUSIC TEACHER. 44

of a young lady. Music is more generally cultivated in the United States than any other accomplishment. It is better appreciated by the mass, and, consequently, becomes more ingrafted in the national element. In a few years our musicians will probably equal the most celebrated of Europe. A skilful musician need never suffer in America. If competent to give instruction in music, there will be opportunities to do so in our cities. Most seminaries require one teacher of music, and often two or more.

36. Teachers of Navigation. "One of the best and most popular teachers of navigation and nautical mathematics and astronomy in England is a lady, Mrs. Janet Taylor. Her classes are celebrated, and numerously attended by men who have been at sea as well as by youths preparing for the merchant service." Not long since, she received a gold medal and a premium of £50 annually from the British Government.

37. Teachers of Swimming. There is a swimming school in Paris, containing as pupils ladies of all stations in life. Swimming schools for both sexes have been established in New York. In the one for ladies and girls instruction is given by one of their own sex, and a charge made of 25 cents a lesson. From the New York *Observer* we copy an article: "A few years ago, a gentleman well known in the philanthropic world established a school in New Jersey, not far from New York, with the intention of making physical training a prominent part of his educational system. He began with his own children and a few others. The school has gradually grown until it numbers eighty pupils, both boys and girls. Every pupil at this school is a gymnast; every one can row a boat; and every one, down to the smallest girl, can swim. The boys and girls are formed into separate boat clubs, seven to each club, rowing six oars, with the seventh for coxswain. So they row races whenever the weather permits, and they do not mind a little rough weather. Every day, too, during the warm season, they all have a swim. The boys swim by themselves; and the girls, in suitable bathing dresses, go elsewhere, with a teacher. One year of such training and exercises will lay up stamina for a lifetime." A school has been commenced in New York for teaching swimming out of the water, by machinery. The prices are 25 cents a lesson in a class, and $1 a lesson for private instruction.

38. Translators. Translations published in the United States are mostly made in England. Some languages are susceptible of a much more correct and graceful translation than others. It requires study to get the exact meaning of some authors, and taste and genius to convey that meaning. A literal interpretation will not always convey the meaning of an author as well as a looser translation getting more the spirit of the original. A person should have general information on the subject to be treated. A translator of history must be a good historian. It requires time to establish a reputation as a translator, but even a translator's career must have a beginning. Dr. G., who has charge of the editorial department of one of the most extensively circulated magazines in the United States, says translations from French and German are not so well liked in magazines as original matter, and anything to be translated for his magazine he does as a recreation from more serious duties. Owing to the international copyright law of England and France, a French author will send his manuscript over to England and have it rendered, securing the right to the translation. The translation often makes its appearance very nearly as soon as the original. Most of the valuable works in French have been translated. Mr. W. told me, however, that there are some scientific French works that might be rendered into English, and some on mechanics; but it would require some one acquainted with the subject, on account of the technical terms. Dr. G. thinks the chances a thousand against one that an individual could find constant employment translating. He has frequent applications from translators for work in that line. So we have reason to think translating is a very precarious occupation. The best way is to find some French book that will be popular in America, and translate it, and offer it to a publisher. Some translators look over catalogues of foreign books and examine such as they think will be likely to please. They take it to the publisher, who, if he thinks it will be available, gives the individual the task, if they can settle on satisfactory terms. A lady, who translates considerably, told me that she receives $5 a page for a finished translation from the French for magazines. Books are generally done for so much, according to the contract of the parties. The price charged for verbal translation would doubtless depend on the amount of time consumed; but for a written translation, the charge would be made by the page or volume. In most of the Government departments translators are employed, and their salaries are no doubt good. Interpreters are also employed in some of the courts, but they usually unite their occupation with that of copyist. In some private establishments interpreters are employed. Where there is sufficient business to occupy all the time of a lady, she would doubtless find her services as an interpreter lucrative.

ARTISTIC PURSUITS, AND EMPLOYMENTS CONNECTED WITH THE FINE ARTS.

39. Actresses. The circumstances under which a play-actor's life are seen are calculated to please the young and susceptible. They put a false estimate on the pleasures it affords. They are apt to forget that the moments in which performers appear on the stage all sparkling as the diamond sands and crystal pebbles of a brook, are the principal, perhaps the only bright ones of their lives. Many a sad spirit, many a broken heart is concealed under the glittering tinsel. We are not among those who denounce the theatre as a school of vice and infamy—nor could we conscientiously laud it as a school of virtue. We think the influence and effects depend very greatly upon the character of the plays; much, too, depends upon the individuals of the audience. There is no amusement that may not suffer in the abuse. Late hours, intoxicating drinks, and bad companions, in many cases form the curse of regular theatre-goers; and for these the plays (perhaps harmless in themselves) are charged with being demoralizing. Good plays have an intellectual fascination. We think the drama might be made more a school of instruction and innocent pastime—less a school of evil tendencies. In China and Japan, the female parts in theatrical performances are never executed by women. No women ever appeared on the stage of the Greeks or Romans. Even the female characters in Shakspeare were not represented by women in his time. The first lady that appeared on the stage took the parts of Juliet and Ophelia in 1660. The publicity attending the life of an actress makes it repulsive to many, and the egotism that the profession engenders is an objectionable feature. That there are good and virtuous people connected with the theatre we cannot for a moment question; but some of the men are worthless and dissipated, and many of the girls and women engage in it because they see no other way of earning their bread. Many a ballet girl has danced to support an infirm mother or orphan brothers and sisters. The roving life of an actress and want of home influences are not conducive to the growth of domestic virtues. Yet some actresses have married advantageously in Europe, and been respected in social life, not less for their virtues than their talents. The craving of admiration incident to the calling is apt to make an actress vain. Her fondness for excitement, and her consciousness of importance in the eyes of those who patronize her, furnish additional fuel to the fire If she makes a failure, she may die of chagrin. Mr. B., a dramatic agent, thinks there is always a supply as soon as there is a demand for dramatic performers. They cannot enter and leave the profession, like any other. They must be actively engaged in it all the time, or leave it. Their talents must be carefully considered, and they placed in the company that requires them, and in such places as suit their talents. If a play in which they excel is to be performed in a distant city, they accompany the troupe to which they belong. A company consists of a combination of various talents. The number employed is not fluctuating, but they change their localities often; that is, go from city to city and town to town, shifting their place as seems best. They are compensated according to talent and proficiency—from $3 a week to $150. They are usually paid according to the contract made with them. I think the voice of actors when off the stage is peculiar. It is deep and hollow, as if trained to be thrown to a distance. By the drama two of the senses which afford most pleasure are entertained—the eye and the ear. Madame Celeste made $50,000 clear in this country; Essler, $70,000. The play, "Our American Cousin," is said to have cleared $40,000 in New York. Mr. P., a dramatic agent, told me that actresses are paid according to their position and talent. A ballet girl is paid from $3 to $6 a week, if by the season. Wallack pays $5 or $6. Utility people are paid from $6 to $10. Prices depend very much on who and what the people are, and the class of theatre by which they are employed. Those of the better class are paid from $25 to $60 a night. When they are not required they are not paid anything. In Europe, some of the theatres are open during the summer. In New York a paper has lately been commenced, devoted almost exclusively to the drama. "Our great star actors, Mr. Forrest or Miss Cushman, command their hundreds of dollars a night. The handsome Brignoli or the ponderous Amodio will not dispense their silver notes short of fabulous thousands of golden dollars per month. Those who try the life of an actor speedily discover that, of all hard-working men, few render more constant, wearing, unceasing labor for their money, than those who conscientiously do their duty in a theatre. Multitudinous and constantly varying requirements are made of an actor who has achieved a leading position. He *must* be a linguist, an elocutionist, a fencer, a dancer, a boxer, a painter (for the proper coloring or 'making up' of his own face and figure is no small part of his art), a soldier (so far as a knowledge of military drill and the manual exercise is concerned); and he should be a singer, and a bit of an author. In a theatre where a drama unfamiliar to the com-

THE ACTRESS.   48

pany is produced every night, or in case of a new 'star,' who plays his own pieces, a day's work of an actor may be set down as follows: To learn by heart a part not exceeding six 'lengths' (a length is forty-two lines), attend rehearsal from ten to one or two, and act at night in one or two pieces. That is, six lengths new study, rehearsal, and playing at night, is what may be required of an actor for a day's work, without giving occasion for grumbling at the managers. There are many actors who, upon an urgent occasion, will study from ten to fifteen lengths in a day, besides attending to their other duties. This, however, is never required except in case of sudden sickness of another performer, or some similar extraordinary event. In provincial theatres the actors are worked much harder than in New York, and paid much less. The starring system universally prevails, which necessitates a constant succession of new plays, most of which have to be studied from night to night, as a play is not often acted two nights in succession in small cities. But when a piece has a successful 'run,' the actors have no new study for several weeks. Actors are usually engaged for certain lines of business; that is, each one engages to perform only such style of characters as he is best qualified to personate. The remuneration of actors comes next into consideration, and the scale has a wide range, from $3 a week up to $200 a night. This last sum was for years the demand of Mr. Edwin Forrest. Other stars are generally content with certain 'sharing terms;' that is, the gross receipts, after a certain specific amount has been deducted for the expenses of the theatre, are equally divided between the star and the manager. Thus, for example, if the expenses of the house are $300 per night, and the receipts $400, the lucky star and the fortunate manager pocket $50 each per night. This is the fairest basis on which to conduct the starring system, because, by this plan, the salaries of all the stock company are assured *first*, and the profit of the star depends on his own power of attracting the public to the theatre. In New York the salaries paid to stock actors are higher, on the average, than those in any other city in the United States. The managers ignore, to a great extent, the technical 'lines of business,' and engage the best artists that can be had, and then have plays especially written, in which each of their leading actors shall have a part suited to his peculiar powers. While this plan secures to the New York public the finest acting that can be seen in the country, it also entails upon the managers a salary list of dimensions that would swamp a provincial theatre in a single week. The leading actors, as Messrs. Lester, Blake, and Walcot, at Wallack's Theatre; Messrs. Jefferson, Jordan, and Pearson, at the Winter Garden;

Messrs. Mark Smith and Vincent, at Laura Keene's Theatre, receive from $50 to $100 per week. Salaries for women are about half, or perhaps two thirds of what are paid to men holding corresponding positions. General utility men, supernumeraries, and ballet girls receive from $3 to $10 per week. When an unusual number of ' ladies of the ballet,' or supernumeraries of the other sex are required, on some extra occasion, they are specially engaged, at 50 cents a night, or sometimes for even less money. The salaries on the east side of the city, at the Bowery Theatre, are lower than on Broadway, the principal actors seldom receiving more than $35 or $40 per week, and the others are in proportion. In smaller cities, as Buffalo, Detroit, Chicago, &c., the highest sum paid to a performer seldom exceeds $25 per week. Actors who have achieved a position which warrants them in demanding it, stipulate for a ' benefit ' in addition to their salaries. On these occasions, a third or a half of the gross receipts of the evening is paid over to the performer, according as his agreement is for a ' third clear ' or a ' half clear ' benefit."

40. Aquaria Makers. One of the most innocent and pleasing amusements that has attracted attention for some time is the making of aquaria. The cases are formed of plate glass, square, oblong, circular, or any shape to please the fancy of the owner. The glass is tightly sealed when joined. The aquaria are of two kinds : one is formed of salt water, and contains marine plants and animals; the other contains fresh water, and such plants and animals as are found in rivers and smaller streams. They form a beautiful addition to a garden, conservatory, or drawing room. Rocks form the foundation, and the soil on them furnishes subsistence to the plants. Zoophytes, mollusca, and fish form the inhabitants of the aquarium. Insects also find a place in this miniature " ocean or river garden." The size for parlors is from one foot to three in length. The largest aquaria in this country are now on exhibition at Barnum's Museum, New York. " They comprise over one thousand specimens of living animals and vegetation. In these tanks the water is seldom changed, the natural operations of the plants and animals keeping it always pure." They are made to order in New York, and we think might afford a pleasant pastime to some, and pecuniary profit to others. A work giving directions for making them has been published in New York. The author is a Mr. Butler, who has got up the mammoth aquaria in Barnum's Museum. There are two establishments in New York where they may be ordered, and specimens seen. " Before we leave the margin of the sea, we must just glance at the smaller occupations pursued there by women. The most considerable of these was once the gathering and burning of kelp; but chemical science has nearly put an end to that. There is still a great deal of raking and collecting going on. In some countries half the fields are manured with small fish and the offal of larger, and sea weeds and sand. Then there is the gathering of jet and amber, and various pebbles, and the polishing and working of them. The present rage for studies of marine creatures must afford employment to many women who have the shrewdness to avail themselves of it."

41. Architects. We scarcely know to what extent this branch of business can come within the province of woman. Yet it is as practicable, perhaps, as some we mention. Civil architecture is the only one open to women. In this art we are as a people little more than novices; yet great improvements are going on. In a century's time, perhaps, the art in this country will have obtained the perfection of ancient nations. Properzia di Rossi, born in Bologna, 1490, is said to have furnished some admirable plans in architecture. The author of " Women Artists" mentions as designers in architecture, Madame Steenwyck, of the Dutch school, and Esther Juvenal, of Nuremberg. She also gives the name of a lady who was a practical architect in Rome, in the seventeenth century—Plautilla Brizio—who has left monuments of her excellence in that species of art. The villa Giraldi, near Rome, is the joint work of this lady and her brother. "The wife of Erwin von Steinbach materially assisted her husband in the erection of the famous Strasbourg cathedral; and within its walls a sculptured stone represents the husband and wife as consulting together on the plan." The most varied and general information is desirable for a first-class architect. A knowledge of drawing and the first principles of geometry are the most important requisites. Some architects select the materials for the building, which of course requires a knowledge of the different kinds and conditions of wood, their fitness for various parts of a building; also, the qualities of iron, stone, brick, and whatever goes toward making up the building. An architect should also select the most suitable site for the erection of the intended structure, which would be decided, to some extent, by the way in which it was to be used. He also should be able to judge the nature of the soil, and the way in which a want of fitness may be remedied. Then he must see that the foundation is securely laid; and, as the building progresses, that the workmen carry out the details of the plan which he furnishes. Much of this work seems unsuitable for women; but the making and executing of plans could be very well done by them. It would give exercise to their taste and inventive talents. Men employed in architectural drawing earn from $1.25 to $3 a day of ten hours. Miss H. told me of a wealthy lady in New York who is quite an architect by nature. Mrs. D. told me of a young lady of her acquaintance who is gifted with talents that would make a superior architect. She has planned several houses for her father, who has sold them at an advance of from $3,000 to $4,000, on account of the convenient arrangement of the rooms and their tasteful decoration. She displays exquisite taste in the selection and arrangement of furniture. She is withal economical in her expenditures. She is a close calculator of the cost of materials, and a great economist of space.

42. Cameo Cutters.   There are two kinds of cameo cutting—one with a lapidary's wheel, of hard stones, as the onyx and the sardonyx.   The shell cameos are cut with small steel chisels, from the white portion of the shell, leaving the chocolate color for the background.   The figures are in relief.   The stone is prepared by the lapidary, and the artist arranges his design according to the capabilities of the stone.   He makes a drawing in paper on an enlarged scale, and a model in wax of the exact size, and the latter is carefully compared with the stone, and such alterations made as the markings on the stone seem to require. The outline is then sketched on the surface, and cut with tools prepared for that purpose.   After it has been properly cut, it is smoothed and polished.   In Mrs. Lee's " Sculpture and Sculptors " we find an account of those that have engaged in cameo cutting in the United States.   Mrs. Dubois, of New York, cut several cameo likenesses of her friends, and so well did she succeed that she went to Italy to acquire proficiency in the art; but the artist to whom she applied said he could teach her nothing—she had only to study the antique.   John C. King, a sculptor of Boston, has also engaged in the art of cutting cameos; and Peter Stephenson, of Boston, had cut in 1853 between 600 and 700 cameo likenesses.   He writes me : " Cameo cutting might be done by girls, especially the finishing process—polishing.   When in Italy, some years ago, I employed girls to polish my cameos, and paid from 12 to 50 cents apiece.   I think they earned about $1 a day.   The employment is not unhealthy, but confining."   Margaret Foley, formerly a member of the New England school of design, resided in Lowell, and cut cameos at $35 apiece.   She was kept busy in filling orders.   The Misses Withers, of Charleston, S. C., are said to cut cameo likenesses with beauty and skill.   I saw Mr. L. a Frenchman, in New York, copying a likeness from a daguerreotype.   He also copies from life.   He learned the business in Paris.   He charges $15 for those large enough for a breastpin, and which it requires him about three days to make; smaller ones are lower in price. He imports the stones, and furnishes without extra charge to those for whom he works. A good intaglio worker can make cameos, but a cameo worker cannot make intaglios. Some men can never learn the business. It would form a beautiful pastime and a profitable and refined occupation for a lady, if sufficient work could be obtained.

43. Copperplate Engravers. In a hasty reading of "Women Artists," we find mention made of a number of ladies occupied at various times, in different European countries, as copperplate engravers: in the sixteenth century, one in Holland, and one in Italy; in the seventeenth century, Germany produced seven, France one, Spain one, and Italy three; in the eighteenth century, Italy two, France one, and Denmark one. It may have been that some escaped my notice. Mr. S. told me he knew a family of copperplate engravers; but the daughters are now married. I saw a lady who engraves on copper; she had an office in New York. She was willing to instruct a lady on these terms: after the pupil had acquired about six months' practice, she would allow her half for all the work she did in six months more; then she could be at liberty to work for herself. She thinks a year sufficient time to acquire a good knowledge and practice of card engraving. She had spent a year at it irregularly, having no instructor, but asking advice and assistance now and then. In that way she did not obtain the custom she would have done by being known to others. The patience and careful attention to details requisite, and the sedentary nature of engraving, render it a more suitable occupation for women than men. To make a good card engraver, an educated eye, a steady hand, and ability to form letters gracefully, are the principal requisites. A card engraver told me he knew a lady who assisted her husband in his work, that of copperplate engraving. As the people of the United States become wealthy, and cultivate a taste for the fine arts, engravers will be more patronized. There is a collection of old and choice copperplate engravings in the possession of Mr. Plassman, who has a school of art in New York; there is also such a collection at the Historical rooms in the same city.

44. Daguerreans. The process consists in concentrating the light of the sun on a metal plate, so prepared by chemicals as to retain the impression of an image that falls upon it. The shadow catcher has become almost interwoven with the every-day realities of life. Prof. Draper speaks of daguerreotyping as introducing a beautiful work, in which "the fair sex may engage without compromising a single delicate quality of woman's nature." Some artists, not content with moving in the ordinary way from place to place, have cars built that roll on wheels and are drawn by horses. The daguerrean sleeps in his little home, and, on the road, far away from a good tavern, can even do his own cooking, or have it done, in his car. The business has also been carried on by men in small boats, floating down rivers and stopping at villages and farm houses. It requires taste and judgment both to make an operator and to color. Colorers of photographs could, if skilful and constantly employed, earn $30 a week in large cities. An operator, if busy, works from 9 to 5 o'clock in winter. A wonderful improvement has taken place in the daguerrean art since its discovery. A lady daguerrean and photographer writes me : " Ladies are employed in the business as operators, and to superintend ; also to repaint and retouch photographs. With care in the use of chemicals, I do not consider it particularly unhealthy; less so, I think, than sewing by hand or machine. No person will do well for himself, herself, or patrons, who commences business without a good knowledge of it. The time of learning will depend upon the individual's knowledge of the sciences bearing on photography, and their talent for the business. It would vary from two weeks to three months. The labor of the learner is usually given while learning, and from $25 to $100 besides. Spring and fall are the best seasons, summer the poorest; but there is no time during the year in which there is not something to do. I operate and superintend in my own establishment, and hire a boy only, who does chores. The principal discomforts of the business are the heat to which we are exposed in summer (being usually and necessarily near the roof), the smell of chemicals (which do not unpleasantly affect any one), and the soiling of clothing, which is more unavoidable with women. The amount of business, and consequently the location, decide the profits of the business. As the business is attended with considerable expense, it is necessary, in order to make it pay, to seek a good location. It is profitable when a person is well established in a desirable location. I think ladies and children usually prefer a lady artist. Upon the whole, I think the business quite as suitable for women as men. There is generally more or less spare time, but a woman is most apt to occupy such time with fancy work or reading." A daguerrean writes: " Women are sometimes employed in the reception room to receive ladies—occasionally, in the operating room. They receive from $3 to $8, according to capacity and address. Men generally command better prices, because they can sometimes perform labor out of a woman's sphere, such as unpacking goods, carrying packages, and other jobs, not suitable for women. I think the business as healthy as any indoor business. It requires from six to twelve months to learn the duties of the operating room; for the reception room, from one to three weeks. Industry, patience, perseverance, shrewdness, and suavity of manners, are the necessary qualifications. Prospect for employment poor, as prices are reduced to almost nothing. All seasons are nearly alike. November and June are dull. Our women work in summer from seven A. M. to six P. M. The work averages about eight hours per day the year through. Men are superior in patience (?) and force of character. Women are easily discouraged, and liable to be petulant. In many instances, there is much running up and down stairs, which is harder on women than men. And there is too much standing for a woman's health."

45. Schools of Design. Schools of design were established 444 B. C., for the purpose of improvement in making statuary. The arts declined when Europe was overrun by barbarous tribes, but in the eleventh century began to recover, and in 1350 several painters, sculptors, and architects formed an academy of design at Florence. In Paris there are seven schools of design for males, and two for females, supported by the city. There are seventy schools of design in Great Britain, and there is an annual exhibition of their work in London, where premiums are awarded. It is about twenty years since the schools were commenced in England. In 1854 nearly 1,500 students had been educated in the School of Arts in Edinburgh. There are schools of design in New York, Philadelphia, Baltimore, and Boston. The object of these schools is to give a knowledge of some industrial branches of the fine arts. "The greater part of the higher order of designs are practically unavailable, for want of knowledge, on the part of the designer, of the conditions of the particular manufacture in question. The economic possibility and aptitude are not studied; and hence, the manufacturers say, an enormous waste of thought, skill, and industry. This want supplied, a field of industry practically boundless would be opened to female artists, as well as artisans; and it would be an enlightened policy to look to this while the whole world seems to be opening its ports to our productions." Mrs. Alice B. Havens writes of the school of design in Philadelphia: "When novelty and jealousy shall have ceased to excite envy and suspicion among those who would keep our sex from honest independence, a wide sphere of employment will be opened by this and similar institutions to educate intelligent women; for surely, if English manufacturers are not content to be under the control of foreign influence, our own countrymen can never be." The largest class of wood engravers is in the school of New York; the largest for designing on wall paper, in Philadelphia. More time has been devoted to instruction in drawing in the New York than the Philadelphia school. Without some practice in drawing, nothing can be accomplished in either wood engraving or designing. Designing, in some of its branches, is taught in all of the schools. Designs for paper hangings, calicoes, and wood engraving receive most attention. Designs for carpets, silks, ribbons, furniture, lace, plated ware, silver, jewelry, &c., have received but little, if any attention—those for casts and moulds, no more. If women of taste and cultivation attain superiority in designing, we doubt not they will reap a very fair harvest for their work. Lithography, wood engraving, drawing and painting, are also taught in schools of design. There are now in the school of design, New York, between 200 and 300 pupils: some are wood engravers, some designers, and some painters. "The earnings of the pupils in the classes of drawing and engraving are as varied as their skill and experience, but are about the same as those of men who have been at those branches of art the same length of time. Engravers and designers are generally qualified to work on orders the second year of their practice. With industry and the use of their *whole time* during school hours, pupils may expect an increase of about a $100 a year for several years. The income from the branches of art taught in the school must always be proportioned to the talent, experience, habits of application, and rapidity of hand shown by the artist. The engravers·in the school who best understand drawing have the best work, and even the highest wages. The pupils have the entire benefit of their earnings." "At Lyons, France, the manufacture of divers stuffs absorbs the hands of thousands of men and women; but the men, only, enjoy the privilege of inventing combinations of forms and colors destined to inveigle the eyes of fashionable caprice." In the school of design, Philadelphia, a charge of $9 per quarter is made to amateur pupils for instruction, and a charge of $4 per quarter to professional pupils. In the school of design, New York, a charge of $4 per quarter is made to pupils who acquire instruction as an accomplishment: to those fitting for a profession, no charge is made. A lady teacher in the New England school of design had a salary of $400. We will copy an article placed at our disposal on the artistic employments of women in America. It was written by a former principal of the school of design in Boston: "The artistic employments of women in this country may be divided into three classes: 1st, those devoted to the fine arts; 2d, those engaged in designing and the business departments of the arts; 3d, teachers of drawing, painting, &c.—1. Under this head comparatively few will be found; the number, however, is fast increasing, and as avenues of sale for their works are found, I doubt not that there will be a marked improvement both in the quality of their work and in the amount paid for their labor. Most who pursue this department are confined to portrait painting or crayon portraits. I have seen beautiful portraits in colored crayons executed by ladies. I regret to say a comparatively small price was given, varying from $10 to $25, while works executed by men not a whit superior in any respect would command from $25 to $50, and even more.—2. *Designing, and the Business Department of the Art.* This admits of several divisions, and first we will take designing for textile materials. When women are engaged in the mills, their labor is very poorly paid for, compared with the payment made to the other sex. I know of about twenty women who are so engaged. The prices paid for their labor varies from $1 to $2 per day—men receiving from $800 to $1,200 and even $1,500 per annum. The difference here, however, is not so great, when the time given by the two to the necessary study is compared. Many of the male designers serve an apprenticeship varying from three to seven years before they are supposed to be fitted to take the situation of designer in a mill, and even this does not include the preliminary instruction in the school. Women, on the contrary, after a year or little more of study, enter the mill on equal terms with the prepared designer, his pay at the commencement of his engagement usually being from $1 to $1.50 per day. The employment of women at all in this department is almost a new thing, and is not yet countenanced to any great extent. Time, however, will remove all difficulties in the way, and, by steady perseverance I think woman will be able to show herself superior to man in this branch, because it is more in her own domain than in that of man. When the designs of women are presented to manufacturers and found acceptable, they will command a price equal to the designs of men. This I speak from experience, having disposed of designs for silver ware, printed coach linings, coach lace, paper for walls, calicoes, delaines, and muslins, and other articles of like nature. These have commanded the same price as the designs of men, but it is difficult at times to find a market for them. I remember presenting some designs to a manufacturer, about two years since, which were very much praised ; but when I stated they were made by ladies, at first it was said to be impossible, and then they sunk in value, were wrong in the mechanical detail, were not adapted to the purpose for which they were intended ; but, unfortunately for the truth of the latter statement, they were disposed of to another manufacturer in the same street, who had formed rather a different idea of the powers of women as compared with men. A second branch of business art is drawing for mechanical purposes and patent inventions. There are in this city many ladies who earn quite a handsome income by drawing for the patent office, patent agents, &c., the drawings chiefly linear mechanical ones, the remuneration varying according to ability. Some are paid by the piece, and others by the day. The day laborers earn from $1 to $2, and in two instances $2.25 and $2.50 per day. The price of work varies according to size, intricacy, finish, &c., the rate being nearly that which men receive, in some instances the same. This requires mechanical knowledge which is not very often possessed by women, but is a branch of study that would be found both pleasant and profitable, especially if they were prepared for it by an elementary course in the public schools. It is not a branch that admits of much display, and is therefore almost entirely neglected, or taught in such a way as to be utterly futile for all practical purposes. A third branch is architectural drawing. I know of but one instance of a woman pursuing this branch, which is both delightful, useful, and very profitable. Perhaps there is not any department of the fine arts to which woman might more successfully devote herself than to this. Such a devotion of woman's power would tend to abolish the gross deformities we so often see paraded before our eyes in the streets, in the form of buildings presenting every possible incongruity of shape and every perversion of the beauty of form. This requires much study, but would eventually repay for all the time and trouble that would be bestowed upon it. A fourth is wood and other engraving. This commands as high a price as men's labor, when brought into the market; but when women are employed in engraving establishments, the grossest injustice is shown them in the inequality of the payments made. A woman will receive, in the same place, for the same amount of labor, a sum not exceeding half of that paid to the men in the same employment. In England this department stands on a perfect equality as regards sex. The quality of the work being the test of price, it is the same to men as to women, if the quality is the same.—3. *Teachers of Drawing and Painting.* This is always most profitable when pursued independently of the schools. When it is so pursued, the rate of payment varies from $5 to $25 per quarter, for each pupil, excepting in the case of very small children, when the prices may be a trifle lower, but the same would be the case with men as with women. In most academies the service of teaching in this department is given by preference to women, and at the same price. When they are engaged simply as assistants, then a gross inequality begins. A man would be paid say $200 or $300 per annum for one half day a week—a woman $100 or $150 at most. The reason for this lies deeper than I can divine, but in other instances when a lower price is paid, it is generally the fault of the individual employed. There should, if possible (and I conceive it to be so), be a fixed rate for teaching a certain number of pupils, and so much more additional for every one added: this would give a general rate for all to make their demands upon. If more branches, or extended time, or any other demand was made upon the individual teaching, then they would have some standard whereby to regulate the extra charges. There is only one feature which requires to be somewhat changed, and that is a tendency to superficiality. Women oftentimes commence to teach before they themselves have taken more than the most elementary steps for their own improvement. Time will, however, regulate this deficiency; and as the resources of improvement open to all, those who devote themselves to the honorable employment of teaching will take all proper steps to fit themselves for the office.—There is no department of the fine arts—painting, sculpture, architecture, or manufacturing design—in which woman may not run an equal race with man, if she takes the same trouble and care to fit herself for it, and, when fitted, is faithful to her own interests and her profession. This will never be accomplished by schools of design as at present instituted, for they lose their character and become designing shops. This must be laid aside, and culture, with a general or specific object, be alone attended to for the time necessary to learn properly and thoroughly what they are about to practise. Men and women both, now expect to learn the art of designing fully in the course of six or twelve months. This can only be done to a limited extent, depending on the powers of the pupil, the mode of instruction, and the capacity of the teacher to win and to guide those committed to his or her care. If the profession is entered upon with unfitness and want of knowledge, then the prices of labor will be necessarily reduced to a low scale; if with fitness, and a certainty of our own capacity, we can demand ' a fair day's pay for a fair day's work.' The interests of this nation demand the production of native designs, and whenever her children are fully fitted to produce them, are competent to put their designs side by side with those of other nations and challenge a comparison, every other obstacle will dwindle into a shadow, and every difficulty that now stands in the way of woman's *natural* place, in art at least, will be finally removed—to which end 'may God speed the plough.' "

46. Miscellaneous Designers. Designing is a peculiar, and more a natural than a cultivated talent. A few years ago, Miss M. drew on stone for the New England Glass Company. She received $10 a page, which she could generally do in four days, working only four hours per day. Two men had at differ-

ent times done the work for the company, one receiving less, and
the other more than she.   Misses L. and R. drew and designed
in the carpet factory at Lowell.   They received $1.25 per day.
A young lady who designed at the Pacific Mills, in Lawrence,
was said to receive $3 per day.   Miss S., who had given but
eighteen months' practice to drawing, designed for ground and
painted glass, and received $6 per week.   Designs for toys, dis-
sected pictures, games, puzzles, &c., are an appropriate filling up
of spare moments for a designer.   I was told by an English
seller of embroideries, that, in England, designing and making
patterns for embroideries is a distinct business.   He has been at
it many years, and does not feel himself perfect yet.   It is not
made a distinct branch in this country yet, because there is not
enough of it done.   Here a few primary patterns can be arranged
and rearranged so as to answer all the demands of trade.   A great
deal of money is expended on monuments, but there is a want of
variety in the designs.   A wide field is here opened to operators
in this department.   Some designers in Boston write me : "Only
a few ladies are employed in our business, for there are not many
who are willing to devote the time necessary to become proficient.
Some are employed in Europe.   The employment is not more
unhealthy than sewing.   Women are paid according to their proficiency, and earn from $3 to $15 per week.   Women receive the
same compensation as men, if they do the work as well and as
fast, but they ordinarily cannot do either.   They are not paid
until they have spent two or three years learning.   A combination of artistic and mechanical talent is required.   The prospect
for employment is good.   There is not much variation in the
seasons for work.   Ten hours is the average time required.
There are now as many in the business as can find lucrative or
constant employment.   It requires not less than five years, generally more, to be a fair general workman in this business.   Boston, New York, and Philadelphia are about the only places
where there is a demand for designers.   A first-class education
and cultivated taste are absolutely necessary to success."

47. Designers for Calico Prints.   This employment
is well adapted to women.   It requires taste and ingenuity.   Its
labors are light, but rather confining.   A person of lively fancy
and nice powers of discrimination succeeds best.   The gay, rich,
dark colors of winter clothing are not suitable for summer; nor
are the light, delicate ones of summer suitable for winter clothing.
This inviting field of labor, now that it is unbarred to woman, we
hope will be well improved.   Let her enter, and she will find
sufficient to "reward a careful gleaner with a valuable sheaf or
two."   We do not speak of inventing and preparing designs for

calico prints particularly, but of the general field for designers. Some proprietors engage a designer (here and there a lady) to stay at their establishments, and devote all their time to the preparing of designs—paying a fixed salary for the month, year, or any time specified. Some adopt the same plan in wall-paper establishments. The price generally paid for a design pattern for calicoes is from $1 to $3.

48. Designers for Wall Paper. One of the most important branches of designing is that of preparing patterns for wall paper, fire screens, &c. In the report of the Philadelphia School of Design it is stated that one of the ladies of that school received $60 for a design some time ago. They seldom bring that much, and all designs prepared will not sell. The usual price for a good hall design is from $12 to $20; and of paper for a room, from $12 to $16. We fear it will be long before the beautiful designs of the French are equalled by Americans. Their taste must be more highly cultivated before such is the case. Mr. C., of New York, employs a designer (Frenchman), paying him $1,000 a year, who receives in another manufactory a salary of $3,000 a year. N. C. & Co. get some of their patterns from the school of design in Paris, because the French have more taste in designing, or, rather, that taste has been more cultivated. Brande gives the merits of designing as follows: " Every work of design is to be considered either in relation to the art that produced it, to the nature of its adaptation to the end sought, or to the nature of the end it is destined to serve; thus its beauty is dependent on the wisdom or excellence displayed in the design, in the fitness or propriety of the adaptation, and upon the utility of the end."

49. Draughtswomen. There are several kinds of draughting, or drawing on stone: architectural, mechanical, letter, figure, and landscape. Very few women have undertaken draughting in any of its branches. But we do not see why it should be confined to men. We suppose the minds of some women are as well adapted to the business as those of some men. Our ideas of the fitness of women for architectural drawing are given under the article Architects.

50. Employés in the United States Mint. A very interesting description of the employment of ladies in the United States Mint at Philadelphia will be found in *Godey's Lady's Book*, of August, 1852. Col. Snowden, Director of the Mint, writes to me as follows: " Women are employed to adjust the weight of the blanks or planchets, preparatory to the coinage— each piece for the gold coinage being separately weighed and adjusted. So also are the larger coins of silver; namely, the dollar

and the half dollar. They are also employed in feeding the coining presses. There are about fifty women at present employed.
This force is amply sufficient for our present operations, and for
any additional amount of work that the mint may be called on
to perform. The employments in which they are engaged are
healthy and pleasant. Some years ago the women received
seventy-five cents a day in the adjusting room, and eighty-five
cents for those employed in the coining room. Since that time
I have increased their per diem compensation to $1.10 in both de-
partments. They are paid monthly. Men employed in labor of
a similar character secure about $2.20 per day. A day's work
is about ten hours; ordinarily the women do not work more than
seven or eight hours; sometimes more, sometimes less, but never
beyond ten hours. There are no other occupations in the mint,
than where they are now employed, suitable for women. I am
greatly in favor of employing women, and I have extended the
employment of them as far as it is practicable. For adjusting the
weight of coins, and attending or feeding the coining presses, I
consider women as not inferior to men, except that they cannot
endure work for as great a number of hours." The adjusting
room is kept very close, as even the breath of a person may affect
the gold dust. The windows are kept closed on that account all
the year. Visitors are not permitted to enter this room. I have
been told that the adjusters wear chamois dresses, which they
change before leaving the mint. They are required to wash their
hands and clean their nails before leaving the premises, lest gold
dust should be in them. A great many applications are made
for situations in the mint. None but a thoroughly honest person
should occupy so responsible a place."

51. Engravers and Chasers of Gold and Silver.
I was told by a lady in Philadelphia, that had been engaged with
her husband for some years in chasing the backs of gold watches,
and had laid by quite a snug little fortune, that from $5 to $6 is
paid for engraving a watch case. It requires many years to
render one a competent gold or silver chaser—I think about five
years. A general engraver told me he thought women could very
well engrave jewelry, silver, and card plates. The superior taste
of women could be exercised to advantage. He thinks a woman
of good abilities could obtain sufficient practice to earn good
wages at the expiration of six months. It is a very confining
business, but one that pays well. It requires more skill in drawing than beauty of penmanship, though the last is a desirable
item. A good engraver calculates to earn $1 an hour. The kinds
most suitable for a lady are so clean that she need not have
her clothes soiled by her work. Mr. C. knew a lady once in

New York who was a beautiful engraver.   She learned the business with her father.   A watchmaker can soon learn to engrave, because he uses similar tools, and knows how to handle them.   A person that can engrave watches could easily engrave coarser work.   Engravers, when employed by the week, earn from $12 to $25; and $15 a week is a fair average of an engraver's wages.   An engraver cannot well work more than nine hours a day.   Ornamental engraving is done in some jewelry manufactories by women.   Engraving is done with gravers, but chasing is executed with punches and a small hammer.   Engraving is more on the surface than chasing.   An article chased is indented on the inner side, one engraved is not.   It requires some time to excel in chasing and engraving.   There are two kinds of watch engraving—that of landscape and that of borders.   I was told by an Englishman that some silver-plate chasing is done in England by women.   A jeweler writes : " We occasionally employ women in engraving—on brass, and we do not find any difficulty.   In this branch of business, we believe, they are more suitable than men." Mr. S., who engraves on gold, silver, and other bright metals, told me that a long time back all the engraving in his branch was done in England by women.   It is light work.   The designing is like a lawyer's work—hard on the brain.   Most engravers in this country do their own designing.   His father was the first engraver in New York.   He takes apprentices for five years, not paying anything the first year, the second, $2 a week and clothing, and increases according to the attainments of the learner.   There are two kinds of engraving in his branch : the line engraving can be done with one tool, the other kind requires several.   He can obtain foreigners who can do both kinds (usually called mongrel engraving), and who would be glad to get work.   Chasing and polishing are about as good mechanical pursuits as a woman can follow.   Some silver chasing is done by filling the article with sand, and striking with proper tools ; some is pressed with heavy machinery.   Soft chasing is done on metals, but the chasing of plated ware requires some strength in the wrists, and is done before being plated.   The patterns are placed before the workers.   It requires a long time and application to acquire proficiency.   More women could find employment as chasers, if they would apply themselves long and closely enough.   A chaser, who employs eight girls in Providence in making and chasing jewelry, writes: " They earn from $4 to $5 per week, but men from $15 to $18.   Women cannot do their work as well as men.   Men spend from two to three years learning, women from one to two months.   Spring and fall are the best seasons.   The prospect of employment for women in this branch is good.   There are

other parts of the jewelry business in which women could be employed, and I think they will be. I prefer to employ women,
because they are cheaper." A jewelry engraver writes: "In
some branches of our style of engraving, women are employed in
France and Germany. The occupation is sedentary. The
average rate of workmen is $12. I think women could command
the same prices as men. It requires about one year to learn.
There are but few first-class engravers. A bold and steady
hand, a ready and quick ingenuity, which would qualify a person
to be a good draughtsman and designer, are the qualifications
most needed for an engraver. About fifteen years ago there was
no demand for engraving, but it is now on the increase, and considered a necessary finish to jewelry. About the Christmas
holidays are the best seasons for work. Ten hours a day are
required. In the Western and Southern States are openings—
in large cities a surplus. I think, women are peculiarly adapted
to engraving, but they would be likely to marry, and then we
would have our trouble to repeat in teaching new learners."

52. Equestrians and Gymnasts. In equestrian entertainments, much depends on the accessories. Without music, artificial light, and paintings, they would be rather tame. The
principal requisites for a circus rider I take to be agility, grace,
and fearlessness. Size and form have not so much to do in
making a successful rider and gymnast as one would suppose.
The athletic exercises require vigor and firmness of muscle.
One should be trained from the earliest childhood. Children
usually begin as early as three years old. In former times, these
children were, many of them, picked up in the streets, and there
is no doubt that these human waifs had a hard time of it; but
now many of the professionals bring up their own children to the
business. All the performers, in addition to their several "star"
or "single" acts in the ring, are required to appear in any capacity
assigned them in the scenic pieces and spectacles, and to attend
the rehearsals of the same; also, to appear and remain on the
stage in proper dresses, for the purpose of filling the scene, and
giving a gay and animated appearance to the stage. Mr. Nixon's
establishment, New York, being the most complete in the country,
and being thoroughly systematized in every department, will
serve as the best source from which to derive information concerning the routine duties required, and the weekly moneys paid
there to circus performers. "The principal performers in Mr.
Nixon's company are paid as follows: Ella Zoyara, equestrian,
in addition to first-class passage from England and back for
self and two servants, medical attendance for self and servants,
carriage and horses whenever required, and a benefit every two

weeks, receives per week $500; Mr. William Cooke, equestrian, manager, passages for self and wife from England and return, and per week, $500; James Robinson, equestrian, for self and three horses, $305; the Hanlon brothers, six persons, gymnasts, per week $300; Mr. Charlton, stilt walker, passage, &c., $125; Mr. Duverey, contortionist, passage, &c., $125; Mlle. Heloise, equestrienne, $100; Mlle. Clementine, equestrienne, $100; M. and Mad. Du Boch, equestrians, $100; Master Barclay, equestrian, ten years old, $75; Mr. Whitby, ringmaster and equestrian, $100; Mr. S. Stikney, equestrian and general performer, $100; Mr. J. Pentland, clown, $100; Mr. Ellingham, ringmaster and general performer, $40; Mr. Armstrong, equestrian and general performer, $40; W. Kincaid, do., $40; W. Pastor, do., $30; W. Bertine, do., $30; Brennan, do., $25; Niel, do., $25; F. Sylvester, do., $20; A. Sylvester, do., $20; W. Ward, slack rope and clown, $30; Prof. Yates, ballet master, $25; Mr. Stark, general performer, $25; S. Ruggles, $20; Davenport, $20; Foster, $20; Peterson, $20; four lady equestrians, per week, each $20; and twenty ballet girls and twenty supernumeraries." We extract from an English paper the following statement : "In Paris, no less than 15,000 persons were admitted yesterday, although the prices were doubled for the occasion, to witness the performance on the tight rope of a woman—Madame Blanche Saqui—who is entering her eighty-fifth year."

53. Etchers and Stamp Cutters. In England, in the seventeenth century, Anna and Susannah Lister were regarded as having much skill in the noble art of etching. They illustrated a work on natural history written by their father. A century later, the Countess Lavinia Spencer and a Miss Hartley became noted for their skill in etching. Rosa Elizabeth Schwindel, of Leipsic, worked at the business of a stamp cutter in the beginning of the eighteenth century; and two Frenchwomen during the same century—M. A. de St. Urbin and E. Lesueur.

54. Herbarium Makers. Herbariums are collections of dried plants. They are formed by gluing to sheets of paper the flowers and leaves of plants, after they have been pressed and dried. To botanists, they are useful; and a choice collection is a frail, but pretty ornament, for a centre table. The largest public herbaria are at Berlin, Paris, and London. It is supposed that some of them may contain as many as 60,000 species. There is not much of beauty or interest in such a collection, but for scientific purposes they may be valuable. It is not unusual to see them made of the plants and weeds of the sea; and a very pretty collection do they make, if got up with taste. A book has been lately printed containing plates, with explanations for making them into pictures and other fanciful arrangements. The making of herbariums of both earth and marine plants, would furnish a pleasant pastime to ladies of leisure, and a source of revenue, perhaps, to those who might wish to make it a matter of profit.

55. Lapidaries. A skilful manipulation is necessary to the business of a lapidary. If woman has sufficient firmness of nerve to perform the duties of surgeon, we see not why she would not have for the cutting of precious stones. It is a business conducted on a limited scale and by few persons in this country. Mr. R., of New York, told me that a lady in Birmingham, England, had a large establishment, and employed women and girls to work for her. He knew of no lady that worked at the business in the United States, except one that used to be in an establishment on Broadway. The employment, he thinks, is not unhealthy. After a lady has learned, she would probably earn from $4 to $5 a week, working for others. He received $12 a week when working as a journeyman. He spent seven years as an apprentice in England, but he learned the manufacture of jewelry in connection. The prospect of employment depends much on the condition of the money market, but there is reason to think the business will increase as the country grows older. All seasons of the year are alike. Money matters only make a change. He says there are many books written on the precious stones and the art of cutting and polishing them. He mentioned a book by a lady of London on the subject. Mr. H., an importer and manufacturer of cornelian and other fancy goods, told me that grinding precious stones is very hard work. Men lie across wooden benches to apply the agate, cornelian, or whatever it may be, to the grindstone. There are eight grindstones, weighing twenty tons each, on one axle. The polishing is done by boys, who sit at small wooden wheels, some of which are covered with leather. Sometimes women do this work. As this method of grinding stones is done by water power, it is done more cheaply than by steam. In Germany, a man who works at precious stones or makes up jewelry at home, has his wife and daughters to assist him, and hires a peasant girl to do his housework. The women and girls make the fastenings for earrings, and file and polish the rings. He pays seventy cents a gross in Germany for them. He says, in the country and villages of northern Germany daughters are considered treasures, for they remain at home, and by their handiwork maintain themselves; but in the south of Germany, where there are no manufactures, girls are a burden on their parents. B., of Philadelphia, used to employ girls to set up jet, garnet, and turquoise for grinding; but those stones are now out of fashion, and so girls are not employed. He says an old lady, whose daughter is connected with the Home Mission, wished them to give instruction to her daughter in cutting stones, that she might, as a pastime, cut those brought by members of the family from the seashore and watering places. He thought it likely she would also teach the art in the Mission School. Cutting facets he thought pretty work for women. They can either sit or stand at the tables. There is nothing unhealthy in the grinding, as the stones are kept wet all the time. But the dust used in nipping glass and stones is injurious to the lungs. When a man has been nipping all day, his nostrils are nearly closed. The amount of work depends on fashion. There are seven establishments in Providence, and the work is done by steam. Some stones cannot be cut by steam machinery, as the wheel must every few seconds be graduated in motion. In hard times, the jewelry business and employments connected therewith are dull, as people dispense with superfluities. Southerners buy most jewelry, but now they do not indulge in such purchases.

56. Landscape Gardeners. Mrs. R. often goes and looks at gardens, directs how to lay them out, and what to buy for them. She then orders the plants of others, and sells on commission, having them arranged according to her own taste, influenced by that of the purchaser. Her purchases are made of a German, living some distance from town, who can raise them cheaper than she could in the city. Her compensation, of course, varies greatly. A landscape gardener writes: " What a lady could do as landscape gardener at the West, I do not know. I am rather inclined to doubt her success at the East. It would require too much time and space to enter here into the details of what are required to constitute a landscape gardener : First, one must have a decided love for it, and a willingness to sacrifice much to the pleasure of the occupation. Nor can I say a great deal in favor of the profits. I have never been able to make a living by the profession, although I have often thought if I had gone to New York, or farther West, the case might have been different. In pages 381 and 382 of ' Country Life,' and in many other parts of the book, you will see what I consider essential to the making up and preparation of a landscape gardener, and better expressed than I can condense into a letter." Mr. C., of Massachusetts, writes : " I have never known a lady to undertake the profession of landscape gardening; and much of the labor which I find it necessary to perform, would be impossible for a lady. Still, there is much in which female taste would find abundant field for exertion, if the labor could be so divided as to make it profitable. My first work on any estate is to make an accurate topographical survey of the ground, and draw a plan of it in its natural state, and then proceed to make my designs for its arrangement; and when that is done, if required, I undertake the superintendence of the work at the ground. A lady would have to employ a surveyor, in the first place, and would labor under many disadvantages in directing the operations upon grounds; and, to judge from my own experience, the business could not be made profitable under such circumstances. Loudon's ' Encyclopædia of Gardening ' will give the best directions I know of for the necessary operations of designing and executing plans, and Downing's work, with Sargent's appendix, comprises enough suggestions, on matters of taste, for the use of any person who is possessed of innate natural taste, without which I would advise no one to attempt to be a landscape gardener."

57. Lithographers. The impression for chalk drawings is made by delicate manipulations with crayon pencils; for ink drawings, with steel pens and camel-hair brushes. It requires one skilled in the use of her pencil, for every stroke of the pencil or pen on the stone remains, and cannot be erased. Consequently, any defect on the stone is conveyed to every copy of the paper. In answer to a letter of inquiry, respecting the time necessary for preparation, the writer says: "A person who draws well upon paper would, I should think, with six months' practice on stone, become proficient. The process differs little from crayon drawing on paper; and the progress of pupils depends entirely on their previous attainments in drawing. The different kinds of lithography are black, chromo, and gold illuminated; also, lithography combined, or uncombined, with embossing. In a report of a British school of design, it is stated that the chromo-lithographic class for females " exhibit the commencement of a series of useful labors." An immense number of cheap lithographs are colored by women ; such as are hung in taverns, country houses, sailors' homes, servants' rooms, &c. At Mr. C.'s establishment, I was told that in France the females are quite as successful as the male artists in lithography. He says lithographs require to be more highly colored than the colors we see in nature. Mr. C. thinks of sending to France for lithographers, as he cannot get enough in New York well qualified. A correct eye, skilful manipulation, and an appreciation of art are required to make one skilful in lithography. Germans excel, because they have so much patience. An American would become nervous at the slow work that they prosecute with the greatest pleasure. At Mr. C.'s they have a forewoman, who superintends the girls, who are paid by the quantity and kind of work they do. He finds that small girls are usually the best workers. Their fingers are more nimble, and they enter into it with more zeal. He thinks it best for them to commence at ten or twelve years of age. Prospect good for employment in that branch. The coloring of all the finest pictures is done by men. It requires some time to become sufficiently expert to earn much. Their girls earn from $3 to $7 a week. The work requires care, and is wearisome, because of sitting long and steadily. Mrs. P., Brooklyn, an English lady, learned to draw when eight years old, and studied lithography with a distinguished artist of London, who executed entirely with his left hand, having lost three fingers on his right when he was a child. She has spent twenty-two years in lithographing—seventeen of them in this country. She is probably the only lady professionally engaged in this business in the United States. She has earned almost constantly, I was told, from $12 to $30 a week. Lithographing is very lucrative to a skilful artist. The remuneration is better than women often receive for their handiwork. We believe some women could find employment in it, if they were prepared. Mrs. P. excels in architectural drawing. She thinks one must have the talent of an artist, and great practice with the pencil, to succeed. She has given instruction to several youths, but never to one of her own sex. One must be articled, and pass through a regular course of advancement, to follow it advantageously. To an apprentice, after two or three years' practice, a small premium is paid. She had one youth to learn of her, who, after four years' time, received $7 a week from her for his work. She thinks there will be employment to a few well qualified. She has always been kept busy. The employment is not more unhealthy than any other of a sedentary kind. Mr. M. says they have no difficulty in finding enough of crayon lithographers, but that there is more lithographic engraving done than crayon lithographing. It is done on stone with instruments, very much as engraving is done on copper. We have read " that an improved method of transferring copies of delicate copper and steel plate engravings to the surface of lithographic stone has been invented. One copy taken from the steel or copper plate, after being transferred to the stone, is capable of producing 3,000 prints." " Lithography, engraving, and especially engraving on wood, would gain in quality by passing from men's hands to the hands of women." " Lithographic works are produced which rival the finest engravings, and even surpass them, in the expression of certain subjects." The first lithography executed in the United States was in Boston, 1826. W. & S. used to employ girls to color lithographs, but found it did not pay. They paid from $4 to $5 a week to women, who did the common part of the work. Men did the finer parts, and earned from $12 to $25 a week; but only those who are expert, have artistic taste, and understand the business, can earn so much. French lithographs are prepared and the coloring done so much cheaper in Europe, they have ceased to have it done in New York. B., lithographer, Philadelphia, employs many ladies—about twenty—in the house. Some associate in companies, and take their work to the house of one of their number ; but the greater part are educated women, who do not wish it known that they earn money by their labor : these carry the plates to their own homes (and even have them sent to the fashionable places of resort in summer), so that many a fair damsel trips along Chestnut street with a roll of something, which seems to be music, but is, in fact, work. The coarse handed take no part in this employment. Very few have ever attained the highest degree of proficiency in it. The most delicate work is done by men. Americans have most aptness for coloring, although the Germans excel in drawing on stone. Women seldom attempt the latter art. It requires long practice for girls to excel in coloring. Many grades of skill are required to color lithographs, and there is much difficulty in making all the copies exactly like the first. Some need a treatment so nearly approaching the artistic, that scarcely any one who has the skill can be found to give his labor for the price, which is necessarily limited. We gained no information as to the amount of wages paid to the colorists, but, judging from the price of a very beautiful specimen (29 cents), it must be sadly inadequate. The scientific societies are the main support of this business. The Government, indeed, gives very extensive orders, but there is always so much competition to obtain them, that the profit is small. Audubon was the greatest encourager of this branch of industry. This employment is very desirable in every respect for educated women; and although machinery for printing in colors is fast encroaching on it, yet it will long offer a field for female enterprise. Our informant employs from 100 to 300 hands, according to the prosperity of the times. A commercial crisis affects this as well as all other trades. One of the firm of the best lithographic establishment in New York, told me they pay their men for drawing on stone from $25 to $30 a week. The time required to learn lithography, he thought, would depend much on natural talent. A good knowledge of drawing is necessary. He thought men would soon get over the opposition of women entering the business; but they did not like the restraint of working where women are. They would soon become accustomed to it; and if they were women of the right kind, it might be a very beneficial restraint. But, as to that, women could do the work at home. Many Germans, well acquainted with the art, are engaged in crayoning. When they first come to this country, they work for lower wages than Americans, but after a while learn their value, and ask as much as any one else. On account of the low wages for which foreigners can usually be had, but few Americans have prepared themselves for this occupation. But when work is plenty, and the individual industrious and skilful, he can earn good wages. Seven eighths of the work done for this country is executed in New York. The agent of a lithographic company writes: " Drawing on stone could be done by women as well as men; and would open to them a very genteel and remunerative branch of business. The drawing is now done mostly by Germans and Frenchmen; but ladies who have a taste for drawing could soon learn this art. The usual price for such artists now is from $12 to $35 per week." Prof. P., of New York, gives instruction in lithography, charging $12 per quarter of eleven weeks—two lessons per week. Special arrangements are made with pupils who intend to devote themselves to the profession as artists or teachers. A gentleman remarked to me that Mr. S., a certain distinguished lithographer of this city (New York), would make an excellent teacher in that art. His forte is heads. A few strokes from his pencil always give a beautiful finish to a piece of work.

58. Map Makers. Women could not well travel about to obtain information of localities for the making of maps, but nearly all the manual labor connected with the business would be very suitable for them. Lithographing maps is said to be a profitable branch of the art, and opens a field to competent women. Attending the machines for making impressions from the stones might very well be performed by women. " In Philadelphia, map coloring gives employment to about 175 females, some of whom display exquisite taste in this delicate art." There used to be 150 girls in New York painting maps, but there are very few now. Freedley tells of a map-manufacturing establishment in Philadelphia that " turns out 1,200 maps weekly. Connected with it are two lithographic printing offices, having twenty presses, and coloring rooms, in which 35 females are employed." I was told by a lady who had colored maps, that it is trying on the eyes and poorly compensated. A map maker said he was always most busy in the fall, and then employed from 12 to 16 women. In winter he employed about half that number, and they principally married women, who have worked for them several years. Mr. W. pays two of his best and most experienced lady workers a certain sum by the week, and they hire girls and women to work for them. The profits of these forewomen, aside from their own work, amount to $1.50 to $2 a week the year round. Girls receive

$1.50 a week while learning. It requires from six months to one year to become proficient. Neatness, a steady hand, knowledge of colors, and fineness of touch, are the principal requisites for a good map colorist. It requires no artistic knowledge. An expeditious and experienced hand can earn $1 a day. There is at present a need of hands in New York, and a surplus in Philadelphia. All seasons are alike in this business, except as monetary affairs are concerned. All Mr. W.'s hands work in the house. They work about nine hours a day all the year, and never take maps home with them, as they are mostly large and heavy maps. Map making is mostly confined to Philadelphia and New York. None are made in the South and West. There is one map publisher reported in Richmond, but he has his maps made in New York. Mr. C. gives his maps to a map mounter, who employs a girl to sew the bindings on with a sewing machine. She is paid at the same rate as any other operator. The paper bindings are of course pasted on. Mr. C. employs one girl to paint the outlines, but all the other painting is done by stencil plates. Map coloring formerly gave employment to many females, but now it is very rare that a map is colored by hand. The stencilling process introduced by the Germans has superseded it, as they are thereby rendered cheaper. Girls used to earn 75 cents to $1 a day for painting maps. If girls would learn stencilling and work on their own responsibility, they might compete with the Germans. The process is very simple and soon learned. At Mr. H.'s, I saw a large room full of Germans stencilling. Men earn $8 or $9 a week, and do it faster and better than girls, as they have more strength. I saw one girl shading, who earned $1 a day. A map manufacturer writes me: " In map coloring I am compelled to employ men to a large extent. A curious fact is, that respectable middle-aged women, who have been coloring for years on piecework, make from $4 to $5 per week; while young men, comparatively unpractised, earn at the same prices, say from $9 to $10." A manufacturer who employs about 80 females, writes: " I employ women in pasting and putting down maps, who receive from $3 to $4 a week, being paid by the week, and working ten hours a day. The difference in prices of male and female labor is about one half. One can learn the business in a few weeks; the only qualifications requisite are sobriety and strength. The prospect for work in this branch is good. There is no difference in the seasons. Some parts of the work can be done more cheaply by women. A supply of hands can always be had. The women do their work less carefully than men." A map publisher in New Hampshire writes: " I employ 28 women and girls in binding, mounting, stitching, and coloring maps, and pay from

$3 to $6 per week, working eight hours a day. The engraving is done by men, who receive from $6 to $20 per week. Women's labor can be learned in a few weeks, and is not so hard or difficult as men's. Engravers spend three years learning. I employ women to color, because they have better taste than men. Draughting surveys, engraving, and lithographing have never been attempted by women. New York is preferable as a locality." A gentleman in Boston writes: "We employ from four to eight women in our map-mounting department. They could not be employed in any other branch, which is varnishing and polishing all kinds of hard wood. There are a large number employed in New York, Philadelphia, and Buffalo. Pay varies from $3 to $5 per week—ten hours a day. We employ no men in this branch. There is something new to learn every day. Business is the same all the year. We pay our girls nothing while learning." A lithographer in Boston writes: "I employ women to color maps and pictures, paying by the piece, the workers earning from $3 to $6 per week. The employment is not unhealthy."

59. Medallists. "Beatrice Hamerani worked at medallions, and in 1700 elaborated a large medallion of Pope Innocent XII., highly praised by Goethe." "Toward the end of the seventeenth century we hear of Madame Ravemann, who executed a beautiful medal, an exquisite specimen of cutting." In the school of design in New York, we saw two very creditable medallions, executed by one of the members of the school.

60. Modellers. An ornamental designer and modeller writes me: "In England I attended my lady pupils at their own residences, except one to whom I gave instruction at my residence. One was the daughter of the Lord Mayor of the city, another the daughter-in-law of the Earl of H. Very few ladies learn any of the higher branches of art, except those that do so for recreation. A person that has some skill in drawing would, without the slightest doubt, soon acquire a knowledge of this beautiful art. Some persons have a natural gift for modelling, while others would not learn it with all the cultivation arising from education and good society. Probably the best source of employment in New York would be to design and model for the silversmiths—such as Ball & Black, Tiffany, &c. One of the most fertile departments in Europe to lady modellers is not carried on to any extent in this country—the making of fine pottery. The fingers, of course, must be soiled in modelling; but such an inconvenience is trifling compared with the pleasure of forming fruit, flowers, and foliage, or modelling the medallions of friends." The modelling of gas fixtures might afford employment to a small number of qualified women. We know of one establishment in

4

Philadelphia where part of the designing for fixtures, lamps, and chandeliers, is done by a lady, and all the copying done for illustrated catalogues of those which are finished. She receives $6 a week, and goes about 9 o'clock A. M. and remains until 4 P. M. Mr P., at his school of art in New York, has a very large collection of casts. He gives instruction to boys and young men in modelling and drawing, charging 25 cents a lesson of 3 hours in the day or 2ʹ in the evening. They are instructed in classes. Some of his casts are gigantic. In one of his rooms is a beautiful, but small model, in wax, for $300, representing a hunting scene. We have been told that some ladies in Germany model wax patterns for the ornamental work on china. Few tools are used by a modeller—the only ones are for the sharp and delicate parts that cannot be formed by the fingers. As clay does not shrink uniformly in drying it is moulded before drying in plaster of Paris, and a cast of the same material taken from that, which serves as a model for the workman. Some artists model in wax. Women might be employed in modelling ornamental and scroll work for brass founderies, &c., and get good wages.

61. Modellers of Wax Figures. Catharine Questier, who lived in Amsterdam about 200 years ago, besides possessing many other accomplishments, was a modeller in wax. Joanna Sabina Preu, who lived in Germany not long after, was noted in the same way. A daughter of a Danish king also modelled in wax. "Professor Anna Manzelino, an Italian lady, modelled excellent portraits in the beginning of the eighteenth century." In England, in the early part of the eighteenth century, Mrs. Samore modelled figures and historical groups in wax. Mrs. Patience Wright, born in Bordentown, New Jersey, 1725, made a great many likenesses in wax. Some were full length and some were busts. They were mostly of the statesmen that were conspicuous in the American colonies at that time—yet some were of Englishmen, as she resided in London, after she became a widow, and supported her family by her handiwork. Her daughter, Mrs. Platt, modelled in wax in New York in 1787. I saw a maker of wax figures who said he had supported his family by his work, and thought a few others might make a living at it. One must be able to draw a model before undertaking wax figures. It requires good perceptive powers, ability to distinguish colors, and a peculiar taste. One must be able to work from life, and it is well to know how to do so from pictures. Mr. G., interested in Barnum's museum, told me that it was impossible to get such wax figures made in this country as they want. He spoke of the miserable imitations that are made, and thought a person well qualified would be patronized. Most of the groups in Barnum's museum were made by Mrs. Pelby, of Boston. Mr. Barnum wrote to Mr. Tussaud, whose mother made those so famous in London (and who is living now), to know if he would instruct some one to send to America; but he is not willing to give any one instruction. He employs persons to make the different parts; one set of workers make the bodies, another the heads, another the feet, &c. The world-famed group of his mother, Madame Tussaud, was first opened in Paris about 1770. After being exhibited in the large towns of Great Britain, it was taken to London, where it still remains. The figures are so life-like that now and then one is mistaken for a living person, while a person is as often mistaken in the group for one of the figures. More than forty persons are kept in charge of the exhibition.

62. Mineral Labellers and Arrangers. A lady could not easily make collections of minerals, but she might find it an absorbing occupation to arrange and label them. Few ladies in our country have given any study to mineralogy, and very few would be competent to form cabinets. Yet, for those that are, we doubt not employment of that kind could be found. The individual wealth of our country has not been sufficient to enable many to make extensive collections. The most that exist are connected with universities and other institutions of learning. They have been collected at different times—in fact, mostly formed by single specimens, added now and then. Individual collections have been formed in the same way. Individuals add to the cabinets of their friends, as they have it in their power. The most extensive collections in the United States are at the Patent Office, Washington, and in the National Academy of Science, Philadelphia. Mr. H., a mineralogist from Berlin, says: "In Berne, Switzerland, a man and his wife are mineralogists. On the husband's death the wife will continue the business." It must require many years' study and an extensive knowledge of chemistry to become a superior mineralogist. I would think considerable time and capital were requisite for a mineralogist to establish himself. Mr. H. makes exchanges of minerals for others, receiving, I suppose, a commission for doing so. A geologist writes me: "No women are employed in my business. It requires one half of a lifetime to become fitted for the duties of a geologist. A knowledge of engineering, and most of the natural sciences, is needed. Draughting in the office is the only part suitable for women."

63. Musicians. Madame Romeau says: "Few women have been engaged in musical compositions, and they have rarely undertaken important works. In painting and literature one is pre-occupied only with the work of the author. In music, it requires the coöperation of two persons—the composer, and the performer. Books and paintings act upon us without any intermediate objects, while the piece of the composer, to be understood, needs the flow of harmony noted on the paper in hieroglyphic signs, and must escape under the fingers from the instrument. It is necessary to animate the inert matter—to make it yield to the wish of the performer and reproduce the inspirations of the composer. Few women compose songs. A musician leads a different life from an artist, who lives in her studio and has few expenses. A musician must face the crowd, and hear its dissatisfaction, and smile at its applause. A cantatrice, or songstress, often travels from town to town like an actress." Some persons think none of the arts can be purely religious except music. " Mozart in music, and Raphael in colors, have taught us the spiritual ministry of the senses." A comparatively small quantity of music has been composed in the United States. The study of a lifetime is bestowed by very few on music. Some American ladies have gone to Europe to perfect their musical taste, and a few have acquired distinction. With musicians, as with vocalists—those who, in this country, have reaped the greatest profits in the shortest time were foreigners. Some were pianists, some flutists, some violinists—some one thing, and some another. The composition of music for soirees, fancy balls, masquerades, tableaux vivants, private theatricals, operas, dramas, musical farces, ballets, &c., might occupy all the spare time of musicians capable of composing. There is a circulating library in London of 42,000 volumes. There is, also, one in New York and one in Brooklyn. Subscribers to the one in Brooklyn pay in advance for one year $12, with the privilege of selecting from the catalogue $6 worth of music at the termination of the subscription; for six months, $6; for three months, $3; for a single piece worth less than $1, 6 cents per week; less than $2, 9 cents per week. Mr. G. thinks a lady can never become a good violinist, because it requires great strength in the right arm. The muscles of violinists are as rigid as a blacksmith's. I have heard that occasionally a pianist acquires such strength in his hands that he could almost prostrate you with one of his fingers. A gentleman told me, ladies could not become superior organists; that they cannot have sufficient power developed. It requires much strength of hands and feet. He remarked, the organist, at the church he attended, was a lady, but made no comments on her qualifications. I have known two lady organists, who were considered superior performers, and received as good salaries as gentlemen would have done. One received $500 for playing twice on Sabbath. On week days she gave instruction. I was told that she supported her whole family for years by her musical talents, and laid by money with which she purchased a comfortable dwelling in a city in New York State. The salaries of organists are small considering the amount of talent and practice required; but most organists teach music, or stand in music stores, or act as agents for manufacturers of musical instruments. "In the summer of 1860, among the Marblehead band of female shoe strikers in the procession at Lynn, Mass., was Miss Margaret Hammond, fifteen years old, who beat the drum in martial style the whole line of march." "In Ohio they have a lady drummer, who has received a diploma for her skill. Her name is Minerva Patterson, a daughter of Major Elisha Patterson, a wealthy farmer of Jersey, Licking Co." The French papers have given some insight to the prices paid great musicians. Malibran received in London, for every performance at Drury Lane, $750; Lablache, for singing twice, $750, and for a single lesson to Queen Victoria, $200. At a soirée in London Grisi received $1,200. Paganini charged $400 a lesson. "Herz and Thalberg each made about $60,000 in this country." There is a female musical society in London which gives concerts for benevolent objects.

64. Music Engravers and Folders. Mr. L. engraves and prints music, and employs two ladies to fold it. There are but few music engravers. The smaller the number of persons in any one kind of business the higher the prices they can command. A lady in New Orleans engraves, whose husband is a music printer. It would require but two or three years to learn it. Some ingenuity, a knowledge of the value of notes in music, and judgment in the arrangement of them are necessary to make an engraver. In New Orleans, eight months are usually considered a year, I believe, in business arrangements. At a music engraver's the young man told me that he never heard of a woman engraving music in this country, but he knows that some do in Paris. The work they turn out, he added, is not good; it will not wear, because women have not sufficient strength in the wrist to engrave as deeply as a man. A person who engraves plates for music can earn from $3 to $5 a day. German work is considered the best, because the quality of the ink used is better. Music engraving is divided into two distinct branches—one is lettering and engraving the title page—the other is engraving the notes. No steam machinery has ever been invented for printing music, because the ink must all be put on the way the work is done. Music is one of the first things dispensed with in hard times.

65. Opera Performers. The first opera of modern times was performed about the close of the fifteenth century. At the first introduction of the opera into France and England, it was much ridiculed by wits and critics. Voltaire, however, and others, came to its rescue, and with what success may be known, when it is acknowledged to be one of the favorite amusements of the fashionable world. The want of adaptedness of the opera to the English language has to a great extent excluded successful efforts at translation. Yet some operas have of late years been performed in English. "In Paris, the Italian opera is patronized by the Government, as a school of vocal music; and the managers are careful to maintain a complete and skilful company." In an opera, the music is the most important part, while at the theatre the music is subordinate to the play. The orchestra in some parts of the opera accompanies, and, in others, seems to respond to the sentiments of the piece. The operatic performance is not so warm, so impassioned, so abandoned, as that of the theatre. The trilling and sudden starting, so common in operas, is rather too artificial to please the unsophisticated. A conversational style is seldom used, but the words are expressed in a recitative style that is graceful and effective. In Germany, however, dialogue has been introduced. Good imitative powers are essential to success. The noble talent of music has been desecrated, in some operas, by the impure thoughts and language expressed. In the United States probably not more than thirty, out of the entire audience of several hundred, sufficiently understand the Italian, to follow the play without considerable effort; but it is so much of a pantomimic character that much is gained by the sense of sight. Much of the zest and interest are lost to those who are indifferent to the accessories. On this account, we suppose it can never become a favorite amusement with the generality of people. The French papers give some curious statements in regard to the salaries paid to great musical artists. We learn that Hummel left a fortune of $75,000, and twenty-six diamond rings, thirty-four snuff boxes, and one hundred and fourteen watches, which had been presented to him at various times. In modern days musicians are quite as extravagantly paid. Alboni and Mario get $400 every night they sing; Tamberlik, every time he sings a certain high note, demands $500; Madame Gazzaniga was paid $500 a night recently in Philadelphia; Lagrange, at Rio Janeiro, is now receiving a princely salary; and Piccolomini cost her manager over $5,000 a month; and these prices are said to be moderate, compared with those often paid in Europe to distinguished musical artists. At the opera house in Paris, for the present season, Mr. Colzado, the manager, pays as follows: to Tamberlik, for seventeen representations, $8,000; Alboni, $2,200 for seven representations; Mario, $15,000 for a season of five months; Grisi, $5,000 for two months; Madame Perer, $14,000 for the season; the Grazioni brothers, $15,400; Corsi, a baritone, $4,000; Galvani, $3,600; Nantin Didere, $4,000; Tecehini, $3,600; Mlle. de Ruda, $3,400. The chorus and orchestra cost for the season $17,600. " Parodi, the American prima donna, receives no less than $30,000 per annum, a larger salary than that paid to the President of the United States." " Miss Hensler, the American prima donna, has been engaged by the manager of La Scala for fifteen months, at the rate of $170 a month." " Sophie Curveth receives $2,500 a month, for eight representations; for every representation beyond eight in the month, $300 more."

66. Painters. " Less prejudice exists against artists than teachers in France. They have privileges that teachers have not. Painting is considered the most desirable profession by parents for their daughters. The girl begins early in life to fit herself for her profession. The work is less severe than that of an author. Painting does not require such close application of mind, nor is it necessary to spend so much time in solitude, nor are the expense and anxiety so great as that of authorship. Gratuitous schools of art exist in Paris, where instruction is given principally in perspective. Most students prosecute the art in studios, paying from $4 to $6 a month. Most of them spend the whole day in the studios, from eight in the morning until six in the evening. The artist that instructs them visits the scholars only two or three times a week. The studio is a sort of mutual school, where pupils teach each other; they are of all ages. All conditions of society are represented. Three kinds of painting are done by them—face or portrait, landscape, and flowers. Most of the girls of the higher classes prefer landscape. Female artists compete with men, and wear their hair short. Few women like the physical fatigue of a painter's life. There is not the same play for coquetry in artists, as in singers or actors. It requires great perseverance for a female artist to acquire firmness of execution; she does not possess it to the same extent as man. Some artists are willing merely to copy paintings, paint portraits, and give lessons. The school of landscape painting is one well fitted for young and original talent. Women succeed in painting portraits; also, in painting flowers and fruit; very few have tried historical paintings." Painting is certainly a profitable employment for a lady artist of superior ability, if she can have enough to do. Miss F., New York, established a life school for lady artists. One subject is used at a time; the classes are limited—two classes—eight or ten pupils in each. Those that need instruction will pay $12 for twenty-two lessons; those without instruction, $6. There will be two sittings a week, of from three to four hours. A person of sensitive, nervous type, susceptible to every impression of a pleasant kind, is most likely to succeed as an artist. Mr. R. Peale told me that many ladies in Europe paint portraits. He considered it a higher style than landscape, or still life. He thinks painting itself not injurious to the health. The turpentine used is sanitary, and the white lead is deleterious only when taken into the lungs. What is inhaled in breathing can do no harm. Mr. Peale thought that the principal reason of artists being so poor in health, is because of their long and close confinement indoors. In painting the first coats are often applied by an assistant, employed by the artist; and in some cases, by the students of the artists. Miss Merrifield, of England, has written a work on the art of painting. A number of ladies in England, and in the United States, are winning a reputation as artists. The prospect to lady artists in the United States is very encouraging. Ladies are allowed the privilege, on proper application, to copy paintings in the Academy of Fine Arts, Philadelphia, the Düsseldorf, and the Bryant galleries, New York. According to the census of 1850, there were 2,093 male artists; but there are said to be not more than 600 or 700 superior artists in the United States. The patronage the best receive is such as to keep them well employed. A meagre support and a long life of labor are necessary to establish a reputation as an artist, even to one that has talent. But the way in which most of our first-class artists live, that are prudent and steady in their habits, and possess any business qualifications, contradicts the opinion, quite common, that an artist's life must always be one of self denial and poverty. We think artists fare as well as most people, and we do think it a life very inviting to the young ladies of our country. Those that have the time, the means, and the talents, will find it an absorbing, a fascinating employment. Women succeed best in painting pictures of their own sex, and of children. The more tender and delicate organizations are best suited to their talents. Most of our artists live in the metropolis, New York; the Western country is too new and crude. There are materials enough, but not much appreciation of talent. Besides there is less wealth, and another thing is, that artists must keep themselves where mention will now and then be made of their pictures, to bring them into notice, and where the most ready sale will be found for them. During the last few years a taste has been developed in St. Louis, that promises some golden fruit. A gallery of paintings has lately been opened there. Why is it that a talent for painting and poetry is so often combined? Is it that the quiet, contemplative state that produces poetical inspirations also favors the visible expression of beautiful thoughts? A poet painter is more frequently to be seen than a poet musician. One, I suppose, of a quick, lively disposition, and very impressible, might be more likely to possess musical talent than one of a quiet, thoughtful nature. But genius is not fettered by temperament. There is a society of female artists in London; the first public exhibition of their paintings took place in June, 1857. It is managed by a committee of eight ladies, and bound by twenty-three articles. A portrait painter writes: "The artist requires a high, well-developed anterior brain, a healthy body; and a brain and body well regulated and balanced; a love of the beautiful that inspires the character with patience and indomitable perseverance, and a contempt for applause; for 'art is long,' and, unless one is willing to 'scorn delights and live laborious days,' he can never meet with real success. If women can attain to excellence as artists, they can command the same remuneration as men receive. Art knows no sex." A professional artist remarked to me: "Amateur painters never attain excellency, because it requires not only talent, but constant application." I think if there is anything that should have its full value, it is a painting, because of the patience and perseverance necessary for an artist to excel, and the long and costly preparation requisite. It commands, too, a certain style of talent that many do not possess. In addition to this, those who can afford to buy paintings are those who can afford to pay a good price.

67. Animals. We know of no artist in this country whose talents have been devoted to the painting of animals, and of but one lady, in any country, that has distinguished herself in that line—the far famed Rosa Bonheur.

68. Banners. We saw an ornamental sign painter decorating a large flag. Stars are painted on the silk, and then sized and gilt. The flag was stretched on a frame like a piece of tapestry, but upright like an easel. Mr. M. had never known of any women being employed in the trade. He decorated banners for processions, political campaigns, &c. This is evidently a field for female industry.

69. Crayon and Pastel. Crayon drawing seems to have been much in vogue in Italy in the seventeenth century; and we read of an Italian lady, as far back as 1700, devoting her time to pastel painting. The soft, light, dreamy effect given by the use of pastels, peculiarly fit the style for the portraits of ladies and children. Mrs. Dassel, of New York, was noted for her excellency in the use of pastels. Mrs. Hildreth, of Boston, is very successful in her crayon portraits. She charges from $30 to $40 a head.

Mrs. M. A. Johnson, of Massachusetts, has spent some years working in crayon. " Her indefatigable patience in the execution of details, the fidelity of her likenesses, and the delicate perfection of finish in her pictures, are remarkable." Miss Clark received $20, and over, for crayon portraits in Boston, a few years ago. Before Miss Stebbins, of New York, became a sculptor, she drew crayon portraits, charging $50 per head. Her execution was said to be clear and forcible.

70. Flowers and Fruit. During the latter part of the eighteenth and the first half of the present century, a number of lady artists have distinguished themselves in flower painting. During the seventeenth and eighteenth centuries, a few devoted themselves to it in Holland, Germany, Denmark, and France. For a few years past some American ladies have turned their attention to flower painting with marked success. A number in England have also obtained distinction.

71. Fresco. The wife of an artist told me her husband knew of a fresco painter in England, whose daughter would assist him when he was hurried. But the lady thought working with men was objectionable. I heard of a young lady in New York, who assisted her father, by filling up the outlines, as he drew them on side walls. Mrs. Ellet states that Angelica Kauffman assisted her father in the interior decoration of a church, in Schwarzenberg. She painted, in fresco, the figures of the Twelve Apostles. Her success in an undertaking so difficult excited considerable attention. Mrs. N., wife of a fresco painter, thought the work unfit for women, because they would be compelled to work with men, and stand on platforms to work on ceilings; consequently are liable to exposure of person. They might paint the side walls, and let men paint the ceilings.

72. Historical. But few ladies have devoted themselves to historical painting. The most lived during the latter part of the last century, and the commencement of the present. Catarina Vieira painted several church pictures, after the designs of her brother.

73. Landscape. In the past century Holland gave to the world the largest number of female landscape painters. America and England bear away the palm for the present century. American scenery opens as wide a scope for the talent of the landscape painter as any on the globe. Mrs. ——, one of the first landscape painters of our country, thinks landscape requires more care and talent than portrait painting, but the latter pays best. She says there are some ladies in Boston, who are very good landscape painters. She thinks it would be very difficult for a young artist to become established in New York, without influential connections, and the means to keep ner until she does become established; but would be more likely to succeed in cities in the South and West. She thinks there are good openings in Baltimore, for artists of every kind. She says art is much more encouraged in the United States during the last few years, and a good artist need not fear starving. The artists of New York have three receptions during the year. The object is to make known their paintings, with a view to selling. At the last annual sale of pictures for the New York Artists' Fund, $2,000 were received. Some artists copy a landscape exactly as they see it; some select the most beautiful parts of different landscapes, and combine them; and a few draw entirely from imagination. Good painters of scenes for theatres, I have been told, often receive from $25 to $40 per week.

74. Marine. Some very good marine views have been executed in this country, but none by ladies.

75. Miniature Painters. "We may run back as far as the twelfth century, and find a few miniature painters among the fair sex. Margaretta von Eyck devoted most of her time to painting miniatures, in the fifteenth century. In the seventeenth century, an Italian lady of Palermo distinguished herself as a painter in oils. Mrs. Wright, an English miniature painter, died in 1802; and Maria Conway was a noted miniature painter, living in London, who died in 1821. In the seventeenth century, Maria Rieger was employed to paint miniatures in the aristocratic circles of Germany. In the same century, a Swiss lady, Anna Wasser, began at the early age of thirteen to win a name in the same branch of painting. In the same century, almost every country in Europe gave birth to one." Mad. Goldbeck, of English birth; Mrs. Hill, of Boston; Miss C. Denning, of Plattsburg; Miss Anne Hall and Miss O'Hara, in New York, are the principal miniature painters in the United States. It was reported that Miss H. occasionally received as high as $500 for a miniature. Mrs. Hill received from $75 to $100 for a miniature. The popularity of photographs has caused many portrait and miniature painters to devote themselves to that branch of art. Some artists succeed in giving an ideal, *spirituel* beauty, truly astonishing. I think it is more observable in miniatures on ivory than any other style. Mr. W. writes: "In the department of miniature painting women find profitable employment and are ofttimes very expert at the work. I know a lady in Washington who paints very beautiful miniatures, for which she receives from $10 to $15. This is very nearly the same rate paid to men. Woman's delicate sense of touch and facility of expression make it a branch for which she is especially fitted."

76. Panoramas, we suppose, have pretty well paid their way, particularly the first that were exhibited; but we know not that any lady has ever engaged in this branch of painting. Mr. D., a scenic and panoramic artist, says the "decorative work-shops" of Paris are 250 feet long, and 50 feet wide. The cloth for panoramas is laid on the floor, and the paint then applied, as it would run if hung up. There are galleries around the walls, some distance above, from which the artist may judge of the effect of his painting. Many dioramas are used, and might be colored by ladies. Panoramas have not been so common since Banvard painted his. Painting them does not always pay for the trouble and expense. It requires a certain order of talent for painting panoramas, and probably as high an order as any other.

77. Portrait. "Lala, though not a native of Rome, exercised her profession in that city during the youth of Marcus Varo, painting portraits of women. Her pictures were better paid for than those of any other painter of her time. Portrait and character drawing have ever exercised the talents of the first-class artists." Mary Beale was a celebrated portrait painter, who lived in the reign of Charles II.; and Anna Killigrew painted the portraits of James II. and his queen. An artist told me that it requires the most intense mental application to bring out a variety in the expression of the countenances of some sitters, and difficult to seize the most happy expression. An ambrotype copy should be kept for the colorist to look at occasionally, while progressing with his work. He thinks seven hours a day enough for an artist, when his mind is exercised with his work. After so long an application, he might turn his attention advantageously to some style of painting more mechanical in its nature, that will be an occupation to his body and a relief to his mind. A portrait painter writes me in answer to some questions: "The artist's labor cannot well be intrusted to another. In France there are female portrait painters, who are said to execute such works with more delicacy and profit than men. The employment is not unhealthy, unless the laborer confines herself too long in a poorly ventilated room. Women are paid by the piece, when employed by artists. I would say, in general terms, why women are not better paid is owing, doubtless, to a very foolish idea that, in all respects, they are not so reliable. Perhaps a remnant of a more barbarous period has something to do with it. In inferior conditions of society women are always looked upon as inferior creatures. Women have done great things in art. See the career of Rosa Bonheur, Angelica Kauffman, Miss Sharp, of London, and, in our own country, Mrs. L. M. Spencer and Miss Hosmer." Some people are gifted with a love for, and success in, one style, and some in another. Our nation, composed as it is of representatives from all lands, will give fair play to the best powers of the portrait painter. Miss G. thinks a lady of talent, by close application, with an extensive respectable connection, can establish herself in New York as an artist, and earn a livelihood by the products of her pencil. She charges as much for a crayon portrait as for one in oil. She succeeds best in crayons. $60 is her price for a large portrait; $10 or $15 more, with hands. " Mademoiselle Rosée, born in Leyden, in 1632, deserves a place among eminent artists for the singularity of her talents. Instead of using colors, with oil or gum, she used silk for the delicate shading. It can hardly be understood how she managed to apply the fibres, and to imitate the flesh tints, blending and mellowing them so admirably. She thus painted portraits, as well as landscapes and architecture."

78. Water Colors. Much improvement has taken place in this style of painting during the last few years. Fanny Corbeaux is mentioned as a superior English painter in water colors, of the present century.

79. Painters of Dial Plates. This is rather an artistic employment, but poorly paid. All the clock faces used in the East are said to be painted by women. Men would not do it for the prices that are paid. In Boston is a large factory where a number of girls are employed in painting hard dial plates— that is, enamelled. I saw a Swiss lady in New York who paints silver-faced dial plates. She and a gentleman in Hoboken (she told me) are the only persons in this country who paint that style. The drying of hard dial plates she thought to be bad on the health, because of the great heat to which a person is exposed in placing the enamel in the furnace, and attending to it while there. Mixing the enamel could be done by women. When learning to paint dial plates in Switzerland, she paid $3 a week for instruction and board, but for a sleeping room separately.

80. Picture Restorers. E. says he has been thirty years engaged in restoring paintings and engravings. He thinks it is more of a natural gift than anything else. He has made money by it. His sons, who have been ten years employed as draughtsmen, cannot succeed, with all the instruction he has given them. To succeed requires the talents and experience of an artist. He never adds paint when any is left, but merely restores it. If it is gone, he supplies it. B. says, restoring paintings is a work of all time. The prospect of a lady succeeding is poor. She can-

not use the heavy iron (twenty-five pounds) necessary for ironing the lining on the picture. (But that part is merely mechanical work, and can be done by a man.) The greatest aim with
most restorers is to imitate the old masters. Mrs. C., whose
husband is a picture liner, says there is a great wear and tear of
mind in that business. A restorer may injure a picture, and
have it thrown upon his hands, and have to pay ten times its
value. Restoring is the most difficult, lining the most laborious.
She never heard of any one being taught. I should think a
restorer would find it desirable, if not essential, to visit the galleries of Europe, and study the works of the old masters. The
business requires considerable artistic taste and knowledge, but,
in our large cities, may after a while present a field for qualified
women.

81. Piano Tuners. I think a piano tuner might form a
class of ladies, and give instruction in the art. $1 is the usual
price for tuning a piano in the city. One should have an acute
sense of hearing, to succeed; and he should commence early to
cultivate that sense. It is very necessary to know how to make
a nice discrimination of sounds. Practice in that is best gained
in a piano factory. Some could learn the principles in half a
day. More depends on practice, and a native talent for it, than
anything else. At Mr. W.'s is a very superior tuner, and he
has been at it but a few months. It requires strength of wrist,
and a rather long arm. The change of posture and strain on the
back is considerable. There is not one good tuner in fifty. Mr.
W. thinks a lady might be a tuner. He says it is not necessary
that a person should know how to play on an instrument, but it
is better. A tuner in his factory receives $3 a day. Regulating
is done by the touch, tuning by the ear. If a lady could obtain
the tuning of the pianos of her friends, they might speak to others,
and in that way she might succeed in obtaining sufficient custom
to make a very comfortable support. It might also bring out
any musical talent the individual possesses. While piano tuners
are learning, if they practise long at a time, they often experience
a confusion of sounds, and are not able to distinguish correctly.
I was told by another manufacturer, it is not at all necessary to
be a player to make a good tuner, as the two are entirely distinct.
There is a great difference in the abilities of tuners. There is
much difference naturally in the sense of hearing in different individuals : there is much from training, there is much from the
aptness of a pupil, and in the application. When they take a
boy as an apprentice, they keep him at first to sweep the room,
and go errands, and give him instruction, probably an hour at a
time, in tuning. Longer time would confuse a learner. They

have had a tuner for three years, that they can now send to tune
pianos for concerts; but, a year ago, they could not.   Two piano
tuners (women) are mentioned in the census of Great Britain.
Mr. W. had two or three ladies to learn piano tuning in his
factory.   They were music teachers, living in villages and the
country, who could not engage a tuner oftener than once in two
or three months, when the tuner would come around.   He thinks
ladies could not make very good tuners, because it requires great
strength in the hand or wrist, and complete control of the key; for
if the key is turned ever so slightly more than it should be, the
wire will break.   A manufacturer of musical instruments writes:
" I think women could be placed in a situation profitable to themselves and the community by learning to tune pianos and melodeons, which I believe they have the skill and capacity to do.
They would also find it profitable, in some places, to instruct ju-
venile classes of both sexes in sacred music."

82. Plaster Statuary.   The few women in this country
who work in plaster of Paris, are, as far as we know, natives of
other countries.   There is an old Italian woman in Baltimore
who makes and sells works in plaster.   Casts are sometimes
taken by women, but rarely.   Casts of living persons are taken
by having the individual breathe through iron tubes placed in
the nostrils.   Casts are also taken from reliefs, statues, and
models.   They require less care than the first mentioned.   Fruit
is imitated in this material, and colored exactly like the original.
I saw a case that had been prepared by a lady for the rooms of
the American Institute, New York.   The librarian thought several collections might be disposed of to agricultural societies and
farmers.   It would pay well, and take but little time to learn.
It would require a nice discernment of colors and shades, and
neat, careful workmanship.   In Brooklyn, I was told by a boy,
that did not look to be more than 14 or 15 years of age, that he
had been working in plaster of Paris for three years.   His was the
architectural branch.   The first year he received $1.50 per
week; next year, $2; and the next, $3.   He thinks a woman
could do any of the work.   The moulds for some parts are made
of wax and rosin; some of sulphur, and some of plaster of Paris.
The moulds are tied together, and the liquid plaster poured in.
It hardens in half an hour.   Mr. W., a plaster of Paris worker,
says the whole of the work could be done by women.   Modelling
requires practice in drawing, and a knowledge of geometrical
figures.   Inventive talent finds a ready field for exercise.   A
good moulder is paid $2.50 a day.   The study of architectural
ornaments and books much facilitates the advancement of the art.
Modelling and casting are distinct branches.   Most employers pay

boys thirty-seven cents a day for casting; but to learn modelling, it is customary for the learner to pay a premium. Another maker of house ornaments said modelling could be learned in six months, and when a person has learned, he can earn from $3 to $5 a day of ten hours. One must know how to draw in order to model. Another proprietor told me he had thought of employing girls to break off the edges of architectural ornaments. They now have boys, and pay from $3 to $9 per week. Modellers can earn $2, $2.50, and $3 per day. He paid $2.50 a day, for a year, to one man. At a large store for the sale of plaster of Paris articles in New York, the proprietor, a gentlemanly Italian, said he would be willing to give instruction to a class of ladies in modelling, moulding, casting, and polishing. He would charge $2 for two hours' instruction, and thinks, after a lesson every day for three months, and some practice in the intervals, his pupils would have no difficulty in prosecuting the work alone. It soils the clothes very much. His daughter learned it, but prefers embroidery. One of the Pisani brothers told me that in Italy and Paris women work at the business. Much ornamental work is executed in alabaster, spar, composition, and plaster of Paris. None of them are unfit for women. A more desirable occupation, with the exception of its want of cleanliness, a woman could not engage in, than plaster of Paris modelling. An Italian plaster image maker in Boston writes me : " We employ about 60 women. Women are employed at this business in Florence, Rome, and Milan. I get about $10 per day, and pay women $3 per day, working ten hours. I pay both by the piece and by the day. As a general thing, we pay men better than women. It requires some genius and a lifetime to learn the business. The prospects for employment are good in Boston, and there is a pretty lively demand for hands. All the women I employ are Italians. Women are decidedly superior workers. The business can be carried on in any part of the United States. Women might be employed in taking casts from the dead, if they have sufficient nerve. I have a peculiar fancy for this branch of the work, and do not consider it unhealthy."

83. Painters of Plates for Books. Hundreds of thousands of plates are annually colored in London, and some in this country. The neatness and patience of women fit them admirably for this work. It is an agreeable, but at present not a very constant or profitable employment. The coloring of lithographs in printing has done away with much hand coloring. The painting of stereoscopic plates has given employment to some ladies, and does not require much skill or taste. The gentleman who prepared stereoscopic plates for the Messrs. A., employed

several ladies, to whom he paid on an average from $9 to $10 a
week, working by the piece. Botanical plates are mostly colored
by hand. The gentleman who prepares the fashion plates of the
Ladies' American Magazine employs women, paying from $4 to
$7 a week, according to application and rapidity of execution.
They work from eight till dark, in winter, and by the week, not
the piece. It requires but a few weeks to learn. He has stereoscopic views also painted by women. They receive rather better
prices, as it requires some artistic taste and more care. The
universal complaint among employers is, that their best workwomen will get married and leave them. If women were better
paid, employers would not be so likely to lose them. A few
years ago, we saw a newspaper statement to this effect: When
maps were colored by hand in New York, girls were paid from
three cents to ten cents a sheet, and they earned from $3 to $5 a
week. A few years back, it was estimated that there were two
hundred female paint colorers at the top of the profession, who
made excellent wages by coloring costly engravings. The colorers of plates in *Leslie's Magazine* pay by the hundred or thousand. The first year, a learner is paid but little. If she succeeds
right well in that time, she is then paid according to the quality
and quantity of her work, earning from $3 to $5 per week. They
must work in the shop, so the superintendent can see if it is
properly done, or reject and have altered such plates as are not.
All seasons are alike. A manufacturer of children's toy books
told me he employed girls for coloring, paying by the piece.
They earned each from $3 to $3.50 a week. They used stencil
plates. He generally kept them employed all the year round,
but the occupation is full. A German print colorer told me he
employed thirty girls till the panic, paying by the piece from $3
to $3.50 a week. Stencil plates of varnished paper were used.
He paid his workers from the first, and they could either sit or
stand while at work. Another paint colorer told me his girls
earned from $4 to $4.50 a week, for coloring the finest prints,
working only in daylight. A manufacturer of valentines and
children's toy books told me his girls painted valentines in winter,
and toy books in summer. He pays two of his girls by the week
$7 each, and none of the rest less than $4 a week. They work
from nine to ten hours a day. The use of stencils by Germans
has reduced the price of such work. He could get girls to do
book coloring for $2 a week, but prefers to retain his old hands
constantly. Most colorers of prints work at home. A getter up
of gentlemen's fashion plates told me he pays ten cents for coloring a large sheet containing several figures, and the worker finding her own materials. No one could earn the salt of her bread

at such rates.   Another print colorer told me it requires from
two to six weeks to learn, according to the ability of the learner.
Sometimes he has Government work that must be done hurriedly.
They have least work from New Year to March.   Some print
colorers pay by the week ; $5 is a good price.   I saw an engrav-
ing on the wall representing an English barnyard, for which the
proprietor was paid $3 for coloring, while he pays the lady who
does it, $2.25.   Some ladies, he says, can earn from $10 to $12
a week.

   84. Photographists and Colorists. Mr. F. says they
would employ good lady artists, if they could get them ; but
ladies do not succeed so well, because they do not have such an
efficient course of training—do not go through the same grada-
tions in a preparation for the work.   They mostly employ men
that are foreigners to color.   A colorist of photographic views
for stereoscopes says he pays a lady to color for him $6 a gross.
English ladies color best.   The firm with which he is connected
cannot get their coloring done in New York, so have most of it
done in London ; and as work is cheaper, it costs them no more
with the addition of transportation.   At one photographic establishment in Philadelphia, the proprietor told us that several
artists now devote their time to the coloring of photographs.
He pays one lady at the rate of $12 a week.   She is employed
on the low-priced pictures, such as are sold for $5, exclusive of
frame.   The portraits range from $75 up.   The lady painter is
daughter of an English artist.   She works all the hours of daylight, when required—sometimes only six hours.   B. has at
different times encouraged and employed female artists ; has
never met with any one who excelled, but does not doubt they
might do so if properly trained.   He had a lady partner in
daguerreotyping and photographing.   She was very poor when
she commenced, but, while engaged in it, supported herself and
children, and educated them, and left $3,000.   He told me of two
ladies making a handsome support by coloring photographs.   His
best pictures are painted by gentlemen artists.   He thinks the
taking of photographs not so suitable for women, because it is
dirty work ; that is, the nitrate of silver that gets on the fingers
stains them like indelible ink—a small difficulty, I think, in the
way of a woman that has a living to make.   There are several
ladies in Philadelphia who make their living by painting photographs.   Some ladies have quitted the profession of teaching to
become photographers.   Ladies are sometimes employed in photographic galleries, to wait upon company, agree upon prices,
deliver the work, and receive pay.   For such services they are
paid from $3 to $5 per week, according to the amount of busi-

ness done. Photographers work from eight to ten hours. Some think the business unhealthy, because of the gases that arise from the combination of chemicals. Women that have had practice in drawing and painting can give a pretty and delicate touch in the coloring of photographs. L., photographist, employs two ladies to color photographs in water colors. He teaches it for $10. A good colorist, with constant employment, can earn from $10 to $15 a week. He thinks there are openings in the South. Some prefer water coloring to oil, because you can see the pictures in any light. Oils are better for large pictures that you see at a distance. Painting in water colors does not pay the artist so well as painting in oils. Misses E., New York, are busy all the time. They execute different styles of painting, but have lately found it more profitable to color photographs. They each earn from $12 to $15 per week coloring photographs, when busy. Their work is all brought to the house. They have had several offers to go South, and better prices than they receive in New York. Miss E., with whom I talked, thought if any ladies would learn thoroughly, and could not obtain painting to do, they could easily obtain situations as teachers of painting. I saw the wife of an artist who gives instruction in drawing and painting. She told me her husband is very conscientious and will not recommend any one to spend their time and money learning to draw and paint, if he finds they have not talent of that kind. Some people think they possess genius, and can excel in painting, even if they commence when thirty or more years of age; but it is best for an artist to commence early in life. The talent of some is developed in a shorter time than others. One may learn in three months what another could not in six. Her husband can advance an American pupil as far in two years as he did his German pupils in four. He thinks the Americans are more apt, and acquire more rapidly. She thought a lady would not find any difficulty in obtaining constant employment as a painter. Miss J., Philadelphia, has as much to do at coloring photographs as she wishes. It takes her about a day to color a small one, for which she receives $1. For those pictures 'on which there is more work, the prices are higher. The painting of ivorytypes is more expensive. An ivorytype the size of a $1 photograph would cost $10. Most photographers send their coloring out of the establishment to be done, and pay by the piece. In several States, women have been successfully engaged as daguerreans and photograph colorers. Some have travelled through the country, stopping in various towns to carry on their business. Some knowledge of chemistry is necessary for a photographer. One photographer writes: "Women are employed in every

country where there are first-class galleries. It is unhealthy in
the operating rooms, on account of the acids and poisons. We
pay $4 a week to ladies to attend the show case and wait upon
customers. We pay men $6 and $7, because they can do more
by one third of the same kind of work than a woman. Any part
of the business can be performed by a woman. We pay girls $4
from the commencement. They spend eight or ten hours at the
gallery, but are not employed all the time. They are as comfortable as in their own parlors receiving visitors. Ladies prefer one
of their own sex in the reception room. There is always demand
for superior work in our line; consequently, a prospect of employment so long as the world stands. In Syracuse, fall and
winter are the most busy seasons." Mr. A. says the occupation of
portrait and miniature painters is gone since the discovery of the
photographer's art. He thinks ladies are as capable of arriving
at great excellence as men in painting, if they will only apply
themselves as closely. Their knowledge of colors probably makes
them excel in that respect. He teaches photographic coloring,
charging $1 a lesson of one hour. A mechanical execution in
coloring is gained in a short time, but a good photographist
ought to be an experienced artist. Mr. R. told me his girls are
engaged in painting and mounting. He pays one $7 a week, and
the other $5. An individual that is bright, intelligent, and
capable of rapid tuition, could learn in six months. They spend
from eight to six o'clock in the gallery. They have but a few
minutes recess at noon, as that is the most busy time. He prefers
women for some parts of the work. Men are more powerful
artists, give a better expression; women are more careful, and
give a finer finish. I talked with a photographic colorist, who
gives instruction to a few ladies in coloring, and employs four.
He thinks women are generally better judges of colors than men,
but some women never learn the shades. (I think, unless it arises
from some physical defect, it is because they are not taught to
distinguish colors when children. It is difficult to teach a person the careful use of any of the senses if they are neglected in
childhood.) The work requires some artistic taste. A knowledge of drawing and colors, and a good education, are essential to
success. A young lady in the business should be social in her
nature, and of pleasing address. I would think an artist of any
kind would need the talent of drawing to the surface the soul of
his or her sitter, for much of the beauty of a picture depends
upon expression. Mr. G. thinks water colors neater for ladies than
oil. The employment is now in its infancy. The taste for photographs is increasing. There are now one hundred engaged in the
business where fifteen years ago there was but one. Photog-

raphists are usually employed from nine to six, or from eight to five. The remuneration is good when constant employment can be had. The best locality is a growing place. The business would grow up with the place. The prices paid enable ladies to obtain boarding in houses that possess the comforts, and even the luxuries of life. Summer is the dullest season, but much depends on weather. French women generally succeed well in coloring. Some English ladies, also, do well. Mr. G. gives a lady colorer $12 a week. Mr. B., a photographist, writes: "Women are employed in my branch of art in England. I would like to find competent assistance, but have been unable to do so. The work is not unhealthy, but it is very trying to the eyes. I should think that in many respects the work would be well adapted to females, but think, from trials that I have made, that the mathematical precision of the work is a feature unfavorable to the feminine mind. Were I to find such assistance as I would be satisfied with, I would pay according to capacity and work. Thorough artistic education and natural talents are essential. In point of taste, as regards color and elegance, I think women might be superior; as regards precision and firmness of minute work, I am uncertain. It would require considerable time and patience to learn the art." One of the proprietors of a photographic establishment in Philadelphia writes: "I employ from two to four ladies in painting photographic pictures, and pay by the week from $3 to $6. They work eight hours a day. I pay men about twice as much, because the men, being longer at the business, work better and quicker. It requires several years' practice to gain a moderate acquaintance with this branch. It is our opinion, that women are well adapted for most branches of photographing, and for some they would be superior to men, provided always, that they bring to the work a certain degree of education, and some natural talent. We suppose the reason they are not more employed in this and similar pursuits, is, that young women of a certain degree of education, are seldom eager for any sort of employment. Besides, in this business, it requires years of earnest application to master it, and before this is accomplished, many marry. The employer feels little security in retaining a woman at the business after going through years of instruction, because in many, or most cases, they marry, and must attend to their domestic duties. With a man the reverse takes place. He becomes a better and more steady worker after marriage." "We have a great improvement in photography by its combination with lithography. By the process adopted, the object to be represented is photographed at once on the stone, and thus the intermediate operations are avoided." In times of excitement, like the present, when soldiers are going from their homes, there is much for the artists to do.

85. Preparers of Scientific Plates. Mrs. B. has supported herself for some time by making drawings of fossils for works on geology. She is now doing one for a work on Niagara. It requires a great deal of care. It is very trying to the eyes as the engraver imitates every line made by the pencil, and a magnifying glass is of course much used for presenting enlarged views of the smallest fossils. I think she is paid by the piece or set, for the work. Of course this pursuit must be limited.

86. Seal Engravers. Seal engraving is cutting in a precious stone, letters or a device. The cutting is done by means of a lathe and sharp cutting tools. Diamond dust and oil are used. The lathe is moved by treadles. The finer the work, the smaller the tools. Taste, good eyesight, and a knowledge of form are necessary. No pattern is used. The hand and eye must serve as guides. It would be a very pretty occupation for women, but would require time, patience, and practice. Seal engravers in New York earn from $10 to $12 per week, but the occupation there is filled. Mrs. Ellet, in her " Women Artists," mentions a Prussian and a German lady as being noted for their skill in cutting precious stones. A seal engraver told me he does not pay apprentices the first year, but the second year $2, and from that up, according to the abilities of the worker. It requires from four to seven years to learn all the branches thoroughly. Another engraver told me the business is not worth learning now that gum mucilage has done away with sealing wax, and consequently the use of seals. The designs for seals are usually taken from a heraldry book; always when for a coat of arms. Such seals are in greater demand in Europe. Seal engravers in this country do not have constant employment. They cut fancy seals when not otherwise occupied. The work can be done at night by a good light.

87. Sculptors. Properzia di Rossi, Maria Domenica, Anna Maria Schurmann, Maria von Steinbach, Anne Seymour Damer, Falicie de Faveau, and in our own country and time Miss Lander, Harriet Hosmer, and Miss Stebbins, are among those who have proved the ability of woman to succeed in sculpture. Sculptors, it should be understood, seldom, if ever, labor with the chisel. They prepare models, which are made in a composition of clay or wax, and then superintend the imitation of these in marble. Sculpture is the chastest imitation of nature and the highest expression of the form and spirit of beauty known to art; and while woman is possessed of the finest sensibility and most exquisite perceptions, there can certainly be no reason why she should not succeed in it. Mr. Lagrange, in urging the establishment of Government schools of design in France, says: "Painting, engraving, and sculpture, encouraged as music and dancing are, promise equal success; they provide a more assured support in its being better acquired, and a more substantial renown, and especially a calmer and chaster existence. Painter, engraver, or sculptor, it is her *works* alone that claim the public eye. Her person is sacred; no one dares to lift the veil that conceals her countenance; no one presumes to call upon her to courtesy to feeble applause. A young girl, chaste and pure, she may watch by the lonely hearthside; a wife, she may not see her smiles and caresses in dispute as the seal of a purchased rite; a mother, she may educate her children under a name they will never be tempted to despise. Exhibitions, open to everybody, will afford the public an opportunity to measure her talent or genius; critics will confine their attacks to her works; and praise, if she deserves it, will reach her eyes and ears in terms that she will be able to listen to or peruse without the accompaniment of a blush." Mrs. Wilson, wife of a physician living in Cincinnati, has executed busts of her husband and children that are said to be excellent likenesses. Mrs. Dubois, of New York, has sculptured in marble several specimens. Misses Lander and Stebbins, and Miss Hosmer, we believe, find their art lucrative. Sculptors should attend anatomical dissections; should learn the structure of the human frame, and the appearance of the muscles under the various conditions to which circumstances may subject them. Indeed the study of anatomy is essential to success. In sculpture, we closely imitate the parent, nature. The most superior specimens of statuary are said to be modelled after nature, as seen in the unlaced, unpinched, unaltered original—just as nature's own hand has chiselled. In sculpture, modelling is the inventive part of the work, and requires taste and genius; copying is a merely mechanical operation. A pursuit of this kind, if followed from the love of it, becomes a soul-engrossing study. Means or friends to rely upon, for at least two years, during the time of study, will be necessary in most cases; for if the artist is to support herself while she studies, only the highest earnestness can sustain her; but then those that are not in earnest should not undertake this art—for "it is better to pursue a frivolous trade in a serious manner, than a sublime art frivolously." Without very decided talent it will be some time before a sculptor comes sufficiently into notice to sustain herself entirely by the filling of orders. "Sculpture has become almost a fashion in Paris; but a woman finds it difficult to devote herself to studies pertaining to the art. Though greater in number than painters, they have accomplished scarcely any remarkable works." Many women who might not undertake sculpture, might learn to work in marble for sculptors. A marble worker in its various branches, writes me: "I think women might be very well employed in the lighter parts of finishing. I suppose they are not so employed, because there has not yet been any organized and extended effort made to introduce them into this line of business. I am not sure, but think it likely, women are employed to a limited extent in *chiselling* marble in Italy and France. Miss Hosmer has done more than mould for others to copy. She has herself handled the mallet and chisel. The employment in general is healthy; but lettering, and indeed fine chiselling of any sort, requiring the eye to be brought near to the work, raises a dust, which is breathed into the lungs—though the injury is not very apparent till the lapse of years reveals it. The qualifications desirable are a good judgment, and eye for form, and a certain slight of hand. The prospect for marble workers is good in all departments." On the other hand, another writes: "Sculpture is too laborious for women, and if women practise the art, they hire all the work done." In Rome, two thousand women serve as models to painters and sculptors.

88. Steel and other Engravers. Steel and copper engraving require a very good knowledge of drawing, and careful manipulation. A great advantage has been gained by substituting steel for copper plates. One beauty of steel engraving is that it can be done at home. Men like easy employments, and so have appropriated this one. An engraver must learn to convey the feelings of an artist. Lithography has seriously interfered with steel engraving, and photography has to some extent. There are very few journeymen engravers. Most go into business for themselves. Some women are employed in engraving copper cylinders for calico prints. Line and stipple are the most expensive engraving. Mezzotint is cheaper. Boys practise on copper, and do not work on anything valuable until they are able to engrave well. One reason that engravers do not like to take apprentices is, that they cannot do any thing under two or three years, of any value to their employer, but expect to be paid from the first. Besides, an engraver seldom has enough of such engraving as a learner can do to keep him constantly employed. Those who receive apprentices in New York take them for five years, and pay something from the first; but very few men in New York, in any branch of work, are willing to take apprentices. Much of the success of a learner depends on his inclination, taste, and individual exertion; and when he possesses these, they render him valuable to his master—so it proves a matter of mutual interest. All engraving is mechanical to a certain extent, but requires some artistic taste. In "Women Artists" we find the names of some ladies distinguished as engravers in Italy, France, Germany, and England, in the sixteenth, seventeenth, eighteenth, and nineteenth centuries. Jane Taylor and her sisters paid their share of the family expenses by engraving. Miss Caroline Watson was an engraver of portraits to the queen in the reign of George III. Angelica Kauffman and Elizabeth Blackwell both engraved on steel. We read: "In London, recently, one accomplished female engraver has turned her steel plates into a pleasant country house, which she means to furnish with the proceeds of her delicate painting on glass." In Paris, during the last thirty years, quite a number of ladies have earned a livelihood by steel engraving, and several are now employed there in card engraving, and engraving fashion plates. There are some engravers in the South and West, but there are openings for more. A card, seal, medal, and door-plate engraver writes: "The usual number of hours for engravers are from eight to ten. The business may be learned in from one to two years, to be of use; but to learn thoroughly requires three or four years. The business generally pays well by jobs, and I see no reason why females may not engrave as successfully as males with the same application."

89. Bank Note Engravers.

"Steel engraving was first practised in England by the calico printers; but it was first employed for bank notes and for common designs by Jacob Perkins, of Newburyport, Mass." The American Bank Note Company, New York, employ about sixty girls, forty-seven of whom are engaged in printing or making impressions; the others in drying, assorting, and laying together the sheets to be placed under a hydraulic press. It requires but a few weeks to learn the part done by girls. Some are paid $3 and some $3.50 per week. They are mostly American girls. A lady told me that she heard a girl, who had been employed to cut up bank notes (done with scissors), say she often earned $9 a week. The company pay a boy $3 a week from commencement until through his apprenticeship, which is usually four or five years. Here a man can earn $100 a week, if a first-class bank note engraver; but in England not more than $10 or $12. There, however, paper money is but little used; a £5 note being the smallest in value. Bank note engraving is both mechanical and artistic. At the office of the National Bank Note Company, a gentleman showed me the various processes. He had often thought ladies would do well to learn bank note engraving. I saw two or three gentlemen engraving. The process is simple, but requires a good deal of patience and practice. Their girls are employed to place the sheet for an impression under a roller, and, after the impression is made, remove it. Some receive $3, and some $3.50 a week. It is dirty work, on account of the oil and ink used. Their girls wash every evening the blankets used on the cylinders. Bank-note engravers of the first order receive a salary of $4,000. Some receive from $2,000 to $3,000 per annum. Bank note engravers work but eight hours a day. Mr. M. thinks there would not be much difficulty, if a lady wanted to learn bank note engraving, from the prejudices of men, for some of them are not only just but generous. One of the gentlemen engraving knew several ladies in England that were bank note engravers.

90. Card Engravers. I was told by a card engraver that it was not usual to pay a learner anything. He gives his apprentice only his board the first year. A card engraver may draw letters well, and not be able to write well, and *vice versa.* One should be steady and patient to draw and form letters, and possess some natural taste, to succeed. It requires also much practice. A card engraver can earn $5 a day, if he is industrious, and has sufficient work. A journeyman is paid in proportion to his abilities, from $5 to $25 per week. Some card engravers earn $2,000 a year, clear of all expenses. The older a city, the more engraving is done. In Europe, first-class merchants never use type cards, but engraved ones.

91. Door Plate Engravers. I was told by a door plate engraver that a skilful person, who would apply himself closely, could learn the business, so that, at the end of one year, he could make a living. For door plate engraving, it is necessary to form letters well. The size of the letters for a given space must be divided by the eye. It requires great care, as one badly formed letter would spoil the whole plate. Engraving of any kind fatigues the back from stooping, and the eyes from straining. In door plate engraving the eyes suffer least fatigue. Of course less strength is necessary for plate engraving if the tools are of a good quality and in proper order.

92. Map Engravers. Map engraving is divided into two kinds: the lettering and plain work. The last can be learned in six months by a person of taste and talent. The most that is needed is practice. A knowledge of drawing is not necessary for this branch. There is not much map engraving done in this country, because of the expense. Most is done in New York and Philadelphia. The best map engraving done in Paris is executed by ladies. There are also some ladies employed in map engraving in London, and card engraving is there quite common for ladies.

93. Picture and Heraldry Engravers.

Engraving pictures pays well—a man often earning $10 a day. A superior landscape engraver calculates to earn $2,500 a year. Mr. R. historical engraver, does the engraving for the *Cosmopolitan Art Journal.* He says : " In England, better prices are paid for historical engraving than here. Those who do the work receive less, but the employer has a greater profit than in the United States. More time is allowed the engraver in England to execute a piece of work." Mr. R. pays his hands from $7 to $10 a week, and the best historical engraver never gets in this country over $30 a week. In England the work hours of an engraver are nine ; here seven. He says the art is dying out both here and in England. It is a something in which we can always be improving. Seven years was formerly the length of apprenticeship in England, and there an apprentice was paid nothing while learning ; on the contrary, the parent usually pays a premium of £100. When an apprentice has finished, he will earn £1 a week, and continue to receive more according to his skill and ability. Some people send pictures from the United States to England to be engraved, saying they cannot do such work in this country as in England ; while, if they would pay the same price, and allow the engravers as much time, it could be done just as well. Such an engraving as you would pay $150 for here, in England you would pay $200 for. In England it is customary for an engraver to confine himself to one style ; for instance, in " Falstaff Mustering his Recruits," one engraver would do the wall, another the figures, and another the drapery. Mr. R. was paid only $2,000 for engraving " Falstaff Mustering his Recruits," and it took three men two years. The business is not unhealthy, and not injurious to the eyesight, although a glass must be used constantly. Mr. J., historical engraver, used to have persons employed that did the different parts of a picture, and he paid them each from $15 to $25 a week. He thinks, of those who learn metal engraving in Europe, not more than fifty per cent. pursue it as a vocation, and not above four per cent. attain perfection. Some engraving, both picture and letter, is done by etching, but the best and most expensive with a graver. Mr. J. M. Sartain writes in answer to a circular : " I have no females in my employment, because I work alone. To direct others or alter what they do wrong, takes longer than doing the whole work myself. Neither do I know of females being employed by others in my branch of business. But if I were willing to be troubled with the teaching of any one at all, I should choose a female. This is from my experience of the males I taught in times past. Women have the requisites more than men—patience, neatness, delicacy ; and the occupation is as suitable for them as any other they are accustomed to adopt. An unmarried daughter of mine is about to learn from me, with a view to follow it as a profession. The chance of employment is however very limited, for the reason that the cost of printing plates separately necessitates, in an extensive class of pictorial embellishments, the use of woodcuts. This wood engraving is equally suited for females, and to a limited extent they are thus employed. The field in that branch is a wide one already, with a constantly increasing demand. In my own branch of engraving, the kind of skill required is that of *drawing*. The mere mechanical skill required in *any* kind of engraving is easily attained; but the art of *drawing* is the great thing, and positively demands aptitude and taste—at all events, quite close application and earnestness. *Skill in drawing* is a key that admits to a wider range of arts than I can readily enumerate, and successful and profitable employment in any engraving depends on *that*. I am chairman of the committee on instruction of the Board of Directors of the Pennsylvania Academy of the Fine Arts, and in that capacity do all I can (as do also the other directors) to encourage female talent. We have seven or eight ladies among our students, and they *certainly* are fully equal to the males in capacity for acquiring art. Some model, others only draw. The whole of our academy studies are gratuitous. For whatever branch of the fine arts is to be followed, the first requisite is *drawing*, and the next is *drawing*, and the third and last is *drawing*." Mr. B., heraldic chaser, says there are several processes in making heraldry plates, sketching, engraving, embossing, chasing, and burnishing. He used to employ girls to burnish. The making of patterns for heraldry is never taught in this country to women, as it would cause the labor of men so employed to depreciate. He pays a man from $15 to $20 a week for chasing. He charges $1 for finding the coat of arms of an individual or family.

94. Telegraph Operators. A new source of employment has been opened by the invention of the electric telegraph. Most of the telegraphing in England is done by women, and in the United States a number of ladies are employed as operators. To a quick and intelligent mind it requires but a short time to learn. An English paper says: "Here women do the business better than men, because of the more undivided attention they pay to their duties; but considerable inconvenience is found to result from their ignorance of business terms, which causes them to make mistakes in the messages sent. However, a short course of previous instruction easily overcomes this impediment." We have been told that, in one telegraph office in London, several hundred women are employed. I hope the application of steam to the operations of the electric telegraph may not interfere with the entrance of women into the occupation. In New Lisbon, Ohio, a young woman was employed, a few years ago, as principal operator in a telegraph office, with the same salary received by the man who preceded her in that office. " I was told by her," writes my informant, " that several women were qualifying themselves, in Cleveland, for the same occupation." The ex-superintendent of a line writes : " I have long been persuaded that ultimately a large proportion of the telegraphists, employed exclusively for writing, would be females, both because of their usually reliable habits, their ability to abstract and concentrate thought upon their engagements, their greater patience and industry, and the economy of their wages. In offices where there is a large amount of business, and, consequently, much intercommunication with customers, I have supposed the arrangement would be to have a clerk to receive and deliver communications, and the corps of operators and writers, composed exclusively of females, in an adjoining or upper room, apart from public inspection. And to this arrangement, I think, there is at this time very little to oppose, except the antagonism naturally felt by male operators, who see in it a loss of employment to themselves, and a want of proper facilities for teaching and obtaining a complement, in number, of female telegraphists. Any female proficient in orthography, with an inclination to useful employment, would make a good telegraphist, and might readily command, under a system above indicated, a salary of from $300 to $500, and be profitable to her employers beyond the ordinary male telegraphists employed under the present arrangement of office. It is in operating by the Morse system that ladies are mostly or entirely employed. The Morse is the easiest. They telegraph in small towns, where there is not much to do, and the compensation is small." The Electric Telegraph Company in London suggests that women should be employed in preference to men, as working more rapidly. All the lady telegraphists we have heard of gave satisfaction to all parties concerned. To Mr. A., connected with the New York and Boston telegraph line, I am indebted for the following information : " Women are employed in operating the Morse instrument. They are paid from $6 to $25 per month, and are paid by the month. For the class of offices in which females are employed, about the same wages are paid both sexes. It requires from three to six weeks to learn, and nothing is paid while learning. The qualifications needed are a fair knowledge of orthography, arithmetic, geography, and ordinary mechanical ability. We may want a few operatives, say six annually. The employment is constant, and about ten hours a day are devoted to work. We employ about fifty women, and they only at small offices. Nearly all are American. The employment is comfortable. There are no parts of our occupation suitable for women in which they are not engaged. They are generally more attentive and trustworthy than men. The price they pay for board depends on the locality, say from $1.50 to $2 per week."

95. Vocalists. This is an important and profitable employment—one that has secured to many a poor foreigner visiting this country a snug little fortune. We have only to cite the cases of Jenny Lind, Garcia, Sontag, Parodi, and Catherine Hays. It was stated in the New York *Tribune* of December, 1853, that Catherine Hays had sent $50,000 to purchase an estate in Ireland. American talent is in some cases very highly cultivated; but we fear the Scripture verse applies to the substantial encouragement of native vocalists amongst us : " A prophet is not without honor, save in his own country, and in his own house." Too much money and attention, we think, are lavished upon foreign vocalists, while home talent is depreciated. An American singer must often go to other countries and acquire a name, before she is received with eclat in her own. It may be that other countries have the same failing, but, we think, not to the same extent. Let us love American talent, and encourage it before every other. Adelaide Patti, Miss Hinckley, and Miss Kellogg are at present the most noted singers of American birth. Mr. C. told me, that in New York, lady singers receive from $100 to $400 per annum for singing in churches. One lady choir-singer of whom we knew, received $500 a year, singing twice on Sabbath. Not more than from twelve to fifteen lady singers in New York receive over $350. One lady in a fashionable church receives $1,000 ; but she is a widow, and somewhat favored. Another lady, leading the choir in a Broadway church, receives a salary of $1,000, I have been told.

96. Wax Work. I called on two Italians that make wax fruit ; their baskets vary in price from twenty-five cents to $2. It would take a day and a half to make a $2 basket. The Italian that could speak some English told me that when he goes out to work, he charges $2.50 a day ; but to give lessons, he would charge $2 a day. He thought an individual might learn in eight, ten, twelve, or fifteen lessons, according to abilities and taste. Miss W., teacher of wax flowers, charges $1 a lesson, and thinks eight or ten lessons sufficient. She thinks in country places there would be openings for teachers. I think, where there are large seminaries, a teacher would do better. She says there is an opening in Troy. If a person has enough to do, it pays well. She makes by hand; they are more natural than those made by moulds.

97. Wood Engravers. Much and long-continued toil is requisite for success in wood engraving. A great deal depends, also, on the talent of the individual. Wood engraving is a business adapted to women, as it requires mostly patience and application, and but little physical strength. Mechanical skill is the most that is requisite, yet, as in everything else, it bespeaks the soul and taste of the originator. "Women's nimble fingers, accustomed to wield the needle, lend themselves quite easily to minute operations in the use of small instruments and the almost imperceptible shades of manipulation that wood engraving exacts." As more publishing is done in our country, of course there will be a greater demand for wood engravers. A great many newspapers now contain a large number of woodcuts, as *Harper's Weekly*, *Frank Leslie's Illustrated News*, &c. Wood engraving has been called into use for Government reports and scientific works, aside from its extensive demands for periodical literature. A lady engaged in the business writes of a class in wood engraving: "The pupils vary so much in ability, application, perseverance, and in the number of hours devoted to it, that it is impossible to judge what any one may do who has not made a trial. My own experience is that the practice of wood engraving brings a sure return for all the outlay of time and trouble spent in acquiring the art. It would hardly be safe to rely entirely upon the proceeds of the second year; the third may make up for it. The best wood engraving is done in England and the United States. In classes of wood engraving in the schools of design in England, the students are required to produce the drawing as well as to engrave it." "For a quarter of a century past, many hundreds of young women, we are assured, have supported themselves by wood engraving, for which there is now a demand which no jealousy in the stronger sex can intercept. The effort to exclude women was made in this, as in other branches of art; but the interests of publishers and the public were more than a match for it." "In 1839, Charlotte Nesbit, Marianne Williams, Mary Byfield, Mary and Elizabeth Clint, held honorable positions among English wood engravers." Miss F., at Elmira, New York, carries on business for herself in wood engraving. She learned it at the Cooper Institute, four years ago. The pupils of that institute canvassed for work, some two and two, but she went alone, and principally in the lower part of the city. They visited publishers mostly—she went to manufacturers. She got an order for $500 worth of engraving at a gasfixture manufactory. I have heard that ladies in the school of design, New York, receive the same price for wood engraving that men would receive. N. Orr, the wood engraver, thinks the prospect very good for a woman to earn a livelihood at it. He knows a lady who has not only supported herself but partially supported her parents by her work. For wood engraving, women usually receive as good prices as men. The business is increasing. There are none West, except a few in Cincinnati, and I believe a still smaller number in St. Louis and Chicago. A person that has any talent for it can earn a living at it in less than two years' practice. A knowledge of drawing is not essential, as the drawing is usually put on the wood by the designer. Mr. Orr takes apprentices, but pays nothing the first year. They are bound to him for five or six years. Some engravers require a premium. I have been told that designing requires a very different and much higher order of talent than wood engraving. One designer can do enough in a day to keep a man busy a week. New York is the principal city for wood engraving. I think most men, while engraving, stand; but all the ladies that I have seen at work sat. "A wood-engraving office in Cleveland employed three girls in 1845, at wages varying from $3 to $7 per week, according to the experience of each in the business, being the same that men receive in the same office."

MERCANTILE PURSUITS.

98. Merchants. Occasionally we hear such complaints as these : "Women who keep stores of their own ask higher for their goods than men, and saleswomen are less obliging than male clerks." Women, as a general thing, do not understand their business as well as men, and that is the reason they are not so well liked. Those inclined to be bold, may become pert ; and those in poor health, peevish. "If women were more employed in stores," said Mr. P., "there would probably be less shopping, but as many goods sold. Young girls that go shopping to whisper in the ears of clerks, would then find something else to do." Woman has a power of adaptedness that fits her admirably for the vocation of a merchant. A friend remarked to me that Mr. Stewart, of New York, she thought, would employ women in his store, if a large number of fashionable and influential ladies would petition him to do so. If the retail merchants of our large cities and towns would combine and employ only sales-women, how greatly would they promote the welfare of the nation! Young men would no longer waste their health, strength, and talents selling gloves, tape, and dress goods, but would cultivate the soil, or find openings as traders, speculators, mechanics, and manufacturers, in cities, towns, and villages of our Western country. They might do something more creditable to their physical powers, while they gave their half-starved sisters a chance to earn an honest livelihood. If ladies would patronize those stores only in which there were saleswomen, and influence their friends to do so, employers who now engage the service of salesmen would soon learn what was to their interest, and make a change. Promptness and regularity are desirable qualifications in a shop-keeper. The business brings those engaged into intercourse with all classes of people. Mrs. Dall makes this statement: "It is a singular fact that there are a great many more women in England in business for themselves than employed as tenders or clerks; while in America, the fact, at the present day, is directly the reverse." A lady who has lived in New York all her life said, if the merchants of the city would employ women, they could find twenty thousand to-morrow, ready and willing to enter their stores. In Paris large stores are owned and conducted by women, and even the importing and exporting of goods is in the hands of some. The tact and address of French women admirably fit them for shopkeepers. Many of the smaller fancy and variety stores in our cities are owned by women, that have by long-continued industry earned a competency. Lady merchants can to some extent control the taste of the community where they are; for such articles as they purchase and keep on hand will be likely to find sale. The taste of the best keepers of dry-goods and fancy stores, millinery establishments, and embroidery shops will be displayed in the dress of their patrons. To merchandize extensively, requires much experience and knowledge of business; but to those that are qualified it presents an extensive opening for enterprise. Barter, or the exchange of one kind of goods for another, is very common in the villages and towns of our country. The Gothscheer (Austrian) women often follow the trade of peddlers, and are absent from their homes many months, travelling about the country with staff in hand and a pack at their back. "Advertising and politeness are the main levers to get customers. Advertising will draw them; ability to fill their orders will satisfy them; and politeness will induce them to buy." Quick perceptive powers and judgment are also essential to the success of merchants. It is very desirable to have a good location for a store. A lady keeping a small dry-goods store told me she sells $100 worth of goods a week on an average. She has been nine years in the business, and constantly gaining trade. She likes rainy Saturday evenings, as she then sells most. She said one must use judgment in the amount of profit to be made on various articles. A person must regulate her prices by others. On some goods she can make but five per cent., and on some others fifty. Many of the fortunes in Boston are said to have been founded by women engaged in trade. And the ladies on Nantucket Island during the Revolutionary war conducted the business of their husbands, fathers, and brothers. A lady wrote, some years back, of some stores in one of our large cities: "The proprietors say they give from twenty-five to fifty per cent. more to the males than to the females of equal talent and capacity, but can give no reason why they should do it, except that it is the custom, and some parts of the business require more physical strength, as some articles are too heavy to be handled by women." Yet why not, we would ask, place women in the lighter departments, and pay them exactly what would be paid a man for the same work? The average wages of females in Philadelphia are $4.50 per week, though some get as high as $7 or $8, but very few above $6. In a few of the stores of New York and Philadelphia the business is conducted entirely by ladies. There is a school of commerce for women at Perth, France. We read an account some time ago of a colored woman on the Island of Hayti, who is a wholesale dealer in provisions, and worth from $15,000 to $20,000, that she has made by her own industry and business tact. She can neither read nor write, but trusts entirely to her memory. She sells on credit to retail dealers, and to girls whom she has trained. The merchants have such unlimited confidence in her, that they will trust her to any amount. Nearly all the commercial business of Hayti is done by women.

99. Bookkeepers. The employment of female accountants is gradually extending in our cities. In female institutions of learning, and in benevolent institutions, lady bookkeepers might be very well employed. Indeed, we think, they would find no difficulty in obtaining situations. We know that many merchants would employ them, if they were properly qualified. We know of some that now occupy lucrative situations in fancy dry goods and millinery stores. We have no doubt but the books of most mercantile men would be more accurately kept, if their wives and daughters had charge of them. In all European countries women keep the books of the majority of retail stores. The books of nine tenths of the retail stores in Paris are kept by women. They are fenced in, and separated from the saleswomen by a framework of glass. A number of women are employed as accountants at hotels in Europe. There is a large school for instruction in bookkeeping in Paris, where the pupils are practically trained. An exchange of articles of a trivial nature, and a cheap coin of some kind, are used as a medium of circulation. At one of the largest wholesale warehouses in Boston, the head corresponding clerk is a young woman, who writes a beautiful, rapid hand, and fulfils the duties of the situation to the complete satisfaction of her liberal employer. A practical knowledge of arithmetic is necessary for bookkeeping and selling goods—two of the most inviting openings now presented to women of ordinary intelligence. The lady who keeps the books of T—'s skirt factory, New York, receives a salary of $400. Mr. M. prefers lady bookkeepers, because they are more particular in keeping accounts, and they are more patient in their calculations. They are, as a general thing, more honest and conscientious. Women are just as capable of becoming good financiers as men. Industry, honesty, and promptness, with the ability to write a plain, correct business letter, ability to calculate rapidly and correctly, with a knowledge of bookkeeping, certainly should insure a situation to a lady, where there is a vacancy. It is well, however, for those who have qualified themselves for bookkeeping, to obtain a certificate : it is a passport that will aid them in securing a place. The salaries of bookkeepers in New York run from $250 to $2,500. At a large store, where saleswomen were employed, I was told they find lady bookkeepers more accurate in their accounts, and not so likely to appropriate money that don't belong to them. Where a gentleman bookkeeper receives $15, a lady usually receives but $8. I know of one lady in Cleveland, assistant cashier, who received a salary of $300. An accountant in Boston replies to a circular sent him : " I think the employment as favorable to bodily health as any sedentary occupation ; but in my particular line of business it is rather trying to the head, as it often requires close application and intense thought. Those who employ women here as clerks, undoubtedly pay them by the day, week, month, or year, where they have permanent situations ; but for transient work, by the piece Women can always be hired cheaper than men, as it costs them less to live. I am fifty years old, and have been figuring ever since I was sixteen ; still, I learn something new about accounts every day. A woman would have to serve a long apprenticeship in accounts and on books, before she could do much in adjusting accounts. For a first-class bookkeeper, practical experience in accounts and bookkeeping of business of all kinds are necessary qualifications. I always prefer the early part of the day for work. My business is as good at one season of the year as another. I attend to business as it suits my pleasure—sometimes four or five hours, and sometimes twelve or fifteen, according to the nature and importance of the task, and depending oftentimes upon the length of it, and the time when it is wanted. As a general thing, men and women everywhere in the United States keep as far apart in business affairs as possible—it is the custom. The counting house, office, and place of business are not suitable for a female. I would state that I charge for making out accounts and adjusting books, as a general rule here in Boston, $10 per day, and sometimes more—never less. I have had all prices, from $10 to $50 per day, for one, two, and three months in succession. Sometimes I take a job by contract, say for $500, or some other specific sum, as may be agreed upon, according to the nature and value of the service rendered."

100. Book Merchants. In many of the new towns springing up in the West, there are openings for booksellers. Many colleges and seminaries are being built up, thereby offering a still better market for the sale of school books. It would be well for those going into the business to ascertain, before doing so, what books are used in the literary institutions of the place. Some booksellers are so mean as to sell old-fashioned, out-of-date school books to country merchants, thereby clearing their own stock, and imposing their unsalable goods on others. No doubt, many established book merchants would be willing to trust, to such as they have confidence in, a stock of books to be sold on commission. When a sufficient sum is acquired, the individual can purchase a stock of her own. Many dry-goods merchants keep a few books, but when there is a sufficient sale of books, a store, if expenses are only cleared for a while, may gradually become a revenue of profit, and is likely to prove a permanent business, where discretion and industry are used. In London and Paris, women sell stationery, almanacs, memorandum books, diaries, and pocket books, on the streets. Public auctions of books are held frequently in cities and towns. Agents do much to extend a circulation of books. In large cities, merchants confine their stock of books to two or three kinds—as those of medicine, law, theology, or school books; but, as a general thing, miscellaneous books are kept. The trade sales which occur in Boston once, and in Philadelphia and New York twice a year, are only attended by booksellers. These sales last but a few days. The prices at which books sell at these auctions are considered a pretty fair criterion of their future worth. Miss. H. told me of a Miss P., niece of Horace Mann, now living in Concord, N. H., who kept a bookstore in Boston, and imported books to fill orders, but was crushed by other book importers, because she was a woman. In many towns and cities, women keep small stores for the sale of stationery, magazines, newspapers, &c. " In large stationery stores, women might be employed to stamp initials on paper," with small hand presses made for the purpose.

101. China Merchants. This business is peculiarly appropriate to women. Who so well able to handle china as careful women? Who so well able to judge what will look well on a table? It comes so entirely within their province, that the mind readily suggests the appropriateness. In Paris, most, if not all the china stores are kept by women. A lady china-dealer, on one of the avenues, told me that she sells considerable at night to working women, who cannot spare the time to go shopping in the day; also, to ladies living in cross streets near, who go out walking in the evenings with their husbands, and call to buy articles in her line. It does not require as many attendants in a china as in any other kind of store. A girl is more careful and steady, and can dust china better than a boy; but a boy answers best to take china home. She sells most about the holidays. It takes time to learn the business well. In an Eastern city, two ladies stood in their father's store, and so learned the business. They married brothers, and each opened china stores, which they attended, while their husbands engaged in other business. They are both widows now, but have raised and educated their children. A son and son-in-law of one conduct the business. They employ saleswomen, paying from $5 to $8 a week. They are now in search of two intelligent young women, from fifteen to eighteen years of age, to grow up to the business. They require a little more readiness in arithmetic, tact, and general business qualifications than they can easily meet with. From their experience they judge the employment to be healthy. A lady in a large china store on Broadway, New York, receives $5 a week. A lady in another store told me that lifting crockery causes quite a strain on the back, and should be done by men. A person gets very dusty who attends china. It requires lifting and dusting, and now and then must be washed—always when first taken out of the crate. Mrs. L. and her husband are English, and have been brought up to the business. She sells most about Christmas. She is on her feet all the time. To learn the names of all the articles sold in a large store, and their prices, and to exercise care in handling, requires patience. A china merchant writes: " Women are generally paid less than men. There is a difference of from $10 to $40 per month in favor of men, because (with few exceptions) women are not so well qualified to do business as men. It would take from six to eight months to learn to sell china. A clear head, common sense, and activity are the qualifications needed. Women are not more likely to be thrown out of employment than men, if as well qualified." A lady told me, the china is a slow business and seldom pays more than twenty-five per cent., but is a sure business for the cheaper kind of goods. The profit is not so much as for fancy articles of ladies' wear; but less is lost from the change of style. China merchants, she thought, seldom employ women; why, she could not tell. Mr. H., who employs a girl, paid her $1.50 a week and board the first year, then raised her wages to $7 a month. He thinks if more girls would qualify themselves for china stores they would be likely to find employment. A girl should commence young, but should know how to read and write, on account of taking orders. He thinks it best to get homely girls, rather advanced in age, to attend store, because the young and handsome ones will get married. He prefers girls, because they are more quiet and steady. Small articles of china he sends the girl home with; heavy articles he takes himself. A lady, whose ware was partly out of doors and partly in the house, said she had dusted it at least a dozen times through the day, and then it was covered with dust. Her breakage is considerable. She sells most about Christmas. Another china dealer told me, she sells most in spring, when people go to housekeeping. E. L., in the Five Points, sells most in summer, because her patrons are poor people, and in summer the men have most work, and their expenses are lighter—consequently the women have more money. Her stand is a good one, but she does not much more than make a living. The business requires some experience in buying and selling. Ladies sometimes come into the store to purchase articles they would not like to ask a man for. A girl keeping a china stand told me she sells most in spring and fall. She pays $3 a month for ground rent, but owns the shelter. She locks it at night, and it is perfectly secure, for her lock is different from all others. It does not take long to learn to sell common ware. She expects to sell all winter at her stand, and has to be on her feet all the time. She sells on an average from $2 to $3 worth a day.

102. Clothiers. In London there are shops confined to the sale of nautical clothes, and some to the sale of theatrical attire. B.'s sewers (New York) earn from $2 to $10 per week—piece work, of course. Most of it is done by machine. Meritorious girls need never be out of work, said Mr. B.; yet he can always get plenty of hands. He has much of his work done in New Jersey. Some men make a business of taking it from establishments, and hire women all through the country to do it. There are two kinds of tailoring—custom and slop work. The last is subdivided into the cheap slop work and that of the best quality, and there are two kinds of establishments for this common work—that which is not better done perhaps than the other, but for which a better price is paid and received, and done by houses of standing and reputation. The other is done by extortionists, Jews and Germans, and patronized by their own class. As tailoring is done now, it does not require a regular apprenticeship as in bygone years, particularly for those who work by machine. I met a girl on the steps, seeking for work, who told me she makes $4 a week as operator, when she can get steady work. One of the proprietors of L. & B.'s clothing establishment told me some of their workmen earn from $8 to $10 a week, working by the piece. Much of their work is for California. They employ hands most of the year, as they work both for the home and foreign market. The great trouble is that the majority of tailoresses are inefficient. Some are widows, striving to support their children. Some have dissipated husbands, and are subject to constant interruption. Some have not the time to properly learn the trade, and, consequently, such workers cannot have that labor which pays best, however much they need it. The character of work done by applicants is judged of by turning to the book of their former employer, and seeing what prices were paid. In hard times, like these, employers try to retain those that are dependent on their labor for their bread. The foreman said, in good times, there is work enough for all the tailoresses in New York. They pay good operators $5 a week—a day of ten hours. All the summer work is done by machines. The pressing and basting is done by men. The foreman of the S. Brothers' establishment says the best place for tailoresses is in the West, where there are openings, and they can make money. The only trouble is, the poor have not money to go West. All their work is done by machines, and all given out. They do not give work more than six months in the year, and that barely keeps the girls while they are at work. P. & C. have their machines worked by hot condensed air. The operators receive from $4.50 to $6. Basters are only small girls, and earn from $2 to $3 a week. B. & Co., clothiers, give work out, and, of course, pay by the piece. Their most busy times are from October to March, and from April to September. They do Southern work. Some of the workers only earn $2.50 if they are slow, even if they are industrious and constantly at work. Some of their best hands can earn $6 a week, but are likely to be at least two months out of employment. The prospect for tailoresses is poor. I have heard that some good hands are wanted in Chicago. A great deal of clothing is sold there to people from the surrounding country and towns. B. does not require any deposit, but a girl must show her book from her other employers. They have thousands of applications for work. The reason more clothing is not made up out of the city is the difficulty in procuring such tailors' trimmings as they need just at the time they are wanted. Most clothing establishments keep a list of those that do not return work taken out, and send them to each other. On persons applying to the foremen, he turns to his book to see if the names are among the delinquents. He thinks girls in service are more certain of making a living, for they are paid from $1 to $2 a week for their work, and have their board, which would be from $1 to $3 a week, and a competent servant need not be out of employment; while slop work is very uncertain, and everything that is made goes for board and clothes. Many of these shop girls sleep half a dozen in a garret, on straw beds, without sufficient covering. Many might go to the country and the West and get employment, but they have not the means; and, if they had the means to go, might not have enough to come back, if they found it necessary. F. D. & Co., clothiers. Their girls earn from $3 to $6 per week, paid by the piece, and done at home. They give most of their work to men who have machines and employ operatives. The prospect for this kind of work is poor. Not more than two thirds of the hands in the city, in this department of labor, will be retained. When business is good they are able to keep their hands employed all the year, except for a few weeks when changing from thin to thick work, and *vice versa.* They sometimes give a girl work to do as a sample. A woman told me of three girls occupying the room above her, that have a sewing machine. Two baste and finish off, and one operates. They work day and night, and one she knows is even now earning $8 a week. They make flannel shirts, receiving 75 cents a dozen, without putting in the sleeves, working the button holes, or putting on the buttons. I saw a girl that receives 87 cents a dozen for making flannel shirts. We have seen it stated that " persons possessed of machines, who make up large quantities of clothing at very low prices, are enabled, by the speed at which they can work the machines, to produce sufficient to remunerate all the parties employed, at an average of $4 a week." One clothier in Albany, New York, pays $3 a week to his hands working eleven hours a a day. He furnishes work steadily through the fall, and pays men better wages, because they can do more work. The proprietor of a mammoth establishment in New York, D., writes: " We employ women in making pants, vests, shirts, and summer coats, both by the week and by the piece. When the sewers take work out, it is by the piece; but when the work is done in the shop, it is paid for by the week. The wages by the week range from $3 to $7. Women thoroughly educated in the trade can make about $6 per week, men about $9—their work is heavier. The number of branches in this trade, and the time of preparation for each, varies. We never receive learners. As the articles are of general use, good hands usually find employment. The work is brisk from November till March 1st, and from May till September 1st. The time of work could be shortened, but at the expense of the laborers' wages. In a city like ours, there is always a full supply of hands. About two thirds of our women are American. Women could not be employed to sell clothing to men." This firm employed, in February, 1860, five hundred hands in the shop, and eight hundred outside. In B. Brothers' establishment, "indoor work is paid by the week. An agent pays for the outdoor work by the piece. Those in the house average $5 per week. Men do heavier work and receive $7. Women make vests and pantaloons; men, coats. They work in the same room. The men do the pressing." (I expect it is a rule that they shall not speak to each other, for not one word did I hear any of them speak in the half hour I spent in the room.) "It requires about six months to learn the business. They do not take learners. An ability to sew well, and neatness with the work, are necessary. They sell most when the country is in a peaceful and prosperous condition. They sell most clothing to Western customers about the 1st of January, and to city retail stores about the 1st of February. They work ten hours a day. There is a surplus of hands in New York. They employ seventy in the house, and between 2,000 and 3,000 outside. The number of Americans is about 20 per cent." Great injustice is done by women in the country, in comfortable circumstances, who do the work at a very low price, merely to obtain pocket money. An English tailor in New York hires girls for making pants and coats. He pays one $4, one $3.50, and another $3, and they work from 7 A. M. to 7 P. M. There is no difference in the prices paid, except when the man's work is heavier. Spring and fall are the best seasons for work. Men can press better, because they have more strength; but women can stitch as well, if they have the experience. He kept one operator at $6 a week in busy times, and $3 in slack times, and another at $5 the year round. Some of the poor tailors in New York rent a room, occupy a spot themselves, and rent out the rest of the room to others at the same kind of work, charging fifty cents for seat room for a man and a girl to assist him; thir-

ty-seven cents for a man alone.   It is not easy to get good hand
tailoresses, for most are employed on machines.   One firm, that
employ about five hundred hands, write they pay from $3 to $5
per week of ten hours a day, and that it requires two years to
learn the trade.   S. & D., manufacturers and venders of boys'
clothing, write : " Their work is done by the piece, so much a
garment, and wages run from $2 to $6 a week, of ten hours a
day—of course, depending on the skill and hours of the worker.
The relative wages between men and women are, as sewers, say
for men, one third more ; that is, as four for the women and six
for the men.   The business of a tailoress is numbered among the
regular trades for women, and requires somewhat more than the
average trade time, say one year.   They excel as vest makers—
a branch almost exclusively confined to them.   There is no uniform usage in regard to pay.   The requisites are good eyesight,
average strength, and if taste be superadded, the better.   Winter is the best season for those who work for wholesale venders.
Women are most apt to be out of employment in summer.   The
demand is, at present, less than the supply.   There is a surplus
of vest makers, and a deficiency, if anywhere, in children's suit
making.   It is an occupation less suited to women than trades
that require more nicety of touch and eye, such as designing or
wood engraving.   The majority of tailoresses in New York city
are German and Irish."   A firm engaged in the merchant tailoring and ready-made clothing business write : " The occupation
is unhealthy, because the workers are constantly sitting.   They
earn from $2 to $4.50 per week, ten hours a day.   We pay men
better, because they are stronger and more capable, and have
more experience.   Men receive from $9 to $12.   It requires four
years for men to learn the business, and two years for women to
learn it so as to earn $4 per week.   The qualifications needed
are common sense, good taste, and strong eyes.   From March to
January is the busy season ; but good hands have work all the
year."   B. O. & S. " give their work out.   Their trade is
Southern.   Their spring work begins 1st October, and continues until the last of March ; and fall work begins in May, and
lasts until September.   They do not require a deposit, but a
recommendation from the last employer, and give some work to
applicants to do as a sample.   Some is done by hand, some by
machinery.   Wages run from $3 up.   Much of their work is
done by Germans, whose wives assist them.   It is sometimes
difficult for them to get good hands.   The foreman dismissed the
Jews he found at work when he went there, for he thinks they
are not reliable.   Some get work out, but intrust it to others to
do, and so it is poorly done.   The foreman said many women

spend a day or two out of every week running from shop to shop to get work. He has never lost anything by girls not returning goods. If they should keep them, they would soon be known at the different establishments, and have no place to go for work." In Maine, New Hampshire, Vermont, Massachusetts, Rhode Island, Connecticut, New York, Pennsylvania, New Jersey, Delaware, Maryland, District of Columbia, and Ohio, during the year ending June 1st, 1860, 36,155 males and 52,515 females were employed in making clothing.

103. Curiosity Dealers. In large cities, a few persons may find employment in this way. To the business of selling coins, medals, buckles, old-time jewelry, &c., is usually added the sale of shells and foreign birds. The same persons might engage in the sale of stuffed birds and animals, marine plants, minerals, and other such articles as are suitable for placing in a museum. Many women on the streets of London sell coins, medals, &c.

104. Druggists and Druggists' Clerks. Some knowledge of medicines and their nature is requisite to an attendant in a drug store. The business is light, and, to some, a pleasant one. In a large drug store, one of the clerks might be a young man, to attend to night prescriptions. The day business could easily be carried on by ladies, if they were qualified. Many articles sold by druggists require a chemical or mechanical combination. Schools for giving instruction in the art of preparing medicines are established in New York and Philadelphia. If enough ladies would unite to form a class, we have no doubt that separate instruction would be given them by the professors of pharmacy. We hope these schools will tend to prevent abuses in the prosecution of the drug business, as those persons will be most patronized who are known as graduates of these schools. Dyestuffs, paint, hair oils, &c., are sold by most druggists, besides the materials directly used in their business. The apothecary's business is more confined to the mixing and putting up of medicines, as prescribed by physicians. Girls that put up drugs are paid by the package, and earn from $2 to $5 per week. Most country physicians prepare and sell their own medicines. Censors in Great Britain visit the stores of druggists, and are required by law to destroy any medicines they consider not fit for use. In France the regulations are equally strict. In some parts of France and Germany, sisters of charity are employed to compound medicines, and some to administer them. Mrs. Jameson, in her " Communion of Labor," describes her visits to several hospitals in Europe, in charge of sisters of charity, where some of their number were employed to fill prescriptions, both homœopathic and allopathic. I find that in most Roman Catholic institutions in this country, some sisters are set apart to perform the duties of druggists. In 1776, when Howard visited Lyons, he found "there were sisters who made up, as well as administered, all the medicines prescribed, for which purpose there were a laboratory and apothecary's shop, the neatest and most elegantly fitted up that can be conceived." Lord Brougham, in a speech at York, about two years ago, after eulogizing the Protestant sisters of charity as nurses, said: "They are the persons who make up, who distribute, who administer all the medicines; they are, as I can answer from my own knowledge practically in the matter, as well acquainted with the chemical preparations as the professional men themselves." In the preparation of fine chemicals in laboratories, women are sometimes employed. A druggist told me that a person in his business need never be idle. When not otherwise employed, he can be making tinctures, compounds, &c. It requires four or five years to become a competent druggist. The business is one on which hang the lives of its patrons. Some druggists put up their goods very neatly, and make them look beautiful; but often sacrifice, to do so, their medicinal properties. The standard of druggists is higher in Philadelphia than New York. In Philadelphia, many young men receive nothing for their services, while learning; but in New York, boys over fifteen are generally paid $100 the first year, and more afterward. Many of the best druggists will not make or sell patent medicines. In some new parts of the Western country, druggists unite their calling with something else; and are often but a poor excuse for druggists, deriving their profits mostly from nostrums. One in the business needs a retentive memory. In the census of Great Britain, three hundred and ten females are returned as druggists. Dr. Brandreth has his pills made at Sing Sing. He employs twelve females, and pays an average of $5 per week to each one. The widow of a deceased druggist and chemist told me that the receipts left by her husband she could easily dispose of for a thousand dollars. We have seen it stated that the average hours per day of a drug clerk are thirteen, and his wages $9. The neatness of women, their delicacy and attention to details, qualify them admirably for the drug business. At the Woman's Infirmary, New York, the apothecary's department is entirely in the hands of ladies. At St. Luke's, a lady of education and refinement (a sister of the Order of the Holy Communion) gives her services to the measuring out and dispensing of medicines. At Smith's homœopathic pharmacy, the lady in attendance told me nearly the whole in their department of business is in the hands of females. They employ men, to press the plants and make tinctures; but the distilling of water and alcohol, the pulverizing, triturating and diluting, cleaning vials, corking, labelling, and stamping, are done by women. It requires neatness, exactness, and quickness, to succeed in putting up medicines. The girls, while at work, wear clothes that will not suffer from their labor, which is not the cleanest in the world. The proprietor of the establishment wrote me : " We employ six ladies, and prefer them to men, as their work is neater. We pay them from $3 to $6 per week, and they work from nine to ten hours. There is no difference in the seasons, as regards our employment. We pay women from the first; and they may learn the part done by them in from three to six months. As their work is essentially different from men's, we cannot make a comparison in the prices paid." At another homœopathic pharmacy, I was told they employ a few girls to wash bottles, to put on labels, and place them in the boxes. They are paid from $3 to $3.50 a week. At a wholesale drug store, one of the proprietors told me they "employ a number of women, and pay by the piece, the workers earning from $3.50 to $6 per week. Different kinds of work have different prices. They pay from the first. Those who put up perfumery earn most. The greater part of the duties in a drug store can be performed by well qualified ladies as efficiently as by men." So few ladies are employed in that way, that they might feel timid about assuming the responsibilities of a drug store in a city. Yet, after they had spent two or three years in a store of others, where they were properly instructed, why need they feel any more responsibility in a drug store of their own ? I was told that no drug broker and no retail druggist employs women. When employed, it is by those in the wholesale business. I called on a German widow keeping a retail drug store, but who employed a young man to attend the store. She regrets that she did not learn to compound of her husband. She can sell simple medicines, and buys all her own medicines. She had heard of one lady druggist, in Switzerland, that performed all the duties of a druggist, and one in Germany; but it is not common to see women in the business there. H. & R., druggists, employ women to put up patent medicines, and pay $4 or $5 per week. Mr. M., maker of patent medicines, employs some girls all the time. When busy, they pay from $6 to $8 a week, but at other times $3. It requires some experience to put up pills. The pills are mixed, rolled, and cut by men, as it is heavy work when done extensively. Their girls get $2.50 the first week of their work, and their wages are increased in proportion to their skill and abilities. Messrs. K. & K., wholesale druggists, employ a woman to put up Seidlitz powders, furnishing all the materials, and paying by the quantity. They pay her about $250 a year, but suppose she is assisted by some of her sisters at home.

Mr. H. employs a woman to put up Seidlitz powders, paid for by the gross. A smart woman can earn from $1.25 to $1.50 a day. A measure is used, containing the right quantity for filling the papers. A house that makes extract of ginger, in Philadelphia, formerly employed women to put it up; but they now employ men and boys in preference, because of the work they can do at intervals, that women cannot do. I called at Mrs. S.'s drug store. The youth that stood behind the counter said drug stores kept by ladies, or where they are employed to dispense, would not be patronized by physicians. He said, if any trouble should occur, from want of knowledge or skill in putting up medicines, and the case was brought into court, the man that employed female dispensers would be punished. Many persons, he says, come to druggists for medical and surgical advice, that could not, and would not think of consulting a lady, even if she were competent to give advice. It would be as unsuitable as for women to shave men, as they do in Germany. I sent for the lady, though the clerk urged that she had a sick child, and could not leave it. I told her the object of my call. She very kindly talked with me, and gave me information, of which I will give a synopsis. She boarded for several years after she was married, and as she had nothing to occupy her time, she spent much of it in the drug store with her husband. Seven years ago he died, and she, by the advice of friends, continued the store. She has employed a young man only part of the time. She says it involves great responsibility, but she is, and feels just as responsible as a man, and would be held so in court; but is not any more liable to indictment, or prosecution, than a man. It is something that requires exactness. It will not do to trust entirely to the memory. She generally refers to the book for directions. A youth of good abilities can, in from six months to one year, put up prescriptions, and a boy, when taken into a drug store, is paid from $1.50 to $2 a week for six months. A druggist of New York writes: " There is but one college of pharmacy in the city of New York, where instruction would be given equally to ladies, if they desired it; although, as yet, none have ever presented themselves. Ladies have never been employed, to my knowledge, as druggists' clerks in this city, or elsewhere in the United States, nor, as I am of opinion, in Europe. In one instance, it was attempted in Philadelphia a few years since, by a leading druggist, with a view of economy, I believe; and although he professed to have engaged the ladies merely as saleswomen in the fancy goods department, they nevertheless were allowed to dispense medicines. It so happened that one of these made a mistake, in giving the wrong medicine, which resulted in the death of the patient, a lady of wealth and wide acquaintance, and the consequence was the ruin and destruction of the whole business of the druggist. This put an end to the experiment in Philadelphia." (This we extremely regret, but know that such accidents have occurred from the incompetency and carelessness of some young men and boys, with less disastrous results to the proprietor.) "The business," the writer adds, "is, in some respects, quite unsuited to females. It requires much real manual labor, its hours are long, and its constant, close confinement wears upon the strongest constitutions. I have myself lost my health at it, and I know of numerous others who have done the same." A lady physician writes: "I do not know whether women are anywhere employed as druggists' clerks. They are not either in France or England, where special education and license are required. I am not aware of any druggist here who would take a pupil, but I have no doubt one could be found."

105. Keepers of Fancy Stores. A fancy store pays well when a good connection is established, but it takes time for that. Business is moving up street in New York, and of course fancy stores with it. Some unite millinery with the sale of fancy goods. The prices paid to those who stand in such stores, vary greatly. They are given under the head of Saleswomen.

106. Gentlemen's Furnishing Stores. A great many women are employed in this business, and many more might be. The making of gentlemen's robes furnishes in itself quite a business in cities; also the making of cravats, collars, hemming handkerchiefs, and odd work to be done. Mrs. M. told me she has a girl that assists in the house, and stays in the store when not so occupied, and receives for her services $6 a month and her board. Madame P. pays $3 to each of her operators (ten hours a day), and to one superior operator $4. She pays $3.50 a week to a button-hole maker. That is made a separate branch of sewing. Fourteen is the usual number of button holes in a shirt, and some employers pay one cent apiece; some, one and a half; and for large ones, in which studs or sleeve buttons are worn, two cents apiece. Some men are very particular about the make and fit of their shirts. Madame P. gets $2.50 a dozen for shirts from a store down street, and $4.50 for shirts from a store up street. Ordered work pays best. Her great trouble is that she does not get constant employment. For awhile she sunk in her business from $4 to $5 a week. Mr. P. says, whenever business is dull in New York city, it is, of course, wherever work is done to supply the city. He takes learners in busy times. Mr. D., who employs 2,000 hands in his factory at New Haven, has discharged them all; also Mr. H., who employs 1,000; and Messrs. M. & H., who employ as many. He thinks, when business revives, there will be work enough for all in this line, and even more. Shirts are such an essential part of a man's wardrobe, that as long as men exist, shirts must be made. With the many improvements in sewing machines, Mr. P. has shirts, when cut out, given to the operator, and turned from the machine complete, with the exception of buttons and button holes. No basters are employed. All the felling is done by a feller, and all the hemming by a hemmer. He furnishes his operators with machines. He employs men to cut, because they do it faster than women. They cut with a knife twenty-four thicknesses of cloth. All factories furnish machines and needles. Troy is the great place for making shirt collars. The girls are paid by the piece in these factories, and the employers will not permit them to work more than eight hours a day, as they do not wish them to lose their health. A girl is not retained in these collar factories that cannot earn $7 a week—eight hours a day. The machines are moved by steam.

107. Furniture Sellers. A French woman that keeps a new furniture store told me that her husband does most of the work, employing some men to help him. She only attends store in his absence. The lifting, repairing, and varnishing, she thought could not be done by women. Called in the store of a woman—a German Jew. Her husband is away most of the time. She has furniture made to fill orders, and, of course, employs several men to make the furniture. I think she sells on credit. I think women are better adapted to the keeping of house-furnishing than of house-furniture stores. I was told in a furniture store by a saleswoman, that she takes entire charge of the store, cuts and gives out damask for making furniture, orders the men, and keeps the books; for which she has a comfortable home with her employer, a widow lady, and $5 a week. She says it requires one to be amiable and obliging, to possess health and energy, and to be a good judge of human nature, to succeed in business; but thinks good conduct and sobriety will insure success in almost anything. The spring she finds best for selling furniture. Small profits and quick sales is her motto. She never credits. She regulates her prices according to circumstances, allowing herself what she considers a fair profit, and yet doing justice to the buyer. She goes into the store at seven in the morning, and remains until ten at night. Only a strong, well-built woman, can move furniture. A lady that keeps a furniture store told me she sold a great deal before the holidays, but will not sell much again until spring. On making inquiry of a lady that keeps a furniture store, about the business, she uttered these practical remarks: "Never credit in the furniture business, or your money and furniture are both gone. You may succeed, if you have an honest, reliable man to attend to the business for you. It is a money-paying business. You should have a man that can attend auction, and buy furniture, and repair and varnish it. Besides, you need a carman, to lift and move furniture in the store, and carry it home." We would state that a woman can just as well attend the sales of house furniture in New York, at residences, as men, and a carman can at any time be hired to move furniture.

108. Grocers. The retail grocery business is one that many women can and do carry on. It is very common to see the wives of grocers in their stores. The store is generally connected with or beneath their dwelling—so that it is very convenient for the man, and the woman is saved from exposure to the weather, passing back and forth from the dwelling to the store. The business is light and generally profitable. Much depends upon selecting a stand. A good stand is not likely to be idle long. The fall, I was told, was a bad season for a retail grocery in New York. Many small groceries in New York are owned by men, whose wives attend the stores while they are at work. I saw a nice little grocer, whose husband is a tailor, and who works at his trade in a room back of the grocery. This seemed to be reversing the general order of things. The husbands of some grocer women keep stalls in the markets, and furnish the groceries of their wives with vegetables. I called in a neat grocery store and bought some apples. The lady in attendance says she never sells liquor, but all the groceries around there do. She goes to market at four in the morning to buy potatoes and apples for her grocery. The baker leaves her bread, and she goes every evening to a baker's and buys cakes. Bundles of kindling wood are sent her from the wood yard, and the milkman leaves her milk. She goes to Washington market for her meat, and to Vesey street for her tea. So she manages. She said, not a cent in the store had been gained dishonestly. A grocer woman told me that peddlers interfere seriously with her business. Besides, the baker next door had gone to selling milk and butter, from which she has always derived most profit. She has least sale after families have laid in their groceries in the fall. Rich people and those in moderate circumstances generally purchase their groceries in large quantities, it being more convenient and economical to do so; hence we find but few groceries in the best portions of a city. Of course a grocer woman must be much on her feet. Most groceries are open until ten o'clock at night. Mrs. A. says it is impossible for grocer women to make more than a living now, paying $6 and $7 a week for rent, and sometimes not clearing more than $3 a week. She opens at five in the morning, and closes at nine at night. She makes most in summer, because then she does not have to burn fuel, and can do with less candle light. What lifting is necessary, her son does when he comes to see her. There are too many small groceries in New York for any to thrive. I have been told that in the majority (even when attended by women) liquor is sold. What a crime, to make ferocious beasts of those who are stupid enough to buy ardent spirits!

109. Junk Dealers. Junkmen go about New York with small wagons, across which is a rod. Over the rod are strung several cowbells of different sizes, and from it fly a number of various-colored strips. Junkmen are not the same as the rag gatherers, or dealers, but a blending of the two, as they buy on a very small scale, and sell again. Part of their rags they sell to shoddy manufacturers. A. B., a female junk-dealer, keeps a shop, where she buys and sells old metals and rags. The first she sells to a man who comes to the door and buys them; the others she sells at a store where rags are bought for making paper. She has no system in buying and selling—buying at the lowest prices she can, and selling at the highest. Another woman told me she buys white rags at three and a half cents per pound, and sells at four. She pays so much a pound for old metals, and sells at an advance. Other articles, as bottles, glass, bones, cold victuals, and grease, are disposed of by junkwomen. The damaged cotton picked up by old women is sold to junk dealers.

110. Music Sellers. Mr. W. does not know of any ladies engaged in selling sheet music, but thinks there may be some in small towns. He thinks it would be a very suitable employment for them. I called in a music store, B—, where a lady was in attendance, and, in the course of conversation, learned she was the wife of the proprietor. According to her report, "it is an arduous business, and one that requires brains and musical talent. People will seldom purchase a piece of music until they hear it, and she must try the pianos before a person will purchase or hire. The business requires great patience. She and her husband keep their store open until ten o'clock at night. They do not sell so much when the weather is bad, nor in summer, when the people are out of the city. A lady so employed must be able to keep accounts, and, when she sells, must require good security, if she does not sell for cash. She must also be able to distinguish bad from good money." She says, "keepers of music stores will not employ women, however great their capabilities," but no reason could I obtain for it. I think it is something, where an opening offers, that would pay a woman well. I called at another music store in the same city, kept by a lady. She said: "She and her sister would not keep a music store, if they had not brothers in the business, for she did not consider it any more appropriate for a lady to keep pianos to sell than to keep a cabinet wareroom. The pianos sometimes need to be repaired and tuned, and no one can attend to that without knowing how a piano is constructed. (?) The mere selling of sheet music, she thought, might do well enough, but selling books would be better. She says it would not do well for a woman to tune pianos, as it requires considerable practice to make one competent." Why might not women acquire that practice? Her selfishness and fear of competition were very evident. It is desirable for a music seller to understand Italian, French, and German, as many of the songs used in our country are in those languages. Many pieces of music have two or three titles. It requires some time to learn to rightly perform the duties of a music seller. The selling of sheet music and the selling of pianos are separate branches, and a person in one may be totally ignorant of the other. The wholesale and retail departments are entirely distinct in large establishments. Clerks that attend in the piano department are expected to be able to play. A lady is now employed in a large piano store in New York to try the intruments for purchasers. A lady in New York stays in the store when her brother, Mr. D., is absent. He paid a boy $1.50 a week for some months while learning, then more. A person of ability could learn the business in six months' time, or less. Music is always arranged alphabetically on the shelves. A boy should be kept to climb the ladder. An extensive music seller in Boston writes: "In our direct employ is only one female—a cashier. Repeated losses of money, and cash continually over or above, induced us four years ago to adopt the plan of employing a female to receive the proceeds of sales. It has saved us a great deal of money, and lessened the temptation to the young men in the store. We would gladly employ more women, but the height of our shelves, and the unsuitableness of female apparel, prevent." Another music seller writes me: "Women are employed in our business, in Germany and France, and are there paid at the same rate as men. We do not employ ladies in our store, because those of their own sex will not buy from them."

111. Sellers of Artists' Materials. The sale of paintings, engravings, and artists' materials, form of themselves a branch of business in large cities. I know of such a store in Philadelphia, kept by a lady. It must be a light and pleasant employment. In London there are seventy-nine print sellers.

112. Sellers of Seeds, Roots, and Herbs. In agricultural and horticultural communities, there is always a demand for roots and seeds. A large number of seeds are raised and put in papers for sale by the Shakers. In stores for the sale of roots and seeds, growing plants in jars might be offered for sale, and evergreens, with their roots in dirt, enveloped by linen or sacking. Orders might be given, and filled, for forest and fruit trees. Bouquets, also, might be kept for sale. A man in New York hires a room about Christmas, and devotes himself exclusively to the sale of evergreens for Christmas trees. As field seeds are usually sold by the measure, and not put up in papers, women have no employment in that line. The proprietor of an agricultural warehouse and seed store writes: "Our seed and grain are put up by men and boys in the winter months. It is work that might be done by women." A lady botanic druggist told me, "there are families in the West that make a comfortable support by gathering herbs; but even the smallest children assist." Those plants that bear flowers she has gathered when they begin to bloom. Those engaged in gathering commence early in life, and gather those growing in their yards and the fields of the neighborhood. Another seller of botanic medicine says there are spring and fall herbs, and, of course, they must be gathered in their seasons. She has a man and his wife gathering herbs, who support their family of five children by it, and two girls of another family, who earn a livelihood by it. Ladies in the occupation of root, seed, and flower selling, would do well to keep garden tools for sale.

113. Sellers of Small Wares. In England, the word "haberdasher" is applied to those who engage in the sale of cord, tape, pins, and such articles. In America there is no synonymous word—so we use the expression heading this article, which we have seen occasionally employed in the same way. The number of women in this business is legion. With many it is a suitable and successful employment. Those whose means will not permit them to engage in any more extensive business—who have a room well located in town, and not too much competition—can, with a small capital, commence a safe and light business. It requires but little effort, and, with enough customers, will well repay time and capital. Many a poor woman, unable to purchase the articles required, has obtained them to sell on commission, and, by industry and economy, earned sufficient, in the course of time, to purchase a stock of her own. I called on a lady that keeps a variety store. She sells gloves, handkerchiefs, suspenders, and such articles to gentlemen, and tape, buttons, &c., to ladies. She would rather sell to gentlemen. She has been keeping store thirty-five years. Her store is near the river, and she sells much to people coming from the ferry and off the boats. She thinks in the South and West there would be many good openings for such stores. Spring and fall, and during the holidays, are her best times for selling. I called in a small store : I was told by the lady that she did not much more than make a living. She depends much on her friends and acquaintances for custom. As they increase in number, which they do from year to. year, her custom increases. She finds herself very closely confined at home by the business. She does not regulate her profits entirely by the value of the articles, for cheap goods sell best where she is, and she puts on a large profit.

114. Sellers of Snuff, Tobacco, and Cigars. A lady, keeping a cigar store, said she makes only one third profit on her sales. Most people make one half, which, she says, is the usual profit on all goods. Snuff gives her the headache, when dealing it out, but she thinks she may get accustomed to it. She sells most from six o'clock in the morning until nine or ten ; and then again in the evening. To know what manufactures of tobacco, snuff, and cigars are most popular, is important. Having acquaintances assists much, and they are the first patrons to one commencing business. A cigar store generally pays well in large cities, and, if well located, is sure to succeed. Fall and winter are the best seasons for selling cigars ; in very warm weather no one cares to smoke.

115. Saleswomen. Women are quite as capable by nature to sell dry goods as men, but are not trained so thoroughly, nor from so early an age. Suavity of manner and perfect control of temper are very desirable qualifications for a clerk. Care, judgment, and taste are requisite for success. A flow of speech and ability to show goods to advantage are also desirable. Some people urge that if females are employed as attendants in stores, they will be exposed to dangerous and demoralizing influences, and something is said about the corruption of female shopkeepers in Paris, by way of warning. Now, it so happens that the corruption spoken of does not exist among the store attendants in Paris, but among sempstresses. Saleswomen and bookkeepers there enjoy as a class a good reputation, but the same cannot be said of sempstresses. Sempstresses, we know from the rates paid them, and the accounts of travellers, cannot make enough to support themselves ; but shopkeepers can. " One fifth of all the female criminals in Paris are sempstresses," says Madame Mallet. Some employers complain that women are too sociably inclined, too much disposed to chat, where several are employed in the same establishment. It may be true ; but are they more so than men of the same age ? The languid appearance of saleswomen, we think, arises from their being on their feet so constantly. It is injurious to a woman; and employers should allow them to be seated, when not waiting on customers. The number of skirts they must wear, and the weight of hoop skirts, does much to bring this about. The kind of ladies that saleswoman mostly see in first-class stores is calculated to improve and refine their manners, and give them a command of language. Besides, it renders them more particular in their attire. They want to dress and look well. Those acquainted with the art, say there are at last a hundred ways of putting up new goods. Some Jews hire a girl to stay in their store, and require her to sew, make hoop skirts, &c., when not waiting on customers. In the United States, women are employed in a variety of stores: dry goods, lace, and fancy stores are the most common. In Philadelphia they attend in nearly all the largest stores—Levy's, Sharpless's, and Evans's; besides, several hundred earn a subsistence as saleswomen in smaller stores. Close observation and much experience are needed to fulfil the duties, but the natural quickness of most women gives them a tact seldom equalled by men. The variety afforded by the occupation is pleasing, and the labors are light. The handling of gloves, tape, ribbon, &c., is undoubtedly best suited to the finer and smaller hands of women. The reason there are so many young men performing the duties of clerks and salesmen, is, that they are lazy, and do not want to perform hard work. Another reason is that the majority want to dress well and make a good appearance, but have no capital. The price paid for a girl to attend store would depend on the size, location, and kind of store, how much they sell, and the abilities of the girl. Lady clerks usually receive from $3 to $8 per week. The best seldom receive more than $6; while men receive from $6 to $12. The ladies are obliged to dress well, and to do so must retrench in other expenses, living in crowded attics or damp cellars, or on unwholesome food. Mr. M., Philadelphia, pays his girls from $3 to $6 per week, it depending altogether on their qualifications. In Bangor and Belfast, Maine, most of those who attend stores are women. They have also been much employed in Buffalo, New York, during the last few years. It is a regulation of some of the stores in New York and Philadelphia, that a salesman or woman shall not sit down to rest; and in some, if they do, they are fined. If there is nothing to do, they must take down the boxes and pull out the articles, then arrange them carefully in the boxes, as if they were closely occupied, to give the impression that much business is transacted in the establishment. In fancy stores on the avenues, New York, girls get from $2.50 to $4 a week. The stores are mostly open from 7 A. M. to 10 P. M. In some localities, most goods are sold in the evening. At a small dry-goods store, where I called to make a purchase, the lady told me she used to employ a girl, paying her $3 a week, without board. She was in the store from 7 A. M. till 9.30 P. M. A girl in a store on Sixth avenue told me, she and her companions get from $2 to $5 a week. They are there at eight in the morning, and remain until ten at night, and on Saturday until eleven or twelve. They are not allowed to sit down. A girl in a lace and embroidery store on Sixth avenue, New York, told me that girls get in such stores from $3.50 to $10, but they must make up laces when not waiting on customers. Some receive a percentage. Women are not paid as well as men, even in such stores. Time of learning depends on the individual. They are seldom paid anything for a few weeks. They have most to do in spring and fall; are in the store from 8 A. M. to 9 or 10 P. M. A lady told me she used to get $7 a week in a fancy store. At M.'s dry-goods store, New York, the superintendent told me they do not pay learners for one month. They have girls who have been in the store but a few weeks, that can do as well as those who have been in it for years. Some again are stupid, and they will not retain such. When girls are qualified, they pay from $1 to $10 a week. They prefer having ladies in the store, thinking they know best a lady's wants. They often have occasion to change—some get broken down and go away, some get tired, some get discouraged, some cannot be on their feet so long, some cannot please customers, some are not satisfactory to employers, &c. ; so, many changes take place. The ladies all looked to be Americans. They are allowed to sit when there is nothing to do, and no customers in; which, I suspect, is rarely, if ever the case. I have been told the openings for saleswomen are better farther East than in New York. A lady told me she used to get $1 a day in R.'s store on Broadway, and the other saleswomen got the same price. Then she was on her feet nearly all the time. She was there at eight and staid till seven : all were expected to take their dinner and eat in the store. Mrs. H. told me she knew a lady that stood in a store on Chestnut street, Philadelphia, who received a salary of $800 a year. When girls first go into a store, they usually get $1 a week during the season (three months), then $1.50, and so increase. A pretty good knowledge of store keeping is acquired by a smart person in six months, and now ladies are relieved in large stores from the responsibility of making change. Many of the ladies in New York stores are Irish. American ladies are more engaged in making artificial flowers, bookfolding, &c. I was told rather a novel feature in the life of shop girls, viz. : that many board from home, for the sake of having company ; and in addition to this, men, earning good wages, but of disreputable character, will often board in low houses, and ingratiate themselves into the favor of the girls, until they work the ruin of one or more.   Mr. D. employs five ladies, and pays them from $3 to $5.   He prefers ladies.   When he takes beginners, he pays $1.50 a week, and better wages as they become more capable.   He has paid $8, and even $9 a week. The ladies are in the store from eight to half past eight.   He allows them to sit when no customers are in and there is nothing doing.   A lady with whom I talked, and who had stood in a store on Catherine street, New York, finds the occupation very injurious, because of having to be on her feet so constantly, and its lasting from 7 A. M. until 9 P. M.   In some stores they are obliged to remain until eleven, and even twelve, in busy seasons.   On Grand and Catherine streets, New York, they keep open very late.   She says, when the weather is dull, and there are but few customers, employers are apt to be cross and vent their bad feelings on the girls.   And in those stores the girls cannot sit down to take a stitch for themselves ; but, when there are no customers to wait on, they must make up undersleeves, capes, and caps for the store.   She now keeps a millinery and fancy store, and pays her girls $5 a week, and the girls are in the store from seven to nine.   They make up bonnets, when not waiting on customers, and so have a change of posture without a loss of time.   She has a friend in a Broadway store, that receives $1 a day.   A saleswoman should know how to make out accounts. Ability to speak the French and German languages is a most valuable acquisition to a saleswoman in our cities.   One discouraging feature in the history of saleswomen is, that their wages are not advanced like those of men.   In Detroit, Michigan, girls receive from $3 to $5 for standing in a store.   " In Cleveland, in 1854, there was one dry-goods store where four lady clerks were employed at salaries from $200 to $350 per annum.   In one shoe store a lady received a salary of $250 ; and one, in another shoe, store, $200.   In a millinery and fancy dry-goods store, kept by ladies, fifteen girls were employed at from $4 to $6 per week.   In another, kept by a gentleman, ten girls were employed at from $4 to $6 per week."   In the same city, gentlemen clerks usually receive from $250 to $600 per annum.   At a store on Grand street, New York, where a number of saleswomen are employed, the owner told me he takes girls in the spring and fall.   He tries them for one month, and such as he finds he can make anything of he retains.   He then pays them something, and increases their wages in proportion to their advancement.   Some never rise above $3 ; but those who are ambitious and desirous to excel and make proportionate effort, he will pay higher.   He has paid as high as $12 a week.   A merchant keeping a large trimming store on Canal street, pays his women from $1.50 to $8 per week, and they are in the store from seven in the morning till dark.   To wait in a store requires experience ; and a lady, in getting a situation, should endeavor to do so through the influence of a merchant.   It is very desirable to have a good location for a store. Mr. M. pays his saleswomen from $2 to $6, according to their qualifications.   At a confectionery the woman told me she gives $6 a month and board and washing ; but as she does not keep open on Sunday, the girl would have to go home Saturday night and stay till Monday.   She would be kept busy all the time, from seven in the morning till eleven at night, waiting on customers, cleaning tables, washing plates, sweeping floors, &c.   On most of the avenues in New York, merchants do not sell as much, nor receive such a profit, as on Broadway, and employ women because they can get them cheaper.   In a small variety store, a lady told me she had paid $4 a week and board to one who had never stood in a store ; but the lady was a friend.   She remarked : "If a person has the inclination, a memory, and common sense, she can soon learn.   Few are willing to take learners. American ladies are not ambitious enough to keep store.   For one month in summer and one in winter there is little doing."   A lady confectioner says : "It requires a very honest person to be in a confectionery, because small sums are being constantly received and no note taken of them.   Girls are paid according to their capabilities from $2 to $5, and are in the store from 7 A. M. to 9, 10, 11, and even 12 P. M., in busy seasons, which are about the holidays.   It requires some weeks to know the prices, where to place the articles, and how to make them appear to advantage."   A merchant, who employs saleswomen, told me he thought women have a better sense of propriety and are more particular than men, but they lack judgment and promptness.   He thinks women do very well as far as they go, but there is a boundary line in ability, beyond which women cannot pass.   The gentleman referred to was indebted to his mother, who had kept the store he then owned, for his education and position in business.   Mr. P., seller of ladies' trimmings, employs from twenty to twenty-five saleswomen, who knit and embroider for the store when not waiting on customers.   A lady who waited in the store told me they change their position frequently, seldom sitting more than ten minutes at a time.   Women are paid from $4 to $10 per week, and are in the store from half past 8 A. M. to half past 6 P. M.   They pay from $2.50 to $3.50 for board.   The business can be learned in from three

6*

to six months. While learning, they receive enough to pay their board. Industry and ambition are necessary for success. The prosperity of the business in the future depends on the fashion and the amount of money in circulation. Winter is the best season for the sale of goods. The women are mostly German; they succeed best in knitting, because they are brought up to it. There are openings in the business, West and South. A saleswoman told me her business is hard on the back, because of the standing, reaching up, and bending. She is paid $6 per week, her store companions $3, spending eleven hours in the store. A person of business qualifications requires only practice to make a saleswoman. She has often heard ladies complain of having to purchase small or fancy articles of men. She thought heavy dress goods could be better handled by men. She says dissatisfaction is likely to arise when an employer boards his work hands. Mrs. D., who keeps a fancy store, told me that fifteen or twenty years ago, it was a rare thing to see a saleswoman in a store in New York. She says nearly all of her saleswomen have relations dependent on them for support, and if they are thrown out of employment for a week it is a serious matter. She pays $5 a week to experienced saleswomen, and gives something to learners; all stay in the store ten hours. She thinks honesty, truthfulness, intelligence, good address, and a knowledge of human nature are the best qualifications. Spring and fall she finds the best seasons for selling goods, and thinks the occupation for a lady next best to teaching. A merchant in New Haven writes: "We employ from two to five women (all American) as clerks, paying from $3 to $6 per week. To learners we pay $2 per week. The employment of women is on the increase. My clerks are employed through the year, and work from ten to eleven hours per day. We employ women to save expense, and because we believe them most honest." A firm in Providence, who sell gloves, hosiery, &c., write: "We employ ten saleswomen on an average, and pay from $2 to $7 per week, ten hours a day. We pay $2 per week to learners. To learn thoroughly requires about six months' practice. We consider the prospect good of the occupation being opened to more women. One third of our hands we send off in summer and winter. We find women neater and more steady than men, but not so energetic." The proprietor of a large establishment in Philadelphia writes: "About thirty women are employed by us in selling dry goods. Their health generally improves by their active occupation, the proper ventilation of our warehouse, and the regular habits to which they become accustomed. Wages are from $1 to $10 per week; they are paid less than men because their time of work is shorter, their

expenses are less, and their channels of usefulness more circum-
scribed. A lifetime is needed to learn the business thoroughly,
although in five years much may be learned. Women are paid
while learning. Quickness of intellect and of body, good temper,
and pleasant manners are very essential. Women well instructed are generally permanent in an establishment. Our most busy
seasons are from February to June, and September to December.
In no season are saleswomen thrown out of employment. In
winter they spend eight and a half hours in the store; in summer, nine hours. Seventy-five per cent. are of American parents.
The work is fatiguing at times, but not wearing on the system.
Another part of our occupation, in which women might be employed, if properly instructed, is bookkeeping. Women are
deficient in generalizing, excellent in concentrativeness. Many of
our saleswomen have been teachers, and some return to it. They
have their evenings as their own from 6 P. M.; they have good
moral boarding places, and a public library open gratuitously.
About one half live with parents; the remainder board at from
$2 to $2.50 per week, perhaps two persons occupying the same
room." In Paris, France, young women in stores receive for
their services their lodging, washing, and board, with from $40 to
$80 per annum.

116. Street Sellers. The number of women alone, in
London, according to Mr. Mayhew's estimate, engaged in street
sales, wives, widows, and single persons, is from 25,000 to
30,000. Girls and women form a large proportion of the street
sellers, and earn from sixty-two cents to $1 a week. The com-
parative newness of our country, the smaller size of the cities,
and the greater demand for manual labor have presented fewer
calls for street sellers. We hope the time may never come when
our streets will be thronged, as those of London are, with street
venders, for we consider it not by any means an index of general
prosperity. More especially do we hope the scanty pittance obtained by their labor, and the consequent privation and suffering,
may never be the portion of any of our population willing to
work for a support. All the wants of a great city can be supplied by the London street sellers. They are patronized mostly
by those in the middle and lower walks of life. All the varieties
imaginable are represented in their sale of articles. Both dressed
and undressed food can be obtained of them. Home and foreign
fruits and vegetables of all kinds have each their separate sales.
Of the eatables and drinkables offered by them for sale, the solids
consist of hot eels, pickled whelks, oysters, sheep's trotters, pea
soup, fried fish, ham sandwiches, hot green peas, kidney puddings,
boiled meat puddings, beef, mutton, kidney and eel pies, and baked

potatoes. In each of these provisions the street poor find a midday or midnight meal. The pastry and confectionery which tempt the street eaters are tarts of rhubarb, currant, gooseberry, cherry, apple, damson, cranberry, and (so called) mince pies; plum dough and plum cake; lard, currant, almond, and many other kinds of cakes, as well as of tarts; gingerbread nuts and heart cakes; Chelsea buns, muffins, and crumpets; sweet stuff includes the second kind, of rocks, sticks, lozenges, candies, and hard cakes; the medicinal confectionery, of cough drops and horehound; and, lastly, the more novel and aristocratic luxury of street ices and strawberry cream, at two cents a glass (in Greenwich Park). The drinkables are tea, coffee, and cocoa; ginger beer, lemonade, Persian sherbet, and some highly colored beverages which have no specific name, but are introduced to the public as cooling drinks; hot elder cordial or wine; peppermint water; curds and whey; water; ice milk, and milk (just from the cow), in the parks. In addition to this information, most of which is derived from Mr. Mayhew's "London Labor and London Poor," we will devote the remainder of the article to information from the same author; and would do so in his words, were it not that we would like to condense as much as possible. For the substance, we acknowledge, therefore, our indebtedness to Mr. Mayhew. In the suburbs of London, some people spend their time collecting snails, worms, grasshoppers, caterpillars, toads, snakes, and lizards, which they sell in the city as food for birds. Some, in collecting frogs, which they sell to French families, at hotels and at hospitals. Some devote their time to the sale of coffee, beer, and baked potatoes. Some engage in the sale of coke, some of salt, and some of sand. Nor is literature forgotten by the street sellers. "There are," says Mr. M., "five houses in London that publish street literature, and six authors and poets that prepare such literature in prose or rhyme." Some streetsellers devote themselves to the hawking of dog collars, and some to the sale of rat poisons. Some collect the nests of wild birds and the eggs, and sell them. Some sell whips; and some, walking sticks; but these last articles, we believe, are sold only by men. In London, some women sell refuse fruits; some, water-colored pictures and cheap engravings; some, coins commemorating public events. Some engage in the sale of children's watches. Some sell implements belonging to a trade; for instance, tailors' implements. Some sell washerwomen's clothes lines, pegs, and props; or kitchen utensils, as tin ware, vegetable nets, kettle holders, &c. Some of the street sellers are blind, with having taxed their eyes too greatly in sewing for slop shops. Some women are co-workers with the men in the sale of crockery and glass ware. They go in pairs (generally husband and wife); some with a large basket between them, others with separate baskets. Some sell spar ornaments, and some, china ornaments; some, lace, and some, millinery; some, thread, tape, needles, &c. Quite a number sell women's second-hand apparel. Some sell umbrellas; some, men's suspenders, belts, and trowser straps. Others again will sell embroidery, stockings, gaiters, shoe laces, blacking, pipes, quack medicines, snuff, tobacco boxes, and cigar cases; and in winter some are seen carrying even kindling wood to sell. Some women sell dolls, spectacles, wash leather, china cement, razor paste, matches, or japanned ware. Some women carry sponge in baskets; they either sell it for money or exchange it for old clothes. A few sell musical instruments. Some offer guide books, play bills, newspapers, stationery, and jewelry. Rabbits, squirrels, parrots, and other kinds of birds are sold by them; and some dispose of dead game. Seeds, flowers, roots, and, about Christmas, evergreens, are sold in large numbers. In shops, some try to resell slops from kitchens, old glass, metal, or worn clothes, &c.; some, exhausted tea leaves, which they dispose of to those that dye and redye them to sell again.—We give this chapter, because it comprises all and many more than the sellers on our streets. The few engaged in street sales in our cities are mostly confined to old women, who sit at the corners, with stands on which rest store articles, tin ware, sweetmeats, and fruits, or a small lot of fancy articles. There are several stands of second-hand books and newspapers, or shelves of candy, kept by men, but the variety in the business is quite limited, compared with the cities of Europe. Mr. Mayhew thinks the majority of street sellers in London have been servants and mechanics that could not get employment. Some street sellers go on foot through the country during the summer, to sell at fairs and races. Many others get employment from the farmers in gathering vegetables and fruits for market, weeding gardens, picking hops, and assisting in haymaking and harvesting. In Paris, some women carry bread to sell, in baskets strapped to their backs. In New York, I saw two women with baskets of vegetables and fruit to sell. I spoke to one, who told me she earns sometimes as much as $1 a day, and sometimes but a few cents. In winter, it is not unusual to see girls with baskets of dried thyme, parsley, and sage, who sell it for culinary purposes. I talked with a woman who carried tin ware in a basket. She often does not earn fifty cents a day, and will be walking all day, not even going home at noon. She buys by the dozen, and so gets the articles a little cheaper. I inquired of a girl selling radishes how many she usually disposed of in a day. She takes them around only in the afternoon, and sometimes sells to the amount of $1.25.

117. Toy Merchants. This is a business better suited to the natural nurses of children than to men. A handsome profit is derived from the sale of toys. The busy seasons with toy merchants and confectioners are about Christmas and New Year. Toys might be more extensively made in our country, thereby giving employment to many now without it. Women mostly stand in toy shops in New York. Even so small an item as the eyes of children's dolls produces a circulation of several thousand pounds in England. Several establishments in London are devoted exclusively to the manufacture of dolls.

118. Wall Paper Dealers. Selling wall paper is a light, pretty business. In cities it affords a remunerative return; in towns and villages it is sold mostly by dry-goods merchants and druggists.. The only objection I see to it is, that a step ladder must be used to get the paper down from the higher shelves; but a small boy might be used for that, and also for carrying paper home to purchasers.

119. Worn Clothes and Second-hand Furniture. Mr. Mayhew tells us that in London thirty persons are engaged in the exclusive sale of second-hand boots and shoes. He mentions one man that, in 1855, was thought to take over £100 ($500) a day. Boots and shoes, too far gone to be repaired, are sold to Prussian-blue manufacturers—so nothing is lost. In Philadelphia, near Penn Square, may be seen ranged, on an open space, a large quantity of second-hand clothes, shoes, dresses, &c., for sale. The business, in this country, of buying and selling again worn clothes is mostly in the hands of the Jews—perhaps altogether. In all countries it is more or less a favorite business with them. The time is past when the Jew was prohibited in other countries from holding real estate; yet the Jews in all countries, so far as I know, generally retain their property in money, or invest it in something movable. Old clothes in our country are generally given in exchange for new china, glass ware, &c.; yet a number in the large cities pay money. In London all kinds of articles are given for them, and then they are taken to the old-clothes exchanges, where they are disposed of for money, principally to shopkeepers who deal in the sale of worn clothes. Some of these articles are made over, some made smaller, some turned, some changed in form; in fact, the greatest ingenuity is exercised to employ to advantage the articles used. Second-hand articles are not so much sold in this country as in older countries, where money is more difficult to get, and poverty greater. Boys' cloth caps and roundabouts, and women's shoes, are made of old coats and pants, so worn in parts as to be unsalable. Coats are also made of cloaks, bonnets of aprons, &c. Men's and women's apparel of all sorts is bought and sold by them. Old umbrellas and parasols are bought, repaired, and sold. Silk dresses, if unfit to be sold, are used for making children's hoods, facing coats, &c. The scraps are used for making quilts. Old woollen dresses, whose waists are much worn, are used for making wadded skirts. Tailors' and dressmakers' trimmings are sometimes purchased for a small sum, and used in making up girls' hoods, boys' caps, &c. In London, most of women's second-hand apparel is (as it should be) sold by women. It is customary for buyers to cry down every article offered them for sale or barter, but those they offer for sale are magnified into ten times their value. Many of the men who go through the streets of our cities buying old clothes or giving china ware in exchange for them, take them home and their wives repair them. I called at a second-hand variety store in Brooklyn. The woman says most people engaged in the business are foreigners. The business is not unhealthy. Clothes brought in are washed and done over, and their domestics are always healthy. Their business is very dull. Ten years ago it was quite brisk, but many stores of the kind have been opened in Brooklyn lately. She and her daughter go and look at any articles for sale; and if they think the person honest and the price suits, they will buy; so that, if any one should come and claim the clothes as being stolen, they could immediately take a policeman to the place where they got them. If articles are bought, they examine and put a price on them, and get the address of the individual. If they find they are not stolen, they then purchase. The poor-est season for the business is midwinter. They keep their store open till ten o'clock at night. I was told at another store they sell most clothes in the evening to laborers' wives. In a store in New York, the lady says she buys her clothes of Jews that go about exchanging china for old clothes. It is very necessary that a good locality be fixed on, near a river or bay, on a thorough-fare, or in a neighborhood where many poor people live. One woman told me she employs two girls and three men to make over and do up worn clothes for her store. She pays her girls, each, thirty-one cents a day, and they work twelve hours. She sells most in the evening. At one place I was told that Mondays and Saturdays are their busiest days for selling. They sell most to the French, Irish, and negroes. Germans do not like to buy second-hand clothes. She regretted that in her present store she had not glass cases to keep the dust off her clothes. Her pur-chasing is mostly done among the rich, she says, and so it brings her a good class of customers. The keeper of a second-hand

furniture store told me that she goes to auction herself and purchases. It is two or three years before the business pays. She
will go to a dwelling and look at furniture before purchasing. It
requires a man to do the lifting. She has old furniture repaired,
chairs reseated, &c., before she attempts to sell them.

120. Variety Shops. Variety shops, for the sale of coal,
wood, kindling, candles, matches, and water, are frequently seen
in the poor districts of cities. They are a great convenience to
those whose means will not admit of their buying in large quantities. It costs them more to buy it in that way, yet the keeping
of shops affords a subsistence to those who do.

EMPLOYMENTS PERTAINING TO GRAIN, BIRDS, FLOWERS, FRUITS, AND VEGETABLES.

121. Agriculturists. With industry and enterprise,
what may not woman accomplish! We have heard of women in
Western New York, Ohio, and Michigan, that not only carry on
farms, but do the outdoor work, as tilling, reaping, &c. It is
said that in countries where the physical labor of women in the
open air is as great as that of men, their constitutions become as
stout and capable of endurance. Agriculture is an employment
safe and profitable, and capable of almost any extension in this
country. There is a great difference usually between the theory
and practice of farming. Many agricultural works and periodicals are published that abound in practical instruction. In graz-
ing countries stock is raised, and the labor of the people is given
to making butter and cheese. A variety of soil and difference of
altitude produce different crops in the same latitude. In the
United States the raising of hops is becoming a branch of national industry, and some women are employed to pick them. In
England and France large numbers of women are employed to
pick hops. In England, 52,000 acres of land are devoted to their
cultivation. There is danger, in picking hops, of getting wet and
taking cold, which acts upon the system very much the same as
the ill effects of calomel. But if proper care is used, the work
is not unhealthy. There is a people's college in New York State,
where females are received as pupils as well as males. No doubt
a horticultural department will be formed. We think it would
be well if more women would devote themselves to agricultural

and horticultural employments. Weeding gardens and attending dairies or poultry yards would each furnish work for more women than are now employed, and save women from running to the cities, which are already crowded to excess with applicants for work. Headley, in his " Adirondack Mountains," says: " Twenty miles from any settlement on Brown's Tract in Adirondack, Arnold and his family of thirteen children—twelve girls and a boy—live by their trafficking, by sporting, and cultivating the field. The agricultural part, however, is performed chiefly by females, who plough, sow, and rake equal to any farmer. Two of the girls threshed alone, with common flails, five hundred bushels of oats in one winter, while their father and mother were away trapping for marten. They frequently ride without bridle or even halter, guiding the horse by a motion or stroke of the hand. They are modest and retiring in their manners, and wild and timid as fawns among strangers." " On the west side of the Scioto, just below Columbus, there is planted a field of six hundred acres of bottom land. Twenty-five German girls follow the ploughs, and do the hoeing, for which they receive 62½ cents per day." There are two sisters in Ohio who manage a farm of three hundred acres ; and two other sisters, near Media, Pennsylvania, that conduct as large a farm.

122. Bee Dealers. A new species of bee, that builds in trees instead of hives, is about to be introduced by Government from Paraguay. In keeping bees there is no expense. The hives can easily be made at home, or purchased for a comparative trifle. Their food they seek themselves. " The bee mistresses gain a living by selling honey in many rural districts of England." Most of the honey used in the United States is collected in the South. That to be carried to the North is put in hogsheads. Merchants who buy it have small glass jars filled, which are sold in markets and groceries.

123. Bird Importers and Raisers. There are establishments in most of the large cities of the United States for the sale of birds. The proprietors import and raise them. Most imported birds are from Germany. They are caught by the peasants living among the mountains, and sold for a trivial sum in small wooden cages. The favorite pet bird has long been the canary. In the South the mocking bird is common, and often seen caged. But few of our most beautiful birds bear domestication. Their wild, free nature unfits them for it. In Germany there is a class of men who make it a separate business to train birds to sing. The bullfinch is the kind most commonly taught —perhaps the only kind. They teach in bird classes of from four to seven members each. It is done by withholding food from them in the dark and playing on a bird organ or a flute. A gentleman told me, he thought few, if any, ladies could be repaid in making a business of bird raising; indeed, he had known several undertake it, but fail. He says, people like German birds best, because they learn earlier to sing; and, you know, a purchaser always wants to hear a bird sing before he buys it. At a bird importer's I priced birds. He asked for a male canary, $3; for a female, $1; an African parrot, $8; green parrot, $5; goldfinch, $3; and thrush, $2. Mrs. L., a German, who raises canaries, told me she could not support herself by raising birds, but she knows several men that do. She says the American birds are the longest lived—the imported die in about two years after reaching this country. Foreign birds are generally devoid of strength, and their limbs are apt to turn backward as they rest on the roosts. I suppose that arises from their being shut up in small cages during the long journey across the ocean, and many of them, being caught birds, cannot bear the confinement and cramped position. Another bird dealer attributed the fact of imported being less healthy than American birds, to their taking cold in crossing the ocean. American birds that are not mated may live fifteen or sixteen years. The breed, form, color, sex, and ability to sing determine their price. It is difficult to tell the age of canaries from their appearance. So one is liable to be imposed upon by unprincipled dealers, who prefer to sell old birds, particularly of the feminine gender. Birds are subject to a variety of diseases. Birds are cheapest in the fall, as it requires more to keep them in winter than summer, and many do not wish to be at that expense. Mrs. L. sells most in February, March, and April, the breeding season. Prices vary from $2 to $7. It does not take long to learn to raise birds, another bird raiser told me, when you know just how to feed them, and the proper temperature for them. She sells most in winter.

124. Bird and Animal Preservers. I notice in the census of Great Britain three women returned as animal preservers; and I know there are some in Germany, three of whom are in Strasbourg. Bird stuffing is a trade in which but few can find employment. It would therefore be necessary to have something else to rely on in case that should fail. It is thought by some to be unhealthy, on account of the arsenic used—particularly to young people. The senior of a firm I called on had been engaged in it fifteen years without detriment to his health. Females mostly prepare the branches of trees, or other fanciful stands, on which the birds are placed. The frames are usually of wood or pasteboard, covered with moss. I called at Mr. B.'s, and saw a young man who works with him. He thinks the work is not un-

THE LITTLE BIRD-CATCHERS.   138

healthy. It is an art in which there is always room for improvement. Mr. B., who has been at it thirty years, says he is always learning something new in regard to it, or making some discovery in the art. The eyes are manufactured in New York. To one practising the art a good eye for form is necessary, and an ability to imitate nature closely. The spring of the year is the best season; but all seasons answer. The only danger in summer is from insects. A bird stuffer told me he would teach the art to one or two persons for $50; but he thinks the prospect for employment poor. It is difficult to get birds to learn on in winter; but in summer plenty can be had. He has had acquaintances commence in New Orleans, St. Louis, and Chicago. The first two could not make a living. He knows of two young ladies that have learned it merely as a pastime. I called on a French lady, Mrs. L., who stuffs birds and animals. She taught the art to a barber, who made a great deal of money by it. He paid $150 for his instruction, spending every other day at it for two months. A Cuban, who owns seven hundred slaves, paid her the same amount. He wished to learn, that he might preserve birds he could obtain while travelling in various countries. She has received several letters from Boston requesting her to come there and stuff birds for a museum that is being commenced. She was the personation of health, but she complained that she suffered with rheumatism. She trembled much—she thought from rheumatism. May it not be that it is the result of arsenic that she has got into a pimple, or where the skin was broken? The work, of course, requires a firm hand. She showed me a parrot, done, she said, in one hour, for which she was to receive $3. A German book is written on the subject that contains directions. The information can be obtained in English from a little work called "Art Recreations." The ingredients are often sold in drug stores already mixed. It can be done at all seasons. Mrs. L. thinks one could become proficient in two months' constant practice. A gentleman went to California, and made a large collection of birds; stuffed them, and sent them to various European countries. In the four years he was at it he made $60,000. She sent six hundred to a museum in Paris a short time ago. She thinks St. Louis may present an opening. Mrs. L. knows a man who has been employed in stuffing birds and animals in the museum of Strasbourg from the age of fifteen to seventy-seven, and is a very corpulent man, being nearly as broad as he is long. That she gave as an indication of its healthfulness; but it may be that he is bloated from the arsenic, as it has that effect. She says even poor people will pay to have a pet bird stuffed, when they have not a dime to buy bread

11

125. Florists. The rearing of flowers has ever been a charming pastime to many of our sex. When the pleasure can be combined with profit, it is well. The cultivation of flowers is a taste whose beneficial results are not sufficiently appreciated. When the cares and troubles of life begin to press upon men and women, they are apt to neglect the cultivation of flowers, when it might absorb some of the cares that burden their hearts. Vines, roses, and ornamental fruit trees cost but a small sum, and yet how much they add to the beauty and comfort of a place! Most of the choice roses of our country are from cuttings imported from France. They are brought over in jars. Many, of course, die on the voyage. The variety is very great. The selling of roots, plants, and bouquets is quite remunerative in some places. Much depends on the knowledge and skill of the florist, the location of his gardens, and the fondness of the people in the community for flowers. It is a delightful business for a lady, if she has men to do the planting, digging, and other hard work. In Paris, there is a market devoted to the sale of flowers. In most of the markets of our large cities, are exposed for sale pot plants and bouquets, also shrubs and evergreens. A florist told me that he employs two women in winter to make up bouquets and wreaths for ladies going to evening and dinner parties, concerts, and other places of amusement. It requires taste and ingenuity. He pays each $5 per week. They can make up wreaths to look like artificial flowers. A woman on Long Island makes a living by raising flowers that are sold in New York. I was told that some lady has established a horticultural school on Long Island. Florists in and near cemeteries are apt to find sale for flowers and plants. Hence it is common to observe gardens and hot houses so located. I rode out to a florist's near Brooklyn. He says the business is not so good as it was, because the Germans in Hoboken raise flowers and sell bouquets for sixpence that he could not sell for twenty-five cents. The man does not send bouquets to the city, as it does not pay. Their profits are mostly derived from the sale of choice fruit trees raised at Flushing. They sell bouquets at their hot houses from a shilling up to $5. They derive most profit from flowers in winter. A florist's occupation is healthy, and affords much pleasure to one fond of flowers. Yet it requires close attention to business. In England it was formerly customary to serve a seven-years' apprenticeship at the business, but three or four years will answer very well, if an individual gives undivided attention to his business, and is with a superior florist. A knowledge of botany is necessary to a florist. It requires considerable taste to make up a bouquet, and therefore is very appropriate to women. A knowledge of colors and their artistic arrangement is

THE BOUQUET VENDERS.   140

essential; also a natural taste for flowers, and some patience. Making bouquets, wreaths, &c., is slow work. The stems of flowers for bouquets are cut very short, as most of the nutriment of the stem is lost to the succeeding ones by cutting long ones. Artificial stems are added to the natural ones, and are usually made of broom straw or ravelled matting. Mrs. F., the wife of a florist, says the wives of most florists assist their husbands in making up bouquets, wreaths, and baskets. She thinks, if a florist had enough to do to employ a lady, he would pay her $3 or $4 a week. She has often thought a small volume might be written on the flower business in New York. She says no one has an idea of the amount of money expended for flowers. Mr. D. used to send out $1,000 worth of flowers on New Year's morning. It is a very irregular employment. Some days she sells a great many for balls, parties, and funerals. One might learn to make bouquets, if they have taste and judgment, by a few months' practice. The flowers that are sold at different seasons vary greatly, and the value of them depends much on their age. Mrs. F. has sold a few baskets of flowers at $50 apiece. She sells many flowers for Roman Catholic churches about Easter. Mrs. R. says florists prefer to have men, because they can work in the garden or green house when not cutting or putting up flowers. The Germans have run the business down in New York. A florist named *Flower* writes: " We employ from two to four women tying buds, hoeing, weeding, &c.; in winter they help about grafting. They are paid fifty cents a day, of ten hours. Women so employed are German born. The employment is healthy. Men get seventy-five cents a day, as they can do more work; but the principal reason for employing women is, that we can hire them cheaper and like them better for light work. Women could do all parts of our business, if they had a fair chance with men, and would improve the chance. One year would give a general knowledge, but five would be better. A good, sound constitution, and industrious habits, are the best qualifications. Women that want such work can find plenty of it; but outdoor work is too hard for American women." Another florist writes : " In Europe, where women are sometimes employed in fruit or vegetable gardens, their wages are usually about half a man's. Women (chiefly Germans) are employed in this country by farmers to pick fruit, vegetables, &c., by the quantity. At light work, done by contract, women, I believe, can make as much as men. Several years would be necessary to learn the business; some branches of it might be learned in a few weeks. The requisite most needed for women to work in green houses, is a change of fashion. Their dress unfits them altogether for moving about in crowded plant

houses. Were their dress similar to the men's, I see no reason
why they would not be equally useful in other departments as well
as this. If that should ever happen, they would, in my opinion,
be worth as much as men; for the work is mostly light, and ladies,
having a natural taste for flowers, would soon learn it. If you
have gone through green houses, you cannot but know the difficulty of doing so without breaking everything. Men, at this kind
of work, are not fully employed in winter." A lady florist
writes: " I sometimes think my nervous excitability is to some
extent caused by an excess of electricity, derived from the earth
or flowers with which I work."

126. Flower Girls. Flowers are the mementoes of an
earthly paradise. They are said to be "the alphabet of angels,
whereby they write mysterious things"—the mysteries of God's
love and goodness. Earth would be a wilderness without them.
Girls sell flowers most profitably at opera houses, theatres, and
other places of amusement. They buy of those who devote themselves to the raising of flowers, and arrange them into bouquets.
A number dispose of flowers on Broadway; and, summer before
last, I observed a French woman at the Atlantic ferry selling bouquets to people waiting for the boat. A florist told me he dis-
poses of flowers to girls who make up bouquets and sell them. One
of them pays $500 rent for her room. It yields a handsome profit
when a person has a good stand. He would like a stand at the
opera house, but a great many others are looking forward to it.
Some pay for the privilege, others obtain it by being known to the
managers. I was told by a man who supplies bouquets that he pays
to florists from $8 to $10 a day for flowers, and then makes up his
own bouquets. I have been told that at some hotels in Germany,
girls pass around the table at dinner, and give bouquets. Such
recipients as feel disposed, pay a small sum.

127. Fruit Growers. If American women would only
turn their attention to the cultivation of fruits and flowers for
market, instead of giving it up to ignorant foreigners, how much
better it would be! A few hundred dollars would make a very
handsome beginning; and those who do not have so much at their
disposal, could get their friends to advance it. At Shrewsbury
and Lebanon, much fruit is put up by the Shakers, and sent to
New York for sale. Women might have orchards, raise fruit,
and send it to market. Mrs. D. owns a farm, and does not disdain to graft fruit trees, superintend their planting, gather fruit,
send it to market, &c.; and she realizes a handsome profit. The
grafting and budding of fruit trees might be done very well by
women, and also the budding of ornamental shrubs. " Miss S. B.
Anthony," says the Binghampton *Republican*, " resides at Roches-

THE LITTLE FLOWER GIRLS.   142

ter, and supports herself by raising raspberries from land given
to her by her father." I have been told that on one acre of land
near New York city a thousand dollars' worth of strawberries can
be grown. In New Jersey and Delaware, women are employed
to gather berries for market. If a lady is within a few miles of
town, and has facilities for raising and sending fruit to market,
she will not be likely to fail in meeting with ready sale. Berries
bring a good price in the markets of a city. In Cincinnati, from
May 21st to June 1st, 1847, 5,463 bushels of strawberries were
sold, and near St. Louis is a gentleman that has some hundreds
of acres of strawberries in cultivation to assist in supplying the
St. Louis market. The drying of fruit affords employment, and
generally well remunerates time so given, if carried on extensively.

128. Fruit Venders. Flowers are formed to please the
eye and indulge the fancy; but fruits are a healthy and important article of food. Some women sell fruit in market; some, at
stalls in the street; some, in fruit shops or groceries; and some,
from baskets, going from house to house. Most dispose of small
fruit, such as berries—some wild and some cultivated. The
ferries in large cities are very good stands for sellers of fruits
and sweetmeats. Places of amusement and the entrance to
cemeteries, are also. I talked to one apple woman, who says
her business is a slavish one. Her stand was at the Atlantic
ferry, New York. When she goes to her dinner, she gets the gate
keeper to mind her stand. She earns, on an average, $1 a day.
She rises, gets her breakfast, and starts to market by five o'clock.
She remains at her stand until nine o'clock at night. She sells
the greatest quantity of fruit in the spring and fall, when people are most apt to be making money, and so permit a little self-
indulgence. She sells least in winter. I saw a woman on the
street selling fruit and flowers. When she is out all day, she can
generally earn from fifty cents to $1. Another fruit seller told
me that she makes a good living. She has been at her stand
eight years. She sells most fresh fruit in summer; and in winter,
about the holidays, most dry fruit and nuts. In the coldest
weather she remains in her basement, heated by a stove, where
she stores her fruit at night. Her grapes are brought in on the
cars, put up in pasteboard boxes. Her location is excellent,
for the working class of people pass in the evening, returning
from work, or in their promenades. I talked with an old woman
at an apple stand, who told me she often sells $1 worth of articles
in a day, but seldom makes a profit of more than half. She sells
most fruit in summer, but most cigars, candy, and nuts in winter.
She says there is a stand on every block, in that part of New

York. Hers is a good location, because so many men pass. In wet weather, she does not sell much. She is shielded in winter, by sitting in a hall near, where she can keep an eye on her stand. She lives near, and while she goes home to dinner, her husband sells for her. An apple woman, in New York, told us, she has kept her stand in Washington park for seven years. She remains at it all the year. If any other fruit vender should trespass on her bounds, a policeman would soon send him or her off. Another old woman, keeping a fruit stand, told me she makes a comfortable living at it in summer; but in winter she stays in a confectionery store, and gets $10 a month and her board. At another fruit stand, on asking the old lady how she got on, she burst into tears, and replied, very poorly, scarcely made enough to keep her alive. A professional honor exists among fruit women, and a desire to sustain each other in their rights. A wholesale fruit dealer writes me that it takes from two to four years to learn the business, when carried on extensively.

129. Gardeners. The strength and energy of people, in northern climates, have led them to excel in the rearing of fruit —not in imparting a more delicious flavor, but in the quantity, the fulness, and the size of the fruit. In the balmy air and under the sunny sky of the South, vegetation develops more rapidly and more luxuriantly. He who adds to the list of beautiful and fragrant flowers, or improves some variety of fruit, enlarging, or rendering it more luscious, will be remembered as a benefactor. Gardening is a pleasant and healthy occupation to those that love outdoor life. A woman can no more be healthful and beautiful without exercise in the open air, than a plant can when deprived of air and light. We learn, from Mr. Howitt's " Rural Life in England," that " there are on the outskirts of Nottingham, upward of five thousand gardens, each less than the tenth of an acre. The bulk of these are occupied by the working classes. These gardens are let at from half a penny to three halfpence per yard." German women are often employed, near cities, to weed gardens, gather vegetables, and other such work. " In Hereford, England, there are no fewer than six annual harvests, in each of which children are largely employed: 1, bark peeling; 2, hay; 3, corn, 4, hops; 5, potatoes; 6, apples; 7, acorns. Add to these, bird keeping in autumn and spring, potato setting and hop tying, and the incidental duties of baby nursing and errand going."

130. Makers of Cordial and Syrups. Women who live in the country, and have small fruit, would find it pay well to make cordials, berry vinegars, &c. There are some establishments where it is made, and women are employed to gather the fruit. The people of the Southern States have depended on the

GATHERING THE FRUIT.   144

North for these articles, but we presume a change will be wrought. The abundant growth of small fruit in the South will enable the South before long to meet the demand. We think there will be many openings of this kind, in the South and West, for many years to come. Some manufacturers of ginger wine, bitters, syrups, cordials, and grape wines, write: "In reply to your circular we say—We do not employ any women in our business, although we indirectly furnish employment for several hundred, during the various fruit seasons, in gathering most kinds of fruit, which we use in our business. Many of these fruits are wild, which we buy at a specified price. The gatherers control their own time, and their earnings will vary from fifty cents to $1 each, per day. It would probably require the labor of about six hundred for six months of each year, in gathering the amount of fruit which we use. But as we do not directly employ them, or know anything about the general business of those thus employed, we are unable to give further particulars."

131. Root, Bark, and Seed Gatherers. When the grass is bowed by the sparkling dew, and the hills shrouded in mist, plants exhale most freely their sweet odors. They are then gathered and sold to manufacturers, who prepare from them oils, essences, and perfumeries. An old Quaker lady on Tenth street, Philadelphia, keeping an herb store, told me that she purchases her herbs mostly of men, but some women do bring them to sell. It requires a knowledge of botany to gather them, and the stage of the moon must be observed. Digging roots, and gathering plants, at all seasons, is a hard business. At another herb store, I learned that the prices paid gatherers depend much on the kind of herb, the difficulty of obtaining it, and the season when it is gathered. A woman may earn $1 a week, or she may earn as much as $10. The roots and herbs are bought by weight. Many are purchased fresh in market, but some of the gatherers dry them. They are sent from different parts of the Union to the cities and towns. One told me that she would rather purchase herbs and seed put up by women, for they are neater and more careful with their work. She sells most in spring and fall. An Indian doctress told me barks must be gathered in the spring and fall, when they are full of sap; and roots, when the leaves are faded or dead. She sometimes makes $20 worth of syrup in a day. She says the business requires some knowledge of plants, experience in the times of gathering, amount of drying, &c.

132. Seed Envelopers and Herb Packers. In a seed store in Philadelphia, we found, they employ women in January and February, at $2.50 a week, to put seeds up in paper bags, seal them, and paste labels on. They go at eight in the

7

morning, and remain until dark. At a large drug store in Philadelphia, we were told they employ nine women. They have
seven distinct branches for the women, and separate apartments
for each branch, consisting of weighing and putting up powders,
sorting herbs and roots, putting up liquids, &c., &c. The
women earn from $3 to $5 a week, and spend nine hours, from
eight to six, having an hour at noon. In busy seasons they remain
till eight or nine, and receive additional wages. There is nothing unhealthy in the business. They are paid $3 a week from
the time they are taken to learn, and deduction made for
absence. A seller of botanic medicines in Boston writes me: "He
employs women in putting medicines in small packages for the
retail trade, bottling the same, and labelling. He pays $5 a
week to his women, and $3 a week while learning, the time for
which is six months. Common sense, neatness, and integrity are
the qualifications needed. The girls work from nine to ten
hours. He will not employ any but American women. He
pays men $8 or $9, because they can take them off, and put them
upon work that girls cannot do. Women would be paid better
if they were stronger, and did not need so much waiting upon
in the way of lifting and arranging their work. Rainy days
they want to stay at home, or, if they come, it takes half a day
for them to dry their clothes. Men they can depend on in all
weather. Women might keep their books, if their crinoline was
not too extensive: that alone would bar them from the counting
room. Women are inferior only in physical disabilities. Girls
are good for nothing until after sixteen years of age; and nine in ten
will get married as soon as they are fairly initiated in work—
hence the time spent by women in acquiring a business education
is to a certain extent lost—lost to their employers, but of assistance to them in the education of their children." Mr. P.,
botanic druggist says: "There are but three establishments in
New York, for this business, and twelve women would be quite
enough for them. They put up herbs in packages. One day's
practice is enough for a smart person. The women are paid
from $3 to $5 a week." At the United States Botanic Depot
they employ one girl, and pay her $4 a week. She only works
in daylight. Mr. J. L. employs two girls to put up botanic
medicines. He has men to cork the bottles. They work ten
months in the year. Nothing is done in December and January.
They pay $4 a week, of ten hours a day. In Louisville, St.
Louis, and Cincinnati, few women are employed in this way.
Some seedsmen and florists near Boston employ four ladies in
enveloping seed. One of the ladies writes: "We presume more
ladies are employed in Europe to put up seed than in this

THE BARK AND SEED GATHERERS. 146

country. The employment is not unhealthy. We are paid 6 cents an hour, and work by the hour. To learn the part the women do, requires about two hours. Judgment is most needed. Employment of this kind is increasing, there is a demand for female labor in the seed department." A seedsman, in Rochester, writes : "We employ six women in making paper bags, paying 25 cents per hundred. Boys are employed at about the same wages. We have work from July to January. The girls take their work home. We use some boys, because their work benefits their families equally as much."

133. Sellers of Pets. In Paris there are stores for the sale of dogs and cats. In London, the sale of dogs is mostly on the streets, or at the residence of the raiser. The aristocracy of England maintain 500,000 dogs and a large number of cats ; conseqently food must be provided for them. The sale of birds is common. Gold and silver fish, white rabbits, Guinea pigs, squirrels, tortoises, fawns, lambs, and goats, are sometimes sold in seed and flower stores. Flowers and birds are the favorite pets of ladies in the United States. Everything of this nature is sold to some extent in the markets and on the streets of our cities, but generally at the houses of those who devote themselves to the business.

134. Wine Manufacturers and Grape Growers. Many persons are becoming interested in the culture of the grape ; and some are spending time and money in experimenting. Longworth of Cincinnati has realized a fortune from his operations. Belle Britain says : " In Longworth's cellars are 700,000 bottles of wine. Mr. L. informed her (?) that we have in this country at least 5,000 varieties of the grape, and his vineyards yield from 600 to 700 gallons to the acre." The color of wine depends on the color of the grapes from which it is made. In several of the States, Ohio, Iowa, Illinois, Missouri, and Alabama, vineyards are flourishing, and many new ones are being planted out. The variety of soil and surface in our country is such that there is every probability of success. As yet, only two kinds have been much grown. No doubt a large number of women will, in the course of a few years, be employed in the cultivation of the vine and the manufacture of wine. One can soon learn, with a few instructions in each season, the proper culture of the vine. A great deal of the work in the vineyards of France and Switzerland is done by women. Women do better that men, because their fingers are smaller and more nimble. The want of intelligent culture has been the greatest barrier in the introduction of graperies into our country ; but such is the number of foreigners now among us that have a practical knowledge of the business, we need fear no want of workmen. Many, too, have not been willing to invest capital in an uncertain enterprise. Wine manufacturers in Orange county, N. Y., write: " We have not employed women to any great extent in our business. There are some branches of the business in which women might be suitably and profitably employed, where those branches are extensively carried on. The bottling process, including cleaning of bottles, filling, putting on foil, labels, &c., could be done by women as well as men. Women could pick the grapes, and cull out the green and poor berries, and prepare them for the press. They are employed for this purpose in Europe. The reasons why we have not employed women in these branches are, we bottle not more than one sixth of our wine; we manufacture principally for church communion and medicinal purposes, and the principal demand for those purposes is by the gallon—consequently we send it out mostly in casks. (Some wine growers bottle all.) The men, whom we necessarily employ by the year or month in the cultivation of the ground, vines, &c., are of course employed in the season of the vintage, bottling, &c.; and in hurried times, such as the time of picking the grapes, we get such additional help as is easiest obtained, generally boys and girls, with sometimes women. Women are in such demand here for household labor, that, unless sought for at the proper time, March and the 1st of April, and hired for the year, it would be almost impossible to obtain them. The wages generally paid are from $5 to $7 per month, mostly $5 and $6." Another grape grower writes, in answer to a circular: " I do not employ female help in my business, except for a few weeks during the time of tying up the vines and in gathering the fruit, for which I pay 50 cents per day, without board. Women might be employed to quite an extent in this business, which is increasing in the country to a wonderful degree."

RAISERS, MAKERS, PREPARERS, AND DISPOSERS OF ARTICLES OF FOOD.

135. Bread Bakers. Nearly all the bakeries in New York are attended by women. I could not learn of any women being employed in bread bakeries to mix or bake, but they are in Germany and France. In France the bakehouse girls enter ovens heated often to 300°, and, it is stated, sometimes to even

400°. Bakerooms are usually of such great heat as to be injurious to the health of any but the strongest and stoutest. Some establishments have day and night bakers. The night bakers are up all night, and must have their bread ready by 5. 30 A. M. The day bakers go in at 7, and turn out a batch of bread at 11 A. M. Bakers spend on an average seventeen hours at their work, and this no doubt accounts partly for the absence of women from the occupation in this country : seventeen hours out of the twenty-four are too many for any woman to be on her feet. In this country the bakers are robust, hearty-looking men, and mostly Germans. Their average wages are $6 a week. Some bakers have a scaly eruption produced by frequent contact of the skin with flour. Inhaling the flour in mixing bread I have heard is unhealthy. Some women might object to working in the same room with men, and baking is certainly very warm work in summer. In most European cities the price of bread is regulated by the Government. The cost of materials and the state of the market regulate the price. A fine is the penalty for a violation of the law. In this country, bakers regulate the price of bread by the kind and quality. No law is enforced specifying prices. Some years ago an attempt was made in New York to have bread sold by the weight, but the bakers all opposed it. They might have been tempted to put something heavy in the flour. In large cities some establishments are devoted to one branch only of the business. Baker's bread is more used in free than in slave States. In Northern cities some families prepare their bread, cakes, pies, and meats, and send them to bakeries, where for a small sum they are cooked. It saves a vast amount of labor. Some bakers use potatoes in making up wheat bread. I never knew of rice being used by bakers in this country, but know it is by some bakers in Paris. The modes of baking bread, and the kinds of bread used, vary not only in different, but in the same countries. " Some bakers give the impression their bread is made by women," said a lady in a bakery, to us, " but it is not. A woman could not make up two or three barrels of flour in a day. Men are just as neat bakers as women could be." At three bakeries I was told by the employers that they pay their girls who attend the shop $7 a month, and board them, but do not have their washing done. From several girls that stood in bakeries I learned that they received from $6 to $10 a month, and their board. Only one of the number got her washing done without extra expense. The girls were expected to keep the counters, waiters, jars, and floors clean. They must be in the bakery by 5 o'clock A. M., and stay until 10 P. M. Some women require the girls to sew when not waiting on customers, and some require them to sweep and keep the room clean, and some even to wash the shop windows.   Girls that stand in bakeries receive no better compensation than house girls.   A foreman of the baking department, generally receives $8 a week, and his boarding.   Girls are usually paid from the time they enter.   A knowledge of reading, writing, and figures is considered sufficient.   I was told by one lady in a shop that girls attending bakeries usually receive from $8 to $10 a month, with board, and some, also, get their washing done.   They are not required to keep the books for those terms, and the bakeries are few in number where female employees keep the books.   I was told by an Irish woman that in Ireland there are few or no women attending bakeries and groceries.   At one bakery a girl told me she finds it very bad to be on her feet all the time.   She could not stay constantly in a bakery for one year at a time, she gets so weak from excitement and fatigue.   She says most Germans keep their bakeries open on the Sabbath; but the Americans have too much respect for the day to do so.   On Saturday night, bakeries are often open until 12 o'clock, and sometimes later.

136. Brewers.   I wrote to a lady, whose name I saw in a directory as a brewer.   She replies : " You wish to know if I work at brewing, personally.   I do not at present, but have done so, and worked hard the man's part; but my means are such now that I can do without.   I have men employed, and a clerk, &c., &c.   I am a widow, and superintend my business, and understand all that is connected with it.   I suppose it is not necessary to dwell longer on the subject, as I am out of the working part now. I am sixty-two years of age."

137. Candy Manufacturers.   " There are three hundred confectionery manufacturers and retail dealers in New York city.   Twelve establishments are devoted exclusively to the manufacture of candies.   In some, as many as a hundred hands are employed in busy times.   During the busy season, there are engaged in the manufacturing houses about five thousand persons of both sexes, though a very much larger number, probably some thousands, are indirectly supported by it, the paper-box makers being generally busily employed, and many children gaining a livelihood by hawking candies through the streets.   The city of New York is the headquarters of the confectionery trade, supplying as much as all the rest of the Union together, and distributing the results of its industry to all parts of the United States, as well as to Canada, most of the West India Islands, Mexico, Chili, and many other places.   It is estimated that fully $1,000,000 worth of confectionery is made annually in this city; and by that term we mean preparations of sugar, chocolate, jujube paste, &c., but exclude many articles such as ice creams, jellies, blancmanges, pastry, and other delicacies, which would sum up this amount to perhaps double. Two of the principal houses manufacture daily between them four thousand pounds of candies, at prices varying from 14 cents to 50 cents per pound, the average being about 20 cents." The coloring matter of foreign candies is generally showy, and of a poisonous nature. That of American manufacture is not of such brilliant and permanent colors, but more regard is paid to health in the selection of coloring matter. At confectioners' in London, classes of young ladies are taken and taught the art of making confectionery. Some candies are made by stretching over a hook, some must be shaken in a pan over a charcoal fire, and rolled on tables with marble tops. I was told at S. & P.'s (a wholesale house) that they are most busy from August 1st to 20th of December, and from March to June. They take learners for a week, to see if they are fit for the business, and if they are, reward them for their time. It takes but a short time to learn the part done by girls. They pay experienced girls from $3 to $6 a week. The girls work ten hours a day, and if longer, they are paid extra. Lately they have kept their girls until ten o'clock at night. It requires taste and invention to envelop fancy confectionery, but is not very reliable for constant employment. S. & P. employ ninety girls in busy times. At another place I was told they will not take Southern orders, for the Southerners will not buy, and have not the money to pay, if they would. The fancy candies go through three or four processes, and so the girls must work in the same room as the men who paint them. The girls sit while at work. R. pays by the month, and keeps his girls all the year. He says labor is more poorly compensated in New York, in proportion to the rates of living, than in any city in the Union. He thinks some girls should go from the cities into country places, and enter into service. H. says a person of any intelligence can learn in two or three months to paint candies. He used to employ girls to put gilding on, paying $2 a week—ten hours a day; but if a girl can paint well, she can earn $4 or $5 a week. He knows several German girls in the city that do. The candy flowers, he says, are made by hand, the fruit moulded. A lady confectioner told me that a woman who ornaments fancy candies is poorly paid, and it is dirty, sugary kind of work. Yet she acknowledged that candies must be kept on a clean table and handled by clean hands—otherwise they would not look well, and consequently not sell readily. The wives of German manufacturers do most of that kind of work. A confectioner told me, candy is never made in this country by women, but it is in England. He said the dust of the powdered sugar and the gases of the coal render it unhealthy. In large establishments most candy is made by steam. The making of candy he thought even too laborious for men. The teeth of candy manufacturers are often decayed from the frequent tasting of heated sugar. One candy manufacturer writes me : " We employ six girls in making candy, and do not think the business unhealthy. Wages range from $1.25 to $4.50 per week—ten hours a day. Men's wages are from $4.50 to $9. It requires from three to five years for men to learn. Women's part is learned in one year. The prospect of employment is good for a limited number. Fall is the best season, but they are always employed except during part of the winter. In some branches of the work women excel." At a manufactory of gum drops and candy rings, I saw a boy who receives $3 a week for making the rings, and a girl who receives $2.75 for picking gum drops, *i. e.*, loosening the sugar in which they are incrusted while being made. They work from 7 A. M. to 6 P. M.

138. Cheesemakers. A great deal of cheese is made in Central and Northern New York, and some in Ohio, Vermont, and West Massachusetts. Making cheese is a chemical operation, and requires experience. It is made in all civilized countries. I talked with an old gentleman who had been in the cheese business nearly all his life. He said a farmer's wife is the best help in cheese making. In making cheese, seven eighths of the work is done by women. A man usually places the cheese in the press, and removes it when it is dried sufficiently. The occupation is healthy. Women are paid from $1.75 to $2 a week and their board. Some people employ men, because they can go to work on the farm when not making cheese. The business can be learned in from six weeks to two months. When learning, girls give their work for instruction, but have their board. Neatness, good health, judgment, and common education, are desirable for a cheese maker. An individual must be able to reckon the pounds, weigh the salt, and regulate the temperature of the milk and curd by the thermometer. The first advice given by a lady who taught to make cheese was, " Keep your vessels clean." The prospect of employment in this branch of work is good, for it is difficult to obtain good cheesemakers. The best seasons are from the 1st of March to the last of November. The number of hours given by a girl to her work depends on the contract made —generally eight hours—sometimes ten. In most places cheesemakers have more leisure than house girls, but some employers expect them to do housework when not employed about the cheese. Some farmers hire girls who devote themselves exclusively to cheese making during the season for it. Some have the afternoon after the cheese is put in the press, and the jars, &c., are cleaned, until time to milk in the evening. The morning milking is usually done before breakfast, and the cheese made after breakfast. It requires until about two o'clock to get through. When cheese is put in a press, nothing further is necessary until it is ready to be removed. It remains in the press twenty-four hours. Most farmers have their cheese made on Sunday morning as on other days. The girls have Sunday afternoon or evening, according to contract. Some farmers do not make their cheese on Sunday, but retain the milk until Monday morning, and make it into butter. Women are best adapted to the work, and employed mostly because they can be got cheaper. The majority are Irish women. They are usually put on a footing by their employers, and eat at the same table. So little spinning and weaving are done now in the country, that the female members of farmers' families generally do the milking, unless the farmers have grown too wealthy and proud to have their wives and daughters so employed. Some dairymen make, with the aid of their families, all the cheese they use and sell. Milk should be drawn from a cow as rapidly as possible and while the cow is eating. One milker should be employed for every ten cows. Milk is very sensitive. Dairymen will make more by having the cream remain on the milk than by taking the cream off for churning, at the rate butter sells this winter (1861). Where the cream is used, an inexperienced hand would find it more troublesome to make cheese. Twenty-three million pounds of cheese were exported last year from the United States. American cheese is, in England, taking the place of English cheese. A German cheesemonger told me he makes the Limburg cheese—a preparation which has been known about eight years in this country. He was putting up some to send to New Orleans. It was very soft, and I thought the smell very offensive. He gets American cheese of a Yankee girl, to whom he pays $80 a year. She uses the milk of sixty cows. She works at it but eight months. During four months of the year but very little cheese is ever made. The arrangements of some cheesemakers for preparing the article are very complete.

139. Coffee and Chocolate Packers. B. S. & W., Philadelphia, employ women in packing parcels of essence of coffee, spices, vermicelli, &c. They make paper cases, pour the article in through a funnel and ram it down, then label and pack the cases in boxes, which are nailed up ready for delivery. One or two persons obtain a livelihood by cutting the labels to paste on the boxes. They are paid fifteen cents a thousand for this work, and are able to support themselves by it. The women are paid by the piece, and earn from $2 to $6 per week. The work rooms are airy and comfortable. Females were formerly more

7*

employed than at present to put up coffee; but as coffee is now ground every day at most factories, and as it is considered best when just ground, less is put up than formerly. Messrs. L. & B., New York, employ girls to put the articles in papers, pasting labels on and sealing them. They work by the piece, and earn from $3 to $7 a week. The odor might be disagreeable to some, but persons get accustomed to it, and it is quite as healthy as most work. There are not over one hundred and fifty women so employed in the State of New York, yet such packing is generally done by women. It is customary to pay by the package. The girls change their dresses on coming to the workroom of L. & B. They do not work with the men, but with some boys who fill boxes with the same articles. L. & B.'s girls have employment all the year. They never have any difficulty in getting hands. I saw a man who makes up essence of coffee. A lady was assisting him to put it in papers. At another factory I was told they pay by the week, from $1.50 to $4, according to the industry, quickness, and practice of the worker. It is not unhealthy work. They give employment ten months of the year, but at present have little to do. It requires but a few weeks to become expert. In some establishments girls stand or sit, as they please, while at work; in others they are all required to assume constantly whichever posture the foreman directs. At W. & Son's two small girls are employed, who each receive $2.50 a week. There is one factory in Cincinnati, one in St. Louis, and one in Chicago.

140. Cracker Bakers. At M.'s the young man said fancy crackers could be made by women. In making soda, oyster, and some other crackers, the dough is kneaded by machinery. In some establishments the dough is rolled out and conveyed to the oven by machinery. In a cracker bakery I was told the women might be employed in packing and selling crackers. It would not require all the time of one woman to pack for a large bakery. A cracker baker writes us: "We employ no women, and do not see that they could work to advantage in our business." Women could do all the work now done by men in this line, but I suppose considerable opposition would be experienced, except by ladies who have sufficient capital to carry on business for themselves.

141. Fancy Confectionery. Most confectioners sell, in addition to their fancy candies, imported fruits; and a few keep cakes. Some also keep fruits preserved in brandy or their own juice; and some keep in addition pickles, oysters, sardines, &c. Some confectioners merely make sweetmeats—some sell them, and some both make and sell. In cities, confectioners usually furnish the refreshments for both public and private entertainments. A manufacturer of confectioneries in New York told me that in busy times he employs fifteen girls; but at that time (January, 1861) only half as many, for they have no Southern orders—the people in the South are doing without candies. The part done by girls requires no special training. He pays girls for their labor from the first. They pack, pick gums, envelop in fancy papers, fill boxes, &c. He pays $3 a week for those that have some experience, and keeps them ten hours a day. He gives the making and painting of fancy candies out to those that have families, and who do it at home. W., of Philadelphia, pays his girls, eight in number, $1.50 a week for the first two or three weeks, then from $3 to $4. Making common candy is said to be too hard for women. They assist in the finishing of fine candies, as rolling and covering chocolate nuts. They put the fancy candies in French envelopes, and cut the silvered or gilt paper that gives the finish. They can sit or stand as they please while at work, but while enveloping mostly sit. They work ten hours. It is rather a light business. M. employs fifty women in putting up and packing candies. He pays them, from the time they begin, $2 a week. They learn in two or three months. He pays then from $4 to $5 a week. A lady told me she was paid in one establishment $6 a month and board. A girl in a confectionery told me the prices usually paid girls are $7 or $8 a month, with board and washing, and the girl is expected to keep the accounts. A lady in another store said summer is the poorest season for confectioneries, as people do not like to eat candies, because it makes them thirsty; but in those confectioneries where soda water and lager beer are kept, there is more or less custom during the summer. They keep open till ten o'clock at night, and all day Sunday. Sunday is their most profitable day. She knows a girl that is paid $5 a month in the Bowery, with her board, or $7 without. To be kind and obliging, and have the faculty of pleasing the little folks, are the best qualifications for the business. Prices paid depend on the responsibility of the employed. Some that keep the books receive $5 a week without board, most others receive $1.50 or $1.75 per week and board. Judgment must be used in the selection of a stand. A lady who keeps a small confectionery and fruit store in Williamsburg, says she does not make much on cakes and bread, only half a cent on a loaf of bread. She says it is best not to trust any one for pay—that children often come and say they want so and so, their mother says she will pay on Saturday; but Saturday comes, and no pay; and if they go for the money, the parents will say, " Come again," and put it off from time to time, until they become discouraged, and give it up altogether. M—s, French confectionery and chocolate cream manufacturers, take learners at the proper season, which commences in August. They employ some girls to paint fancy candies. H. says one must commence at the very first step, and gradually advance—that to learn the business requires a long time. He pays four girls $5 or $6 a month each, and gives them their board, for selling confectioneries and waiting in his saloon. At S—'s confectionery I was told that the small fine candies are made by steam. They are made in pans, which are shaken back and forth over fires, the gas of which is very injurious, and cannot be carried off by flues. Their girls make so much noise, laughing and talking with the men, and waste so much time, that they are required to work on the first floor, the same as the store. They are paid from $1.50 to $2 a week. They are paid by the week, because they do their work better than if paid by the quantity; besides, it is less troublesome. They are paid for overwork (regular hours being ten), and some earn as much in that way as by regular wages. The girls pick gums, separate gum drops, put candy in boxes, &c. C. employs girls to paint, put up candies, and attend store, and pays $1.50 and $2 a week. Most of the painting is done by French and German men, who are paid from $10 to $12 a week. It requires a long time to acquire taste and experience; one, in fact, can be always improving. C. thinks girls are not likely to find constant employment in the kind of work he gives to females. A French confectioner told me he had employed a woman to make chocolate cream, paying $3 a week for ten hours a day, and could employ her all the year, as the demand for chocolate cream is very great. S. employed one girl to sell candy, paying $5 a week. She was at the store at 7.30 A. M., and remained till 6 P. M. in winter and 8 P. M. in summer. She did not keep the books, but washed the jars and case, and swept back of the counter, and dusted several times a day. Talked with a girl who stood in a confectionery store on Broadway. She knew a girl on Chatham street who received $12 a month and her board. She herself received $9 a month and her board, but not her washing. The proprietor told her she must sew for his family, when not waiting on customers. It seems that it is not an uncommon requisition. They have but few customers until about 11 o'clock, and he expected her to accomplish more sewing than a sempstress who gives all her time to it. The young lady is in the store by 7 o'clock in the morning, and remains until 11 o'clock at night. Any one wishing to commence a confectionery can learn from the wholesale dealer of whom she purchases how to regulate the prices of sweetmeats. Mrs. W. wants a girl to wait in her saloon, will give $8 a month, with her board and washing. She would be required to sew, when not waiting on customers, and would have to wash the jars and cases, keep the counter clean, and dust and arrange the articles in the window every morning. She would have to be in the store at seven, and remain until twelve (seventeen hours). In large confectioneries girls stand while picking gums used in making gum drops. They are mostly made in summer. There is now (December) a great demand for girls, as there always is about the holidays. Those now at work are kept three hours over time—from seven to ten—and paid extra. The chemicals used in making some confectioneries are unhealthy, but women have nothing to do with that, except in painting candy toys. A confectioner in Boston, who employs four American girls in attending store and making goods, writes: "We consider the occupation very healthy, never having had a case of sickness with girls while working at this business. Some are paid $3 and $4 per week, working ten hours a day; others by the quantity, averaging $1 per day. Male labor is paid for, according to the knowledge of the business, from $6 to $15. Girls could not do the work, and the work that women do it would not pay to have done by male labor. It requires a long time and a great deal of practice to learn the whole business, but that part done by women is learned in a few weeks. They are paid something while learning. Honesty, industry, and a good education are the most desirable qualifications. Spring and fall are our most busy seasons. In midwinter we do not have many at work. Retail stores require most help in summer. New York requires most hands, especially women; but the demands are now very small, the trouble at the South being the main cause. They are not strong enough to do some parts of the work. The large towns are best for our business." A lady in a fancy confectionery on Broadway told me she receives $8 a month and her board, and is paid by the month. She thinks many diseases are brought on women by having to stand so much, as they do in confectioneries, bakeries, and dry-good stores. Women that have stood in any kind of a store before, and have business qualifications, are paid while learning. There is never any difficulty about obtaining qualified hands. She finds the work very laborious, and complained of having to be in the confectionery and saloon from seven in the morning until twelve at night. In some saloons the attendants are up until 1 o'clock (eighteen hours !), and are on their feet most of the time. A confectioner in Concord, N. H., writes: "We employ from five to ten girls (because we find it most profitable) for helping make, rolling up, and packing lozenges and pipe candy. Also for standing in the confectionery. The work is very healthy. We pay about sixty-seven cents per day, and they work from six to ten hours. No man employed, except one who takes charge. There is a prospect for employment so long as children cry for lozenges. The girls are American, and work at all seasons. They are as well paid, according to the cost of living, as mechanics in this place. Women are superior to men in rolling up and packing lozenges. They pay for board $1.75 per week."

142. Fish Women. In the United States, where every one has a right to fish in the rivers and lakes, there is a fair opening for those in this line of business. But it is only in the spring and fall that fish are much eaten. They are not considered healthy in the warm weather of summer. A pound of fish is said to be in nutritive power equal to eight pounds of potatoes. In the United States, according to the census report of 1850, there were engaged in fisheries 20,704 males and 429 females. The fishwomen of Philadelphia have long engaged in the selling of shad, and are to be seen in great numbers on the streets of the city, and even when not seen are likely to be heard crying fish. At one time they had a large market devoted exclusively to the sale of fish, but it became a nuisance, and the city authorities had it torn down; yet the women, possessed of strong local association, were not to be so routed. They are still seen sitting before their tables of fish in the neighborhood of where the market stood. Much money has been realized by the fishwomen, some of whom are said to own property of considerable value. What a lesson to patient industry! "From the time of Louis XIV. to the present, fish have been sold in Paris exclusively by women. They are now remarkable for the urbanity of their language and propriety of their conduct, having risen high in the scale of respectability during the last half century." "On the coasts of the department of Somme there are certain fish, the shrimps and 'vers marius,' which are exclusively reserved to the young girls and widows." On the coast of Great Britain thousands of women are employed in the herring, cod, mackerel, lobster, turbot, and pilchard fisheries. Women and children rub salt on the fish to be cured, with the hand. When cured, women pile them in stacks from four to five feet high, and as wide. Women are paid, at Newlyn, for this labor, 3d an hour, and every sixth hour receive a glass of brandy and a piece of bread. Many are also employed in obtaining oysters and canning them; and on the return of whaling vessels, numbers of women assist in preparing the cargoes for market. In New York, fish are mostly sold by men, who drive about in a little wagon containing fish, and blow a horn, crying out now and then the kind of fish they have for sale.

143. Macaroni. Macaroni is moulded and dried. Girls then pick out the whole sticks, and put them in boxes. The broken pieces are all thrown together in a barrel, then ground and moulded over. It is very easy work, and requires no learning. They are paid from $2 to $3.50 a week, working ten hours a day. The girls I saw, stood while at work.

144. Maple Sugar. The cheapness of sugar made from sugar cane has almost annihilated the existence of maple sugar, except as a sweetmeat. The peculiar flavor of maple molasses and sugar makes them much loved by some people. The trees are tapped early in the spring, when the sap first rises. After sufficient water is collected, it is put on and boiled until of the consistence required. It is slow work and pays poorly, but can be performed by women capable of the heavy labor involved in carrying, lifting kettles, and stirring.

145. Market Women. Mrs. Childs says, in her " History of Women," " On the seacoast of Borneo fleets of boats may be seen laden with provisions brought to market by women, who are screened from the sun by huge bamboo hats. In Egyptian cities, the country girls, closely veiled, are frequently employed in selling melons, pomegranates, eggs, poultry, &c." In the southern countries of Europe it is common to see women riding to market on donkeys, laden with marketing. We learn from " London Labor and London Poor," that there are 2,000 persons employed in the sale of greenstuff in the streets of London, as watercresses, chickweed, groundsel, turf, and plaintain. The cresses are eaten by people; the other articles are sold for birds. We may divide market women into two classes—those that raise or have raised the products they sell, and those that buy to sell again. The articles of the first are generally genuine and of fair price. Vegetables, poultry, eggs, and butter, with fruit, both green and dried, are carried to market, and there the market women, placing them on stalls or retaining them in their wagons, wait for purchasers. This class mostly supply the markets of towns and villages. Their articles are usually fresh and wholesome. There are thirteen markets in New York city where everything is obtained at the second or third remove from the producer. It is estimated that there are 1,300 huckster women attending the New York markets. The members of some families are engaged in the sale of different articles: one will sell eggs; another, vegetables; another, poultry, &c. It is said that better meat and vegetables are brought to Philadelphia than to New York markets. In New York there is a larger population requiring articles of a cheap kind. We think market women, considering their habits and modes of living, probably do as well in a pecuniary way as any other class of women. Their wants are few, their habits simple, and their occupation—though an exposed one—healthy. The variety of seeing new faces, and chatting with those similarly employed, yield more comfort and content than most women's work. They take in but a few pennies at a time, yet have their regular customers, and, in prosperous seasons, many besides. I will give an extract from my diary of a visit made to several of the New York markets: " I saw some women selling fruit; some, vegetables; and some, tripe and sausage. I judge, from the appearance of most dealers, it is not unhealthy. Most of the women were far advanced in life, particularly those who sold vegetables. They all complain that they do not sell so much since the commencement of the hard times. How is it? Do people buy less, and so eat less? or is less wasted in their kitchens? or are some unable to buy meat and vegetables at all? Here I would state the remark of a druggist: that, as times are hard, people do not indulge in so much rich food, nor in a surplus of it; consequently there is less sickness, and so little medicine sold that the druggists are discouraged. This druggist has since sold out, and moved to the country. Most of the market women looked to be Irish. One strong Irish woman told me that American women cannot bear the exposure in cold weather, and rent their stalls through the winter to men. They make their appearance in March with the flowers and early fruit. Butter is sold exclusively by men in Washington market, New York, and is more profitable than anything else. There is considerable difference in the class of custom in the different markets in New York; but the poor are usually more in number than the rich—so the markets frequented by them may receive as great a profit as where a smaller number of better customers attend. Some women regulate their sales to have a percentage, but many sell for what they can get, without regard to the amount of profit. I find those selling vegetables, buy of farmers who come early, and leave a supply for each seller in case she is not there. Any vegetables they may have left are locked up in boxes, or barrels, or covered over and left on the bench. The gates of the market house are closed and locked up at one o'clock every day except Saturday, with the exception of Washington and Fulton markets, which are open all day, and the first mentioned all night. Watchmen are about the markets at all hours of the day and night, and in some markets an extra fee is paid by the sellers to secure attention to their stalls. At two o'clock in the morning, Washington market is fully lighted, and the farmers begin to arrive to sell to grocers. The grocers usually buy from four to five in summer, and from four to six in winter. Boardinghouse keepers mostly buy from seven to nine o'clock. Families buy during any of these hours, or later. All the markets are open by half past three. Fulton market is rather warmer than the others because of the stoves and ranges used for making coffee, cooking oysters, &c. Ladies do not come to market so much in winter as in spring and summer. I think the vocation of market selling must be very healthy, when the venders are comfortably clad, and have stoves, as many of them do. Market women live to a great age. Vegetables injured by frost or long keeping are sold at a lower price. As a general thing, less is sold in market during January and February, than any other months. In spring time the market presents the most inviting appearance, for the stalls are then freshly painted, and flowers and fruit exhibited to advantage on them. Mrs. B. told me that a woman who sold flowers in Fulton market had made a fortune at it. Some of these sellers let other women have flowers and fruit to take over the city to sell, and reap a profit in that way. One old lady told me she always made 12½ cents profit on her goods, they being pocket-knives, combs, &c. The stalls are sold or rented. One woman told me she paid 12½ cents a day for her stall; another, 9 cents; and this must be paid for even on days when they are absent from market. Another woman told me that she got a permit for the use of a stall in Washington market when it was first built, and not long since she sold it for $1,500, and the owner pays a tax of $2 a week besides. She paid $200 for the stall at which she stood in Fulton market, and pays a rent of 75 cents a week. She makes a living by selling smoked salt fish. The processes through which produce must pass from the producer to reach the consumer, might be avoided by permitting farmers to remain longer in the city, and furnishing them with a place for their teams and produce; but now they must all leave by ten o'clock, and can scarcely feel that they have a place to put anything down while they are in the city. In England are women who shell peas and beans at so much a quart. I have seen books, spectacles, canes, pocket-books, caps, shoes, hose, china, and even old clothes for sale on the streets, and around or in the market-houses of Philadelphia and New York.

146. Meat Sellers. In markets and in meat shops of the United States, women may occasionally be seen selling meat. They are generally the wives or the daughters of butchers. They no doubt assist in cleaning tripe, and making sausage and souse. On the streets of London are nearly one thousand sellers of dogs' and cats' meat. Most of them are men. This meat is the flesh of old worn out horses, which are bought, killed, cut up, boiled, and sold by those who make it a business. Mrs. M. told me of a woman that sells meat in the New York market. She has made a fortune by it. She stands in market, and sells, and orders her hired men to cut it up as desired. Mr. W. told me that women are employed at the pork houses in Louisville, in putting up hogs' feet, to send to New Orleans. Less meat is sold in summer than winter. I have been told that curing meat is too heavy work for women, on account of the lifting. Besides, they would get wet from the brine used; but some German and English women do pickle meat, and some even buy and sell stock. The late census of Great Britain reports twenty-six thousand butcheresses.

147. Milk Dealers. Kindness to animals always indicates something good in the heart. Life, in its every form, should be precious to us. Cows yield much less milk, and of an inferior quality, on the eastern than western continent. In Canada and some countries of Europe, the milk of goats is sold, and considerably used. In some parts of Rome it is customary for dairymen to drive their cows in every morning, and around to the houses of their customers, when the milkman draws from the cow into the vessel the desired quantity. In Belgium it is not uncommon to see milkmaids following their little wagons, containing vessels of milk, and drawn by dogs. Mayhew stated, in 1852, that in St. James's Park, London, eight cows were kept in summer to supply warm milk to purchasers; four in winter, and the number of street women engaged in the sale of curds, was one hundred. A lady called with me in a milk depot. The man has his milk brought in on the cars. Milkmen pay their women from $6 to $7 a month. They begin to milk about five in the morning, and the same hour in the afternoon, so that it may cool before being placed in the cans. Those hired to milk do house work or kitchen work in the intervals. When milking is done in the afternoon, the men that work on the farm, and the proprietor himself, assist. In some places where butter is made for market, the churning is done by horses and dogs. A milk dealer told me he sold to those who wished to sell again at cost price, four cents a quart; to other customers his price is six cents. At one depot, Williamsburg, the dealer was counting over an immense pile of pennies. His milk comes from New Jersey, seventy miles from New York. He crosses two rivers every night at twelve o'clock, to receive his milk at the Jersey depot. He sells at six cents a quart. To those who buy to sell again, his price is five cents a quart. He told me a separate freight agent is employed on some trains to take charge of the milk sent on the cars. Milk does not often sour while being brought in. Cream is brought in cans placed in large tubs of ice. He pays for freight, forty cents a can. Cream usually sells at twenty-five cents per quart. He sells twice as much milk in summer as in winter—he supposes, because it sours so easily. At shops, milk is usually sold at five cents ; when delivered, at six cents. Milk is less rich in winter than summer. A milkman told me that in dairies in and near the city, men mostly milk. He mentioned one quite near a distillery. Women that take milk about in buckets to sell, have a cow of their own, and feed her on swill from the distillery, and slops from kitchens. The milk they sell is not healthy. Some of them buy a little good milk and mix with theirs. If a dairy woman's time is not entirely occupied with her business, she might in some places find it profitable to have an ice house, and send ice around with the same horse, wagon, and driver used for the sale of milk. Borden's condensed milk is boiled at a temperature of 112°, I think, and prepared in Connecticut. The American Solidified Milk Company, in New York, employ some girls in rolling, packing, and labelling. The superintendent writes : " The employment is healthy. Women receive from $7 to $8 per month, and their board. They spend twelve hours per day, including meal times, in the establishment. An intelligent person may learn in a week. There is a prospect of more being employed. All the girls we employ are Americans, except one. It is a very comfortable occupation. I find little difference between male and female labor. When I have hired men or youths, I have found them to be more habitually attentive, and less irritable ; but women are usually neater. The women all board at a house, subject to the control of the Company. The price is $2.25 per week, washing included, and is paid for by the Company. The character of the house is unexceptionable, and the table is much better provided than that of most farmers living here."

148. Mince Meat and Apple Butter. The preparation of mince meat might be performed by women. And it might be sold by them in stores where poultry, eggs, and butter are disposed of, or in clean, well-kept groceries. With a machine for cutting the meat, and another for paring the apples, it could be easily accomplished. Apple butter is an article that meets with ready sale in market. People that are very particular about their food only buy of those they know to be cleanly in their cooking. Stewing apple butter is laborious work. If a farmer has a cider press and an apple parer, much labor is saved in preparing the materials. In some places, apple butter is kept for sale in groceries, and in establishments for the sale of the products of the dairy. The apples that are partly decayed, and those picked off the ground, furnish an abundance from large orchards. And from orchards not accessible to market where de-

fective fruit can be sold, there will be no want of a supply.   It
is sold by the pint or quart, or put up in jars holding more.

149. Mustard Packers. Most of the mustard in this
country has been imported, but some planters are now turning
their time and attention to it.   Mustard is cultivated to some
extent for the oil pressed from its seed.   Some factories exist in
the United States.   I have heard of a man in New York that
used to be engaged extensively in grinding mustard with vinegar,
and employed women to put it in jars, paying $3 a week.   In
some dry mustard factories women are employed to put the
mustard in papers. A manufacturer of mustard writes : " Women
are employed at some large establishments.   The business is
severe on persons with weak lungs, as a large quantity of steam
or dust arises from packing.   The work is paid for by the quantity, not the day.   Women of good judgment would soon become
mistresses of their work—in six months they would become good
workwomen.   They would probably spoil as much as their wages
were worth for the first few days.   When cholera and yellow
fever are about, is the best time for the sale of mustard.   Ten
hours is the usual time for work, but in busy seasons the hands
work longer."

150. Oyster Sellers. I called on a woman who makes
a living for herself and five little children by selling oysters.
She sells most about tea time, and on until twelve o'clock.   She
thinks oysters are wholesome all the year.   Physicians recommend them for their patients, and many can eat them when they
cannot eat anything else.   Of course a real oyster saloon can
only be kept in places where fresh oysters can be had.   Oysters
are rather hard for a woman to open.   In summer nothing is
done.   The room, vender, and oysters should be clean, to draw
decent customers.   It pays well ; but too often, in small concerns, the profits are derived from the sale of liquor.   At a little
oyster shop the woman told me she barely made a living.   She
keeps boys to open the oysters.   She supplies families with fresh
oysters, and when she receives an order, prepares them for families and sends them to the house.

151. Pie Bakers. " Many of the young Swabian girls
of thirteen or fourteen years old are sent to Stuttgard to acquire
music, or other branches of education, among which, household
duties are generally included.   A matron, who keeps a large
establishment there, gives the instruction, which they voluntarily
seek.   They may often be seen returning from the bakeries, with
a tray full of cakes and pies of their own making ; and sometimes young gentlemen, for the sake of fun, stop them to buy

samples of their cookery." The foundation of Miss Leslie's culinary knowledge was laid at a school of cookery in Philadelphia. In England, women make pastry for confectioneries. At the W. pie bakery I was told they employ women to prepare the fruit. They used to employ them to roll the dough; but they are not such fast workers as men. One man remarked, the shoulders ache from rolling by the time evening comes. The women are paid fifty cents a day, and board themselves. One woman boards with them, and receives $1.50 a week, with her board. M. & Co. pay their women five cents an hour, for preparing the fruit and making pies. They sell most to retail stores and hotels— consequently sell most in the spring and fall, when the largest number of strangers are in the city. They keep three wagons running part of the time, which start at six in summer, and, in busy seasons, sometimes do not get in to remain till twelve at night. When it rains or snows they do not sell so much, as those who sell at stands on the street are not out. The drivers come back several times during the day for pies, when very busy, and they mention how many are ordered. So the manager knows how many to have baked. They always sell most on Saturday, and I think sell least on Wednesdays and Thursdays. When the women work over ten hours, they are paid extra at the same rate, five cents an hour. C. and wife pay their best woman $9 a month with board and washing. It is her duty to roll out pastry, put the fruit in, and put the covers on. They employ some girls for $6 a month, to wash dishes, cook fruit, chop apples, pick dried fruit, &c. The work requires more strength than skill. There are only four large pie bakeries in New York. Madame L., who sells French pastry and confectionery, says very few women are employed in Paris, in making pastry, except for families. It requires too much strength and too long labor, to do so for a saloon. The saloons are usually open until twelve o'clock at night. At a bread bakery an attendant told me she prepares the fruit for pies, but the bakers prepare the crust, make and bake them. She says their men do that in the morning, when not otherwise employed, and it would not pay to have a woman for that purpose alone. Mrs. H. employs fifteen women. She pays $3.50 a month, with board and lodging, to those that slice apples and carry pies to and from the oven. Men place them in the oven and take them out. She pays $6.50 to those that roll out pastry and wash dishes, &c. She has three thousand pies made sometimes in one day. It requires more care to bake pies than bread. At another pie bakery, the lady told me she has the fruit prepared for pies in her kitchen and taken to the bakehouse, where they are made up by men, to save the women from working where the men are. She pays a woman for preparing fruit $5 a month and her board. In a pie bakery in New York, one of the attendants said in the old country women learn to bake pies and cakes for confectioners. They pay £30 for instruction, and spend two years' apprenticeship. They learn the whole process, including the stewing of fruit and preparing mince meat. In this country that is followed as a separate branch, and mostly done by women for bakers. She said in the bakery where she stood, girls were required, not only to wait on customers, but wash the counters, shelves, and windows of the store. The other attendant told me she found the smell of the pastry, and being so constantly on her feet, very injurious. They each receive $8 a month, and their board and washing. To succeed, a person should be quick in her motions and calculations, and a good judge of money. They are in the shop fifteen hours. In some bakeries the girls spend eighteen hours in the shop. The time could be shortened, if all the establishments of the kind would unite and make regulations to that effect; but it could not be done by one or two stores on account of the competition in the business. Such a store would lose its patronage. The majority of girls board with the bakers' families, on account of rising early to be in store. Summer is the poorest season on Broadway, as most of their customers are out of the city at that season; but in localities where the working classes are supplied, the summer is the best season, as most of them do not go to the expense of making up a fire to bake their bread and pastry.

152. Picklers of Oysters. An oysterwoman told me that girls and women are employed at most places where oysters are put in cans to send away. They are paid by the gallon for opening the shells; and near New Haven, some girls make $4 a day. On the Great South Bay, they do not earn so much, as the oysters are smaller and rougher. It requires considerable practice to become expert, but not much physical strength. The business is considered healthy, and women are paid at the same rate as men. Miss B. told me that at Fair Haven some women are paid for opening oysters two and a half cents a quart.

153. Poulterers. Much attention has been paid in this country, during the last ten years, to the breeding and feeding of poultry. All that read this will remember the hen fever that spread through our country a few years ago. Chinese chickens sold at from $40 to $100 a pair; and the usual price of one egg for a time was $5. The saving of feathers off poultry will be found profitable, for they bring a high price and ready sale.

Poultry are best disposed of in large quantities at hotels, steamboats, and restaurants. Houses for poultry should be warm and tightly made. When there is a variety of poultry, each kind should be separately lodged. Plenty of space, water accessible, gravel, living plants and loose soil are the principal things to render poultry comfortable. The worms and insects obtained from the loose soil furnish them animal food, and sand or gravel is necessary to promote digestion. It is best not to draw poultry when preparing it for market, as it keeps longer when the air is excluded. In winter some farmers let their poultry freeze, and pack them in boxes of dry straw, and send them to market. They will keep so for two or three months. I was told of an old lady, back of New Albany, Ia., that has made several thousand dollars by the sale of poultry. The egg trade is a very extensive one. It requires a knowledge of the state of the market, and promptness in supplying its demand at the right time. Several establishments in Cincinnati entered largely into the business some years ago, and, we suppose, still continue it. Eggs are often shipped from Cincinnati to New Orleans and New York. " In France and England 6,000,000 eggs are used annually in preparing leather for gloves."   In New York the poultry sold in market is mostly purchased from the wholesale commission merchants, who have stands in some parts of the market, or stores near the market. Poultry is there sold by the pound : chickens, 9 and 10 cents, and turkeys from 10 to 12 cents. It requires experience to learn the quality of poultry, but those in the business can judge of it by seeing the poultry when alive. The best time for selling is through the fall up to February. Some market women sell poultry in winter, and flowers in summer. Those who engage in raising poultry, could unite with it the raising of rabbits, pigeons, &c. About a hundred persons (mostly women) are employed in a henery near Paris, where thousands of chickens are annually hatched out by keeping eggs in rooms, heated by steam to a uniform temperature.

154. Restaurant Keepers. In London and Paris, young and pretty women are employed in the best class of tobacco stores and in restaurants. This should not be so on account of the number, and often the character, of the men that resort to these shops. Indeed, we think it best not to employ them in any stores that men only frequent. Besides, the unseasonable hours that restaurants are kept open, make it objectionable for women. They are often not closed until midnight or after. In Great Britain girls and women are frequently employed as bar maids at inns.

155. Sealed Provisions, Pickles, and Sauces. The plan is now almost universally adopted in the United States, of putting up fruit and vegetables in cans from which the air is excluded. It is one of the greatest inventions of the age for housekeepers. It saves labor and expense; and if well put up, the fruit and vegetables are as fresh and taste as natural as we have them in the growing season. Quite a number of large houses are engaged in the business in New York, and a few in Philadelphia. E. Philadelphia employs women to put pickles and preserved fruit in jars, sealing and labelling them. They can earn from $2.50 to $3 a week. They sit while at work. The season begins in July, and is over in October. K. & Co., New York, employ about a hundred females during the fruit season. The occupation consists in preparing the articles to be preserved; that is, peeling, seeding, washing, &c., labelling bottles, and painting cans. Those they employ are mostly Irish, and not capable of any very elevated position of labor. The fruit season lasts six months, after which only about thirty remain the rest of the year. The hours of labor are ten, and the compensation from $2.50 to $3 per week. In another establishment they employ only small girls, to whom they pay $2 per week, and occasionally $2.50. Mrs. Dall suggests that farmers' daughters put up candied fruits like those imported from France, which bear a good price and yield a handsome profit. Some women engage in making pickles on their own responsibility. Owners of gardens not convenient to market would find it profitable to put up fruits and vegetables, and to make pickles and sauces. The spices they would have to purchase; but if they had an orchard, they could make good vinegar. They could either sell the articles in the nearest large city, or pay a commission for the sale of them. Mr. D., in one of the New York markets, employs women for putting pickles in jars—gives $8 a month and board. The number of hours they are employed depends on the quantity of work they have on hand. B., New York, employs for six months from six to eight women; for four months, some twenty-five; and the remaining two months, from ninety to one hundred and twenty-five. B. has always had his work done in the city, but contemplates having it done hereafter in the country, as the articles will then be on the ground, and save the trouble of transportation. They send South. He thinks the South must for a long time be dependent on the North for pickles. They even furnish some of the pickle houses in Baltimore. They fear they will lose much because they have now no demand for pickles from the South, and they are likely to spoil by keeping. They are most busy in summer and fall. They keep some steady hands all the year. They find it difficult to get good hands, and pay learners from the first. Many girls go from New York in the summer, to the country, to put up pickles, gather berries, and weed gardens; and it pays them pretty well. B. pays his women fifty cents a day of ten hours. It is not unhealthy, and requires but a little time to learn. In this, as in most other mechanical work, practice makes perfect; consequently, experienced hands receive the preference. At most places men attend to fruit while it is being cooked. The preserving is mostly done in large kettles, around which pass pipes containing steam, encased by larger vessels. Lifting the kettles would be too heavy for women, when they contain, as in some cases, thirty-five gallons of fruit. And the steam used would require some one that knew a little of such matters, yet a smart woman could soon learn. M. & M. have their work done in the house, paying from $2.25 to $4. They can always get hands. W. & P. have their pickles, preserves, and sauces put up in the country. Their girls get from $3 to $6 a week. They employ two hundred girls, and take most of them from the city in the busy season from June to October. G. pays $3 a week. Any one that can use their hands can do it, and become expert in two or three months. Another pickler pays $2 per week. His wife does most of the work. Mrs. M. lives near Washington market. She employs some women to preserve, and some to put up pickles. Most of her preserves are put up by an old lady who does it at her own home. She pays her women from $2.50 to $4 a week. It requires long experience to become proficient. Nearly all the work is done in her house, and of course is done only in the summer. Her custom is mostly confined to the city. If she is preserving a very large quantity of fruit, she has a man to stir it. He spends most of his time taking purchased articles home. She uses only the best articles. She can always get enough hands. An extensive pickle manufacturer writes: " I employ women in packing pickles and all goods of the kind into glass— labelling, corking, making jellies, jams, &c., packing, labelling catsups, bottling syrups, &c. Women are so employed wherever these goods are manufactured. The employment is *healthy*— so much so that I have known invalids gain their health. I pay $3 per week—men $6 to $10; all work ten hours a day. Women can learn in from three to twelve months. Some learners receive $2, and some $2.50 per week. Quickness, neatness, and skill are required. Summer and fall are the busy seasons. The females are mostly young Irish, born in the United States. Women are superior in handiness, inferior in strength." A gentleman in the business writes from Newburyport : " I employ usually from eight

8

to ten women. I pay eight cents per hour, and they work from four to seven hours. The men's work is worth more than women's, and entirely different from it. The prospect for this kind of work is good. There is no work in winter or early spring. Seaports are the best localities for the business. My women pay from $1.50 to $1.75 for respectable board."

156. Sugar Makers. When the part of the sugar cane to be pressed, is cut, it is tied in bundles and drawn to the mill in wagons. It is deposited in heaps outside, and negro girls carry the bundles on their heads to the mill door. After the cane has been subjected to pressure by cylinders, to obtain the juice, it falls through an opening in the mill walls, and is carried off by negro women and spread in the sun, to dry for fuel. The work in sugar mills is very warm and heavy. The work in sugar refineries is very laborious, and requires the workers to be subjected to great heat. Several refiners have informed me that the business does not admit of the employment of women in any department. The business is said to be very trying on the constitution, and produces an unhealthy increase of flesh. It is said to be good for consumptives on account of the great nutriment in sugar. A sugar refiner died not long ago, whose salary received from the company amounted, I was told, to $25,000 per annum. I have thought there is one part of the work a woman might do—it is enveloping the sugar in paper cases. At a sugar refinery a man told us, some women are employed to make bags for containing char, i. e., burnt bones, and earn several dollars a week. The sewing is done by hand; making the bags requires but a short time, though it is heavy work. Most refiners buy theirs at bag factories, or have their men to make them.

157. Tea Packers. A boy fitting himself to be a tea broker told me, the business is best in the spring, fall, and winter. The quality of tea is principally decided by smelling—which is done before it is moistened, by blowing on it with the breath and then putting it to the nostrils. Boiling water is then poured on it, and tasted. The boy said, it is a paying business. It is not healthy on account of the dust inhaled. It does not take more than a year to learn to judge of the quality of kinds of tea. Boys learning the business do not live long. They are paid $2, and $2.50 a week. In busy seasons, they sometimes work as late as nine o'clock. There are not many tea packers in the city, and one told me, most of them cannot make a living. We called on Mr. N., a teapacker, who charges for putting tea out of the large boxes, in which it is imported, into canisters and packages, according to the way in which it is put up; whether in paper covers, or canisters of lead or tin. The facing or labelling varies some. He says, packing could be done by girls. He employs men and boys, paying the boys from $2 to $4 a week. There are only two tea packing establishments in New York, and not more than one in any other large city. It is not at all unhealthy. Packing is done most in spring and fall. Mr. N. thinks it would be best to have the girls work in separate apartments from the men. He complains of the want of promptness in girls. A tea packer of Boston writes : " I employ from six to ten girls to cover and line boxes, &c. They are American, of Irish descent. There is nothing in the business, that the girls do, that can be considered unhealthy. Wages run from $2.50 to $3 per week. It does not take a long time to learn, and full wages are paid while learning. I employ my help the year round, though less hours are used for a day's work during the winter. Ten is the number of working hours during the summer, spring, and autumn ; and eight, during the winter months." In London, a number of men and women, principally women, buy exhausted tea leaves of the female servants and sell them at establishments, where they are dried, and a fresh green color given them by a copper preparation. They are sold for new tea. The quantity so renewed is thought to amount to 78,000 lbs. annually. The Chinese women assist in gathering tea leaves and drying them, but men do the packing.

158. Vermicelli. Vermicelli is moulded by passing through a machine and being laid on frames until the next day to partially dry. Then girls cut it in short pieces, and twist it. The twisting requires a little art acquired by practice. They receive from $2 to $3.50 a week. It is cruel for females to be kept on their feet all day while at work, when they might sit. At a factory I saw a French lady, the wife of the proprietor, cutting and twisting vermicelli. A young Frenchman was at work, who told us he was paid 75 cents a day; but women, he said, would not be paid as much, because he had to attend to the machinery. The lady sat, as girls in factories should do if they wish.

159. Vinegar. A plant is now grown from which vinegar is made. " In addition to the consumption of vinegar in culinary uses and the preparation of preserved food, it is indispensable in several branches of manufacture, as in the dressing of morocco leather, and in dye and print works." The labor of making vinegar is too hard and heavy for women. The handling of barrels, changing of liquids, and constant exposure to heat and cold, without cessation of labor, are too great for the female frame to sustain. The workers often pass from a temperature varying from 92° to 105°, to one of extreme coldness." A Boston vinegar manufacturer, writes : " Women are never employed in making vinegar in large quantities. They are not adapted to the occupation. It does not agree with some constitutions. It requires but a short time to learn the business. The prospect for future employment is poor." Some women make vinegar from parings of fruit, tea leaves, &c., for family use.

160. Yeast. A manufacturer of yeast powders writes: "There is but a small part of the work that women can do. It requires the strong, muscular arm of a man to do most of it." We know women are sometimes employed for putting up the powders, and are paid by the number of packages.

TEXTILE MANUFACTURES.

161. Cotton Manufacturers. Only so far back as 1789, doubts were entertained whether cotton could be cultivated in the United States, while now the amount of calicoes annually produced in the United States is supposed to equal twenty millions of yards. "The number of females employed in the various factories of Lowell, in which textile fabrics are produced, will exceed 12,000. Those engaged in weaving can earn, upon an average, from $2.50 to $4 per week. Those who labor as spinners and spoolers make only from seventy-five cents to $2, but they are generally very young." In the cotton mill at Cannelton, Ind., there were " in 1854, about 200 females. They worked by the job, and their pay was the same as would be given to men for the same work. They earned from $1 to $5.50 per week." We believe, in the majority of factories, the plan of paying some hands by the piece, and some by the week, is adopted. B., manufacturer, told me quite a number of his weavers earn from $5 to $6 a week, being paid by the piece. It requires two or three months to get in the way of weaving well. His hands are busy all the year. His factory is in New Jersey, twenty-five miles from New York. The laws of New Jersey prohibit the employment of operatives more than twelve hours out of the twenty-four, but some evade it. The law, also, forbids the employment of children under ten years of age. The smaller children are engaged in spinning, and not so well paid. It requires but a short time to learn to attend the spinning machinery. There is generally a full supply of weavers to be had, because it pays well. Manufacturers usually have their work done in the country, because living, and consequently labor, are cheaper there. A cotton manufacturer in Rhode Island, who employs about 100 operatives, writes: "I pay both by the piece and the week. When by the week, from $4 to $5. When by the piece, the women are paid at the same rate as the men, but the men are able to make from fifty cents to $1 per week more. It requires from three to six months, to learn. Girls are paid while learning, if they grow up with us. They are employed through the year, and work sixty-nine hours per week, twelve hours per day for five days, nine hours on Saturday. All classes of laborers must work during mill hours. Women keep the rooms and machinery neater than men. About seven eighths of the women employed in our mill are Americans; one half would be the nearer proportion in mills generally in this section, three fourths in some instances. There are other parts that women might be employed in, but the custom has not been introduced in our section, on account of their dress. They pay from $1.50 to $1.75 for board, and are all in private families." The Lawrence Manufacturing Company, at Lowell, write: "Women are employed in carding, spinning, dressing, and weaving. The employment is not unhealthy, and they earn from $1 to $4 a week, clear of board, according to capability and skill—average, say, $2 per week. They work eleven hours a day; men average about eighty cents a day clear of board; their work is altogether too hard for women. The women learn in from one to three months. They are paid, usually, $1 a week, besides their board, while learning. The qualifications needed are respectable character and ordinary capacity. They are employed all the year round. The scarcity of hands is greater in the departments requiring most skill; there is an abundance of inferior sort. We employ 1,300 women; perhaps one third are Americans. They are employed in all branches where it is expedient. The Americans are well informed; the Irish, improving, though low in the scale of intelligence. They have churches, evening schools, and lectures. Work stops at 6.30 and 7 o'clock. They live in boarding houses under our care, well regulated, respectable and comfortable, and pay $1.25 per week." At the New York mills, "361 adult and 99 minor females are employed in the manufacture of fine shirtings and cottonades. Wages of adults are $3.99, and minors, $2.12½ per week. Price of board, $1.50. They work 12 hours per day." The Naunkeag Steam Cotton Company, Mass., "employ 400, and pay by the week, from $2.50 to $3. Those that do piecework, earn on an average, $3.50 per week; six months will enable intelligent hands to earn three fourths pay. Their board is paid for two weeks, while learning, then they receive what they earn. Desirable hands find steady work; they are employed all the year; they work eleven hours a day. We prefer women, because neater and more reliable. They have more time for improvement than is made available. Board, $1.50 to $1.75. Good boarding houses are provided." At Kingston, Rhode Island, a man employing nine girls, pays by the yard, and the girls earn from $4 to $6 per week. Men receive the same wages as women. They work from sun up to sun down, except at meal times. If other mills ran but ten hours, they would. They have work all the year. Hands are rather scarce in that State. All are American. They prefer it to general housework. Women are the best in mills for light work. Female operatives pay $1.50 for board, lodging, and washing. The Jackson Manufacturing Company of New Haven writes: "Women are employed in the various branches belonging to a cotton mill Average wages of our females are $2.30, and board money $1.25, making $3.55 per week received by them. Some females in our employ earn eighty cents per day; average price of male labor, about eighty-four cents per day. Women are paid less, because they cannot do such work as is done by men. In regard to the time required to learn to do the work in the different departments, much depends upon the dispositions of the learners. Six months would ordinarily be sufficient time to render one competent. Women are usually allowed their board while learning. A good character and good health are needed. There is much changing among help during the spring and summer months, say for four months in the year; but we almost invariably keep our supply good. Our working hours are eleven and a quarter per day. With the exception of our weaving department, but little work is done on Saturday afternoons aside from cleaning, so that our working hours will not average over ten and a half per day. By giving a suitable notice to the overseer, it is so arranged that the help can be absent from their work one day or a month. The largest proportion of American help is found in the weaving and dressing departments. We have in our employ 140 men, 310 females, about one half American. We have good boarding houses, carefully watched, and kept clean in all respects. Our American help are quite intelligent, also some of the foreign. Some of our help attend school during the winter months. Board $1.25 per week—the keeper of the house not paying rent. The houses will each accommodate about twenty persons comfortably." Another manufacturing company pay from $2 to $4 per week, mostly by the piece. The work can be learned in three or four months. Their hands are paid small wages while learning. They have constant employment. They usually work twelve hours per day; three fourths American. From a manufacturer in Gilford, New Hampshire, we learn he employs forty women, who work by the piece, and whose average pay is $3 per week. They work eleven hours. Females are paid the same as men for the same kind of work. Some parts of the business can be learned in one day, others ten, and some hands will learn in one day what others would not in ten. Work at all seasons; spring and fall most busy. It pays better than housework. Board of males, $2.50; females, $1.25 to $1.50. A manufacturer in New York writes: "I employ about twenty women in weaving, twenty-five in spinning, spooling and other branches; boys and girls from fifteen to twenty each, and ten men. Women average about $2.50 per week. Women are paid the same price as men. Weavers earn about $3.50 per week. My mill runs twelve hours per day, the year round. Women are mostly American. The girls have an hour for each meal." A medical man has stated, that the health of operatives is promoted by occupying rooms with large windows on each side of the room, so that the sunlight will penetrate the apartments during the entire day. And those rooms with white walls are more healthy and better for the eyes than those with colored walls.

162. Batting. A manufacturer of cotton batting writes: "Women are employed in our factory to tend machinery. They are employed in Europe. It is only unhealthy from being indoor work. We pay, per week, for best hands, $2 and board. They work twelve hours. I think there is a surplus of hands at this time. The work is light and does not require an expenditure of strength. The work is as comfortable as any can be. All parts will not answer for women. Board $1.42. Men are paid $1 more than women, but perform a different part of the work. Learners usually command wages after two weeks. The summer is the most profitable time to manufacture."

163. Calicoes. Calico takes its name from Calicot, a town in Malabar, where the art has been practised with great success from time immemorial. Calico printing is the art of producing figured patterns upon cotton. They are transferred to its surface by blocks, or engraved by copper cylinders, by which the colors are directly printed, or by which a substance having an affinity for both the stuff and coloring matter is employed, which is called a mordant. "In England, calico printing employs a vast number of children of both sexes, who have to mix and grind the colors for the adult workpeople, and are commonly called turners. The usual hours of labor are twelve, including meal time; but as the children generally work the same time as the adults, it is by no means uncommon in all districts for children of five and six years old to be kept at work fourteen and even sixteen hours consecutively. They begin to work generally about their eighth year, as in Birmingham and Sheffield, but often earlier." Calico is printed mostly in Lowell, Philadelphia, Saco, Dover, and some other towns. A manufacturing company of lawns and calicoes in Providence, R. I., write : "We employ fifty women in stitching, folding, and tracing pantograph designs. The employment is healthy. We pay from fifty cents to sixty-seven cents per day of ten hours. We have one woman who does a man's work at folding, and is paid a man's wages—$1 per day. The time to learn the business is according to natural ability; very soon with ordinary capacity, say, two weeks. Cool weather is the best for work, but the women are not thrown out of employment at any season. We have more applicants than we can accommodate. The light, clean work, is best for women; the rough and heavy for men. We adopt female labor as far as practicable. Ordinary board is from $2 to $2.50 yer week."

164. Canton Flannels. A manufacturer of Canton flannels in Holden, Mass., writes: "We employ from twenty to twenty-five women in spinning, spooling, drawing, and speeder tending, warping and weaving. We like them because they are neater, and more reliable, and the work is better adapted to females. They earn from fifty cents to $1 per day of twelve hours. Women are paid the same as men, except the overseers, who get from $1.25 to $1.67 per day. It requires from one week to four to learn the business. We sometimes pay their board while learning, if they are attentive to work. It is as reliable as any business. There is no difference in seasons; we work the year round. The time could not be shortened. In weaving there is no surplus of hands. I would say, that with the present prospects for business, it would be well for many of the females in want of employment to learn to weave. They can make from $4 to $6 a week, but mostly average $4.75. It is healthy work. The labor is not hard, but confining; and the girls are generally happy and contented. Three fourths of ours are Americans."

165. Carpet Chains. We were told that in the manufacture of carpet chain, "women are employed in spooling. We saw women employed in weaving various kinds of binding for carpets, webbing for girths, reins, and harness. The hours of labor are nominally ten, which, indeed, seems reasonable, in Philadelphia; but in the suburbs, and some parts of New England, both men and women work fifteen hours. Our informant uses no artificial light on the premises, and when the daylight fails, his workpeople leave off labor. The wages are the usual fifty cents a day. Steady hands are kept in work the year round; but unskilful workwomen are dismissed after fair trial. Men earn double what women earn, though they do not produce double the work, nor do it any better. When machinery is used, women frequently require assistance from a workman."

166. Cord. C., of Philadelphia, manufacturer of black and white cord, employs about thirty women in spooling, twisting, balling, and making into skeins. He keeps his hands all the year. He did not permit us to see them, saying they object to being seen by strangers, on the ground that they are " en deshabille." We can bear witness to the probability of this statement, for almost all the women we have seen at work are very untidily clad, and dirty; indeed, in the present total disregard of cleanliness in the workrooms, if they wore better clothes, they would spoil more than they can afford. Ought not employers and workwomen to consider this subject, since it undoubtedly degrades a female, even in her own estimation, as in that of others, to be habitually in what is mildly qualified "deshabille?" The spoolers receive the highest wages, viz, $5 per week; the other hands from $2 to $5. The *fine* cord is made farther East, as it can there be produced cheaper; the *coarser* can be made in Philadelphia, at a lower rate. Mr. J., of New York, employs six women, two of them earn $7 each—the others less. It is paid for by the quantity. Prospect for work, good. There are but five factories in New York city, but they do seven eighths of the city business. In Philadelphia most is made. It takes but two or three months to learn. They give employment all the year, and learners receive something from the first.

167. Dyers and Bleachers. Dyeing may be divided into seven branches: 1, calico and cotton; 2, fur; 3, fustian; 4, leather; 5, linen; 6, silk; 7, wool and woollen. Silk and wool are of animal origin, and require different treatment in dyeing from substances of a vegetable nature, such as cotton and flax. All the various colors and shades of dyed goods were originally derived from the combination of the four simple colors—blue, red, yellow, and black. Cotton is more easily dyed than linen, and the colors are brighter. Much of what is said under "Print Works" will apply to this subject. They are so similar, a distinction is scarcely necessary. In large manufacturing cities, dyers usually confine themselves to one kind of goods, as wool or silk, and some to certain colors. Dye houses, in other than manufacturing cities and towns, are mostly for the coloring of goods that are worn, or new goods that have been damaged. A great deal of dyeing is done in our large cities. Frequently, persons going into mourning have articles of dress dyed. Steam has taken the place mostly of hard labor. When goods have been well dyed, a casual observer could not detect it. Permanency of color is a

8*

desirable item in dyeing. Some women make a living by keeping a little shop, where they receive goods to be colored, and have the work done at dye houses, making, of course, a profit. There is generally a dye house connected with every large factory of woollen goods. A girl who was employed in a dye house says the work is far from being neat. The work of most of the girls is light. It is to put letters or figures on the articles sent, and when dyed, fold and tie them up, and place the numbers on. In the dye house where she was, one girl received $3.50—the others, each, $3 per week. They worked ten hours a day. One girl was employed in finishing the goods—that is, running them over a heated cylinder to smooth and dry them. She says the floors of dye houses are so wet that women would find it not only filthy, but injurious. Mr. Y. says women are not employed in the mechanical department of his dye and print establishment—that the business requires the workers to stand in liquids, and the atmosphere is very damp. A woman would be liable to suffer from exposure of that kind. A girl employed at another place to mark goods, told me she received $3 per week. Was told at C.'s dye house that he employs four girls, paying $3, and $3.50 a week. They put numbers on goods, and do other work of that kind. They work ten hours. A cotton goods bleacher and dyer told me the work was too wet and dirty for women. Most of the winding of cotton for dyeing is done by machinery. By steam power one person could do ten times as much as by a wheel. At one place they paid thirty-five cents for basting together two pieces of cloth eight yards long to be bleached; and a woman could earn from seventy-five cents to $3 per day; but the work could not last long. We called at a dyer and bleacher's. He said: "Very few women are employed in dyeing in this country, but in the old country they are. He has seen them at it in Scotland, and there it is rather better paid than most women's work. They are also employed in bleaching, both by chemicals and exposure to the sun. It is not unhealthy, although in a dye house a person must be wet from the knees down. By wearing thick boots, and leggins of India rubber, they would not be likely to suffer. Occasionally, dyers get some of the chemicals they use into sores on their hands and feet, which may injure them some, but not seriously. He says the work must be done in a certain time, and so they cannot be particular about keeping their feet dry. He pays old women for hanking cotton $37\frac{1}{2}$ cents a score, and so they may earn $2.25 a week." There are mechanical modes of printing textile fabrics. In the Staten Island Dye and Print Works, "there are a good many women and children employed. The latter are principally confined to the printing department, each of the sixty printers engaged there being allowed a child for the purpose of adjusting or distributing the color evenly, previous to the application of the block. The rate of wages paid in this establishment is, we understand, as follows: the printers and block makers are paid by the piece, and when in full work can earn from $60 to $70 a month; the dyers and other workmen receive from 37½ cents to $1.25 a day; the women $6 to $12 a month, and the children from $6 to $8." A dyer writes: "Women are sometimes employed in the finishing department, and are mostly paid by the day. Spring and fall are the busy seasons." One in Walpole, Mass., writes: "I think more than an ordinary degree of intelligence is required for the business, because of the thought and observation necessary." A dyer in Buffalo, N. Y., writes: "I employ two, and sometimes three women. Women are employed in basting work together, and in finishing it after it is dyed. In some places they have charge of the office, and receive and deliver goods. For a healthy person it is not injurious. In finishing, the individual is on his or her feet all the time. I pay from $1.75 to $5 per week, and hands work from ten to sixteen hours. The time could not be shortened, owing to the nature of the business, and the loss during the winter. The comfort and remuneration of the part done by women is very good. Women of equal intelligence with men do better, as it is of female apparel the business mostly consists. In winter they have considerable unoccupied time they could devote to mental improvement." The proprietor of the Chelsea Dye House writes: "We employ about seventy-five women to wash, iron, and finish dyed goods. About one eighth are Americans. It is not unhealthy, to my knowledge, or in my experience. Average pay is $3.50 per week. Those that work by the piece can earn from $3.50 to $6 per week of eleven hours per day. Women are paid all which the business they do will afford. It requires a woman of fair capacity a few weeks to learn. Work is constant for good hands. Work is nearly uniform through the seasons. Large cities are the best localities for business. They pay about $1.75 per week for board in private families of their own standing." A member of a firm at Astoria, L. I., writes: "We employ from seventy-five to one hundred women in washing and dyeing yarns and cloth. We know them to be so employed in Berlin, Prussia. The employment is not unhealthy. We pay by the week from $4 to $5. They work ten hours. We pay men $7 per week for the same work that the females are employed at, because they do more. It requires about four years to learn fully that portion of work done by females. They are paid $2 per week while learning. A good public school education is needed, and temperate, steady habits. The prospects for females are good—eventually they will supersede the men in one branch of the business. The spring and fall seasons are the best. The winter is not so good. About two months in the summer our works are partially stopped. There is a surplus of dyers in Lowell, Mass. We employ women in preference to men, because we believe them to be more intelligent than men—especially emigrants. About two thirds are Americans. They have evening schools, lectures, and church services. Those that board pay about $1.50 per week."

168. Factory Operatives. The larger number of operatives in our manufactures are females. They are of all ages. They do not remain so permanently in our factories as in those of older countries. They make skilful and active workers. The factory operatives of this country are more favorably situated than those of most countries. Most of them have wholesome food and comfortable homes, or boarding houses. They are not confined in factories from early childhood until they lie down to take their last, long sleep; consequently, they are not stunted and deformed, and prematurely old. The activity and variety attending life in the city are likely to produce great restlessness, and insatiable thirst for excitement. This must be checked, or its results may be ruinous. Vent of the feelings in harmless, wholesome amusements, recreation so far as is possible in the quiet of the country, reading good books, and social intercourse with the virtuous and worthy, will form a good substitute for this artificial excitement. So greatly is the manufacture of materials into cloth, and cloth into goods, facilitated by machinery, that wool taken from the sheep's back to-day, can be worn as clothing to-morrow. The number of factories has greatly increased since the introduction of machinery; nor is it strange, for goods have become cheaper and the demand is greater. The materials for manufacturing are abundant in this country; but the want of workmen acquainted with this business, and the want of capital, have prevented some branches of American manufacture from equalling those of older countries. The improvements in machinery for removing dust and floating cotton in the work rooms, no doubt renders it more healthy than it was. "In proof of his assertion that factory labor shortens life, Dr. Jarrold deposed, that having examined, in the schools, all the children whose fathers had ever worked, or were still working in factories, he found that from one third to one fourth were fatherless." "Out of about two thousand children and young persons taken promiscuously, who were carefully examined in 1832, two hundred were deformed. These were factory operatives." These statements refer to operatives in England. Some women are employed in the manufactories of Birmingham, England, as overseers in the departments where women work, but the number is small, and in our country it is still more uncommon. Cotton and woollen goods are extensively manufactured in the New England States, New York, and Pennsylvania. A gentleman told me that a little more than a year ago, as he came from Vermont, he saw a young man in the cars with about twenty girls, that he was bringing down from Canada to a cotton factory in Massachusetts. The manufacturers had offered a bonus of $5 apiece for girls, and to pay their travelling expenses, and this young man was making a business of it. He says, in busy seasons there is a scarcity of hands in the New England factories. We believe that when men and women do the same kind of work, such as weaving, and are paid by the quantity, no difference is made in their wages. In comparing returns from several factories in Massachusetts, I find weavers earn in them from $4 to $5.50 per week; warpers, $3 to $5; dotters, $3 to $4. Irish women, by working for less wages, have pushed American women out of factories. In Lowell, a few years back, nearly all the operatives were young American girls from the country. Many worked from the most honorable, self-denying motives; some to educate younger members of the family, some to assist widowed mothers or hard-working fathers, some to lay by a sum to support themselves in old age, and some to acquire the means for obtaining a more extensive school education. A manufacturer of printing cloths, Reading, Pennsylvania, writes: " In all countries where there are cotton mills, women are employed as weavers, fly and drawing tenders, spoolers, warpers, dressers, and cloth pickers. The work is not more unhealthy than any indoor employment. Workers earn from $2.25 to $6. Men and women are paid the same for the same kind of work. Our kind of work may be destroyed a year or so by the unsettled state of the country—otherwise it is good. The hands work about eleven hours at present prices, one hour less would reduce wages about 10 per cent. There are openings in cotton mills along the Hudson River, and farther East, and a surplus of hands in mechanical towns inland. The work is lighter than most of womanly employments. Women are superior in attending faithfully to their work, and are more easily managed than men. Board is from $1.50 to $1.75 per week, and is much better than their homes would be, if they were the daughters of day laborers, as many of them are. I would say further, in our branch of business women are treated in all respects as regards their work the same as men, paid the same, and under the same rules and restraint. In our dressing department the women make from $6 to $8, while the men make from $8 to $10, with the same machine at the same price. There are but few mills that employ women dressers, except in Pennsylvania. They are not strong enough ; but here the descendants of the old Dutch stock are more masculinely developed, and are taking the place of the men in this branch." A gentleman who has been manufacturing cotton cloth in North Adams, Massachusetts, between twenty and thirty years, writes : " We employ women and girls in our mill. Some of the work requires constant stepping and walking. Wages for spinning girls, $2.50 to $3 per week; for boys the same, for spooling ; from $2.75 to $3 for speeder and drawer tenders ; $3 for warpers, or $4; all the rates of labor include the board. Farther East, women are employed as dressers, earning from $4 to $6 per week. Weaving is paid for by the piece— most other work by the week, as it cannot so well be let by the piece. To learn to spin on the throstle frames requires from six to eight weeks. The qualifications desired in an applicant are expertness, good behavior, ability to read and write, industry, and a desire to be useful to the employer. In midsummer, hands are most scarce. Good workers are never thrown out of employment except during panics. In this place (North Adams), hands usually work from twelve to twelve and a half hours ; Saturdays we close at four o'clock in summer. Farther East, a number of operators work eleven hours ; some, twelve ; and some, even twelve and a half. The legislature of the General Government is, and has been for many years, against encouraging the industry of the country. Whatever revenue laws would promote the making of iron, wool, cotton, or cutlery, would assist and support agriculture, the making of shoes, and all other branches of labor. The cotton mills can merely subsist. The hours could not be shortened. Those employed in watching, warming, oiling up, superintending, repairing, &c., have the same hours. There has been a demand for hands everywhere in Massachusetts, Connecticut, and adjoining States. Women are more orderly, more easily governed, and more cleanly than men. Their slim fingers enable them to be more expert. They are more attentive, as a general thing, where the labor requires only looking after, creating no fatigue, except that which arises from close attention. For these reasons women are preferable. Their labor is somewhat cheaper than men's of the same age. In Western Massachusetts, about three fourths are American women ; in Eastern Massachusetts about one half are, and the other half foreigners. The women have good boarding houses, and live and dress well. Here, a hand can leave his employer by giving two weeks' notice ; farther East, four weeks' notice is required. In both places, effort is made to spare them at once, if they desire it. My American work people are above mediocrity; the others, rather below. Children under fifteen years of age are required by law to be kept out of the mills for at least three months in the year, to attend school; more if the parents choose, as the schools are free. Employers, as a general thing, press and urge the children to school, as intelligent hands are worth more than ignorant ones. For good board, women pay $1.50 per week ; with lodging and washing, $2. Many hands lay up sums in the savings banks; very many more might do so, if they chose. Good female spinners, speeder tenders, spoolers, warpers, twisters-in, and weavers are always rather scarce. They command from $3 to $6 per week. Widow women, with families of girls to support, can get a good living by such work, and lay up some money if they try."

Hitherto few manufactories have been established in the Southern United States: but now that the South will depend more on its own resources, no doubt manufactories of cotton goods will be built up very rapidly. From "Northern Profits and Southern Wealth," we make an extract: "One third of the hands employed in factories at the East are females. At the South, female labor is taking the same direction. At the North, this element of labor is supplied by immigration in nearly its whole extent—a very large proportion of the females employed in the factories being Irish. The Eagle mills in Georgia have one hundred and thirty-six looms, and employ seventy girls, who earn 50 cents to $1 per day. The operatives in all these factories are white people, chiefly girls and boys, from twelve to twenty years of age. On an average they are better paid and worked easier than is usually the case in the North. Country girls from the pine forests, as green and awkward as it is possible to find them, soon become skilful operatives; and ere they have been in the mills a year, they are able to earn from $4 to $6 a week. They are only required to work ten hours a day. Particular attention is paid to the character of the operatives, and in some mills none are received but those having testimonials of good moral character and industrious habits. Churches and Sabbath schools are also attached to several of the manufactories, so that the religious training of the operatives may be properly attended to. In 1860, 45,315 males and 73,605 females were employed in cotton factories. The woollen manufacturers employed as operatives in 1860, 28,780 males and 20,120 females.

169. Gingham. From the Manchester Gingham Manufactory, we learn 149 American women are there employed in weaving, winding, spooling, piecing, drawing, reeling, and spinning. "Spinners' maximum is sixty cents per day. Weavers receive twenty-six and eighteen cents per cut. Women receive for winding ten cents per cut, nine cents for spooling, forty cents per day for piecing, for drawing $2.50 per week, and for reeling $1\frac{1}{4}$ and $1\frac{1}{2}$ cents per doff. We pay the same to men and women for the same kind of work. They are usually about two months learning. Prospect for work is very good. We make a staple article. Summer is the best season; we have steady work the year round. Hands work sixty-nine hours during six days—twelve hours, five days; and nine on Saturday. There is some demand for them; we prefer women for weaving. They pay for board $1.40 per week." The agent of the Gingham Mills, in Clinton, Mass., in reply to a letter seeking information, says: "We employ four hundred females, young and old, in the various branches of cotton manufacture. They are paid from forty cents to $1.25, according to skill and ability; they work $11\frac{1}{2}$ hours. They are paid partly by the piece, and partly by the day. By the piece, and for the same kind of work, women receive as much as men. Some branches are learned very quickly, and some slowly, according to capacity. Women are paid while learning, much to our loss. Ordinary intelligence and complete use of the physical faculties are necessary qualifications. We work at all seasons. The women are very careful to select their times for absence, visiting, &c., when we are preparing the winter style of goods, which are of darker colors, and possibly less profitable to them. They are sure to come back during the manufacture of lighter styles. It is clearly a womanly way of doing business, but *the men do the same.* The kinds of work women do in mills do not require the strength of men, and so women are employed. It is cheapest to employ women; because, if we employed only men, half the village would be idle. Boys can do all the work that the females do. We have four hundred males also. One third are American. In weaving, where men's and women's work is most justly and fully compared, men do the most and the best in quality. In other branches there is no decided difference. Board $1.50 per week; the houses are of good moral character, and very comfortable."

170. Hosiers. The invention of machinery for making hose is ascribed to William Lee, of England, 1589. Some trace the invention of knit stockings to Spain. The number of hands employed in the manufacture of hose in Saxony amounts to 45,000. Cotton, woollen, linen, and silk are the kinds of hose common to us. The manufacture of hose worn by Americans is mostly English. The amount of capital required, and the small number of good operatives in our country, cause the products of some of our manufactures to be of an inferior quality. Years back knitting was much done, particularly in the country, but

the general use of machinery has superseded the knitting needle.
In our large cities, the great amount of hosiery worn might make
the sale of hose and half hose a payable business. In making
cotton and woollen hose, some children wind the cotton, some
join the seams, and others sew them on the boards, to put them
in shape. We called to see Aiken's knitting machine. It is
quite an ingenious affair ; price, $65. I think if any two women
would buy one, and one should knit, while the other formed the
feet and finished them off, it would pay better than sewing. Large
quantities of hosiery are made in Germantown, Pa. It gives
employment to many women, who, at their houses, finish them
off. The United States Government have usually obtained their
clothing, shoes, hats, and socks for the army and navy at Philadelphia, but since the war commenced, most of the clothing has
been made up in New York. The manufacture of hosiery is very
limited in New York. At the principal hosiery establishment
we were told they only employ women to seam that are the wives
of the weavers, and they do the work at home. It is very poor
pay, and is done almost altogether by English women who have
been brought up to the business. It would not pay a person to
learn it. An English stocking weaver told me that he does
theatrical work, as it pays best. He has known two women from
his own country that wove hosiery in the United States. One
did journey work with her husband in New York. She earned
from $4 to $5 per week. Such work is paid for by the piece or
dozen. The work pays poorly. A woman cannot earn at it
more than thirty-seven or fifty cents a day, being paid eighteen
cents a dozen for seaming socks. To seam shirts and drawers
pays better, six cents being paid for each article. Weaving
stockings by hand looms will not pay in this country—they can
be imported so cheaply. It is rather light work. Work done
by steam power is not so neat ; the selvages are not well made,
and the goods must be cut and sewed in seams. Many women
are employed in hosiery manufactures where steam is used. A
stocking manufacturer in Lake Village, N. H., writes: "Seven
hundred girls and married women are employed in this village to
make stockings. Wages run from 50 cents to $1 per day of ten
hours; some are paid by the day, others by the piece. Men's
work, being harder, is better paid. It requires from three to five
weeks to learn. Women have their board paid while learning.
Spring, summer, and autumn are the best seasons for work. Some
work at the business to maintain their families; others, because they
have nothing to do. All are Americans. They pay for board
from $1.25 to $1.50 per week." A manufacturer writes : "We
employ twenty-five females in the mill, and from one hundred to

one hundred and twenty-five who take work to their homes. Nine tenths are Americans. We pay from $3.50 to $6 per week. It requires but a short time to learn in some departments. They are paid from the time of entering the factory as a learner. It is considered a permanent business. Men and women do not work on the same branches." At the Troy hosiery manufactory, "sixty women are employed in tending knitting machines, winding yarn, and sewing by hand and by machines. The employment is healthy. Their wages run from $3 to $6 per week, average $4.50. They work mostly by the piece, a few by the week. Males and females usually work side by side, and the wages are alike. They are continually learning, from 18 years old to 40. The prospect is good for future employment, and the employment in factories is generally constant. They work twelve hours per day. If shorter time was universal, it would not affect the profits. About one half are Americans. The rooms are well ventilated, and the temperature from sixty to seventy degrees summer and winter."

171. Men's Wear. A gentleman in Darby, Penn., writes: "Women are employed in factories equally with men, throughout this section of country, as weavers. They are paid just as well, for the same kind of labor. The employment, for aught I can see, is entirely healthy. They receive from $18 to $25 per month of four weeks. They are paid by the piece. It requires about three months to learn weaving, dependent upon the facility with which the learners acquire knowledge. Learners are never paid while receiving instruction; but on the other hand, they more often pay their companions for the privilege of being taught. Industrious habits and quickness of perception are essential to complete success. By a law of Pennsylvania, sixty hours constitute a week's labor in factories. There is neither a demand nor surplus of hands at present, though a number of factories are in course of erection in this section of country; but they will doubtless be filled as soon as ready, for American women especially prefer factory to household labor. About one half our hands are American. Women have more stability of character than men, and are generally superior to them in the neatness with which they bring the cloth from the looms. Board for operatives is from $8 to $9 per month."

172. Print Works. The Calico Print Works, New Hampshire, report: "We employ about 24 girls. The employment is healthy. We pay girls about fourteen years old, thirty-three cents a day for 10½ hours in summer; in winter they work till dark, averaging ten hours. To girls about twenty years old, we pay fifty cents per day. The men and women do different work. The prospect of future employment is good. Hands work all the year the same. The price of good board is from $1.25 to $1.50 per week." The agent of the Pacific Print Works, Lawrence, Mass., gives the following reply to inquiries: "We employ one thousand women in carding, spinning, spooling, warping, and weaving, on sewing machines, sewing by hand, measuring, knotting, ticketing, &c. The employment is generally healthy, but the workers are more or less exposed to bad air and to dust. They are paid from twenty-five cents to $1 per day, according to age or skill. They work from ten to eleven hours per day. Some work but 5½ days, from choice. It would doubtless be a pecuniary loss to shorten the hours. Women are as well paid here, generally, as men, when comparative strength and power of endurance are considered. It requires from three to twelve months to learn. While learning, they usually receive enough to pay their board. The more strength and intelligence they have, the better. The prospect for this employment is good. They work during all seasons. Women are not usually as well fitted as men to attend large machines, but are better for smaller ones. From three hundred to four hundred of our women are continual readers of our library. They pay $1.50 per week for board. It is as good, for the class of people to be accommodated, as any I ever saw." The agent of the print works, Manchester, N. H., writes: "Women are employed in all departments. They average sixty-five cents a day, and work eleven hours. They are paid by the piece, and at the same rate as the men. It requires from one to four weeks to learn. This kind of business is increasing. There is a demand all through New England for female labor in our branch of business. We employ 1,200, and three fourths are American. They are more steady than men. Some of our girls go West to teach, and some teach here. They have separate boarding houses, and pay $1.37 per week, including washing and lights. The houses are kept with as much order as any female school. No operative is received until they certify that they will comply with the regulations," a copy of which we examined, and found to be very good. From the print works at Haverstraw, N. Y., we receive the following information: "Women are employed in sewing, measuring calico, and in the engraving department, in running the pantograph machines, which dispense entirely with hand engraving, die making, and machine engraving. Women are employed in England, but only partially in other European countries. The women earn from $2 to $4 per week. Men receive double the pay of women: I know of no reason but usage. Only a few weeks are necessary to become proficient in our work, except in the engraving department. Men serve seven years to

learn the art of engraving and printing. Women learn to trace
by the pantograph in three months; become proficient in one year.
Ability and good judgment are necessary. The prospect for the
employment of females is good in many other departments, particularly *designing*. We are decided that females could successfully acquire the art and trade of designing and drawing patterns
for calico. Wages of males for this work are from $10 to $40
per week—few at the former, more at $20. Ten hours constitute
a day. The time could be shortened an hour or two without loss.
We employ about forty females, because their labor is cheaper,
and they are more reliable. We find women superior in all
branches in which they are employed. The trade society forbids
their employment in other parts of the work. Ability to read
and write are indispensable in some departments. Men pay for
board, $3; women, $1.50." The Suffolk print works pay by the
piece, and average eighty cents per day. One of the proprietors
at the print works in Pawtucket, Mass., writes: "Women are
employed in tracing pantograph designs, and receive from fifty to
sixty-seven cents per day. We have one woman who does a man's
work at folding, and is paid a man's wages. The work is soon
learned, with ordinary capacity. A good physical condition is
needed. There is prospect for employment as long as calicoes
are used. Cool seasons are the best for work—in very warm
weather, work is suspended a short time. We employ fifty. The
work is light and clean. The number of American women is very
small. We adopt female labor as soon as the aid of machinery
renders it practicable. Men are superior in strength and endurance. A locality is desirable where a free circulation of air is
furnished on all sides. For ordinary board, women pay $2.50."
The agent of the Fall River print works writes: "We pay women
by the piece. They earn from $18 to $20 a month; have work
the year round. For five days in the week they work $10\frac{1}{2}$ hours;
on Saturday, $8\frac{1}{2}$. We employ women because they can do more
and cost less than men. Localities are sought where there is a
good supply of soft water. Board from $2 to $2.50." A lawn
manufacturer in Lodi, N. J., writes: "We employ women in engraving, in stitching, and in finishing goods. The work is very
healthy. We pay women $5 per week for engraving; from $2.50
to $5 for other branches. The work can be learned in from four
to five weeks. The business is increasing. The women are
never out of work. One half are Americans. Women are employed ten hours a day; on Saturday, eight. Women are employed, to help the village along. Very comfortable board, $5
per month." The proprietor of some works in Rhode Island
writes me: "We employ about twenty women and girls in meas-

uring cloth, sewing the ends together for bleaching and fulling, knotting the ends of the pieces of cloth when folded; also in engraving copper rolls for printing calicoes, with a pantograph engraving machine. The prices vary from $1 per week to $3 and over, working ten hours a day. For the same work, females are paid the same as males. The work is easily learned. Women are paid while learning. Women will be more employed in future. Work is constant, so far as seasons go. There is probably no other branch of this work, in which women may be employed, than those in which they are. Where women are employed they are as valuable as males. Board of women, $1.50 per week."
"In the calico mills of Great Britain, girls grind and mix the colors. They are called teerers. They begin at five years of age, and labor twelve hours a day, sometimes sixteen; and are kept late into the night to prepare for the following day."

173. Spinners. " Each of the workmen at present employed in a cotton mill superintends as much work as could have been executed by two hundred or three hundred workmen sixty or seventy years ago; and yet, instead of being diminished, the numbers have increased even in a still greater proportion." Again, we read that " a single person can spin as much cotton in Lowell in an hour, as could three thousand Hindoos, by whom at one time cotton cloth was principally manufactured." The wages of cotton spinners in Paris are only from twenty to forty cents per day of twelve hours. We read in the *Monthly Review*, that " the masters of mills are unanimous in asserting that girls, and they alone are trained to flax spinning, never become expert artists, if they begin to learn after eleven." The small particles set loose in spinning affect respiration, and in the course of time do so very seriously. In many parts of Europe women carry portable distaffs, and spin as they walk. Two kinds of wheels are used for spinning—one for spinning cotton, tow, and wool— the other is used for flax. Steam machinery is mostly used for spinning cotton. The prices usually paid spinners will be found under factory operatives. I inquired of a girl spooling cotton for a weaver of coverlets, what wages she received. She replied: " $1.50 a week, working five hours a day."

174. Spool Cotton. A manufacturer at Fall River, Mass., writes: " We employ twenty women in spooling thread, and preparing it for market. The average pay is $3 per week, and they work eleven hours per day. It requires from one to two months to become expert. When learning, they are paid for what they do carefully. The qualifications needed are neatness, and dexterity in their manipulations. They are employed at all seasons. The demand and supply of work people are about equal. We employ twenty females, because the work is adapted to them, and they are quicker in motion than men. They pay $1.75 per week for board."

175. Tape. At W.'s, New York, I saw several women weaving tape for hoop skirts. They looked dirty and sad enough. They earn from $2 to $3.50 a week. It does not require long to learn, but they must stand all the time. W. finds it difficult to get good workers. The incessant hum of the machinery in such a low-roofed room would deafen me. I think it must affect the nerves of females. He pays a learner the first month $1.50 a week. After that, if she is competent, she will receive full wages. At the Graham Buildings, I saw the girls putting up tape for skirts. They earn from $3 to $4. The weavers earn from $4 to $6. It requires but a few days to learn to weave, and but a few hours to learn to measure and tie up tape. Most of the girls were Irish. Sixty were employed, and received work all the year.

176. Weavers. Weaving is an occupation that was followed by all classes of women in primitive ages. The story of Penelope's shroud has been read as far as Homer is known. In Africa spinning is mostly done by women, and the weaving by men. The invention of machinery has very much done away with manual weaving. Fifty years back all woollen and most of cotton goods were made in that way. Some jeans, coarse flannel, rag carpets, coverlets, and other similar articles are still woven by hand. Now, shawls, dress goods, gloves, hosiery, fine carpets, cassimere, and cloth in all its varieties, are woven by machinery. The uniting of threads, and a constant attention to the machinery, are all that is necessary. The wages vary according to the places, the capabilities of the operatives, the goods woven, and the price of living. "A practical working machine is now in activity, weaving silk by the motive power of electricity. It is applied at Lyons and St. Etienne to the Jacquard loom." Children are extensively employed in Great Britain as drawers to weavers. "The great majority of hand-loom cotton weavers work in cellars, sufficiently lighted to enable them to throw the shuttle, but cheerless, because seldom visited by the sun. The reason cellars are chosen is that cotton, unlike silk, requires to be woven damp. The air, therefore, must be cool and moist, instead of warm and dry." In Philadelphia, the average payment of female weavers is from $2.50 to $4 per week. Spinners and spoolers make but from 75 cents to $2. They are generally unskilful adults or very young girls. The number of female operatives engaged in the manufacture of textile fabrics in Philadelphia exceeds twelve thousand. A manufacturer in Providence writes me : " We do not consider weaving particularly unhealthy. We pay on an average $1 per day, by the piece. They work eleven hours a day; the time could not be shortened. Men spend from three to twelve months learning ; women, from three to six weeks. Women are not paid while learning; men are. All seasons are alike. There is always a demand for weavers. We employ twenty-two women, one fourth are American ; they are not inferior to men as weavers. Men pay $2 for good board ; women, $1.75." A manufacturer of negro cloth in Connecticut writes : " The employment is very healthy. We pay weavers from $3.75 to $5 per week, and some make more by the piece. We pay men and women the same for their labor. Some parts are learned by women in two or three weeks. We generally pay women while learning. We sometimes stop a few days, in July and August, for water. They work eleven hours and a half, except Saturday ; then from eight to ten hours. The time could be shortened by adding extra help and looms, equal to difference of time. We prefer women, because they weave more than men. All Americans. They are superior to men in tying knots. Good board, $1.25." A manufacturer of cotton cloths for calicoes writes : " Women and girls are employed in power-loom weaving. Weaving requires a little more labor and skill than the other departments. None under sixteen years are allowed to weave. Women are so employed over New England, much of New York, and Pennsylvania, but mostly in Massachusetts, Rhode Island, and Connecticut. There is always a demand for girl weavers. It requires from one to three months to learn to weave. They will continue to grow more expert for three years. They weave by the cut from thirty to forty pounds. The wages of an expert weaver are from $4 to $6 per week; board, $1.50 per week. Men weavers are paid per cut the same. An expert weaver attends four looms, weaving from 150 to 160 yards per day. Seamers generally pay their way at the end of four weeks. The employment is not thought unhealthy.

177. Linen Manufacture. Very little flax has been raised in this country. The quantity grown was mostly for the seed and the fibre. Ireland grows and exports large quantities. The soil is not adapted to its growth. It is the result of the most severe labor and high culture. In France, almost every peasant woman has a flax plot. She tends its growth, reaps, dresses, spins, bleaches, and weaves it herself. Some women are there employed in rotting flax and hemp. Generally, the manufacturers of flax goods confine themselves to special departments. Some take the raw flax, and convert it into yarn, and then stop. Some take the yarn and weave it, and when woven, bleach it; and some only take the unbleached woven cloth, and bleach it. In D. & Co.'s establishment in Ireland, all the departments are combined. Eight thousand people are dependent on this firm for support. Of these, four hundred females are employed in spinning and weaving flax. Hand-loom linen weaving is carried on chiefly in the north of Ireland, and, for the most part, made subsidiary to other employments—therefore, not the sole dependence of families. Women are employed in flax mills, in this country, England, and Canada West. A manufacturer writes from a village in New York: "The business is healthy, and women can do any part of the work, as well as men. Here, men receive from $9 to $14 per month. While learning, I pay my men $11 per month, and board them. The work is done in cold weather, away from the fire, and requires strong, healthy persons, warmly clad. The business is increasing in this country. The best season for work is from October till May, and sometimes later. It is not heavy work. I would pay women $5 a month and board, while learning; but to men would pay $11 a month and board." (Justice!) The treasurer of the Boston flax mills writes: "Dear Madam, women are employed on the different machines in preparing the stock, and in spinning and weaving. They are employed largely in England, Scotland, and Ireland, but not much in the United States. They are paid from fifty to seventy-five cents a day, and from fifty cents to $1 for piecework. Ordinary female hands are paid about one half as much as men of the same stamp; best workwomen about two thirds of same grade of men. Men are employed where it would be too difficult and laborious for women. For most work, a very short time is needed to learn; for the higher grades, often many months or years, according to capacity of worker. Common hands can earn fifty cents at once, and we would pay about that, or more, while learning the better description of work; but should not continue it, if they did not improve. A quick eye and hand, and a desire to give satisfaction, are the best qualifications. The prospect for employment in this branch is good. All the year work is furnished. Average time through the year for work is ten hours forty minutes. It is probable that a mill, where all hands were interested to do their best, would turn off as much work in ten hours as a similar mill would in eleven or twelve hours, where the hands were indifferent or careless. There are but few linen mills in this country, and probably in none of them is there a superfluity of good hands. We employ one hundred and twenty women and children. The work is different from that of the men. Our workwomen are mostly foreigners—Scotch, English, and some Irish. There is as much comfort in this occupation as laboring people would expect. The women pursue different branches. We find a great difference in the capacity of different women, but cannot suggest any superiority or inferiority as regards sexes. The general intellect among our women is very fair for foreigners, but would not be considered remarkable for Americans. Their evenings are their own, although there have been times, occasionally, when we have worked till nine o'clock, paying, of course, for extra work. The mill has a good library, and there is usually evening school in winter for those who wish to attend."

178. Sewing Thread. A manufacturer in Andover, Massachusetts, writes : "We employ about one hundred women, who receive about $3 per week, working eleven hours per day. Women are sometimes paid while learning. Morality, industry, and intelligence best fit them for their work. They work at all seasons. Very few are Americans. Women are inferior only in strength to men pursuing the same branch." The secretary of the American Linen Thread Company writes : "We employ about sixty women in spinning, twisting, reeling, rolling, skeining, &c. Those that work by the week receive $3; those by the piece, more or less. Women do the lightest work, and are paid about half as much as men. There is a prospect of this branch of labor increasing. They have work all the year. Those that are paid by the day work twelve hours. The time could not be shortened without serious loss. Most are foreigners. Board, $1.50 to $2." A member of a firm in Schenectady writes : "We have thirty women in our flax and tow factory, because they are best adapted to the work. The work is healthy. We pay from $3 to $4.50 per week, working twelve hours per day. The working time could not be shortened. A superintendent would require from two to three years to learn. A girl, say sixteen years old, would require about a year. Learners receive half wages. Summer is the best season, but they have work all the year. There is no surplus of female workers in the business. Two thirds of our women are American, one third English. Women could not perform that part of the work done by men, and *vice versa*. One third board, and pay $1.50 per week. The Americans have a common school education, and are intelligent. The larger ones are teachers in Sabbath schools ; the smaller ones scholars. The best localities are in the Northern and Western States."—SHOE THREAD. A manufacturer told me, most or all the flax used for shoe thread in this country is imported. "The

9

greater part of the shoe thread used in the United States is spun
by machinery, at Leeds, in England, from Russian flax." The flax
of this country is not fine enough; and, for bleaching, the climate
of this country and Scotland is too changeable. If the bleachers succeed in getting it of a pure white, they extract the substance—the life of the plant—so that it will not retain its strength.
Flax is not much attended to in this country, but it is because
the tariff is so low that no encouragement is given to manufacturers. Pennsylvania makes more woven goods of coarse linen
than any other State, and Philadelphia more than any other
city. Labor is so cheap in Europe, that linen can be made there
more cheaply than here. Mr. A. employs a number of small
girls in his mills for winding the thread into balls, as it is imported in skeins, and pays them from $1.50 to $2 a week. They
work only in daylight. He thinks the occupation is well filled.
Most factories of the kind are in small towns where living is cheap.

---

179. Woollen Manufacture. Women and children are
not so much employed in the woollen as in other manufactures,
owing to the severe labor required in some of the processes. Wool
growing is increasing in the United States, particularly in Texas.
We doubt not but many woollen manufactures will spring up
when business revives. We called on the widow of a wool puller,
to ascertain what the business is, and learned that it consists in
steeping sheep skins in lime water, then rinsing them in clean
water, then removing the wool from the skin, and packing it in
bales to send away. The daughter of a wool puller in Utica
writes: "Part of the work of a wool puller could be performed
by women—that of removing the wool from the skin, and sorting
it according to the quality. In Gloucester, England, women were
at one time employed as wool pullers. The business is healthy,
owing to the presence of disinfectants employed in manufacturing.
It could be made respectable and remunerative." A wool puller
in Buffalo writes: "I employ some girls in sewing sheep skins.
They are paid by the piece, and earn $4.50 a week. Board, $2. It
requires a week for a woman to learn her part—a lifetime for a
man to learn his. A steady hand and good eyesight are essential.
There must be work of this kind as long as boots and shoes are
fashionable. The most busy seasons are fall, winter, and spring.
The best location is where sheep are raised and bark to be had."
People employed in the making of cloth are wool sorters and pickers, scourers, carders, slubbers, spinners, warpers, sizers, weavers,
burlers, boilers, millers, giggers or dressers, croppers, singers,

THE WOOL-GROWER'S DAUGHTER. 194

fuzers, glossers, drawers, and packers. Some of these are women. I am sorry to say that carding—the most unhealthy process of all—is performed almost exclusively by women, and at low prices.

180. Blankets. "Blankets were first made at Bristol, England, by a poor weaver named Thomas Blanket, who gave his name to this peculiar manufacture of woollen cloths." One hundred and twenty-two women are reported in the census of Great Britain for 1850, as blanket manufacturers. A blanket manufacturer in New Hampshire writes: "Women are employed in carding, weaving, and binding. The work is not unhealthy. Average wages are seventy cents per day of eleven hours, and they are paid by the piece. Women receive about two thirds of the wages of men, because they do less laborious work. It requires from one week to three months to learn. They are paid small wages while learning. The manufacture of blankets will increase. Business is the same at all seasons. There is a demand for hands in many of the manufacturing villages, and a surplus in country towns. We have twenty women, all American. They do light work faster than men. They pay for board twenty-one cents per day, in private families."

181. Carpets. Mr. Lagrange writes: "The carpets of Smyrna and Caramania, so widely esteemed, are evidence of what woman's genius can produce. They are all woven by feminine hands." In 1858 there were 2,500 persons employed in the manufacture of carpets in and near Philadelphia. Ingrain and Venetian are the kinds mostly made there, but some of a very cheap quality are also manufactured. Those made at Hartford and Lowell are all worsted goods. The business, we believe, has been a successful and lucrative one. It is said that much carpeting is sold in this country, as English, that is in reality American. Our finest carpets are imported. I visited Mr. H.'s carpet factory, New York city, and saw the entire process, from putting the wool in to its coming out in various kinds of carpeting, ingrain, velvet, Brussels, tapestry, &c. From that manufactory we have the following report: "Females tend carding, spinning, spooling, weaving, and other machines, in the manufacture of carpeting. The employment is not unhealthy. The branch of manufacture and the capacities of females vary the wages from 50 cents to $1 per day of eleven hours. Three fourths work by the piece. Males and females are not employed at the same kind of work. The time required to learn any branch of the carpet trade depends on the natural talent and application of the learner. Many never become proficient enough to pursue the business profitably. The prices paid to learners depend on their success. Health, natural talent, and application are essential.

The prospect of employment in the business is good. They have work the whole year, except during unusual depressions of the trade. Whether the work time of eleven hours could be shortened would depend on the profit on the quantity produced in ten hours, compared with that produced in eleven hours. There is no demand for female labor at the present time. We employ from 500 to 600 females, because their labor is cheaper. About one third are Americans. The comfort and remuneration is better than the average of other employments in this city. They are employed by us in all branches they can be. Females perform some branches better than men. They have free evening schools, libraries, lectures, and churches in abundance. About one half board. The majority board in private families, the comfort depending generally on the price paid." Carpet manufacturers in Wrentham, Massachusetts, write : " We employ women in winding yarn. It is unhealthy only because of sitting so steadily. Women average $14 per month, and are paid by the piece. They work ten hours a day. It requires but a few weeks to learn the business. Women are paid something while learning. They are employed all the year. We employ eight, because the work is better adapted to them. All the workwomen are foreigners. Men, as a general thing, do not want to be confined to indoor work, unless the wages are high. Good board can be had at $1.50 per week." A gentleman, who was once superintendent of the carpet factory at Lowell, informed me all the weavers were females, when he was there, and earned from $3.50 to $4.00 on an average. They had about thirty pickers (females), whose business it was to pick the knots and loose wool off the carpets.

182. Carpet Bags. K. & M., carpet-bag makers, have a factory in Newark. The carpet bags are sewed up and the buttons put in by machines. The lining is put in by hand. It is piecework, and the girls earn from $3 to $6 a week. It requires but a short time to become sufficiently expert to make it pay. The busiest times are from February 1st to June, and from the middle of July to the 1st of November. One of the proprietors thinks the prospect to learners is good, for the business will extend. It has increased five hundredfold in the last five years. Their girls are mostly Americans. Making trunk covers is piecework. The linings could be put in trunks and valises and the varnish put on by girls. The linings could be better put in valises than trunks by women, as they are lighter and less difficult to handle. At H.'s carpet-bag factory, I was told they employ seventy girls, and make from ninety to one hundred dozen bags a day. They keep their hands all the year, with the exception of three weeks. Some work by machine and some by hand. They take learners when busy. A smart girl can learn in making two or three dozen bags—of course, is not paid while learning. They used to allow a few hands, accustomed to the work, to give instruction to learners, having the profits of their work for their time. Those that work by machine can earn from $3 to $4.50; hand sewers from $3 to $6. These work by the piece. Those paid by the week work ten hours, and earn from $2.50 to $5. The gentleman thinks the prospect for learners to enter the business is poor. I think differently, if the statement that he made is true, that there are no manufacturers West or South. A regulation that struck me as being very unjust was, that if a girl learns in their factory and goes elsewhere to seek work, she cannot be taken into their factory again, unless she makes eight or ten dozen bags for them without pay. A manufacturer of carpet and oil-cloth bags writes : " We pay by the piece, and women earn from $4 to $6 per week, working ten hours a day. Women can learn in one month, if skilful with the needle. Spring and fall are the best seasons, but we find work for our hands through the winter. They work at home."

183. Cassimere. A manufacturer of cassimere in New Hampshire writes : " We pay mostly by the week, $3.50, working eleven hours a day. We pay the same to women as men. It requires from two to twelve weeks to learn. They are paid what they can earn while learning. There is no surplus of workwomen in this branch of labor. Our girls board in families, and pay $1.34 per week." A manufacturer in Vermont says : " Twenty women are employed by me. They are all American or English. They are paid according to the amount of work they do. Girls that weave make $3, besides board. Some are paid by the yard, and some by the week. They are paid as much as men for the same kind of work. It usually takes four weeks to learn to weave. Learners give their time. Work is performed ten hours a day all the year. Women prefer factory to housework. They pay $1.50 per week for board." A manufacturer in New Hampshire writes : " We pay from $2.50 to $4.50 per week. For the work that women can do in our establishment, they are worth more than men, as they can work quicker. Women soon learn to weave, but for the first six months they are not worth more than half pay. The prospect for future employment is good. The best seasons for work are spring, summer, and fall. They are usually employed ten hours a day. We employ none but American women. Some parts of our business are suitable for women, but we can get boys cheaper. Board $1.25 per week." B. Brothers, of Proctorsville, Vermont, write : " We employ from thirty to forty American women in preference to men, because the work is more suitable for them. Prospects for increase of employment in this line are very flattering. The women average $2.50 per week with board. They work twelve hours a day, and can be employed all the year. They are superior in all respects to men. If they were not, we should employ men. Their facilities for mental and moral culture are good. Women are paid less than men, on account of the work being light. Board $1.50 per week." The Globe Woollen Company (Utica, New York) write : " Our women, seventy-five in number, earn from $3 to $6 a week, and are paid both by the piece and week. Men and women work together in the weaving room. It requires but a few days to learn to weave, although experience is valuable, both on account of wages and excellence of production. Mental and physical ability ought to be combined to insure success. The prospect for future employment is good. Continual employment is given. Our hands work 12 hours each day, Saturdays 10½. One fourth are Americans, and they live and dress well. The demand for labor is good all through the country. There is no part of our business where women could be advantageously introduced, where not now employed. The women have all the facilities a city affords for mental and æsthetic culture."

184. Cloths. A manufacturer of gray cloth in Vermont writes : " Women are employed at spinning, carding, burling, and weaving. We have ten, because they are more easily obtained than men. We pay women from $2 to $3.50 per week, and board them. They work twelve hours per day. The work done by men requires more than double the experience of that performed by women. Women can learn in four weeks, men in sixteen. Women are paid half wages while learning. They are busy except in the winter. All board with me." C. & Sons, of T., N. Y., write : " Experienced hands receive $3.75 per week—inexperienced $3—board included. Women are not employed at the same work as men. It requires two years to learn our business—six months for women. We adopt the ten-hour system. There is no difference in seasons as to work, except in case of low water. Our labor yields sufficient to keep them until they find an opportunity to marry. They have a good library— ten periodicals every week. They pay for board from $1.50 to $1.75 per week." A manufacturer in Derby, Conn., writes : " We employ about fifteen women, because they are cheaper and more easily obtained; but many are now using male weavers. They earn from $3 to $6 per week, and are paid both ways.

They work eleven hours. To work ten instead of eleven hours, we would lose that amount of the product of those who work by the day. I think there is a demand for such labor all through New England, and I do not know where there is a surplus of such help. We have had but few whose parents were born in America. Women might be employed on shearing machines. They are not, because it is as easy getting boys. Women have less strength and endurance, and are less constant at work, but quicker in motion and less liable to bad habits. Board for females from $2.25 to $2.50 per week." A manufacturing company of satinets and printing cloths, Troy, N. Y., give the following information: "We pay from $2.50 to $6 per week, average $4.50. Men and women get the same wages for the same work. Women learn in from two to four weeks. At best it is but partially learned. Some are paid while learning, and some are not. There is now, and always will be full employment. We furnish steady work all the year. The hands work twelve hours per day. The time could be shortened, but the workers would lose by it. There is a demand for female labor of this kind in Cohoes, N. Y. We have sixty-nine women, and one half are Americans. They are well fed and dress better than any other class of working people. Women are more steady and neater than men. They are all Protestant, and their intelligence is about the average. They pay $1.50 per week for good board." The Monsoon Woollen Co., Mass., say: "We pay fourteen mills per yard for weaving. The women make just the same as the men, and perform the same kind of work. They earn on an average eighty-three cents per day of twelve hours. The work can be done without apprenticeship. The prospect is that our business will be on the increase for years. Our help are employed the year round: three quarters are Americans. They have their evenings after seven o'clock. They pay $2 per week for board." The agent of Shady Lee Mills, R. I., writes: "Women are employed in woollen mills in England, Germany, France, and this country. They are paid in our mill by the piece, and earn $5 per week on an average. Women weavers earn as much as men. It takes a lifetime to learn; some learn better than others. Learners are paid. The business is improving daily. Women work all the year round, unless broken down. They work twelve hours a day. The time could not be shortened. The supply of hands about equals the demand in this manufacture. We employ seventy-five women, because they are better for weavers. Nearly all our work people can read and write. Board $1.75." Mr. H., a manufacturer in Massachusetts, writes: He "pays from $14 to $18 a month, working by the piece. While learning they are paid for

what they do.   They can earn fair wages after two weeks' experience.   They work thirteen hours a day, and are employed through
the year.   There is no surplus of weavers.   He employs twenty-
five, because they are better adapted to the work.   Women are
superior in hand work.   Board $6 a month."   A satinet manu-
facturer in Maine, writes: " Our women weave by the cut and
earn about $6 per week.   A person can get an insight of the
business in a few years; but to get a thorough knowledge requires
at least the English term of apprenticeship—seven years.   Women
are paid half price while learning.   Summer is the best season,
but our women are employed the year round.   They work twelve
hours—which is the usual time here, and less would be a loss.
Women are handier than men, and can be boarded for less.   We
have churches in the village and a good moral influence.   Board
$1.50 per week; comforts quite equal to those of their homes."
Manufacturers in Pittsfield, Mass., inform us " they have a number of women employed in weaving and sewing, mostly weaving.
The employment is considered healthy, and the condition of
weavers is entirely comfortable, as this is, of course, for the interest of the employers as well as the employées.   The average
time of work is thirteen hours.   The wages paid them is from $4
per week to $6.   They are paid by the yard, and their earnings
depend upon their attention, activity, and capability.   They are
paid $3 a week while learning.   Women weavers earn quite as
much as men, and can stand the confinement as well, if not better.
We have no difficulty in keeping our looms supplied, and frequently have applications which we are obliged to reject.   We
employ sixty women, nearly one half Americans.   In this place
they have every advantage for moral and mental culture.   Those
who have parents or friends working in the establishment usually
live with them; and those who have not, live at our boarding
house, which is as comfortable and well regulated as any house
in the country.   The price charged for board is from $1.25 to
$1.50 per week."   A company in North Berwick, Me., writes:
"We pay both ways; when by the week, from $2.50 to $4.
Males and females do not perform the same kind of work with
us.   The time of learning varies with the capacities of the women.
Some of our hands have been with us more than ten years.
Seasons alike.   They work eleven hours.   We employ twenty-
five women, because it is more economical.   Not one of our women
will do housework.   Our employées are Yankee girls—can all
read and write; and, so far as we know, converse intelligently on
general subjects.   They have their evenings and a portion of each
Saturday.   Board $1.33⅓ per week."   We would add that every
cotton and woollen manufacturer from whom we have heard, ex-

presses the opinion that their occupation is healthy. All, we believe, pay some hands by the week and some by the piece, and most pay men and women at the same rate for the same kind of work. It will be observed that the rates paid for labor decrease the farther you go North, but that board is also something less.

185. Coverlets. A manufacturer of woollen coverlets in Allentown, Penn., answers inquiries in regard to prices paid, &c., as follows: "I employ eight American girls for spooling wool and cotton yarn in my coverlet manufactory, and pay two cents per pound. They earn from $2 to $2.50 per week. I pay girls the same as boys. The prospect for increase of work is good. There is a surplus of hands here. I prefer girls, as they have more patience than boys."

186. Dry Goods Refinishers. A. & Co. employ women when busy to put up dress goods, cravats, ribbons, &c. They pay $3 a week. I was told by a satinet printer and refinisher, that he employs one woman to sew the ends of the cloth together. She does it with a machine, and earns $5 a week, working ten hours a day. The coloring matter rubs off on the hands. S. employs some women, and pays $3 a week. He gives them about eight months' employment. During two months in summer and two in winter, there is not enough doing to employ them. He says some women, like some men, know nothing but how to eat. He finds it difficult to get women of intelligence and judgment to do his work. (I should think he would, for such wages.) The girls fold, label, and pack. There are but three large houses of the kind in New York. At another place we saw a girl who gets $3 a week for such work—ten hours a day.

187. Flannels. Flannels differ much in color and quality. Employers are unanimous in pronouncing the work healthy. If the sum paid foreign countries for flannels and blankets were invested in manufactories in our country, it would give employment to many, and tend to encourage home industry. A flannel manufacturer in Stockport, New York, writes: "We employ women at weaving and spooling. Women and girls are paid mostly by the piece, and earn from $3 to $5 per week. No males are employed at the same work as females. It usually takes about a week to learn to weave. We do not pay learners. We will increase the number of women as we increase our product. All seasons are alike as respects employment. Our hands work twelve hours per day. The time could not be shortened without loss to both employer and employed. We have about forty females, and prefer them, as it gives the whole family work. Eight tenths are American. The work is as light and comfortable as any in the mill. There is no other work suitable than that in

9*

which they are now engaged. All our women can read and write, and are already quite intelligent, particularly the Americans. We do not employ many under sixteen years of age, and those younger are usually sent to school a part of the year. Board is $6 per month in good, respectable families." A manufacturer in Dover, Maine, replies to a circular asking information: " I employ women as weavers, carders, spoolers, and one as a warper-on to draw the web. Women earn from $2.75 to $5 per week, eleven hours per day. Weavers are paid by the piece. I pay men from 83 cents to $1.50 per day. Women do the lighter and easier work. Some parts are not adapted to women, that is one reason why we pay less, and perhaps custom has something to do with the prices of labor. Women learn their part in from one to six weeks, but it requires some years of experience to be a manufacturer. For some kinds of work we pay from the beginning; for others, after one or two weeks. The prospect is fair; work, constant. In large manufacturing places, there is a demand for labor of this kind Women are employed because they work cheaper. Women do their kind of work better than men. Our women are Americans, and appear to enjoy life well. They have the early morning and evening, and the Sabbath for themselves. More than one half are church members. Those that have relations living near the factory, board with them, and pay $1.50 per week." A manufacturer in Conway, Massachusetts, writes: " We employ women in weaving, burling, sewing, and numbering flannels. They receive from 50 cents to $1 per day of twelve hours. Women doing the same kind of labor as men receive the same price. It requires from one to four weeks to learn. If our business does not pay better in future than the past, we had better stop. In the more difficult part of our work there is a demand for hands. Men make better work than women. One fourth are American. Board, $1.50, to $1.75." A manufacturer in Morgantown, New York, writes : " The employment is as healthy as any indoor work. The wages average about $5 per week, they being paid by the piece. It takes about four years to learn the business, so as to conduct it in its several branches. I pay their expenses while learning. The best season is the fall. Work lasts ten hours—if obliged to run longer, we pay extra. We think women more to be depended on than men. We have no department suitable for women but what is filled by them. Board, $2 a week—quite good. In the cities board is seldom over $2 per week for workwomen. The rent and price of provisions are too high to keep a boarding house as it should be on such terms. Our wages may be lower in the country, but expenses are much lower also, and consequently the laborer is able to save more money." Manufacturers in Keene, N. H., write: "We pay one half $3, the other, $3.80 per week, twelve hours a day. We pay the same to both sexes when the quantity and quality are the same. A carder will learn in one month, a weaver in three months.· The qualities wanted are industry, sobriety, perseverance, constructiveness, and amiability. All seasons alike good. To shorten the time of thirteen hours would be a loss to both parties. All branches are well supplied with workers. Women have more patience, tact, neatness, and are more reliable than men. All our women are well fed, well clothed, well housed, and some possess the luxuries, and even elegancies of life. We have six places of worship, a public library, book stores, and newspapers in abundance. Board, $1.50."

188. Gloves. Kid, silk, cotton, and woollen are the kinds of gloves most used. They differ much in quality. Kid and leather are most numerous. The price of labor, the difficulty in obtaining the best kid, and the want of experienced workmen, are such that the finest kid gloves have not been made in the United States. An immense number of kid gloves are annually imported. In Paris, women are paid from sixty cents to $1 a dozen for sewing gloves. The French excel in the manufacture of kid gloves. French workmen are very economical in cutting out the kid. In France 375,000 dozens of skins are cut into gloves every year. Nearly 3,500 female glove sewers are employed in Vienna. Immense quantities of buckskin gloves and mittens are made in Johnstown and Gloversville, New York. "Most American manufactures have been introduced by sending the goods into the country by peddlers, or the manufacturers themselves selling them in that way. This trade was commenced so." The manufacture of buckskin gloves and mittens is mostly confined to small towns and the country. The cutting is done by men. The sewing is given out to those who do the work at home, and receive for their labor from $4 to $6 per week. It requires but a few weeks to learn. A manufacturer of kid and buckskin gloves, in Philadelphia, has all his sewing done by hand. He will not use machines for cutting out and sewing, as it would throw many of his workwomen out of employment. Those who are neat and intelligent obtain a very good livelihood by it. They take the work home, and earn $6 a week or more; beginners only $1.50 or $2. The kid is imported from South America, and not so fine as French kid. A glove manufacturer, New York, who lived in Johnstown eighteen years, told me that "girls can earn at glove sewing from $3 to $6 a week. Those who board in the families of their employers receive less, because of their board. Many gloves are made up by farmers' daughters at home, both

by hand and machine. A good sewer would not find it difficult
to make gloves. Most of the gloves made in factories are
stitched by machines. Singer's and Grover & Baker's are preferred. Handworkers do not receive quite so good wages.
Women used to cut out gloves with scissors, but now men cut
them by striking with a hammer a tool the shape of a glove.
The plan is preferred, because of being cheaper. The knowledge
of dressing kid seems to be lost to foreigners in coming over the
ocean." A manufacturer in Springfield, Mass., writes: "We
employ some women in making buckskin gloves and mittens. Some
work by the piece, and some by the week, and earn from $3 to
$5. Those who work by the week spend ten hours, sewing. It
takes females from two hours to four weeks to learn. Patience,
perseverance, and taste are needed by learners. The best season
for work is from February to November. They are out of work
about two months at times. Most are Americans. They can
use a needle better than a man." A glover in Salem writes :
" Our women sew by hand, and earn $3 per week. Men spend
three years in learning—women six months. The prospect for
work is poor, as importation is destroying the business." A
manufacturer at Gloversville writes : "Women earn from $3 to
$5 a week, ten hours a day. Males get as much again as women.
A smart woman will learn in eight months. Prospect of work
in the future is good." Manufacturers in Broadalbin, N. Y.,
write me they employ twelve American women at the shop, and
about one hundred out of the shop, finishing up. When paid by
the week, they receive from $2 to $4.50, and work ten hours a day.
The comparison in prices in male and female labor is about $2
to $1, for the reason that it requires more strength, labor, and
skill to perform the man's part. Men spend two or three years
in learning—women, six months. Punctuality, sobriety, and a
liberal education, together with a steady nerve, will insure success
in our business. (Some one else suggests, mechanical talent.)
As long as there are feet to wear moccasins, and hands to wear
gloves, our kind of business must thrive. Board in neat and
commodious houses, $2 for women." A glover in New Hamp-
shire writes : "Women sew by the piece for me; most have families, do their own work, and sew when they can—so I cannot
say how much they would earn, if they sewed constantly. A man
would have to spend from two to four years qualifying himself
to superintend; the part done by women can be learned in from
two to six weeks. Summer is the best season, but good workers
have constant employment. All are Americans. Any locality
is good where water power may be had. Ladies pay for board
from $1.50 to $1.70 per week." Another in Perth, N. Y., says :

" Some of our workers use sewing machines; others fit and prepare the goods for them. They earn from $3 to $4.75. The
male and female labor is different in our establishment. I think
the business permanent. Best time for work is from 1st of
March to 1st of November. They work all daylight, except at
meal times. When a certain amount of work is required in a
given time, the women are apt to overwork themselves and slight
the work. The wives and daughters of mechanics and farmers
do the piecework at their homes. All Americans. Board, from
$1.75 to $2." " At Gloversville the men cut, and machines do
the sewing. Five pair of mits and two pair of gloves are a heavy
days work. Gloves are worth 75 cents per day to cut; and to
make from 12½ cents for a light article, to 18 cents for heavy
ones."—*Woollen Gloves.* I was told by a man who employed
eight girls to crochet woollen gloves for him, that he pays fifty
cents a dozen pairs. He makes over five cents profit on a pair
when selling to the wholesale stores; and in retailing, nine cents
a pair. He says a right expeditious girl can make one dozen
pairs a day. He employs his girls all the year. Most that attempt to learn find their progress so slow that they get discouraged, and give it up. It is best to learn early in life. The
Germans excel.

189. Linseys. An agent for a manufacturing company of
linseys and flannels in Rhode Island, writes : " I employ fifty-eight
women in spooling yarn and weaving, and pay from $3 to $5 a
week. Our men are paid $1 per day, because they are able to
do more. Men run three looms; girls, two. The organs that
manufacture vitality in women are not allowed, by lacing strings,
to attain more than two thirds their natural size. If nature could
have her way with them, especially when young, they would earn
more in the weaving shop than men, because they are naturally
quicker and smarter. They are paid something while learning,
which requires three months. Good female workers have always
been scarce since I have been in the business—twenty years.
We might employ more, if we could get them. April, May, and
June are the most busy seasons. They work twelve hours. To
shorten the time two hours would make one sixth difference,
which the work people would not be willing to lose. We have
more families than single help. Those who board pay from
$1.75 to $2.25 per week. The boarding houses have to be helped
by us, to enable them to take boarders at these prices." Mr. T.,
writing from Rhode Island, mentions, in addition to the branches
stated above as performed by women, that of warping. He informs us, the work is not more unhealthy than housework, but
complains that his women are careless, in bad weather, going to

and from the mill. " Wages, when running full time, average from $3.75 to $6 per week. Weavers are paid by the yard, spoolers by the bunch, warpers by the web, and extra hands by the week. Men's wages are from 75 cents to $1.25 per day, but men's board is from 50 to 75 cents per week more. The prospect for work in the future depends upon the state of the country. Spring and summer are the best seasons for work. From March 20th to October 20th, the hands work from seven to seven; from October to March, until 8 P. M. Their wages are according to the number of yards woven ; so of course it is to their interest, as well as our own, to run full time. We find male labor scarcer than female. Most of our hands are Americans. Our mills are well ventilated and well warmed. The company have a boarding house under their own supervision, but the women are at liberty to board in private families, and some do. The majority of young ladies in our employ are farmers' daughters, not really compelled to work, but prefer to do it, and in most instances use the means for obtaining an education. Instrumental music is taught in a seminary near the mill, by a young lady, who obtained her education with the means gained by working in this mill. We have from one to three nights every week devoted to literary societies, reading circles, &c., in all of which, the ladies from this and neighboring mills take an active part. Some eight or ten who worked at the mill during the summer are now attending school. Board $2.25 for men; $1.75 for women." The proprietor of the Kenyon mills, R. I., writes : " Probably one half the operatives in mills, in this part of the world, are women. Weavers are paid by the yard, and earn from $3 to $6 per week. Men are generally hired by the day. An intelligent woman will be able to run her loom after two or three weeks' practice. It is common to put learners on looms with experienced weavers for two or three weeks. From 20th March to 20th September, my working time is from sunrise to sunset, the remainder of the year, until eight o'clock in the evening. My weavers prefer to work full time as they are paid by the yard. There is generally a demand for good weavers in this part of the country all the year. Weavers make most money in summer. Large mills are being supplied with foreign help. Very few Americans are willing to work with them. Women are employed in mills on all kinds of work which they can do, and are preferred because they are more steady. Nearly all my mill girls are daughters of farmers in the neighborhood, and have had a fair common school education. Several of my weavers take newspapers or other periodicals, and carry them into the mill to read, when they can do so without interfering with their work. Some take sewing or knitting.

Board $1.75 for women; $2.25 for men. If we did not keep comfortable boarding houses, our help would find employment in other places. Any smart, good girls, who want work, need have no hesitation in coming to Rhode Island to look for work in mills."

190. Woollen Shawls. The secretary of the Waterloo Woollen Shawl Company writes : " Women are employed by us in weaving, carding, &c. The work is not unhealthy. It is paid for mostly by the piece, and hands earn from $2.50 to $3 per week. Most of them earn as much as males; and some, more. They are employed twelve hours. Skill, industry, and good character are necessary. The prospect of future employment is good. There is no difference in the seasons for work. In weaving there is no surplus. We employ two hundred and fifty women, because they do better work than men. We employ but very few young girls, and they generally work at home under the eyes of parents, and attend school at least four months in the year."

191. Shoddy. At flock or shoddy manufactories, girls are employed to separate rags of different qualities and colors, and to cut the seams and buttons off. The rags are placed in machines and cut to pieces, then put in other machines that grind them to flocks. From them satinet is made. Women are paid so much one hundred pounds, and earn from $1.50 to $3 per week. They are busy all the year. It is dirty work, and, I think, unwholesome on account of the dust. Boys attend the machinery for cutting and grinding, and are paid about the same wages as the girls, and probably a little more. Girls could just as well attend the machines. Modern improvements have made wool shoddy susceptible of receiving a fine dye, and it is made into cloth for soldiers' and sailors' uniforms, and for pilot coats; into blanketing, drugget, stair and other carpeting, and into very beautiful table covers. A manufacturer of wool shoddy in Massachusetts writes : " I employ Irish women at $3 per week, of eleven hours a day in winter and twelve in summer. Men receive $6 per week. Women cannot perform their labor. It requires two weeks to learn. They receive small wages the first two or three weeks. The business is probably permanent. The work is hard. Women do best for picking and sorting stock and tending cards. They pay $1.50 a week for Irish fare."

192. Yarn. A manufacturer of stocking yarn, in Spring Valley, New York, writes : " Girls are employed in twisting and reeling yarn. The employment is not unhealthy. We pay some by the piece, and some by the week; those by the week receive $2.50. The wages are the same for men and women. To learn the whole business requires from three to five years; that part done by girls, from one to two months. They are paid while learning. The prospect of employment is as good as that of business generally. Our girls work the year round; they work eleven hours. To shorten the time would be a disadvantage to us, and a loss in wages to the hands. Boys would do for us, but are not so easily governed. The work is easy and comfortable." A yarn manufacturer in Stoughton, Mass., writes me: "I pay $2 per week, and furnish board to those that twist and card. The labor of the women is much cleaner and easier than that of the men. Men receive from $1 to $1.75 per day, board included. I charge them $2.50 per week—women $1.75. Much of the men's labor requires strength, knowledge, and skill. It requires two or three months to learn it well. Women work, on an average, eleven hours and a half. I should like the ten-hour system, but cannot adopt it, unless others do the same. The supply of hands is adequate to the demand. Ladies have done some parts of our work, now performed by men, and have received equal wages; but the labor being hard, and women's dress being inconvenient, we have abandoned the plan."

---

183. Silk Manufacture. The duty on raw silk is so very great that it will not do to import it into the United States for manufacture. We suppose, if a duty in proportion to their value were levied on silk and linen goods, we would no longer be so dependent on other nations for these articles. Or if a reduction were made on the duty of the raw material, capitalists would establish silk manufactures in the United States. Individual failures here are attributed by some to ignorance and want of experience; by others, to the nature of the climate. The support afforded by our Government to the culture of silk has been very fickle—to-day encouraged, to-morrow neglected. The experiments that have been made prove the feasibility of growing the mulberry, and raising the silkworm in this climate. The silk produced was of good quality, and, but for imperfect implements and want of experience, might have done well. The cheapness of labor in older countries affords an advantage that we have not. Most of the raw silk manufactured in the United States comes from China. The women there rear silkworms; they also reel and weave the silk. Not many years back silk winding was done by men in England. "In the silk factories in France, there are two unwholesome processes entirely carried on by women: the first is the drawing of the cocoons, when the hands must be kept constantly in boiling water, and the odor of the putrefying insects constantly fills the lungs; the second is carding the floss, the fine lint of which affects the bronchial tubes. Six out of every eight women employed, die in a few months. Healthy young girls from the mountains soon develop tubercular consumption; and, to complete the dreadful tale, they are kept upon the lowest wages, being paid only twenty cents, where a man would earn sixty." "One silk manufacturer in Valencia, Spain, gives employment to 170 women and young girls." In Lyons, France, many women are employed in the silk manufacture, for particulars of which see *Revue des Deux Mondes*, Feb. 15th, 1860. Silk weavers mostly work in attics, where they can have the best light to distinguish shades of colors, and where the silk, which moisture would damage, can be kept perfectly dry. In Spitalfields, the silk manufacture is mostly carried on by the workmen at their homes, their families assisting. Each child has his own branch, and the wife hers. It is the same case in the making of lace, artificial flowers, embroidery, straw braiding, &c. The strength of silk is greater than that of cotton, flax, or wool. Machinery is now employed for winding the silk off of cocoons, but formerly it was done by hand. Mrs. O. told us her husband employs a few girls to spool silk, which he dyes for a large dress trimming manufactory next door. The girls earn from $2 to $3 a week. The pasting of patterns of floss silk upon cards was done by men a few years ago in England, but women, after great effort, have succeeded in gaining the work, so much more suitable for them. "A lady in Jefferson county, Ia., has made herself a handsome silk dress from cocoons of her own raising." A manufacturer of silk goods in Paterson, N. J., writes: "We mostly employ girls from twelve to eighteen. The work is not unhealthy. Average pay is $3 per week. To learn, a girl must be about twelve years of age; it takes about two months. Pay begins after two weeks. To learn, one should be smart with her hands, and careful with the material. There is a good prospect ahead for weavers. All seasons are good, except during a panic. They work twelve hours. The time could not be shortened conveniently. If other States worked less time, we could too. We employ a hundred girls and twenty-five boys. Seventy-five per cent. are American. Board, $1.75. Women could be employed more extensively in weaving. Men are employed upon the spinners, women in winding, &c."

194. Ribbons. In England, formerly, a woman was not at all engaged in ribbon weaving, as the men thought it an encroachment on their sphere of labor; nor were they even allowed to wind silk preparatory to its use in weaving. Manufacturers of ribbon in West Newton, Massachusetts, write: "We employ from forty to eighty women, and prefer them to men in all departments they are fitted for. They are paid by the week, and earn from $2 to $6, according to the value of their work. It requires from six months to a year to learn the business. Women are paid something while learning. Good character and fair capacity are needed. Our women work eleven hours. If the time was reduced to ten, the loss would be the use of machinery. There is a surplus of hands in New York, by reason of immigration. Women are inferior in mechanical skill, superior in steadiness."

195. Sewing Silk. The first factory for spinning silk in this country was established in Northampton, Massachusetts. There are 156 hands in Massachusetts, engaged in the manufacture of sewing silk. Two other factories have been established since then in Paterson, New Jersey ; one for the manufacture of the raw silk, and the other the manufacture of sewing silks, fringes, gimps, and tassels. There is a manufactory in Mansfield, Connecticut, and one in Newport, Kentucky. Most of the sewing silk used in this country under the name of Italian silk is made by American manufacturers. An agent for the manufacture of twist in Paterson, New Jersey, told me their best hands do not earn over $3.50 a week and work eleven hours. They try girls, that wish to learn, two weeks, and if they find them fitted for the work, pay $1 a week. There is no danger from the machinery as in cotton factories, nor has it the unhealthy tendency of cotton, as there are no particles flying from the material like the lint that flies from cotton. It does not require an apt person long to learn. The girls stand all the time. They have to watch the machinery, and tie the threads that break. The agent said, in the Eastern States girls are paid better in silk factories, but they are more competent workers. There some earn from sixty to eighty cents per day. The work is neat and clean. Some manufacturers of sewing machine silk and twist write me from Boston : "We employ fifty women winding and twisting silk. They work eleven hours in winter and twelve in summer, and earn from $3 to $6 per week. Some are paid by the piece and some by the week. Men are paid from $1 to $2.50 a day. Integrity and activity are wanted. The prospect for future employment is good. They work at all seasons. One fourth are Americans. No parts of our occupation are suitable for women but those in which they are engaged." A sewing silk manufacturer in Paterson, N. J., writes : "Our women are engaged in winding and doubling the raw silk and finishing, in skeins and on spools, the dyed material. The work is generally considered healthy. Many children, boys and girls, from ten years and upward, are employed—say forty per cent. of the whole force of help; children at $1 per week—women at $3 and $4. They work sixty-nine hours to the week. State rights prevent the shortening of the time. Each State makes its own laws on the subject, and no unanimity exists. Males and females are employed up to a certain age, say fifteen years, indiscriminately; girls always preferred. The time of learning depends upon the quickness of the hand; some learn in two or three days, some again can scarcely learn at all. The rule of the trade is not to pay learners. It depends on circumstances whether we pay. In brisk times we have about sixty (including children)—women about forty—perhaps less. About half are Americans. Crinoline is in the way to prevent women from performing other parts of the labor. Women are cheaper. Men could not be got, and could scarcely do the work, if they could. Yet no particular qualifications are required. The prospect for an increase of this manufacture depends upon congressmen and the tariff. The best seasons are immediately after the New Year's and Fourth of July holidays." In France, some girls are employed to wind the raw silk from cocoons, and some spin it into skeins of silk. In Dublin, many women are employed in the winding and picking of silk used in making poplin. Near Algiers is an orphan asylum, from which a large number of girls have been apprenticed to a gentleman who owns a silk winding mill in the vicinity. The girls work twelve hours a day.

---

195. Lace Makers. Large numbers of women are employed in lace making in Belgium, France, Ireland, and England. A normal lace school was established in Dublin in 1847. Lace makers are very closely confined, and in busy times many spend from twelve to twenty hours at their work. Lace making requires care, quickness, and dexterity. Rev. Mr. Hanson mentions the fact that, in Liverpool, there are three Roman Catholic institutions aided by the Privy Council for the industrial training of girls: one, attended by forty pupils, is a laundry; another is a lace school, attended by one hundred and sixty-six; the third, attended by twenty-six, trains domestic servants. Lace making is so injurious to the eyes that, at forty, very few can carry it on without spectacles. In England the process of winding is conducted by young women, while boys are mostly employed as lace threaders. Their condition is a wretched one. Women are mostly employed as lace runners or embroiderers. Mending, drawing, pearling, and joining are mostly done by young children. An interesting account of the business is given in

Charlotte Elizabeth's story of the "Lace Runners": "It is proved by unquestionable evidence, that in lace making it is customary for children to work at the age of four or five and six years; and instances are found in which a child, only *two* years old, was set to work by the side of its mother." The present condition of most of the laboring classes in England is far more depressing and exhausting than the slavery that exists among the colored population of the United States. "The powers of production of a machine for making laces are to hand labor nearly as 30,000 to 5." C. says he and his wife are the only makers of hand lace in the United States, and he has been nine years in the business here. He says, making the figures is most difficult; and he showed me one figure he asked but twenty-eight cents for, that he stated it would require a day and a half to make. I wish I had offered to buy it. He employs a number of girls to put the figures on some kind of a foundation for collars, sleeves, and capes. They also transfer, mend lace, and do other such work. He says, making figures does not pay as well as the other parts, and it would not pay for the salt you use on your potatoes. He does not have lace made, except now and then a figure that cannot be obtained, to fill out a piece that is being transferred or altered, and for which the lady is willing to pay a good price. He says laces are made so much cheaper in the old country, that when imported, paying even a duty of twenty or twenty-five per cent., they are sold as cheap as those he makes. He says he pays his girls nearly twice as much as they are paid in Europe. His report I thought contradictory, and supposed he feared competition. I was told by an English woman, who had been accustomed to making lace from six years of age until the last ten, that it takes seven or eight years to learn lace making in all its parts. She says there are twenty-one processes gone through with in making every kind but pillow lace, in which there are but five processes. When she was a child, none but common laces were made in France, and the making of their finest laces they learned from the English, who went over to France.

197. Lace Menders. I called on M. W., a lace mender. "In New York, she has received from one store, Mme. G.'s, from $20 to $25 a week for work. She thinks in a few years very little work will be ordered from the stores; it will be done by those who make a business of it. The stores derive a handsome profit. She did a piece for one store for $3, that she knows the lady paid $5 for having done; and another piece at $3, that the lady paid $10 for—the storekeeper having such profits for nothing but merely sending it to the lace transferrer. She makes a comfortable living, but works at night as well as through the day. It has injured her eyes and made her nervous. She has had two little girls learning to mend, alter, and transfer lace; one received her board and clothing for her work for three years. One girl, that spent two years with her, is now obtaining a livelihood by her work. She thinks if a bright, steady girl of thirteen should spend two years at it, and then have friends to start her in business, she would be well able to support herself. Lace mending is a separate branch from lace making. In England, if a person can obtain the names of one or two wealthy families, it will at once establish them in business. In doing up lace, little girls can put the pins in the edges to keep it in place until dried. C. and Mme. G., she says, pay her as her customers would, but she prefers establishing herself, and does not so well like store work. Her customers recommend her to their friends, and so she will gradually become known. Lace mending is a nice, clean, respectable business, and can be done at home."

---

198. Hair Cloth Manufacture. "There is some competition in the sale of foreign and domestic hair cloth. The American is of a better quality, and on that ground only are manufacturers able to compete with foreigners, the duty on hair cloth being low. When the hair has been separated from the short hair used for curling, it goes into the more delicate fingers of the hair drawers, who sort it into lengths, each length corresponding to the width of the cloth to be woven. We have seldom seen any mechanical operation requiring more dexterity or constant attention than this. The girls engaged in this work make from $3 to $3.50, and sometimes $4 a week. The weaving is done by hand looms, each worked by two girls—one to handle the hook (answering the purpose of a shuttle), and the other to serve the hair. The prices paid for weaving vary from twenty to thirty-two cents per yard. The average, including plain and figured cloth, is twenty-four cents. A fair average day's work is four or five yards. But this requires two hands, you must remember; so that perhaps a fair estimate of the wages of hair cloth weavers would be from fifty to sixty-two and a half cents per day. The labor is severe, and we should think it impossible, without injury to the health, for young women to work at it more than two thirds of the time." At a hair-cloth manufactory in New York, I was told they employ one hundred girls. The proprietor says they have work all the year. He never knew a woman at the business that could not find employment. 'The first month they do not receive anything for their work, but after that can earn from $3 to $5 per week. It is paid for by the yard. The more practice a worker has, the better she succeeds. I think it must be dirty work.   Another manufacturer told me it does not require long to learn to weave hair cloth, but some time to do it well. He pays $5 per week, but their time is not limited to ten hours. The girls, I saw, were pale and filthy.   He thinks the business is likely to extend, and, consequently, the prospect of employment to women in that field of labor is good.   He keeps his girls all the year.   The Providence Hair Cloth Co. write: "Women are employed in weaving our hair cloth.   Every hair has to be put in separately by the fingers of the girl.   The only disadvantage to the health of the girl is the close application in sitting so long. We pay our girls thirteen cents per yard for weaving.   It requires about two weeks or one month before a girl becomes sufficiently accustomed to the work to weave on full speed.   We pay them while learning.   No qualifications needed, only general neatness and upright moral character.   All seasons are alike.   We work only ten hours.   Thirty girls have each one loom with which to work; one girl mends the cloth, and three shave and trim the same—making thirty-four in all.   One half are American. Women are in all respects superior to men in weaving—same as in cotton looms."

METAL MANUFACTURES.

199. Iron.   "The great heat to be endured and the severe muscular power required, preclude women from the manufacture of iron goods.   They are not directly employed, and to a small extent indirectly.   We think when women have to perform what is unquestionably man's work, it lowers the standard of female character instead of elevating, and nothing is more disagreeable than to be constantly employed at labor uncongenial to one's nature."   From the United States census we learn that in 1850 there were engaged in the manufacture of pig iron 20,298 males, 150 females; in the manufacture of casting iron, 23,541 males, 48 females; in the manufacture of wrought iron, 16,110 males, 138 females.   We do not know exactly how these women were employed.   The work in rolling mills is very severe and the heat intense.   The men have their limbs cased in tin sheaths above their knees.   The vast capital required to develop the mineral resources of a country, and the comparative newness of our country, have hitherto prevented more than a partial development of its resources. Many women are employed in dressing and sorting ore in Great Britain.

200. Files. The notches in files are made by a chisel acted on by a hammer held in the hand. The edge thrown up in making the notch assists the workman in putting the chisel in the right place, and keeping it there while he cuts the next notch. " It is peculiar that hitherto no machine has been constituted, capable of producing files which rival those cut by the human hand." From a manufacturer in Massachusetts, we learn that " he employs from four to six girls in cutting fine work files, cleaning, and wrapping up, &c. They are largely employed in England. The work is considered healthy. They receive from $3 to $4.50 per week of ten hours a day. Men and women are paid equal wages for the same kind of work. It requires from six months to two years to learn. The prospect for a small number in each factory is good. There is work every day in the year. It is quite a new business in this country. Women are neater and more particular with their work than men. They could do some other parts that are suitable for them, but they would soil their hands too much." A file manufacturer writes me : " Women are paid by the piece in cutlery—in other departments by the day ; when by the piece, they receive as much as men; when by the day, one half. It would require three or four years to learn. Most women cannot cut any but small files as well as men, as they have not sufficient muscular power in the hands and fingers. Women are taught in Sheffield, England, by their fathers and brothers, and have what they earn. Good eyesight and stout nerves are the requisites for a learner. No prospect of employment in our business at present. The best localities for manufactures are where files are wanted, in New England and the middle States."

201. Guns. One manufacturer writes : " I hardly know whether the work could be done by women. It is difficult to learn and hard to practise." A gunsmith told me, guns could be polished by women. They are polished by hand. A manufacturer of guns writes : " I have no women employed in my factory. It is not common for them to work at this business in America, although many of them are employed by gun makers in foreign countries."

202. Hinges. A manufacturer of hinges writes : " We employ no women in our manufactory. There are portions of the work that might be done by females as well as male labor. Still we have not adopted the plan." A manufacturer writes from New Britain, Connecticut : " We employ women in packing goods, and making brass hinges, and pay from thirty-eight to sixty-five cents per day of ten hours. We formerly paid women

$1.50 per day. We now get the same amount done by girls for sixty-five cents. We employ them because the work is light, and we can get it done at that price. The part done by women requires one month to learn. The prospect for this work in future is good. Spring and fall are the best seasons, but our hands are employed the year round. Other parts of the work could be done by women if they were willing, but the work is dirty. They are superior to men in the same branch, as they handle the work quicker, and are, as a general thing, more steady and reliable. The housework here is mostly done by Irish girls, while American girls prefer working in shops, even at less wages. There are many other branches of our work that might be done by females, for which we pay men $1 and $1.25 per day; but the work is rather dirty, and few here would do it, as they can have cleaner work, and we have never sought that kind of help on that account."

203. Locks. " The Newark Lock Company " employ eight American girls in packing hardware. They are paid by the week, from $3 to $5, and average half the pay of men, who do more laborious work. Women spend six or eight months learning. Activity and neatness are desirable qualities. Women excel in both qualities. We expect to double our business in a year or two. The women work ten hours per day, and have steady employment. Two thirds of all the locks used in the United States are made in the five large lock manufactories of Connecticut. The best locality is near the great emporium, and on tide water, to save freight. Board $2.50." The secretary of the Eagle Lock Company writes : " We employ from one hundred and fifty to two hundred men, and only twenty girls. Our work is not suitable for females, except to pack our locks in paper ready for market. They work by the piece, and can earn from $10 to $25 per month, according to how they employ themselves. They are mostly daughters of men employed by us, and board at home. They are all Yankee girls. We only work ten hours, unless business is driving." " Hardware manufacturers in Cromwell, Connecticut, pay eight women from 50 to 62½ cents per day for packing. They work ten hours a day. The work can be learned in one month. The prospect of work in future is good. Board $1.62 per week." Manufacturers in N. Britain write : " We pay by the day from 50 to 60 cents, ten hours' work. Women are not generally better paid than they now are, because they compete with each other so much in the light, easy, and clean branches of labor, and meet competition in light work from boys. Their time of learning is from six months to a year, and half never learn. They are paid while learning. An eye for putting up work *true* to the square, and quick fingers, are the most essential qualifications. The business is constantly increasing. Work is the same, or nearly so, at all seasons. Girls employed by us have every personal comfort and convenience that is possible, and are paid as much as men for the same labor. Most of our work is more or less greasy and dirty from iron and brass filings. Girls usually have less natural *mechanical* intelligence, we think. It may be, however, that the want is from their inexperience in mechanical branches. Our impressions are that New England is the place for manufacturing small wares, requiring great activity and industry. Our workers have the use of a public library and lectures free. Board, $7 to $8 per month—thirty to thirty-one days." A manufacturer of trunk castors, in Massachusetts, writes me that he once employed girls to paint castors, and put them in packages for the dealers.

204. Nails. Making wrought nails is too hard work for women. A manufacturing company of nails, in Boston, write me there are no women employed in the nail factories of New England. The work is exceedingly heavy. Another manufacturing company write, they have never known of women being employed in making nails in any country. But we know that in France, women are employed in turning the wheel in making nails, and at Sedgley, E., and the neighboring villages, the number of girls employed in nail making considerably exceeds that of the boys. In England, the part done by girls is attending machinery that splits iron into the proper widths for nails.

205. Rivets. A manufacturer writes: "We believe no manufacturer employs women in our particular branch of industry. The business requires great strength and exposure to furnaces. The writer suggests that in *iron moulding*, perhaps a new career might be opened for women. "Innumerable small castings are now being made, such as buckles, eyes, rings, &c., for harness making. As this work is exceedingly light, requiring skilful manipulation, it might be within the scope of women to undertake this branch of industry." The casting is dangerous. The mixture of gases in the hot metal sometimes produces a blowing—that is, the metal is thrown into the air, falling oftentimes on the workers, penetrating their clothes and burning them. A woman's clothes would be unsuitable for this work. The moulding is very light, easy work, and we think as suitable for women as most mechanical labor.

206. Screws. The processes in making screws are forging, turning up, nicking, worming, and tipping. The cutting and polishing of screws, in Birmingham, are chiefly done by women. The machinery used requires care and delicacy.

10*

207. Skates. Skate manufacturers in Maine write: "We employ from ten to twelve ladies to stitch skate leathers, for about two months in the year, November and December. They are paid by the piece, and average 50 cents a day. All are Americans. Board, $1.50 per week. In the New England States, more American women are employed than foreigners, particularly in country towns."

208. Shovels. A shovel manufacturer says he employs boys to clean the handles, by holding them as they run over emery belts. He pays the boys $3 a week. For varnishing the iron part of the shovel he pays 10 cents a dozen, and "yesterday a youth was able to do twenty-one dozen." This branch of work, we think, might be done by strong women.

209. Wire Workers. I was told at a wire manufactory, New York, that women are never employed to draw wire. If it be true that wire drawers are a very rough, coarse set of men, it is well girls do not work in the establishments; as the work is such, we presume, that all must be employed in the same apartments. The labor of drawing is such that the hands of the men become almost like iron. Mr. S., Philadelphia, employs a woman to weave fine wire. She learned it in her native country, Scotland. She also sews pieces of fine wire cloth together. She receives $5 a week, and seldom works ten hours a day. Most men and women engaged in wire work are English or Irish, who learned the trade in their own country. I was told it requires some years to attain excellence. Weaving requires considerable strength in both upper and lower limbs. Men wire workers are paid from $1.50 to $2.50 a day. Mr. C., New York, employs a number of women weavers and seamers. They are paid $4 a week. Formerly their girls would want a day to go to a picnic, to get ready for a party, or help their mothers at home. The steam would have to be stopped unless they could get hands to fill their places during the time, which was very difficult and often could not be done. For a while their women gave them so much trouble, they had to stop the machinery altogether. It caused him such annoyance that some of the female members of his family learned, and are now employed. He employs women to cover steel for hoop skirts, and pays $3 a week. A few women are employed at wire weaving in Cincinnati. The wiring and making of bird cages seems to me a field of industry open to female hands. They can be made in any place, and the work is light. Wire could be woven in fenders by women, I think. Mr. C., maker of patent rat traps, employed a number of girls to lace the wires. Some he paid by the week, some by the piece. They mostly earned $3 a week. A small girl could learn it in two weeks. I saw a manufacturer of wire stands for cloaks, mantillas, &c. He employs a few ladies to dress them, paying 25 cents apiece. One of his hands is very expeditious and can cover six in a day. Those that know nothing of the work, he employs in making skirts only, and of course make less. February, March, August, September, and October are the busy months. There are only three places in New York where the work is done. A wire maker, in Lowell, writes : " I employed a girl four years ago in wire weaving, that gave unqualified satisfaction. She left, to obtain a college education. I paid by the piece when I employed her, and at the same rates as I paid men. She used to earn $1 a day, and even did so while attending school; but of course worked before and after school—probably seven or eight hours a day. Most of my work is too laborious for women ; but some wire workers that make meal sieves, corn parchers, &c., can, and I believe do, employ them to advantage, by reason of the price of labor being much less for women than men. This kind of business is limited. There are not more than one hundred and fifty men and women, probably, working at the business in New England. A maker of sieves, and wire goods in general, writes from Worcester, Massachusetts : " The business is quite healthy compared with needle work. I employ six women, who earn from $4 to $5 per week of ten hours a day. Men earn from $7.50 to $12. Some goods we manufacture will not justify us in paying women higher prices. (The women should not do it. They would then have to employ men and pay better prices, when women could come in and claim equal wages.) Our kind of work they learn in a few weeks. There will be no falling off, in future, of this work. Most girls like the work. Board, $2 per week in families." A wire manufacturer in Belleville, New Jersey, writes : " We employ females in sewing and winding wire. The employment is not unhealthy. We pay from $2.50 to $4.50 per week. Learners receive $2.50 per week. Board, $2 to $2.50. Men in our establishment average $2 per day. I would say that in some branches of our business, women might take the place of men."

Brass Manufacture. In some branches of the brass manufacture women are not at all employed—in a few others, they are. At a brass bell foundery, we were told the work is not healthy, and is too heavy for women.

210. Candlesticks. A manufacturer of candlesticks in Vermont " employs from three to four women, because they are better adapted to the work than men. He pays by the piece, from

$13 to $15 per month, and employs them the year round. Women are paid as well as men or boys at the same kind of work. It requires from three to five years to learn the business—from one to two years, that part done by women. Women are paid small wages while learning. It is a clean, comfortable business. There are no parts of our work suitable for women in which they they are not employed."

211. Hooks and Eyes. The agent of the Waterbury Hook and Eye Company says : " The hooks and eyes are given out to families to put on cards, for which they are paid by the gross. It pays poorly—probably not more for a child than 50 cents a week. The country and villages around supply plenty of girls for the factories. In good times the hands in the factories are kept employed all the year. We employ three females to pack our finished light work, which is as neat and healthy work as can be in any pleasant factory—pay is $3.50 to $4.50 per week of sixty hours. No males are employed on similar work. Supply and demand regulate prices. Only a short time is required by a competent girl to learn to do our work properly; and pay commences when they commence. Every good qualification which 'flesh is heir to' is needed to make the *right* sort of help. Prospect for employing more females than heretofore is not flattering. Girls are preferable for any light, neat, tasty work. Ours are Americans, and I believe as comfortable and happy as people are likely to be on this sinful globe. I doubt if much of our other work can be done by females. A place nearest to a large market, where good air and water prevail and means of living are reasonable, is the most desirable place to locate a factory, ordinarily. Churches, schools, libraries, lectures, &c., afford ample means and opportunity for mental and moral culture, for those who work ten hours a day, and can board for $2 a week, and are free from any special cares or anxieties." N. S. & Co., North Britain, write: " We employ nine women to make paper boxes, and pack hooks and eyes. They earn from 60 cents to $1 per day of ten hours, but are paid by the piece. The men earn from $1.15 to $3 per day; but their work is different from the women's. The women learn their part in two or three weeks. Industry and self-respect are the most desirable qualities. The prospect for future employment is good. They work all the year. Board, $2 per week."

212. Lamps. Mr. J. " used to employ girls to cement the glass body on the marble stand, and the top of the body on the metal through which the wick passes. He also employed them in papering to send away. The prospect for workers is poor, because the business is limited. He paid his girls $3.50 a week.

No manufactories in the West or South." In 1860 the manufacture of coal-oil lamps formed the principal business of sixteen companies, who employed 2,150 men and 400 women and boys."

213. Pins. The pins made in the United States are not so high priced as English pins. They have not until lately been so well finished. In pin making in England, the drawing and cutting of the wire, the cutting of the heads from the coils, and the trimming are mostly performed by men; the other operations, by women and children. Sometimes, in trimming the pins, a man, his wife, and child work together. For pickling and trimming the pins the price usually paid is two cents a pound. A skilful and industrious worker can head 20,000 pins per day, for which in England they are paid about 30 cents of our money. Pin heading is very sedentary work, and children seven or eight years of age are often kept at it for twelve or thirteen hours, with merely time for hasty meals. Girls at Sedgley and Warrington begin as early as five years of age to work in the pin factories. It is said that at Wiltenhall they are treated with much cruelty, if at all refractory. In Sedgley more women are employed than men, and receive the same treatment. The secretary of the American Pin Company at Waterbury, Connecticut, writes: "Women are employed in tending machines, and in sticking and packing pins, and packing hooks and eyes, and making paper boxes. The work is not unhealthy. The lowest wages by the week is $3.25 while they are learning; afterward $3.50 and $3.75 per week, ten hours a day. Some work by the piece, and earn from $14 to $21 per month. The supply of woman's labor is equal to the demand, at the prices we pay. We work through the year, generally without stopping, except for the holidays. Our average number is fifty. Girls can do the work as well or better than boys, that could be hired at the same price. Most are Americans. They have their Sundays, holidays, and evenings—also a public library and institute lectures at a very small cost—besides religious privileges afforded by six churches. Board, $1.50 to $2 per week." The Albany Company, at Cohoes, sends the following information: "Women, and girls not younger than twelve years of age, are employed in sticking, folding, wrapping, &c. The same work is done in England and Germany. Wages from $6 to $20 per month, working twelve hours a day. Those having had the most practice can usually do the work faster and better, consequently obtain higher wages. They receive pay while learning. The qualifications most desirable are care, attention, and activity. The business is not likely to increase greatly, as the work is mostly done by machinery and the demand for the article is limited. We are busy at all seasons except in extremely hot or cold weather. The hands work twelve hours—by so doing they obtain higher wages. We have more applicants than we wish. We employ from twelve to fifteen, because they can do the work more readily than men. The work is light, and the condition of the women quite equal to that of women otherwise employed to obtain the necessities of life." The agent of the Howe Manufacturing Company, in Connecticut, reports : "Our work is all done by the piece. The earnings of the workwomen vary according to their skill, diligence, and the number of hours spent at work. Average in April last, $11.09—in four weeks. Highest earnings of one individual $22.09 (equal to $5.54 per week). Small girls earn from $1 to $1.50 per week, and work six or eight hours. Men and women do not perform the same kind of labor in our establishment. Why all persons are not paid equally for equal labor, I do not feel competent to explain. A knowledge of our work is soon acquired. Learners are paid for what they do. A good character and reputation, honesty, fidelity, common mechanical ability, and diligence are desirable qualifications. We generally find the hands we want in our own immediate neighborhood. Our work is considered desirable, and much sought for. In all seasons the hands are equally employed, except dry seasons, when we are short of water to drive our machinery. Our *stock* hands generally stay with us till they get married or lay up so much money that they are able to get along with less labor, or become too old or infirm to work to advantage. Some have stayed with us over twenty years, many over ten years. The number of hours for work is discretionary. We seldom request industrious hands to work more hours than they choose. Our hands sometimes work twelve or fourteen hours, at their pleasure. Small girls, of whom we employ but five or six, seldom work ten hours. The number of women and girls employed in our establishment heretofore has been variable, averaging perhaps thirty. We are using improved machinery, which has already reduced the number, and will reduce it still more. Our work is peculiarly adapted to female labor. Nearly all our hands are American born. In twenty-two years' business, we have seldom, if ever, had an adult woman employed who was unable to sign her name to the pay roll. Our adult women have the churches and lyceum lectures, which I believe they generally attend. Their time for reading, for the most part, will be evenings and Sundays. Small girls can attend our district school free of cost." A manufacturer, in Seymour, Connecticut, writes : "We pay from $3 to $4 per week. We employ no men in sticking and packing, and, if we were not particular as to whom we employ, we could reduce the amount of our monthly pay roll a large per cent. It requires very little practice to learn the part of our business done by women, and in most cases we pay them full wages upon entering the mill. No special qualifications are needed. The kind of business we pursue will always be carried on, but of course can never become very common. No difference in the seasons, and the girls are never thrown out of employment. Under the present regulations they work eleven hours, and the time could not well be shortened, as that would tend to derange the other departments of our business. We have but ten employed at present, but in the course of a few days expect to have about twenty. They are employed because they are peculiarly qualified for the business, and on account of the lower rate of wages as compared with the labor of men. We employ women in all cases when the work is suitable for them. Women as employed by us are superior to men, being more expert and active. The New England States are doubtless the best locality for our business. The females employed by us are all intelligent and of good mental ability."

214. Rings. The American Brass Ring Co. " employ twenty women at presses, in packing, &c. They are all foreigners. Board, $1.50 per week. The work is not unhealthy. Women are paid fifty cents a day of ten hours. Women are paid $2 a week for four weeks while learning. The prospect of future employment is no better than the business now offers."

215. Scales. H. T., manufacturer of scales and weights, Philadelphia, Penn., writes : " We employ women in making metallic weights. The work is not unhealthy. They earn from $4 to $6 per week. No comparison in the price of labor. Women can make as much as men, if they are willing. It requires almost a lifetime to learn the business ; but the part the women work at requires but a day or two. We pay learners. No extraordinary qualifications are needed. A good prospect for increase of employment. No difference in seasons. They work from four to ten hours. Women cannot be employed at our heaviest work, on account of the great physical strength required." I was told at F. & M.'s, New York, that the beams of the scales could be burnished by women. It is done with steel instruments. I suppose the pans could also be burnished by them. Burnishing the back of the plates could be done by women also, but it is somewhat dirty work. Women would have to work in the room with the men, for while the foreman was employed, he would like to keep an eye on the employees. The work is rather heavy for women, but not more so than some in which they are engaged.

216. Stair Rods. A manufacturer of plated stair rods told me " he employs a woman to burnish the rods. She can make from $4 to $7 a week, not working more than ten hours a day, being paid from fifty cents to $1 a hundred. It is work hard on the chest, but he thinks not hard on the eyes. He had one lady who did it at home. In large establishments, rods are now burnished by machinery. The polishing of stair rods is very hard work, and requires strong, stout lads." Another stair-rod manufacturer told me " he has employed a boy to tie up stair rods, but would employ a girl and pay the same price, $1 per day."

217. Steel Manufacture. No women are employed in the conversion of iron into steel in this or any other country. It is rough, heavy work. It requires great physical strength, and is unsuitable for a woman. No women are employed in the manufacture of axes in this country. It is rough, coarse work, and done by stout, strong men. In one of the largest cutlery establishments in the United States they employ six hundred men, but no females; except six, for wrapping up goods. In the finishing of metals there are three branches: turning, filing, and setting up. In turning, jagged particles of metal fly off, and often enter the eyes of the workers, doing them great injury. Goggles of magnetized iron might be used to prevent this. The magnetized wash is used to prevent the filings from getting down the throats of grinders and polishers. For learning the two parts, turning and filing, four years of apprenticeship are served. The turning requires more skill than physical strength. It might be done by women that were willing to serve so long an apprenticeship.

218. Buckles. G. Brothers, of Waterbury, employ six women in riveting and other light work on bell clasps. They write: " The girls earn from $3 to $5 per week, ten hours a day. The labor of women is paid twenty-five per cent. less than that of males, because they are not able to do as heavy work. It requires about three months to learn the part of males or females. Our branch of trade is not increasing. Spring and fall are the most busy seasons, but the women are not thrown out of employment during the year. They are superior in light work. Board, $2 per week." A manufacturer in Attleboro' writes : " I employ from twelve to fifteen at packing, at light press work, &c. They are paid from four to six cents per hour. Women are not paid higher, because they are not worth more. I pay men from seven to twenty-five cents per hour. The time of learning depends on the ingenuity of the employed. They have steady work most of the time. They are full-blooded Yankees—have a good deal of fun when the boss is out, and work in a pleasant room. The labor is easy, and they are satisfied with the remuneration. (Perhaps because they can do no better!) A healthy climate, convenience to market and to places where the raw material is made, are advantages. All New-England girls have the advantages of a good education in the common branches." A manufacturer in Middletown, Conn., replies: "Girls are employed by me, springing in the tongues of buckles and packing them—also making paper boxes. They earn from forty cents to $1 per day, being paid by the piece. Their employment is not so heavy or laborious as that of males. It takes from six months to one year to earn full wages. Women will probably always be employed in these branches. Good box makers are always in demand. We employ thirty—all Americans. The balance of my work is rather objectionable for women, unless it be foreign or second-class girls. Women are usually more neat than men. Either water or railroad communication is desirable in seeking a locality. Board, about $2 per week. There was never so great a demand for female help in this part of the country as at the present time. They have started a shirt manufactory about nine miles from here, and are in want of girls; but the greatest trouble there is to find boarding places at reasonable rates." The West Haven Co. report " the employment to be very healthy by giving exercise to the limbs. The pay is from seventy-five cents to $1.50 per day—average $1. Some learn the business in two days, some in two weeks. The hands are paid from the first, and are seventeen in number, all Americans. Women are superior in this branch, because they are quicker with their fingers."

219. Edge Tools. The Humphreysville Edge Tool Manufacturing Co. inform me they do not employ females. For polishing they hire strong, rough boys, that they can get cheap, who stand while at work, and stoop over the articles, which produces a strain on the back and compression of the chest. Many find it so injurious they have to give it up, and the majority of those who do keep at it do not last long. The majority of the metal workers in Birmingham do their work at home. Each member of the family has his particular part to perform. An English writer says: " In various branches of the hardware manufacture, both in Birmingham and Sheffield, women may be seen by hundreds in some places, comfortably secluded from the male workers; in others, working side by side with them at the same mechanical process. They are never given to intoxication, and rarely, if ever, to strikes; and it may be very much the absence of these propensities that has recommended them so largely to the notice of the employer. In London the practice is gaining ground."

220. Electrical Machines. From the office of Davis & Kidder's magneto-electric machines we receive the following intelligence: "We employ women in covering wire, spools, sewing velvet, papering boxes, &c., &c. They earn from $12 to $24 per month, and are paid by the month. Women are paid nearly one half as much as men—can form no reason why women are not as well paid. It requires about three months for females to learn; they are paid while learning. All it requires is energy. There is no prospect at all for future employment in this branch. We employ our hands through the year; do not deduct from their wages when absent for a week. They work ten hours a day. We employ four, because the work is light and better suited for them than males. All Americans. Those in my employ are well educated. Board in respectable families, $2.50." C. Brothers, of New York, employ two girls for the same kind of work. They pay one $5 a week, ten hours a day—the small girl $3. They have had them but six months, but expect to keep them all the year. Mr. C. thinks the business is so limited that the prospect is poor for learners.

221. Fire Arms. From the Arms Manufacturing Co., Chicopee, Mass., we receive the following information: "We employ women in burnishing plated ware. The employment is not unhealthy. We pay generally by the piece. Some are paid about eighty cents per day. There is a prospect for steady employment for the few we have, and for no more. They are in no season entirely out of work. Ten hours a day are devoted to work when paid for by the week. All Americans. Easy work and much sought after. Women are inferior in point of strength, superior in cheapness." Sharp's Rifle Co. write: "We employ from ten to thirty women in making cartridges and inspecting primers. We pay about $1 each day, as the business requires good skill and care, and is hazardous. It is generally piece work. Males do the heaviest part of the work, and are paid $1.25 to $1.50 per day. If an individual is skilful, it requires but a short time to learn. Hands are paid while learning. Prospect good of future employment. We have constant work for ten. They are usually employed nine hours. All Americans. They appear very comfortable, and are quite tidy. No other parts of our occupation are suitable for women. Women are superior in forming and folding. $2.50 per week is the price of board."

222. Knives and Forks. The metals used for knives and forks are iron, steel, and silver, according to use or expense.

USED TO FIRE-ARMS.

The dust that arises from the grinding of steel knives, coats the lungs with stone. A German manufacturer of small cutlery told me that in large establishments in some European countries, women put the rivets in the handles of knives, and polish the handles of ivory and pearl. In the grinding of penknives and razors the inclination of the body forward is greater than in any other branch; hence, while less injurious in regard to the amount of dust than the fork and needle branches, they are fraught with greater evil from the position of the body alone. Articles of cutlery are glossed by holding them to a wooden wheel, on which is emery powder. They are polished by holding them to a wheel covered with leather, charged with crocus. Both of these processes are within the range of woman's toil. In a cutlery establishment, I was told the work was too hard for women. The polishing of their cutlery is done by machinery. The Hardware Manufacturing Company, Berlin, Conn., write: "We employ one hundred and forty men, making shelf hardware, and five or six girls to pack it up. They get from fifty to seventy-five cents a day, work ten hours, and all live at home. The work of papering up the goods is light, and requires little skill. The other part of the work about our factory is too severe for women." The Empire Knife Company, Conn., "employ four girls in packing and sharpening. They are paid by the day (ten hours), and earn from $3 to $4 per week. Women receive about the wages of men. It requires from six months to one year to learn. Women are paid while learning. The prospect of future employment is fair. The comparative comfort and remuneration of the work are good. Comfortable board, $3 a week." A company in Northfield, Conn., inform us: "It requires from three to five years to learn the men's part of the work. Some of the women work by the piece, and some by the day, receiving from $3 to $5 per week. The same price would be paid to men. The prospect of future employment is good. They work throughout the year. Women are superior in quickness. A locality should be fixed on where good water power may be had."

223. Needles. Most of the needles used in Europe and America are manufactured at Redditch, fourteen miles from Birmingham, where there are about a dozen very large factories. The number manufactured in Redditch amounts to about seventy million per week. The process is a very long and painful one. The drilling is done by young women. The constrained posture and rigid gaze of the women on the eyes of the needles as they drill, is distressing. It requires a perfect steadiness of hand. In addition to this, the small channel observed on each side of the eye is made by women with a suitable file. The picking out of defective needles, and laying perfect ones with the heads one way and the points another, is performed by children. Dr. G. C. Holland writes: "We candidly admit that the physical evils produced by needle grinding exceed all that imagination has pictured." The needle grinders in England are said to be ignorant and dissipated. One half can neither read nor write. The dust which is evolved in the process of needle grinding, contains a much larger amount of steel than is produced by any other grinding. Mr. Aiken, inventor of the knitting machine, has the machines and needles both manufactured. He says "he supposes he could teach women to do most of the work on needles, if he would give the time and trouble. He pays $1 per day to hands in the needle room." In the manufacture of Bartlett's sewing-machine needles, but a few small girls are employed, at from $1 to $1.50 per week, for smoothing the eye by running an oiled thread through it. Formerly they employed girls to perforate the eye, but it is now done by machinery. A manufacturer of knitting needles writes us: "The winter season is the best for work, and the Eastern States furnish the best localities for manufactories." A maker of sewing-machine needles told me the tools are rather heavy, files and a lathe being used. They pay a boy of fourteen years $3 a week, and one of eighteen, $5.50. C. employs girls to envelop and label needles. They earn from $3 to $4 a week, and do it at home. It takes a long time to become expert. They are paid from the first, but not much. The business is limited. They could have it done for less in England, but prefer to put labels on for parties in this country, who want to be considered manufacturers. G. & B. employ some girls to label and paper needles they import. They pay two cents and a half for putting the labels on forty papers. The labelling is done in the latter part of winter and early spring.

224. Pens (STEEL AND QUILL). A thousand million steel pens are said to be produced annually at Birmingham, England. We are indebted to some writer in an English paper for a description of the part taken by women in the manufacture of Gillott's pen in Birmingham. The number of women employed in his factory is four hundred. "If not altogether manufactured by woman, she has had, by far, more to do in its manufacture than men. He may have forged and rolled the metal, but she cut it from the sheet, gave it its semi-cylindrical form, stamped it, ground it on a wheel to make it flexible, split it, helped to polish it, and finally packed it in a box, or sewed it upon a card in readiness for the market. And whoever wishes to see her thus employed, may find her seated in an airy and comfortable chamber, with two hundred or three hundred companions similarly engaged—all healthy and merry, and singing at their work, while pens in all stages are clicking and glittering through their fingers at the rate of something like one hundred gross a day, each." An attempt has been made to manufacture steel pens in this country, but, I think, as yet without success. The makers of the Washington medallion pen had some girls to come from England to work for them, but found they could not keep up the factory, because of the prices they had to pay for labor. The duty on steel pens is thirty per cent., yet they can be imported for less than it would cost to make them here. Some one writes to the editor of the *Englishwoman's Journal* as follows : "Madam, I have been told that quill pens made by hand are far superior to those made by machinery, and are therefore used in some of the principal offices of London. Besides which, very many persons are unable to write except with quill pens ; rejecting the best and most expensive ones made of any kind of metal. Might not the making of them be a suitable occupation for some young women, who, from lameness or other infirmities, might be unable to follow a more active life?" In New York, some quills are made into pens by machinery, but women, we believe, are not employed.

225. Philosophical Apparatus. K., in Brooklyn, told me that in the old country it is customary to spend seven years learning to make philosophical apparatus, but in this country boys do not like to be apprenticed so long. The business is not fast enough for Americans. It requires close and constant application. The burnishing is quite hard work. The occupation has a tendency to render one intellectual and scientific. Most young men leave it to become physicians and preachers. Dr. McG., of China, is one of the number. The work is mostly done by lathe, but the polishing by hand. I think women could do it, if they were brought up to it. Instruments are made in Europe, and imported for less than they could be made in the United States. Business is now very slack. K. used to have several apprentices, that he boarded and paid $1 a week during the first year. The next year he increased their wages to $1 a week more, the next year another $1, &c. In small establishments an instrument is carried through all its processes by the same workman. The business is done in the United States on so small a scale as not to afford a sufficient subdivision to furnish any part suitable for women. P. does not know of any women being employed in this country in this trade. He thinks there is much of it they could do, and in process of time it will be done in the United States. In France and England, there are many women who learn with their fathers and husbands, and work with them. Many women are employed in making small compasses, that require a nice adjustment and care in pasting, but a separate room would be necessary, and that he has not. A manufacturer of nautical instruments writes me, he does not know of women being employed in any part of his business in any portion of the world. The brass on philosophical instruments is polished by hand, but a manufacturer told me he would not have even the polishing done by inexperienced hands, as they are very particular with the finishing off of their work.

226. Saws. A saw maker says, in England women are employed in lacquering the handles and polishing the blades of saws. An Englishman, who did a very extensive business in New York, employed girls in the same way, but he failed in business, and none have been employed since. W. pays boys for such work $2.50 a week. Another informant writes me that in England women are employed in the saw manufactories.

227. Scissors. In France, women are employed in the manufacture of cutlery. The blades of scissors are polished by women on lathes supplied with emery powder and oil, and subsequently on lathes supplied with crocus.

228. Spectacles. S. says there are women in England and France who make spectacle frames for them. He employs a woman to grind the glasses of spectacles. She can earn $15 a week, and has earned $23 a week by taking work home with her to do at night. On Nassau street, I saw a French lady who grinds glasses for spectacles on a lathe. She works from nine to five o'clock, and earns about $9 a week. There is not the danger some might apprehend of glass flying into the eyes while at work. Yet it requires great care and skill. I called at a manufactory of silver-plated spectacles and saw the whole process. Several parts are done by women. One was shaping the frames for the eyes, another setting them up, another preparing them to solder, another soldering, and three others were scouring. The soldering must be uncomfortable in warm weather. The employment, I suppose, is not more unhealthy than any other of a mechanical nature. One girl told me she earned seventy five cents per day. They are paid by the quantity. She said the rest could earn as much, if they were industrious. One considerably older, at another branch, said she could earn $4 a week. It would not require more than a few weeks, I think, to learn any branch pursued by women—to learn all the parts performed by women, would require six months or more, even for an apt and skilful pupil. A spectacle maker, J., said a smart person could learn to make silver spectacles in a year, but it would require something longer to learn to make gold ones, as gold is a more difficult metal to melt and work than silver. An apprentice is not paid the first year, because of the metal he wastes. To learn it, one should at first look on and see how the work is done. A manufacturer of spectacles writes : " Women might make and repair spectacles. The heavier parts of the business require foot lathes to be worked, where skirts would be out of place, but the most could be done by hand in making spectacles." (We have seen several women at foot lathes, polishing watch cases—so the use of foot lathes need not be an objection with women.) A spectacle importer writes : " We use a great many spectacle glasses, and in their manufacture in England females are generally employed. In France and Germany the women do the same kind of work." P., in Meriden, Conn., writes : " We employ women in making spectacles. The work is not more unhealthy than any other labor in shops. Most are paid by the piece—those who work by the week usually receive $4, and work ten hours a day. They receive about three fourths the price of male labor, because they perform the lighter work. They earn their board in one week—get good wages in eight. They usually do about the same amount of work through the year. We employ about fifty, because they are more active on light work, and can be had for less wages. Most are Americans. Girls prefer this to housework, and make better wages. The nearer New York, the lower are freights; the farther from New York, the more permanent our help. Good sense and religious principle prevail among them. Those who board pay $2.25 per week." A manufacturer in Brooklyn, of fine gilt, silver, plated, and German silver spectacles, writes : " The employment is healthy. Young girls earn $2 per week, older ones from $3 to $6. They are generally paid by the piece. Girls and boys earn about the same wages, but those who have spent years to acquire he trade are entitled to better prices. A smart girl or boy will earn in the course of six months to do a specific part. Wages are usually paid from the time they commence. A fair share of common sense and willingness to labor are the principal requisites. As long as people grow old, and need spectacles, they will be manufactured. Our work continues about the same through the season. They work ten hours a day. In burnishing, the demand is pretty good. We employ ten women, because they can do the parts of work required better than boys or men. Half are American. We find women rather more ready and apt than men. It is advantageous to be in or near the great markets. Board, $2."

I was told by an English maker of spectacle frames, that most spectacles are made in France and Germany. Men and women are paid in England 37½ cents a dozen for grinding the best quality of glasses. The makers of frames should know how to make figures, to put them on the frames. Women would be most likely to find employment as grinders of glasses in New York, and no doubt a small number could get work of that kind. Gold and silver frames are polished on a lathe with leather and rouge. Common frames are burnished with agate and steel. It is done more quickly, and is cheaper than polishing. Most spectacle frames of a common quality are made in the country, because it can be done by water power, and more cheaply.

229. Surgical Instruments. T., manufacturer, told me that some steel surgical instruments are burnished by hand. He thinks there is not enough in that line of business to do, to justify women in learning. He said the polishing of surgical instruments could be done by women. It requires judgment and experience, but is simple, requiring the worker merely to hold the instrument on lathes and turn every few seconds; but burnishing requires more strength. I was told that perhaps women are employed in polishing silver surgical instruments.

230. Telescopes. G., an optician, says much of the light work in making telescopes might be done by women. They could French-polish the wooden frames, lacquer the brass work, and grind the glasses, if properly instructed. He thinks making microscopes is more suitable for them.

231. Thermometers. The construction of the thermometer is quite simple. Women, if taught, could put the parts together, and mark the scales. I have been told that some girls are employed in Rochester, New York, in marking the scales. The same remarks will apply to the barometer.

---

232. Copper and Zinc Manufacture. So far as we can learn, no women are employed in copper and zinc mines, or in the making of copperas. Twenty-five women are employed in packing copper powder flasks, by the Waterbury Manufacturing Company, and making percussion caps. One fourth of them are American. They earn from $3 to $4 per week, and the work is reported not unhealthy. The women are paid about one half as much as men. It does not require long to learn, and learners are paid something during their apprenticeship. Ten hours are devoted to work. All seasons are alike. The agent says the women do better for light work than men, but require more watching.

———

233. Tin Manufacture. A youth, that was working in a tin shop for a widow, whose husband had been a tinner, told me that a female relative of his, who lived about one hundred years ago in Ireland, could do all the various parts of work as well as a man. She learned the trade regularly. Women are paid nearly as well as men for such labor in the old countries, but cannot work so fast. He says, even now in Europe a few women learn the trade of a tinner. It requires four years to learn it thoroughly in all its branches, because there is such a variety. One or two branches may be learned perfectly in a short time; so may several be learned indifferently in the same period; just as a violinist may know how to play a few tunes very well, but cannot play any others; or may know how to play a great many indifferently, but none perfectly. In England, where women are employed in tin shops to solder, they receive for this work their board and thirty-seven cents a day.

234. Lanterns. I visited a large tin establishment in Brooklyn, and saw the girls at work; some soldering the corners of the lanterns, some assorting the pieces, some putting glass in the sides, some fastening conductors' lamps in the framework, with plaster of Paris, and some enveloping them to send away. There is nothing unhealthy in the work. The smoke of the charcoal stoves used in soldering is carried off by pipes. Girls putting glass in the tin frames, sometimes get their fingers cut. The girls all wear aprons. The plaster of Paris part of the work is very dirty. The girls earn from $2.50 to $4.50. They are all employed at first in papering, as it is termed—that is, putting the articles in papers ready to be packed; and receive, for a few weeks, $2.50 a week, then more, according to ability and industry. Some are paid by the week and some by the piece; they work ten hours. Girls prefer mechanical labor to domestic service, because they have the evenings to themselves. It requires but a few weeks for a girl of ordinary abilities to learn the part she is to perform. The proprietor said he could have a hundred times as many girls as he has, if he had employment for them. But few American women will work in factories with men. Most women are neater with their work than men. At a lantern manufactory in New York, I was told they employ eight or ten girls to cement the metal parts on the glass, to varnish, to wash and wipe and paper them. They are paid $3.50 a week.

235. Britannia Ware. Some Britannia is burnished by hand, and some by lathe. Women occasionally do the first kind.

---

236. Silver. "The artisan who forms certain articles of gold and silver is called, indifferently, a goldsmith or silversmith. The former denomination is most commonly employed in England, and the latter in the United States." A manufacturer of silver ware in Providence, Rhode Island, writes: "We do not employ women, and for the same reason that females are not employed in machine shops." Chinese women do filagree work. A lady told me she had seen it done in a factory near Paris, by women.

237. Burnishers. At M.'s, Philadelphia, they employ from thirty to fifty women on plated ware; would employ more if they had room for them to work. They spend three months learning, and receive no wages during that time. They then earn from $3 to $6 per week, according to skill and industry. They work by the piece. Another set of women are employed in scouring the ware. It is wet, dirty work, and the women receive somewhat higher wages. The burnishers work in a light, comfortable room. The scourers work in a cellar. The business of burnishing is not hard on the eyes; nor would it be on the chest, M. thinks, if the burnishers sat upright, which they could do if they chose. We were told by some one else, that the demand for laborers in that field is very limited in Philadelphia. I was told by a silversmith in New York, that a good burnisher can earn from $5 to $7 a week, and he thought it took about a year to learn to become a good worker. Burnishing is a laborious and perfectly mechanical process. With some, the stooping posture is found trying to the breast, and constantly poring over the bright surface is injurious to the eyes. The business is poorly paid, and a silversmith can employ but a very small number of burnishers, but manufacturers of plated ware employ more. F. employs two girls for burnishing silver ware, who can earn from $5 to $9 per week. It is piece work, and does not require long to learn. C. L. pays burnishers from $3 to $6 a week. At a manufactory of silver service for Roman Catholic churches, I was told they are most busy just before Christmas and Easter. They pay by the week, because it is less trouble, and to them cheapest, as many of the articles they make are small. They pay from $2 to $5 a week. Y., in New York, who employs a number in burnishing silver ware, told me he pays learners nothing for a month, then by the piece. A good burnisher could earn from $5 to $7 a week. The prices are better than are generally paid to women for mechanical work. A lady burnisher told me she likes the work because it can be done at home. She thinks the work not injurious to the eyes. To learners she pays nothing for two months, then $1 a week, and so increases as the learner advances. At the end of a year, the learner is considered proficient. Silver platers mostly employ their operatives in factories. Silver ware requires more taste and neatness than plated ware, and pays better. It is like vest making. One that can make good ones, gets a good compensation; but those who slight their work are paid proportionately. A good burnisher can earn $6 and upward. Mrs. —— thinks after a while there will be manufactories of plated ware in the South and West. I saw a man making silver and brass faucets. The burnishing is first done with steel, then with agate. It requires some strength, but a woman of muscular force could do it. The majority of burnishers work upon plated ware, as less silver is used since plated ware has been brought to its present state of perfection. M. pays by the piece. A woman receives from $4 to $7 per week, according to competency and industry. It requires from two to four months to learn. The large cities, or places where the goods are manufactured, are the best for burnishers. The work soils clothes, so girls generally change their dresses or wear large aprons. Spring and fall are busy seasons. Hollow ware is generally burnished by men, as it requires more strength. At H.'s, I saw a few women scouring the ware with sand, and nineteen burnishing. They earn from $3 to $6 a week. A man in B., that does hand plating, employs girls to burnish, and pays them by the piece. They can earn from 75 cents to $1.50 per day; they work at home. In New York there are some ladies who teach burnishing, and at some establishments a premium is paid for learning. In some large factories, girls are paid by the week from $3 to $5. C. pays by the piece, and from the first, but a girl cannot earn more than $1 a week for two or three months. It requires from four to six months to become a burnisher. The prospect for learners is good, because girls will get married, and so leave vacancies. The business is increasing. Good burnishers earn from $4 to $12 a week. He employed a girl to stay in his office and burnish, paying her according to what she did, from $1 to $1.25 a day. Women, he remarked, receive the same price for burnishing that men do. (He may pay them so, but I know all do not.) About the holidays are the most busy times. There are not two months in the year a good burnisher cannot get employment. Merchants are slack longer than manufacturers. C. is a practical plater, and not so much at the mercy of his employés as those that are not. His burnishers begin on knives and forks, as they are most simple. A burnisher told me it is not customary to pay a learner during the first two months. Most burnishers wear a shield. He thinks it is not bad on the eyes unless done at night. A northern light is best for judging of the work, just as a northern light is best for seeing the imperfections of a painting. About four months of the year, January, February, July, and August, burnishers find it difficult to get work, except in very large establishments, where they are kept busy all the time. A man working at coach lamps told me girls used to be employed in the factory to burnish plates, and received $3 per week. The Porter Britannia and Plate Co., Conn., "employ women in burnishing, washing and packing. They earn from $3 to $5 per week. Men and women have the same price for their work, but men earn from 50 to 75 per cent. more, because they accomplish more. Men and women spend three months learning. Women could not endure more than ten hours such work. The supply rather exceeds the demand generally. On many accounts, women are preferable. They are superior in care and nicety of execution. The labor is too exhausting for tropical climates. There are some parts of the occupation suitable for women in which they are not now employed." Information from three other establishments corresponds with that given. Silversmiths in New Orleans write me, February, 1861: "Women are much employed in Europe as well as in this country, burnishing silver ware. It is not in the least unhealthy. Most are paid by the piece, and here some receive as high as $50 a month. For silver burnishing, women are paid the same as men. The time of learning depends greatly upon capacity—usually about six months. There is a very slight prospect, at present, of employment. The best season for work is winter; there is none in the summer. In the higher branches of such work, women acquire superior skill."

238. Thimbles. P. was kind enough to make an entire silver thimble, that I might see the process. The whole of the work could be done by women, but no women in any country are employed at it, so far as he knows. I was told by one or two other thimble makers, that no women are ever employed in that branch of business. It is usual for a boy to serve an apprenticeship of four years. While doing some parts of the labor the workers sit, and while doing other parts they stand. The polishing is done on a lathe, and there is not enough of it to furnish work for a separate person, except in very large establishments, and even then it is so connected with the other processes that it could not be well divided. There are not so many thimbles sold now as formerly, because of the sewing machines that are used.

There are not more than from eight to twelve thimble makers in the United States. There are none South or West of Philadelphia.

---

239. Silver Plating. Women cannot well do the close or hand plating. It is done by soldering and ironing. Door plates are made in this way. Electro-plating is done with a battery. The business includes a variety of work, and requires some knowledge of chemicals, but could be learned by an intelligent person in a short time. The Americans are noted for excellence in this department. H. knew a lady plater in Connecticut, and a very good one she was. I have been told women are employed in silvering metals in France.

---

240. Bronze. Some statuettes are made of the finer metals, gold and silver, while busts are made of other simple metals, as copper, iron, zinc, lead, &c. They are generally made, however, of the mixed metals. It requires some years' experience to make bronze statuettes. Women are employed in France, in ornamental bronze work. Mlle. de Faveau has succeeded in having a bronze statue of St. Michael cast entirely whole, instead of in portions. It is the resuscitation of a lost art.

---

241. Gold and Jewelry Manufactures. Those that manufacture jewelry in the United States form a small body. The articles sold by different houses vary as much in price and quality as any other kind of goods. Jewellers often have connected with their business persons who work in ivory, jet, hair, and such materials. " Felicie de Faveau, as a worker in jewels, bronze, gold, and silver, as a designer of monuments and mediæval furniture, stands without approach." Much common jewelry is made in Rhode Island, and women are employed to some extent in its manufacture. The New England Jewelry Company in Providence employ women to solder, and pay $4 a week, ten hours a day. It does not take long to learn. They have work usually all the year. In the Eastern manufactories, women suffer some from dust, on account of their working in the same rooms where the men are employed at the machinery. In the manufacture of jewelry, the fumes of charcoal are usually permitted to fill the workshop; and the fusion of saltpetre, alum, and salt, used in dry coloring, induces general nervousness and pain in the head and chest. This has been to some extent remedied, by having pipes that carry off the fumes partially, or it may be, in whole. There are many departments in the jewelry line that might be successfully filled by women : the sale of jewelry is one. It requires several years for one to become well acquainted with the jewelry business, and that is longer than many women are willing to spend in fitting themselves for busineess. Mr. B. said : " One to set jewels should be able to mount them. But few people make setting a separate business. When he learned, a woman was not at all employed by jewellers in this country. He pays some of his workers $10 a week, ten hours a day." A jewelry manufacturer in Pawtucket, Rhode Island, writes : " Women are employed in the manufacture of jewelry—also in casing and packing the same for market. The work is not more injurious than weaving or sewing. They are paid about the same as men. Some pay by the piece, some by the hour. Women are not paid as well as men, because they cannot do all parts. The time of learning depends upon their ingenuity. Some may learn in one week, others in four. They are paid while learning. Women are employed in the lighter branches because they are quicker. The advantage of a locality is in having natural water power, in a community where there is plenty of capital, and the capitalists are willing to invest in the business." Some manufacturing jewellers told me " they pay from $3 to $8 per week to their women. They work ten hours a day. The time of learning is six months, but, as in every thing else, much depends on the capacity, aptitude, and particular genius of the learner. More women could be employed in this business, if properly qualified. All their women are Germans. New York is the best place for selling jewelry, but other places are as good for manufacturing."

242. Gold Assayers. Assaying by acids and other reagents could be done by women. Tests are now imported, but most assayers prefer to make their own tests. Assaying requires patience, a knowledge of metals, and endurance of heat. It also requires instruction and considerable experience. Some assayers move from place to place wherever new mines are discovered, and reap the benefit of their skill and knowledge. A gold refiner informs me " that his business is mostly heavy fire work, requiring the most able men. None of it is sufficiently light for females." I find, however, that women are reported in the census of Great Britain as gold and silver refiners, cutters, and workers.

243. Enamellers. The experience, taste, delicacy of touch, and fineness of finish required, make the art of enamelling one very suitable for women. The richness of coloring and exquisite workmanship render some specimens very beautiful.

Simple metals are mostly used as a base. I saw a man enamelling jewelry, who told me he employs small girls to enamel, paying from $2 to $3 a week. It requires but two weeks to learn. I saw some jewelry that had been enamelled in Germany by women. In France, women are employed as enamellers, at from 8 to 16 cents a day. " Gold of the standard quality is the best metal to enamel on, as it imparts something of its own glow to the ground, and assists materially the richness and delicacy of the coloring, particularly in the flesh tints. Copper gives a cold greenish hue to the enamel ground, but it is more commonly used than gold on account of its cheapness. For large enamels it is necessary to use copper, as they require a heat which would melt plates of gold." A highly polished enamel is passed through the fire a number of times in the process of painting; otherwise it would be impossible to imitate any great delicacy of tint—as the colors are considerably changed by burning. " As the plates are every time subjected to a high red heat, it is obvious that enamels must be the most durable of all kinds of paintings." At an enamel factory for lining metal vessels with a porcelain coating, I saw a woman who has been employed for four years to mix enamel in the consistency of buckwheat dough, and pour it into vessels to form an enamel lining. The articles are then baked in a furnace that the enamel may harden. She stands while employed. She goes at half past seven in the morning, has half an hour at noon, and returns and works until four, for which she is paid $4 a week. She has a sister-in-law in Williamsburg that does the same kind of work. It is not at all unhealthy.

244. Gold and Silver Leaf. The iron hammers used for beating gold leaf are very heavy. For the first beating, hammers weighing twelve pounds are used ; for the second beating, hammers weighing six or eight pounds. Strong women could perform the second beating of gold leaf, but I do not know that they ever do—I think never in the United States. Lads serving as apprentices receive $1.50 a week for six weeks, then $2 a week for a time, and then more, according to ability and industry. A goldbeater told me a youth could get a pretty good insight into the business in a year or two, but the usual time of apprenticeship is either three or four years. Goldbeaters earn from $1.50 to $2 a day. We visited several gold-leaf manufactories, and found more uniformity in the time of learning and the prices paid than in any other branch of business. It requires from two to twelve weeks to learn to book gold leaf, depending on the abilities of the learner and the requirements of the establishment. Six weeks is the length of time usually given. It can be learned in two days, but requires practice to become expert. The girls are not paid while learning, as the materials are costly, and the quantity wasted comes to as much or more than the learner's services are worth. The standard price for laying gold leaf is one cent and a half a book. Bookers can earn from $2.50 to $5 a week, according to skill and expedition. The tools of a worker are very simple. I think, most of the women employed in the gold leaf factories of New York are Americans. Gold leaf is so light that even a breath of air will move it. In some factories, the booking is done in a room with the doors and windows closed—consequently the room is very warm in summer. The seasons of the year do not affect this business like most others. The demand for gold leaf regulates the supply. Where business is not systematically conducted, the beaters will sometimes not have the leaf ready to book, and so the girls must lose their time waiting; and in some cases the men's work is retarded by the absence of the bookers. All the manufacturers I talked with thought the prospect good of employment to learners. K. & Co. take learners in the spring, but will not take them unless they can insure them work when the six weeks of learning have expired. Neatness is required. No talking is allowed in the work room, as merely a drop of water falling from the lips might spoil from $3 to $4 worth of leaf. The leaf is weighed when given to the booker and when returned, so there is no opening for dishonesty. W. employs his hands all the year. The girls always sit while at work. Lightness and delicacy of hand are required. The prospect of employment is tolerable, but most prefer to retain those they teach, as there is much difference in the style and expedition. In some shops great care is taken with learners, and they acquire proportionate proficiency. We think this a very neat and genteel employment. It requires honest workers with nimble fingers. There are but very few manufactories South and West.

245. Jewellers' Findings. D. & Co. manufacture tags for all kinds of goods. They employ girls and women in the country to string their tags, because they can do it in their spare moments, and consequently work cheaply. It pretty much takes the place of knitting, and a person could not earn more than twenty-five cents a day at it. They so employ thirty or forty persons. They also engage a number in box making. It requires care and neatness to make small boxes for jewelry. Workers are paid by the piece, and can earn from twenty-five cents to $1.25 a day, but those who earn the latter amount work from five in the morning until ten at night. This work is mostly done in families. D. & Co. are very strict in their regulations, and particular in the kind of work people they employ.

246. Pencils. In Williamsburg, Mass., two women are employed in making gold and silver pencil cases. H., of New York, employs one girl for engine turning—an ornamental dotted work common on pencil and watch cases. He employs her by the week, and pays $3. She works ten hours a day. It requires but a few days for one of ordinary intelligence to learn. It is sedentary, but not unhealthy. He has employed nine women : they cannot do the work as well as men, but cheaper. He would employ boys, but they are so fond of changing their employment, and so anxious to engage in one that will advance them, that it is difficult to keep them at that work. It is very clean work. There is no prospect of future employment, as one woman can keep up with twelve other workers, and so very few are needed. Women have to work in the same room with the men, on account of the foreman having to regulate the machinery if it gets out of order.

247. Pens. I saw a gold-pen manufacturer in Brooklyn. He will take ten or twelve learners shortly, and pay them from the commencement. He must have honest girls, for a dishonest girl will take $5 or $10 worth of gold at a time, frequently without its being missed. He will have a separate apartment for his girls. The best hands can earn from $5 to $6 a week, working ten hours a day. It requires only about a month to learn, but practice greatly improves and expedites work. He thought the prospect rather poor for learners. The part done by men could be done by women, but it is dirty work. That done by women is rather neat work. W., of Brooklyn, employs a number of girls in watch-case polishing and in finishing off pens. The majority are Americans. Some are paid by the piece, and some by the week. They work ten hours a day, and have employment all the year. Some girls learn the art in a short time, and some never. Some girls are paid while learning as much as $2.50 a week. W. thinks the prospect good of employment in that branch. He wanted several girls more. From the nimbleness of their fingers they can do their work better than men. More gold pens are made in this country than steel ones. A jeweller said learners should be paid from the first, and you may know he is not much of a man who would be willing to receive a woman's work for nothing. On Nassau street, N. Y., I saw a manufacturer who employs girls for stoning, frosting, and polishing pens. They are paid by the quantity, and can earn from $3 to $5 a week. They stand at a lathe while polishing. The only trouble is that their dress is likely to catch on the wheel. That might be remedied by wearing Turkish costume without hoops. It requires care and some judgment to do the frosting. They are paid something while learning, and in two or three months receive full wages.

11

When business is good, the factory is going all the year. To make a good finisher requires that the individual have some mechanical talent and be a good penman. Some never succeed. In stoning and frosting, girls sit. The finishers are men, and the stooping required sometimes produces consumption. So many gold pen cases are not used now as formerly—probably not more than one tenth as many. Gutta percha has become a substitute. N. employed women seven or eight years ago in polishing, stoning, and pointing pens, and paid $5 a week of ten hours a day. Manufacturers in Williamsburg, Mass., write : " We employ women to make gold pens, pen holders, and jewelry, and pay from $3 to $4 per week—some by the piece and some by the week. It requires from one to three years to learn, according to the part they do. They are paid small wages while learning. We wish honesty and ingenuity in our workers. The business is permanent. Work is given at all seasons of the year. The hands work eleven and a quarter hours per day. We employ from ten to twelve women, because they can do the work equally as well as men, at about one third the price. Half are Americans. No other parts of the occupation are suitable for women than those in which we employ them. Help once settled in the country, if married, are likely to be permanent—in cities, *vice versa*, changing about. Our workmen have a fine reading room. Board, $1.50 for women, $2.50 for men."

248. Watches. A watch is said to consist of 992 pieces. We have seen it stated that two hundred persons are employed in the entire process of making a watch, and that, with the exception of the watch finishers (who put the parts together), not one of the workmen could perform any but his own specific part. In Switzerland, families, for generation after generation, devote themselves to making particular parts of watches. Women have proved their ability to execute the most delicate parts. Twenty thousand Swiss women earn a comfortable livelihood by watch making. They make the movements, but men mostly put them together. I think a few women work as finishers. We quote from the *Englishwoman's Review* : " Geneva has always refused to employ women, and has now totally lost the watch trade. None of the Geneva watches, so called, come from that part of Switzerland, but are manufactured elsewhere, and principally in the canton of Neufchatel, where women have been employed from the first." Mr. Bennett, of London, " states facts relative to the mental culture of both sexes, which is deemed requisite in Switzerland to prepare the intellect, the eye, and the hand for watch manufacture, and he refers to the salubrious dwellings of the operatives." A traveller states : " We see women at the head of some of the heaviest manufactories of Switzerland and France, particularly in the watch and jewelry line." In England, women have been until lately excluded from watch making by men, but some are now employed in one establishment in London and in several of the provincial towns. "There is a manufactory at Christchurch, England, where five hundred women are employed in making the interior chains for chronometers. They are preferred to men, on account of their being naturally more dexterous with their fingers, and therefore being found to require less training." From the November number of the *Knickerbocker* we quote: "All imported watches are made by hand, the American watches being the only ones made by machinery in a single establishment by connected and uniform processes. The Waltham watches have fewer parts and are more easily kept in order than any others; and are warranted for ten years by the manufacturers. They have over one hundred artisans employed, more than half of whom are women." The manufactory occupies a space more than half an acre in extent. Hand labor is cheaper in Europe than this country, but American watches are cheaper, because made by machinery. Making the cases is a distinct branch from the interior work, and furnishes employment to some women. Cleaning watches would form a pretty and suitable employment for women. I was told of some Swiss women living in Camden, New Jersey, that make the inside work of watches very prettily and very accurately. A manufacturer of chronometers in Boston writes: "We employ women in cutting the teeth of watch and chronometer wheels, polishing, &c. They are generally employed by the week or year, and work nine or ten hours a day. Women might be employed in large establishments in merely cleaning or polishing the parts of watches repaired, without putting them together; and they might learn to do it in a short time, a few months perhaps. We pay our women for such work from $4 to $6 a week, according to their capacity. The qualifications needed are delicacy of touch, patience, and great carefulness. The employment will be very limited. Work is steady the year round. The principal objection to employing women is that they are very apt to marry just as they become skilful enough to be reliable; therefore, what does not require long apprenticeship or a great expense to learn, is most desirable for them. A good degree of intelligence is indispensable. The more, of course, the better." We would add to the requisites for a watchmaker, patience and ingenuity. The secretary of the American Watch Company at Waltham writes: "Women are employed at our factory. The employment is entirely healthy. We pay from $4 to $7 per week for intelligent girls, and women's average pay is $5. About half are paid by the piece. Men earn about double the wages of women, because, first, they do more difficult work, are more ingenious, more thought-ful and contriving, more reliant on themselves in matters of mechanics, are stronger, and therefore worth more, though not perhaps double, as an average; second, because it is the custom to pay women less than men for the same labor. Women and girls are paid from $2.50 to $4 per week during the first four months, while they are learning the particular part of our business we set them at. The requisites are a good common-school education, general intelligence, and quickness; light, small hands are best. The business is new to the country. We work every working day in the year, without detriment to the health of women, who seem to endure their labor as well as men. We work ten hours a day. There is little demand for labor in the watch-making business generally in this country, but we think women could be taught successfully the art of watch making, so as to be able at least to earn a living as watch repairers. We employ seventy-five women out of two hundred hands, and because there are many parts of our work they can do *equally* well with men; but it is generally light and simple work, for which no high degree of mechanical skill is requisite. Nine tenths are American born. Our hands are all made perfectly comfortable in their labor. We employ female labor, where we can, as being cheaper; but we find women do not reach the posts where a high degree of skill is needed, as of course they do not those for which their strength is insufficient. They have abundant facilites for mental culture in the evenings. About half live with parents or relatives; the rest board, and pay from $2 to $3 a week, according to quality."

249. Watch Case and Jewelry Polishers. Quite a number of women are employed in polishing watch cases, and a few in polishing jewelry. It requires some time to learn to do the finest work, and some can never learn. The polishing of good gold is done by hand and the lathe—common jewelry, by the lathe alone. A good polisher can earn $1 a day of ten hours' work. C. & Co. employ girls, because they do not have to pay them so high, and they do it as well. B. & H., who have a fac-tory in Jersey City, employ a number of lady polishers. The rouge renders it dirty work, but not unhealthy. Very good hands can earn $7 or $8 a week. They employ four sisters, French girls, who have bought a farm for their parents. They have generally paid $23 a week to the four sisters. The prospect for learners is good. They generally pay by the week, and have their hands work ten hours a day. They take learners, and pay something from the first. It requires two years' practice to become very good polishers. They prefer to make an agreement with the learner to retain her some time, as the material is costly, and considerable is wasted by a learner. In good times they have work steadily all the year. Polishers can either sit or stand while at work. Burnishing and polishing are different. Burnishing is done with steel, polishing with buffs. Plated ware is burnished, silver and gold are polished. S. thinks several girls might, in busy times, find employment in polishing jewelry. He often advertises for workers, but receives few answers. It requires two or three years to learn, and four or five to become perfect workers. In Germany and France, girls have polished jewelry for many years. In the Southern and Western U. States, there are no manufactories of any extent. They have not the machinery for such work. What little is made and repaired is done in the jeweller's shop, or above his store. F. & P. employ small girls about thirteen years old to polish, paying $1.50 per week, while learning. It requires about a year for young girls to become expert. We were told women are the best polishers of jewelry. A maker of gold buttons, who has employed girls to polish, paid $2 a week to small girls, and $3 to older and more experienced hands. The girls are also employed in putting them up. Care is needed in polishing, that the work be evenly done. A watchcase polisher told me a woman cannot earn more than $2 or $3 a week at polishing. (It may be all he pays.) Mrs. C. is teaching a girl to polish watch cases. She boards her, and pays her $30 the first year, and furnishes her with a certain number of dresses. A good polisher may earn from $6 to $8 a week. She told me a lady in Philadelphia, that she taught, is making $27 a week. C. has most of his polishing done by a lady. He pays boys he takes as apprentices, $2.25 a week, from the first. He says a good lady polisher can earn $1 a day. He pays his men from $10 to $15 a week, because they do more, and do it better than women. In good seasons there is so much polishing to do that experienced hands are very much hurried. The work is not confined to seasons. It does not require long to learn to polish. Such work is mostly done in New York, but considerable is done in the small towns around. At S.'s we saw a girl polishing, who told us she received $1 a day. She says there a girl spends six months learning. For three months she receives nothing, after that $3 a week. At B.'s, the lathes are moved by steam, but have treadles also, that the work may not cease when the engine or machinery is out of order. Less and less watch work is done by hand in the United States every year, owing no doubt to the large number imported and the increased use of machinery. The work in the business has fallen to European rates. A good

polisher has been earning $6 or $7 a week, but very few can do
so now, and the prospect of employment is poor for a learner.
Some years ago he employed a lady at $15 a week, for fitting
movements to the case. The sister of a watch-case maker and
importer, in Brooklyn, told me that she worked at the business
some years ago, and received seventy-five cents apiece for polishing watch cases—now but fifty cents is paid. The lady often
polished four cases in a day of ten hours, and so earned $3. In
the European countries, some years back, a man was paid $1 for
making a watch case; in the United States, $5. Prices have
fallen greatly in the United States for this kind of work, because
the duty on imported goods is so low. She says the work is not
very clean, because the oil and rouge get on your clothes and person. Everybody should wear working clothes, if their labor is
such as to soil them. The motion of the foot in moving the lathe
tries the back greatly. When the polishing is done by steam, it
is not so. As men and women are paid by the piece, women receive as good wages. A smart person can learn to polish in a
few days, but to learn it thoroughly would require three months.
Women are paid in this country while learning, but in Europe
they are not. In prosperous times, work is good all the year.
In summer, work is done for the North; in winter, for the South.
A locality in or near a large city is preferable. Prices vary in
different establishments. Usually, where the best quality of work
is done, the best prices are paid the work people—where cheaper
work is done, lower wages are paid. The usual price paid to
girls as polishers, when they are employed by the week, is $6—
a better remuneration for mechanical labor than most women
receive.

250. Watch Chains. In Birmingham, several hundred
women are employed in making chains, and we suppose fifty or
more in this country. The gold wire is prepared and drawn out
by men, as it requires too much strength for women. All the
work after that is performed by women. The wire is cut into
pieces of the right length, then bent into the proper form by
means of a die worked by a hand press; each link is then soldered
together by means of a jet of gas, a blowpipe, and a tiny piece
of solder, when it is finished by polishing. D. & S., Philadelphia,
employ three girls in soldering. The wages of the girls vary from
$3.50 to $8 a week. They work ten hours a day. It is not an
unhealthy business, D. and S. think, and can be learned in two
months. M. F. & Co., New York, employ girls in soldering
and polishing chains. Those that solder earn from $3 to $8 a
week. Some of the girls are paid by the week, and some by the
inch. It can be pretty well learned in three months. After two

or three weeks they are able to earn about $2 a week. To those
girls who instruct learners they give the profits of the learners.
Polishing is not clean work, but the women can generally earn
more at it. They earn from $3 to $9 a week. They work ten
hours a day, when paid by the week, in summer; but in winter, not
so long. The building is never lighted. The women have a
separate apartment to work in, and change their clothes on entering and leaving the work room; and the polishers tie up their heads,
to prevent their hair being covered with rouge. The girls wear
the same clothes every day while at work, that they may not carry
away any gold. The proprietors sell their waste scraps for $8,000
a year. They require boys to spend five years learning the business, taking them at the age of 16, and retaining them until 21.
Men that learn a trade expect to follow it until death. M.
thinks women will not spend long learning a trade, for nearly all
women look forward to something else than working all their lives
at a trade. The heat and fumes of gas used in chain making are
said to render the occupation unhealthy, but an extensive manufacturer assured me that the fumes are not inhaled, as the flame
is blown from the worker, and that it is not more unhealthy than
any other sedentary occupation. I would have thought the mi-
nuteness of the particles composing some chains would be trying
on the eyes, but the girls said not. The chain makers sit while
at work. In summer they cannot sit near an open window, lest
any of the gold be blown away. Chain making looked to be very
nice, delicate work, requiring care, judgment, and some skill. The
Europeans have not got to using steam in any part of the process,
and are astonished at the superiority of the American chains.
There are no manufactories West or South. I was told at Tiffany's,
the making of some kinds of chains can be learned in two or three
years, while other kinds require five years. S., at Tiffany's, told
me he was the first person that introduced women into the manufacture of jewelry in New York. The hands at chain making receive $1.50 a week at first—as they become more skilful, they re-
ceive more. The average payment is $5 a week. They have one
woman who has been at the business six years, and earns $8 a
week. Another manufacturer told me chain making is not unhealthy. It requires a year to learn to do polishing well, and
during that time a learner can earn only from $1.75 to $2 a week.
While polishing at a lathe, workers stand. Men do most polishing now. They do it by machinery propelled by steam, and one
man can accomplish as much in a day as a woman by a treadle
lathe can do in two weeks. Manufacturers in Providence write
me, " their girls, from six to fifteen in number, work at home, and
are paid by the piece. They earn $1 a day of ten hours on an

average. They do not employ men in that department of the business. It requires men five years to learn the business—females to solder, thirty days. Good eyesight is necessary. The business will probably increase with growth of country and increase of wealth. Spring and fall are the most busy seasons. They are all American." Some manufacturer in New York writes: " The work is not more unhealthy than any other so sedentary. It is generally paid for by the piece, the workers earning from $2 to $8 per week. The men average from $10 to $12. Men spend seven years learning—girls, one. Quickness of motion, perseverance, and attention are desirable qualities. The prospect for work in future is moderate. The busy seasons are spring and fall. In July, August, January, and February, the women are employed. We have from thirty to forty females, because the work is light."

251. Watch Jewels. I called on a Swiss lady who sets jewels in watches. She supports her family by it, but complains of a scarcity of work, because watchmakers can import their jewels at four shillings a dozen from Switzerland, and set them themselves.

----••·-----

MISCELLANEOUS WORK.

252. Indian Goods. Any one that has ever visited Niagara, knows something of the immense quantity of Indian goods offered for sale. Moccasons and reticules (made of buckskin, and ornamented with beads), pincushions, baskets, &c. (made of birchwood, and ornamented with figures and flowers of party-colored porcupine quills), can be had. Fans of feathers and a thousand little fancy articles may be bought in a dozen different shapes at Niagara. The Indians make most of them, but quite a number are made by fairer hands. The duty on goods purchased in Her Majesty's realm, and brought into the States, is ten per cent. So, if a person is careful of his purse, or disposed to encourage home manufactures, he had as well purchase on the American side. On most of the steamboats and cars of the Western waters, while in port or at the depot, genuine Indian women may be seen, with (we suppose) genuine Indian articles for sale.

253. Inkstands. Manufacturers of inkstands in Connecticut write: " We employ from twelve to fifteen American women in painting, varnishing, and bronzing inkstands, and pay from fifty to sixty cents per day of ten hours. Females do not perform the same kind of labor that the males do. The wages of women are less, because there is a surplus in consequence of there being so little diversity in female employment. The occupation is learned in from one to two years. That part done by females may be learned in one month. They are paid while learning. Some mechanical ingenuity is required. The business will depend on general commercial prosperity. Summer and fall are the most busy seasons. No cessation of employment during the year. The other parts of the work are too laborious for women. Our location is preferable, as we have water power and are convenient to market. Board, $1.75 per week."

254. Lithoconia, or artificial stone, is being used as a substitute for terra cotta, papier-maché, &c. It is composed of mineral substances, and is insoluble in water. It is used for making photograph frames, busts, and statuary, and for architectural purposes. It is made in Roxbury, Mass. The proprietor and inventor writes: "I employ fourteen women in manufacturing and finishing lithoconia photograph frames. Their wages average $5 a week, ten hours a day. Some are paid by the piece, and some by the day. Men earn from $1 to $2 per day. Women learn in from one to four weeks. Cultivation of the eye and finger, and great neatness are desirable in a learner. Girls accustomed to drawing or fine needle work answer well. The prospect of more work is good. My women work the year round. Women, I think, are more reliable than men; that is, if told to do a work in a certain way, they will do it. Men are more apt to experiment in a new business. Women might be employed in gilding the frames. We have twelve men in New York doing that for us now. My girls pay from $1.75 to $2 per week for board. I hear no complaint of their houses; but, judging from my Scotch experience, the accommodations in Scotland are far superior in an intellectual point of view; but so far as pies and doughnuts go, American boarding houses have the advantage."

255. Marble Workers. The rough parts of marble working are wet, dirty, and laborious, but not the finishing. Constant standing on the feet, and having the hands wet much of the time, would not do for very delicate females. A marble worker writes: "Sawing marble is heavy and wet work, and performed in the night as well as the day. I do not see that women could be employed at it to any advantage." Theodore Parker mentioned seeing a woman, in a marble yard in Paris, sawing marble. I have been told that in Italy whole families engage in chiselling the beautiful marble ornaments brought to this country. "As a stone cutter, Charlotte Rebecca Schild, of Hanau, worked

11*

in Paris. Miss McD. told me that she got situations for two girls with a marble cutter in Hollidaysburg to do the fine part of marble chiselling.

256. Mineral Door Knobs. Manufacturers of mineral door knobs write: "We have women to make mineral door knobs, and to pack locks. They are paid by the piece, and average $5 per week. They work from nine to ten hours a day. It requires six months to learn. The prospect for further employment is small. Seasons make no difference in the work. We find men better adapted to the work. Our business affords little or no opportunity for the employment of women to advantage. We have about two hundred women in busy seasons. When men and women are employed in the same department, they talk too much."

257. Paper Cutters. We read in "Women Artists" of a Dutch lady, "Joanna Koertin Block, who produced from paper very beautiful cuttings. All that the engraver accomplishes with the burin, she was able to do with the scissors. Country scenes, marine views, animals, flowers, with portraits of perfect resemblance, she executed in a marvellous manner." "Mrs. Dards opened a new exhibition with flower paintings in the richest colors. They were exact imitations of nature, done with fish bones."

258. Papier-Maché Finishers. Papier-maché is made of paper ground into a pulp, and bleached if necessary. It is moulded into various forms. It has been cast into figures of life size. It is made into mouldings for the ornamental parts of bronzes. It is lighter, more lasting, and less brittle than plaster. It can be colored or gilt. Another article of the same name is made by gluing and pressing together, very powerfully, sheets of prepared paper until they acquire the thickness of pasteboard. They must be shaped while moist into the articles desired. When dry, they will be very hard and firm. They must be covered with japan, or other varnish, and may be beautifully painted with flowers, birds, landscapes, &c. Workboxes, portfolios, waiters, miniature cases, clock faces, and many other beautiful articles may be made of it. The varnishing, painting, and inlaying is done by women in the factories of England. Papier-maché manufacturers in Boston write: "We employ women in pressing and painting. The work is healthy. We pay $4 per week of ten hours a day. Men and women do not perform the same kind of work. We pay learners $2.50 the first month, $3 the second, $3.50 the third, and $4 afterward. The prospect of future employment is good. We find women have not a mechanical eye. Board, $2 per week."

259. Pipes. Meerschaum means " foam of the sea." The pipes are made from earth found in the island of Samos. They are light, porous, and not easily broken. Some pipes are sold as genuine that are made from the clay left after forming and cutting the real pipes, but are of an inferior quality. A manufacturer of meerschaum pipes told me he employs a woman to polish the pipes. It is done by hand. She is paid $1.25 a dozen, and can do two or three dozen a day, but they have not enough of work to give her more than a dozen a week. A maker of white clay pipes told me : " The clay is brought from England. Nimbleness of fingers is most that is required for success. There is not much of that kind of work done now in our country, because pipes are imported from Germany for what the labor costs here. They are retailed at one penny apiece. Women used to make them here, and do now in European countries. They can do all parts of the work. Putting them in the furnace and baking them is warm work, but not more so than any other baking. The work is paid for according to the number of pipes made. A woman can earn about fifty cents a day for moulding, yet a man can earn $5 a day, because he can mould faster, and also attend the furnace." Besides, the man owns the tools and furnace, which do not cost a great deal, and I suppose would last a lifetime. We have seen it stated that white clay smoking pipes are made in Philadelphia by one person, who recently sent to England to procure additional assistance.

260. Porcelain. Porcelain partakes of the nature of both earthenware and glass. It is a connecting link between the two. Few men are willing to run the risk of establishing porcelain and china-ware manufactories in this country, for they have nearly all proved failures. The porcelain of China and Japan is harder and more durable than that manufactured in Europe, but in beauty of form and elegance of design the European excels. Our best articles of household ware are mostly from England, those of an ornamental kind from France. Much of the work in a porcelain factory could be done by women, such as cutting the porcelain with wires, moulding the articles with a press, and washing them over with dissolved porcelain to produce a gloss. They could also bake them. Some do decorate and burnish them. (See China Decorators.) Women and children are employed in Cornwall, England, in preparing clay from china stone to be used by porcelain manufacturers, paper makers, and calico dressers. Miss B. told me that much of the fine lacework seen on Dresden china is executed by women. It is very beautiful and delicate. At Greenpoint, L. I., the proprietor once employed girls, but now employs boys in preference. The men earn about $10 a week on an average for their work, being paid by the piece. The best of materials for making porcelain are found in this country, particularly in New Hampshire, where porcelain, parian, and enamel flint are manufactured. Porcelain earths are also found at Wilmington, Del., near Philadelphia, and in Alabama and Texas.

261. Pottery and Earthenware. "In Africa, in the manufacture of common earthen vessels for domestic use, the women are as skilful as the men." In the making of stone and earthenware, women could, if properly instructed, perform most of the processes : those of throwing, turning, attaching handles, &c. Pressing might perhaps tax their strength, and burning prove rather warm work. In Germany, where the finer clay is used, women tramp the clay with their feet, and cut it with wires to remove any small stones it may contain. One of the disagreeable parts that fall to women in the potteries of Great Britain is that of washing and straining the clay. For turning large articles it requires men of a peculiar make. They must be tall and have long arms, to enable them to reach to the bottom of the vessels as they are being turned. Small articles made by the hand are stronger than those formed by pressing. The construction and management of wheels differ in Germany, England, and the United States. The materials for making earthenware are obtained in almost every part of the globe. At an earthenware factory I was told they pay $2.50 a week to a boy the first year he is learning, and increase that according to ability and industry. Flower pots are paid for by the piece, and a man can earn from $1.50 to $5 a day. At C. & M.'s factory I saw girls and women at work. Some were treading the lathe. It was done with the right foot only, and must be very fatiguing. I noticed the hoops of the girls were very much in the way. The girls receive one third as much as the men working at the wheels, which is generally $3 a week for the girls. A woman cutting claws of the clay with a hand press, told me she is paid by the piece, and can earn about $4 a week. She can sit while at work. It requires strength of hand. In another room girls were cutting clay with a wire, kneading with the hand, and giving it to the potter, and, when the vessel is turned, taking it off the wheel and placing it on a board to be baked. They are paid fifty cents a day. In another room a woman was employed dressing the ware, that is, selecting any that is imperfect and removing any surplus clay that may have been accidentally left on, and setting aside any too defective for sale. She receives about $3 a week. The proprietors have been thinking of getting girls in place of some of the boys who are wild and difficult to manage. A firm in East Boston write : " We employ four girls, paying $3.50 a week. Girls are more generally employed in the old countries at potteries than in this, but women will eventually be more employed here in that way. Pottery is now in its infancy in this country. My girls work ten hours. The employment is not unhealthy. My girls are all English. We employ them to do light work only, that boys would do, if we had no women. Board, $2.50. We employ them all the year. Spring and fall are the best seasons for work. We hope to live to see the time when we shall have twenty women and four men, instead of *vice versa*, as they are more steady and less expensive."

262. Stucco Work. "Women are not employed at this trade in this country; in England there are some instances, but rarely. It is not unhealthy. The time spent in learning depends altogether on the taste and natural talent of the learner. Boys generally serve from three to five years. For ordinary work the qualifications need not be of a very high order; but for moulding, &c., a knowledge of drawing is essentially necessary. Summer and fall are the best seasons for this work. Ten hours a day are the usual number. Women may be employed at trimming and cleaning ornaments—also at making moulds for casting the same." Rosina Pflauder, in Salzburg, assisted her husband in stucco work.

263. Terra Cotta. The list of articles made of this substance is comprised under two heads, vases and garden pots, and ornaments for architecture. A Gothic church was built of it in 1842 at Lever Bridge, England. The pulpit, reading desk, benches, organ screen, and the whole of the decorations were made of terra cotta. In the making of figures, women could do all except moulding. The finishing up would be suitable and pretty work for them. "Mlle. de Faveau has been peculiarly successful in her adaptation of terra cotta to artistic purposes."

264. Transferrers on Wood. We do not know whether a distinct class of people engage in this business, or whether it is considered a branch of cabinet work. It is a light, pleasant business, and if there is sufficient demand for it, women would do well to engage in it.

GLASS MANUFACTURERS.

265. Glass Manufacture. All the materials for making good glass exist in the United States, and a great deal of glassware is made from them. The largest manufactures are in different parts of Massachusetts and in Pittsburg. The best glass for windows and mirrors is imported. I think glass making is not altogether suitable for women on account of the great heat, and necessity there would be for mixing with men, and men there must be. Yet it need not be so in all departments. Of the different kinds of ornamental window glass are enamelled, embossed, etched, painted, white, and colored. At a glass factory in Greenpoint, I saw some girls employed in breaking off the rough edges of mustard cruets, cementing the metal tops on, wiping them clean, and wrapping them up. They also cemented the tops on glass lamps. Occasionally they are employed to tramp with their feet and knead with their hands the English clay of which the vessels are made for holding the materials that are fused to form glass. In a factory I saw a girl washing glass, for which she is paid $3 a week—a day of ten hours. Two others were tying up glass, and were paid $4 a week of ten hours a day. At one factory in the East, they employ some girls to do the rough grinding, making stoppers for bottles, &c. People who silver mirrors are very seriously affected by the fumes of mercury, and more by the touch of the substance. A trembling disease is produced, which carries off its victims early in life. In France, some women are employed in this work. In blowing, moulding, and pressing glass, women of strong lungs and ability to sustain great heat could be employed. Casting glass requires greater physical strength than generally falls to the lot of women. A glass-bottle manufacturer in Stoddard, N. H., writes: " I employ twelve women willowing demijohns. They are paid by the piece, and can make about $3 per week, and board themselves. Men and women are paid the same. The work can be learned in from four to five weeks. They are paid at the same rate while learning. Half are Americans. Price of board here, $1.25." The Bay State Glass Co. " employ seventeen women for selecting and papering ware. They are paid by the week, from $3 to $5. It requires from one week to one month to learn. The prospect for employment depends somewhat upon the secession movement. The women are employed the year round, and work ten hours a day. Board, $1.50 to $2 a week." The Suffolk Glass Co. inform us they "employ one girl in capping lamps, &c. The work affords plenty of air and exercise. Their girl is paid by the day, and earns $4 a week, working ten hours a day. The work done by women could not be given to men. The reason they employ a woman is that women are employed by others for the same work. Men could accomplish much more in their work, but not enough to pay the difference in their wages. Boys are sometimes employed for such work. Women receive $2 while learning. Spring and fall are the busy seasons, but work is furnished all the year:

Board, $2 to $2.50." The Union Glass Co., Boston, write: "We employ women in assorting the different qualities of ware, in cementing glass and brass parts together, and in cleaning glass. Their average pay is $3.50 per week, ten hours a day. There is no comparison in the prices of male and female labor, as they do not perform the same kind. The laws of supply and demand regulate pay, excepting that very valuable women get twenty-five to fifty per cent. extra pay. Men spend from seven years to a lifetime learning the business—women a year or so to learn the best paid kind of labor. There is little chance of women rising above $5 per week, as they perform only a certain department of labor. There is generally constant employment to good hands all the year. We employ fifteen, because it is customary and found expedient. Men can be employed at a better profit in other departments. Remuneration twenty-five to fifty per cent. less than men would require. The glass manufacture is carried on chiefly in the New England and Middle States."

266. Blowers. I called in a factory where men were blowing glass bells to color and gild for Christmas trees. The man, a German, said in Germany women make them. The women there earn fifty cents a week at it, while men earn $2, though they do the work no better, and no more of it. There a person can live as well on $3 a week as on $10 here.

267. Beads. Beads are made to a limited extent in this country, but nearly all are of French or German manufacture. Some cheap beads are made of potato and colored, and some made in imitation of coral. E. employs girls to make baskets, head-dresses, &c., of beads. They cannot earn more than $2.50 a week of ten hours a day. He has most of it done in winter. Another gentleman, who has beads made into bracelets, necklaces, &c., gives the work mostly to married ladies, who do it in their leisure hours, and to school girls. They do so, because they can get it done more cheaply than if they employed those who do it to earn a living. They pay for such work by the gross, and a person could not earn over $3 a week at it. Putting the necklaces on cards is done by some ladies they employ by the week. Spring and winter are the busy seasons. The importation and selling of beads have formed quite a business in New York for some years. G. judges from the appearance of the applicants whether they are to be trusted with materials, takes an account of the kind and quantity given, and the address of the applicant, requiring them to be returned in a week's time. B. has children's coral bracelets and armlets made up, for which he employs two English girls, who each earn $1 a day at their work.

268. Cutters or Grinders. It requires strength, firmness of nerve, and cultivation of eye to grind glass. One man told me he spent seven years learning the business in England. In this country, apprentices seldom spend more than three or four years at it, but do not of course learn it so thoroughly. A glass cutter told me that two girls, daughters of his boss in Jersey City, made drops for chandeliers. They were ground on a lapidary's wheel. As drops are no longer fashionable, they are not made. They also cut stones for breastpins. Glass cutters in New York earn from $9 to $10 per week. Glass cutting could be done by women. No women in this country have yet engaged in it. It is not very neat work, as the wet sand will of course get over the clothes. The number of straps and wheels is very numerous, and if any women desire to engage in it, we would advise them to lay aside hoops and don the Bloomer costume. Grinding is tiresome to the lower limbs, which are kept in motion, like a person operating on a sewing machine. It requires taste and ingenuity, as the figures of an experienced workman must be made by the eye, no pattern being used. Apprentices usually receive $2 a week the first year, $3 the next, $4 the next, and so on.

269. Embossers. In preparing gas and lamp globes to emboss, they are first covered with a dark-colored substance. Girls then trace figures on them with a chemical which corrodes the glass. The tracing is learned in a few hours, and could be done without much practice. At a glass factory, I saw a girl who received $2 a week for tracing. Those who have worked at it for some time become very expeditious, and do piece work. They receive fifty cents a dozen, and a fast hand can do two dozen a day. The operatives work nine hours.

270. Enamellers. A glass stainer and enameller in Utica writes: " In reply to your circular, I give what information I can. My daughters assist me in staining and enamelling glass. Their wages are worth from $5 to $8 each. Learners are paid from $2 to $4. To learn the work requires from three to five years. Spring and fall are the most busy times. The business will increase. I consider eight hours a day long enough for women to spend at this kind of work, as they have to be on their feet most of the time, but men can work ten hours. All parts are suitable for women except drawing (?) and the heavy parts of the work." A large manufacturer of enamelled glass told me that in England hundreds of women are employed in enamelling glass. He employs a number in Newark, N. J., paying by the week from $4 to $5. He thinks it not more unhealthy than working in any other paint. He thinks the opinion existing that the business is prejudicial to health, arises mostly from the girls being so very careless of themselves. One should be as careful in that work as in any other. He said he knew girls working at it in England for eighteen years, who never suffered any bad effects from it. It requires but a short time to learn to put the enamel on, but some time to acquire proficiency. He and his partner expect to increase the manufacture of it, but think of using a machine that will do away with women's work in applying the enamel. He complained that their girls lacked promptness. They keep them employed all the year. They work nine hours in summer, and eight in winter. He thinks a few women with artistic taste might learn etching, and execute their own designs. He would be willing to pay a good lady designer $8 or $10 a week—yet he pays his men for that work from $12 to $15. (!!!) He thinks, in a factory, a lady so employed would find it most pleasant to have a separate apartment. My opinion is that one or two lady designers and a few enamellers might find employment in this line. M. says enamelling is very deleterious. The enamel is made of three fourths lead and a fine sand, with a small quantity of tin. It is of a softer nature than glass, and is applied with stencil plates and brushes. As the enamel dries a dust arises, which is inhaled, and is more or less injurious to the lungs, producing something like the painter's colic. It also affects the eyes some. A glass stainer in Boston, who employs some women to enamel, writes "he pays them by the day, and they earn from $4 to $6 per week. They receive as much as men would for the same class of work. It requires but a few days to learn enamelling; eight or nine years for glass staining. He sometimes pays part or two thirds wages to learners. The prospect for future employment is uncertain, as little of the above work is done in this country. To get near the materials is an item in selecting a location."

271. Engravers. An engraver on glass told me there are only from ten to thirteen glass engravers in New York. In Bohemia, whole families engrave glass; and women do so in other parts of Europe also. A good glass engraver is paid $3 a day.

272. Painters. Painting on glass was practised by nuns and monks some ages back. H. said he used to employ ladies to paint on glass. His wife would give instruction in painting and transferring on glass, for $20—$10 to be paid on entering, the other $10 when the learner feels that she is thorough. To paint on glass, one must understand colors, as opaque paints would not answer. One must have some knowledge of shades to attain excellency in decorative painting. Embellished glass is cheaper than stained glass, and does not require a furnace; yet if burned, has the pigment rendered more durable. In England, many wealthy ladies buy traced glass and paints, and color and shade it. Pictures transferred on glass can be finely finished up and burnt. Painted glass is more brilliant than stained. H. thinks to learn the art is a safe investment. He thought a few ladies might learn painting and transferring on glass, Grecian painting, and wax flowers, and turn it to account by travelling through the country, stopping in small towns, exhibiting and selling specimens and giving instruction. Painting glass need not be merely a source of amusement, but prove an art of utility. H. spoke of some people as speculators—not practitioners in the art (such I would say he would make of ladies). He thinks, among connections and at fairs a lady might meet with ready sale for painted glass. The pieces could be framed to hang at a window or place on a table. Painted glass is less costly than stained glass. A glass gilder can easily earn $2 a day. Women can do the filling in with very little instruction. It would probably take several months' practice to learn to form the letters perfectly.

273. Stainers. Stained glass is now generally used for churches, and to some extent for dwellings. The Germans are the most successful in staining glass. There are two kinds of stained glass—the pot metal, the coloring substances of which are fused in the glass and then burnt. The pictures of the other kind are formed of small pieces, each one painted separately, burnt, and united with blacklead. Frequently a window is formed of hundreds of these pieces. A picture of stained glass looks on the right side like a rich oil painting on canvas. I have been told there are 18,000 shades of stained glass. G. charges $6 a square foot for stained glass of a fine kind. There is a lady in England, that fills large orders for the stained glass windows of churches and cathedrals. Madame Bodichon writes as follows of a convent of Carmelite nuns she visited at Mans, France: "By the direction of the sisters, glass windows of all sorts, and in every stage of progress, were shown to us by an intelligent young man—one of the artists in the employ of the convent. He told us there were twenty-seven employés, two of them German artists; but the sisters arrange everything, carry on all the immense correspondence, and execute orders not only for France, but for America, Rome, and England, and other countries. Three of the nuns are occupied in painting upon glass themselves, but the principal part of the work is done by the artists, under the direction of the ladies." It requires a person of artistic skill and taste to excel in staining glass, and the work is best appreciated by people acquainted with art. It would require at least three or four years to learn the art well. A knowledge of other styles of painting is not of much assistance.

The paint must be put on very thickly, but very evenly. There seems to be a combination of arts in the business to one who performs all the parts. A man must be enough of a glazier to cut glass, enough of a chemist to understand the colors to be used and the length of time the glass should be exposed to heat, enough of a designer to prepare his own patterns, and enough of an artist to color with taste. A man can earn at least $18 or $20 a week, who is proficient in the art. The business has increased greatly during the last few years in the United States, and is continuing to increase. Much of the stained glass used in the United States is of home manufacture. The designs for stained glass are usually made by the proprietor of an establishment. Skill in drawing is very desirable for any one working at the business. The art is one that affords exercise for inventive talent, artistic skill, and good taste. In a few glass-staining establishments, girls do the tracing. It requires an apprenticeship of four years to learn the grinding, enamelling, and staining of glass. A boy is usually paid $1.50 a week the first year, but he is expected to grind colors, clean brushes, go errands, &c. An employer informed me he pays from $1 to $3 a day to men for staining glass. S. spent about seven years in England learning the business. He painted a window not long ago for $5,000. He does his own designing. He says it would not pay to have separate designers. He is acquainted with some secret in coloring, that he would not impart for a great deal. Great progress has been made in the art in this country during the last few years. It requires more skill than painting on canvas.

274. Watch Crystals. M. told us there are two kinds of watch crystals made in this country the English and Dutch. The English are the best. The Dutch make them in a cheaper way. Men bend, cut out, and clip them. Females grind the edges. The Dutch can be known from the English by a more sudden rounding near the edges, while the English round from the centre equally. In Williamsburg, German women can be seen at work in watch crystal factories. B. told me he used to "employ girls to grind and polish glasses. They were paid $3 a week—ten hours a day. It requires but two or three weeks to learn, and during that time they are not paid, because of the time lost in giving instruction and the material wasted. Now it is all done by Germans, and Americans need not expect to get in." V. confirmed the statement. He says it is mostly done by German families, and the women that are hired are never paid over $3 a week. It is light and steady work, and they are employed all the year, and do not work in the same apartment as men. In some of the factories of Europe, from one hundred to one hundred and fifty women are employed.

CHINA DECORATORS.

275. China Decorators. We find that in France, some years back, many females earned a livelihood by painting on porcelain. During the last century, a Madame Gerard, "who possessed a large fortune, had a hotel furnished with facilities for painting Sevres. Her splendid cupboards of polished mahogany were gilded and bronzed, and their contents looked like a rich collection for the gratification of taste rather than for sale. She purchased some pieces for sixty and eighty louis d'ors. A pair of vases, not very large, painted with sacred subjects, sold for 26,000 livres." "There are two distinct methods of painting in use for china and earthenware : one is transferred to the bisque, and is the method by which the ordinary painted ware is produced; and the other transferred on the glaze." In the former process, women called transferrers and cutters are employed. The cutter trims away the superfluous paper around the pattern, which the transferrer applies to the ware, and rubs with flannel to produce an impression. She then washes the paper off, and the ware is ready for the hardening kiln. Women are excluded from that department termed ground laying, though, from the care and lightness of touch required, it is very suitable. In Staffordshire, E., great opposition was made some years back to women becoming decorators, and even now they are not permitted to use a hand rest. In France, and to a limited extent in England, decorating, gilding, and burnishing are done by women. This is probably one reason that imported China is cheaper. Most of those in France and England who attain respectable skill in decorating, are the wives or daughters of working manufacturers. Besides the mechanical skill, it requires a very exact knowledge of the effects of the coloring matters employed, as they are much changed by being burnt. Decorating is certainly a beautiful employment for women, but few in this country have the opportunity and are willing to apply themselves long enough to learn the art. At K.'s china warerooms, Philadelphia, I was told, no establishments of any size in the United States are engaged in the decoration of china, because they can get it done more cheaply in England and France. K. employs Englishmen to do what decorating he wishes to have done. He employs women to burnish. The following contradictory statement I found in the " Manufactures of Philadelphia :" " Decorating porcelain and china ware, which had been imported plain, is done in one establishment in Philadelphia to an amount exceeding

$75,000 per annum." At H.'s, New York, I saw women burnishing china. It is merely a mechanical operation, consisting in rubbing the gilding with agate, after being burnt. The girls earn from $3.50 to $4.00 a week. It requires care and physical strength. One girl was cleaning superfluous paint off the china. Women might learn to make impressions for letters, flowers, and other patterns. I saw an English lady in New York decorating china. A lady took lessons of either her or her husband, to teach in the school of design. S. employs one woman for painting, and fifteen for burnishing china. China decorating is usually paid for by the piece. Mixing the colors for china painting is not more unhealthy than mixing them for canvas, and putting them on not more so than any other sedentary occupation. A French decorator told me that in Paris he gave private instruction to some ladies who learned it for a pastime, and a few who made a business of it. Boston, New York, Philadelphia, and New Orleans are the only places where china is painted in the United States. L. thinks a person of taste and abilities could learn in one year, earning nothing during the time, and after that earn from $5 to $10 a week. He pays his burnishers $3 a week. Another decorator told me he pays his burnishers (girls) from $2 to $2.50 a week. The foreman of a large establishment in New York told me that it requires several years to learn to decorate perfectly. Most decorators design their own patterns, and usually earn $12 a week. He says, in busy seasons it is difficult to get enough of good burnishers. His girls work only in daylight, and earn from $3 to $5 a week. They are busy all the year—most so three months before New Year. It requires three months' practice to become a good burnisher. A learner receives $1 a week from the time she commences to learn burnishing: he thinks it is not hard on the eyes. The work is paid for by the piece. If there was a higher protective duty, more decorating would be done in the United States.

LEATHER.

276. Leather. A leather dresser, somewhere in New York State, writes: "Leather dressing is a disagreeable, wet business, fit only for men. After leather is dressed, all the other work can be done by women. We cut by measure and by pattern.

A person cutting and making should earn one hundred per cent. Women can cut, make, and sell as well as men, I suppose even better."

277. Currying. The currying of skins might be done by women. Cutting it of the desired thickness, soaking it in water, and working it with a small stone, cleaning it with a brush, and, in the drying shed, applying oil and tallow, would not require very long practice for one of any mechanical talent. The skin is softened by being doubled and washed with a grooved board. It is then carefully shaved, and worked again, after which it is blackened and grained. The work would require some strength, but not more than the ordinary process of washing clothes. All the work must be performed standing. The process of converting the skins of sheep, lambs, and kids into soft leather, is called tawing, and is somewhat lighter work than currying; yet the leather requires much stretching and rubbing. I am sure the work would not be more, if so offensive, as morocco sewing.

278. Harness. A harness maker told me that a lady who stitches harness of the best quality, can earn from $1.25 to $1.50 a day. He pays $1 a set for stitching the blinds. The perforations are made by a man, and they are stitched by hand. Not a great many are engaged in it, and he thinks the prospect good of learners obtaining employment. Many earn $6 or $7 a week. He employs two women all the year. A person that can sew well, can learn in two or three weeks. It requires some instruction. A maker of horse collars told me his women stitch collars by machine; formerly by hand. He pays six cents a pair. The wife of one of his workmen stitches twelve an hour, with one of Howe's machines. B. employs from fifty to seventy-five girls to make fancy harness, horse blankets, and coach tassels. Fancy bridles he has stitched by Singer's machine. Good operators can earn from $5 to $7 a week, and for leather work are paid by the week. Spring and fall are the most busy seasons. The fashions of fancy leather work change. One gentleman, who employs many girls in making harness trimmings, says the cloth pieces are made by hand, the leather by machinery. In Newark, Bridgeport, and New Haven, much of the stitching for the South is done by machines, and women are employed. The English harness is considered the best, and is done by hand. In England, men called "bridle cutters" get large quantities of bridles to make up, and employ from one hundred to two hundred girls to do the stitching. A lady who has quite an establishment in New York, and employs a number of work people, told me that she pays them each from $2 to $6 a week. She thinks machine operating is trying on the health, but not so bad as sewing with a needle. She pays by the week. Women do as well as men, except for heavy work. The trade can be learned in a few weeks. She pays learners something. Her hands have work all the year, but are most busy from October till the end of December. They work ten hours. She prefers men for most of the work. She would like American women, but cannot get them. She says girls think more of having a beau than laying up a few dollars in a bank, and consequently spend all they make on dress. A manufacturer writes: "Working on leather is considered very healthy. I employ thirteen women in the manufacture of fancy bridles, riding and driving reins, riding martingales, &c. They average $1 per day. Three of them run stitching machines. All are paid by the piece, except one, who does the overseeing and writing. We think the girls receive as good pay as the men. Considerable practice is necessary to do the work well. Learners are paid for all work that is sufficiently well done to be salable. Good judgment, accurate eye, and nimble fingers, best fit one for the occupation. As our business is wholesale, it depends upon orders. Spring and fall are the most busy seasons. Sometimes the women are entirely out of work for a short time in winter. They never work over ten hours. We will not employ foreigners."

279. Jewel and Instrument Cases. At a manufactory, I was told they employ some girls, paying by the piece. The girls can earn $4.50 to $5 a week, of ten hours a day. It does not require long to learn. In busy seasons it is difficult to get good hands, and they have to advertise frequently. At another place, the proprietor told me he used to employ girls who earned $4 or $5 a week, but he prefers boys, because they can do all parts of the work. At a manufactory of morocco and velvet jewel cases, the man told me he pays girls $4.50 and $5 a week, of ten hours a day. In busy seasons it is difficult to get good hands.

280. Morocco Sewers. At a morocco manufactory, I was told by the proprietor, a German, that he employs girls, paying twelve cents a dozen, and they can sew from five to twelve dozen a day. He wants hands, and of course would speak favorably of the occupation. He says they can have work all the year except one or two weeks. At an American manufacturer's, I was told it is wet, dirty work, and requires considerable time and practice to learn to do it quickly. After working at it constantly four or five years, a good hand may be able to earn from $5 to $7 a week. Most of it is done in the families of tanners. Some women undertake it, but give it up because they do it so slowly it will not pay. The man said nearly or quite all who work at it are Germans, and the wives and daughters of those in the business. They are paid twelve cents a dozen. The occupation he thinks is full in New York, for women. Beginners are apt to hurt their fingers, as needles are used, the sides of which are triangular. Sewing five skins a day is considered very good work. Dr. Wynne says: "Exhalations from animal substances, which are very offensive to the senses, more especially to that of smell, not only appear to be in most instances innoxious, but often of absolute advantage in affording a protection from disease." Most morocco is made in Philadelphia, none South or West. S. employs sixteen women, and pays good hands from $4 to $5 per week. He thinks there are at least two hundred morocco sewers in Philadelphia. It does not take long to learn. He pays from the first. They have work all the year, but the prospect for learners is poor. At A.'s, Philadelphia, I saw some women sewing up goat skins, which were to be tanned. It is extremely disagreeable work, as the skins are wet and smell offensively. The women are paid twelve cents a dozen, and find their own thread. A steady hand can earn from $3.50 to $6 a week, and can always find work. They are most busy in spring and fall. A morocco dresser writes: " He pays by the piece, and his women each earn about seventy-five cents a day. A woman can learn in two or three weeks. The prospect for future employment is very poor, as skins are mostly tanned now without sewing. A location must always be had where pure water is abundant."

281. Pocket Books. One man told me he employs a woman to make portemonaies, paying $5 a week. On Broadway a firm employs four or five women, paying from $3 to $6 a week. It requires but two or three months to learn the business. The women sew with a machine, paste morocco on, and varnish some parts. C. pays his girls from $3.50 to $4 a week. At another place one of the firm told me their girls earn $3, $4, and $5 a week. It is piece work, and requires but three or four weeks to learn. A smart girl can earn $2 the first week. The busy seasons are spring and fall. They find it difficult to get enough good hands in those seasons. The business is mostly confined to New York and Philadelphia. A manufacturer in New York told me, about two hundred women are employed in making pocket books, &c., in that city. He pays $4.50 a week, but they have a certain quantity to do in that time. It requires but a short time to learn to do the stitching only (which he has done by hand), but about a year to learn to do all parts. He pays $2 a week while they are learning, and then he increases at the rate of twenty-five cents a week after a few months, and at the end of the year some are earning $3; some $3.25. Neatness in cutting and fitting the parts together is desirable. He keeps his hands

employed all the year. There is a scarcity of good hands, but
an abundance of indifferent ones. A manufacturer in Maine
writes: "We employ from eight to twelve American girls. They
are paid by the piece, and earn from $12 to $16 per month.
Boys earn about the same as girls. They are paid while learning, if the work is well done. It requires about a year to become
proficient."

282. Saddle Seats. In Philadelphia, I was told at a
large saddle store that they employ women to stitch saddles,
paying from fifty cents apiece for common ones to $1.25 for
those of a better quality. At a large saddle and harness manufactory in New York, I was told they employ women to stitch
by the machine and by hand. They are paid by the day, as there
is a variety of work, and their girls are not confined to exclusive
branches. In prosperous times their hands are employed most
of the year. Spring and fall are the best seasons for work.
There are small factories in most of the Southern and Western
cities. The hand sewers earn but $3 and $5 a week; a few operators can make $6. At S. & M.'s they employ about twenty
women in the different branches, and, when business is good, have
work all the year. It does not require long to learn. They are
paid by the week, from $3 to $4. Prospect dull. This kind of
work is mostly done in Newark.

283. Tanning. Leather can now be tanned by a chemical
process in a few days. Leather has been made so thin, and received so high a polish, that it has been used for making bonnets
in Paris. Buckskin is used for making many articles in this
country. Shoulder braces, drawers, shirts and gloves, are made
of it. A tanner writes: "I know of no country where this business exists in which females are employed, unless perhaps in some
of the smaller German States, where female service is not deemed
incompatible with the services of the ox and the horse. The
tanning business in all its departments is laborious and offensive,
and although not unhealthy, is dirty and disagreeable, requiring
a great amount of muscular power. I know of no employment
less congenial to the taste of women, or less suited to their elevation. Morocco is polished by hand, and in some places is done
by women." A tanner writes: "It requires strong and healthy
men to perform *any part* of a tanner's trade, and they do not
get very highly paid at that. The business is decidedly dirty,
and oftentimes very disagreeable, not fit for women in any particular. In order to conduct the business successfully, one needs
to be located by a good stream of water, or where it can be easily
obtained, plenty of bark, and not far from market." Among the
Cossacks, some women are employed in tanning.

12

284. Trunks. A trunk maker said he thought women could not well put the tacks in trunks, because the trunks are first put together, and are heavy lifting; but I think it could be done by them. Putting the linings in trunks could certainly be done by women. The man referred to said he thought some women are employed in a large trunk factory in Newark, because the proprietors thought they could get their work done cheaper, and he hoped they failed, because of their motive. The employment of women, he urged, cuts down men's labor, and so all labor is reduced below its worth, just as it is now in England. There a woman must neglect her home duties, to help make a living. If women, he added, were paid at the same rate as men, and so there was a fair competition, he would not object to women being employed.

285. Whips. V., of New York, says he and his partner have whips manufactured in Westfield, Mass., and some in the House of Refuge, Charlestown. Westfield is the principal manufacturing place for whips in the United States. The daughters of farmers for miles around the town braid lashes. The covers are put on the handles by machines attended by girls. That part is usually done in factories. The part called buttons is also made by girls, and done by hand. Girls can earn from $3 to $5 a week. They receive about three fourths the price paid men, because the work is not so laborious. It requires from three to nine months to learn, according to the skill of the person. They are paid what they can earn while learning. They have been able to keep their hands employed all the year, but fear they cannot this winter (1860). In 1857, there were probably but one half the working class able to obtain employment. The prospect for work in this line is better than in most others, for the whip market has increased twofold in the last ten years, and is likely to extend. The work done at home is piece work, and that done in shops is usually so. The business suffers in hard times, for people then think they can dispense with whips. V. said the Philadelphians and Yankees have different views in regard to woman's labor. The Yankees know they can get it done cheaper by women, and the Philadelphians think they cannot get it so well done by women. The American Whip Company write "they employ eighty females; about one half are American, and one half Irish. Women are employed in any department where they can labor with propriety and advantage. The prospect is that the business will always continue as good as now. All seasons answer equally well for the work. During working hours, one of the women often reads aloud for the benefit of the others in the room. Board, $2 per week." " The reason why women are employed at making whips is, the work being light, they can do as much as a man, and competition compels the employer to get his work done for the lowest wages." P. & S., in Philadelphia, employ some girls to braid lashes. It requires about six weeks to learn. Some earn $3, and some $4 a week, working from nine to ten hours, but are paid by the dozen. All their girls are Americans, as are the generality of females in this business. "In London," says Mayhew, "the cane sellers are sometimes about two hundred in number, on a fine Sunday, in the summer, and on no day are there fewer than thirty sellers of whips in the streets, and sometimes—not often—one hundred." The branch of finishing in whip making has been entered by women in Birmingham, England, and created some opposition. Sellers of large, coarse whips usually frequent market houses —those with fancy whips stand on the sidewalks.

WHALEBONE WORKERS.

286. Whalebone Workers. The natural color of whalebone is nearly the same as gray limestone rock. The black ones we buy are colored. Whalebone is exported from New York. About four hundred American vessels are employed in whaling, and about ten thousand men. Enough whalebone can be prepared in one factory to supply the whole United States, I was told by one of the proprietors of a whalebone factory. He paid a boy $2 a week for tying up whalebone for parasols and umbrellas (which work could be done by a girl). Small holes are punched by machinery in the ends of bones to be used for stays. A woman runs a thread through, and ties them in bunches. She is paid one cent a bunch, and, as she ties up five hundred or six hundred a week, earns $5 or $6. At another factory, I was told they employ girls and women in tying up some whalebones, and stringing others. They sit while at work, and are paid by the week, working ten hours a day. They keep their hands all the year, but are most busy in the fall. Tying up whalebones looks simple, but it requires practice to become expert, and requires discrimination to select the indifferent from the salable. The woman we saw earns $4.50, but she has been at it several years, and is very expert. Women seldom earn more than $3. Girls might polish the bones—a something I saw a boy doing.

BRUSH MANUFACTURERS.

287. Brush Manufacturers. Women have from the earliest period been employed in making brushes. In France, women are employed in preparing bristles for brushes, bleaching, washing, straightening, and assorting them. If they are so employed in this country it is at Lansingburg, N. Y. Indeed the finer bristles are all imported. The process of preparing bristles is simple, merely washing them and placing them in a preparation of sulphur to bleach them. " The great art in making brushes for artists is so to arrange the hairs that their ends may be made to converge to a fine point when moistened and drawn between the lips ; and it is said that females are more successful than men in preparing the small and delicate pencils." In shaving brushes the bristles must be so arranged as to form a cone. This requires skill, and commands handsome wages. A large number of bristles are imported from Germany, Russia, and a considerable quantity from France ; yet the United States furnish some. We think the owners of pork houses, and farmers in the Southern and Western States, would find the saving of bristles to justify the trouble of doing so, as they bring a good price. In this country, the process in making finer brushes, called drawing, is mostly done by women. The heavier kind of brushes is seldom made by women. Persons working in horn, wood, whalebone, ivory, gutta percha, pearl, &c., prepare the handles. Few if any brush makers have them prepared in their own establishments. I called on a brush maker whose manufactory is in Boston. The clerk says they never have any difficulty in getting plenty of good hands. They work by the piece. He says, if you advertise there, you are sure to have hundreds of applicants, many of whom are already in business, but hope to get better wages for the same amount of work, or less work for the same wages. A manufacturer told me that he employs boys, who do piecework and earn from $5 to $10 a week, but thinks he will employ girls, as he could get drawers for from $3 to $4 per week. The girls sit while at this work. H., a maker of tooth, nail, and hair brushes, told me his is the only tooth brush manufactory in the United States. His girls looked clean and orderly, and had intelligent faces. Those working in the house were of Irish extraction—those who worked at home, Americans. Most of them attend night school. H. finds his girls more careless about their work Monday morning than at any other time. He attributes it to their talking and thinking of what they saw and heard the day before. Those that sew well he finds work best for him. (I expect that principle generally holds good—those that work well in one business are likely to in another, because they are industrious and give their attention to it.) If the work is not well done, he takes it out and makes them do it over. As it is done by the piece, it of course is their own loss. They engage in trepanning, wiring, and trimming brushes. The trepanning and wiring are done altogether by women in England. They are paid by the piece. Those wiring and trepanning earn from $3 to $4. The lady that trims earns $6 a week. The work is very neat and well adapted to women. It requires about three months to learn. Women are paid something while learning. Care and nicety must be used to fill the little cavities in the brush with bristles closely and firmly. The business is not good, on account of competition in the manufacture with European countries, where labor is cheaper. Women cannot polish the ivory well, as it is done by hand and is very hard work. Women are superior in the branches pursued by them. $2.50 is the usually price paid by workwomen for board in New York. A brush maker in Philadelphia writes: " I pay from eighteen to twenty cents per thousand holes. No men employed by us in this branch. Boys spend four or five years at this trade. Girls spend six months learning one branch. The prospect for more work of this kind is poor. Our women are all Americans, and work the year round. Women are superior in their branch." P. & M. employ girls to make ostrich feather dusters, and they earn from $4 to $6 per week. They have had employment all the year. While at work the girls can sit or stand, as they please. Their girls also paint the handles. A manufacturer of ostrich feather dusters told me, he pays girls from $2 to $3 a week for coloring and putting the feathers in handles. They can always get enough of hands. The girls work in daylight only.

IVORY CUTTERS AND WORKERS.

288. Ivory Workers. Ivory is generally turned in a lathe—a machine that differs some in size and shape, according to the material worked. Ivory, wood, and metal can be cut by it into almost any shape. The ivory nut is now much used as a substitute for animal ivory. In a store for the sale of ivory goods, the lady in attendance told me some of their articles are imported from Germany, and some they have made. In Germany,

some women are employed in ivory carving. The lady thought
it could not be done to any extent in this country, because labor
is so high. (But if men can afford to do it, pray, why cannot
women?) The carving is done with steel instruments, and requires considerable strength. " Barbara Helena Lange, of Germany, earned celebrity in the seventeenth century, by engraving
on copper, and carving figures in ivory and alabaster." "Barbara Julia Preisler was skilled in various branches of art; could
model in wax, and work in ivory and alabaster, and added painting and copper engraving to the list of her accomplishments."
H. & F. have four or five girls to count and pack their ivory
goods, but none to polish. An ivory worker in Providence
writes : " Women are employed in carving and turning in Russia,
and carving in England. I can say for myself, that I have known
many women to transact the business equal to the smartest in the
trade in England, when the husband is deceased, and the widow
has been left to support a large family, and they have never failed
to do so creditably. I know of but two in this country, one in
Providence, R. I. ; the other in Westfield, Mass. They earn
from $4 to $6 a week. The labor is light for women, and they
could earn the same as men. Carving could be learned in six
months, turning in one year. To be able to superintend, two
years' practice is required. The prospect for employment is not
flattering. In this country, women work eight hours ; men, ten.
In England, France, and Scotland, they work eleven hours. In
New York, principals could employ twenty-five carvers and one
hundred turners, and I can see no objection to employing women.
Women excel in the business, if to their taste. Large cities or
manufacturing districts are the best localities. They must have
cultivated minds, or they are not suitable for the business, as it is
necessary to invent and execute new styles and patterns." In
Connecticut, some hundreds of families labor in the ivory comb
manufactories, and are paid per week $4.50, and by the piece
earn from $5 to $6 a week. An ivory turner in Essex, Conn.,
writes : " I usually employ two girls ; one packing goods, the
other on fancy turning. They earn from $10 to $20 per month.
My help consists mostly of men. The work is very healthy. It
is piece work. The girls earn $1 per day of ten hours. They
are paid by the piece, the same price as men, and earn as much.
A learner receives $1 per week and board. A woman can do
nearly as much as a man after working one year or more. The
work is very clean and easy. A girl to succeed should be active,
intelligent, and ingenious." A gentleman who has ornaments
made of vegetable ivory, told me he could hire Germans to turn
them for him at from seventy-five cents to $1 a day.

289. Combs. The comb is an article of primitive date, and has been frequently found in use among nations when first visited by civilized men. Madame de B. told me she had frequently seen women in Europe, making, mending, and polishing combs of tortoise shell, bone, and ivory. In Leominster, in 1853, 264 men were employed in the comb factory, at an average of $7 per week, board $2.50—women at an average of $3 a week, board $1.50. A firm in Lancaster, Penn., write : " We employ seven women, because they are better adapted to the work. They are paid by the week, from $2 to $3.50, and work ten hours a day. They do not perform the same kind of work as men. Boys are apprentices until twenty-one years of age—females spend but a few weeks learning. All seasons are alike. Women do the light work best. Board, $1.25." Some manufacturers of ivory combs write : " Our establishment, which has been in operation over thirty years, formerly gave employment to a large number of female operatives; but of late years, so many labor-saving machines have been introduced, that the number employed is very small. At present, less than a dozen women are engaged in our factory, while we employ some forty men. We expect all who are employed by us to work eleven hours each day, except Saturdays during the winter, when we close before sundown. Most of our girls work by the piece, and earn from 70 cents to $1 per day. To the others we pay $4 per week. The time required to learn the business varies with the character of the work—in some cases two months, in others not more than one week. The only qualifications needed are carefulness, activity, and common sense. The work is light, and not particularly unhealthy. The only reason why it should be unhealthy at all, is its sedentary nature. Board, from $1.75 to $2 per week. We have uniformly, since the commencement of our business, refused to employ any but American girls of known good moral character. There have been few or none of them that have not possessed a good common-school education, and some of them have enjoyed and well improved the advantages of such schools as those at South Hadley, Pittsfield, and New Haven. It is a source of gratification and pride to us, that we are able at present to call to mind no less than seven of our operatives who have married clergymen ; one is now a missionary at the Sandwich Islands, and numbers of them are respected and useful members of society." A manufacturer of horn or bone combs writes : " The part assigned to women is the staining and the bending or shaping of the comb. The business is healthy."

290. Piano Keys. I cannot learn of any women being employed in sawing piano keys, but I think they could do it, if

they were properly instructed, and they certainly could polish
them. The turning of the ivory in the sun to bleach is usually
performed by a boy, and occupies several hours a day. The
assorting of piano keys and putting them in small paper boxes
could certainly be performed by women, but I was told it requires
considerable experience and judgment. The sharps are made of
ebony, sawed by circular wheels moved by steam. When large
blocks have been sawed into smaller pieces, women could then
saw them into keys. It would only require care. The noise of the
machinery and the black dust flying might be disagreeable at
first. A manufacturer of piano keys writes : "No women are
employed in the piano key department of our business, and none
are employed by other manufacturers, to our knowledge. We
suppose the reason is, that most of the labor in this department
is either quite severe or dirty, wet, and unpleasant. Assorting
and matching the ivory requires so long a time to learn, that we
cannot afford to hire any person for less than two years. Girls
are generally unwilling to engage to remain so long, especially
if they are at an age when their judgment and discretion make
their services really valuable." A Massachusetts manufacturer
of piano forte, melodeon, and organ keys writes : "I employ a
lady bookkeeper, but my business in the manufacture of keys for
musical instruments is such that it requires men alone, although
the work is very light and clean."

291. Rules. The materials for rules are ivory and wood.
The prices of rules have fallen during the last few years—so
the profits are less. A rule manufacturer in Vermont writes :
"We employ women graduating rules by machinery and stamping on the figures. We pay 7 cents per hour. Women are
paid proportionately while learning. Common sense and a
slight knowledge of arithmetic are the only qualifications needed.
They work all the year, ten hours a day. All are American.
Women are quite as rapid as men, and, in application, better."
A manufacturer in Connecticut writes : "I employ but one
woman, and she takes the work home. It is paid for by the
piece. There are many parts suitable for women, but it is more
profitable to employ men. The great demand for female labor in
the domestic employments in this section of the country is becoming intolerable, on account of the general desire to obtain employment in the factories." The machines are small and easily worked,
for making lines and figures on rules. The rivets of rules might,
I think, be inserted by women. I was told, men employed in
working at rule manufacture are paid $8, and some $9 a week.
The ruler stands while at work.

PEARL WORKERS.

292. Pearl Workers. At S.'s, we saw a man grinding the outer and rougher coat off of pearl shells. It requires some strength, as it is done on a stone wheel moved by steam, the shell being kept in its place by a wooden rod held on it. It is wet and dirty work. The water is cold, too, even in winter, for warm water would soon become cold on account of the rapid motion of the wheel; and it would not do to heat the pearl, as it would cause it to split. The polishing was done on a wheel covered with leather, and could as well be done by a girl as a boy. S. had never known women to work in pearl, except to make paper cutters, and then only in Germany. The inlaying of pearl is in some places done by women. A worker in pearl writes me: "The pearl button branch is separate from the pearl shell work. In the first, females are employed; in the latter, they are not, as it is unhealthy and laborious. In Birmingham, England, where pearl buttons are almost exclusively manufactured, upward of two thousand hands are employed. Pearl buttons are made in Newark and Philadelphia." A manufacturer of pearl buttons in Philadelphia writes: "I employ women in finishing, and pay from $2 to $3 a week. It requires from one to three weeks to learn. The prospect of the business increasing is good. The work is regular, and the hours ten a day. I employ women because they are cheaper." To polish pearl buttons is very simple— merely placing the button in a pair of tongs, and holding it against three revolving wheels successively. The carving of pearl is wrist work, and S. thought women have not sufficient strength in their wrists to do it; but I think many have.

TORTOISE-SHELL WORKERS.

293. Tortoise-Shell Workers. Shell is made into clock cases, cigar cases, card cases, writing desks, and other such articles, but is most used for combs. In Brooklyn, a manufacturer of shell combs told me they had several times thought of employing women. Gutta percha and vulcanized india rubber have become, to some extent, a substitute for tortoise shell. On tortoise-shell combs the light carving might be done by women;

12*

the heavy cutting requires more strength. The sawing out of the figures is suitable for women. The finishing could also be done by them. To learn the finishing would not require a person of ordinary talent more than a week, and either of the other processes probably not more than six or eight weeks. Workers could earn from $6 to $7 a week, if they could have constant employment. The business is very dependent on fashion. P. & B. used to employ girls in rounding the teeth of shell side-combs, and paid each $4; but gutta-percha combs have done away with shell ones. A worker of shell combs told me he had employed girls, paying some by the piece and some by the week. They earned from $3 to $6 per week. It requires about six months to learn carving and sawing—polishing, not so long. Care, judgment, and a good idea of form and proportion, are necessary. The business is now very dull. The style of carving on combs is very different from that worn a few years back. It is now of a heavier kind, and the work not so suitable for women.

GUM ELASTIC MANUFACTURE.

294. Gum Elastic Manufacture. "In nearly all the manufacturing branches of this business, females are employed. After the articles are moulded, females join them; also paint the toys, pack the combs in boxes, &c. In most establishments they are employed the whole year, while some only retain a small proportion during the dull season, which is in the winter. All are paid by the piece, varying from $4 to $7 per week. They learn very quickly, and are paid for what they do as soon as they commence, although it takes six months or one year's practice to equal the best workers. The manufacturing is almost exclusively confined to the country, and, as a class, the women are in no way exceptionable, many of them being considerably cultivated. There are plenty found to learn the business, and it gives employment to several thousand." In Massachusetts, Rhode Island, Connecticut, New York, Pennsylvania, and New Jersey, 1,825 males and 1,058 females were employed, in the year ending June 1st, 1860, in making india rubber goods. I talked with one of the most extensive gum elastic manufacturers in the United States, for the purpose of gaining some idea of the number of female operatives in that department, their wages, if the occupation is unhealthy, &c. This manufacturer has realized millions from his business; and, after repeated efforts to learn how his women were paid, I succeeded in learning that those who work out of the house are paid by the piece, and earn *only* from $2 to $3 a week, working from dawn until midnight. Some worked in the establishment, going at 7.30 A. M., and working until 6 P. M., receiving about the same wages. They were employed in making suspenders. More women are employed in the shoe department than any other. The hard india rubber goods are labelled and packed by women in some manufactories; but most of the making is done by men. At a city in Western Massachusetts, ten girls were employed by one man, at an average of $2.50 each per week, to mend imperfections in india rubber goods. I went to Harlem, and was permitted with my attendant to go through the manufactory and see the process of making up a variety of india rubber goods. Some of the girls are paid by the piece, and some by the week. They earn from $4 to $6 a week. It does not require a girl of good sense more than from one to four weeks to learn. I inquired of one of the proprietors and three of the foremen, if they thought it unhealthy. The proprietor said, not; but the foremen were not very positive in their assertions. I inquired of a girl in the sewing room. She said she found it so in the cementing room, and had secured work in the sewing room on that account. She attributed it to the evaporation of the camphene, and the flying of the powder,. made of pulverized soapstone and flour. The odor, no doubt, is very disagreeable at first to most workers. One foreman said he thought it would not be well for a consumptive person to confine him or herself to that kind of work. One of the proprietors said, if a nice, genteel-looking girl comes along, they will take her as a learner, even if they do not wish a learner, that they may have good hands when they need them. They have a great many applications. They used to take learners, and permit old hands to instruct them, paying them for the time spent in doing so. They are most busy in the spring and fall, but have something to do all the year. Those in the first cementing room were working at large tables, and stood. They were paid fifteen cents for cementing the seams of a gentleman's coat, and some at that work make $1 a day of ten hours' labor. Most of the girls prefer to stand while at work. They were very neat, quiet, and good looking. In the second room we saw women making rubber cushions, small tubes, &c. One of the girls making tubes said she was paid by the hundred, and could not earn $1 a day. All in the second and third room sat. In the third room the ladies were finishing off coats, sewing in the sleeves, binding, and putting on buttons. Most india rubber factories are in New Jersey. There are none in the West or South.

295. Men's Clothing. The Rubber Clothing Company at Beverly, Mass., "employ from seventy-five to one hundred women. They report the work as being light, and therefore requiring nimble fingers. Their girls are paid both by the piece and week, and earn from $3 to $6 per week, usually working ten hours a day. One half are American. Women are paid as well as men in this branch. It requires four weeks to learn. Prospect of future work is good. Activity and intelligence are needed. The work is very easy, and is given at all seasons. Girls are usually not so steady at work as men. Board, $2 per week." The superintendent of the American Hard Rubber Company writes: "We employ ten women in making hard india rubber goods. We prefer them on account of their small fingers. It is piece work, and women are paid from $4 to $6 per week, ten hours a day. Our women could not do the work of men, who have to be mechanics, having learned a trade. Men receive about thirty-three cents more per day than women. The time required for men to learn our business it is impossible to answer. Women can learn sufficient in four weeks to earn seventy-five cents per day. Carefulness and nimble fingers are necessary. The business is new, but the prospects for the future good as could be counted upon in any ordinary business. The business is not sufficiently extended to furnish a particular set of people depending upon it with labor. Some of our women are quite intelligent and refined. There is a good library connected with the factory, and on Sunday they have ready access to church."

296. Shoes. The application of india rubber to the making of boots and shoes originated in the United States. B. & S. "employ seventy-five girls, who earn from $3 to $6 a week. They are employed all the year, and it is not unhealthy." The business has been on the decrease for two years. The treasurer of the Boston Shoe Co. informs me: "The company employ about seventy-five women, who work by the piece. The employment is not unhealthy. Average wages from seventy-five cents to $1.25 per day, of eight or ten hours. Our women earn full as much as men, in comparison with the work done. Three fourths are American. A smart girl will learn in a couple of weeks to make from fifty to seventy-five cents per day; in two or three months, she can earn full wges. The prospect of future employment is fair. The fall of the year is the most busy season. Good board, $2 per week."

297. Toys. The New York Rubber Co. write: "We employ women in making and ornamenting toys. Little of the work is done in other countries. The girls earn from $3 to $8 per week, but are paid by the piece. Men and women do not

perform the same kind of work. In a few weeks learners earn
$3; in a few months, $5 or $6. They have work at all seasons.
The work is pleasant. Board, $2."

GUTTA PERCHA MANUFACTURE.

298. Gutta Percha Manufacture. A manufacturer
of gutta-percha goods told me that the firm to which he belongs
employ twenty-five girls. One of their girls earns $1 a day,
making handles. The others close the seams of coats, and other
articles of dress, with cement. Some work by the piece, and some
by the week. When by the week, they are paid $3.50 and $4;
and those by the piece earn about the same. He thinks, if it is
unhealthy, it is because the sulphur used opens the pores and renders the person liable to take cold. I visited a gutta-percha
comb manufactory. The girls receive $2 a week, while learning.
They can learn in a few days. They polish and pack the combs.
They work ten hours a day, and receive $4. Few of them get
$4.50. The employer thinks there may be more work in that
line hereafter. A woman acquainted with machinery could superintend the machine that cuts the teeth of the comb. Rounding
the teeth is done by men, but could be performed by women. I
was told there is a manufactory at Stratton, L. I., where seventy
women are employed.

HAIR WORKERS.

299. Artists. The making of hair ornaments is a distinct branch of labor. Some very beautiful and ingenious
pieces of workmanship have been executed. Bracelets, earrings,
breastpins, and guards are the most common articles. The work
is nicely adapted to the nimble fingers of women, whether engaged in it for pastime or profit. A foreign lady, that does ornamental hair work, told me that it is a right profitable business to
one that can do it well, but American women have not patience
to learn to do it in a superior manner. A hair jeweller in Philadelphia told me he employs six girls—all Americans, and he
thinks they do better than foreigners. He pays a girl seventy-
five cents a week, for three or four weeks. By that time she has

learned enough to earn $3 or $4 a week. Formerly he required a girl to spend two years learning, and paid her nothing during the time. He mentioned one firm that required three years' apprenticeship. But the girls often became discouraged, and went at something else. Now the business is not so much of a secret. He has now and then paid as high as $12 a week, for a hand that was very ingenious and successful. They pay high for their designs. The gentleman had paid $50, the week previous, for a design. His girls all work in the establishment, and spend about nine hours at their work. It is done altogether by hand. The only disadvantage attending it is the confinement that pertains to it, or any other employment of that kind. An artist on Fifth street gives work out of the house. The average rate of wages he pays is $4 a week. Hair artists, when employed by the week, receive from $4 to $5. At S.'s, New York, they pay a good hand from $4 to $5 a week, ten hours a day. A person of good abilities can learn most of the patterns in three weeks. An ornamental hair worker told me she charges fifty cents a lesson of an hour. A lady was taking lessons who had recently married a jeweller, and was going to Louisiana to live. A good price can be got for such work in the South, for Southerners have had all such work done in the North. A German, who made very pretty ornamental hair work in New York, told me he charges from $25 to $50 for teaching the art—those that wish to learn in a short time, and so require much of his attention, pay $100. It can be very well learned in six months. He pays $10 a week to good hands. The work is the same at all seasons. Strong eyes, nimble fingers, and a clear head are the essentials for a learner.

300. Dressers. The business of a barber was performed by females among the Romans, about the time of the Christian era. I have read that there are now women barbers in Paris, Normandy, England, and Western Africa. In the reign of Louis XIV. it was not unusual for ladies of rank and wealth to dress the whiskers of their favorite friends. Both men and women are engaged in the United States in the business of dressing ladies' hair. We think women most suitable for it, and should be patronized to the exclusion of men. The business requires practice and taste. Some ladies of wealth have their dressing maids to learn the art and perform that office of the toilet. Most hair dressers charge 50 cents to $1.50 for dressing the hair. The price is regulated by the style in which it is done and the reputation of the dresser. The demands for a hair dresser are sometimes such, in a fashionable season, that a lady must have her hair dressed as early as noon, to wear to the opera at 8, or to a party at 10 P. M. Mrs. W., New York, charges 50 cents for dressing hair, 75 for shampooing and dressing, and $1 if she sends out. She never sends any one out to dress hair where she is not acquainted. She thinks there are about 200 hair dressers in New York. At an establishment in Broadway they give instruction in hair dressing—price, $1 a lesson. A person of ordinary abilities can learn to dress hair plainly in three or four lessons. C. says he thinks more women could find employment as hair dressers in New York; but I think, from the number of signs I saw, no demand can exist. He thinks it strange that they do not make engagements by the week, as they do in the cities of the old countries, where there are 200 or 300 in every large city that go out daily to the houses of their customers. I have since learned that there are some in New York that do. Mrs. G. goes out by the week, and receives $3 per week. She makes such engagements for the morning only, as she is likely to be called in the afternoon to prepare ladies for parties. From the middle of June until September she is at Saratoga. C. had a woman four years learning the styles of dressing and making up hair. The third year he paid her $4 a week, and the fourth year $5 a week. He says it requires so long to learn it that women generally get discouraged and go at something else. Women employed by the week to dress hair receive from $4 to $5. A lady told me she charges 50 cents a lesson, and a person can learn in from fourteen to twenty lessons. Two years' time is generally given to learn hair work in all its branches, weaving, mounting, &c. It takes time and capital to establish a business for one's self, as hair is a costly article. I saw one lady who teaches hair dressing for $10. A young woman told me it requires two weeks of constant practice to become a hair dresser. Nearly everything at it is done in winter. Practice makes perfect. The best plan is to get regular customers, and go to their houses every day, including Sunday, for which it is usual to charge from $1.50 a week up, for one head. She charges 50 cents a lesson. Some chambermaids at hotels take a few lessons, to enable them to dress hair plainly. For shampooing, most of which is done in summer, she charges 50 cents; for braiding front hair, 50 cents; and with the back hair, 75 cents. Miss S. told me many female hair dressers board with the family of the employer, because of being up late at night, and receive their board and $10 a month and up. For weaving hair her mother pays 6 cents per yard; for the finer kind, 12 cents per yard. Her mother earns from $1.75 to $2 per day. A person that can weave and make front pieces can get work at any time. There are only three months dull time in a city—June, July, and August. Some ladies pay a hair dresser $10 a month for dressing the hair every day but Sunday, when a separate and higher charge is made.   For dressing a bride entirely, $5 is charged.   One needs taste and ability to please; at any rate, one must be civil and obliging.   Fashionable watering places present the best openings.   Saratoga and Newport present favorable ones, at the first of which there is but one permanent hair dresser. D., hair dresser and wig maker, requires learners to be bound for four years.   The first year he gives a girl her board, lodging, washing, and $4 a month.   The next year he gives the same, with an increase of $1 a month; and so continues that increase each succeeding year until the apprenticeship expires.   He gives to journeywomen their dinner, supper, and $4 a week.   The business is not confined to regular hours, on account of hair dressing, which is done mostly in the evening.   He charges 50 cents for dressing a lady's hair at his rooms, and $1 at her house.   A Frenchman, under Fifth Avenue Hotel, pays $5 a week to a girl who receives the pay of his customers.   She is there at 8, and can leave at dark.   He charges 75 cents a head at the saloon, and at the ladies' residences the same.   He has rooms fitted up, and has many customers from the hotel.   He employs three girls, paying them one half of what they earn.   He keeps but one there constantly.   The other two live near, and when he needs their services he sends for them.   He is going to teach hair dressing, and charge $1 a lesson; forty or fifty (?) lessons are usually taken, according to the extent it is learned.   Mrs. B. told me men teach ladies wig making, but ladies give instruction mostly in hair dressing to those of their own sex.   It is usual to pay learners something after a few months' or a year's practice. Those that work for others get most to do in winter.   Those that have establishments of their own can of course work all the time. Most employers pay by the week.   Mrs. Dall has the following sentence in her " Woman's Right to Labor : " " I think there is room in Boston for an establishment from which a woman could come to a sickroom, to shave the heated head or cut the beard of the dying; a place where women's and children's wants could be attended to, without necessary contact with men."

301. Dyers. B. will want some nice women to dye ladies' hair.   Now he has it done by men.   He wants but one at first —one who has worked with hair—for instance, a lady's maid would be most suitable.   She must not be afraid to color her hands, or to work.   When not working at that, she will spend her time making wigs.   He will teach her how to do both, and, if she proves herself competent, he will give her fair wages. For two or three weeks he will board her and pay all her expenses.   Then he will pay her $5 a week.   He will take another when needed, and so increase the number as he has occasion.

He employs some women to put up hair dye and perfumery, and pays $3 a week.

302. Growers. Dr. Gardner says : " At Caen, in France, there is a market, whither young girls resort, and stand hour after hour, with their flowing hair, rich and glossy, deriving additional lustre from the contrast with their naked shoulders. This is the resort of the merchant barbers, some of whom come even from England. The merchants pass along among them, examine the color, texture, evenness, and other qualities of the beautiful fleece, haggle for a sou, and finally buy. The hair then, after being cut as closely as possible to the head, is weighed and paid for, and the girl goes home to let another suit grow out for shearing time."

303. Manufacturers. The woman at S.'s says they have constant application to receive hands, and have to turn a great many away. They have trouble to get good workers. The girls will not take time to learn to do their work perfectly. They ought to spend some years learning. At C.'s, they employ a number of women in making wigs, scalps, and toupees, who can earn from $4 to $5 a week. It requires six months to learn that branch. At another place I was told it requires but a few weeks to learn to make wigs only. Workers at it earn from $3 to $5. This branch of work is profitable. Mrs. R. told me that those who make wigs can be at work all the year, but hair dressing is mostly confined to seasons. In different stores, the wages of employées vary. It is well for a person to learn all the branches, if she has time, so that if one fails her, she can take up another. Her work is mostly done in the country—no doubt because she can get it done more cheaply. Weaving hair pays best. It is paid for by the yard, and generally done at the home of the worker. If done in the house, it is most likely to be paid for by the week, and ten—the usual number of working hours—spent at it. American women form a majority in the business. It is a good business, for a small capital, when living near the importers. It is extending West and South. A hair manufacturer in Rochester writes : " The occupation is permanent, and my employées have work at all seasons. There is a demand in many places for workers in this line." A hair manufacturer in Newburyport, Massachusetts, who has three women braiding hair for jewelry, and making wigs, pays by the day, of ten hours. They receive from $3 to $8 per week, and work the same at all seasons.

304. Merchants. Most of the hair made up in this country is bought in France and Italy. The price paid for each head of hair ranges from one to five francs, according to its weight and beauty. From one of the cyclopædias we learn, that 200,000 pounds of women's hair is annually sold in France; that the price paid for it is usually six cents an ounce." "Whether dark or light, the hair purchased by the dealer is so closely scrutinized, that he can discriminate between the German and French article by the smell alone; nay, he even claims the power, 'when his nose is in,' of distinguishing accurately between the English, the Welsh, the Irish, and the Scotch commodities."

WILLOW WARE.

305. Willow Ware. Great quantities of willow ware have been imported from France, but of late years some attention has been paid to the growing of it near Philadelphia. Our climate is said to be well adapted to its growth, and the willow raised to be of a superior quality. Willow grows in damp places. Most basket makers buy the willow, and split it themselves. All the most tasteful and elegant baskets used in this country are imported from France. Basket making is one of the principal employments engaged in by the blind. It requires some strength, but more skill and practice. A basket maker's tools can be bought for $5, and last a lifetime. On looking for women basket makers in Philadelphia, we found a German widow, who could not make herself understood in English, but my companion conversed with her in German, and learned that she had supported herself and son for six years, by making baskets for the trade. She buys the willow ready for use at seven cents a pound. She sells small round baskets, with covers and handles, at $2.25 a dozen. She looked very poor, but clean, and had evidently a room to sleep in besides the one we saw, where she works and cooks. A German woman, in New York, making small fancy baskets on blocks, told me she could earn from fifty cents to $1 per day. Her husband dyes the willow. A German woman asked me $1.50 for a basket she had paid fifty cents for making—at that rate her profits were considerable. I met a German boy with baskets, who said he could make from seventy-five cents to $1 a day by his work. His father, mother, and sisters also work at the trade. I saw a woman who merely colors willow. She could make a comfortable living at it, if she could give all her time to it; but she cannot, as she has two small children, and must give part of her time to them. In Williamsburg, I had a long talk with a basket maker. He says it is best for an apprentice to learn basket making of a practical worker who has not many hands, and who will give instruction himself. He can give the more time to his learners. He spent seven years learning the trade in England. It requires knowledge of form to make the baskets of a handsome shape. He showed me a book giving directions how to proportion baskets. He thinks a right smart person might learn the business in two years, when they could earn from $10 to $15 a week. The basket makers have a society in New York that discourages the work of women in that line, by not allowing its members to sell to any store for which a woman works. The excuse is, it throws men out of work. Yet the man told me that there are probably not more than two hundred basket makers in the United States, and that it is a good business. He has more work than he can do. (Oh, what injustice to woman!) The Dutch, he says, make baskets at a lower price than the members of the society, and consequently they are discountenanced by the members. Inexperienced or careless workers are apt to cut their hands with the willow while at work. A woman who sells baskets told me that basket making is a poor business now. A man that worked for her during the summer said that, working from early in the morning till late at night, he could not make more than $4.50 a week, and if his wife had not worked out, they could not have made a living. She says the duty on willow is high, and transporters ask any price they please, as it occupies considerable room, and does not pay very well as freight. When American supplies are brought in, it is cheaper. The women that supply her do the lighter parts of the work; and their husbands, the heavier. A willow ware manufacturer in Waterbury, Vermont, writes: "The work is light and healthy. It is paid for by the piece. Women are paid less, because they are not so strong, and can live cheaper. It requires about one year to learn the business. Learners are paid by the week, about $2. Ingenuity and some taste are needed for a basket maker. A great many women might advantageously learn the trade, if they would. They can work at it all the year. We should like to employ a few girls to learn the trade and make baskets, but have been unable to do so yet, as it is very difficult finding help enough to do housework in this vicinity." A German, who learned his trade with the basket maker of his Majesty, in Dresden, replies to a circular asking information on willow work: "Women are employed at this trade at several places in Germany. They are paid by the piece. In this country, if they are able to finish the work as well as men, they are usually paid the same wages. Coarse work can be learned in much less time than fine. It is in some places the custom to have five persons to make a basket, each doing a separate part. I think the prospects for work good. Women can make the finer work quicker than men, but men succeed best in making coarse work."

––––•••––––

WOOD WORK.

306. Carvers. The word " carver " is rather extensive in its application, being applied alike to one who cuts stone, wood, or metal. Carvers of stone and metal we treat of elsewhere. The art of carving is quite ancient. There are five kinds of wood carving : house, ship, toy, furniture, and pattern making ; to these we may add the cutting of wooden letters for ornamental signs. Pattern making is the reverse of architectural carving : the first being in bas relief ; the other, alto. Architectural carving is mostly done in pine, occasionally in oak. Ship carvers cut figure heads for vessels ; some of this carving is done in oak, some in pine. For some kinds of carving the design is drawn on paper and cut out ; then it is placed on the block, which is prepared of a proper thickness, and the outline drawn with a pencil. The portions of wood outside the design are then cut off with carving implements. The plan of marking the wood is not practised by all carvers. It may be that it is used for beginners only. Ingenuity in planning and skilful drawing are desirable qualifications for a carver. The tools used by carvers are very simple, being merely a hammer, and gouges of different sizes. When the wood is carved, it is smoothed with sand paper, then gilded or painted and varnished. During an apprenticeship, the usual sum paid a boy is $2.50 a week the first year, and more afterward. A journeyman can usually earn $1.50 or $1.75 a day of ten hours. It requires three years to learn the trade. " In wood sculpture, all that belongs to its simple ornament might receive a special grace from the inspiration of women." We have seen architectural and ship carving done by women ; and it is our belief that almost any and every kind of carving could be done by them, if the wood were properly prepared, and they were carefully instructed. Some kinds of carving require considerable muscular strength. An architectural carver writes : " Our employment is healthy. Part of our business is suitable for women, but there is not enough in our establishment to keep one constantly employed." A carver told me that furniture carving is sometimes done by women. Though it is done in harder wood

than most other kinds, it does not involve the lifting of heavy
blocks, like architectural carving. The widow of a ship carver
carries on the business in New York. Her son told me that
eight persons could do all the work necessary for that city. There
are a few ship carvers in Boston and Philadelphia, but none in
the South or West. (Would not New Orleans present a good
opening?) A. told me, a boy in learning ship carving is apprenticed for five or six years. He receives $1.50 a week for the first
year, then $2, and after that $2.50, but no more. A carver told
me that he had an Englishman working for him, that showed him
some work done by his daughter, which was superior. He knows
the wives of some carvers who finish the work of their husbands
by rubbing it with sand paper. " Louisa Raldan, of Seville, was
known as an excellent sculptor in wood." " Anna Maria Schurmann, of Sweden, carved busts in wood." " Anna Tessala, an
artist of the Dutch school, was eminent as a skilful carver in
wood." "Properzia di Rossi, an Italian sculptress, carved on a
peachstone the crucifixion of our Saviour." Many toys are
made in Germany by women and children. They are purchased
very cheaply, we know, from their low prices in this country.
Mrs. Dall says : " I would direct the attention of young women
to the Swiss carving of paper knives, bread plates, salad spoons,
ornamental figures, jewel boxes, and so on. On account of the
care required in the transportation, these articles bring large
prices ; and I feel quite sure that many an idle girl might win a
pleasant fame through such trifles." Articles might be cut of
wood, as mementos of some great event or pleasant association.
The small wooden cages, in which we see canaries for sale, were
made by women in Germany. There labor is cheaper, and they
probably receive only two or three cents for a cage, while in this
country they could not be made for less than a shilling. I saw
some pretty wooden toys, made in Switzerland by the shepherds
while watching their flocks, and some which were made by
women. It is a favorite pastime with them in the evening, when
the family is gathered around the hearthstone. The small
carved boards, used for the support of music in pianos, are carved
by a delicate saw, moving perpendicularly and driven by steam.
The carver has the pattern marked on the board, and moves it
under the saw, as the workman does the back of shell combs.
One species of carving common in Europe is that of saints and
virgins for small churches.

307. Kindling Wood. Some little boys putting kindling wood into bundles told me they are paid fifteen cents a
hundred bundles, and can do from two hundred and fifty to three
hundred in a day of ten hours. Most of them take the strings

home at night and tie them, to save time in the day. Girls could do it, but they would be liable to accident from the carelessness of those at work.

308. Pattern Makers. The wife of a pattern maker told me it requires ingenuity, patience, and a knowledge of drawing to become a pattern maker. C. thought general pattern making would not do for a woman, as it would require planing, cutting, and turning wood. He said some of the finer parts of pattern making, as forming models on a small scale for the patent office, could be done by a woman who is qualified. It would require a knowledge of arithmetical proportions, ability to turn a lathe properly, and aptness at catching the ideas of others. A gentleman who makes models for the patent office, patterns for machinery, steam and gas fittings, &c., writes : " The varnishing might be done by women, but in most shops there would not be enough to keep one at work all the time." S. told me that a part of the work of pattern making could be done by women, but it would be advisable they should have a separate apartment in founderies. The variety of ornamental iron work is so great that it affords scope for inventive talent. We suppose the business of pattern making is not more laborious and is very similar to block cutting. If women were prepared for some branches of this business, we doubt not it would prove remunerative and furnish steady employment. A pattern maker writes from Hartford : " We do our own draughting, but there is considerable done independent of a shop. For such work we pay $2 a day. A knowledge of geometry and mathematics is a prerequisite."

309. Rattan Splitters. Formerly, rattan was thrown from the ships that landed in New York, as something useless; now it sells at from four to nine cents a pound. The centre of the rattan is used for hoop skirts. The outside is split off by a strange-looking machine. The strips are then shaved thin by another machine, for making chair seats and ornamenting buggies. They are bleached in a close room with ignited sulphur. The refuse is used in some way in the manufacture of gas—also for making coarse mats and filling beds. At N.'s factory, I saw girls shaving rattan. The work was dusty—one sat, but the others stood. The girls had merely to attend to the strips as they ran through small machines moved by steam. Each girl received fifty cents a day of ten hours, for her services. In Fitchburg, Mass., fifty girls are so employed.

310. Segar Boxes. I called in a segar-box factory where the man had four boys at work. The trade requires care, and some ability to calculate proportions. The work consists in driving small nails, gluing on tape, planing the edges, and similar labor.

Women could do it, and I expect do in Germany. If boys from ten to fifteen years of age can, why cannot girls? After two months, a boy earns something. Two of the boys had been working at the trade two years, and were earning each $3 a week. The wood is cedar, and so easily managed.

311. Turners. I saw the process of wood turning. The flying of the chips I thought disagreeable. The trade can be learned in three years very well. A boy learning is paid $2.50 a week, the first year; the next year, $3; the next, increased fifty cents more, and so on. A good hand can earn from $1.75 to $2 a day. Some women do the turning of small wooden articles in France, and quite a number are employed in bone and horn turning in the old country, which is not so hard. Turning is more nearly perfect than most mechanical operations, and consequently is employed in all those branches susceptible of its use. In most work of this nature the article operated on is stationary, and the machinery in motion; but in turning, the article is kept in motion, the tool merely pressed upon it by the hand. "There is said to be but little difference in the management of turning different substances. The principal thing to be attended to is to adapt the velocity of the motion to the nature of the material." Rosa Bonheur, when a girl, was apprenticed to a dress maker, whose husband was a turner. His lathe stood in an adjoining room. Rosa delighted to slip away from her work and employ herself at the turner's lathe. The making of bone and wooden handles for canes and umbrellas could be done by women. Removing the surface of the bone is dirty work, and requires some strength. The polishing could be done by a girl. The bones are bought at glue factories, slaughter houses, &c. In New York, for a small new bone, two and a half cents is paid; for a large one, five cents.

AGENTS.

312. Express and other Conveyances. We saw a description, a short time ago, by some traveller in Scotland, of ladies acting in the capacity of railroad officials; that is, one sold tickets, another collected them, and a third was telegraphing at a station. I have been told that some of the ticket agents in Boston are women. Women are also employed at some of the railway stations in France and Germany, not only to sell tickets, but to guard the stations and crossings. I have heard that on those

roads where women are switch tenders no accident has ever occurred. " In Paris, omnibus conductors submit their way bills
at the transfer offices to women for inspection and ratification.
Women book you for a seat in the diligence. Women let donkeys for rides at Montmorency, and saddle them too." The St.
Louis *Republican* mentions that there is one feature about the
steamer *Illinois Belle*, of peculiar attractiveness—a lady clerk.
" Look at her bills of lading, and ' Mary J. Patterson, Clerk,' will
be seen traced in a delicate and very neat style of chirography.
A lady clerk on a Western steamer ! It speaks strongly of our
moral progress."

    313. General Agents. " The walks of business become
more manifold and extended as the luxuries of civilization and
the skill of human inventions become more multiplied and more
widely displayed. Every description of commercial, mechanical,
and executive business excited and created by the new wants and
new imaginations of advancing society, will call for the creation
and extension of new agencies to accomplish the labor which
they must demand. Thus the variety and number of business
agencies of every kind must spread out in a constant increase."
We think there is great imposition practised by some people who
secure lady agents, and we would advise ladies who can undertake an agency to learn something of the parties who would employ, and the character of the article, before they engage in any
undertaking of the kind. A conscientious agent is likely to have
her interests suffer by a want of honor in those whom she represents. With a liberal discount on the retail price of most goods,
agents might be enabled to make a handsome return for their
services. I saw a man that manufactures indelible ink, and
employs agents to sell it and stencil plates. He allows them
half they receive. One lady in Boston, he said, made $20 one
day. I think it probable it was in a large school. Ladies, he
says, will not stay long at it, because it tires them very much to
go up stairs a great deal. An agent should be one that can talk
well and has tact and judgment. She should select those parts
of a city where she will be most likely to meet with success. If
her article is something for ladies' use, let her go where the best
dwellings are. If it is something for universal use, if she selects
but part of a city, the largest quantity will probably be sold in
those parts most densely populated. A manufacturer of fancy
soaps and perfumery told me he has employed ladies as agents to
go around selling those articles. Some have cleared $2 a day.
He allows one hundred percentage. C., of Boston, manufacturer of needle threaders, wick pullers, and pencil sharpeners,
offers a liberal discount to agents; but we presume it would re-

quire some Yankee tact to make the sales amount to much. He states that some of their agents make from $200 to $300 a month. A stencil cutter in New Haven writes: "I have made tools for ladies to do the work of making embroidery stencils. It is necessary to travel to sell them. One lady may make the work at home, and another sell it. One young man, whom I furnished with tools, told me that he sold $14 worth of plates in five hours." Dr. B. employs twenty ladies making shoulder braces, and pays them from $3 to $4 a week. The sewing is done by hand. He allows lady agents to have the braces at $1 a pair, which can be retailed at $2 a pair. Boarding agencies have become common in some of the large cities. Some agents charge the keepers of boarding houses a percentage for every boarder sent them, but do not charge the applicant. In some offices a person records his name and pays $2, for which he has the privileges of the office one year. The boarding-house keeper pays a percentage to the agent in proportion to the rate of board, without regard to the length of time the boarders remain. One agency charges $2 for registering a name, and fifty cents for each boarder it secures. Some agents in New York have purchased articles of every kind on commission for Southerners, receiving a commission from both parties. Southern ladies have always preferred New York goods, but we suppose they will now wish to patronize their own people.

314. Literary, Book, and Newspaper Agents.

By literary agents we mean those that are willing to take the compositions of others, review, correct, prune, polish, mend, and present them for publication. We suppose there are not a great many ladies, in our country, of sufficient experience in this way to be prepared for the business, and probably a smaller number that would wish to undertake it. Yet, we think, to a competent and reliable lady, it might yield a handsome profit. We know there are a few gentlemen so engaged. Proof readers are sometimes employed by authors for this purpose, or some literary friend of ability does it as an accommodation. Ladies have been agents more for magazines than standard works. Indeed, only new books claim the privilege of having their merits set forth by agents. In towns and cities, ladies could act as agents without any difficulty. The business, of course, requires one to be on her feet a great deal. In sparsely settled portions of the country, it could not be so easily done. Yet we were told in New York of an educated lady that wished to earn a livelihood, and, not seeing any other way open, she became a book agent. She got a horse and buggy, and rode through the country, and was very successful. She met with a young lady who was very anxious to join her. They made a great deal of money, and

13

wrote a book of their travels. There are said to be many book and paper agents in New York city—both men and women—and they are paid the same percentage. The time of work is confined to daylight. If newspaper advertisements for book agents can be relied on, we suppose the business would pay well. We can scarcely glance over the columns of a newspaper without finding a call for agents to present the merits of some new work, with the promise that, if active and diligent, the individual will clear from $30 to $100 per month. It requires judgment, taste, and a knowledge of what is popular in the book market. I was told by the editor of a ladies' magazine, that he pays his agents fifty cents on the dollar, and would be glad to secure the services of more lady agents. He stated that one of his lady agents in Brooklyn obtained in two weeks twenty subscribers, so making $12.50. Some sell books on subscription, but if the books are printed, the surest and most speedy way is to deliver the book and receive the money, when the individual decides to buy. A lady who earns her living as a book and newspaper agent, told me that she gets a percentage for the agency of books and papers. She has been an agent eight years in New York. Her health is poor, and she thinks it is from being out in all kinds of weather. She does not go to every house, but calls on one friend, who recommends her to another—so that she has as many to visit as she can. She says the qualifications needed are health, tact, judgment, courage, pleasing address, perseverance, with faith in the work, and in God. Ladies are more likely to be well received than men, but cannot walk as much. She prefers the agency of books, because she then gets the money, gives the book, and that is the last of it. But there is a responsibility attending the agency of papers. The editor may require prepayment for his magazine. If he is not an honorable man, he may discontinue his magazine during the year, and not refund what is due to his subscribers. The agent is then blamed, as well as the editor, when it may be totally out of her power to remedy the matter, or to have prevented it. A lady news agent, that has a good location and a small circulating library, told me she has occupied the place for several years, and so has regular customers. She does it to aid her husband in supporting and educating their children, but thinks an individual could earn for self alone a comfortable living by keeping a news depot. In the large cities of the North are newspaper agents (men) who solicit advertisements, for which they receive a commission from editors. There is a Miss S. in New York, who makes a very good living by obtaining advertisements for the principal city papers. She goes to stores and offices, and solicits advertisements of business men, for which she receives a percentage from the conductors of the papers.

315. Mercantile Agents. At the office of a mercantile agency on Broadway, New York, one hundred young men are employed in writing. Why could not women do it? An agent who travels for C.'s paper-hanging manufactory, exhibiting specimens and getting orders, and has a commission also from another house for another kind of business, makes $4,000 a year. Ladies were employed writing for one mercantile agency in Boston one winter.

316. Pens. The inventor of Prince's Protean pen thinks a lady would do well to act as agent for the sale of his pens. A man who was agent made $3,000 a year, but he could not stand such exertion over a year. This pen is so constructed as to furnish a flow of ink for ten consecutive hours. It is very convenient in travelling, on account of the ink being in the case. Physicians would find it very convenient. An agent would receive a very good allowance; for instance, a $5 pen she would receive for $3; one style of $4 pen for $2.50, and another style for $2.25. Mr. Snow, of Hartford, an importer of steel pens, offers to pay $2 a day to all agents who sell five gross of pens per day, at the list of prices furnished, and at the same rate for any larger quantity.

317. Sewing Machines. H., manufacturer of low-priced sewing machines in Newburyport, Massachusetts, desires to secure some local and travelling agents. In his circular he says: "In order to ascertain who would prove an efficient and reliable agent, we have concluded that each applicant shall sell thirty days on commission; and after that time, if he proves as before stated, and prefers it to a commission, we will pay him a salary of from $30 to $80 a month, according to capabilities, and travelling expenses. The commission allowed will be thirty-three and one third per cent. on the machines sold." We know nothing of the merits or demerits of the machine, but give it as a criterion by which to judge what sewing-machine agents may expect in the way of remuneration. The manufacturer of the universal hemmer, which can be attached to any sewing machine, retails them at $2.50, but to agents a deduction is made of seventy-five cents. (It probably costs ten cents apiece to make them.) They require agents to buy what they wish to sell. It being a cash business, they have few lady agents. Their agents confine themselves to towns, on account of the time that would be consumed in travelling through the country. At a manufactory of children's spring horses, I saw a lady employed to sell the horses and make saddles for them. Some she stitched by hand, and some quilted and stitched by machine. She got $6 a week.

318. School Agents. A lady properly qualified might, we think, conduct a school agency. As there are few school agencies in New York, we suppose it must be a business that pays. The prejudice that will probably be created by the difficulties in our country, will no doubt open the way for the preparation and employment of slave State ladies as teachers in their own States, and consequently one or more agencies in the South will be needed. The terms of one of the best agencies we know of, are as follows: " To principals who have their schools registered for the purpose of obtaining scholars by making known the terms, locality, and advantages of their schools, a fee of $5 is charged; and for each yearly renewal, $2; and for the introduction of each pupil into a registered school, where the board and tuition does not amount to $120 per annum, the fee is $5. When over that amount and under $160, $7, &c. For the registration of a teacher, in advance, $2. When the situation is obtained, and the remuneration is under $1,000, three per cent. If $1,000 and over, five per cent. When desired to examine and personally assume the responsibility of selecting teachers for important positions, an additional fee of from $3 to $5 will be charged."

319. Telegraph Instruments. A manufacturer of telegraphic instruments in Boston writes: " We do not employ women in the mechanical part of our business, but we employ them as agents to sell our instruments for medical use. They fit themselves as lecturers by studying the science, and travel about lecturing, giving instruction, selling machines, &c. A very handsome income is derived therefrom."

320. Washing Machines. At a washing machine establishment, I was told they make a deduction of twenty per cent. to agents who sell for them; but to agents who sell for themselves and buy six or more, they make a deduction of thirty per cent.

————•••————

MANUFACTURERS AND COLORERS OF LADIES' APPAREL.

321. Artificial Flowers. As in everything else, the price for making artificial flowers is very much regulated by the quality and taste displayed. Many flowers made in the United States are equal in beauty and delicacy of finish to genuine Paris flowers, but they are mostly made by French women, and so are in reality French flowers. In France, the preparation of the

materials used in the manufacture, forms several distinct branches
of trade, and the quality of the flowers depends in a great measure
upon the care used in the getting up of these materials.   The
modes of coloring flowers are exceedingly various.   The materials
used in the United States are mostly imported from Paris.   Some
stores in New York are confined to the sale of materials for artificial florists.   There are said to be between sixty and seventy
flower manufacturers in New York, and about a dozen in Philadelphia.   I have been told there are probably 10,000 women and
children employed in making flowers in New York : I know there
is great competition in the business.   The work is mostly done
by women and children, who receive as wages from $1 to $6 per
week.   It requires care and patience, united with good taste and
much experience, to succeed in this pretty art.   There are said to
be about twenty processes in the making of artificial flowers.   The
employment is one easily affected, consequently fluctuating.   The
New York manufacturers have sold large quantities of American
flowers to Southern merchants, but have had no orders lately.
In New York, flower peps are made by men and boys.   A man
at the work said it requires some time to learn to do all the parts.
Boys, he said, do some parts that girls cannot well do ; but from
my observation, girls and women could as well do it all as workers of the other sex.   One maker of flower peps told me that at
one time he employed girls, but found they had not strength
enough to cut the wires.   To cut the wires might be hard, but
they could get accustomed to it ; at any rate, they could dip the
pistils and stamens into the coloring matter and place them in
the frames to dry.   H. told me he employs about 600 women
and 400 men in his business, that of making flowers and dressing
ornamental feathers.   The women earn from $4 to $12 a week ;
the average is from $6 to $7.   They only work eight hours in
winter.   There are several distinct branches, and it requires
longer to learn some than others.   The washing and dyeing of
feathers is done by men, the curling and dressing by women.   A
few of his women are French.   He thinks it a business that must
increase as the country grows older.   T. imports all his flowers,
but employs one girl to mount them, that is, make them into
clusters, wreaths, &c.   Not more than one in eight or ten of
those employed in the city in making artificial flowers devotes
herself to mounting them.   It requires excellent taste and some
ingenuity.   He pays by the week, from $8 to $10.   I called on a
German lady who makes artificial flowers of paper and coarse
muslin.   She arranges them in wreaths, and sells them to decorate
small stores, particularly German book stores.   She and her
daughter make a comfortable living at it.   It requires long prac-

tice in the artificial flower business to earn good wages, and very good wages are earned at only a small number of establishments. The trickery of mean people in every occupation, it is desirable to avoid. In this business much is said to be practised. One of the unprincipled acts referred to is this: Learners are told they must spend six months acquiring the trade, and during that time will receive nothing, but after that get fair wages. One branch is learned in a week or ten days, but the apprentices remain, according to agreement, six months doing the same kind of work, when they are dismissed on the plea there is no work to give them, and new apprentices are taken. Some will keep their apprentices at but one branch of work for a year or two, so reaping the benefit of their work, without giving the instruction they promise. Girls who have served several years at artificial flower making can seldom earn over $3.50 or $4 a week. G. & K., one of the oldest and most extensive firms in New York, prefer to take girls from thirteen to fifteen years of age. Older girls are not satisfied with such wages as learners receive. While learning, for the first month, they are paid $2; after that, by the week, according to what they can do. They teach their girls all the different parts, and they make the finest French flowers. They give their girls work all the year, and they earn from $1 to $6 a week. In summer, they work ten hours; in winter, nine and a half. In this, as in every business, the best hands are most sure to obtain employment. Mrs. P. thinks only little girls should learn it, as it takes a great while to acquire proficiency. She and her partner pay fifty cents a week for two months to a learner, then $1 a week for a time, and then increase according to what is done. They usually give employment all the year. They pay altogether by the week, wages running from $2 to $5. At another manufactory, I found the arrangements the same, the girls working nine and a half hours in winter, and ten hours in summer. At another place I was told that it was best for a learner to begin at ten years of age. By the time she is eighteen, she will be able to make $4 or $5 a week. In some of the first-class houses for the sale of fine French flowers, a few superior hands may earn $6 and $7 per week; but for common flowers, particularly in the cheap establishments, the prices paid are very low. It is said to be common among some manufacturers of flowers to mix in a few imported ones with their own, and sell them all as foreign flowers. At another place, I found the same arrangement, fifty cents a week for a learner; $4 a week is the price paid for a very good hand. At an importer and manufacturer of flower materials, I was told their season commences about the first of February. It requires but two or three weeks' practice to earn something—then learners are paid by the piece. Their girls make centres. They manufacture stamps and veins. At a clean-looking place, where the flowers were of a superior quality, I was told their girls earn from $2 to $7. At a Frenchman's, I was told, in two months a smart girl could begin to make fine French flowers. He pays nothing for two months; after that, seventy-five cents a week, and increases that as the worker acquires speed and proficiency. A good worker, he said, can earn $9 (?) a week. His girls work nine hours a day. They make all parts and different kinds of flowers. Some girls never learn to make flowers. At another place, the girls, I was told, are paid nothing for three months, but at the end of that time are paid $5. They learn all the branches. Workers are paid by the piece, earning from seventy-five cents to $6 a week. It requires taste and a peculiar aptitude.

322. Belts. B. & H. have ladies' and children's belts made, dolls dressed, fans trimmed, &c. Their business is wholesale. They manufacture for houses here that sell to the Southern trade. They have employed at some seasons from twenty-five to fifty girls. The belt trade is merely making the goods into belts. A person that can sew neatly can learn belt making in a day. The girls earn from $3 to $4 per week, and are paid by the piece. The belt room is superintended by a man. The busiest time for belt making and for trimming in the wholesale business, is in July and August, January, February and March. Spring work begins in January and ends the first of June, and fall work the first of August and ends the first of December. Their hands have work most of the year. They have a variety of work done; so if there is not enough of one kind for their hands, they put them to doing something else. They pay by the gross. The sewing must be done by hand. The business is confined mostly to New York. When business is good, the foreman will allow those he knows to take work home, and get their mothers and sisters to help them. The factory is in Newark. It is difficult to get girls to go there from New York.

323. Bonnet Ruches. At some factories, ruches are made entirely by machinery. They are not as well nor as neatly put together, and do not sell as high as those made by hand. It does not require long for a girl with any brains to learn, but she should commence when young, and gradually rise to the more difficult processes. A manufacturer told me girls must be at it a year before they are good pressers. For making ruches he pays by the week, from $1 to $4.50. Ruche makers are not apt to be out of employment more than from two to four weeks. P., New York, told us his workers are of all nations. Some work by the week, sewing ten hours a day. Girls sit in his factory while at work, but stand in most places. Standing is thought to be the easiest position, as it allows of change. He told us that some girls earn as high as $6 a week. It is piece work. Joining, sewing, and pressing are done by females, fluting by men and boys. It is best for females that wish to learn the business to commence quite early, say when twelve or fourteen years of age. P. thinks it would not be advisable to introduce more workers into the occupation but I would advise any one desiring to learn the trade to make further inquiries into the condition of the business. T., of Philadelphia, who has been in the business a great many years, employs over one hundred females.

324. Dress Trimmings. In London, many women and children are employed in making dress trimmings. The children wind the quills, and the women wind the silk on reels, and weave it, knit covers for fancy buttons, make fringes, tassels, buttons, and other trimmings. In this country most of such work is done by women and girls, the majority of whom are Germans, as are also the proprietors. They are the best for hand work, but English trimming makers are best for power looms. All large cities contain more or less manufacturers of dress trimmings, but the business is mostly confined to Boston, New York, and Philadelphia. Many who manufacture, also keep for sale the different varieties of sewing and embroidery silk, zephyr wool, patterns, and canvas, braid, and such articles. It is only within the last twenty-five years that fringes and tassels have been manufactured in this country, but quite a number of houses are now engaged in it. The goods are said to equal those of Europe. " There are over 1,000 hands employed in this branch in New York, at least three fourths of whom are females. Girls at reeling earn $2.50 ; at braiding, $3.30 ; and at weaving, from $4 to $6." I called at a factory where eighty girls are employed. They earn from $1 to $6 per week, doing both day and night work. No girl, the foreman said, can earn $1 a day of ten hours at that work. When the snow is on the ground, the girls can take work home with them to do at night, instead of remaining at the factory. He says there are different seasons for different kinds of trimmings, as buttons, fringes, gimps, &c., and the styles of these trimmings change. Work is slack in the early part of the winter for a few weeks. It would take three or four years to learn all the branches perfectly. Some sit and some stand while at work. At a manufactory in New York, I was told the season begins in September and lasts through the winter. Their hands earn from $3 to $5 per week. There is an over supply of hands in New York. At another place I was told the work is nearly always paid for by the piece. Their hands earn from $3 to $5 per week. Men receive from $7 to $10. Women's part can be learned in from four to six weeks, and learners are paid if they do not spoil too much material. June, July, December, and January are dull months. In busy seasons good hands are very scarce. The clerk of Messrs. B.'s factory told us the wages vary greatly. We glanced over the account book, with his permission, and observed that the lowest wages were about $1 a week, and the highest $4. It is piece work, and they will not promise employment all the year. He says, if a girl that learns cannot earn something in a year, she is not worth having. Their work is for wholesale houses. At one place I was told the girls work nine hours a day, and receive $4 a week—six months learning. After the first week they were paid $1.50 a week for six months. They make up a stock when not doing ordered work. N. employs from fifty to one hundred women, and sometimes more. They can learn in fourteen days. He pays from the first, and pays by the week, they working from six to six, having an hour at noon. It requires but a few weeks to learn one branch. One girl told me she works by the piece, and sometimes earns from $3 to $6 a week. She works from seven in the morning till gaslight. Girls, when reeling and braiding, stand. To those engaged in this kind of work, there is employment all the year to twenty-five out of every hundred; the rest are occupied from July to January. When paid by the week they seldom receive more than $4, though by taking it home and working more hours they sometimes make $5. Prices in this kind of work have fallen considerably in the last few years. I have been told by a manufacturer that the class so employed is usually of not so elevated a character as some others. The prices paid and work given for so short a time, prevent the best class of workers from entering the business. M—s, Philadelphia, employ about seventy females, including bookkeepers, saleswomen, and trimming makers. In the dull seasons their operatives are not likely to be thrown out of work, as the wholesale dealers will always require them. The workers are paid by the piece, according to the degree of perfection they have attained. When a girl presents herself for employment, the foreman immediately sets her to work on some easy kind of trimming, but she receives no wages until her work is fit for sale. The loss of time on her part and the risk of materials on the part of the employer constitute the apprenticeship. A smart girl will of course soon be able to earn something, and has always the stimulus of increasing her gains. The class of girls in the store seemed to be superior to those in the workroom, more intelligent and refined. The workrooms were large and airy. The weavers, button makers, &c., work from eight to ten hours a day. Another

13*

proprietor said a person to learn the business should *go* to a small place, where only a few are employed—not to a factory, as they will not be troubled with learners in a factory. Some of his hands work slowly, but execute in a superior manner; others work rapidly, but make the article in an inferior manner. At another manufacturer's, one of the firm told me a good hand can earn from $5 to $6 a week, ten hours a day, when times are good. They pay, after a learner has spent a week at it, according to what she can accomplish. The prospect for work is good, but he would not advise a lady to learn it; he thinks millinery better. In a town not far from New York, where he lived, a milliner could earn $20 a month and her board. Crocheting pays better. For crocheting the heads of silk fringes, a girl may earn $5 a week. I saw the agent of a lady who has trimmings manufactured. He says girls spend about two weeks learning, and are then paid by the week, from $1 to $4. He thinks the prospect for work very poor at present, for their work has been for the South almost exclusively, and now the Southerners will not purchase, particularly as such articles can be dispensed with. They have employed hands all the year, but are most busy spring and fall. The busy season commences in February. A manufacturer told me he pays his learners $2 a week for a time. His girls have work most of the year. Good hands can earn $5 a week. Some of his hands take work home with them to do in the evening. From the arrangement of the conveniences in the room, I think the air must be not only offensive but unwholesome. I observed this in two or three other workrooms. At another factory, I was told it takes but four weeks to learn, and girls during that time are paid fifty cents a week. Girls earn from $3 to $5. One man told me he pays as soon as the work is done well enough to sell. The largest manufactory in the world of dress trimmings, curtain trimmings, carriage laces, and military goods, is that of W. H. Horstman & Sons, Philadelphia. They employ four hundred hands, the majority of whom are females. In R.'s dress-trimming manufactory, Philadelphia, seventy females are employed, at an average of $2.75 a week.

325. Embroideries. Embroidery was a favorite employment of the ladies of ancient times. In the days of Grecian prosperity it was a pastime among all ranks of ladies, and in the middle ages it was no less popular. The French excel in embroidery. Much of the embroidery sold in New York is done in Ireland. "A French manufacturer has invented a process of applying the electric spark to piercing designs on paper for embroidery." There now exists a machine by which one lady can accomplish as much as fifteen hand embroiderers. There are one hundred and fifty needles attached, all of which can be in use at the same time. By it the most difficult patterns can be executed. Many of the machines are now in operation in Germany, France, Switzerland, and England. " The canton of Neufchatel employs more than 3,500 females in hand embroidery, but this branch of the trade is principally carried on in the eastern parts of Switzerland, where manual labor is extremely cheap." In 1851, 250,000 females were employed in Great Britain in muslin embroidery, and the larger number of the women did the work at their own homes. About a million and a half of dollars then passed out of the United States in payment for a portion of this embroidery. We would be pleased to see a greater demand for these articles from a home, and less from a foreign market. The increased facilities for stamping impressions on the muslin, and the consequent cheapness of doing so, tends to render the business more lucrative to those employed. The prices earned depend on the skill and experience of the worker. Embroidery may be divided into two kinds, cloth and muslin. The first is used for thick goods, furniture covers, ottomans, chair seats, tapestry, &c. The other kind consists in the embroidery of ladies' caps, collars, handkerchiefs, and other light articles of apparel. The materials used are cotton, linen, silk, and silver and gold thread. Embroidery is paid for by the piece, according to the quality of the material and the amount of work. For stamping muslin to embroider, four, six, and eight cents a yard are paid, according to the width and style of pattern. Some stamping is done with wooden plates, some with copper plates, and some by a paper impression. The wooden plates cost from fifty cents to $2.50. Metal tools for stamping cost more. It would be well, in establishments where embroidery is kept for sale, to keep patterns on hand for braiding, needlework, and embroidery. Such patterns have met with a ready sale, and always will, when such a pastime is fashionable. I find fifty cents a lesson is the usual price paid for instruction in embroidery, and a person accustomed to using the needle can learn in a few lessons. One lady told me she charged twenty-five cents a lesson. An embroiderer told us but little of such work is done now. A good deal of money was made at it, when fashionable for outer garments and for children's flannel skirts. A gentleman that has such work done told me that good medallion workers would find employment. B., who employs some embroiderers, thinks there is not a surplus of such labor. He could employ more hands. He pays by the piece, from $3 to $7 a week. Taste and skill with the needle are required. Embroidery pays poorly—one could not make a living at it now, unless they had constant work, and were rapid with the needle : very few in New York depend on it for a livelihood. D., a gold and silver embroiderer, thinks a person of ordinary abilities could not get to embroidering well in less than one year's practice. He pays something after a few weeks—as soon as the work is done well enough to sell. Many Germans and French have taken the custom. The Germans do it for less, and consequently root out other embroiderers. So there is not much prospect for work in New York. He has considerable done for cap makers and flag makers, who send South and West. He pays his girls from $4 to $5 a week, and they work from eight to six o'clock. I was told at another place that gold and silver embroidery pays well. The lady that works for W. earns $25 a week. A man writes: "You are aware that women are unable to make the very finest kind of needle embroidery, and that wherever the highest skill is required, men are needed?" We are aware there are some womanish men in France that embroider, but we must have facts before we are convinced that women cannot equal men in embroidering. A young lady, keeping an embroidery store in New York, told me her father cuts stencil plates with chemicals for embroiderers. In some establishments they are cut by steam power. Her father made wooden plates, but it would not pay. It takes but a short time to learn stamping, which pays better than embroidering. Those that do embroidery cheapest, get most to do. The greater part of it is done in winter evenings, as a pastime by ladies. Many ladies have stamping done before they go to the country in the summer, and embroider while they are in the country, putting out their plain sewing. Ladies that embroider, generally do their own stamping. M. knows one lady that embroiders for two or three stores, and makes a very good living. But she thinks very few have enough embroidering to do to occupy all their time. The Broadway stores have considerable embroidery ordered, and get very good prices; but their embroiderers, I have been told, are not better paid than those of other people. Some stores give it to ladies who do it for pocket money. Some of these ladies talk about embroidering for their friends, but, lo and behold! they expect their friends to pay them. It requires considerable practice in embroidery to keep the stitches even, and properly shape the leaves and flowers. A French woman told me she used to get $1.20 a day for embroidering fine collars in Paris.

326. Feathers. Mrs. M., Philadelphia, has served an apprenticeship of five years at dressing and dyeing feathers, and is now (and has been for fifty years) able to perform every part of it herself, including the preparation of the dyes. She employs women, but they do not give themselves the time or trouble to learn enough of it to carry it on on their own account, but are satisfied to acquire enough of it to enable them to earn a day's wages. From the information obtained from this veteran, we concluded that this trade can be very well carried on by women alone ; and farther, that there will always be considerable demand for feathers and plumes, at least in large cities. Ladies' plumes pay best. She prepares plumes for the military. At a feather store in New York, the lady said the season commences in May. Learners are paid $1.50 the first week, and, if they become good workers, may in a few months earn as much as $6 a week. Mrs. D. says she would like to teach some one the business, and establish them where she is. She would turn over her custom to them. She would do so for $200. Her location is a good one. She would instruct how to curl, mend, sew, and color the lighter shades, for $5. She says it is not unhealthy, but requires one to be much on her feet. Taste, both native and cultivated, are required for success. I saw turkey feathers made into a light, delicate plume, and those of geese into flowers. Some feathers from the tails of roosters formed large, dark, rich-looking plumes for children's hats. This I mention to show what the poultry of our own barnyards can produce. Mrs. D.'s work was not confined to the feathers of domestic poultry. In dull seasons she prepares feathers for busy seasons. Connected with her business might be the making and selling of artificial flowers and head dresses. She says a superior feather worker can earn $6 a week, and a few even $8. Mrs. N. told me she takes learners, paying $1 a week for one month, then more if the worker is worth it, and so on. She will not teach to dye. All the American feathers used in the United States are sent from New York. A colorer and curler of fancy feathers told me it does not require more than a few weeks to learn, if you can see the process constantly during that time. It is easier to learn to curl than dye. To dye feathers on a small scale is troublesome, for if you have a feather to be dyed one color, another of a different shade, &c., you must mix up just enough coloring matter for each one. A lady, that would learn the business well, might make a living at it in the South or West.

327. Hoop Skirts. There are now hundreds of women employed in the manufacture of hoop skirts, that will, when the fashion ceases, be thrown out of employment. What resource will they have ? It may be that some other fashion will spring up requiring their services, but we doubt it. D. & S., New York, employ from 600 to 1,000, and once had 1,500 girls working for them. They have large well-aired rooms. We passed through and saw their girls at work. They were neat, well dressed, and cheerful looking. Nine tenths are Americans. Most of the girls have homes.   D. & S. have established a free library of two thousand volumes for the girls, but owing to the negligence in not returning books taken out, they lost so many that the library is no longer accessible to them.   The trade of D. & S. is Southern. Their girls earn from $4 to $8 per week, and work 9½ hours a day in winter.   The girls can change their position frequently. Women are superior to men for this kind of work.   While learning, girls receive enough to pay their board.   The continuance of this occupation depends entirely on fashion.   S. thinks the fashion as likely to last as the wearing of bonnets.   Most of the small establishments in this business have been absorbed by the large ones.   From December to April are the best seasons for work; from June to September the most slack.   T., a large manufacturer, says the average pay is from $4 to $4.50.   His forewoman earns $400 a year.   Some girls are dull, and some are smart—so the time of learning depends much on that.   They pay the girls something from the time they begin to learn.   They work ten hours a day.   As a general thing the girls and women spend all the money they can spare for dress.   The firm have thought of establishing a savings bank in connection with their manufactory, for the benefit of their workwomen, but have never yet found time. Some they pay by the piece; some, by the day; and others, by the week, or year.   Some seasons they employ about one thousand work people, of whom nine hundred and fifty are women and girls. I saw, at a factory, some girls covering wire for hoops.   The machinery was very ingenious.   They are paid $3, and a few $3.50. They have to stand all the time, and watch their work constantly. They work ten hours.   The man can always get enough of hands. It requires but a short time to learn.   They have work all the year.   The spooling, respooling, and covering, are all done by women.   Girls can earn from $2 to $6 a week, working ten hours. I saw an old woman who spools cotton for covering hoop skirts. She receives five cents a score, and cords six scores a day, earning thirty cents.   At a factory I was told the girls work by the piece, and get from $4 to $5 per week.   Owing to the want of proper management on the part of the proprietor, I found the girls do not have work steadily.   Sometimes they get out of clasps, or tape, or hoops, and cannot get them immediately, because of their distance from the stores.   At B.'s hoop-skirt factory, he told me he pays from $2 to $7 a week to his girls, and he employs between two hundred and three hundred.   It takes but a few days to learn.   The season commences about the middle of November.   The twelve o'clock bell rang, and I heard one girl say: "Let's swallow our dinner, and, when we have time, chew it."   I called at A.'s factory.   He has about two hundred girls, and they receive from $2 to $5 a week—working ten hours a day. They were nice, bright-looking girls. More hoop skirts are manufactured in New York than in any other city. I was in a factory where hoop skirts were woven by hand. The weaver girl we spoke to, said she did not get tired now, but did when she commenced. The girls are paid by the piece, and a good weaver, when industrious, can earn $1 a day. They do not sell so many as formerly. At O.'s, they have employed two hundred girls, but discharged one hundred the day before, and the girls earn from $3 to $4. Last year they sold more than ever before. They pay from the time a learner enters, but of course the pay is small for a time. They begin at the lowest branches and gradually rise. Those at machines sit, and those at frames stand. Some skirts excel in elegance of shape, some in durability, and some in elasticity. Many improvements have been made since their introduction into this country. The prices paid were better at first than since there has been so much competition. At S.'s factory, I was told the girls are paid every Saturday night. They are not paid while learning, but, when they have learned, can earn from $3 to $5 per week. Some of their girls take their work home. The amount of work depends on the market. So they cannot tell what amount will be done next spring. They are making up to send to New Orleans. Prices have fallen for this work, and so a smaller number are employed than formerly. Spring and fall are, of course, the best seasons for work. The bindings are sewed on by machines, and operatives get about $5 per week. A. writes from Massachusetts: "Women are employed in Europe in making hoop skirts, principally in London and Paris. In our country they earn from $4 to $6 a week. I pay my men higher wages, on account of the labor they perform, requiring more exercise both of body and mind. The work of a woman can be learned in a week or ten days, but constant practice for months gives greater skill and success. The employment is very neat and clean, and gives exercise to the whole system. Women are quicker in motion than men, and their powers of endurance greater. A sound mind in a sound body, and ambition to excel, together with a tolerable love of money, are qualifications necessary to render a girl desirable in this business." This branch of business has given employment to upward of twenty thousand women in the city of New York, and States of Massachusetts, Connecticut, and Rhode Island. The business is usually suspended for the winter months. In New York city there is always a surplus of girls seeking labor; they are daughters of the poorer classes, and live in tenement houses, in close quarters —are shabbily clad, and their wages go to support perhaps a

22

drunken father, or a widowed mother and fatherless children. This class of girls contrast sadly in looks and health with country girls, accustomed to breathe the free air of heaven. Their flattened chests, pale faces, and scanty wardrobe tell too plainly of the competition of labor among girls in that great city. I am told by manufacturers, in New York, that the daily applications of girls for employment, at their counting houses, is a source of annoyance, and that they are obliged to paste placards on their doors to avoid them. This business can be best prosecuted in localities where the materials can be purchased, and near markets where they are sold. The fact that workwomen are not paid as well as men, is owing to competition. In New England, men laborers are scarce, but women compete with each other. Board, $2 for ladies, $3 for men." A manufacturer in Connecticut, employing from fifty to one hundred, writes he " pays from $3 to $4 per week. The best seasons for work are from Jan. 1st to April 1st, and from June 1st to Nov. 1st. They work eleven hours per day. Women are superior to men, in the more ready use of their fingers. Board, $1.50 to $2. Quickness and dexterity are qualities most needed. " O. & C., Connecticut, write, their girls, "above one hundred and twenty, work by the piece, and earn from fifty cents to $1.12 per day, in proportion to their skill and industry. A very few in one branch earn more. Living on fashion, is of course uncertain. Business months, May, June, October, November, and December. Women are generally inferior in construction and skill. Board, $1.75 to $2.50." Manufacturers in Ashfield, Mass., write : " We employ about one hundred and twenty women. The greater part of them do the work at their own homes. Some baste the work together, some work the sewing machines, some draw the bastings, and others sew on the buttons and finish the work. Our work is all done by the piece. Those who work the machines can easily earn eighty-three cents a day of ten hours—the others earn from thirty-three to fifty cents, according to age, activity, and capacity. We pay men $1 a day for cutting the work and packing the goods. Neatness and despatch are desirable for workers ; and for operatives, sufficient ingenuity to keep the machines in good order and condition. The work is as comfortable and pleasant, perhaps, as any employment whatever. Board, $1.50." I find some firms work ten hours, some eleven.

328. Muslin Sets. Many girls are employed in large cities in making up lace goods, as collars, undersleeves, &c. S. employs two women to make up undersleeves, caps, &c., and pays from $3 to $5 per week to each. They stay from 8 to 6 o'clock. There are too many in that business who are not well

qualified. Very few are Americans. Miss A. used to make up
sets, and earned $10 a week often (piecework), before the South-
ern trade became so poor. Girls earn from $3 to $5 a week for
this kind of work. It is cut and prepared by a forewoman.
Some women sell lace goods on the streets of London. I called
on a man who employs a number of girls to make crape collars.
He says experienced hands can earn from $20 to $26 a month.
They work by the piece. It does not require long to learn. Mrs.
H. called on a Frenchman who advertised for hands for that purpose. He offered her $1.50 a dozen for making ornamented
ones.

329. Parasols and Umbrellas. The parasol was used
by the ancients more in religious ceremonies than as a protection from the sun. In some of the warmest countries, they are
as much used by men as women. The manufacture of parasols
and umbrellas is quite extensively carried on in this country,
and is one that pays pretty well. At S.'s umbrella manufactory,
Philadelphia, great numbers of women are employed—one hundred and seventy-five in his principal establishment, and nearly
as many in its branches, and some at their homes. They make
and sew on the covers, and are paid by the piece, according to the
material and workmanship. It requires about six weeks to learn
umbrella making. The girls we saw leaving the premises looked
tidy and cheerful. S. remarked that those who live at a distance from the workshop, generally arrive earlier than those who
live near. He thinks, if they would abstain from excessive use
of tea and coffee, they would enjoy better health. They used to
employ Americans principally, but now have foreigners, mostly
Irish. They can come and go during work hours as they please.
Last summer there were twelve hundred females, in Philadelphia,
engaged in making umbrellas and parasols. In most umbrella
factories in New York, girls are paid eight, nine, and ten cents
an umbrella. For silk umbrellas, they receive only two cents
more than for cotton ones. Parasols range in price from four to
twenty-four cents, according to size, style, and quality of material. Old hands, in some houses, take apprentices for two or
three weeks, and receive the proceeds of their work for the time
given in instructing them. March, April, and May are the
busiest months for making city parasols; and August, September,
and October for umbrellas. Where I purchased an umbrella in
New York, the man said he employed two women in spring and
one in winter to work. The parasol work pays best. His girls
earn, when making parasols, from $5 to $6 per week; but umbrellas seldom pay more than half that. The wholesale parasol
work commences about the middle of December, but his, being

retail for the city, does not begin until May. A girl in the trade told me that umbrella sewers can earn from $2 to $6 per week. Of course they have not work all the year steadily. She is paid to stay in the store, and is expected to spend any unoccupied moments in sewing for the shop. An umbrella maker told me his girls earn from $2 to $6, according to the kind and quantity of work they do. He thinks the occupation well filled. In New York city, in 1853, there was one parasol and umbrella firm that employed two hundred and fifty girls, and their average wages were $4 a week. In the umbrella business the work is invariably paid for by the piece. A gentleman told me that girls in that branch of work become very immoral from association with men while at work; but in large establishments the females have a separate workroom, and there is no need of their ever seeing any man while at work, except the foreman. (Why might they not have a forewoman?) S. Brothers say their girls earn from $2 to $8 a week. They keep them employed most of the year—their best hands all the year. Most of the work is done at the factories, but some girls run up the covers at home, and come to the factory to put them on the frames. I was told that in Philadelphia, work can be done as well for lower prices, because living is cheaper. My experience as to the price of living was to the contrary. I talked with one girl who had been making umbrellas seven years, but thinks she will die of consumption in less than two years, from the long and close confinement; but I think the detriment to health arises more from the dust and coloring matter that rubs off the umbrella muslin, particularly in summer, when the coloring matter is absorbed freely by the openness of the pores. A manufacturer told me his hands could earn from $4 to $6 a week. A learner must spend three weeks without remuneration; then she is paid according to the quality and amount of work done. About one fourth of his girls are Americans, that have worked out, but desire to do something they think more respectable. His hands have work all the year, with the exception of six weeks. The busy time commences in January. Most of his girls run them up at home, but put them on the frames at the factory. S., New York, says the business is bad in July, and part of August—also in February. In his factory, some tailoresses, and girls that sew for milliners and dress makers, get employment until the busy seasons of their trades come round. His women get for sewing from $2 to $3 a week; those that cut get from $5 to $8. It requires about two weeks to learn the business. A good use of the needle is necessary in a sewer, and economy in the use of the cloth for a cutter. The business is likely to increase. In busy seasons there is often a demand for good hands. In Paterson, Newark, and other towns where the Irish prevail, they usurp the labor even in umbrella making. In New York city a foreign influence predominates, and many Irish have come into the business there within the last year. The importation from England of umbrellas (like almost everything else) is less and less every year. Some manufacturers have the hemming done by machines. S. will not, because it throws many women out of employment. A Broadway manufacturer informs me he pays the ladies who attend his store, each $5 per week—those who sew are paid by the piece, and average $4.50 per week. He pays while learning, the time of which is one month. A good maker will always find employment. The best season is from January to June. Those who attend store are there from 8½ until 7 P. M. A manufacturer in New York, who employs eighty girls, informs me " he pays by the piece, and each earns about $4 per week. Spring is the most busy season. Men and women pursue different branches. Board, $1.50 to $2." An extensive manufacturer, a Jew, in New York, complained to me that women do not stick to one trade. He has often had women who have been sempstresses, cap makers, &c. Some, too, will not remain long at this work—they want to go at something else. Now, I would ask what a woman is to do, when her trade gives her work but part of the year, and her wages for that are merely enough to keep her alive during that time? Is she to be blamed for going to another trade in the interval? No—she is to be commended for her prudence and good sense. Do men confine themselves to one trade, if they find they can do better in another? The proprietor said he would not receive any applicants but those that are of good families and bring certificates of character. He pays by the dozen, and his women earn from $3 to $4 per week. Some parts of the work, he says, is done by machinery that women cannot manage. They receive enough to pay their board while learning. A woman that has been a milliner has acquired a skill with her needle, a smoothness and softness of touch, that enables her to become a very good umbrella maker. Such a one is best fitted for sewing on silk umbrellas. One that has been a tailoress and accustomed to sewing on heavy cloths is deficient in fineness of touch, and cannot succeed so well. The secretary of the Waterloo Company writes: " The girls of the factory are all paid by the piece, and earn from $3 to $5 per week. Men receive $1.25 per day, and are practical mechanics. The work of the females is easy, and requires little or no experience. Work hours average ten, the year through. The women are all American. Men's board, $3 ; girls', $2.50." A manufacturer in Concord, New

Hampshire, "pays his girls from $10 to $12 a month. Women can learn their part in from one to three months. The best seasons for work are spring and summer—the poorest, winter. Board, $6 a month." Manufacturers in Boston write: "We employ one woman the whole year in cutting out covers of umbrellas and parasols, and pay her $6.50 a week the year round—to another, who performs the same kind of work, in busy times, say from November 1st to July 1st, we pay $5.50. A superintendent, who gives out and receives back the work and keeps the pay roll, receives $5.50 part of the year, and $4.50 the other part. From March 1st to July 1st we employ thirty girls to sew up covers and put on frames, and pay by the piece. They average $4 per week. We keep ten girls, for this kind of work, through the winter. It takes four or five years for men to learn the business; women well versed in the use of the needle, two or three years. From December 1st to March 1st, some of our women work on furs, or upholstery, and some are unable to obtain any kind of work. The supply is more than the demand, particularly this year. As a location for this business, the advantages are in favor of New York, because of the large market, and on account of the principal part of the material being made there. Most of our hands board with relations or friends, because they find it difficult to get boarding places at such prices as they are able to pay. Board, from $1.75 to $3.00." Umbrella stitchers in New Britain, Connecticut, "have some girls tending machines, to whom they pay from 50 to 75 cents per day of ten hours. They have some to sort and pack goods. Women can do the light work somewhat cheaper than men, and are somewhat quicker. No other parts of the work are suited to their strength and dress."

330. Sempstresses. In 1845, there were in New York ten thousand sempstresses, and now there are probably many more. "The following are the prices for which a majority of these females are compelled to work—they being such as are paid by the large depots for shirts and clothing, on Chatham street and elsewhere :—For making common white and checked shirts, six cents each; common flannel undershirts the same. These are cut in such a manner as to make ten seams in two pairs of sleeves. A common fast sempstress can make two of these shirts per day. Sometimes, very swift hands, working from sunrise till midnight, can make three. This is equal to seventy-five cents a week (allowing nothing for holidays, sickness, accidents, being out of work, &c.) for the first class, and $1.12½ for the others. Good cotton shirts, with linen bosoms, neatly stitched, are made for twenty-five cents. A good sempstress will thus earn $1.50 a week by constant labor. Fine linen shirts, with plaited bosoms,

which cannot be made by the very best hand in less than fifteen
or eighteen hours' steady work, are paid fifty cents each.   Ordinary hands can make one shirt of this kind in two days.   Duck
trousers, overalls, &c., eight or ten cents each; drawers and
undershirts, both flannel and cotton, from six to eight cents at
the ordinary shops, and 12½ cents at the best.   One garment is
a day's work for some, others can make two.   Satinet, cassimere,
and broadcloth, sometimes with gaiter bottoms and lined, from
eighteen to thirty cents—the latter price paid only for work of
the very best quality.   Good hands make one a day.   Their coats
are made for from 25 to 37½ cents apiece.   Heavy pilot-cloth
coats, with three pockets, $1 each.   A coat of this kind cannot be
made under three days.   Cloth roundabouts and pea jackets,
twenty-five to fifty cents.   These can be made in two days."   In
a large town, in Massachusetts, we read, not many months past,
of overalls being made at thirty-seven cents per dozen, or three
cents a pair, and shirts at forty-eight cents per dozen, or four cents
apiece.   When the times are hard, prices fall from their usually
low standard.   Our hearts sicken within us as we read the prices
paid needlewomen.   The trifling remuneration and wasted health
of most needlewomen is a bitter reflection on those who employ
them.   Some clothing merchants and cap and shirt makers pay
their women such prices as enable them to live—better than those
mentioned above.   They are houses of a more respectable class,
that have a position, and deal with a more liberal class of people.
The occupation of sempstress is crowded to overflowing in New
York.   In business times it is impossible to get a working person
to leave New York, but in hard times they are very willing to
go.   One firm told me that they often have applications for
operators and sempstresses in busy seasons, but then they will
not leave; and when the times are dull there is no demand, and
they cannot.   The supply of labor has been greater than the demand, and hence the competition that has arisen among clothing
merchants, and the low price of made clothing as sold in slop
shops.   The use of sewing machines has to some extent done
away with sewing by hand.   Many a woman has been thrown out
of employment by it, to which many of our newspapers can
testify, and have borne witness during the past two years.   We
have heard of some slop shops in large cities offering to pay the
highest wages to good shirt makers, each applicant to take a shirt
and make it for nothing, as a sample of her sewing.   From one
hundred to two hundred, perhaps, apply, and, of course, that many
shirts are made.   It meets the demand of the unprincipled shop-
keeper, and he has, perhaps, employment for a dozen or more.   A
man that has a ladies' furnishing store, told me he pays girls that

sew neatly by hand 37½ cents a day. Many clothing merchants have their work done in the country, because they can have it done more cheaply. The sewing done by French linen makers is very beautiful. The majority of sempstresses have no time they can call their own. Those that sew twelve or fourteen out of the twenty-four hours, without any relatives or friends even to be protectors for them, and often in bad health, have no time for mental improvement or social intercourse. " The habits of the sempstress are indicated by the neck suddenly bending forward, and the arms being, even in walking, considerably bent forward, or folded more or less upward from the elbows."

331. Sewing Machine Operatives. There has probably been no invention in which so large a number of persons have realized fortunes as the sewing machine. All the first manufacturers of them have amassed money. In the United States 150,-000 sewing machines are in use. Miss P. says, a sewing machine and baster do the work of ten hand sewers and five basters. We hear of some sewing machines in London, each of which can accomplish as much as fifteen pairs of human hands. At several highly respectable establishments we were told their operatives earn from $4 to $7 a week, according to the abilities of the operative, the kind of machine, and the style of work. In houses of lower standing, operatives earn from $3 to $5. I was told of one man who hires a number of girls to work on machines at $2.20 a week. At Y. & Co.'s, operatives earn from $2.50 to $4. Machine stitchers of leather generally get $6 a week. The usual number of hours for operatives is ten. I have been told that the secret of its being so difficult to get basters is, they are paid poor wages. A clothing merchant in the Bowery says he has a family working for him that earn $28, and sometimes $30 per week. They use two machines. The machine-made clothing for men sells at about the same price as hand-made, and is generally liked as well by purchasers. We think, the sewing of ladies done by machine does not pay quite so well as hand sewing; but if we sewed for a living, we would give the machine the preference, because of its rapid execution. C., who employs about four hundred hands, says their dull season begins the 4th of July. L., who sells sewing machines, told me he frequently has applications for operatives to go into clothing manufactories. G. & B. occasionally have applications from other places, but always give the choice to those who have learned with them. L. thinks the employment of operatives will not amount to anything as a permanent reliance out of cities. He thinks in one or two years the sewing machine will be used in almost every family—as much domesticated as the wash tub. In cities where clothing, bagging, &c., are made in large quantities, of course, there will be a demand for some. L., superintendent of E. S.'s machines, employs from three to twelve ladies, and pays from $5 to $10 a week. They stay from eight to ten hours. A lady, who hires sewing machines, and sends out operatives, told me she charges $2 a day for a machine and operative, sending both, and giving twelve hours' time, or from $1.25 to $1.50 for an operator only, according to the number of hours given. If they are hired for a week or more, the prices are still lower. I think the usual hire of a machine only is $2 a day. A man that hires machines told me that he rents for from $3 to $5 per month, keeping the machine in repair during the time, if it is not badly used. Singer's principal machine is a strong, heavy one, most suitable for cloth, and requires much strength to work long at a time. According to D., a clothing merchant, a woman with one of Singer's machines can do all the stitching of twelve pairs of cloth pantaloons in a day; and a coat that formerly required two days to make by hand, can now be made in one sixth of a day. W., agent of W. & W.'s machine, says the lady that has charge of L. & S.'s sewing department, told him ladies prefer to have their sewing done by machines, and that B. will not have his mantillas made by hand. He told me of a woman that takes in $30 a week with the aid of two girls, to whom she pays $6 a week each, leaving the profit of $18 a week; and of another who makes $8 a week with her machine. Now that machines are more plentiful, work done by them is not so well paid. The sellers of machines say it is not unhealthy. Some people suppose the machine to be much more injurious than the needle, if worked as long and constantly. The tax on the muscles of the lower limbs and the weaker parts of the system is certainly very great; yet those with treadles are thought by some to be less injurious than those moved by steam. I talked with a lady keeping a depository connected with an influential church for the supplying of poor women with work. She thinks sewing machines are very injurious—says a girl of seventeen will give out in three or five years at most. It produces a pain first in the hips, and the jar affects the nerves; and the sameness of the stitch on white or black goods produces a constant strain of the eye. She mentioned a young woman who came a few days before to get sewing, who had worked at B.'s five years on a machine, and her sight had so failed her that she cannot see to work now by gaslight. She was but twenty-three, but looked to be thirty years of age. Sewing by machine, I have been told, injures some kinds of goods. The needle being large, threads of the cloth are liable to be broken. Changing the kind and quality of goods in operating injures a machine. The utility and profit of sewing machines have to a great extent been usurped by Jew men, that are tailors and cap makers. I have heard that many respectable men in New York, after coming home from business, spend nearly or quite all the evening in operating on machines, doing the family sewing that has been cut and basted ready to stitch. What can we say of such effeminacy and meanness, when done by those that are able to give such work to poor women? A lady remarked to me: "When sewing machines were invented, it was said new occu-pations would be opened to women as the machine came in use, and deprived some of a livelihood; but it is eight years since, and I have not heard of one." The sewing machine has certainly thrown many women out of employment. Those who are able to purchase one may get along. It is in this as in every other branch of labor—a capital, however small, is an assistance in business. One advantage always gained by machinery is that it enables the poor to purchase more cheaply the materials used by them. Free-masons often buy machines for the widows they help to support. In some of the large manufactories of Dublin, where sewing ma-chines are used, from fifty to two hundred women are employed.

FUR WORKERS.

332. Dyers. Dyeing furs is wet and dirty work, and the odor is very disagreeable. I was told by a lady that girls at such work can earn $4 a week, or if by the piece, from $5 to $6. There are very few indeed at it. She thinks it not unhealthy. She sometimes cleans furs, mostly ermine, with a powder of some kind. In the fur business, people must sell enough in three months to keep them the other nine months of the year. In the summer they take time to examine, purchase, and make up furs. C., a fur dyer and dresser, told me he once employed an English-woman to flesh fine skins—i. e., take off the flesh that adheres to a skin when removed from an animal. It is done with a sharp knife. She earned as much as a man, $1.50 a day. But men object to working with women in that business; and no American women, to his knowledge, know how to do it.

333. Sewers. From conversations with a number of fur dealers in Philadelphia and New York, I find the rate of wages for sewers runs from $2.25 a week to $8. Forewomen get good wages. Some sewers and liners are paid by the piece, and some by the week. Those who work by the week are paid for extra hours. A small number of the women employed in New York are English, but the majority are Germans, who have learned the business in their own country. In Germany most of the men learn to sew, and most of the men engaged in the fur business know how. Quite a number in New York are married women, whose husbands are connected with the business. Furs are sold only in the fall and winter, but made up in the summer. In a few places they give work all the year to a small number of workers, but the majority do not give work more than six months, from May to December. Some fur sewers have another trade for the other six months, as hat binding, &c. It does not require long for a good sewer to learn—from one week to six. There are some kinds of fancy fur sewing that require rather longer. No women are employed in preparing the skins : that is done at different establishments, generally in the suburbs, and exclusively by male hands. The usual number of hours of sewers employed by the day is ten; but many of those who sew by the piece take work home with them to do at night, and so are enabled to earn considerably more. Men working in the fur business in New York earn from $8 to $12 per week. The quilting for linings is done by machines, but the linings are sewed in by hand. Liners are generally better paid than sewers, and earn from $6 to $10. In extensive establishments, a cutter and a certain number of sewers and liners confine themselves to one kind of fur. Some furriers pay their learners enough to board them ; some do not pay anything. I think the supply of hands in New York is equal to the demand. The best workers, of course, are most sure of employment. New York is the great fur depot of the United States, but some business is also done in Boston, Philadelphia, and Baltimore. Furs are sent from St. Louis and Chicago to be made up in New York, and part of them returned to be sold in those cities. Those that sew furs at home can most conveniently take learners. There are a number of middlemen in the fur business, who get work from the stores and make a profit by employing women to do it at lower wages. Mrs. G., an importer and manufacturer, cuts her own furs, particularly ermine and sable. She says furs are sometimes cut in Germany by women, but people in this country think a woman cannot properly cut them. Work at the fur business in England is said to pay better than any other. G—s, the largest firm in New York, write : "We pay women from $2.50 to $6 per week. Some work by the week, some by the piece. Men get about double wages, but their work requires more physical strength. Men do the cutting and matching, and it requires several years to be a good workman. Sewers receive about half price while learning. Some women

14

can learn all that is necessary in a few months. The prospect of employment is not so good as heretofore. The women work the year around. Work hours are 9½. Board, $2 to $2.50 per week." Most furriers report the employment healthy, but it is not, on account of the dust and loose hairs flying, for persons predisposed to consumption. A furrier in New York writes: " I pay mostly by the piece. It takes about one year and a half for women to learn the parts they do. The amount of work hereafter depends some upon fashion and the weather. The best seasons for work are from May until February. We could not shorten the hours of work unless the business had a longer season. Board, from $1.50 to $2." A furrier in Boston writes: " Women are employed for sewing and lining furs here, in England and France, and partially in Germany, Russia, &c. Week hands get from $4 to $4.50, ten hours a day; others, from $2 to $6. Business in future is uncertain. I am busy from July to Christmas. The best location for the business is where furs are fashionable." A fur dealer in New York, who employs from 10 to 15 women, gives the following answers to questions concerning the fur business: " The work is very easy, and not unhealthy. I pay women from $3 to $6 per week, ten hours a day. They are as well paid as males, in proportion to the amount of work done. Any apt female can learn in three months, and is always paid by me $2.50 per week while learning. The business is better and there is more of it every year. Work is steady from May to December; very little at other times. The comfort and remuneration of the employment is satisfactory among working classes. Women are more capable of handling a needle for light, fine work than men. The colder the climate, the better the location for business, provided people have money to buy furs." In some establishments where men and women work in the same departments, they are allowed to talk while at work; but the practice, some complain, is not conducive to good morals. The character of the people and conversation, however, would decide that.

FITTERS, CUTTERS, AND SEWERS OF LADIES' AND CHILDREN'S WEAR.

334. Bonnets. The making of silk, crape, velvet, and other fancy bonnets gives employment to many females. Connected with this is the bleaching of straw, Leghorn, and hair bonnets. In large cities this is a separate branch of business. The making and selling of bonnets has long been one of the few employments open to women in the United States. If a milliner gets a good run of fashionable custom, she can do well. Most proprietors of millinery establishments make a handsome profit on their goods, but some of the girls employed receive but a scanty pittance. I have been told that in Holland men milliners are common. From a newspaper we take this pithy article : "A stranger in Mexico is struck with the appearance of the milliners' shops, where twenty or thirty stout men with mustaches are employed in making muslin gowns, caps, and artificial flowers." The cruelty exercised by some milliners and dress makers toward those in their employ, by requiring of them too long and severe application, is very great. Many girls suffer, as the effects, diseases of the spine and the eyes. "In the case of the milliners and dress makers in the London Metropolitan Unions, during the year 1839, as shown by the mortuary register, out of fifty-two deceased, forty-two only had attained the age of twenty-five ; and the average of thirty-three, who had died of disease of the lungs, was twenty-eight." But the length of time required of their employés by milliners and dress makers in London is longer than in the United States. A number of women are engaged in the sale of millinery on the streets of London. Girls usually spend from six months to a year learning the millinery business. Unless a girl has taste and talent, she is not likely to be benefited even by a year's apprenticeship, for it is rarely the case that they are instructed in any but the mechanical work. No pains are taken to instruct them in what is becoming or stylish, what shades are most harmonious, how to make a graceful bow, and turn a well-trimmed end, to arrange a face trimming, and render attractive the *tout-ensemble*. A hundred small minutiæ are essential to a first-class trimmer, among which is a nice discrimination of colors and shades. A knowledge of the languages is, in cities, desirable for milliners' saleswomen. A love of dress is said to be created by working at such articles. Many bad effects must result from the indulgence of such a taste by those who receive the small wages of most girls working at the millinery and dress-making business. Over four hundred women are employed in the large straw-goods and millinery establishments in Philadelphia. W. had, in 1854, three hundred girls making and trimming bonnets, and twenty-six in the store as saleswomen. They were paid from $2.50 to $6 per week. W. & L., his successors, employ about twenty-five women constantly all the year, and about one hundred and twenty-five on an average of six months in the year. Their best workers and saleswomen receive about $1 a day; some get a little more, and some rather less. The business has increased greatly during the last few years. The only kind made by that firm are silk and fancy bonnets. One of the firm told me that the largest establishments of fancy bonnets in Paris employ only about fifty women. They have girls spend three months learning, and pay nothing during the time. A girl does well to earn seventy-five cents a day. Six years ago a good worker could earn $8 or $9 a week. C., Philadelphia, employs twenty-six girls in the store and millinery department, and pays about $4 a week, according to their capacity and diligence. Learners spend six months with him. Some time ago I saw it stated that there are "450 millinery establishments in New York city, and 1,800 milliners working in shops, and 900 at home;—35,000 silk and velvet bonnets are turned out of the workshops of New York city, in the three months of the fall, and the five months of what is known as the spring trade." "Of straw bonnets, one million two hundred thousand are sold annually to the milliners of New York for their trade alone." A tasteful and dexterous trimmer can generally secure a good place and fair wages, but the majority of milliner girls are apt to be out of employment, except in the spring and fall. Most in the millinery business are Americans; yet French, German, and English are well represented. The prices paid for bonnets vary greatly in New York, according to the locality and establishment from which they are obtained. No one who has not priced them could believe the difference would be so great for bonnets of the same material and make, merely because purchased on such a street or at such a store. The milliner girls of New York are said to be good looking. The time milliners and dress makers spend at their work is such as to preclude (except in a few first-class establishments) any time for exercise and mental culture. Their wages are so low that they could not indulge in any recreation if they had the time. Those girls that live at home can afford to do work cheaper generally than others. Such girls are drawbacks to those who pay their board. Western merchants do not purchase as much as formerly in New York, because milliners have gone West. Southerners have purchased, until lately, nearly all their bonnets at the North. There are, or will be openings in the South for milliners. In 1845, "apprentices at the millinery business in New York gave one year to learn, boarded themselves, and, in some of the most aristocratic establishments, had to pay a bonus." Now it is different. The time given is usually six months, and an apprentice receives her board for her work. Mrs. S., Broadway, employs about fifty hands in the busy season—all American girls, very genteel looking. It requires six months to learn. They are not paid during the time; and, after that, are paid according to abilities. I called in one establishment where there were two girls employed, American. They received each $6 a week. A milliner told me she wanted a first-class workwoman, and would pay from $6 to $7 a week, according to her swiftness and taste. I called in a small store of dry and fancy goods, with which was connected a millinery. The young lady waited on customers, and, in the intervals, trimmed bonnets for the store. She received $1 a day, and is at the store by half past seven, and leaves at nine at night. She lives near, so she goes home to her dinner and supper. A lady told me of a Miss M., on Canal street, who commenced the millinery business five years ago with twenty dollars, and is now worth $3,000. A milliner in New York told me she could, by piecework, sewing early and late, make $7 per week. Mrs. T. has learners spend six months, during which time they are not paid. After that she gives them from $3 to $7, according to competency. The number of hours spent in the store depends on the agreement of the parties. One can best learn where there are vacancies by inquiring at the millinery shops and of girls working at the business. At a fashionable millinery, on Broadway, the lady in the showroom told me the girls receive from $3 to $12, working ten hours a day. There is one that selects, arranges, and invents, who receives $12 per week. A surplus of indifferent hands can always be obtained. Sometimes good hands fail to get employment, because in busy times some indifferent hands are engaged, and it is difficult to get rid of them. She has had to turn away many nice-looking girls seeking for work. On back streets and avenues in New York, women work longer, and the stores are kept open later than on Broadway. On Division street, large cases of bonnets are exposed for sale in summer on the sidewalks. In the poorer portions of a city, people live much and sell mostly out of doors. Their crowded apartments and the high price of rent account for it. D., on Broadway, informs me that he knows of an invention connected with his business—the sale of straw goods—that will throw ten thousand people, mostly men, out of employment. He says his girls spend all they make on dress. He has two forewomen, to each of whom he pays $500 a year. They never save a cent. He had one to whom he paid $1,000, but she never laid by a dollar. Women, he thinks, have not as much originality of thought as men. They seldom invent. He would give $1,000 a year to a woman that would think for him, and originate styles, and combine and arrange the trimmings of his bonnets with taste. He walks on Broadway, and studies the fashion of bonnets; but none of his women ever do. (Perhaps they have no time.) Women, he thinks, never acquire such proficiency as men. They advance to a certain degree in the art, and ever after are stationary. He thinks it is partly because the majority look forward to marrying, and partly because they are so constituted that they are not susceptible of acquiring the highest degree of excellence. (I fear that D. does not consider that women have not had as much time nor so many opportunities for improving themselves as men, nor have they as much to stimulate them.) He pays women from $3 to $8 per week. His girls spend four months learning. B., another Broadway bonnet-dealer, told me " good workwomen could at any time find employment by going to the country towns around, but they do not like to go from the city. Milliners often come to the city, and spend two weeks trying to get hands, and then pay them more than they are worth to go. His forewoman directs some of the trimmings, but part are left to the taste of the girls. His is a wholesale business, and he trims many bonnets before sending them away. Some of his girls earn on an average $7—a forewoman more. The occupation is not entirely filled by good hands, and pays well. He employs his hands about eight months." One of the proprietors of a straw-goods warehouse told me " his women earn from $6 to $10 (average $7 a week), ten hours a day. The season commences December 1st, and runs to March 15th, and again from July 1st to September 1st. Taste, industry, and imitative powers are the qualities most needed. He employs about sixty in the busy season. When that is over, some go to millinery shops and work, some to the country, and some to towns in the surrounding States. The girls that work in cheap shops are mostly Germans, and earn from $2 to $4. Some women, while learning, receive their board for their work. By quilling ruches and such work, if not by their bonnet work, they can earn their board. He does not pay learners, because the waste of materials amounts to the worth of their work. Girls of Irish parentage often make good milliners, and display very good taste in trimming." A Boston milliner writes : " The wages of the women I employ vary from $3 to $15 per week, of ten hours a day, according to the amount of custom they can bring, and their aptness for the business. There are comparatively few persons that make good milliners. As a milliner, one must have good taste and nimble fingers ; as a saleswoman, she needs to understand human nature, have activity, an honest heart, and good disposition. The best seasons are from March to July, and from September to January." A lady in Reading, Pa., who employs girls, informs me " she pays $3 a week, ten hours a day, to some ; to others, $1.50, but the latter she boards. A knowledge of reading, writing, and arithmetic is desirable." A milliner in Auburn, N. Y., pays from $2.50 to $5 per week, of ten hours a day. A girl spends six months learning, if she boards herself; one year, if boarded by her employer. The dull months are July, August, January, and February. A lady in Poughkeepsie writes "she gives from $2.50 to $3.50 and board to some, and from $4 to $4.50 and dinner to those who lodge and otherwise board themselves. It requires one year and a half to learn the business thoroughly, and during the time they receive only board. None should learn millinery except those who have homes, or design to carry on the business. Her girls work from 7 A. M. to 7 P. M. The business is easy and pleasant to the industrious and to those who can sit much. Out of work hours, they have time for study, attendance on lectures, meetings, &c. Board, $2." Millinery is often carried on in connection with some other business, in small towns. A lady who combines millinery and book selling, in Easton, Pa., furnishes board and pays from $1.50 to $2 per week, of twelve hours per day, to her girls. She pays about one half the price of male wages. If they spend six months learning, she pays their board. Two or three first-class milliners could find employment in Sacramento, California.

335. Bonnet Frames. Bonnets, of course, are worn in all civilized countries, and as long as bonnets are worn there must be bonnet frames. Several hundred women are employed in bonnet-frame making in New York. K. employs two hundred girls, and H. one hundred and fifty. The time of learning is from two weeks to two months, but some never learn. The more practice a worker has, the better she succeeds. Learners are paid nothing. Some women working at the trade, take learners for their labor. Workers earn from $2 to $12 a week, but it is a rare thing any earn the last-mentioned sum. Fast hands, to work constantly from 6 A. M. till 10 P. M., sometimes can. The usual price, in all respectable establishments, is fifty cents a dozen. In busy seasons there is sometimes a scarcity of hands. There are no factories South and West, consequently they present openings for the business. Apprentices generally commence in March. The busy seasons are from January to June, and from August to December. Some houses are not busy until in February, and their fall business lasts till January. The art of making the wire part of the frames is learned in six weeks. The crowns are made by machinery attended by women. Some manufacturers have all their women to work in the establishments, but the majority have the work taken home. H. says "the business is the same, so far as confinement is involved, as making up clothes at home. The girls come two or three times a week for their work; so they

have that much walking. The prospect of work to competent
hands is good. He has a great many to reply to his advertisements for learners, but for hands he has lately advertised seven
times and got but five. Some leave the business for places as
saleswomen in millinery establishments; but that is more uncertain,
for it is more difficult to retain the same place long. It requires
a year to learn thoroughly. It is necessary that the work be
uniformly done; for instance, one hundred and twenty bonnet
frames should be so uniform that one would not differ from another. Buckram frames are used to shape them on. The wages
paid, he said, vary as much as the rainbow. They range from
$2.50 to $8. He knows one woman that earns $10 a week now
and then. He sends goods away to California, and other parts
of the Union. He also manufactures for the city trade. The
season for work to send away commences about the 20th of
January, and ends about the middle of May; the fall season
begins 20th July, and ends 15th December. The city trade gives
work in the intervals. A girl of intelligence and ability can make
enough to keep her when out of work. Some employers keep
their hands all the time, for the sake of having them the next
season. The girls employed in the business are mostly Irish and
Americans. He boarded some of his girls, but they would asso-
ciate with the servants. What was said before them was repeated
to the servants, and *vice versa*. They got the impression that
he was making money off their board, though he charged but $2
a week. He thinks the result of large numbers of girls congre-
gating in the same house is bad. The influence of one depraved
one may be exerted over every fourteen good ones, and discon-
tent and rebellion be the consequence. Few persons are willing
to board working girls, because the remuneration is small, and
the girls are expected to be furnished with nearly the same advantages as higher-priced boarders. Those that work in their
rooms are about the house nearly all the time, and all expect the
privilege of using the laundry for doing their washing."

336. Bonnet Wire. At a bonnet-wire factory, I was
told but little of the work could be done by women; but, if my
eyesight did not deceive me, it could all be done by women.
Covering the wire was done on a steam-power machine, which
only required attention. The spooling is done by females, and
also tying it up, when covered, into bunches of twenty yards each.
A manufacturer of bonnet wire writes: "We employ some girls,
and pay from $3 to $3.50 per week, of twelve hours a day. Females cannot do all parts of the work. It requires from one to
four weeks to learn, and they receive while learning enough to
pay their board. The business is best nine months of the year,

during fall, winter, and spring. We prefer girls to boys, for such work as they can do. Board, from $1.50 to $2."

337. Children's Clothes. Quite a number of stores are devoted to the sale of children's clothes in large cities. A handsome profit is generally made by the merchant. At Mrs. C.'s, between three hundred and four hundred females find employment in making up children's clothing of all kinds (mostly infants'); also under-garments for ladies. A large assortment is constantly kept on hand, and they are ever busy filling orders; giving employment about nine months in the year to all, and to some the year round. The work is mostly done by hand, and to sew neatly is the only requirement. The work is all cut in the establishment and given out, being piecework. The sewers earn from $3 to $6 per week; cutters, the last-mentioned sum. Aside from these, a few girls are employed in the establishment, who wait upon customers, and sew when they have leisure.

338. Cloaks and Mantillas. Mayhew says: "In London, the workwomen for good shops, that get fair or tolerably fair wages, and execute good work, can make *six* average-sized mantles in a week, *working from ten to twelve hours a day;* but the slop workers, by toiling from thirteen to sixteen hours, will make *nine* such mantles in a week." At a wholesale store, Philadelphia, where sixty women are employed, I was told they earn from $3 to $6 per week. The head cutter has $6, the assistant, $5. When the work is finished at the wholesale houses, the good hands can find work at the retail houses. The best and most steady hands are kept in work all the year. Miss S., New York, has her stitching and seaming done by machines. She pays $5 a week to a good operator. She does her own cutting. The prospect of employment to learners is good, even in the city, in prosperous times. She has sold a great deal to Southern ladies stopping at the hotels. She estimates one machine to do as much as seven sewers. M. pays his girls $5 a week, and they work in daylight only. A cutter designs, and consequently should have taste, judgment, and experience. A good cutter can earn from $7 to $10 a week, and usually has one assistant, who superintends the girls while at work. Several mantilla manufacturers have failed, and he could get fifty thousand mantilla makers to-day. G. & Co. make for wholesale houses. They pay by the piece, and a girl can earn $4 a week, taking work home with her at night. It requires from six weeks to three months to learn. Nothing is paid during that time. Mrs. M., who makes mantillas for S., Broadway, says she takes learners, but they do not learn anything, for most they do is to pick out basting threads, run errands, &c. Good sewers can make from $3 to $5 per week,

14*

ten hours a day. Cutters can earn from $6 to $7. She thinks
the prospect for a few, that would properly qualify themselves,
would be good in the South or West, provided they find openings,
take hands from New York, and be willing to incur some expense
for a short time. In Richmond, Savannah, and Charleston, it has
been almost impossible to get good hands. S. wanted a woman
cutter, and would pay from $8 to $10 for a competent one. His
work is done mostly in the house, and continues all the year. It
is almost entirely done by machine. B—s (German Jews) employ
German girls mostly. They prefer to keep old hands that have
been with them several years. They think German girls most
industrious, and love best to make money. American girls, B.
charged (I think unjustly) with working just enough to get along,
and spending all their spare time promenading. According to his
account, cutters earn from $15 to $20 a week. He employs his
girls most of the year. The occupation of mantilla making, he
says, is more than filled in New York. Board, $2.50 to $3. At
H.'s wholesale mantilla depot, I was told it is best to learn to
make mantillas with those who sew for the mantilla merchants.
Some of their girls sew in the building, some take their work
home. If they do not know applicants for work, they require
some one as security, who has property or is in business for himself. A gentleman told me that, not long since, he saw an adver-
tisement by a mantilla manufacturer for men to make mantillas
and cloaks. A manufacturer in Boston writes me he " employs
seventy-five women, and pays them mostly by the piece ; some
receive as high as $12 per week, average $6. They are paid by
the piece from the first ; but until they acquire dexterity, they
can earn but $3 or less per week. Cloak and mantilla making
is constantly increasing, like the ready-made clothing business.
The busy seasons are from February to July, and from September
to December. Many are out of employment about three months
in the year. As sellers of goods, he finds men better qualified,
because of having been educated from children with views to
business. The New England States are the best for manufacturing, as in other localities it is more difficult to obtain female help.
Board, from $2 to $3." Another cloak maker in Boston writes :
" I employ from twenty to thirty women (mostly American), and
pay by the day. They work nine hours a day, and receive from
$4 to $10 a week. A good sewer, with taste, will learn in six
months. Some learners I pay, some I do not. Spring and
autumn are the most busy seasons. The girls are not out of employment two months. I employ three ladies as saleswomen.
Board, from $2 to $5 a week." A cloak and mantilla maker in
New Haven writes me " he employs twenty-five American girls,

and pays by the week, from $4 to $8. He pays learners when they have spent six months at the trade. His girls are principally farmers' daughters, who are rapidly taking the place of men in stores. Board, $2.25 to $3.50." A manufacturer in Providence writes : " I employ women in making and trimming bonnets, making cloaks and mantillas, and as saleswomen in my store. I pay by the week, from $3 to $8—average, $4.75—ten hours a day. Six months is the time usually spent in learning either trade. In January, February, July, and August, some of my workers are out of employment. All are Americans, and pay for board from $2 to $2.50." P., of Providence, " employs about twenty girls making dresses and cloaks, whose wages depend upon their ability as sewers; average price per week, about $4."

339. Costumes. P. pays his girls (five in number), each, $3 a week. They work from eight to five o'clock. He has no difficulty in getting hands. Anybody that can sew can make costumes, but it requires taste for the design and arrangement of such as his—theatrical. B.'s girls sew at the house, $9\frac{1}{2}$ hours in winter, and the best earn from $3 to $4 a week. Their costumes are theatrical, and are very slightly put together. A slow, careful sewer would not answer for them. They want their work done so that it will rip up easily. They have many costumes on hand for sale. They have a lady cutter. They give employment but four months, and they are in winter. W., employed in both flag and costume making, has been in the business since 1822, and employs six girls all the year. Flags, costumes, &c., used in the South, have always been ordered in New York, so there will be some openings in the South for such work. W. pays $3 and $4 a week to his best hands, and has his sewing done in the house. His work is of a superior quality, and, consequently, commands a good price. He employs only correct and fast sewers. He thinks there are openings for girls of good moral character, properly qualified. A lady cutting out costumes told me that it requires judgment to make the two halves alike—sleeves, for instance ; also to know in how short a time an article can be made up, where and how to get workers, &c. It is difficult to get good hands, and some of the materials are costly—so they do not like to give work to any one they do not know. A spangler receives from them $62\frac{1}{2}$ cents a day. Mrs. T. employs a number of hands, paying $3 a week to those that work in the house—ten hours a day. Those that take their work home are, of course, paid by the piece. She does all her own cutting out. It requires ability to fit, ingenuity to design, and taste to execute. Spangling pays best. She had a lady tinselling and spangling for her, that made a good living at it. She

does opera and theatrical work, mostly. She makes some ball
costumes also. Equestrian work she does not like, as it is pretty
much made up of horse trappings. The prospect for those who
would learn it well, she thinks very good. She finds it difficult
to get superior workers. The girls that sew for costumers are
mostly those who prefer that to going out to do housework, because they can have their evenings as their own. It is usual to
have a costumer travel with an opera troupe, who directs and
superintends the making up of costumes, and dresses the prima
donna before she makes her appearance on the stage. Mrs. S.
takes learners, paying them half price for two or three months,
while learning. She makes up most after Thanksgiving, for the
Christmas festivities; but in summer she makes up some ball costumes, and apparel and drapery for tableaux, and operas at water-
ing places. She has from one to two hundred women and girls
sewing for her at different times. Frequently she is very much
hurried, and must employ a great many to assist, for bills announ-
cing operas are often out before the costume is brought to her.
At W.'s, they pay $3 a week—ten hours a day—and are most
busy about Christmas.

340. Dresses. In Germany, many dress makers are men,
and there is one on Broadway, New York. France is the fountain head of fashion for ladies' dress. Most of the fashions,
however, are Americanized when introduced into this country.
Dress is, to some extent, an index to the mind of the wearer.
Judgment and good taste are the best guides. Several things
are to be taken into consideration—age, complexion, proportion,
means, station, comfort, and decorum. A lady, with command
of a full purse, can dress as she pleases. Rich and elegant clothing, appropriately made, is an ornament, and well becomes those
that can afford it. With a scant purse, a lady cannot dress very
handsomely, yet she may always observe neatness and propriety
of costume. A passion for dress is apt to betray an empty mind
or great vanity. Much of the beauty of a dress depends on its
tasteful make. If the figure is bad, it improves it. If good, it
adds to the beauty of the figure, which is one of the most im-
pressive modifications of beauty. In dress making, a lady has
only to establish a reputation as a successful fitter and fashionable trimmer, and she will be sure of a run of custom and handsome profits. I am sorry to say, in the majority of dress-making
establishments, no reliance can be placed on the word of the
principals, in regard to the time work will be finished. While
many of those at the head of dress-making establishments are
realizing dazzling profits, the poor sempstress, working in busy
times from twelve to sixteen hours out of the twenty-four, re-

ceives the generous allowance of from $1.50 to $4.50 a week. But few, and those only of much skill, taste, and dexterity, ever gain better prices. Fitters and forewomen, in some places, gain from $4 to $7 per week. I believe it is generally thought men fit better than women, so many ladies have their basques and riding habits made at tailors' establishments. We do not see why the plan used by tailors, of fitting by measure, is not more generally applied to dress fitting. Dress making is more fatiguing than millinery work, because you have to sit at it more steadily and there is more sameness in it. Spring and fall are the most busy seasons. Those who can secure sewing in good families, and have some decent place to go in the intervals, are better off than most others. They receive from 50 cents to $1.25 per day and their dinner. It would probably require a little time to become known; and one, to succeed, must know how to do all parts, from the fitting to the finishing off; so it requires skill and a thorough knowledge of the business. A lady who sews by the day told me she often gets her system out of order by the different food of the several families she is in, and the different times of taking it. We think there are no regular hours for those who work by the day in New York. The length of the day depends on the mercy of the employer. "Dress makers in Boston, some years ago, adopted the ten-hour system, and now average $1.25 per day. Previously they received but 75 cents or $1." The demand for dress makers in the Northern and Eastern States is fully met, but throughout the South and West there are openings, here and there, for good dress makers. There is probably no occupation in which there are so many incompetent persons as that of dress making. Many persons take it up without having learned the trade at all, and many who become reduced in circumstances immediately resort to it without any preparation, and are destitute, not only of experience, but of skill, ingenuity, and taste. In New York, the conditions on which apprentices are taken vary greatly. Some pay nothing for six months, and even receive $10 or $15 for instruction. The girls are kept at making up skirts, sewing up sleeves, and such plain work, and so learn nothing during the time. Some are taken for a year, and boarded during that time for their work. Some live at home, and are paid from $1.50 to $2.50 for their work. Some are taken for two years, to learn the trade thoroughly, and work from eight to twelve hours a day. Some apprentices have not the ability to become good fitters and sewers, and are destitute of artistic taste; but women seldom change from one employment to another on discovering their incompetency. The majority, probably, have not the time or means of doing so. Miss B. says those who sew for dress makers receive from $2.50 to $4 a week, working ten hours a day. Apprentices that can sew right well when they commence, receive at some houses $2 a week for six months, but they are not taught to fit unless the employer is a conscientious woman and there is a special contract. When the busy season is over, the inferior hands are turned off without an hours' warning. It is desirable to get a good class of customers, that the pay will be sure, and that the dress maker may know what to rely on. Some dress makers in New York have kept the patterns of ladies in the South, and made their dresses for years. If a slight change was needed, for instance, the length increased, or the waist made smaller, or *vice versa*, the lady wrote accordingly. Miss B. never works for servants. They do not pay as well, and are just as particular as their mistresses. She never works for a stranger, unless recommended by one of her customers. Mrs. C. told me that a girl of fair abilities can learn dress making in six months. The first three months she does not pay anything, but the last three $1 a week. After they have learned she pays according to their taste, skill, and industry. One girl, that has good taste in trimming and finishing off, she pays $4 a week; another, that sews well and is industrious, but deficient in taste, she pays $2. They all live at home. Those girls that live at home are often willing to work for less than the ordinary wages, as they are not at the greatest of all expenses—boarding. They work from seven in the morning until six, having an hour at noon. They prefer it to the hours of some of the Broadway shops, which are usually from eight to seven. By the first arrangement they are enabled to get home early and go to any place of amusement. Miss H. told me that three years ago she earned $7 per week, ten hours a day, sewing for a French lady on Broadway, who had a great run of Southern custom. There were many strangers in the city at the time. " Servant girls seldom pay over $1 for making a dress; yet 10,000 servant girls in New York city, will have from three to six and eight new dresses a year." At Wilson's Industrial School, New York, some of the older girls are taught dress making.

341. Dress Caps and Head Dresses. The making of ladies' dress caps is an extensive and important branch of business. The rates at which they are now put together, enable most ladies to buy them already made. In large cities there are separate establishments for the sale of them, but in smaller towns they are sold at milliner shops. Much taste should be, and generally is, exercised in this department of business. In London, on the streets, the caps and bonnets exposed for sale are placed in inverted umbrellas. On summing up what was told me by eight manufacturers of dress caps and head dresses, I find the prices they pay the women who sew for them, run from $2 a week to $10—the average $4. Some pay by the week, but most by the piece, which is usually most profitable to the worker, and most satisfactory to both parties. Superior hands prefer to work by the piece, and, when working for first-class stores, earn from $6 to $8 per week. There is a scarcity of good hands in New York, and I would advise some ladies to learn. Taste, and swiftness of fingers are required. The finer and more delicate the hands of a worker the better. Some are employed all the year, but the majority are not. The busy season begins in January and lasts till the middle of May, and begins in September and lasts till the middle of October, when city work usually commences. Some houses, in the intervals, make up for the city trade. The South has depended almost entirely on the North for the supply of these articles. There will be openings in the South for establishments of the kind. One keeper of a large fancy store said to me, there are not more than ten first-class makers of dress caps in New York. He thought the Irish succeed, many of whom learn in the convents of their own country to use the needle well. Hands employed by the week usually work ten hours a day. Most people prefer to employ the hands they have had. The best place for learning is in a shop confined to the city trade. Mrs. D. devotes herself to making up caps for the dead, but employs sewers to make ladies' dress caps. It requires time to get to making them tastefully and rapidly. An experienced hand can earn from $4 to $6 a week, piecework. It is thought three months' time is necessary for learning, and during that time a girl cannot earn over $1 a week. Mrs. D. says some can earn but eight or nine cents a day while learning, and become discouraged and give it up. She will not trust any but experienced hands, on account of the loss of materials, for when badly cut, they cannot be altered into anything else, and, when they have to be ripped, lose their stiffening, and are only fit for the scrap bag. They can soon judge of hands by their appearance, the way they sew, and knowing for whom they have worked, and the kind of work that house turns out. They always require reference or deposit. They keep their hands all the year, making caps part of the year to send away, and the remainder of the year for city trade. Ladies' dress caps have been superseded to a great extent by fancy head dresses and flowers. Miss C., Broadway, told me her best hands earn, by the piece, from $6 to $7 per week. It requires three months to learn the business. Learners, that have some knowledge of sewing, receive from her $1 a week. Judgment, in size, form, and manner of putting together, is desirable. The busy seasons are spring and fall. There is rather a deficiency of good hands in New York, and in busy seasons it is sometimes difficult to get enough of indifferent hands. The French are very successful, on account of their cultivated taste. I was told that Mme. D. employs two Austrian girls that invent beautiful styles of head dresses. Mr. D. says the person that has the taste and ingenuity to invent pleasing styles will receive a good price. He had to pay $4 a dozen more for a new style of head dresses imported not long ago from Paris, merely because it was of a new design. He playfully remarked : " Fancy goods must bring fancy prices." A woman that has lived in Paris, and been engaged in the business there, and accustomed to observing the fashions and inventing them, would receive a high salary. He pays from $6 to $9 a week, according to qualifications. The abilities and taste of a person have much to do with the time of learning—six months are usually given. He pays $3 a week to smart learners. He sells rather more goods in fall, as ladies are then preparing for balls and parties. He prefers to have foreigners to work for him, as he is himself a foreigner. His store girls leave at 6 P. M. Those that board pay $3 a week. In most stores for the sale of ladies' fancy articles, the ladies in attendance make up such articles, when not waiting on customers. From a larger establishment, the superintendent sent me the following report : " Women earn from $4 to $10 per week, being paid by the piece. It requires from three months to one year to learn the business. After six weeks, the hands are paid a small trifle. Women are employed about eight months in the year, but first-class hands find employment always. In busy seasons the work must be done —so hands cannot limit themselves to time, but must be employed late and early. The demand for first-class hands is great, and enough cannot be found. I employ from one hundred and fifty to two hundred on an average. Most of my hands are foreigners, and married women that live at home."

342. Fans. In most ages, and in most countries, the fan has been used as much by gentlemen as ladies. In Japan, every body carries a fan. " In M. Duveleroy's fan establishment—the largest in Paris—each fan, from the commonest to the most costly, passes through fifteen hands before it is ready for use and the retailer." The palm-leaf fans, which have been so much in vogue for years past, are made to some extent in the Eastern States. Fans are sometimes made of feathers. Peacock, duck, turkey, and those of small birds are employed. As in other manufactures, the capital required, the risk run, the want of operatives acquainted with the business, and the comparative highness of wages have hitherto debarred any one from undertaking the manufacture of fans extensively in the United States. Taste is necessary for a fan maker. A man that has been making fans for two years in New York, told me he took it up from repairing fans. He cannot keep materials enough on hand, because suitable feathers are high and difficult to get. He is raising some peacocks and white turkeys, that he may have the feathers for making fans. The women he employed last year he paid by the piece, and they earned from $5 to $6 per week. He will employ more women in the course of a year or two.

343. Ladies' Under-Wear. A sempstress in New York can seldom earn more than seventy-five cents a day—fifty is the more usual sum. At Mrs. C. & Co.'s, all the work is done by hand. They employ by the week and by the piece. They will not allow goods to be taken out unless they know the person to be reliable, because they find it difficult to get work back at the time promised. They sell most articles made up, about Christmas, and in the spring. People do not have half so much sewing done out as they used to, because so many own sewing machines, and they are not willing to pay the same prices that they formerly did. Some women that live and dress well in New York, take in sewing to obtain pinmoney. She mentioned one lady that came dressed in her elegant furs and point lace, and got sewing, she said, for a sick young friend; but when she came back, she said the friend was not able to do it, and so she did it herself, and would like to have more. She lived in style on —— street. The cutters of under-wear, who are competent and responsible, can earn $6 per week, and even more, but it requires considerable experience. A lady that has sewing done told me that nothing pays so poorly as white work. She requires a sample of work and a deposit from any one that takes sewing out, to the amount of the value of the article. A lady that has most beautiful under-wear made up for ladies in New York and in the South, told me her Southern orders have all ceased. Her work is mostly done by hand. She has a forewoman that bastes and cuts. She has not less than ten or twelve applicants every day for work. Some of her hands earn $5 or $6 a week, and others work just as long and do not earn $3. Some of her workers can earn $4 by embroidering, but sewing generally pays best. She pays her operator by the piece—so much a yard. When she had Southern orders, she sent goods by express, and the express collected the money on the goods. If the money was not paid by those who had ordered the goods, the express would not deliver them, but returned them. They were responsible for their return, in case they were not paid for. In the first place, something was paid for transmitting and collecting; in the latter, for transmitting both

ways. Many ladies used to send their measures and directions,
and she would make up accordingly. She finds bridal apparel
most profitable. In large cities there is a small demand for the
costume of artists, sea bathers, and practisers of gymnastics. At
the Employment House, B., I was told they have more applications
than they can attend to, for plain sewing; but fine sewing it is
more difficult to get done. Fine sewing pays for itself very well,
but coarse does not. At L. & T.'s, New York, they have every
branch done, and pay sewers by hand as good prices as operators.
A right neat and fast sempstress can earn $6 a week : it is piece-
work. Operators can earn $5 or $6. Part of the work is done
in the building, and part is given out. At first they found it difficult to get superior sewers, but they have plenty now. They
have sometimes employed 375 hands. About half their women
are Americans. It is usual for the forewoman to do the cutting,
and she can earn from $6 to $12. When they pay by the week, the
girls work from 8 A. M. to 6 P. M., and have three fourths of an
hour at noon. They pay by the week for making mantillas and
cloaks. It is most profitable to the employées to pay by the
piece. Their customers can rely on their work, and are willing
to pay a good price for hand sewing. A lady that supplies under-
wear told me that she finds it difficult to obtain any one that is
reliable to give her work to—one that she can be sure will do
her work well at the proper time. She pays those that work in
the house $3 a week, of ten hours a day. Neatness, care, and ex-
pedition, she requires of her hands. There is an abundance of
indifferent hands, but a scarcity of superior ones.

344. Over Gaiters. R., Philadelphia, employs fifty girls.
Some of the gaiters are made by sewing machines, and some are
stitched by hand. Makers earn from $3 to $5 a week. Most of
the work is done in the establishment—some is taken out.

345. Patterns. In large cities there is a constant call for
a supply of new patterns; consequently stores are kept for the purpose of cutting and selling them. A dress and cloak making establishment is frequently connected with them. The sale of patterns
to dress and cloak makers in the South and West is considerable
—greater, perhaps, than that in the city. T., and Mme. D., are the
leaders of this branch in New York. Mme. D. has in pattern
making mostly young girls. A large room of young girls requires
but two or three ladies to assist and direct. It takes but little
time to learn. She does not pay until they have learned, and
then pays young girls $1 a week and upward. T., son of the ed-
itor of the *Bon Ton*, told me their fashion magazines have a circulation of three thousand, mostly among milliners and dress
makers. The plates are colored in Paris. Leslie's and Godey's

plates are colored in this country. T.'s takes six French publications devoted to the fashions. They look over plates and select such styles as they think will be popular. They have a lady in Paris who writes to them from there, describing the fashions. They employ a lady in connection with their pattern making who, by looking at the plates, is able to cut out a mantle, sleeve, &c., exactly like the plates. Some ladies could never learn to do so. They employ ladies, both in pattern cutting and dress making, and pay from $3 to $5 per week—to a competent forewoman, $10 and $15. Women are paid small wages while learning. Their business is advancing—has advanced most during the last few years. Their trade is Eastern, Western, and Southern—mostly Southern. Their girls are employed from 8 A. M. to 6 P. M.; having an hour at noon. In the pattern business, there are just about enough of hands in New York. Spring and fall are the busy seasons. E. G. says the busy season commences the middle of January, when she is willing to receive learners. She gives instruction for nothing for one month; after that, she pays $2.50 a week, if successful, and continues to increase salary according to the abilities of the individual. A good hand can earn $5 per week, working ten hours a day. Another lady told me that in pattern making she gives instruction two months, paying nothing, but then they can earn $2.50, and, as they become more expert, can earn $3, 3.50, and $4. They are paid by the week, and it would be impossible to pay by the piece. It requires practice to become an expert cutter. She prefers, for pattern cutting, young girls from twelve to fifteen years old. In large cities, some women go around to cut patterns, sell stays, embroidery, &c.

346. Shoes. The business of making and selling shoes opens a wide field of employment to women. The fashion, a few years back, of ladies making their own shoes, raged like a fever. Those that had leisure did so with economy, as the lasts and implements for working cost only $3, and the materials for a pair of shoes from sixty cents to $1. Afterward no further expense was needed but the materials. The fitting of shoes is basting, stitching, and putting them together. Fitting is generally done by females, and is so simple that children can work at it. A good deal of this work is done in families at the East. Crimping and bottoming are done altogether by men. Some firms in cities confine themselves to importing and dealing in shoe-manufacturers' tools, materials, &c. In Massachusetts, most of the shoes are made in country towns, where living is much cheaper than in the cities; and the business in cities is very much absorbed by foreigners, that can live much cheaper than Americans. The principal defect in ready-made shoes is their imperfect shape. It would be well for every adult to have a last made the exact shape of his or her foot, and keep it at the shoemaker's. "The application of machinery to the manufacture of shoes has made so vast a difference in the ease and rapidity of their production that those engaged in the business can scarcely realize the advantage they possess, and before they are aware of it they are in the way of creating a surplus. The effect of this change in their production will be to lessen the number of manufacturers and operatives." Says a writer in the *Pennsylvania Inquirer :* "Individuals that are prominent in the shoe business assert that about 2,000 females are employed in Philadelphia in binding shoes or sewing uppers; but they do not obtain steady work, and the average of their wages is only $75 to $100 per annum." Four thousand two hundred men are employed in Philadelphia in making women's shoes. Might not a large part of that work be done by women? Yes; the cutting, binding, stitching—indeed, the entire making of ladies' shoes might be done by women. Most of the stitching is now done by machines. The most depressed trades in New York, in 1845, were those of shoe and shirt making. From the New York *Tribune* of May, 1853, we take the subjoined extract: "The binding of children's shoes is paid for at the rate of two pairs for three cents, or eighteen cents a dozen pair; while for the full size, five cents a pair. Now a first-rate hand may succeed, by the closest application—say from fourteen to seventeen hours a day, if uninterrupted by domestic cares—in making, during the week, four dozen pairs, for which, after delivery and approval, she will be paid $2.40, that being the maximum paid, and representing the value of not less than eighty hours' labor ; and from this miserable dole the cost of light and fire is to be deducted. We are not prepared to say this sum is never exceeded, as some houses may pay a slight advance on these prices; but it is more than sufficient for us to know that this is *above* the average that hundreds of women and girls in this city (New York) are earning from that source." We have seen it stated, elsewhere, that good shoebinders, in New York, usually earn from $4 to $7 a week. I talked with a shoe fitter in New York, who works for a large and fashionable store and employs a number of hands. Some of her operators have $6 a week, and have better wages than hand workers, because they can do more work in the same time. As sewing machines become cheaper, wages for work done by them will fall. Shoemakers made more money before ladies wore heels on their shoes, as they wore out more. Mrs. I., a shoe fitter, told me that she pays one of her hands $7, another $6, and none less than $4. It requires about six months for most women to learn the trade. The business is one that will extend.

Spring and fall are the best seasons for work. Her hands usually spend but nine hours a day at labor, as stitching shoes is heavy work. Men usually do the cutting in the back of the store, and receive better wages than the women. The cutting is done by hand. Her workers pay $2.50 for board. There is a scarcity of good operators on uppers. Plenty of indifferent hands can be had at any time. She says American women are too fond of pleasure and dress. They make money, and then must have a day or two to rest. She was an Irish woman. The journeymen shoemakers of New York have an association for regulating prices and hours of work, and a lady branch was started, but has become extinct. A shoebinder in Brooklyn told me that he employs a number of girls, paying his operatives $3, $4, $5, and some even $6 per week. The machines have taken work from many, and lowered the prices of those that do it by hand. To make fancy shoes requires taste and judgment. The late strikes have given us, through the newspapers, some reliable information in regard to the starving rates paid for work, and wages have been somewhat increased by it. I heard a shoemaker say he knew one sewer that received forty cents for a week's work, stitching sixty pairs of gaiters. Two cents is what some of the Massachusetts women received for binding a pair of boots. Yet the consumer must pay as high for boots and shoes as ever. The reason given is, that leather costs more than formerly—a statement we are led to doubt when considering the increased facilities for tanning. An intelligent shoe fitter told me the prices of work were formerly much higher than now. The work that would formerly have brought fifty cents is now not paid more than twenty-five cents. Mrs. B. says well-dressed women sometimes come and bring what they say is a sample of their work. A few pairs will be given them to make, which they will bring in poorly stitched. She thinks any one in the shoe-making business that does her work well can always find employment. "In Ohio, several women are employed as shoemakers, and others are working independently and successfully, evincing both taste and ability in their elegant and substantial work." A manufacturer in Albany, N. Y., writes: "I employ ten women running sewing machines, binding by hand, and stitching with wax-thread and awl. I pay mostly by the piece, and my hands earn from $2 to $5 per week. Women cannot do men's labor in our branch. Learners are paid what they earn. Mechanical talent is a desirable qualification. The prospect for extension of the business is necessarily poor. Prison work is interfering much with our craft. Women can have steady work, if employers manage prudently. Women that work with awl and wax thread are mostly foreign." The returns of 1860 give 56,039 males and 24,978 females employed in making boots and shoes in New England; and in all the States, 96,287 males and 31,140 females. In Dublin, about five hundred women are employed in eight of the large establishments of that city in boot closing, and earn on an average eight shillings per week, of nine hours a day.

347. Stays and Corsets. At Mrs. B.'s, Philadelphia, I was told women are paid by the dozen for making corsets, and earn from $2 to $3 a week. They mostly take their work home. At a place in New York, I was told they have sewing machines, and they pay operators $4 a week, working from $7\frac{1}{2}$ A. M. to $7\frac{1}{2}$ P. M. Those that sew for them by hand do not earn so much. It is difficult to get enough of good hands; so the lady thought there must be openings for competent workers. Girls get $4 a week for basting. Their girls are of all nations. Every store, she remarked, has its own way of doing business. It takes some time to learn to do all parts, as a girl usually works at some special part. A man does the cutting. One corset maker thinks it a valuable gift to be able to fit well. She considers corsets necessary to the preservation of health. American children, by their restlessness, counteract the effects of their rapid growth. Miss C. told me those that work for wholesale houses can, if good hands, find work all the year. They are paid by the piece, and can earn from $3 to $6. It requires three or four years to learn all parts. Her girls cannot take their work home. Few are willing to take learners. At another place, I was told a good operator can get $6 a week. They sell most women corsets of French and German make. The French fit American ladies nearly as well as those made to order, but the German do not. At another place, I was told it requires but a short time to learn. There are but few manufactories in this country. The imported corsets are mostly sold, because cheapest. The basters get $3 a week, ten hours a day, and operators $4, and $4.50, according to abilities. Mrs. B. thinks it difficult to become a good fitter. She employs men to cut, put bones and eyelets in, and press. Anybody that can sew well can soon take up corset making. All her sewing is done by hand. She sends her work to the country, because she can get it done more cheaply. The work pays poorly. She says the form is retained much longer by wearing corsets. A lady who employs women to stitch corsets for her by hand, pays from $2.50 to $3.50 a week—ten working hours a day. It requires six months to learn, and a just eye, a knowledge of figure, and an ability to sew by hand and stitch by machine, to succeed. She says most corset employers in New York are French, and employés Irish. She thought, if a lady has good apartments in a genteel part of the city, she may do well. Mrs. B., who has been twenty-three years carrying on the business on Broadway, says "she has applications constantly, but finds it difficult to obtain competent workmen. Men are practical corset makers, and do the cutting. They are better able to cut the goods, so as to make a handsome fit. They receive better wages than women. It is a business as much to be learned as cutting gentlemen's coats. She pays both by the piece and week, and her hands receive from $3 to $8. Some of the stitching is done by machinery —some by hand. It requires about the same time to learn corset as dress making. Learners receive from her from $1.50 to $2 per week. She thinks the supply of hands just equal to the demand. She employs from 100 to 150 hands. They are mostly from Great Britain. The business is dependent on fashion. Spring and fall are the busy seasons. In summer, she does not sell so much, because ladies are then out of town; but the employés can work all the year, and do so, as she keeps a stock on hand. Corsets are more worn now than a few years back. A manufacturer in Boston writes: "I employ ten American women in sewing on corsets. They work by the piece, and average sixty cents per day. The prospect of future employment is not flattering. Board, $2.25." Another manufacturer in Boston "pays from $3 to $4.50, and says it is all he can afford to pay. His hands work ten hours a day. The prospect for this work is good. July and August are the dullest months. He has found women equal to men in all branches of business they conduct. Board, $2.50."

STRAW WORKERS.

348. Bleachers and Pressers. I called in a place where I saw the pressing of bonnets and children's hats. The rims of the hats were pressed by a woman with a large iron, the crowns by a man with an iron attached to a lever fastened in a frame. It is all piecework, and some can earn from $4 to $5 a week. I have been told that Mrs. K., New York, employs women pressers. The iron is not so heavy for bonnet pressing as for hats, but requires too much strength for a woman. Shaping straw bonnets is done by women—that is, placing them on blocks and pinning them around the edge, after they have been bleached, until they acquire shape. A man pressing straw hats, told me he is paid 5 cents a hat, and can press sixty in ten hours. The time for learning either to sew or bleach, I find, is usually six weeks. Mrs. M. pays learners nothing for six weeks. Her busy seasons are from October to last of November, and from December to spring. It is all piecework, and her girls earn from $3 to $4. A bleacher of straw hats employs a lady at $5 per week to alter and wire bonnets, after they have been bleach-ed, which is done by her own family. She works ten hours a day. The work is mostly confined to spring and fall. The bleaching process is very deleterious, owing to the sulphur used. It pro-duces a loss of vitality and shortens life. A stout, healthy man, in the course of a year, becomes quite pale and thin. The bleach-ing does not require all the time of any one. The bonnets and hats are put into the bleaching room, and, when they have be-come white, are taken out.

349. Braiders. The following is from the New York *Tribune*, of 1845 : "The Amazonia braid weavers—a large and ill-paid class of working females—begin work at seven in the morning, and continue until seven in the evening, with no inter-mission save to swallow a hasty morsel. They earn, when in full employment, $2 and $2.50 a week. Out of this, they must pay their board and washing (for they have no time to wash their own clothes), medical and other incidental expenses, and pur-chase their clothes—to say nothing of the total absence of all healthy recreation, and of all mental and moral culture, which such a condition necessarily implies. They have, many of them, no rooms of their own, but board with some poor family, sleeping anyhow, and anywhere. For these accommodations they pay $1.50 per week, some of the lowest and filthiest boarding houses charging as low as $1 per week. The living here must be imagined." At Foxboro', Franklin, Middleboro', and Nan-tucket, Mass., are straw manufactories. "In 1855, 6,000,000 straw hats and bonnets were made in Massachusetts, giving employment to ten thousand of her people." Rye straw is raised in all the New England States. It is cut, soaked in water (I think split), and then dried. It is sold by the pound—then braided by women and children for 10 or 12 cents a day. It is mostly done in farmers' families, who are at but little expense for living. In this state, it is mostly sold to merchants or agents, who sell it at manufactories, where it is trimmed by machinery, and then sewed. It is then shaped into bonnets, wired, pressed, and bleached, the crowns are lined with paper, and they are packed ready for exportation. The women earn on an average $5 a week. In England, wheat straw is raised, which is inferior to rye straw. N. says the largest straw-bonnet establishments of Eng-land are not as large as those of the United States. For making straw hats in Philadelphia, men receive $7.50 a week, and women

$4.50. Philadelphia is said to spend $6,000,000 annually in the manufacture of straw goods. At H.'s, New York, they employ from fifty to one hundred hands. It is usual to have learners six weeks for nothing, and then pay full wages, if they prove competent. Work is given about ten months. They are paid by the piece, and can earn from $4 to $6 per week. In December, they begin to make up hats and bonnets for spring. A milliner told me she pays her braiders by the yard. Some earn $4 a week, and some even $5. They work at home. The summer season is over by September. H. writes: "In my opinion the best arranged industrial establishment is the Union Straw Works at Foxboro', Mass. High wages, cushioned arm-chairs, a literary society which carries on the lyceum lectures of the town, are all far above any of our factories. The proprietor would not call it a factory, to make it more attractive. Out of three hundred operatives, sometimes, seventy-five have been teachers."

350. Sewers. Mrs. K. employs about seventy-five girls for bleaching and sewing braid and straw bonnets. She pays some $3, some $3.50, and some $4 a week. They work ten hours. All live at home, but bring their dinners. She bleaches by the old-fashioned process with sulphur, and has men to do the pressing. N. & Co. employ about one hundred and twenty-five on an average six months, and about twenty-five all the year. The bonnet business has increased very much during the last few years. At B.'s, I was told the wholesale work for the South begins in November; but the city work, the last of March, and continues to July. It is light work, and does not require close application of the eyes. Machinery can never be used for sewing straw, because long stitches answer, and straw is too brittle. Persons of a nervous temperament are often the most intellectual. Such females make good straw sewers. It requires a peculiar adaptability, as every other occupation does. Everybody cannot learn to sing or to paint—just so some cannot make good straw sewers. He thinks most young work-people in New York do not live at home, and considers obedience to parents and observance of the Sabbath the foundation of success in life. B—s, of Connecticut, write: "Women are employed in this country, and in Italy, France, and England, in sewing straw. Our girls (150) are mostly paid by the piece, and earn from $3 to $7 per week. They also trim straw hats. They spend four weeks as learners, and are paid $2 a week while learning. To be a fast sewer is the most important requisite. The prospect of a continuance of this work is good. The busy season is from September to June. The best locations are near New York and Boston." "About 200 persons are employed in the straw

15

factory at Nantucket. Some of the operatives are daughters of the leading men of the town, and make $5 a week at the business." A firm at Middleboro', Mass., write: "We employ 850 women, and have them in preference to men, because they are more dexterous with the needle. They receive from 30 cents to $1.62 per day, and are paid mostly by the piece. Women are paid five eighths what the men receive, but could not perform their labor even at the same price. Learners make enough to pay their board the first three weeks. Good mechanical talent is needed in a learner. They have work about nine months in the year—generally stop July, August, and November. Nine tenths are Americans; seven eighths live at home. A large number of them are not dependent upon labor for a living. Board, $2 to $2.25." From a factory in Wrentham, Mass., we have the following report: "We employ during the winter season, in the factory, from seventy-five to one hundred females, and in families who work at home about six hundred, whose pay is not so good by about one third. Some of our workers are paid by the piece—some by the hour. Most of them can earn $1 a day, twelve hours being a day for females. Men are paid 15 cents an hour; good help extra, and poor, less. They work ten hours. For the part done by women, we pay the same price from the first, but their work is not received until it is well done. A person is employed to give them instruction; five or six weeks' practice mostly makes a good sewer of one who can learn at all. During this time most girls earn half wages. To good help we usually give work nine months in the year. Busy seasons from December 1st till June 1st, and from July 15th to October 1st. The rest of the year, work is given out at reduced prices—sufficient to earn about half wages. All American women. It is desirable for manufacturers to be near New York city, so as to keep posted on styles. Many ladies choose this business after teaching school for years. Most of our hands come from Maine, and board in houses provided for them, paying $2 a week." Another straw manufacturer informs me "the girls in straw shops earn more than in most other kinds of business, they being, as a general thing, smarter girls, and such as would not work in cotton and other large mills. Their work varies much, as the styles and materials change." A firm employing about eighty American girls write: "They are paid according to their skill and smartness, from $2.50 to $10 per week. Two thirds work by the piece—half will earn $5 to $6.50—average about $4.50 per week. Male labor will average double. It cannot be done by females—they are not strong enough. The reason of women's being paid low wages is the surplus of female labor. They cannot be hired to do housework—it is too confining. It requires one month, more or less, according to taste and genius, to learn the work. Good references as to character are required, and some skill with the needle, and an idea of form. Busy from December to June, and from August to November. We do nothing for about three months. Hands hired by the week are paid extra for overwork. If we could not give them the amount of work they have, the *best* help would go elsewhere. There is always plenty of help in this branch in New York, and they get work done for much less, but by a different caste of girls. In the New England States, girls are generally brought up to work, whether rich or poor, and we can get help from the best families, well educated and intelligent—while in some States we could not find them. Board, $2.25 to $2.50." A straw firm in Franklin, Mass., write: "We employ about 400 females—60 of them in our manufactory—the remainder work at their homes. The former have the privilege of working from 6 A. M. to 9 P. M.; but as they work by the piece, they are not confined to any particular time. The latter accommodate themselves. Few get less than 80 cents per diem, and many can earn over $1—some over $1.50. All are paid by the piece, except overseers. Males and females are never employed in the same kind of labor. Females make and trim bonnets and hats—males bleach, block, and press them, which is too laborious work for females. Some years would be required to learn to conduct the straw business successfully. Some females will make a very good bonnet or hat after a few weeks' practice. Others take a longer time, and a few will never make a good bonnet. Our practice is to pay all while learning. The qualifications required by us are a good character, good health, skill in the use of the needle, and a desire to acquire proficiency. The supply of hands is always greater than the demand. All the females employed in straw factories are American. Our girls have access to a good library, lectures, &c. Those employed in manufacturing board at $2.25 per week, including washing. Boarding houses attached to the different straw manufactories in this town are of good character and comfortable."

———•••———

RENOVATORS.

351. Gentlemen's Wear. A dyer and scourer of gentlemen's clothing told me she charges 37 cents for scouring and pressing a pair of pantaloons; 75 cents for a coat, and $1 for an overcoat.   A woman could make a comfortable living at it if she had constant employment.

352. Ladies' Wear. The cleaning of kid gloves saves quite an item in the purses of the wearers.   Wooden frames, the shape and size of gloves, are used for drying them on.   The renovating of silk shawls, dresses, and other goods is best done by the French. They are sometimes made to look almost as bright and clean as if they were new. Woollen goods, too, that will not bear washing, are beautifully cleaned by those that rightly understand the business.   All that profess to, by the way, do not.   Prices vary, of course, according to goods, places, and renovators. Women are mostly engaged in this business.   A cleaner of kid gloves writes : " I employ some women with pens and needles at $3 per week, working from four to six hours per day.   Cool weather is the best for work, but they are employed all the year." Mrs. C. told me that her husband and his men clean most gloves in winter ; they can clean them in two days.   I noticed they are free from any offensive odor.   They pass through the hands several times.   She charges individuals 12½ cents a pair—store-keepers less.   She has been many years at it. They used to send a wagon and collect them from the stores, but their business does not warrant it now—so they send a messenger. As many have attempted that do not thoroughly understand it, the business has been injured.

————•••————

GENTLEMEN'S CLOTHING.

353. Army and Navy Uniform. Our Government might do something toward bringing about a reform in the prices paid women. If those who have clothing made for the men of the army and navy would pay good prices to men of standing, that pay their workwomen well, we think some good might be done.   At any rate, they would set a good example.

354. Buttons. The making of buttons is chiefly done by women, and affords employment for a great many. The proportion of women to men in this branch of industry is six to one.   Some kinds of buttons are made by hand, but most by machinery, moved by steam.   The manufacture of cloth for buttons is a distinct branch of business.   It was estimated in 1851 that five thousand persons were employed in Birmingham in the manufacture of buttons of different kinds, more than half of whom were women and children.   In the manufacture of buttons a variety of hands are employed—piercers, cutters, stampers, gilders, and varnishers. "In a factory employing five men and thirty females, from six to seven hundred gross of buttons can be turned out daily." I called in a factory where buttons were made of vegetable ivory. I think all the work could be done by women, but it is a trade, and requires three years to learn all the parts. One man might be needed to put the machinery in order when it would get out of repair. Boys that polish buttons are paid from $2 to $3 a week. Polishing looks simple, but, no doubt, requires practice. A little girl, whose father makes common horn buttons, says he employs some small girls who, by presses, cut out the buttons and make the perforations. They are paid seven cents for a thousand. Her parents assort them. H. & C., manufacturers of cloth and gilt buttons, say it requires some weeks to learn to chase the gilt buttons, which are done with small metal tools and a hammer. Chasers are paid by the piece, working ten hours a day, and some can earn $1 a day. Those that make cloth buttons work by the week, eleven hours a day. They pay nothing while the person is learning. They think the prospect of employment in that branch is good. (I think it must be, for it is a manufacture likely to extend.) They employ their hands all the year. The girls sit while at work. S. has girls to do most of the work in making men's coat buttons. They cut out the iron and cloth with machines, and also cover the buttons with machines. The girls require but a few weeks to learn. They are paid from $1.75 to $3 a week. Some of the girls are not more than twelve years of age. The average of the oldest girls is $2.75. They work ten hours. Learners are paid half wages. Good eyesight and smart fingers are needed. The gilding of brass buttons is called water gilding, though no water is used. The mercury and nitric acid used in gilding metal buttons renders the business pernicious to the health, the fumes of the nitric acid affecting the lungs, and the mercury producing its peculiar disease. A manufacturer of tin buttons writes: "Our women earn from 75 cents to $1 per day, and are paid by the piece. It requires but little practice to learn. All are American girls from neighboring families." A manufacturer in Middlefield, Conn., writes: "We employ from twenty-five to thirty girls in cutting, drilling, sorting, and packing buttons. They work by the piece, and average $15 per month. While learning they are paid $1 per week, and their board. They have regular work, and pay for board $1.50 per week. The prospect for an increase of the manufacture is fair." A button company in Waterbury write: "Our hands receive $3 and upward, as they are worth. The business is good when times are good.

The majority are Americans.   Spring and fall are the best
seasons."   A buttonmaker in Morrisville, Pa., writes: " We pay
our girls by the gross, and they earn from $1 to $4 per week.
Men earn from $3 to $9.   The women's work is lighter.   Beginners are paid small wages.   The prospect of future work is
poor.   Seasons make no difference in the work."

355. Canes. Walking canes could be painted and varnished by women.   I have been told that, in France, women are employed in making ivory, gold, whalebone, and wire heads for
canes.   Mrs. F. makes whalebone heads for canes.   She offered to
teach me how for $20.   P. says he pays from $6 to $100 a dozen
for the heads of canes—ivory, silver, and gold.   The work is mostly
done by Germans.   The business will not pay except in large cities.
There are only six in the business in New York, which is the
main depot.   He sells most to Southerners and Canadians.   The
business requires a regular apprenticeship.   Making and putting
on the heads could be done by women, if they were instructed,
but there would not be enough of it to justify more than a few
in learning.   The South offers the best opening.

356. Caps. Cap makers receive very different prices for
their work, depending on the quality of the material and work,
and the house for which the work is done.   There are between
eight hundred and one thousand capmakers in Philadelphia.
They are said to average $3 a week.   Freedley says: " In Phila-
delphia, there are a large number of concerns occupied exclusively
in making caps; those of cloth constituting the chief part of the
business, though plush, silk, glazed, and other caps are also
made.   The cap manufacture employs a large number of females,
whose wages in the business will average about $4 per week.
Sewing machines are largely employed; being, in fact, indispensable in consequence of the expansion of the trade.   The annual
production is about $400,000."   A few years ago there were
five thousand cap makers in New York city.   Many of the cheap
caps in New York are furnished by Jews, who get them done
very cheaply.   They not only do much to supply the home demand for caps, but export large quantities.   They sell some caps
for from $1 to $1.50 a dozen.   B. pays his cap makers, some $5,
some $6 a week.   When business is dull the work is divided, so
that all hands are retained, and have something to do.   Caps
are mostly made by German men on sewing machines.   Some
Germans take fifty or sixty dozen a week from a store, and employ
girls to make them up.   They are middlemen, and cut out the
goods.   In New York, almost every branch of business seems to
have its own locality—that of the hat and cap manufacturers is on
the lower part of Broadway.   A good hand can earn about $3.50

a week of 10 hours a day, or by working fifteen or sixteen hours, which many of them do, can earn $8 or $9. Working girls generally receive about $3 a week. They pay $2 for board. The remaining $1 is almost consumed in shoes. Nearly all are at times out of employment. In New York, by constant labor, fifteen or sixteen hours a day, some cap makers can earn only from fourteen to twenty-five cents. " We were told by an old lady who has lived by this kind of work a long time, that when she begins at sunrise, and works till midnight, she can earn fourteen cents a day. A large majority of these women are American born, from the great middle class of life, many of whom have once been in comfortable, and even affluent circumstances, and have been reduced by the death or bankruptcy of husbands and relatives, and other causes, to such straits. Many of them are the wives of shipmasters, and other officers of vessels. Others are the widows of mechanics and poor men, and have children, and mothers and fathers, &c., to support by their needle. Many have drunken husbands to add to their burdens and afflictions, and to darken every faint gleam of sunshine that domestic affection throws even into the humblest abode. Others have sick and bedridden husbands or children, or perhaps have to endure the agony of receiving home a fallen daughter, or an outlawed son, suddenly checked in his career of vice." S., of S. & Co., told me they take learners when they can make good use of them. The business, some time back, in New York, was over done, but for the last three or four years the supply has not more than met the demand. It is piecework. A first-class hand can, in busy seasons, make $10, but many are not swift with the needle, and cannot earn more than $3 a week. They give out some of their work. All that can be, he has done by machines. R. & H. have their caps made by machines. It is piecework, and a good hand can earn from $6 to $9 a week. In a cloth and fancy cap store, I was told the girls earn $4, $5, and $6 a week. Few people are willing to take learners, as the season, six weeks, is nearly consumed by the time the trade is learned, and the instructor gets nothing for his time and trouble. Children's fancy caps cannot be made by machine. They are usually piecework. To make them requires taste. Six weeks is the length of time usually given to learning the trade. A.'s caps are made by machines. Good hands earn $5, $6, and $7. His hands are busy only in spring. He takes learners at that time, and pays from the first, $2 or $3 a week. D., formerly a cap maker, told me that P—s have some of their caps made on Blackwell's Island, by the convicts. B. told me the greater part of the cap is made by sewing machines tended by men, but the finishing, lining, &c., is done by women, either at home or on the premises. They are paid by the dozen, and can earn from $5 to $6 a week. Some have received even more, but as the work was taken home, it cannot be known with certainty that one person did it all. The first year they work at caps of an inferior quality, for which they receive fifty cents a dozen; girls of average ability, can then take the better kind of cap, and of course the wages increase according to the degree of proficiency. A cap maker told me, good hands can have steady work all the year. The best season for work is when manufacturing for the fall trade, which is generally in the months of June, July, August, September, and part of October, and, for the spring trade, in March and April. Another told me he pays by the dozen, and his hands earn from $4 to $7 a week. A maker of cap fronts, New York, told me he pays his girls from $3 to $7, working ten hours a day. From July to November are the best seasons—May and June the poorest months. Cutting out is done by hand, and requires too much strength for women. Some men cut out fifty dozen caps a day. It is done with a knife of a peculiar shape, and several thicknesses of the cloth are cut at once. Women are not so employed where the business is done on a large scale. Some cutters earn $24 a week. A cutter should have taste and skill, as he is also expected to design patterns. The English style for caps is sometimes adopted, and the most of gentlemen's clothing is of the English style, in New York; but the ladies prefer French fashions for themselves. An extensive manufacturer of cap fronts and other trimmings, in New York, writes: "I have about twenty-five females employed, the majority of whom sew at home. The occupation is perfectly healthy, easy, and comfortable. I pay by the piece, and the workers earn from $3 to $6 per week. Any woman that can sew and has ordinary intelligence can learn it in three hours. There is no prospect for increase, but constant employment for those already engaged. Spring and fall are the busy seasons, but employment is given all the year. I can always get ten times the help I require in this branch: four or five years ago we paid much better wages, but competition regulates (unfortunately) the scale of wages. Experience tells me women are inferior to men employeés, in regard to promptness in coming to the shop, and in having the articles completed at stated times, when required for shipment. But I find them superior to men in refinement, temperance, decorum, attachment to the interest of their employers, &c., when unmixed with the male sex. I formerly employed women on sewing machines, and when first started in that branch, they made from $8 to $10 per week, although, since the last three years, goods are sold so much cheaper, as to reduce the wages from $5 to $8. In Detroit, Mich., cap makers get from five to twenty-three cents a cap for making, and can earn from $2 to $4 per week.

357. Coats. We were told by one that ought to know, that many of the gentlemen's coats seen on Broadway are made by women. We believe that women of intelligence and judgment, if properly instructed, could make the greater part, if not the whole of gentlemen's coats. Much of the tailors' work of New York is distributed through the country, because it can be made cheaper. Many men make it a business, as agents, to distribute, collect, and pay for such work. Men press seams and sew the heaviest cloth, because they have more strength. What magnificent buildings there are in New York devoted to the sale of gentlemen's wear! But to think they are made of the sinews and muscles and tears and sighs of hardworking women, and to see the clerks in the stores, with nothing to do but receive and wait on customers, while those poor girls on the fifth floor are toiling from early morn to dark to earn less than one half of those clerks! What a hard life most women lead!

358. Cravats. W. & D. usually employ fifty hands. Part of the work is done in the store, on the fourth and fifth floors. Cravats pay well, and a good hand can earn from $6 to $18 a week, piecework. Most of their work is done by machine and finished by hand. Those of their hands who take work home, do it when not occupied with home duties. The gentleman with whom I talked, thought a person would not be able to support herself by that kind of work alone. They have been able to keep their hands all the year. Another cravat maker told me he has employed hands all the year, and had most of his cravats made by machines. A great many have been made in Baltimore. M. & Co. give some work out and have some done at the store. They are most busy in spring and fall, but keep some hands all the year. They can always get plenty of hands. They take learners, and pay from the first, but not so much, of course. Week workers earn from $4 to $5—ten hours a day in summer, rather less in winter. Those that work by the piece can earn from $8 to $9, for they work faster at home and sew in the evenings. Part of their work is done by machine and part by hand. They usually import the material. Most of this work is confined to New York, and has been a separate branch but a few years. In Detroit, girls earn from $2.50 to $3.50 a week making cravats.

359. Hats. We will give an extract from "The Art and Industry of the Crystal Palace": "In the manufacture of hats in the United States, there are twenty-four thousand persons employed: one half of them are men, and the remainder women.

15*

The consumption of straw hats amounts to about $1,500,000, about half of which are imported. The capital invested in the hatting trade in this country is little short of $8,000,000. The number of trimmers in New York are four hundred. There is no branch of industry in which the rate of wages is so fluctuating; no trade reflecting so faithfully the depressed or prosperous condition of the country. There are between fifty and sixty finishing shops in New York. There is no general understanding between the shops as to a fixed rate of payment. It is a peculiarity of the trade, that a person seeking employment never addresses himself to the principal; he goes direct to the foreman." Silk and felt hats are most worn in the United States. We find there is great objection by the workmen to the use of machinery. Some factories confine their work exclusively to the making of hat bodies. The manufacture of hatters' trimmings forms, in large cities, a distinct branch of business. " In C.'s hat manufactory, in London, fifteen hundred hands are employed, two hundred of whom are females. Among the processes by which a beaver hat is produced, women and girls are there employed in the following: Plucking the beaver skins; cropping off the fur; sorting various kinds of wool; plucking and cutting rabbits' wool; shearing the nap of the blocked hat (in some instances); picking out defective fibres of fur; and trimming." Women in our country could be employed in bowing the fur, pressing it with a hatter's basket, folding it in a damp cloth, rolling, rubbing, working it with the hands, and dipping it in hot water. The last operation is a very warm one. As it is, we know of no department in which they are employed, except that of carding, binding, lining, trimming, and tip gilding. Binding and lining are much done by them. The work is light, genteel, and rather profitable, and can be done at home. When done in factories, the workers cannot be so neat, on account of the dust, the large number of operatives in a room, and the coloring matter that rubs off the hats. All employers have reported it healthy, and I suppose it is as much so as any sedentary occupation, unless from causes mentioned in the preceding sentence. A hatter in Philadelphia told us he employs girls to line and bind men's hats. They are paid 75 cents a dozen for felt hats, and $1.25 for silk hats. Girls can earn as much as $6 a week at it. It requires a couple of months' apprenticeship. There is work for steady hands all the year. We have seen it stated that " hat trimmers in Philadelphia average $3.50 per week. They number from eight hundred to one thousand females. Hat binders usually spend six weeks learning their trade." The war department, about two years ago, closed a contract with S , of Philadelphia, to furnish sixteen thousand felt hats for the army, at $2.75 each." They make all qualities of hats at P.'s, Brooklyn, from those at 75 cents a dozen to those at $50 a dozen. The linings of the cheapest felt hats are put in by machines operated on by steam, the others by hand. I saw girls also laying gold leaf on muslin, which was stamped by a machine, forming the ornamental work and figures seen in the crown lining of cheap hats. These workers were called tip gilders. All except the box makers and tip gilders sit while at work. Girls at lining and binding can earn from $2.50 to $7. (I think he set his last mark high.) It is piecework, as everything, I believe, in that line is. Some girls have worked in P.'s factory eight years or more. The business is learned in a short time. Operators are paid at the same rate as hand sewers; but if any difference is made, it is in favor of operators. For hand workers, care and ability to sew well are the principal requisites. The hands have work all the year, but in midsummer and midwinter may do only three fourths of the usual quantity for a week or two. Hatters who manufacture in Brooklyn and sell in New York, told me they employ five hundred women, who are paid by the piece. Those that sew receive from $5 to $6, machine operatives from $8 to $9. A knowledge of sewing and taste, in finishing hats, is desirable. The business will extend. Three times as many hats are sold as fifteen years ago. Some parts of hat making are performed by machinery that could not be managed by women. The West and Northwest of the United States present good openings for this business. Manufactories, of course, must be where there is plenty of water. At a hatter's in New York, I was told that they pay 14 cents for trimming a hat of any kind, coarse or fine, silk or felt; but sometimes pay only 10 cents. Their binder often makes $7 a week. At B.'s, New York, the girls earn from $5 to $7, and are paid by the piece. They sew in the establishment. Sewing the crowns in and wires on of plush hats is a distinct business from trimming, yet one in which they employ some women. It pays rather better than the other part of women's work, but requires great care and neatness. Sewing the leather linings in hats is the least profitable part. More women might find employment in hat work. A lady said to me she has an acquaintance that sometimes earns $2.50 a day at trimming hats. (?) L. employs some girls for trimming in the spring and fall. It is piecework, and some earn $9 a week. It is sometimes difficult to get very good hands. There are some factories in the West, but none in the South. Another hatter told me he pays 12½ cents for trimming a hat. He has noticed that the swiftest are the best workers. A hatter told me a smart trimmer could earn from $8 to $10 a week, six months of the

year; but not more than $3 the other six months, because work
is slack. A salesman in D.'s store told me a brisk hand can trim
a dozen hats a day. The children's hats they have trimmed for
the wholesale trade are not so neatly and carefully done as those
for the retail trade. In selling a single hat, a purchaser examines
closely, and if there is any defect, condemns it. The occupation
is well filled in New York, and the work requires care, taste, and
expedition. D. has constant employment for his hands; but for
four months they have not as much as the hands wish, yet enough
to yield most about $4. The women work above the store, because
the blocks are there. They are allowed to take home and sew in
the evening the linings of those hats that have the rims faced
with leather. The plan is, generally, for a learner to spend six
weeks' apprenticeship with an experienced hand, giving her work
for instruction received. At Sing Sing prison, New York, of the
one hundred and fifty female convicts, a majority are employed
in binding hats, at 15 cents a dozen, made by the male convicts.
The usual price in St. Louis is 14½ cents a hat. At this rate, a
lady can bind and line in a day a number amounting to from $1
to $1.25. There are two hat factories in St. Louis, but they are
not enough to supply the demand. A firm in Danbury write us,
they "employ from seventy-five to one hundred women trimming
hats. They pay by the piece, and their hands average $5 per
week. Males average $9 a week. By the rules of trade, males
spend four years learning; females, five weeks. Women are not
paid while learning. The prospect for a continuance of the business is good. The busy seasons are from July 1st to April 1st.
Time of work does not exceed ten hours. The majority are
Americans. There are advantages in being near the great centre
of trade in this country, New York. Board, $2." A firm manu-
facturing wool hats in the same place—Danbury—write they
"employ ten Irish women in a card room, and sixty Yankee girls
in trimming hats. The first receive $3 per week, the others
$5.50. Women in the card room work ten hours. The American
girls are intelligent and pretty." Another wool-hat manufacturer
in Connecticut writes: "My women earn $1 each per day, on an
average. It takes male operatives two years to learn. Work,
on an average, ten months in the year. Board, $2." A firm in
Milford, Conn., write: "Women earn from $3 to $7 per week.
The reason why women are not better paid, is because the supply
is greater than the demand. The employment will last as long
as people wear hats. Fall and winter are the best seasons for
work. The nearer you get to the market, the better the location." In reply to a letter, a firm employing from sixty to eighty
women give the following intelligence: "The females employed

by us are generally from fourteen to twenty-one years of age.
They are paid by the piece, and earn from $4 to $9 per week.
The labor of women is entirely distinct from that of men. It
takes a good needlewoman about two months to become proficient.
Women give their labor to the person who instructs them, from
two to eight weeks. The business is good six or eight months.
The rest of the year, they average about one half of what they
can do. Busy times are from January 1st to May 1st, and from
July 1st to November 1st. The demand is about equal to the
supply, except in very busy times, when we could employ more;
but I think there are plenty, as an increased supply would tend
to lower prices. Most of our women are foreigners. The proximity to large cities is advantageous to this business, as the goods
are mostly sold in New York, Philadelphia, Boston, &c. I should
say there is little difference between the women employed in hat
manufactories and others who have to earn a livelihood, such as
dress makers, tailoresses, &c. Board, from $1.75 to $2. There
is an objection amongst boarding-house keepers to females generally, and strangers frequently have great difficulty in obtaining
good board. This is certainly the fault of their own sex." A
wool-hat firm in Yonkers, N. Y., write they pay by the piece,
and workers earn from $5 to $7. Male and female labor do not
compete. A gentleman and his son, in New York, who import
and manufacture children's fancy hats, write me they pay from
$5 to $12 a week, according to ability. Women are paid while
learning, the time for which depends upon capacity and taste.
There is regular employment with them in all months but June
and December. Good operatives are always in demand. Large
cities are the best localities.

HAT BRAIDERS, &c. Most hats called "palm leaf" are made
of straw grown in the Northern States. P. & Co., of Boston,
write me : "The occupation of braiding hats is one that employs
the odd moments and hours of almost every Yankee farmer's sons
and daughters, throughout Massachusetts and New Hampshire,
from one year's end to the other. We employ women, but not
exclusively, and pay by the piece, from $1 to $1.50 per dozen. A
wide-a-wake Yankee girl or boy, with nimble fingers, will learn
in a few hours." A manufacturer in New Hampshire, employing
"from 300 to 400, pays by the piece, and his workers earn from
$6 to $8 per month. They learn generally when children, by seeing others braid. The future prospect is not flattering, as the
demand for palm-leaf hats is decreasing. The braiders work at
home." $60,000 worth of palm-leaf hats were annually manu-
factured at Nashua, N. H., a few years ago. C. told me they
never employ women, except, in winter, to bind and put the oil-

silk lining in gentlemen's straw hats, for the spring trade of the South. For the work they pay 12½ cents a dozen. A woman can do from six to ten dozen a day. The best workers find employment. The prospect of obtaining work to those who may learn is good. B. thinks but few American girls are employed in trimming straw hats. He pays by the piece, and some earn as much as $5 per week. They should spend about one month learning, and they do well to earn their board during that time.

360. Oil Clothing. I was told at L. & Co.'s oil clothing depot, that they have their sewing done by women at their homes. It is done by machines. They do not require any deposit. Since the panic, a number of girls and women have come in and offered to do their work at under prices. The oiling is done after the goods are made up. The garments are laid on tables, and the oil applied with brushes. The clothes are then hung on frames to dry, and it requires six months. Oiling the goods is greasy, dirty work, but might be done by strong women. The work is not at all unhealthy. L. & Co. sell $150,000 suits a year. Their best sewers can make up six or eight dozen shirts a week, for some of which they are paid $1 a dozen, and for others, $1.25. The manufacture of oiled goods is confined to New York.

361. Pantaloons. In making pantaloons, as in most other tailor's work, what is most neatly done commands the best prices. Custom work pays best. Making pantaloons is not quite so remunerative as making vests. The prices paid in cities by good-class tailors for making summer pantaloons, runs from 75 cents to $1.25. For winter goods the prices are higher, ranging from $1 a pair to $1.50. Some tailors have their pantaloons made by men, and some even employ men to make their vests.

362. Regalias. "Five American women are employed at Chicopee, Mass., in stitching military goods. They are paid by the piece. They never get their work perfect. Learners are paid something. Men are preferable, because it takes too much time to wait on women. There will be work as long as there are wars." A regalia maker, in New York, told me her girls earn from $3 to $5 a week. The sewing is done by hand. Those who embroider in silk receive about the same; those with gold and silver thread, something more.

363. Shirts. "Women who make shirts by hand, are paid for fine shirts from eighteen cents apiece to $1. Those who make at the lowest prices appear to have no other mission on earth but to sew up bleached muslin into shirts. The only time which they economize is their sleeping time; and their food is economized for them by circumstances over which it would appear they have but little control. In some instances we have been informed, that where there are two or three or more women or girls engaged in this enterprise of making shirts to enable gentlemen to appear respectable in society, they absolutely divide the night season into watches, so that the claims of sleep may not snatch from the grasp of the shirt manufacturers an iota of their rights. In this way, by working about twenty hours a day, the amazing sum of $2.50, and sometimes $3, is earned per week. Sewing machines have so reduced the amount of labor required for shirts, as well as the price, that they can in some places only earn twenty-five cents by working twelve hours; and they cannot get steady employment even at these prices." Between 2,000 and 3,000 women are supposed to be engaged in shirt making in Philadelphia. Competition has depressed prices fearfully low. A shirt maker in that city told me he pays by the week. He gives the bodies out, and they are done by hand; the collars and bosoms by machines. They are cut out by men with knives, and the cloth is from twenty-four to thirty-six thicknesses. They pay basters now mostly by the piece. B., of the same city, who carries on general shirt making, puts the plain parts out in the country to be done. It, of course, costs less than the finishing off. Good workers can earn from $3 to $4 a week for plain sewing—more for fine. At a shirt-bosom manufactory in Philadelphia, P., the proprietor, told me he has the bosoms and collars made by machinery, employing seventeen girls all the year. Some establishments employ them only in the busy season, spring and fall. His women earn from $3 to $5 a week. To one machine are employed three girls: one to cut out, one to baste, and one to stitch. The fine plaits of bosoms are laid by machinery. Cutters and button-hole makers are better paid than basters and stitchers. A shirt maker told me in New York (December, 1860), that the only houses there supplying the article were those that made up for the California market. Operators, good ones, he said, usually earn $1 a day, of nine hours in winter, and ten in summer. Those that work at home can earn more, because they do more. On Dey street, I was told by a gentleman that he has shirts made in Connecticut, and he often finds it difficult to get good hands. He has shirts cut out with scissors. He used to employ a forewoman to cut and superintend. Most shirts sold in the South, West, and California, have been made at the North. New York, Troy, and New Haven are the principal places. Operators usually earn $1 a day, of eleven hours; but as the work is generally paid for by the piece, they may earn only from fifty cents to $1. Making button holes is a distinct branch. He pays half a cent apiece for those of ordinary size, and one cent for the larger ones of the wrists. In good times he employs girls all the year. The spring sale commences in January, the fall sale in July. S., another manufacturer, has common drawers and shirts made by machine. A brisk hand can make two dozen pair of drawers a day, and are paid fifty cents a dozen (?) He keeps workers in prosperous times all the year. A lady who makes shirts by hand told me she could barely make a living, though her work is done for customers. She does most in spring and summer. The trimmings she makes by machine. Madame P. pays eighty cents for making a shirt, except the bosom, which is imported. She does her own cutting by hand. A shirt maker says girls that can finish a shirt neatly get $3 a week of ten or eleven hours a day. Work of that kind is not confined to seasons. J. has most work to do in summer. The girls are paid by the piece, and can earn from $3 to $4. His are made by machine, but finished off by hand. He has girls of all kinds; idle and industrious, easy of temper and obstinate; in short, the variety always to be met with in help. A lady told me she cuts shirts by measure, and has a variety of styles. She pays an old lady fifty cents a day for basting, and from $5 to $6 a week to an operator. The neatness of machine sewing depends much on the way in which the basting is done. W. told me his basters earn from $3 to $4; operators from $5 to $6; button-hole makers from $4 to $6. He gives employment all the year. No demand, except in busy seasons for good operators, and they can be obtained by advertising. The owner of a shirt-collar manufactory and laundry said his collars were stitched by machines, and the operators earn from $3 to $9 per week. It is piece work. The washers are paid by the hundred dozen. Six weeks, I believe, is the time usually given by one that can sew neatly, to learn the trade. At L. & G.'s, I was told the best seasons in the wholesale trade are spring and fall; but in the retail trade there is little difference. Men and boys cut out with a knife, and are able to cut through seventy-two thicknesses of cloth. Women have not the strength to cut such quantities. The prospect is fair for good hands. There is a superabundance of indifferent hands. Their best sewers are English. Many of them are married women. They used to employ young girls, but they wasted material and were not steady at work. They have lost much by women that would come and take out a dozen shirts to make, and never return them. On inquiring at the place where the women said they lived, they would find they had never been there. Few, except the Jews, require a deposit. It is difficult to obtain one from sewers of the value of the material taken out. They could obtain one hundred and fifty hands any day by advertising. Button-hole makers earn $5 a week; some operators, $9. A factory in New Haven employs eight hundred women; two hundred work in the establishment, the others work out. The indoor work is done by machines. The other is finishing off, and is sent through the country. It consists in gathering and sewing in the sleeves, felling down the facing around them, stitching on wristbands, sewing in the bosoms, putting on the collar, and working the button-holes, for which they receive ten cents a shirt. A firm of shirt manufacturers in Troy, N. Y., write: "We employ from three hundred to four hundred women; some with sewing machines, some with needles, and others in various kinds of labor connected with our manufacturing. They are paid by the piece, and earn from $3 to $10 a week. While learning they are paid according to what they do. Spring and fall are the best seasons, but they have some employment all the year. The supply is fully equal to the demand in this locality. About half are Americans; board, $2 to $2.50." Another firm in the same place writes: "We employ four hundred, and pay from $5 to $10 per week to about one hundred hands, and from $3 to $7 to those who do not depend upon it for a livelihood. Women spend a few months learning; men, years. Midwinter and summer are the best seasons for work." A shirt-collar firm in Troy write: "In reply to yours we would state, we are employing in and outside of our manufactory, from six to eight hundred women, in running, turning, stitching, banding, marking, and boxing gentlemen's collars. Most of our workwomen are Americans, and live with parents or relatives. Those boarding pay from $1.75 to $3 per week. Many of our workwomen are very intelligent. All are required to be steady and industrious. Some parts of our business can be learned in two or three weeks, while other parts will take as many months; but each one is paid while learning. Our work is all done by the piece, and women earn from $5 to $8 per week during business seasons, which are summer and winter. They are usually thrown out of employment one month during the fall, and one in spring. The employment requires from eight to nine hours per day, in our manufactory. The making of gentlemen's collars must increase in proportion to the increase of the male population of our country; and, as styles are becoming more and more varied, this also must tend to increase the manufacture. There is, however, no demand for help in any department of the business, yet. We have but five or six women in all our establishment who are required to stand upon their feet while at work. All others can make their positions quite comfortable. We employ but few men (from five to eight), and they are in departments which women could not fill: nor could men well fill the women's department." Manufacturers in Boston write: " The prospect of future employment is good. Our women (fifty in number) are nearly all Americans. There is no competition between male and female labor in this branch, which, probably, is the cause of women receiving less wages. The work is healthy, only as it involves want of fresh air and exercise. Girls in the shop are paid from $4 to $7 per week, and work from nine to ten hours. Good sewers are getting scarcer every year. We are always ready to employ a really good hand—one who can do *nice* work. There is a growing demand for articles of all kinds. There are a great many women unable to sew well, who compete with each other for the work given out by the slop shops." Shirt makers in Ithaca, New York, write: " The work is very healthy in well ventilated establishments. What we employ men for, women cannot do as well. There is a demand for collar finishers, a surplus of machine operatives." Shirt manufacturers in Watertown, Conn., write: "We employ in our establishment from twelve to twenty girls and women, all Americans. They work in winter about nine hours; in summer, ten. Most of them work on sewing machines, and can earn from $4 to $5 per week. For board they pay $2 per week. There is no season of the year when our work is entirely stopped." L., in Lynn, Mass., engaged in custom-shirt manufacturing, writes: " I pay fifty cents apiece for making shirts, and $4.50 per week for a machine girl. My workwomen are widows and married women, and they average five shirts or $2.50 per week, besides their house work. But a woman that makes five shirts a week cannot have much spare time." A lady in Massachusetts, who has shirts made to order, informs me she pays by the piece, and her girls earn from fifty to seventy-five cents a day. She employs the most skilful. She says the nature of the employment is such that no woman could enjoy health long, who did nothing else, and the wages are so small that anyone must work all the time to make a living; hence the work does not suit any, except those who have homes and have recourse to this as a secondary employment. The demand for the articles in the market is limited, and she has never been able to carry it on in a wholesale manner except by the aid of friends whose sympathy has created a demand for the work.

364. Suspenders. J., New York, says his girls can earn from $4 to $5, and are paid by the piece. There are but four suspender factories in the United States, of any size. The factories at the east are mostly supplied by the daughters of farmers from the vicinity. The one in Easthampton is of the best standing.

The girls are intelligent and well behaved. Board too is lower. They like to employ families, father, mother, sons, and daughters. A suspender maker, in New York, told me he buys the woven goods, then cuts it the right length, and shapes the leather for the ends, which his wife sews on. I expect, from the appearance of their room, they earn but a meagre subsistence. The agent of the American Suspender Co., at Waterbury, told me " they employ a large number of girls to spool, weave, and pack. The straps are sewed on by farmers' daughters, who take them home. They are paid for by the gross. They earn less than weavers, who can make from $4 to $6 a week. They have had constant work until this fall (1860). The bindings are sewed on by hand. It requires some time to become a good weaver. A man serves a regular apprenticeship—women will learn for ten years, if they continue. Ingenuity and mechanical talent are desirable. A learner is not paid while in with another weaver. The amount of employment in future depends on European competition. The hands work ten hours a day, and they employ about fifty women, one fourth of whom are American. Women are superior to men in activity, and will handle thread much better than men. Board, $1.75."

365. Tailoresses. The tailors of London have a pension society. All the tailors' work of this country might be performed by women. It is most suitable for them. Some say women cannot do the nice sewing of a coat. Give them the same training, and pay them the same wages as men, and we are confident they can. All of the clothes sold in the slop shops of cities are made by women. Many can sew beautifully, but have not learned the art of cutting out. This they will find an important part of their trade. It will greatly assist those who make boys' clothes. It is ascertained that at least 4,800 females are supplied with work by the ready-made clothing establishments of Philadelphia, which enables each industrious sewer to earn from $1.25 to $5 per week. A large number of women are now engaged in making clothes for the soldiers. At most large clothing establishments, work is done both by hand and machine. Some is done in the house, but most is given out. At O.'s, New York, they employ a large number. The majority are Americans, but some are Germans, and a few Irish. The foreman finds those that are dependent on their work for a living, do their work better than those that merely do it for pocket money. The best work is always best paid. A good hand can earn $3 per week. They work by the piece. Some women hire a room and employ girls to work for them. S. says the principal reason that women do not get as good prices as men, is that they do not learn to do their work so well. He spent five years learning, but a girl expects to learn it in so many weeks, or months, at most; but many women that sew for a support are very poor, and cannot afford to spend much time learning. T. pays his women from $5 to $10 a week, according to the work they do. R. says girls do not feel the interest in their work they should. They forget that three minutes lost by twenty girls amounts to an hour. If a procession is passing, they think it very hard if they cannot have ten or fifteen minutes to look out of the windows. The girls that sew earn from $3 to $4.50, except those who fasten the ends of threads and take out basting threads, who receive $2.50. They all work ten hours. They have some who take their work home, and are paid by the piece. Those that do their work best have the highest prices, and are most sure of having constant employment. Some of their women become mere machines, and that in his opinion was a recommendation. They have no life or spirit, but plod on day after day in the same way. Such, when they do their work neatly and thoroughly, he thinks most reliable. They find it difficult to get their work well done. It is computed by Dr. L. that one thousand needlewomen fall victims annually to overwork at the needle. A city missionary told me that he knew of many sempstresses that spent sixteen hours out of the twenty-four, stitching. I was told in D. & B.'s clothing store, that the women who sew by hand, earn from $3 to $4 per week. P. measures and cuts, and he employs women to operate on machines, paying from $3 to $4 per week, working from 8 to 7 o'clock. It is done under Mrs. P.'s supervision. The work is mostly for boys. They give work out, and of course pay by the piece. Their most busy times are from October to March, and from April to September. They do Southern work. L. & Co. make boys' clothing, and pay by the piece. They require a deposit from those that are doubtful. If business is good, they give work all the year. He thinks there is enough of work, in busy times, for all the tailoresses in the city. The best way to learn is to receive instruction from journeymen who employ hands and take learners. Some require an apprenticeship of three months, and some of six months, in children's clothing. The busy season commences November 1st and runs to March 1st, and from March to September 1st.

366. Vests. First class vest makers receive better prices than women in the other departments of tailoring, and are more sure of work. Superior hands can earn from $4 to $5 a week. Clothing, cap makers and shoe binders are often crowded together from forty to fifty in a room, where it is stitch, stitch, stitch from daylight to sundown. Some slop shops in New York pay only fifteen cents for making a vest, and only ten cents for pantaloons!!!

There are over nine thousand tailoresses doing custom work in New York, and of these 7,400 are vestmakers.

UPHOLSTERERS.

367. Upholsterers. Some branches of upholstery are hard work in consequence of the heaviness of the materials. At some upholsterers in Philadelphia, when a girl applies for work, she is taught during a fortnight, and receives enough to pay her board—usually $1.50 per week. At the end of this time, if found faithful and diligent, she is put upon full wages, $3.50 a week. In this trade there is the serious drawback of remaining a great part of the year unemployed, as it is only in the spring and fall that the business is brisk. Men usually put up tapestry, and lay down heavy carpets. The price to girls by upholsterers is about on a par with other work done by females. H., Philadelphia, employs several women. The forewoman receives $5.50 per week; the next best hand, $5; the less proficient, from $2 to $5. The business requires a good amount of intelligence, and about a year's application to acquire it. H. is not exacting as to the number of hours his operatives work. When business is slack they have easy times. He employs his good hands all the year. In one of the principal importing and manufacturing upholsteries and carpet establishments in New York about seventy females are employed. They make up a great many lace and damask curtains, and are under the supervision of a forewoman. Seventeen sewing machines are kept, though most of the sewing is done by hand. Any person that can sew well can do all the work, as it is cut out and prepared. With a very few exceptions all are paid by the week, receiving from $3 to $4, working ten hours a day. The piece workers can sometimes earn $5. They are employed the whole year. An upholsterer told me that his work is done to order, and consequently the measure for beds, mattresses, curtains, &c., is always taken. There are many women in Boston, I have been informed, working in sofa, chair, and lounge manufactories that earn from $1 to $1.50 a day. A firm in Boston writes: "I employ women to sew and attend sales, and pay from $3 to $4 a week. Men are paid two thirds more than women, because it is the fashion. It requires three months to learn. A knowledge of the needle and figures is desirable. Learners are paid. Females work nine hours and a half. Some parts of our work are in wood, and too heavy for women; the rest they can do better than men. Board, $2 to $4." A firm in Boston, "employing two women to make sofa cushions, pay them $4 each per week, working from eight to ten hours a day. They pay women less than men, because female help is generally cheaper. Men spend three years learning; women, one month. Learners have their board paid. The prospect for work is good. Spring and autumn are the most busy seasons, but they have work all the year." Another firm in the same place write they "employ fifteen women, pay by the piece, and their hands earn $5 per week. The prospect for work is good, but there are plenty of hands there."

368. Beds. At a feather store I was told feathers for stuffing beds are bought from merchants, who employ agents to travel through the country, and buy them up. They get their feathers from the West. Live geese feathers are the best. All imported are from Russia. It requires great experience to buy feathers. At another store I was told feathers must be baked to render them light—otherwise they are flat and heavy. The salesman never knew of a woman being employed in baking— thinks it not suitable, for the down gets in the mouth and nostrils, as the feathers must be constantly stirred. In the spring and fall, when most people go to housekeeping, most beds are sold.

369. Carpets. Two thirds of the inhabitants of Saxony are employed in weaving, It requires from two to three years to become a good carpet weaver. To prepare warp and rags for rag carpets is very suitable, but the weaving is rather hard for women. Mrs. W. says it does not require a great deal of strength to weave rag carpets, when the loom is a good one and in proper order. In weaving, both the arms and lower limbs are exercised, particularly the latter. She wove when she was only thirteen years old. The exercise tends to develop the chest. The price for weaving in small places is from 12½ to 18 cents a yard. She knew one lady that often wove fourteen yards a day, amounting to $1.75; but her health failed, and she changed her occupation. I called in a weaver's, in Brooklyn. He charges 18¾ cents per yard for weaving, and can weave from eighteen to twenty yards a day. Some rags are much more difficult to manage than others. The dust from the rags in spooling and weaving must be disagreeable. When not working for customers he makes carpets to keep on hand for sale. He buys the rags of old women, who get the scraps at tailors' shops every Monday morning, and cut them into strips, then wind and sell them at $7.50 a hundred pounds. The women are mostly Germans, and make a scanty living at it. In the Old Ladies' Home, Brooklyn, some of the inmates pass part of their time in preparing rags for weaving. Some old women buy of junk dealers the rags they sell to weavers. A woman whose husband was a carpet weaver in New York, continues the business since his death, employing two old men to weave. She charges eighteen cents a yard for weaving. She says that kind of weaving could never be done by machinery, as it would pull the rags all to pieces. She buys listing and cloth of old women who get it from the tailors and bring it around to sell. She pays twelve cents a pound for listing, six for cloth. She cuts them herself. A weaver told me he charges eighteen cents a yard. He buys pieces of cloth from the tailors for making up a stock to keep on hand. A pile of listing lay on the floor, for which he had paid nine cents a pound. He can weave from eight to sixteen yards a day. I have seen the average price of weaving carpets stated at nine cents a yard. The dust that flies in preparing carpet rags is disagreeable, and injurious to the eyes and lungs.

370. Curled Hair Pullers. Hair pullers are mostly Irish women, the wives of foreigners and laboring men. A few are women of a better class reduced in circumstances. In Philadelphia, at the shop of a kind old man, I saw women picking hair for mattresses. He pays two cents a pound for picking. The women earn from forty to sixty cents a day. The dust that flies from the hair is injurious to the lungs, and the constant watching is trying to the eyes. At one curled hair factory in New York I saw women employed at one cent a pound, at another two cents. A smart woman can pick twenty-five or thirty a day. An upholsterer in Boston writes: "We have women to sew, pick hair, &c. We pay by the piece. Men receive one third better pay than women. Women receive less, because they have not brass enough to ask more. Any woman can do our work. The prospect of work in our line is very fair. We have twenty women who work all the time. The demand for hands is small, surplus large. Large cities are best for our trade. Board, $2.50."

371. Curtain Trimmings. I saw two girls, in New York, who work at the trade. Their employer does not pay learners for two weeks, then according to what they do. Some are paid by the week, and some by the piece. The last plan pays best. The girls earn from $3 to $5 per week, some even as much as $7. Plenty of hands can always be had. They have most work in summer. At another place I was told it takes three or four months to learn. Good hands can earn then from $4 to $5. Mrs. B., in New York, told me her girls work by the piece, making curtain trimmings, and earn from $5 to $6 a week. They

work from 6 A. M. until 7 P. M. They can learn it in a few weeks.
At Y.'s, in New York, I saw a plain, genteel-looking woman engaged in making tassels. She pays $2 a week for board—wash-
ing extra. She spoke very well of her employer, for whom she
had worked twelve years. She mentioned an old lady upstairs
who had been in his employ twenty years. He has fifteen women
in the tassel department, and fifteen making gimps and fringes.
Some of the hands are paid by the piece, and some by the week—
ten hours a day. They are paid every two weeks on Saturday
afternoon. In the old country women make twisted cord, but
not in this. Cordmakers are on their feet all the time. Y.'s
women get from $2 to $5 per week, ten hours a day. Men get
from $6 to $9. It requires six months to learn, and learners receive $1.50 per week. In winter, just before the holidays, is the
best time for work; but Y.'s hands have employment all the
time. When not filling orders, they make stock work. They have
a great many applications for work.

372. Furniture Goods. "At Seymour, Conn., are
manufactured brocatelles and cotalines, a fabric composed of
silk and linen, or cotton, and used for furniture draperies and
carriage linings. Each loom is worked by a girl, who requires
very little previous experience to manage it perfectly. There
are about 60 persons employed at present in the work, two thirds
of whom are females from the age of fourteen upward. The
rate of wages paid by the company is higher than that given by
the neighboring factories, the nature of the work requiring a
superior degree of skill and intelligence."

373. Mattresses. A girl engaged in making mattresses
told us they are mostly sewed up by machines, and operators
earn from $3 to $6, working ten hours a day. In some factories
women sew the mattresses, and boys and men prepare the hair
and fill them. A mattress seller told me he employs girls to
make mattresses in the spring and fall, paying $3 a week, of ten
hours a day. One bed furnisher told me her work is mostly done
by old ladies. She says some girls down street earn $6 a week,
making mattresses. One large manufacturer told me that his
is piecework, and some of his girls earn from $8 to $12 a week.
He furnishes the sewing machines. In April and May, he finds
it difficult to get enough of hands. At another large store, I
was told they pay from $6 to $7 a week to good operators, and
have their work done in the building. At another large bed and
mattress store, I was told they pay women for making ticks with
machines from $4 to $5 a week. It is not very steady work.
At another place they occupied a room back of the store, and
earned from $4 to $6 a week. A firm in Nashua, N. H.,

write me "they employ fourteen American women in making mattresses, cushions, &c., and pay from $3 to $3.50 a week, including board, and work ten hours a day. Men are paid about $5 a week, and do different work from the women. Some of the hands are employed all the year. There is no great demand for mattress makers at present anywhere. Board, $2."

374. Venetian Blinds. At W.'s venetian blind manufactory, in Philadelphia, I was told they generally employ several women. They earn about $3 a week, and take their sewing home. The work is sewing tapes on the main pieces to support the slats. The business is best in the spring, from January to May, and is good in the fall, but they endeavor to furnish some employment all the year to their girls, who are American. A manufacturer of venetian blinds in Boston employs some women in writing, sewing, laying out work, &c. They are mostly paid by the piece, and earn from $3 to $6 per week. Male and female labor is not of the same kind in his establishment. Men spend two years learning; women, one month. The last part of spring and the first part of summer are best for work. He could easily find more sewers, if he had employment for them. He finds them cheaper and more suitable for the work than men. The means of mental and moral culture are those common to the residents of Boston.

375. Window Shades. At an establishment in Philadelphia, a few women are employed in the busy seasons, spring and fall, in laying the gilding on the borders of linen shades. They earn from $1.50 to $3.00 per week. The painted linen window shades (landscapes, buildings, &c.) are executed entirely by men, who receive $12 a week wages. Our informant said these men could paint (I think) 6 pair a day. I am sure there is no reason why a lady could not paint landscapes and other ornamental work on shades, if they would only qualify themselves. It would probably require two or three years' practice to acquire proficiency, for a person unaccustomed to painting of any kind. The design of common ones is invented as the painter proceeds, as he has no pattern to work from. It requires a knowledge of colors, and some taste and ingenuity. A man is paid from $1.50 to $2 a day. K., New York, has a number of women stencilling shades. The women earn about $4 a week. B., New York, usually employs two girls in putting elastic over the bands of pulleys and tying them up, for which they each receive $4 a week. I saw a girl in New York, engaged in stencilling. She is paid by the piece, and can earn $6 or $7 a week, when she has constant employment. It does not take long to learn. I called at a factory where they pay three cents a piece for painting the

16

centres of common shades. It is done with cloths. They pay $2 a piece for fine ones. The fine ones have the principal parts drawn before being painted. A smart man can earn $20 a week at that work, but shades are not much used now. At a store on Broadway, they used to employ girls for painting shades and putting on the gilding. They had American girls mostly. German men are mostly employed at that work. If American men learn this business, they have so much energy and ambition they are soon able to get an establishment of their own, and then employ foreigners, many of whom work for less, to obtain employment, and then cannot raise their prices, and so are apt ever to retain a subordinate position. Their girls worked in the room with the men, but it was a large room, and they worked at the far end. Part of the work ought to be done by men. They had one woman that put on the flowing colors and earned $9 a week. But they found it necessary to have the girls wear Bloomer costume, to prevent their dresses touching the shade while painting; but they would not even then consent to lay down their hoops, and as their skirts would touch the painting and injure it, they altogether abandoned the employment of females. L., New York, told me he met with great opposition when he first employed women to gild window curtains, and he could not have held out if his house had not been established and he very firm. He lost one or more of his customers by doing so. The work is very suitable for women. L.'s men and women work in the same apartment, but the men are required to be very respectful. The women have a dressing room attached to their workroom. They move about on their feet all the time, while at work. Men put size on, but women could do it. The women receive $5 a week, and never work over ten hours. The work can be learned in a day. The Southerners are doing without fancy goods now, so the trade is very poor. L. has saved about $1,000 the past year by employing women. Men are in such haste to get through their work, that they are careless and waste the gold leaf. A window-shade manufacturer in Boston, who employs some girls in stencilling, informs me by letter that "he pays by the piece from $3 to $6 per week. A smart, active girl can earn more than a man of medium abilities. Cleanliness and endurance are the most essential qualifications. The prospect for continuance is as good as that of any other fancy business. Best seasons for work are from March to July, and October to January, but at other times hands can make enough to pay their board. They work from seven to twelve hours; for over hours, are paid extra. Board, $2.50; (washing extra) but they have not a room alone." One shade manufacturer writes: "There are parts of my work that could be done by girls as well as men, but their style of dress is not adapted to it." Another in Boston writes: " I would employ women, if my shop was convenient, as I could get them for less price than men. Men are paid thirty-three per cent. more than women: one reason is they are capable of more endurance. We work ten hours in summer, eight in winter." Another firm in the same city employs from four to eight women, paying from $3 to $6 per week, working from nine to ten hours a day. Six months is the average time given by a learner. Spring and fall are the most busy seasons."

Wire Window Shades. Mrs. C. said a lady used to paint wire shades for her husband. He also employed men. He has most work done in summer. It requires care to keep from filling the niches with paint. Miss —— acquired boldness and freedom of execution in oil painting by the practice. Rapidity and lightness of touch were also acquired. Her hand had got a stiff, cramped feeling, from painting on canvas constantly. The price paid for shades depends on the fineness of the cloth, the size, and design. Miss S. says her father has the landscape painting done by Germans, and pays good prices. It is paid for by the square foot. He charges $2 a square foot, for a shade in the frame, ready to put in the window. The artists take them to their studios. Germans are preferred because they work most rapidly. One makes a great deal of money, but he works late at night and on Sundays. Several coats of paint are put on before the landscape is painted. Some copy engravings, but enlarge the scale. They make to order. The business is increasing. He sends a great many to the South, particularly Havana and Baltimore.

MANUFACTURERS OF BOOKS, INK, PAPER, AND PENCILS.

376. Bookfolders. I know of no work in a bookbindery that could not be performed by intelligent women that were properly instructed. Forwarding, marbling, gilding, stamping, and finishing could be done by them, in addition to presswork, folding, gathering, and sewing. The female bookfolders of New York number several thousand. The women in Philadelphia binderies are between 1,000 and 2,000. The most bookfolding and sewing, out of New York, are done in Washington and Philadelphia, and some in Cincinnati. The busy seasons for book makers are from September to January, and from March to July. In this business there is a union among the men regulating prices, hours, &c. There is a great difference in the character of the binderies in New York—every shade and grade is to be found. In seeing the size and comfort of the workrooms, and the manners and conversation of the employer, it would not be very difficult to judge of the pay and condition of the workgirls. The trade is well filled, and, no doubt, with quite as many women of worth, self-respect, and education, as any other. At the Bible House, Tract House, Methodist Book Concern, and Harper's, New York, the faces of the workers are bright and cheerful. Every precaution is taken to secure only those who are respectable, and the associations surrounding them are calculated to elevate, rather than degrade. Most of them are able to pay enough for their board to secure the right kind of home associations. These establishments, except in emergencies like the present, retain their hands all the year; while those in a majority of other houses fluctuate with their business and are unoccupied three or four months in the year. Bookfolding is paid for by the 1,000 sheets, depending on the size of the sheet and the number of times it is folded. A good, fast folder can earn from 50 cents to 65 cents a day, whether folding with a machine or by hand. A few can earn as much as $6 per week. Folding and collating pay the best of woman's work. Collating is usually paid for at 20 cents an hour. Men in bookbinderies get from $8 to $20 per week. Some employers are much more kind and intelligent than others. Some bookbinders in New York impose on girls by taking them to learn the business, requiring that they stay from six weeks to six months to do so, and paying nothing during that time. During the most of the time their work is efficient, and they earn money for their employers. When the time has expired they are turned off, and others taken on. Some bookbinders employ those who will do their work at a very cheap rate, often thus exposing them to influences that are pernicious. Favoritism is often shown by employers and foremen. At H.'s, 200 women and girls are employed in folding, sewing, and gilding. Either of the branches is light and pleasant, and soon learned, after which the remuneration depends upon the abilities of the learner. Their hours are from 7½ to 6, but it is piece work. All of his workpeople are temperance people. The work of bookbinders is not more unhealthy than any other indoor work. At the Tract House they take a few girls to learn to fold, and have them work until they earn $6 before they pay anything. An English woman told me that she used to earn $7 a week, as forewoman, but they never allowed her to be absent a day. A publisher in Philadelphia employs about fifty girls in his bindery, but complains that as soon as they make a few dollars they will take a holiday to spend it. He says the better he pays the girls in his bindery, the more they are absent from their work and the more difficult are they to manage. That, I think, arises from defective moral training. We know that people of right principle (both men and women), whose wages enable them to dress comfortably, and provide wholesome food,and well ventilated, healthy apartments, are not only better able to work well and constantly, but do so. It stands to reason they should. If the poor cannot make a proper use of their scanty compensation, they are more to be pitied than blamed, for we know well they have nothing to spare. The manufacture of blank-books is an important branch of business. A blank-book manufacturer in Troy writes : " I pay both ways, and the wages are from $3 to $4.50 per week. Men's wages are from $6 to $12, but their work is different and heavier. Women's part of the work is learned in from six weeks to one year. A ready hand and quick eye are wanted by a learner. Busiest time from December to July. There is a surplus of hands, so far as I know. When men work at the women's branches (which is very seldom), they do it more substantially." In France women do much of the work in blank-book binderies. In M. Maitre's book bindery, Dijon, France, " No apprentice, boy or girl, is received until after they have made their premier communion, and received a certificate that they can both read and write, and also a medical certificate of vaccination. The workpeople are thus of a respectable class. The young children of most of the married women are either sent out to nurse in the country, according to the very common custom of France, or else the married pair form one household with the grand parents."

377. Book Sewers. " Trades in general require a large share of mechanical ingenuity, in combination with strength, mathematical skill, and other qualifications. Strength is requisite to the success of a bookbinder." Women employed in sewing are paid by the piece, and as soon as they are competent, which requires but a few days, are paid according to their application from $3.50 to $7 per week. The work of women in binderies is clean, and about as comfortable and remunerative as any other of a mechanical nature. At the Methodist Book Concern we saw girls folding, gathering, sewing, putting plates in books, gilding the covers, and feeding the presses. They were well dressed and intelligent looking, and evidently felt an interest in the welfare of the establishment. The majority were Americans. The superintendent told us, " girls earn, in the sewing department, from

$3 to $9 per week. A good sewer can earn, without difficulty, from $5 to $5.50 per week. They have about thirty, most of whom work by the piece. They have one strong woman who sometimes earns $10 a week. They never work over ten hours, as the house is only open for work that long. The folding and enveloping of tracts and papers admit of a change of posture. There is no similarity in the male and female labor. The comparison in prices is about one-half to one-third. It requires a lifetime to learn a man's branch ; an intelligent woman can learn hers in a week. The result of a bookbinder's work is not for a day, but for all time. Bookbinders have more constant employment than those in most other trades. The work is most dull in summer. There is constant employment in New York for first-class hands, and always a surplus of second-class. Large cities offer the best localities—those in the South and West will probably furnish many openings to publishers." A. & S. employ girls to fold, stitch, and sew. They are paid by the piece (customary), and earn from $3 to $5 per week. Sewers can earn more than folders and stitchers—say from $5 to $7. They work until six o'clock and commence when they please, as they are paid by the quantity. A bookbinder told me his girls work from seven to six o'clock, He gives work all the year. They are paid by the piece, and can earn from $5 to $6 a week. I have been told folders and sewers are taken as learners only where the cheapest work is done. At some binderies three cents 100 is paid for folding, three cents for sewing, and six cents for stitching. At some places five cents 100 is paid for folding 12mo. sheets. The proportion of hands employed in the different branches of bookbinding is somewhat as follows : About two thirds are folders, one sixth gatherers, and one sixth sewers. A process has been invented by which books can be strongly bound without sewing. I fear it may be the means of throwing many sewers out of employment. At W.'s bookbindery I was told they sometimes take learners. They expect them to stay six months, and pay them half that they can earn during that time. They pay workers by the piece, and they can earn from $4 to $6 a week. Some of the girls are employed to remove the covers from old books and magazines that are to be rebound. M., who does the printing of the A.'s, informs me that his girls work by the piece, and average over $4 per week. His learners receive one half their earnings—the teacher the other half. Spring and fall are the most busy seasons, but the women are never entirely out of employment. There is no surplus of good hands, but many imperfect ones. He employs from 125 to 150. The superintendent at H.'s told me that the girls in the sewing-room earn from $3.50 to $8. He says their women are intelligent and ladylike, and would adorn the best society. They change their dresses when they come to work, and then before leaving. If they are at all hurried in their work, their hands, both men and women, come early and stay late of their own free will. Males average $10, females over $4. The reason of the difference is, that men serve an apprenticeship of five or seven years—women five or seven weeks. The former are the mechanics; the latter merely assistants. The latter cheapen the labor of the former, without having the strength or physical ability to perform their work. (I cannot see how it should be so when the branches performed are entirely distinct.) The foreman at B.'s told me a very brisk worker can earn $6 a week, but few do. They do not average over eight hours a day. They never light their building. S.'s girls, in good times, are employed all the year. He pays by the piece, and his girls earn from $3 to $5. In most small book binderies in New York men and girls work in the same room. A girl at the Tract House told me they pay better for sewing there than in most other places, and have work all the year, in ordinary times. A printer boy told me his sister earns, in a bindery, from $8 to $10 a week. D. has newspapers printed and folded, and pays his women for folding from $4 to $5 a week. A manufacturer in New York, having a bindery in New Jersey, pays his girls mostly $3.50 a week, besides their board and washing. He boards them, and he is very particular in having them attend church on the Sabbath, and keeping an oversight of their morals and habits. Most of the binding done South and West is that of blank books. There is not so much machinery at the South and West as at the North. F. says the binding of blank books pays best. A good folder may earn $6 a week, but a sewer not so much. The majority of both do not earn more than $4. They pay from the first. One woman can stitch enough to keep three men employed. So there are not as many women employed in factories where blank books are made, as where printed books are. I was told on Fulton street, at a blank-book manufactory, that their girls earn from $5 to $7. They give steady work all the year. The binding of blank books pays best. They have one girl that sometimes earns $9 a week. At jobbing houses girls generally earn $6 a week, when paid by the week for binding.

378. Card Makers. For about eleven hundred years women have been more or less employed in the manufacture of cards. At N.'s, New York, I saw two girls who each earn $6 a week, and work only in daylight, and have work all the year. I went through D. & Co.'s work rooms, and saw the process of making playing cards. A large number of girls were at work, who receive average wages of $4 per week. It requires six months to learn well. They do not like to take any learners with whose character they are unacquainted; for many, when they have learned, will go off where they can get better pay. Six girls that learned with him last summer were drawn off by an employer who offered them twenty-five cents a week more; but when his busy time was over, they came back crying to be taken in again. So he made a rule that none should be taken back that once leave. (Do not men go where they get the best prices?) They keep all their hands at work, because many of them represent three or four others, who are dependent on their labor for bread. They give work all the year, and pay a learner according to what she accomplishes. They sometimes find it difficult to get good hands. They will not take hands from another employer unless they bring a note saying they have been honorably discharged. It is to avoid getting bad and dishonest workers. (If employers in that line of business, or any other, should agree never to receive hands from each other's places of business, it would cast workers entirely at the mercy of employers.) D. says their regulations are strict. I thought the girls looked to be comfortably situated. Some were cutting cards, some assorting, some counting, and some enveloping. Nearly all sat. He thinks the business so limited that it is not likely to furnish employment to many more. He says girls working at bookbinding and hoop skirts are out of employment a great deal; two thirds of the hoop-skirt makers are now out of employment. S. & P. make fancy and business cards. S. told me he pays his most experienced girls $3.50 a week. Learners receive $2.50 a week for four weeks—after that, according to activity and capability. He has hundreds of applicants, and always selects those who seem most destitute. They work ten hours a day. He has had some girls several years. To the small girls he pays less. He often has two or three girls from the same family. Foreign goods are so much preferred by Americans that they put French labels on some.

Visiting Cards. A., New York, employs two girls to put up visiting cards, and pays $3 and $3.50 per week. It does not require any time to learn. He now uses a machine for cutting that does the work of several girls. I was told by a very obliging girl, working in a visiting-card manufactory in New York, that to some the occupation is unhealthy, because of the lead inhaled, which injures the lungs. In that factory learners are paid $2 a week. It requires but a week to learn to cut the cards, which is done with a small hand press. The girl knew of two places in the city where the work was paid for by the piece; but in that factory they were mostly paid by the week, receiving $3.50 and

$4, working ten hours a day. It requires from four to six weeks to learn. Nimbleness of fingers and ability to count are the most desirable qualifications. They have work all the year, except in November and December. They sit while cutting, assorting, and packing. This work is confined to women, as they are best adapted to it. Those in the brushing room stand. Several hundred girls are employed in New York in the card business.

379. Card Stencillers and Painters. A stencil engraver told me he cannot use acids in his work, because his lungs are weak, and it is very injurious. The business is dull in winter, but good in spring and fall. It pays very well when there is enough to do. His work has to be done hurriedly, as it is generally for merchants who are going to ship goods, and frequently do not order the plates until the barrels are headed and the boxes are nailed. The making of embroidery stencil plates, he thinks, would do better for a woman, and that could be done without any regard to seasons. A visiting-card writer told me he charges $1 a package of fifty-two for plain marking. Mrs. H. saw the advertisement of one who writes one hundred cards for $1. I. G., who makes show cards, says a boy for filling the letters is paid six cents a sheet. For designing, a person could get twenty-four cents a sheet. He could both design and fill thirty a day, so earning $1.87½. He knows that the merchants of the South used to purchase their cards in New York, and so there must be openings in the South for writers of show cards, and probably in the West. It requires about one year to learn to design well, and two weeks to learn to fill in neatly. Employees are paid by the piece. I was told that card painting must be done by women, judging from the prices paid—some cards costing but twelve cents a piece. I am sure women could do all the work. Making the letters is very simple, and filling them up is a mere mechanical operation. They can earn, I am confident, over $2 a day, if they have enough of work. It is peculiarly adapted to women, and some of them should learn it. I saw the wife of a German stencil engraver, who assists her husband by cutting out with scissors the parts that form the letters. He is paid three cents a letter. He can cut forty letters in two or three hours. A coat of wax is laid on the plate, and an instrument used for working out the letters, figures, or design, then an acid poured on, and when it has stood for a time removed with the wax. It can then be cut out with scissors, or into large letters and figures with other tools. Writing plates are cut by hand, as they can be most neatly and delicately done in that way. They are twice as high in price as stencil plates. S., who manufactures show cards, has several times thought of employing

16*

women. They could with a brush fill the outlines, which is now done by men, who earn from $2.50 to $18 a week. It would require about a year to acquire proficiency in drawing the outlines of the letters and using the brush to fill them. He thinks it a very suitable business for women, and will probably employ some before long.

380. Cover and Edge Gilders. I think burnishing the edges of books could be done by women after they are put in the frames, but considerable strength is required in the preparatory processes of shaving and screwing up. The burnishing is done with agates. I doubt whether it requires more strength than many other things women do. Laying gold leaf on the edges could certainly be done by them. Men that gild the edges of books receive from $7 to $9 a week. Men will not fold or stitch, because it does not pay well enough. G. says gilding the covers of books requires a longer apprenticeship than either folding or sewing; and at H.'s, workers are paid at first eight cents an hour, afterward ten cents an hour. It being piecework, the girls are not strictly confined to hours. Book and card edge-gilding is done both in England and France by women.

381. Electrotypers. Electrotyping is now more used than stereotyping by those who expect to have many editions of a work published. It costs but little more than stereotyping, and is either four or six times as durable, I forget which. 2,000,000 impressions can be taken from an electrotype plate, but only 800,000 from a stereotype plate. A boy learning the business receives $4 a week the first year, and after that more. A journeyman receives $2 a day, and some $2.50. A journeyman told us he had spent seven years at it, and he felt that he had yet much to learn; in fact, a person could be always learning. Electrotyping would be a useful and profitable occupation for women. An apprenticeship of three or four years is given to it.

382. Envelope Makers. At B. & G.'s, New York, girls work by the piece all the year in busy times, and can earn from $3 to $6. Most of those who get in factories, do so through the influence of friends or acqaintances in or connected with the establishment. Their business is increasing. They keep their girls all the year. They give lessons in the busy months, August and September, February and March, and pay from the first. A good hand can earn from $3 to $5. P. & Co. usually employ sixty girls. They are paid by the piece, and earn from $4 to $4.50 a week. The envelopes are made by machines, attended by women. They employ five or six girls making envelopes by hand, as they have not machines of some sizes. P. thinks the occupation is full. They have employed their girls all the year. They used to take learners, and give the teachers their profits. My companion, Mrs. F., inquired if envelopes could not be more easily made where the paper is manufactured. He replied, they could not, because paper (and, I believe, all other goods) are delivered free of freight in New York, and he can make more by being here in the centre of trade, than if he had to send his goods here to be sold, and employ some one to sell them. He prefers the girls that can be obtained in the villages and country, for he thinks them more honest and truthful. He thinks the grade of morals altogether superior in the country to that of the city. He spoke of the want of moral obligation in the lower classes, arising from the want of proper instruction, and the lower you descend the worse you find it. The makers of boxes for containing envelopes they got were such a common set, that they instructed some nice American girls how to make them, and now employ them. He says the box makers are a common set. So I have heard bookbinders, umbrella makers, and hoopskirt workers spoken of. But I frequently hear one trade speak disparagingly of another. W. told me their girls are paid so much a thousand. The envelopes are cut by a machine attended by a man. They are folded by a machine managed by two women, who of course stand. They are pasted and enveloped by girls who sit. The girls earn from $3 to $5 a week. It requires but two or three weeks to acquire the trade. A learner is paid nothing. The envelopes are tipped or gummed by a girl, who stands. This is the most difficult part of the work done by women, and pays best. There are eight factories in New York, one in Philadelphia, and one in Connecticut. Nine tenths of the business is done in New York. There are probably between two hundred and three hundred girls employed in the business in that city. W. requires references. Some employers are particular in their selection of hands—others advertise, and take them as they come. 2,700 envelopes have been made in an hour by machinery. A manufacturer in Massachusetts writes : "The work is considered particularly healthy. Girls from 12 years up are employed, and earn from thirty-three to seventy-five cents a day of ten hours. Men are paid from $1 to $2.75 per day. Two are machinists, two overseers, and two cutters of envelopes. Women are not strong enough for this kind of work. Some parts can be learned in a month, some in six months, and in others it requires a year to excel. We give the same employment and pay through the year, whether our profits are larger or smaller. I employ about sixty, one sixth of whom are American. The work is light, and we have constant applications from girls, who prefer this to any other manufacturing business in town.   Board, $1.50."

383. Folders and Directors of Newspapers.   The lady at F. & W.'s who directs the papers for them, says the business has been followed by women in New York for fifteen years.   I called at the office of the *Independent*, and saw one of the editors, who, on learning my business, kindly invited me into the room where the young ladies were employed in directing strips of paper to envelop newspapers.   It is a pretty business, and well adapted to women.   Some learn it easily, and some never learn it.   Dr. C. remarked : " A person may have a willing mind, but not an obedient hand."   They had one young lady who spent five months at it, and then gave it up, because she could not succeed.   It requires a peculiar aptitude, aside from an expeditious movement of the pen.   It was followed more by women eight or nine years ago than now.   Many ladies would like to get employment of the kind, but cannot.   I think all the young ladies in the *Independent* office were American, and were certainly very pretty and lady-like.   They have a separate room to write in.   They spend about eight hours directing envelopes for papers to send away.   One earns $6 a week, another $5, and another $4.   The one that first came is permitted to have as much work as she can do.   The next has what she leaves, and the third the remainder.   The objections made by some men to employing ladies are that they do not like to have women work in the same room where they are.   They feel under more restraint, and not so free to say what they please.   Such a restraint may be a wholesome one.   Many women make the same objection in regard to working with men.   Again, if a lady does not work as they wish, or is idle, they do not like to correct her, because women are more quick to resent.   The last excuse is a poor one. They also waste much time by having their beaux call on them. Some urge they find a boy more useful, because they can put him to doing something else, when he is not busy writing.   In the *Tribune* office, men are employed because they can do it more rapidly.   It is said some direct eight hundred envelopes in an hour.   In some offices the girls are expected to seal the papers, but not in all.   At the Cosmopolitan Art Association, I saw a lady that is employed in directing the *Art Journals* that are sent by mail.   The covers are put on by a boy.   She receives $9 a week, and spends about eight hours writing.   At the rooms of the A. C. Association, we saw three ladies directing envelopes for the report of the society.   The Association issues a monthly magazine, and at the time of its issue employs the same ladies for the purpose of enveloping and directing them.   At other times they

employ but one. She has been there ten years, and is very efficient. She attends to the books containing the names of subscribers, assists the treasurer sometimes, writes letters for the
secretary, and makes herself generally useful in that way. All
the ladies complained of women being so poorly paid. The one
who has been there ten years says, for the $250 a year she
gets, they could not secure a young man's services for less
than $700 or $800. The others are paid 63 cents per thousand
for directing, and ten cents per hundred for sealing and directing.

384. Ink. A large quantity of writing and printing ink is
used in this country. There are factories for making each kind.
Making printing ink is hard and dirty work, unsuitable for women.
Some persons cut stencil plates and make indelible ink, and employ agents to sell the ink and plates. Indelible, and all writing
inks, could be made and bottled by women. Care should be
taken that the acids used do not touch the flesh. Common clothes
should be worn while at work, as both the ingredients and compound are of a kind to injure clothes. A maker of writing ink
in New York, employs three girls in summer for bottling and
labelling, and pays $3.50, working from seven till dark. He
never employed any in winter, but if his business extends, he will
employ his girls all the year, paying the same price in winter.
He has found it difficult to get good hands. The prospect for
learners is poor. A manufacturer of ink writes : " I have never
yet employed female help, though I am satisfied that most of the
work in my laboratory might be as well done by women as men.
The employment is not unhealthy. My men work ten hours a
day, and are paid by the month.

385. Label Cutters. At P. Brothers', I was told some
of their labels are cut by hand, and some by machinery. The
first are square or oblong, the others are of different shapes.
Those cut with shears are most neatly done. For cutting by
hand the price is one cent per hundred. They take them home.
A lady and her two daughters, who work for them, often receive
$50 a month. Those cut by machinery could not well be cut by
women. It requires practice to make one expert. B. pays a
girl by the hundred to cut labels at home. He would employ a
girl to cut and attend his store, paying $3 a week from the first,
but she must not be absent a day. If her health is such that
she cannot always be there, he does not want her. He had one
three and a half years, who was absent only ten days during that
time. S. says cutting labels is always piecework, and a good
worker can earn from $4 to $6 a week. He gives them out, and
they are cut by hand. Common ones, for spices, mustard, &c.,

are cut by machinery. It does not require long to become expert. The business is always dull in December and January.

386. Lead Pencils. The young man at the agency for the sale of Faber's pencils, says they are made at Steinway, Germany, and he thinks women there are employed in varnishing the wood of the pencils and tying them up. The pencils are either painted or the simple wood varnished. " A man in New York is reported to have made $60,000 by selling lead pencils about the streets at a penny a piece, and safely investing his profits." Some large pencils, such as are used by carpenters, were some time back made in Massachusetts. The writing part of lead pencils is made of lead and clay, mixed, pressed, and burnt. The wooden part is in two pieces that are united when the lead is put in. In Germany each man has his own part to do. Children do some parts of it, such as joining the wood.

387. Operatives in Paper Factories. Paper is of various qualities and colors, and is adapted to different purposes. At least one half of the operatives in paper factories in the United States are females, amounting to several thousand. Water power is used in some paper mills, but in most large mills steam is used. Women are employed in paper mills to sift, sort, and cut up rags. It is dusty, disagreeable work, and we presume not particularly healthy, as much of the dust is no doubt inhaled. In some factories, women attend the picking and cutting machines and calenders. They are also employed for hanging, laying off, reeling, folding, assorting, counting, enveloping, and labelling the paper. The inability to meet fully the demand for rags in the manufacture of paper has led to experimenting with a variety of articles. One agent for the sale of paper made in New Jersey, and the foreman of the same establishment, told me their girls get from $2.50 to $3 a week. The majority receive $2.50. Part work six consecutive hours, have a rest of one hour, then six consecutive hours more, that is from six at night till seven in the morning, having one hour at midnight; the other half from 7 A. M. till 6 P. M., having an hour at noon. The day and night workers take week about. They board for $1.50 a week. In Lee, Mass., women get $3.50 and $4, and the men twice as much. Women are paid best in the ruling department. In the paper factories in New York, women receive from $3 to $5 per week. Paper maker's girls, $1.50 to $2.50 per week. S. says, in some paper factories girls are able to earn $6 a week. All the labor in paper mills, except attending to the fires and machinery, could be done by women. All manufacturers report the occupation as healthy, except one in South Adams, who states that small pox is sometimes taken from the rags—*not often.* A paper manufacturer in Lee, Mass., writes: "Women are employed in all countries where paper is made. The time of learning depends upon their skill and developments in certain directions in the business. They are usually paid by the piece. Men are paid more because their labor is greater. Boys learn the business in about five years, girls in about one year. In learning they generally receive enough to pay their board. They work at all seasons—sometimes have nothing to do in July. There is a demand for hands in the loft, a surplus in the rag room." The New England Roofing Co. manufacture a felt, which is similar to sheathing paper, but made of a fine stock. They employ six females in sorting rags and other materials for the felt, and pay from $3 to $5 per week, one half the price of males. They work eleven hours, and pay $2 per week for board. A manufacturer of wrapping and wall paper, in Connecticut, writes " he employs a few females, and pays fifty cents per day of from eight to ten hours. He prefers them because most economical. Those working by the piece can earn from fifty to seventy-five cents per day. He pays men $1 per day for doing like work. They require less attention, and can perform other work when wanted, that is not suitable for females to perform. He usually pays beginners the same as others when they work by the day. His most busy time is when there is most water for power. An active person can usually earn as much in from six to eight hours as a house girl is paid for a full day's work." A manufacturer at Niagara Falls " employs between forty and fifty women, paying each from $2.50 to $4 per week, without board. They are paid about one half less than men, because boys would do. The prospect of employment is good. They are most busy in summer, although they run the whole year, day and night (except Sunday). They are twelve hours on, and twelve hours off. Board, $1.25 to $1.75." A firm in South Adams, Mass., write me: " We pay by the piece and the day. The prices for female labor, we think, compared with work done, better than for male. It requires no time to learn to cut rags, but experienced hands can earn more wages. For finishing, from four to six months are given. Women are paid while learning. We employ women always, when they can do the labor. Women are superior in the neatness with which they do their work. New England, and such States as have abundance of clear *spring water*, are the best. Board, from $1.25 to $2 per week. We think, perhaps, that at present the business of paper making is pretty fully supplied with laborers, male and female, in this section of the country, yet *good* help finds ready employment, at fair wages." Manufacturers of bank-note paper, in Lee, Mass., inform me by mail, they " pay by the piece, to women, from $3

to $4.50 per week. It would require five years for a man to
learn the business, so as to properly superintend it. That portion
done by women can be learned in one month." A newspaper
manufacturer in Taunton, Mass., writes : " Fifty or sixty women
are employed by me, in manufacturing cotton goods and news
paper. I pay by the piece and the week, from $2.50 to $6 per
week; depending on the age. I give equal pay to both sexes for
the same work. They are employed the year round, and work
eleven hours on the average. The climate of New England is
best adapted to indoor labor." Paper manufacturers in Dalton
write : " We pay women by the piece, from $12 to $16 per
month, and they have work all the year. No men are employed
for the same kind of work. For other branches of the business,
men are paid from $25 to $35 per month. Women are paid
while learning for what they accomplish. The prospect for work
is good. We employ women because they are cheaper. They
pay for board $1.25." A firm in Russell, Mass., write : " We
employ from forty to fifty ; one tenth are Americans. They can
all live comfortably and earn good wages. New England is the
best part of this country for fine paper mills, on account of the
purity of the water. Board, $1.50 to $1.75."

  388. Paper-Bag Makers. At a paper-bag factory in
Brooklyn, the man pays from $1.50 to $2 a week to his girls. They
work ten hours. The work is all done by hand. The bags are
considered better than those made by machinery. He has twenty-
six girls at work. Some he pays by the quantity ; for some kinds,
twenty cents a hundred ; for some, thirty-seven cents. Those that
work by the piece have a forewoman, with whom he makes a contract. She cleared $14 one week. It takes but a week to
learn. Work is furnished all the year. Some have worked for
him five years. Paper-bag manufacturers in Watertown, Mass.,
write : " We employ six women in tending bag machines, and
pay seventy cents per day of ten and a half hours. To males
we pay one third more. It requires about one month to learn,
and all that is necessary are care and application. Summer and
fall are the best seasons, but they can have work the year round.
We will not have any but American girls. Women are more
accustomed to sitting, but cannot keep the machine in order.
Their dress is objectionable, particularly their hoops, which take
up much room, and are in danger of getting in the machinery."

  389. Paper-Box Makers. Though this may seem a
trivial business, it is one very extensively carried on. Every
size and shape is called for. The most are made, we suppose,
in New York and Philadelphia, as greater demands exist there,
owing to the variety and quantity of goods manufactured and

offered for sale. Boxes are almost entirely made by women. I think most of the men in this trade in New York are Germans. The occupation for women is pretty well filled. The bandbox manufacture is a distinct branch. Some women, who make small match boxes, receive but one cent for thirty boxes. At a place in New York where seventeen girls are employed, I was told they are paid by the piece, and some can earn as much as $5 a week. The calling can be learned in three or four weeks. At one place, where they make bandboxes also, the girls earn from $2 to $5. At another, they earn from $2.50 to $5. Some seasons of the year are better than others. They have mostly American girls. It is sometimes difficult to get good hands. They keep their hands all the year. Spring and fall are the most busy seasons. Very little sewing is ever done—mostly cutting and pasting. In some large factories, machinery is used for much of the work. K. employs a number of hands all the year. They work by the piece (customary plan), and earn from $1.50 to $6. They are paid $1.50 per week from the time they begin to learn. He thinks there are not more than from five hundred to six hundred females in New York employed in his branch. There were three hundred in Philadelphia about fifteen months ago. One-paper-box maker told me he pays fifty cents a hundred, and a smart girl can make one hundred and fifty in a day. He gives employment all the year; his brother, in the spring and fall. The work is always, I think, cut out by a man. B.'s girls are paid by the piece, and earn about $4 a week. While learning, his girls are paid $2 a week. It requires but two or three months to become skilful. I noticed the girls in some work rooms sat, and some stood. I was told those making small boxes sit, but those making large boxes stand, because of the time consumed in rising to reach the parts needed to be joined. Learners work with F. fourteen days for nothing, and then are paid by the hundred. Some can accomplish more than others in the same time, because they are quicker with their fingers and apply themselves more closely. In putting on labels, it is best to stand, as it can be done more expeditiously. It is best for girls to learn where the cheap kind of boxes are to be made. Those that make fine boxes are seldom willing to take learners, because of the materials that are wasted in learning. Good hands can get work all the year; indifferent hands are likely to get out of employment for one or two months. The girls in the trade are mostly Irish and German. For three months, the past year, F. was out of hands. He deserved to be all the time, for his factory was on the fifth floor, and the steps of the open wood kind. So girls must have been very much exposed in going up and down stairs, as every flight of stairs led to a floor on which men were at work. At C.'s, I was told his best workers earn from $4 to $6 a week, and are paid by the gross. They never work over ten hours, as his work is of a large kind. In some factories, where the boxes made are small, the girls are allowed to take work home with them to do in the evening. He keeps his best hands all the year. He requires two weeks of learners, and then pays them according to the amount of work done. Another box maker gives his work to three or four families in an adjoining city. His workers earn from $3 to $4 per week. A girl sewing small bandboxes told me she is paid six cents a dozen, and can usually sew ten dozen a day. It takes but a week to learn. They are most busy in spring and fall. In pasting, girls can earn from $4 to $5 a week. The girls sewing, sat; those pasting, stood. At another factory I was told April and September are their most busy months, and then they take learners. Most box makers have steady work. If they are not making boxes for one branch of trade, they are for another—confectioners, candle makers, &c. The business is increasing. Girls can earn from $3 to $7. There are openings in New Orleans. It is difficult to get good hands in busy times. It takes some time to become expert. A boy remarked to me that paper-box makers are a hard set; but I find there is considerable jealousy and envy existing between some members of the different trades, and consequently always make some allowance for what I hear. A firm of paper-box manufacturers in Connecticut write : " Women are employed by us to run machinery, making paper boxes, &c. It is healthy, clean, neat work. Average wages are seventy-eight cents per day, including board. Our male help are employed at some laborious work, which females could not perform. Average price paid men is $1.25 per day, of eleven hours. No time is required to learn the paper-box business, but practice makes it more remunerative. There are advantages in being in large cities; but, having no market near, we prefer the country, on the ground of better advantages for our help, and its being easier to procure trusty, intelligent girls to labor. Our women have constant employment, and are superior to men in their work. Most of them are well suited for making good wives, being from eighteen to twenty-five years of age. Board, $1.75." B., of Philadelphia, writes : " We pay women from $2.50 to $5 per week, working by the piece. Men's wages are double, as they generally have families. Neatness and to be good sewers are desirable. They generally have work the year round. The demand is greatest in Philadelphia, New York, and the Eastern States. We employ them because of their ability to use the needle. Women are superior in their own branch." A manufacturer of hook-and-eye and button boxes writes: "We employ twelve women, and pay by the piece, from $4 to $6 a week. Women's wages are low, because of the competition in the article manufactured. Time of learning depends upon the natural skill of the learner—one can learn for years. The prospect for a continuance of this work is good. The price, and fittedness for the work, recommend women to us."

390. Paper Marblers. I saw the process of marbling—something very suitable for women, if they would properly qualify themselves for it. The young man said a paper marbler in Philadelphia used to employ some women to assist him, but he had to mix their paints. A paper marbler in Boston writes: "I do not know of any females being employed as marblers of book edges in the United States. Some are employed in marbling paper for the covers and linings of books."

391. Paper Rulers. In ruling paper for blank books and ledgers, females are employed in some establishments to feed the machine. It is not difficult to learn, though there are not many willing to take learners, as considerable paper must be wasted before they can become proficient. Only a few weeks are required, and they are seldom paid while learning. $4 a week is a fair average for female workers. Very closely connected with this branch is that of paging blank books. It may be learned in from ten to twelve days. This is a limited business, and would not justify many in learning. K. thinks thirty girls would supply the demand for the whole United States. The most busy season is from the first of July to the last of October, and they seldom refuse any applicants during this season. March and April are also busy months. About half the hands are retained through the dull season. The girls earn from $5 to $6 a week; the forewoman something more. All are required to be orderly and respectable, and there are no associations that would have an immoral tendency. A journeyman paper ruler in Boston writes: "There are a few girls employed in this city at ruling, i. e., where they feed on the paper, watch the work, fixing it when it requires attention, &c. The paper is trimmed for them, it being hard work, and requiring a man's strength to do it. The wages are from $3 to $4.50 per week—$3.75 about the average—and when they board away from home, pay $2 to $2.25 per week. I work by the piece, and make sometimes $10, sometimes $16 per week; can make $12 and $13 per week well enough, nine hours to the day. One disadvantage females have, is, that some of them are inclined to marry when a good opportunity is offered. I wish to be understood that this is a disadvantage only as keeping down the price of female labor. The young man learns his trade, then he marries. He does not quit the shop, but still improves in skill in his trade. The female, when she marries, bids farewell to the shop and her trade. Nine or ten hours a day is as long as girls work at our trade here. One great objection girls have to our trade is, they do not like to soil their hands with the ruling ink, and one cannot get through much ruling without soiling their hands more or less."

392. Press Feeders. "The number of women who feed power presses in printing offices in Philadelphia may number one hundred and fifty. They can earn, upon an average, $4 per week." At the Methodist Book Concern, New York, they pay to press feeders the usual price, $4 per week. It requires about six months to become a good press feeder. When work is scarce, they retain all their hands, if possible, but work a less number of hours, and pay in proportion. At a blank-book manufactory I was told their girls are paid $6 a week for feeding. Their girls think they make poor wages when they earn but ten cents an hour. Some embossers, in Boston, who employ thirty women in binding and press feeding, write: "They pay both by the week and by the piece. Their women, on an average, earn $5 per week. Female labor is thirty-three per cent. cheaper than men's, and the part done by women is too effeminate for men. Women spend from one to two months learning. Prospect of employment in this branch is good. The women work ten hours. They are out of employment in summer. Board, $1.50 to $2.50." At a printing office where from forty to fifty women were employed, I was told the girls were mostly German, because the foreman was a German. It requires four weeks to learn. They work ten hours a day, and are never thrown out of employment. The demand seems to be fully met in New York.

393. Printers. "In 1476, Fra Domenico da Pistoya and Fra Pietro da Pisa, the spiritual directors of a Dominican convent, established a printing press within its walls; the nuns served as compositors, and many works of considerable value issued from this press between 1476 and 1484, when, Bartolomeo da Pistoya dying, the nuns ceased their labors." In the Victoria Printing Office, of London, all the compositors' work is done by women. The Printers' Unions in the United States have done all they could to prevent women from entering the occupation and obtaining employment. Men's employments in the cities, they say, are now filled, and if women enter, men's wages will fall. They do fall, at any rate, because women will work for less than men. To obviate this difficulty, I would suggest that more men engage in agricultural and other occupations that will take them out of the cities. At present, the war demands large numbers. A printer told me that type setting could be carried on more easily by women in towns and villages than in cities, where men are slaves to the Unions. In the latest rules of the Printers' Union, New York, a printer is not prohibited from working in the office with a woman. Yet few publishers are willing to employ them, because it is supposed they are employed for less wages. At a printers' convention, held recently in Springfield, Ill., the following resolutions were adopted: "Whereas, the employment of females in printing offices, as compositors, has, wherever adopted, been found a decided benefit, both as regards the moral tendencies inculcated and the dependence to be placed in their constant presence and attendance upon the duties required of them, and as a means of opening a wider field of remunerative labor to a deserving class of society; therefore, be it resolved, That the Association recommend to its members the employment of females in their offices, wherever and whenever practicable." Printing is mostly paid for by the thousand ems. More is paid for printing from manuscript than for reprint. Newspaper is paid rather higher than book printing, and morning papers more than evening. Much has been said of the unhealthiness of a printer's work. The majority of causes that render it so are not confined to the occupation itself. Some printers must work during the night. Their habits become irregular, and many run into dissipation. The rooms occupied by some are poorly ventilated, and so poorly lighted as even in the day to require artificial light, which helps to absorb the oxygen of the atmosphere. When type are heated they emit an odor that affects respiration, and will in the course of time paralyze the hand. But there is no necessity for using them when heated. The standing position of compositors weakens the organs of digestion; but compositors can as well sit as stand. Stools may occasionally be seen in the offices of men. Bending over the stone to correct is not more tiresome than bending over cloth when sewing. A good education and general intelligence are necessary for a printer. A gentleman connected with a printing office remarked to me that printers generally possess much desultory information, but have not their faculties more fully developed than people in most other trades. Women's fineness of touch and quickness of motion will fit them for type setting. "They might be instructed, not merely to compose and distribute, but to correct, make up, impose forms, and prepare the type completely for the press or stereotype foundery." A man should be employed to carry the chases to the press room. When the pressman has had the type inked and used them, he should have the form

washed and returned to the compositors' room. When women
have had as much experience as men in the printing business,
they will be fair competitors. In most large cities, and even
towns, many are now employed in type setting; but they are
much scattered, and consequently not much is known of them.
In Boston, women have been engaged in type setting for nearly
thirty years, in New York eight years, and in Philadelphia five
years. More girls are employed as type setters in Boston than
any other city of the United States. They set type for nearly all
the large periodicals. They are paid less than men; but some
earn $8 a week. F., of Boston, who employs some women as
type setters, writes : " I pay twenty cents per thousand ems,
which averages to a good hand about $6 or $7 per week. It requires about six months to learn type setting. I pay my learners, because I consider it to my advantage in the long run to
do so. Type setters with an ordinary education will improve
as they progress. In a few years, women will work in many
branches that to-day would be termed innovation. I consider
winter the best season for printing books and periodicals. On
account of neatness and taste, women are well suited for the ornamental branches of printing." The proprietors of a printing
house in Boston, who have some thought of employing females,
write me : " The printing business is considered rather unhealthy,
on account of its being both mental and physical. It requires
from two to three years to become good workmen at our business
for males, and would take about the same time for females,
although our business is now classed composition room and press
room, and females are sometimes employed in other offices in
both rooms. Our business does not vary much, except in the
month of August, when it is generally dull. Our number of
hours for work are ten, the year through. Our business is not
considered very laborious, and females make from $4 to $8
per week. Men are generally superior to women in education and judgment. The printing business is almost a school for
learning. Board, from $1.50 to $2.50." The largest number of
printers in New York are employed on books and periodicals. I
think it likely there are more Americans employed in the book-
making trade in New York than any other trade. From an article on " Printers," in the New York *Tribune* of April, 1853, we
extract the following : " We estimate the services of a competent
young woman at type setting as worth in this city $2 per week,
after a fortnight—$4 per week, after three months—$6 per week,
after a year—$8, after two years. Every compositor on the *Tri-
bune* at work at the case has thirty-seven cents per thousand
em , and thirty cents per hour for steady time." The present

price required by members of the New York Typographical Union for newspaper work, when employed by the week, is $12—ten hours constituting a day's work. For book and job work $11 is required. At the *Day Book* office I saw one of the editors, who thinks women do not correct so well as men, and they want self-reliance. Besides, they cannot lift the forms. Men are paid better for these reasons. He thinks more women might very advantageously be employed in setting type for papers. Job printing he thinks not so well adapted to them, because of the variety in the work, and the judgment and self-reliance required. Two of the girls in the *Day Book* office have with their earnings bought their mother a home in the country. Their girls are more intelligent, have more pride, and dress better than most working girls. To set type requires more intelligence than most shop girls possess. The foreman of the same paper writes : "We employ ten women, whose exclusive business is type setting. Seven are American women. I deem the employment of type setting unhealthy, but not more injurious to women than it is to men. We pay women twenty cents per thousand ems. Men receive thirty-one cents per thousand ems in our office. Women are not as competent to do all kinds of work as men, particularly in a newspaper office; hence the difference in wages. The time of learning depends almost wholly on the aptitude of the new beginner. Some persons (men as well as women) would or could not learn the business in a lifetime. Women have been paid while learning in this office. A knowledge of the English language, and a disposition to improve that knowledge on all suitable occasions, are the principal requisites. The general order of intellect did not amount to much, when we first tried the experiment ; those who have worked steady have improved wonderfully. They work ten hours per day. Average wages $6.50 per week in this office. With proper training and instruction, they would be competent to do any portion of the work not requiring too much physical exertion. The best seasons for a printer's work depend almost wholly on circumstances. Large cities are the best places for the printer who wishes to have steady employment." T., of New York, told me "he employed girls for a while, and would have retained them if he could have had time to attend to the composition department. He paid his girls the same price he did his men. He thinks it strange that more broken-down ministers and worn-out school teachers do not turn to type setting, as it is learned in a very short time, requires intelligence, and demands no outlay of muscle. On the principle that a stout muscular man should be a blacksmith, and a small delicate one a watchmaker, a woman should be a type setter. A girl should begin when young. Women are no more thrown with men in type setting than in feeding presses. In all large establishments, type setting and press work are done in separate rooms." I think if some lady teachers would learn the art of printing and get places as forewomen, they could from girls obtain as much work as a foreman does from boys; but he thinks it difficult for a foreman to be exacting with women, particularly with those who are old enough to be sensitive and self-willed. He thinks, "in New York, women are not so much employed in intelligent occupations as in Boston. In the cities printers make most all their profits off two-thirders, as they are called—boys who have not attained their majority, and do their work as well for much less than journeymen. His son, a boy of sixteen, earns from $5 to $6 a week as type setter." H., in New York, employs three girls. They get $6 a week of ten hours a day. They can sit if they choose. They have a room to work in, separate from the men. At W.'s, opposite, a youth told me a fast worker could earn $8 a week. The girls there were working in the same room with the men. J., of Philadelphia, said he used to employ women to print his labels, but they demanded $6 a week, and men he could get for $9. He told the women they were cutting their throats in asking so much. He said women should not expect as high wages as men, even if they did their work as well, and as much of it, for they would thereby displace men; and besides, you could not order women about as you could men. B., editor of the Pittsburg *Commercial Journal*, employs six girls as compositors. Connected with his office are two journeymen, who set type after 6 P. M., reporting telegraphic and local news. All type setting should be done by women in the day, unless they board very near, or in the house of the printing office, because of the exposure of going home late at night. Three fourths of the work of a printing office could be done by women. Afternoon and weekly papers could be very well printed by ladies, as they are printed in the day. One of B.'s lady compositors receives $7 a week, another $6, and the others $4 and $3.50. They work eight or nine hours a day; and to a learner they pay $1.50 a week, until she can set type correctly—then more; and in two years she will be very nearly or quite perfect in the art. It requires quickness of eye and finger to succeed. At the office of the Detroit *Daily Democrat*, girls as apprentices are paid from $3 to $4 per week, and those advanced twenty-five cents per thousand ems. "The compositors' office of the *Ohio Farmer*, at Cleveland, has four apprentice girls. Compensation light at present, but after the first year they will have the same that journeymen are receiving in this place, i. e., twenty-five cents per thousand ems."

A lady learning to set type in Indiana writes : " I think the reason of the printers objecting to my learning was that I was not required to run of errands, or, in other words, be the 'devil' of the office, as boys are who learn the printing business. Besides, my compensation is better than theirs, in consequence of my ability to do more than they. I receive my board and $50 a year while learning ; after that, journeyman's wages by the week or by the thousand ems, as I prefer. In this time I can learn to do all, except the press work, making up, &c. The girls employed as type setters in the office receive $3 per week while learning." I have been told that in Rochester, Buffalo, and New Haven, printing is done more cheaply than in New York, and some publishers send their printing to those towns to have it done. A great deal of raised printing is done for the blind in the United States, but women do not work at that. Printers were wanted some time back in Charleston, S. C., and when affairs become settled in the South, we doubt not there will be many openings for printers. An institution has been founded in Edinburg for teaching girls the art of printing. Monsieur P. says in many of the villages of France it is difficult to get printers. He proposes that a certain number of girls be qualified for the work, as women are well suited to such work, and it is of a kind that pleases those who have tried it.

394. Sealing-Wax Makers. D., sealing-wax, ink, and mucilage manufacturer, employs two girls in putting up carmine ink and gum mucilage, also in rolling, stamping, and boxing sealing wax. To one he pays $5 a week, to the other $4. He employs his girls all the year. Making sealing wax is too heavy work for women, D. thought, and there is not much demand for the kind used in sealing letters. Self-sealing envelopes and mucilage have done away with both wafers and wax. In the United States, one pound is sold where formerly one ton was sold. Had the use of wafers increased with correspondence, it would have been an extensive business; but the making and baking of wafers, D. thought, was too heavy work for women. I expect it is not more so than making and baking bread. But little ink is made in the South and West. C. said women could not make sealing wax, because of the danger of being about the fire. I suggested there is not more than in cooking. He said lifting the vessels is very heavy.

395. Stereotypers. All the first plates in this country were moulded by a Mrs. Watts, the wife of an Englishman, who introduced the art from London. Stereotyping could be learned by women. It is an interesting employment, but requires intelligence and judgment. In stereotyping, one department of labor

17

is that of correcting metal plates. If a letter is wanting, a type is soldered in the plate. If any of the letters or spaces are filled with superfluous metal, it is removed. I think stereotyping an occupation well adapted to skilful and educated women. It re-quires an apprenticeship of three or four years.

396. Type Rubbers and Setters. At P. &.Co.'s, I saw the whole process of type making. They employ some women to rub type, and some to set them up. The setters earn from $1.50 to $2 a week. It is very simple, but there is much difference in the quantity done by different individuals. A care-ful and rapid manipulation is desirable for the worker, as it is paid for by the number of types set up. The rubbers are paid by the pound, and earn from $8 to $9 a week. Some people can rub 2,000 types in an hour. The fingers become hardened. P. & Co. do not employ many American girls, for American girls do not like such dirty work, and most of them dislike to work where men are. Breaking off the jets is in some places done by women. It is a mechanical operation for removing the inequalities of the metal, caused by the imperfect chasing of the moulds. It requires a very rapid movement of the hand, but is not a laborious opera-tion. It is said that some fast workers can break off 5,000 in an hour. Girls are employed at type rubbing and setting, in the same room with men. Type are cut of a soft metal, from which copper moulds are taken for forming printers' type. It requires a steady hand, a correct eye, and some practice to cut them, but not much strength. It could be done by women. B. thinks the work is not unhealthy. I suppose the same objection as regards health might be made to breaking off the jets, type rubbing, and type setting, that is often made to the business of a compositor—that the lead in the metal has a tendency to paralyze the arm; but I have never heard the objection offered. B. does not pay learners. Prospect for employment tolerable. When times are good, he keeps girls all the year. They are paid by the quantity. The little girls can earn $2.50 each, and some of the larger girls, who are very expert, can earn $4.50. Girls always sit in rubbing type. In setting up, I think they can sit or stand, as they please. There will be a demand for type so long as books and papers are printed. I suppose there will now be an opening in the South for type founderies. W. takes learners, and pays by the quantity from the first. All his women sit while at work. It is not healthy work, because of the lead floating in the atmosphere be-ing inhaled. He can always get hands by advertising. Setters get about $2.50 a week, and rubbers $3, and $3.50. C. says, if type rubbers are industrious and attentive, they can earn from $3 to $7 a week. Rubbing pays better than setting, but is quite laborious. Setters earn from $2 to $3.50, and are generally small girls. They are always paid by the quantity. It does not require long to learn. The prospect is good for employment. In ordinary times they are employed all the year. At H.'s, I was told that girls are never taught rubbing until they have learned setting, as rubbing pays best, and it is not fair to give a learner the advantage of an old hand. Setters cannot earn more than $2.50 a week; rubbers, from $4 to $6. He gives work all the year. Some of his girls are always absent on Monday. He thinks there are from 700 to 800 girls in founderies in New York. His girls earn from $3 to $6 a week. Printers, he says, are always first to suffer in a panic. A type founder in Buffalo, writes: " I employ fifteen American girls in finishing type, and pay by the piece. They earn from $3 to $5 per week. One day is sufficient to learn, and nimble fingers greatly assist. Seasons make no difference with the work. The work is easy in a warm room in winter." The proprietors of the Boston Type Foundery sent me the following intelligence by mail: " We employ about twenty women in breaking, rubbing, and setting type. The metallic dust from the type is considered unwholesome. We pay by the piece. The girls are from ten to twenty years of age, and average from $1 to $6 per week, working from six to nine hours. But a short time is required to learn the parts, except rubbing, which occupies some months. They are paid while learning. All other parts of our business, except those mentioned, are too severe for women. The prospect for a continuance of work is tolerable."

397. Wall Paper Gilders. Most of the wall paper used in the United States for many years past has been made in Philadelphia, and I believe it is still thought to produce the best qualities. There are three modes of impressing wall paper : one by printing, another by stencilling, and the third by painting with a brush. In the cheapest paper, the outlines are printed and the colors put on by stencil plates. For printing, large blocks are used that are cut by hand, and for each color a separate block must be used. This work forms a separate occupation, that of a block cutter. For the finest papers, the outlines are printed, and then filled by the use of the brush. The ailments of colorers of wall paper arise principally from the coloring matter, much of which is very poisonous. " By laboring upon arsenical paper in the finishing department, small tumors are produced, and some have to change their occupation in consequence." At H.'s store, Philadelphia, the young man told me they employ girls from twelve to sixteen years of age, for putting gilding on paper. They work ten hours, and earn from $3.50 to $4.50 a week.

They merely lay gilding on, which is fastened by the pressure of machinery. Some manufacturers have the gilding put on with a size. At C.'s, New York, the foreman told me they employ two girls, at $3 a week each. A powder is sprinkled on by boys, which, by the way, could be done by girls. The girls then lay the gold leaf on the powder. A machine then passes over the gold leaf, making an impression by a die, of the pattern desired. Another branch of labor in which they employed girls for a time, was the rolling of paper for the store. It requires a peculiar tact acquired by practice only. They are paid seven cents for 100 rolls, each roll containing eight yards. It would take a brisk and careful hand to become at all expert three months, at which time she could earn about sixty cents a day, of ten hours' work. At the end of three months more she would, perhaps, be able to earn an additional twenty cents a day. It makes the fingers very sore, as considerable force is thrown into the tips of the fingers. Some fingers cannot become hardened to it, and the individual has to give it up. C—'s have work all the year, except a week in summer, and one in winter, and when the machinery is out of repair. They have most to do in winter, getting their paper ready for spring sale, and to send away to the West and South. It is not unhealthy labor. Many girls might be employed in departments now occupied by boys. At N. C. & Co.'s, I was told by a young German that from one hundred to one hundred and fifty boys are employed in that building, but no women or girls. There are several parts that could be done by women. The common paper is rolled by machinery, the fine by hand. In one factory in Boston, girls are employed to roll, and in one in some other part of Massachusetts. Paper stainers in Nashua, New Hampshire, write: "Women are employed in coloring and finishing papers. The work is healthy, though all cannot use green. We pay some by the week and some by the day: $3 per week for day hands. It requires two or three months to learn. A light hand, quick motions, &c., are desirable qualifications. The prospect of employment is the same as all other branches of manufacture. Warm weather is our most busy season. The hands spend a few weeks in the country in midsummer. We employ from twenty to twenty-five women, and they work ten hours a day. They have the advantages of libraries, religious services, &c., and pay for board $1.50 per week." A wall-paper manufacturer, in Boston, writes: "The different kinds of work and a fair knowledge of the manufacture of paper hangings must be seen to be appreciated. For one to be capable of taking charge of a manufactory in my line, he must devote many years of close application, and must be a man of fine taste, in order to get up a *taking* style of goods, as the success of the business, in a great measure, depends upon that, coupled with a fine finish. The perfection of the manufacture may be all that could be desired, but if the arrangement of the shadings of the colors were faulty, there would be a very limited sale of them. A woman might perhaps make a color mixer (as we call them), if the work was not too hard and too dirty. We employ three girls to roll paper. It is light work, and they are paid from $2 to $4 per week—day hands, ten hours. The time to learn depends upon the capacity of the learner—say a month. The women are not out of employment long. The women are mostly foreign, and can make a comfortable living if they choose. Women have not sufficient strength for some parts of our work."

CHEMICALS.

398. Chemicals. One chemist wrote me that some part of the work in the manufacture of chemicals is wet and disagreeable. Another writes that " women are not employed in that branch in this country, but may possibly be employed in England, Germany, and France; but if at all, only to a small extent. The employment is not generally unhealthy. To learn it in all its details, a pretty thorough knowledge of chemistry ought to be acquired. But a short time is required to learn the ordinary part of the business. The prospect of the employment of women is slight, but your inquiries have, however, suggested the idea and possibility of employing women to a small extent. Men in chemical works are employed at all seasons, and constantly for eleven hours per day. No particular locality has advantage over another, except its proximity to market. Uneducated persons, of ordinary intellect, can be employed to some extent in the labor." Another informant writes: " The manufacture of those chemicals most largely used in the arts, requires laborious work. It is, besides, rather severe on the clothes and hands, and is entirely unsuitable for women. There is, perhaps, room for the employment of women in the manufacture of the finer chemicals, but rather in the way of putting up than in the manufacture itself. We are not engaged in this branch. The demand for pure chemicals is so very limited, that only regularly educated chemists engage in the business, and they do most of the nice work themselves. There is nothing to hinder women from studying practical chem-

istry, but there are few chances for educated chemists; and there
are more than men enough to take all the places that are to be
filled." A manufacturer of acids writes: "We employ no female
labor in our establishment, it being heavy work, not suitable for
them." The present style of female dress would be inconvenient,
if not dangerous, in the preparation of such chemicals as require
the operator to be near the fire. This difficulty, however, could
be obviated.

399. Baking Powders. D. employs girls to put up
baking powders, spices, &c. It is piecework. A very brisk
hand can earn $5 a week, but few can do so. They work longest
in summer days. They like to close early enough to give their
girls time to get home before it is very late. Mechanical talent
only is necessary.

400. Bar and Soft Soap. Large quantities of soap are
made in the United States. That sold in groceries is made mostly
in towns or the country. It is hardened by muriate of soda, and
called bar soap. That used by people in the country is generally
of their own make, and called soft soap. In New York, we observed in some groceries barrels of soft soap of a very light color,
almost white. Vegetable substances were used previous to the
invention of soap, for washing the person and garments. A plant
growing in California is said to yield a very good substitute.
Some kinds of earth, mixed with lye ashes, have been used.
Making soap in large quantities would be very heavy work for
women. A machine has been invented for cutting soap into bars,
which will doubtless in time do away with the primitive plan of
cutting it with wires. At a soap factory, a man told us that
women are never employed in factories in making coarse soap.
Attending the kettles could not be well done by them. The
only part that could be done would be cutting it in bars, but
that is rather too hard, on account of the strain and change of position. It is cut with wire after it has become hard.

401. Blacking. In London, in 1852, there were, by Mayhew's estimate, one hundred and fifty women and girls selling cake
blacking. M., manufacturer, Philadelphia, occupies a four-story
granite-fronted building. He employs about fifty women in
making tin boxes, filling them with blacking in paste, and labelling them. It requires but a few weeks for a smart girl to acquire
dexterity. We saw the women at work in two large rooms (each
being the whole floor of the house). They looked cheerful, though
somewhat grimy. They work ten hours, and earn about $3 a
week. The steady hands are kept in work the year round. The
tin boxes pass, almost with the swiftness of thought, through eight
hands, three of these operations being performed by steam ma-

chinery, tended by women. The boxes are soldered by men, who receive $6 per week. It was once done by women, but is right warm work, particularly in summer. All stood while at work, except the women sorting bands. The premises had been rendered as healthy as possible. All the small pipes of the soldering stoves led into one large pipe, which carries off the fumes of the coal; and a cylinder has been made to confine a white powder which is used in the business, and which formerly floated through the atmosphere of the work rooms. The women are sometimes employed in bottling ink, and earn from $2 to $3 a week, working about the usual time—ten hours.

402. Candles. Candles are made of different materials, of which wax, tallow, and spermaceti are most common. Some candle makers employ women to prepare the wax for candles. Candle manufacturers write us: " Women are never employed in our business, and we never heard of their being so employed. We consider the work too heavy, and too cold. The principal part of the work is done in winter, and the manufacturing rooms must be kept cold. Women were at one time employed in cutting and preparing the wick for candles; but since the introduction of machinery, that part is dispensed with." A manufacturer writes from another city: " Men sometimes work all night, at the season when the nights are long. The only place, I think, where there can be a demand for female labor in my branch, is where there are no men." Another informant writes: " I think women could not be to any considerable extent employed in making soap and candles, for several reasons: 1st. It is for the most part a heavy business, requiring more than female strength. 2d. It is objectionable on account of the dirt, which is the result of coming in contact with tallow, &c." Another says: " Our plan for moulding is too heavy for women to work at." At an oil and candle manufactory, New York, I was told they used to employ some women in putting wicks into moulds, drawing candles, and packing them. Machinery is so much used now, that women cannot do as much of it as they did. Besides, candles are not used so much as they were, owing to the introduction of gas and various oils. They paid their girls $4 a week. They now employ one woman in putting the wicks in moulds for wax candles, and drawing and packing them. J. employs two women in making sperm candles, but they have been at it twenty years. They each get $4 a week. M—s, New York, write: " We employ six women in making and packing candles. They are so employed in France and England, and very likely in Germany. The work is not unhealthy. Our women are paid from $2.50 to $4 per week, of ten hours a day. They are generally paid by the week, though

sometimes by the piece. Men's wages are from $9 to $12. We
know of no reason why women are paid less, except that it is the
general custom. It requires from two to three weeks to learn.
Women are paid while learning. Dexterity of the hands is the
best qualification for a worker. The occupation is gradually decreasing. There is no material difference in the seasons for work.
Women are sometimes thrown out of employment in the summer
months. We employ women because they are more nimble fin-
gered than men, and female labor is cheaper. Workwomen are
more apt to get in trouble among themselves, where many are
employed, and are more difficult to control. We have generally
found them more careless and less uniform in their work than
men; so much so, that their employment is constantly diminishing
in our work, being replaced by machinery. We find them in no way
superior to men, except their nimble fingers." We place against
this the preliminary report to the United States Census of 1860,
where one hundred and forty-two women are returned as being
employed in soap and candle manufactures.

403. Chalk. I saw a man making prepared chalk. He
sometimes employs small girls to put it in boxes, and pays from
seventy-five cents to $2 per week. They work ten hours a day.
There is nothing unhealthy in it. He thinks there are but few
manufacturers of it, and consequently there is not much prospect
for employment.

404. Emery Paper. G. would be willing to employ
girls to pack and tie up emery paper, paying $3.50 a week. It is
dirty work, on account of the glue that is used, and is very severe
on the fingers, causing the blood to flow often, and unfortunately
does not harden the fingers by practice.

405. Fancy Soaps. Some of the fancy soaps of American manufacture are equal to any in the world. Those of Bazin,
Philadelphia, are considered best. Those of Jules Hauel and Har-
rison are nearly equal. There are other manufacturers of fancy
soap in the United States. On Spruce street, Philadelphia, is a
place where they employ girls to put up fancy soaps, and pay by the
piece, from $2 to $5 per week. L., New York, employs girls by the
week, for from $2 to $3.50. It requires practice to put up either
soap or perfumery. They are most busy in spring and fall. None
made South or West. L. has lost the custom of shop girls by the
hard times. They have no money now to spend for fancy soap
and hair oil.

406. Fire Works. Two hundred and eleven females are
reported in the census of Great Britain as being employed in making fire works. S. & Co., New York, employ ten or twelve women
for pasting the paper covers on fire works, but not for filling with

powder. All the work is done in daylight. They are paid something while learning, and then from $3 to $5 a week. For overwork, they are paid by the hour. Their factory is in Greenville, N. J. There is one in Cincinnati, one in Boston, and one in Philadelphia. Girls sit while at work. The prospect for learners is good. S. & Co. are most busy in spring and summer but able to keep their hands employed all the year. They have a great many children employed on Long Island, in making torpedoes, who cannot earn more than $1.50 a week.

407. Flavoring Extracts. Manufacturers in Rochester write: "We have about twenty women engaged in putting up and packing perfumery, &c., and pay from $2 to $3 per week. A smart girl will learn in a week. Quickness of movement and steadiness of habit are the best qualifications. The prospect of work in this line is good. They are employed all the year, and work ten hours a day." C., of Boston, employs a number, "because they can work cheaper than men. They are paid by the day or week, according to their experience. Good workers earn 50 cents a day, of nine hours. To thoroughly understand the business requires a lifetime. Women's part of the work is learned in six months. Women are paid while learning. All seasons are alike. The work is easy, and the pay good. Board, $1.50." H. C. & Co., of Boston say: "In compliance with your wishes, we give below answers to your inquiries. We manufacture perfumery, cooking extracts, hair oils, &c. We employ females to bottle and label them. We pay by the amount of labor done, and the average earnings are about $4 per week. Why women are not generally better paid is a difficult question to answer. We think, however, the argument is good that they do not as a general thing have family expenses to bear. If they were taxed (are not those that own property?) and also bore a proportionate share of family expenses, there is no good reason why they should not have the same pay for the same labor as males. (Have not the majority of workwomen some one dependent upon them, even with their scanty wages?) The work may be learned in a few weeks. An aptness and tact to handle small bottles, to tie ribbons, and cut corks quickly, best fit one for this work. There is a constant demand for the kind of goods we manufacture. Our females work ten hours a day, and their employment is steady. The work is clean and comfortable; the remuneration, we think, just. Women are superior to men, from being quicker in their movements and displaying better taste. Board, $2.50." Other manufacturers in Boston write: "We employ ten American women, because they do the work cheaper than men could. We pay by the piece. They earn $6 a week, and receive three fourths

17*

of the wages of men. They are paid $3 per week while learning. Women are inferior in business capacity, superior in details. Board, $3 per week."

408. Glue. Glue is made from the parings of hides, and refuse leather. First they are put in alkaline water to be cleaned, and then boiled in large vessels. The liquid is poured off from the gelatine which coats the vessel and forms in sheets. I think women might spread the substance on nets in drying rooms, and, when dry, cut it and pack it. It is cut by wires having handles, which are held in the hand, to assist in pressing the wire with more force across the glue. S. employs several girls, who earn from $3 to $6 per week. He pays by the gross. Most of the girls have been with him ever since he commenced manufacturing, eight years ago.

409. Gunpowder. The agent of the Hazard Gunpowder Company told me they employ at the manufacture as many of the widows and children of those killed by explosions as they can, in making linen covers for kegs, and putting gunpowder in envelopes, and cutting labels, and putting on them. D. writes to an acquaintance for us: "We employ women at times in labelling canisters, and then only two."

410. Oils. A manufacturer of machine oil says a lady that understands the business could give men orders, and keep the office, and so carry on the business; but the work is too warm for women, and too laborious. It is certainly greasy work, and therefore hard on clothes. A manufacturer of oil writes me "he thinks the business not at all suitable for women: the only part that could be done by them is such as pertains to the office, which would be the same as that of other merchants." The manufacture of hair oils forms an extensive business. A manufacturer of linseed oil told me he could employ a woman to remove the seed from the bags, after the oil has been pressed out, but it would be greasy work. Some oil manufacturers told me they would employ girls to put oil in bottles for sewing machines. They would also be willing to employ female agents to sell oil for sewing machines. If a lady could sell twelve bottles a day, at 25 cents a bottle, she could make $1.75.

411. Paints. Oil paint is so disagreeable to handle and put up in such large quantities that it is unsuitable work for women. An English workman in B. & I.'s factory told us that women are employed in the paint factories in London and Hull as extensively as men. What they do we could not exactly learn, except that they put the powder for paint in cans, and label them. The man said the business is pernicious to the health. Ex-Mayor T. employed some women in his color factory at

Manhattanville to label. At O.'s, Philadelphia, a few women are employed in moulding the cakes of water paints, and stamping them, and in tubing and packing fine oil paints. A paint manufacturer in Brooklyn writes: "The only way we can employ females is at putting up paint dry in six-pound boxes or in cans. This last is ground in oil. We have generally employed boys for this purpose, but I think females would suit better, provided they were kept by themselves. If this could be done, we might be able to employ from four to five hands. The work is rather unhealthy, as it affects the lungs. We pay one woman $4 per week, working ten hours a day. It requires a week to learn. We do not work for four months in winter. Cleanliness and tact are necessary for putting up goods. Women would attend to their work better than boys."

412. Patent Medicines. Women are very extensively employed in putting up patent medicines. At H.'s, Philadelphia, where extract of ginger is made, they once employed women in the summer. They prefer boys and men, because in intervals men and boys can do other work that women cannot. Women were only employed by them to put up, seal, and label. Where H.'s bitters are made, women are employed to envelop, seal, and label, and paid according to the industry and skill of the workers. They receive from $3 to $4 a week. Dr. Ayres, I have been told, has his medicine put up by females in Canada, because he can have it done there more cheaply, although a duty of 15 per cent. is paid for importing.

413. Pearlash. Women could make pearlash in the country, where large quantities of wood are burned in clearing off land, and would no doubt find it pay very well for the trouble.

414. Perfumery. Perfumeries have been used in oriental countries from the most remote ages. The finest and most costly perfumes are still brought from the East. They were much used in England about the time of Queen Elizabeth. The essential oil of plants confers their odors. This oil may be obtained by expression, infusion, or distillation. In some cases, it may be pressed out of the cellular structure that contains it. Roses and such plants are mostly steeped in water, but some plants are steeped in wine and similar substances. There is a difference in oils obtained from different parts of the same plant; for instance, the leaves, flowers, and fruit of the orange tree yield distinct oils. The perfumeries of France have the best reputation of any others. Considerable perfumery is manufactured in this country, that meets with a ready sale at a good profit. At J. H.'s, Philadelphia, the woman who superintends others employed in putting up perfumery, told me that the hands work three months before they are paid. They then receive from $1.50 to $5 a week. It would require two years, she thinks, to acquire proficiency. J. H. finds employment for his hands all the year round. The girls cut kid for the tops, tie them on, label the bottles, lay them in cotton in small boxes, and then put them in large boxes ready for nailing and sending away. The girls each perform the entire process. It is not divided into separate branches. Sometimes they are employed in putting up fine soaps. The labels are all imported from France. They sit while employed, and spend from ten to twelve hours at it, according to the work on hand. R. says some perfumery is made by machinery and some by hand. He thinks a woman should spend from six months to one year learning to put up perfumery, as it must be done very neatly. He pays his girls, while learning, $2.50 a week, and after that according to ability and industry. The business is now dull, for people cannot afford to indulge in luxuries. At P.'s perfumery manufactory, I learned that the girls work from 7½ to 6, and earn from $2 to $8 per week—the average, $3.50. They are mostly Americans. Spring and fall are the best seasons, but they keep them all the year. They have many applications, but are often puzzled to get enough of good hands. Girls do better than men for putting up perfumery. It requires some taste. Poor workers are very destructive, for the articles of which some perfumeries are made are very costly. There are employed in packing fancy soap and preparing perfumery, between six hundred and seven hundred girls, in New York; average wages, $4. A manufacturer of hair oil pays his men from $10 to $15 per week. Good taste and a quick hand are the requisites. Near a city is the best location. At H.'s perfumery and fancy soap manufactory, one of the firm told me they "import" Frenchmen to make the perfumery, who impart to them the secret, and they furnish the materials. Their busy season commences in January. They pay their girls from the first, but not much until they get to working well. It requires some time to become expert and tasteful in putting up perfumery. They are paid by the piece (customary plan), but do not work over ten hours, as it is all done at the factory. They can earn from $3 to $9 a week. They keep their hands all the year, but in busy times employ extra hands. They employ a number of girls in making boxes, who earn about $3 a week. P. & F. employ one woman, paying $3.50 a week. P. told me such work is usually paid for by the gross, and workers earn about $4.50. The business is likely to increase. No manufactures West or South. It requires six months to become expert. Vacancies are often occurring among the hands. Some are employed in label cutting some in filling bottles, corking, tying,

WOMEN AT WORK IN THE PACKAGE ROOM OF THE MEDICAL LABO-
RATORY OF DR. J. C. AYER & CO., LOWELL, MASS.   396

labelling, and boxing, while others envelop and seal the soap. They sit most of the time, but change their position every little while. There is but one establishment of the kind west of Philadelphia, and that is in Cincinnati.

415. Quinine. At P. & W.'s laboratory, Philadelphia, they employ a number of girls in weighing and putting up quinine, calomel, &c., to send away. The girls work eight hours in winter and nine in summer, and receive from $3 to $9 a week. The employment is thought not to be healthy. It changes the fairest complexion to a sallow, just as the taking of the medicine would. The air of the room where we sat, and where the girls were corking, sealing, enveloping, and labelling, was strongly impregnated with the quinine. It was so offensive that I could not rid myself of the taste for several hours after I left the room. In one apartment a man and woman were weighing the article. The woman wore a bandage over her mouth and a muslin cap on her head, and spectacles with large, dark, convex frames, to prevent the quinine from getting in her eyes, as it turns the white of the eye yellow. The women had each their own apartment of labor. They looked as healthy as you generally see, but I do not know how they may have looked when they commenced working there. The lady who accompanied me, said her friend had fallen off very much and lost the beauty of her complexion while working there during the last two years.

416. Salt. " In certain cities, especially at Dieppe, France, women have the business of carrying salt; it is a monopoly which has belonged to them from time immemorial. They form a corporation, have a syndic, and salt in the sack cannot, in this city, be transported from the vessel to the depots or warehouses by any but them." According to the statistics of the salt manufacture in 1850, there were 2,699 males employed and 87 females in the United States. Water from the ocean, lakes, and salt springs, I suppose, could be boiled by women. A rock-salt manufacturer writes : " Women might do some of our work better than a man ; but one man can tend the hopper and tie as fast as another can fill. The best salt for dairy purposes is imported, and therefore a seaport is the best place for our business." A manufacturer in Barnstable, Mass., writes : " Women are not employed in my branch of industry, as far as my knowledge extends, *in making salt;* but, when it is ground for table use, women are sometimes employed *in making the bags* to put the salt in. They formerly made good wages in this business; but, since sewing machines have come into almost general use, the price of labor has fallen, and I am not posted as to the price now paid, as most of the ground salt and the bags are manufactured in Boston.

Working with salt is very healthy. We manufacture our salt between the 1st of April and the last of October, by solar evaporation; but very little if any salt can be made in this way after the latter month, as the sun runs too low for salt making. Our works are provided with covers, which require too hard labor for women to shove on as rain approaches, and to be opened every fair day. Women can, and occasionally do lend a hand in this business; but it is too laborious. Then, the salt has to be taken out by men with shovels, and this is too hard labor for women. They might assist in drawing the water from one room to another, by simply taking out and putting in plugs; but under a hot summer's sun, we think our business entirely unsuitable for them. In the winter, we manufacture epsom salts; but even this work we consider too laborious for women." A salt manufacturer in South Yarmouth, Maine, writes : " I believe women are employed in the mills in Boston for grinding salt, in making the bags, putting it up, &c., for table use. Otherwise, the service is too hard." Manufacturers in Syracuse, N. Y., say "they have but a limited number of women employed in making sacks. The most of their sacks are furnished by the manufacturing establishments." Salt clarifiers in Burlington, Vt., write : " We employ one woman, because it is cheaper to do so. We pay her $4 per week—a man we would have to pay $6. The work is healthy, and women's part soon learned. Spring and summer are the best seasons. The prospect for work in this line is good. Board, $1.70 per week." A gentleman in the salt business at Geddes, N. Y., writes : " There used to be employed far more women than now in making bags to hold dairy or bag salt. Now, sewing machines have entirely superseded them in this branch of our business. During the summer season, formerly, there were from one hundred to three hundred women at bag making. There are now, say one hundred or more women engaged in packing and filling the barrels with salt. They are all foreigners. It is dirty, heavy, and laborious work, and not suitable for women, but is extremely healthy. No difference is made in the price paid men and women, all being paid by the piece, and earning from 75 cents to $1 per day. A strong woman can learn very soon. The amount of work, probably, will not change much in future. The work is done only in the summer season. A large proportion of all the salt made in this country is made here. The annual product of our salt springs is about seven million bushels salt, produced at an expense for *labor* of not less than ten cents per bushel. Nearly all is paid to men, Irish and Dutch getting the most of it. A very small part of the work, if any, is adapted to women. Most of our women workers are the wives or mothers of men and boys who fasten hoops on barrels. Most of the salt at Syracuse, N. Y., is made by boiling down the water that springs from artesian wells. At Turk's Island, salt is made by simply digging vats in the meadow and throwing the water into them. As it rarely rains there for a number of months, they require no covering to their works, and have only to take out the salt and stack it up when it is made."

417. Soda. I find that in factories of this kind, girls are not employed in this country, except for putting the article in papers. They are paid from twelve to sixteen cents per hundred, according to the size. At a factory I saw many at work. They looked very neat. All wore clean calico dresses, and snow-white handkerchiefs over their heads, to prevent the soda from lodging in their hair. They must inhale considerable of it, as the atmosphere was strongly impregnated. One of the workers told me they are paid eighteen cents per hundred packages, which were rather large. A box contained sixty packages. Some are able to put up as many as seven hundred packages a day. The proprietor and one of the girls said it was not unhealthy work; but it is my impression that it is, if worked at constantly. It requires but a week to get in the way of doing it, and expertness is gained by practice. They work all the year, but sometimes there is not much to do. They are most busy in spring and fall. Some of the hands live near; so, in slack times, if the proprietor receives an order to be filled, he sends immediately for his girls. At another factory, I was told September and October are the most busy months for their hands. They cannot send much away in winter, because the rivers are closed and railroad freight is high. Soda, I was told, is more used in the South than saleratus. Some of their girls are paid by the week, and some by the box. They earn from $3 to $4. The gentleman said the dust was disagreeable, but not unhealthy. Their girls stand while at work.

418. Starch. A large number of plants and vegetable substances contain starch. Wheat, potatoes, rice, and maize are the principal. It is also found in the seeds and stems of plants. It is not soluble in cold water, consequently may be easily washed out of any vegetable substance. For those from which it cannot be so removed chemical decomposition may be employed. Manufacturers write us: "The making of starch is hard and unsuitable work for females; but girls are employed to put up the starch in papers and label it, receiving from thirty-seven to seventy-five cents a day, according to what the worker accomplishes." The following intelligence we received from the Oswego factory: "We employ from fifteen to twenty women, because we find them more attentive than boys. They paste labels on packages of starch, and receive thirty-seven and a half cents per day, of from eight to ten hours. A smart girl can learn in a few hours. The prospect of employment in future is good. They are paid the same that boys would be, and have work the year round. There are no parts suitable for women, in which they are not engaged. Board, $1.25 to $1.50."

419. White Lead. At the store of a white lead manufacturer, I was told they employ a number of girls, when busy, to label the tin cans. The making of white lead is unhealthy, and, I suppose, very disagreeble work. Women are employed in England in the manufacture of white lead.

420. Whiting. This article is used for cleaning silver, and one preparation of it for the face. There are not more than from twelve to twenty women at the work in the United States. B. used to employ women, and paid by the pound. The women earned about $3 a week, of ten hours. They were employed merely in putting up the article.

COMMUNICATING MEDIUMS BETWEEN EMPLOYERS AND OTHERS.

421. Assistants in Public and Benevolent Institutions. There is a wide field of usefulness open to ladies, as matrons in charitable institutions. Blessed is the influence a woman exerts as a matron, if she is a kind, good woman. Her responsibilities are great, but a consciousness of the vast amount of good she may accomplish should reconcile her to them. The discharge of her duties will often cast her in the society of visitors, many of whom are refined and educated people. In *reformatory institutions for children*, a matron may do incalculable good. *The female department of almshouses, lunatic asylums, hospitals, prisons, workhouses, and all other public and charitable institutions*, should be in the hands of women. They can exert a better influence. They know better the wants of their sister women. They can enter into their feelings. They can check familiarities with the male inmates, and exert more influence when temptation is offered. In short, they are women, and know a woman's heart. *Orphan, and deaf and dumb asylums, houses of refuge, eye and ear infirmaries, schools for imbecile* *children, and all such places,* should be managed by women, as far as practicable. The managers of the home department of such institutions should be firm and efficient, yet kind hearted. Nor should merely the filling of these offices be given to women, but there should be a number of lady visitors to coöperate with the managers. They can often suggest many improvements for the comfort and health of the inmates, that would escape the notice of men. I was told by a friend, now deceased, who took an active part in establishing and advancing benevolent institutions, that she found it very difficult to obtain matrons, seamstresses, and tailoresses, willing and competent to instruct the inmates of the institutions in their various branches of labor. She thought it would be well to instruct women so thoroughly in their business that they might efficiently impart a knowledge of it to others. She thought there should be a house where women and girls could be properly prepared to perform the duties of cooks, nurses, and house servants. A lady friend suggested that many of the situations in the public institutions of New York might be filled by some of the women who are now keeping boarding houses, and so, the pressure in that quarter being removed, there would be fairer and fuller play to those that are left in the occupation. A principal reason of the order and cleanliness of the workhouses in Holland, is the attention and humanity of the governesses; for each house has four, who take charge of the inspection, and have their names painted in the room. For the moral management of convicts, men are systematically trained in some countries of Europe. In the hospitals, prisons, and reformatory institutions of England, supported by the government, women are employed. They are even eligible as overseers of the poor. The President of the Board of Public Institutions in New York city furnished me with answers to questions in regard to the women employed therein, as follows : " Women are employed as matrons, nurses, and laborers in this city, and on Blackwell's and Randall's islands. They receive from $5 per month to $430 per annum, and are paid by the month. The labor performed, properly belongs to women, although we employ some men for part of the same labor, but their pay is about the same. There is no need of an apprenticeship to become familiar with their employments, and the only special qualifications are health and strength. There is no difference as to seasons with us. They work only as many hours as are necessary. The demand for those occupying this position grows out of the number of the destitute and criminal thrown on our hands. About twenty-five per cent. employed are Americans. We employ women in all work for which they are suited. The more intelligent are selected for the most responsible positions.   If so disposed, they have ample time for mental and moral culture.   They live where they labor, and their places of residence are comfortable."   Each of the janitresses of the public schools of New York receives a salary of from $100 to $400 per annum.   At the Tombs of New York, a woman has charge of the department where the female convicts are.   At a meeting of ladies in Dublin, for the employment of women, Mr. McFarlane said that "for the last twenty-five years, the Grangegorman Penitentiary had been under the management of a lady, and it had been most admirably conducted."

422. Commissioners of Deeds.   There are about two hundred in the city of New York, and, with a moderate run of custom, each can make several hundred dollars per annum.   Their duties are very light, and, I have been told, could as well be performed by women as men.

423. Housekeepers.   A kind, yet decided manner, will more effectually govern a household than fretting and scolding. A portion of time should be regularly set aside for servants to feel as their own.   It will often prove a matter of economy to those who exact work of them.   Those of principle will work more diligently.   Everybody needs some rest.   Gain the good will and confidence of servants, and they will reward you in the labor of their stronger muscles.   But avoid familiarity, by all means.   Much of the long, wearing toil of servants might be avoided by consideration and management on the part of a housekeeper.   Domestics labor hard, and much of the comfort of a family depends on them.   Do not accuse on suspicion those in your employ of doing or having done wrong.   Be careful of the reputation of others, particularly dependent females.   A man of standing, to whom I expressed the desire that more occupations should be opened to women, expressed the wish that our domestics should be Americans, and of a more intelligent class.   An effort should be made to elevate the standard of servants, he said, to induce more respectable and intelligent women to enter domestic service.   Those engaged in it, he thought, should find something else to do, and will be pushed out as a more competent class enter. I would prefer to see our present class of servants fit themselves better for the discharge of their duties, and American girls enter occupations of a more refined and exalted nature.   The same gentleman referred to, stated that his servants each receive $2 a week, dress handsomely, and lay by money. (?)   They do better for themselves, he remarked, than the girls in his bookbindery.   In some of the convents of France, the sisters go through a course of training to prepare them for the duties of housekeepers, and are then sent to take charge of religious and charitable institutions connected with their church. Why might not some such plan be pursued by Protestants ? Says an English review: " In Germany, the employment of women in the offices of house-steward, maitre d'hotel, butler or lackey, sanctioned by universal custom, is not considered so incompatible as it would be with us, with the other branches of a first-rate establishment."

424. Keepers of Intelligence Offices. Intelligence offices are established for the purpose of giving information to or respecting persons seeking employment. They are individual enterprises. From fifty cents to $1 is paid by an applicant for information of persons desiring one of such capacity as they seek to fill. The same price is paid by the person seeking an assistant or domestic. Most offices are limited to supplying domestics; but one or more might be established for the supply of seamstresses, saleswomen, milliners, dress makers, &c. Girls often find it an advantage to apply at an office, if they have not friends to interest themselves and secure them situations. But they should be particular to know the character of the office they patronize. A lady remarked to me, if a girl was willing to spend a year in a family where she could be well instructed for her work, she could then be sure of a good home and fair wages. Servant girls are universally complained of at the North. Many of them are very exacting. Most are raw Irish girls, who think, when they come to this country, everybody is equal. Consequently, they do not know their places as they do in the old country, where there are distinct grades in society. Another thing that makes some so trifling is that such swarms come, and they are so ignorant, and many of them so corrupt, that they instigate each other. I was told, by the keeper of an intelligence office, that girls and women always ask more than they expect to get. Some cooks get as high as $20 a month. They are mostly French and German. Now and then he has a good American. He has a lady in attendance that can speak French and German. His terms are fifty cents a month from the employer, and the same from the employée. It gives the privileges of the office for one or two months. Few are willing to go to the country. Many girls come from the country that do not know where to board. The keeper of the office sends them to a cheap but respectable house. His office is open from eight to five. To employers he sends a blank certificate of character, to be filled when the servant leaves. There is a Protestant office in Philadelphia, and one or more in New York. At an intelligence office on Grand street, where girls pay fifty cents and the employer fifty cents, the girl has the privilege of being supplied with places for two months, if she remains on trial the time specified by agreement with her various employers. If not, she forfeits the privilege. This office had a servants' home connected with it, that is, a boarding house for servants out of employ. The girls paid $2 a week. A training school was connected with this, in which the servants received instructions in cooking and the various details of housekeeping. The cooking of the boarding house was done by some of the number. He failed in his enterprise, he said, from want of capital. One has been in operation in England for eight years very successfully, connected with which is a training school. They have few Americans to apply for places; for Americans like lighter work, as nursing, sewing, being lady's maid, &c. In summer there is a scarcity of girls, for they go to the country and watering places to cook and do housework. In the fall they flock to the city, and there are more applicants than situations. At some offices the privilege is accorded for three months, and at some only one month. A lady who keeps an office in Williamsburg told me, when the girls come to her, she takes their names and qualifications. She receives the calls of ladies wanting girls, and also records their wants. After five o'clock, and on Saturday after two o'clock, the office is closed, and she then compares the wants of employers and employées, and makes out a corresponding list. Next day she sends girls to their places. I could have got a lady's maid for $5 a month with board and lodging. I saw a lady securing a nurse for her child at the same price. Fifty cents is the fee for the privilege of her office for three months. She furnishes girls during that time until the mistress is satisfied; and the girl pays the same, and is furnished with places for three months until she is satisfied. She does not require references from her girls, but sends the lady to the last employer of the girl. I called at Mrs. Y.'s office, New York. Girls, she says, get different prices in different States. In wealthy States, as Massachusetts, Connecticut, and the Southern States, they get good prices. In Cincinnati, and the States of Wisconsin and New Jersey, poor prices. She sends many from the city to every part of the United States. People write to her, inclosing the money for the girl's passage. She then buys her a ticket and provisions, and sends her on; but the arrangement is always for a year or six months, as people are not willing to incur the expense of paying the passage of a girl for less time. She could get many more places for girls, if they would go to the country; but they do not wish to go, and, if dissatisfied, be at the expense of returning. The girl may be deceived, by finding there are twice as many in the family as represented, or the work is much harder. Mrs. Y. learns the character of a girl that applies to her, and then registers it in her book. So ladies applying for a girl have from her the true character. She has no difficulty in finding places for her girls. She is always busy but on a rainy day. People object to having an intelligence office near them, as the girls are inclined to stand about the door. It is said that the majority of the keepers of intelligence offices furnish the best places to those by whom they are bribed. A few years ago, the number of white female servants in New York city was estimated at 100,000, that of Boston 50,000, Philadelphia 30,000, and Baltimore 20,000. There is a lady in Boston who goes around among her friends and secures to them good domestics, receiving some compensation for her services—I think, fifty cents a domestic. When the influence of servants over children is considered, I think parents cannot be too careful in the selection of their servants; and to obtain good ones, they should be willing to pay a fair price. There is a waste of time to girls sitting in offices, and a risk run of being sent, by a person of whose moral character they know nothing, to a house that may prove the wreck of their virtue. At a boarding house and intelligence office for workwomen, the lady told me they charge $2 a week for board, allowing the privilege of the wash room, and of sitting in the parlor in the evening, which is warmed and contains a piano. To those who cannot pay as much as this, they charge from $1 to $1.25, giving them rooms in the attic. They have been applied to often for persons of a higher class than usually frequent intelligence offices, but only until since the times have been so hard have they had such applicants. I was told, at another office, they seldom have American girls apply for places, except as house girls, and they are mostly girls who have worked in factories. They send girls to California and all parts of the United States; and they have some who travel through Europe in the capacity of ladies' maids. Their office is open from nine to five o'clock. When a girl is sent for from another place, the money is sent by express and a receipt taken, or by mail, and a receipt taken at the post office. One of a high order for cultivated women, who desire places as bookkeepers, copyists, secretaries, &c., is quite necessary. We would suggest the establishment of such an office for furnishing female workers to different parts of the United States, where they are wanted in the higher branches of woman's labor. It would confer a blessing on virtuous and industrious women, and be an accommodation to employers. A paper devoted to the same interests might do much good also; but we think it doubtful whether it would pay its way.

425. Lighthouse Keepers. Miss H. told me of two young women whose father keeps a lighthouse, but he is very feeble and infirm. They attend the lights, and often row out, if

they see a wreck, and do what they can to rescue the passengers.
We observed this newspaper paragraph a few years back: " A
Mrs. Lydia Smith has been appointed assistant keeper of the
lighthouse at Manitou Island (Michigan) at $250 per annum."
" They have a Grace Darling at Bridgeport, Conn. On the night
of the 13th inst., Miss Moore, an accomplished young lady, the
daughter of the keeper of the lighthouse on Fairweather Island, just
below Bridgeport, heard cries for help at a distance from the
shore, and determined that an effort should be made to rescue
whom it might be. It was too dark to tell the direction or the
distance, but, summoning two young men to her aid, she launched
the boat belonging to the lighthouse, and ordered them to pull
out in the direction of the cries, herself holding the tiller. About
two miles out in the Sound, they found a sailboat capsized, and
clinging to it were two men nearly exhausted. One of them was
entirely helpless, and with great difficulty got in the boat; but
both were finally rescued from death by the courage and efforts
of this brave girl, and brought safely to shore. Mr. Moore, the
keeper of the lighthouse, has been for some time afflicted with
ill health, and when unable to see to the details of his office, this
daughter assumes the entire management, and, through the lonely
watches of the night, it is her fair hand that trims and tends the
beacon that guides the mariner safely on his way."

426. Pawnbrokers. I suppose this business requires a
general knowledge of the value of goods. Some pawnbrokers
profess to make liberal advances, but a very heavy percentage is
usually charged. Indeed, some pawnbrokers extort an incredible
interest on money loaned to the poor. S., an intelligent Irish
pawnbroker, into whose office I went to ask something of the
business, told me he never knew of but one woman in the business.
She was nominally a widow, and employed a young man to stay
in the shop. When women are employed in pawnbrokers' establishments, it is nearly always as auxiliaries, being the wife, sister,
or daughter of the keeper. He thinks it not a suitable business
for a woman, as the class of people that come require a strong
man to deal with them, who can use their slang language, and
drive them away if they become very rude. No doubt, many go
to pawn what they have when under the influence of liquor, or
to pawn their clothes to get liquor. The broker retains what is
pawned for a year, if it is not redeemed in less time. It is then
sold at auction. There is a law that permits it. His shelves
were filled with bundles, on which were pinned numbered papers.
Another pawnbroker told me that the fashion and quality of
goods decide the price put on them, particularly wearing apparel.
There may be a difference in the value estimation of pawnbrokers,

THE LIGHT-HOUSE KEEPER'S DAUGHTER.   406

just as there is in different establishments where the same kind of new goods are sold. I saw the name of a female pawnbroker in a business directory, and called. I did not see her, but the young man who was employed to assist her in attending the store said they have most business to do in summer, and that it is a business requiring experience. They pay on articles taken to them what they will be likely to sell for at auction. They must make some allowance for what they may lose on the article. They charge at the rate of twenty-five per cent. for a year's time, which is as long as anything pawned is kept. They lose more on clothes than other goods. They allow a depositor to draw any sum of less amount than the estimated value of an article; and when the article is redeemed, a percentage is paid on the amount of the money drawn, and not on the full value of the article.

427. Postmistresses. There are (1854) 128 postmistresses in the United States. They receive the same salaries that postmasters do. The clerks in post offices sometimes count at the rate of sixty letters a minute. There are 29,000 post offices in the United States, ninety clerks in Chicago, and, I think, nearly three hundred in New York. Might not a large number of these be women? I have read that it is in contemplation to place in the general post office in London a number of lady clerks. I called on Mrs. W., who was for nearly two years at the ladies' window in the general post office, New York. Very few approved of a lady being there. She found some advantages, but many disadvantages, arising from her position. In the first place, it yielded her and her child a support, the salary being $600. She was treated with respect by all the attachés of the office except two—one of whom was immediately dismissed, and the other removed. But the class of women who go to the general post office constantly for letters, are of a kind a respectable woman would not like to come in contact with. The majority receive letters under fictitious names. Some of them were very impudent to her. And sometimes men would come to the window and insist on her getting the letters of their lady friends for them. Besides, there were about fifty clerks immediately around her, and altogether in the office between two hundred and three hundred. They were men of all classes and nations. The office is one influenced by political motives, and a man has the advantage as candidate by gaining the votes of his friends. She says she was kind and courteous, but found it necessary to be very decided, and keep at a distance from every one. The men in the office did not like it, because they had to guard their tongues. She remained there from 8.30 A. M. to 4.30 P. M., and was on her feet all the time, with the exception of a few minutes. There were no conveniences or comforts for a woman. So she suffered severely from the effects. She thinks the plan of employing ladies in the post offices of towns and villages might be done more easily. Even here it might be done more advantageously, if the office was situated farther up street, the regulations were different, and a number of ladies were employed instead of but one. A lady could not well use a ladder to reach down letters from the upper boxes. A young man did that for her. For a postmistress we might enumerate the qualifications of quickness of eye, strict integrity, a retentive memory, and patient industry. "Unmarried females only can hold the office of postmistress. They are appointed, give bonds, and are commissioned in the same manner as postmasters, and receive the same compensation. There is, however, a larger number of females, generally the wives and daughters of postmasters, employed as assistants; but as the latter are appointed and paid by the postmasters themselves, to whom alone they are responsible, their names are not recorded on the government books."

428. Sewing-Machine Instructors. In many of the stores of New York, where sewing machines are sold, we notice that many of those who give instructions to buyers of machines are men. Shame on the men that teach women to sew! When such is the case, to what may not a woman resort for earning a livelihood? Shame on the man that engages in such an effeminate employment, save he who is deformed and cannot engage in harder work! Shame, I say, on the man seen at a sewing machine, or with a needle in his hand! Surely the muscles and bones and sinews of men were never given for such a purpose. W. & W. employ five young ladies as instructors on machines, paying each of them over $6 a week. They have one to sell thread, and two to go about the city adjusting machines. It is something difficult to do, as it requires almost the mechanical talent of a machinist. They have no applications for instructors on sewing machines out of the city, but have for some in the city. They employ females because the purchasers of machines are generally ladies. G. & B. employ a lady for adjusting machines, as they find ladies prefer one of their own sex for the purpose. I was told at S.'s, by the bookkeeper, they do not employ female instructors. They used to employ both young men and young ladies, but they spent so much time talking to each other, that they found it necessary to dispense with either the one or the other. So they gave up the girls eighteen months ago, and have not employed any since. They paid girls $4 a week from the time they took them, and increased their wages to $5 or $6. Many of the women earned $6. They worked, on an average, ten hours a day. Ladies are employed in Boston to sell machines. The ladies of New York (said a young man selling machines) prefer to buy of a gentleman. (?) Yet, he thinks the crying sin of civilization is, not furnishing remunerative employment to women. Simply learning to sew with a machine is by no means difficult, though the time required depends very much upon the abilities of the learner. Some become proficient in all its accomplishments of hemming, tucking, gathering, preparing work for the machine, &c., in from three to six months, while others do not become efficient workers in less than a year. The time required to learn depends very much on the machine used, as some are more complicated than others; and a thorough knowledge of the machine is desirable for every good worker. It is more difficult to learn to operate on one kind of machine after learning on some other kind. By paying $1.50, a person can receive six lessons on sewing machines at S.'s. At W. & W.'s, and at G. & B.'s, purchasers and those who cannot pay are taught free of charge. Some people charge $3 for teaching to operate. L. & W. will teach any one to operate who buys a machine, but they charge others $2.

429. Shepherdesses. Boys who keep sheep in Scotland, knit while so employed. Girls and women who tend sheep, might perhaps do the same. Sheep are being raised to considerable extent in Texas, and the raising of them is on the increase in the Western States, but we do not know that females have ever been employed in this country to tend sheep.

430. Toll Collectors. It is not unusual to see women receiving toll at the gates, but they are mostly foreigners, or poor widows, or the wives of the gatekeepers.

* * *

CONTRIBUTORS TO THE COMFORT OR AMUSEMENT OF OTHERS.

431. Bathhouse Attendants. There are some people that cannot afford to have bathhouses in their dwellings, and for such it is well there are houses where, for twenty-five cents, they may enjoy the luxury of a bath. Particularly is it well for hardworking people, on whom the dust and perspiration collect, and who are refreshed and rendered more healthy by frequent baths. Where a bathhouse is used for women alone—there being no department for men—we think it might be owned and superintended by a lady, just like any other branch of business. Females,

18

of course, would be in attendance to wait on those that frequent the bath rooms. Quite a number are employed at water-cure establishments, which are open for patients at all seasons of the year. Not only does cleanliness promote comfort, but it is conducive to health. Many of the diseases of the poor arise from a want of cleanliness. Even the morals are improved, and the mind freed as it were from its cobwebs. Most medicinal baths should be superintended by some one that has a knowledge of medicine and the human system. And those employed, if unacquainted with the business, should be particular in observing directions given. For baths, a person should have means to fit up rooms neatly, and enough to live on until their establishment becomes known. I called on the wife of a gentleman who has electro-magnetic baths administered. He is a physician, and gives medical advice as to the kind of bath required. He does not give much medicine, thinking the article that would be prescribed had better be administered externally in the form of a bath. The baths are $3 for a single one; $10 for four. More people take the baths in summer than winter. After a vapor bath the system is stimulated, not relaxed; it is then better prepared for the reception of medicine. The charge at one establisment I know to be 50 cents a bath, or $5 for twelve. In New York, I saw the People's Washing and Bathing Establishment, which was put up by some philanthropic citizens, for the benefit of the poor. A man is employed to take charge of it; and in summer, several women attend to bathers, and some wash and iron towels. They pay $3 a week to a bath attendant, and from $3 to $3.50 to washers and ironers. They have had 1,500 bathers a day, in summer. For a bath in a small room and one towel, six cents are charged; for better accommodations, twelve cents. A swimming bath for boys is attached, and a charge made of three cents a swim of half an hour.

432. Brace and Truss Makers. I went to M. & Co.'s, New York, who are surgical and anatomical mechanicians, inventors, and manufacturers. They want to employ several good female workers. They will not take any to learn, because it requires time to teach them; yet a person of moderate abilities, that can sew neatly, can learn in a few days, or weeks at most, to do the cutting out and stitching. Part of the stitching is done by hand, and part by machinery. The workwomen are paid $3 a week, and work ten hours. At L.'s truss and bandage institute, I learned that he employs a number at $3 a week. He cannot get as many good hands as he wants. He drew several hands from his former employer by paying them a little more. His wife does the fitting for ladies. A truss maker in Middletown, Conn., pays his women by the piece, and they earn from $3 to $4 per week. A., Brooklyn, pays a girl that sews neatly, but has never worked at the business, $3 a week. Any one that can sew well or operate on a machine, can do the mechanical work. He pays experienced hands over $3, according to what they do. His girls work but nine hours a day. Manufacturers of surgical apparatus in Boston write: "We employ women in sewing exclusively, generally about twenty, and all American. The work is not more unhealthy than any sewing. We consider any steady sewing, and the consequent confinement, more or less injurious. Average wages, perhaps $4 per week—something depends upon capabilities, however. Some have earned $6 per week, though such cases are exceptions. All our work is done by the piece. Females are paid about half the price of males. There appears to be an ample supply of female labor. On this basis, prices, details, &c., are governed accordingly. That portion of the work done by males, it takes three years to learn; that done by women, three months, presuming they were good sewers at the start. Learners are paid the same as old hands. Of course, they are slower, and accumulate less until well learned. To be a neat sewer and possess some mechanical skill will prepare one for this employment. We are seldom idle more than two weeks in the year. The male portion of our work would be no more adapted to women than horse shoeing. Our hands work from eight to twelve hours each day, and have none too much time for the improvement of their minds, considering they must be occupied more or less upon their own private sewing in addition to their business." A truss maker in Boston writes: "I pay by the week, from $4 to $6 to women; to men, from $7 to $12, because they can do more. They work from nine to ten hours. All are Americans. It requires from three to six months to learn. Some portions of the steel work would not be suitable for women. Board, $2 per week." "W. & F. employ eight women for making braces, bandages, &c. They pay $3 a week to those who are employed by the week. Those that work by the piece can earn from $4 to $6, and sometimes by overwork $7 a week. Their work is steady in good times, and they are able to employ their girls all the year. All sew by hand but one, and she receives but $4 as an operator. The business is mostly confined to cities."

433. Chiropodists. W., of the firm of L. & W., was quite a gentlemanly man in his manners, conversation, and dress. He mentioned three women, each in different cities, engaged in this occupation. He thinks his pursuit preferable to dentistry. Both depend on the class of patients. To follow the calling professionally requires a knowledge of anatomy and surgery.

There is a great deal of charlatanism practised by some in the calling. A knowledge of how to extract corns is not sufficient. Bunions, inverted nails, &c., require scientific treatment. He charges $1 for removing one corn, fifty cents apiece for two, and proportionately less for three or more. There are a great many itinerant doctors. If any individual fits himself properly for the calling, he may, after three or four years, in a large city, living from hand to mouth during the time, succeed in establishing a name and gaining respectable practice. The number of ladies suffering from corns has not decreased, judging from his experience. Men are more liable to have corns than women, because of more severe and constant exercise. He thinks it would not do for women to work at men's feet. I think it would not be more agreeable to a woman to have a man work at her feet; and as far as propriety goes, one is no better than the other. He would discourage any lady friend of his from undertaking the business. I called on Mme. K., a French lady. Her father is a chiropodist in Paris, and what she knows of the business she learned from seeing him. She found it unpleasant at first, but now she does not mind it. She goes to the house of the patient for the same price as she operates at her own room, namely, fifty cents a corn. She has as much to do as she wants. She thinks, in other places there are openings, and a woman that thoroughly understands the business is in every way as fit and capable as a man. She knows of but one other lady in the business in this country, and she is quite aged. She thinks, by three months' study and practice with a skilful operator, one might do very well to commence for herself. She would as soon operate on a gentleman's as a lady's foot. It might be well for one commencing to practice to travel, or get custom in several towns and villages in the same vicinity. I think she would instruct any one for a satisfactory compensation. A chiropodist says, as long as people are fools enough to abuse their feet, the prospect for his employment is good. L. is the oldest practitioner in the United States, and has practised in New York for twenty years. He would be willing to instruct pupils, charging $100 for each student. He would give thorough and systematic instruction, and teach to make the material used. People have not had much confidence in ladies, because of their deficiency in surgical skill. Incompetent persons have injured the business. Times do not affect the amount of practice. There are openings in Boston, Baltimore, and Chicago. Many ladies come to L. to have their finger nails trimmed, polished, and tinted. They would no doubt be as willing to have a competent lady.

434. Cuppers and Leechers. This business is sometimes connected with that of a barber. But in cities, some women
engage in it, and, no doubt, are as competent as men. Indeed,
for their own sex and children they are better fitted. Mrs. A.,
a cupper and leecher, told me the best way to obtain custom is
to form the acquaintance of some of the best physicians, as they
will then recommend you but you must always be ready to attend their patients, or they forget you. Her father was a physician, and in that way she learned the treatment of leeches.
It is well to get into the favor of persons that serve as leechers at
the infirmaries—they may be willing to instruct you. The Germans have killed the business in New York. Some charge but
twenty-five cents for cupping, and proportionately low for leeching. Leeching is sooner learned than cupping, but there is much
less of both done than formerly. Homœopathy has interfered with
their use. She used to be out all day and up all night, but now
she seldom has a call ; and yet she must be always at home, and
ready for a call. She never goes to take a cup of tea with a
friend, and is frequently called out of church. Leeching and
cupping require a steady hand, and ability to use the scarificator.
A person in the business must go into all kinds of sickness, without even asking what it is. Accidents give considerable custom,
and in the sickly season there is most. It has become common
for lads in apothecary shops to be sent out to apply leeches.
When they are to be applied to any hidden part of a lady, a female leecher, of course, is preferable. Mrs. A. charges twenty-
five cents a leech, if more than one is applied—if not, thirty-
seven cents. For cupping she charges $1. One lady in New
York charges not less than $1 apiece for applying leeches, and
in some cases more. Mrs. L. thinks a lady could not make a
living at the business in New York, because the Germans have
killed the trade by working at half price, and, as might be supposed, do not properly understand it. A good location should
be fixed upon for an office. A cupper and leecher is expected to
go in all weather, and in all hours of the day and night, and in
any kind of sickness. Most of it is done in fall and winter, because there is then most inflammation. Judgment must be used
in the quantity of blood to be drawn. A leecher should be a
good judge of the quality of leeches, and the proper treatment of
them. Particular attention should be paid to the directions of
the doctor in applying leeches. Mrs. L. says there is an opening for
a cupper and leecher in Albany, N. Y. A friend of hers there
had to pay exorbitantly for the services of a leecher.

435. Fishing-Tackle Preparers. In Philadelphia,
I was told at the store where most fishing tackle is sold, that one

woman is employed by them in fastening small hooks, with silk thread, on the end of worm gut. Large hooks are prepared in the same way for other kinds of fishing. It would seem that few women know of the existence of that kind of work in Philadelphia, for when the proprietor advertises for a female hand, he never has any applicants. It is clean, healthy work, and the materials can be easily carried home. Fifty cents a day a woman earns at it, but a man $1. There is but a small demand for fishing tackle in Philadelphia, but in New York the trade is much more important. C., of New York, says most engaged in this work are English women. A fast and correct worker can earn $6 a week at it. They are paid for by the dozen. He finds women more honest than men, and therefore prefers them. Men will steal some of the line or some of the hooks. For making flies, a superior hand may earn $8 a week. Something of a mechanical turn is all that is necessary to make a good workman. They have more work of that kind done than any house in New York, and pay a better price to have it well done. Nets pay very poorly, because all the large nets are now made by machinery, and the smaller ones are made by infirm people, who do it to keep employed as much as for the compensation. When the coarse netting is done by machinery, it can be obtained at 12½ cents a fathom, and a fathom of the same kind done by hand would require a day. The peculiar system of the business is that the work is all done in winter, and the goods sold in summer. It is a luxury, and consequently dispensed with when times are hard. C. pays for putting hooks on the lines by the gross. The silk lines are manufactured in England. G. & B. employ four women who work at home in making fishing tackle and artificial flies. They are made in winter. An experienced hand can obtain $15 a week, working from six in the morning till ten at night. He thinks, there are so few in the business, workers would not give instruction without good pay. A woman may possibly earn $4 a week making nets. They employ Irishmen to weave the silk worm gut on the hooks. The three or four large fishing-tackle establishments in New York could furnish all that is needed for the United States. Mrs. R., who makes artificial flies and fishing tackle, says she has now and then earned $9 a week—a difference of $6 in the report of the clerk. But there is considerable difference in the amount of work of the different kinds; and as they are paid for by the gross, some kinds of work pay better than others. There is now considerable competition in this work, because of the many that are out of employment. Girls apply at the store, offering to do the work at forty-two cents a gross. None are prepared South or West—so there may be openings before long in St. Louis, Chicago, New Orleans, &c. Making artificial flies is mostly in the hands of Irishmen.

436. Fortune Tellers. In London is a class of men and women called Druynackers, that take goods around in baskets to sell, and profess to tell fortunes. This magic power gives them influence over many silly girls, that are tempted to buy of them on that account. We cannot believe that God would vouchsafe to a mortal the power to foretell future events—to unite the present and future—time and eternity. The constitution of all nature and the teachings of the Bible confute such a belief. "The veil," says some one, "which covers futurity is woven by the hand of mercy. Seek not to raise the veil therefore, for sadness might be seen to shade the brow that fancy had arrayed in smiles of gladness." Wherever there are people tempted to pry into the future, there will be some to take advantage of it. Many a fortune teller sells her soul to Satan for the power of imposing the belief that she reveals future events. The prices charged by fortune tellers for their services vary from 25 cents to $5.

437. Guides and Door Attendants. "In Paris, the box offices of all the theatres are tended by women—not only those of the evening, but those open during the day for the sale of reserved places. The box openers and audience seaters are women." "The proprietor of the London Adelphi advertised, at the opening of the last season, that his box openers, check takers, and so on, would all be women." We have seen it stated that in some of the Roman Catholic churches in Paris, ladies of the congregation pass around the plates to take up a collection. Women in some of the old countries are occupied as doorkeepers at museums and galleries of paintings. In Great Britain, many of the door attendants are females, where the houses are occupied by several families, as is often the case. In England, some women are employed as pew openers. To come nearer home. Those who have visited the Academy of Fine Arts, in Philadelphia, will remember the pleasant face of the janitress who receives the tickets of the visitors, and that an obliging young woman checked the canes and parasols. In New York, most of the picture galleries have female doorkeepers.

438. Lodging and Boarding House Keepers. Patience, a spirit of forgiveness, and an ability to overlook faults, are very necessary for gliding along smoothly in this difficult and often ungrateful calling. A cheerful disposition, too, is almost indispensable, for everybody likes smiles better than frowns. A love of society is desirable. It is a principle that has been wisely implanted in the human heart, and one that affords numerous and important advantages to mankind. It is one that tends to produce a desire for the comfort and happiness of those around. Yet too great a fondness for society may cause a neglect of duty and a love of gossipping. It is sometimes the case that light, frivolous talk and too great fondness for excitement characterize the keepers and inmates of a boarding house. Yet such, of course, is not always the case. Keeping a boarding house is an office that will give to one of a kind and benevolent nature a good opportunity of exercising her native qualities. Sympathy closely binds such to the unfortunate, and pleasures are doubled by participating with others. Whether those who keep boarding houses happen to have by nature more idle curiosity than others, or whether the business is one calculated to create and foster such a quality, I cannot say, but favor the latter opinion. The tempers of those who keep boarding houses are apt to be very much tried. They need great firmness and uniformity in deportment. The price paid for boarding is usually proportioned to the comforts enjoyed, but not always. In early times, houses of entertainment for travellers were kept mostly by women. In a region of country where hunting and fishing are good, or the scenery fine, and the roads pleasant, ladies often accommodate, for the summer and autumn, families from the city. It is a very general fashion for people in the cities to go during the warmest weather to the country, seaside, or springs. Boarding house keepers usually find it most .profitable to keep a large house, as only one kitchen and parlor are needed, and many other expenses attending a house are proportionately diminished. Good boarding houses for workwomen are scarce in all large cities, particularly New York. Most keepers of boarding houses prefer men, because they are less about the house. I have been told that it is very difficult for work girls to get board in well kept houses. I think several respectable boarding houses should be established in large cities by wealthy and influential ladies, or religious societies, for working women. In New York are some houses where none but merchants' clerks board. Why might not one or more be established for shop girls? A list, as given by employers, of the prices paid by work girls for their board, I will annex at the close of this work; but I would add that comfortable rooms and wholesome food cannot be furnished *in cities* at these prices, and afford a reasonable profit to the keepers of the houses. And I would further say, the prices paid women for their labor does not enable them to pay higher rates for their board.

439. Makers of Artificial Eyes. The science of supplying defects in the physique is such that an artificial man can almost be manufactured. Artificial teeth, hair, eyes, ears, noses, chins, palates, arms, hands, and legs, are some of the missing parts of the frame that can be supplied. In the census report of Great Britain for 1850, we find four women under the head of artificial limb and eye makers. G., of New York, knows two or three ladies in Paris, and one in London, that are engaged in making the whites of glass eyes. G. may be able to give employment to a lady in making the white of the eyes, in a few months. It is done by blowing the glass, and requires but a short time to learn. He says he would pay a woman well for the work. I called at D.'s, a manufacturer of glass eyes, and saw D.'s son, a youth about eighteen years of age. He says there are but two other makers of glass eyes in the United States, and only two or three in London. D. spent fourteen years in London and Dublin, manufacturing eyes at the infirmaries, and giving them away. He did it to get in practice. He prefers to insert the eyes himself. They move as a natural eye does, and certainly were very natural in color. He sells them at from $10 to $20. Some physicians furnish their patients with them, charging $60 or $70 for one, and so making a handsome profit. When a person that does not understand the form of the glass eye and the anatomy of the human eye inserts one, the inside of the eye is liable to become inflamed, and proud flesh is farmed. D. spent a fortune experimenting. It requires an extensive knowledge of chemicals, and the effect produced on them by heat. A small furnace is used for burning the colors in the glass. Some people would give thousands of dollars to know the chemicals used, and their proportions. The young man says his father has never even imparted to him the information. Some people that wear glass eyes take them out at night. D. judges of the shape and size required by merely looking at the remaining eye of the individual. We think a competent person in this business might establish himself at the South. I called on an Englishman who has been at the business twenty years in New York. He is over sixty years of age, and has been in the business fifty years; learned it with his father in London. He had a number of certificates on his walls. He says a woman would go into a decline directly, if exposed to the heat of a furnace in baking eyes. It is necessary to stay in the oven while the change is taking place in the chemicals. In summer it is intolerable. His son would not continue the business on that account. He says the French eyes are made of glass, covered with porcelain, and break easily; the white is made by being blown. The English are not blown, and are made entirely of porcelain. He says they will not break unless very cold water is applied in bathing the eyes (a common fashion in the United States). He has had eyes worn for a year

18*

without being taken out. He takes the dimensions of the eye by fitting in different sized ones. If an eye is too small, it will slip out, fall, and break. It requires long experience to become proficient in making glass eyes; but it is a beautiful art, and not inappropriate to competent women.

440. Artificial Limbs. We had thought, perhaps, a few women could be employed in this vocation, and accordingly addressed a circular to a gentleman so occupied. He thinks no women are engaged in this business in the United States or any other country; but says they could be, and the reason they are not is, there is not enough of the kind of work connected with it, that could be done by women, to employ them. "It requires some men one year to learn, some five years, and some never can learn. It depends on natural ability and skill. The qualifications required are skill, judgment, sobriety, morality, pleasing address, dignity, imitation, industry, love of the beautiful, and anatomy. The prospect of work is good; superior workmen will succeed. The best seasons for work are from September 1st to July 1st. There is a demand for the work in California. Large seaport towns are not good localities—patients generally charity cases. Inland cities surrounded by a populous country, the best localities—patients better able to pay."

441. Artificial Teeth. It is said that 3,000,000 artificial teeth are made in the United States annually. The materials are all found in the United States. Each tooth passes through ten different processes. I called at J. & W.'s, Philadelphia. They employ sixty-two girls, all American. They pay a learner, after two or three weeks' practice, according to the quality and quantity of her work. Their girls earn from $1.50 to $7 per week; average $4.50. They have but one hand earning $7. They would be glad to get more such at the same price, for it is difficult to get good hands. They have to turn away a great many applicants. The prospect is good to learners. They keep their hands all the year. The business has advanced rapidly during the last few years, and is likely to continue increasing. There are constant improvements in the business. Consequently a hand may be always improving. They will not receive a girl without reference, or credentials of moral character. They do not want any but intelligent girls, for the hand is guided by the mind. There are three or four processes carried on in different rooms. They work at the establishment, and never carry work home, unless a mother or sister is sick and requires their attention. It is a light, genteel business; and one well adapted to women of some education and intelligence. A lady in the cars told me she knew a lady who received $7 a week for making teeth in Baltimore. She came to Philadelphia, but could not get as good wages; so she returned to Baltimore. The New York Teeth Manufacturing Company pay from $3 to $5 a week. Learners are paid $2.50 a week, from the first, for six months; and then, if competent, paid more. The work is not unhealthy. Men average $10, but their branch is different; the work is heavier. It requires about two months to learn, in one department. Neither men nor women are often taught more than one branch. All seasons are alike, and they are never out of work. The supply of hands is greater than the demand everywhere. Small hands, nimble fingers, and good eyesight are important to a worker. In the establishment of R., New York, four processes in the making of artificial teeth are performed by women. Some branches require a longer time to learn than others. It takes six months to learn any one perfectly. R. pays $3 a week to his learners, and $5 a week to experienced workers. Careful manipulation is the most that is needed. Judging from the increase in the last five years, the prospect for employment is excellent; yet the openings in New York are limited. Women are the best workers, but some prefer men. The only manufacturers are in New York, Philadelphia, Hartford, and Bridgeport. It is desirable to have careful workers. R. had a girl ruin $500 worth of teeth for him. The parts performed by women are cleaning the moulds, setting the pins, filling the moulds with the tooth materials, and trimming, and putting on the pink color answering the place of gums; also placing them on slides preparatory to baking and carding.

442. Nurses for the Sick. Attention to this subject has been awakened during the last few years, by the heroic conduct of Miss Florence Nightingale and the ladies who went with her to the Crimea to wait on the sick and wounded. When the people of England proposed making some testimonial of regard to Florence Nightingale, she proposed that, with the means expended in doing so, they should establish an institution for the training of nurses. We would not fail to notice a fact that reflects much credit on Miss Anne M. Andrews, of Syracuse, N. Y. While the yellow fever raged in Norfolk, Va., she left her home and went alone to Norfolk, devoting her time and services to the sick of all conditions. She received the medal that is usually awarded to a physician on such occasions, and the citizens talked of placing a statue in a conspicuous part of their city, as a memorial of her goodness and their indebtedness. In Berlin, Vienna, Turin, and Halle, hospitals have been established for the education of nurses. In Germany, there has been óne for many years. A number of good ladies connected with that institution are now in Pittsburg, where they form an order of deaconesses. Some take care of the sick, and some have charge of an orphan asylum. St. Luke's Hospital, New York, is under Episcopal supervision, and connected with it is an order of Protestant deaconesses, who attend the sick. Most of the hospitals in this country have been established by the Roman Catholic Church, and are under its guidance. We think Protestant hospitals for the sick are greatly needed, especially in the Western and Southern cities—Chicago, St. Louis, Louisville, Cincinnati, and New Orleans. It may be that some exist in those cities; but, if so, we think they must be quite limited in extent. Asylums for sick children are established in some of our largest cities. A number exist in Europe. A nurse should have a kind, sympathizing nature, good health, strong nerves, great powers of endurance, ability to sit up all night, and bear exposure to extremes of temperature. In addition, she needs a good memory, that she may give the right medicine at the proper time. If she has not, she should commit to paper such orders, and consult them frequently. A long and thorough training is needed by an attendant on the sick. Great self-control is necessary, for many persons are very impatient in sickness. A bright, cheerful spirit should be cultivated. A sweet voice is pleasant in a nurse, because a sick person is sensitively alive to the smallest matters. It requires a woman of education, consideration, and delicacy of feeling, to be an acceptable nurse to people of refinement; and such an one must become attached to those she serves, if treated kindly. To make a kind and sympathizing nurse, one must have waited, in sickness, upon those she loved dearly. A nurse should use the precaution of wearing camphor, or something of that nature, on her person, particularly where there is contagious fever. The room should be large and well ventilated, and preventives used to keep the infectious air from spreading. A better class of women are employed to wait on the sick than formerly. The infirmary for women, established by Dr. Blackwell, in New York, is designed partly as a school for nurses. There is also an institution in Philadelphia for training them. Nurses earn from $4 to $10 a week. Some wait only on male patients, some only on ladies; some attend incurables, but the most serve in general sickness. Mrs. B. gets $7 and sometimes $8 a week and her board for monthly nursing. She knows some that get $10 a week. She stays in the room with the lady and her infant, and takes care of and waits on them. When food is to be prepared, the child's clothes washed, or anything of that kind done, she rings a bell and gives orders to a servant. Mrs. B., another ladies' nurse, charges from $8 to $10 a week, according to the amount of rest she loses at night. She told me that most good physicians keep a list of the best nurses. A nurse is expected to be able to make all the nice dishes required by her patient. In most small places, she is not expected to have the assistance of any one else, unless the sickness is very protracted, or the patient is delirious. In some places, a nurse is expected to close the eyes of the dying, and wash them after death, and perform any other service of that nature. But it is not uncommon for an undertaker's wife to be sent for to perform these duties, and take a measure for a shroud. For these services she is paid from $3 to $5. A nurse runs the risk of contracting a contagious disease; but, if the system is in a good condition, there is not much danger. As long as people are sick, which will be as long as there are any, nurses will be employed. Of course, there is most to do in sickly seasons. I called on Mrs. P., who charges $5 a week for her services. She does all that is required for the patient, except give medical advice. She would rather wait on men than women, as they are sure either to pay better wages or make presents. As she has had children of her own, and raised them all, she feels competent to take care of children in sickness. It is well for a woman to have a home to go to, when relieved from the labor and anxiety of nursing.

443. Steamboat and Railroad News Venders. Boys and men are much more frequently engaged in the sale of newspapers, than women and girls. They are more disposed to sell edibles. We have seen some little girls selling papers on the streets of New York and Philadelphia; but we do not remember ever to have seen women selling papers at railroad depots or on steamboats, though many are seen with baskets of sweetmeats. Many, perhaps, cannot read, and do not wish to sell papers with whose contents they are unacquainted. Others may think they will be less likely to make any profit by their sale. Some women sell papers at stands on the streets of New York, and about the hotel doors. I saw a newspaper boy with an armful of *Ledgers*. He had sixty that he had bought at three and a half cents apiece, and was selling at four cents apiece. A girl that sells newspapers at the door of a hotel on Broadway, told me that she and her mother take turns about in being at the stand, and the profits of their joint sales are from 50 cents to $1 a day. She has several Sunday customers, to whose houses she takes ordered papers.

444. Street Musicians. Organ grinders and street harpers have ever found a fair representation in the softer sex. Such representation is, however, among our foreign population—

German and Italian, mostly.   Last summer, in the streets of
Philadelphia, might be seen, from day to day, a German woman
with an organ on her back, and a baby in a hand-wagon, going
from street to street, stopping now and then under a window to
play.   And in New York was another, whose organ was placed
in a small barrow, which she wheeled through the streets of the
city.   We have seen two old women going through the streets of
New York, one playing an organ, the other a tambourine; and a
few days since, we observed one drawing very creditable music
from a violin.   Girls in the Swiss costume are sometimes seen
walking from place to place, with a harp and tambourine.   Some
people say that, by the encouragement of street musicians, we
encourage idleness.   Most such people would treat a musician
with scorn, and close the door in their faces, but step out where
they could enjoy the music and save their pennies; or they would
stand behind closed shutters, that their neighbors might not think
them capable of having such vulgar taste as listening to a street
musician.   Now, we may encourage a disposition to roam, but
scarcely idleness.   This propensity to roam may be unfavorable
to the cultivation of business habits; but the class of listless
Italians who engage in it could never become business people.
In the first place, harpers, violinists, and flutists must depend on
their own skill and knowledge of music, to perform.   They must
prepare for their particular vocation, as others do.   Those who
play on organs, harmonias, and similar instruments, where no
knowledge of music is necessary, we must admit, require no training; but walking, as most musicians do, from eight to twenty
miles a day, is in itself laborious.   We have been told that in
New York most street musicians are employed by two or three
individuals, who furnish the instruments, and allow the carriers
to have so much of the proceeds.   In older countries, there is a
greater variety in the instruments used by street musicians.
"There are sometimes fifty persons engaged in the sale of second-
hand musical instruments on the streets of London."

445. Tavern Keepers.   The keeping of taverns in small
villages, or on the roadside in the country, furnishes some with the
means of gaining a livelihood.   Women engaged in this business
should be wives whose husbands can attend to receiving travellers,
settling bills, ordering horses, and such duties, or widows with
sons old enough to do so.   It is laborious enough for a woman to
superintend the table and bed rooms, and the man must be in
wretched health, or good for nothing, that cannot attend to the
out-door duties.   Much money has been accumulated by some
people keeping taverns in the Western country, where fifty cents
is the usual price for a meal.   Indeed, the accommodations are

often such that a person cannot be rendered comfortable, and yet the price paid would command all the comforts of a good boarding house in a large town. It is the same case with the hotels, or saloons, at some railroad depots. At others an abundance of life's good things is furnished. The tavern keepers of London have a pension society.

446. Travelling Companions. Travelling alone, is most favorable to thought, but not to pleasure. How much more we enjoy a lovely scene in nature, or the novel and brilliant sentiments of an author, when in company with one to whom we can talk freely! Good conversational powers, and an ability to appreciate the beautiful, are desirable in a travelling companion. Conversation should flow in a free, easy, unrestrained current. Will it not promote the entertainment and edification of rational, responsible, and immortal beings, to engage in wholesome conversation—to exchange sentiments in regard to books and the improvements of the age—to learn of the heavens above and the earth beneath? In talking with strangers, might not much be learned of their various countries, and a thousand things pertaining to them? Conversation exercises the imagination, gives play to a talent of invention, and strengthens the reasoning faculty. It sharpens thought as fermentation does wine. It tends, also, to restore the diseased imagination of the secluded and morbidly sensitive.

MISTRESSES AND DOMESTICS.

447. Mistresses. We scarcely know that it is in place to say anything to this large and influential class of ladies. Yet, as we treat of servants, and endeavor to impress their duty upon them, we hope we may be excused for saying a few words to those who have charge of them. From the relation existing between a mistress and her servants, the mistress is supposed to have had superior mental and moral advantages. Then let that strongest of all incentives, a good example, be given. In some cases, the only good influence likely to be exerted over the servant, is by the mistress. No woman of right feelings can look upon her servants as mere beasts of burden. She knows and feels that they have souls, and are accountable beings; that each one is capable of extremes of misery and happiness. Should they not therefore receive kind and careful instruction in what is right? If the same regular system of domestic service were employed in this country that exists in Europe, housekeepers would be saved much labor. There, each department, even of kitchen labor, is distinct, and a servant is promoted according to her industry and improvement. But the expense of a large number of servants is one that most people in our country feel unable to support. Difficulties often arise from labor being required of servants that they have not stipulated to perform; and no definite understanding as to the extent of the privilege of receiving visitors, is likely to prove a source of trouble. The thousand petty annoyances to which a mistress is subject, renders it necessary that she have a perfect command of her temper. A mistress must make great allowance for ignorance of what is right and wrong, for untamed passions, strong appetites, unimproved reason, and want of self-control. Many domestics are foreigners—ignorant, dull, and unacquainted with our language. We are sorry to say some mistresses expect their servants to be faultless, when they themselves, with their superior advantages, are not so. Mistresses are responsible, to some extent, for the spiritual, as well as the mental and physical good of their servants. They are in charge of immortal souls. The tendency of their influence and example must be either elevating or depressing. The quiet of the Sabbath, we think, might be granted to those in most departments of domestic labor. Cooks, we think, might prepare a dinner on Saturday, to be served cold on Sunday, with tea, if the weather be cold, or the habits of the people require it. Sabbaths have been called "milestones in the journey of life," and has not the poor cook, steaming over the fire day after day, need to count the milestones in the journey of her toilsome life? Says Mrs. Graves, in her "Woman in America:" "Is it not strange, that, among all the societies of the day, not one should have been formed for the intellectual and moral improvement of domestic servants, and for instructing them in household employments?" At the House of Protection, a Roman Catholic institution, New York, girls and women of good character, out of employment, or strangers in the city, are received on application. The girls are taught to wash, iron, do housework, sew, and embroider. Would that the Protestants would imitate this noble charity more fully! I am happy to add that in connection with the Child's Nursery (a Protestant institution), Fifty-first street, New York, has been commenced a servants' school. Young girls taken into the institution receive a year's instruction in washing, ironing, house cleaning, and sewing.

448. Domestics. We think an important work of benevolence presents itself in Free States. It is providing homes for

AMERICAN MISTRESSES.   424

servant girls, when they are out of employment or sick. Many of them are in a strange land, unacquainted with the language and the ways of the people. When sick, some of them are immediately sent off by their mistresses to save the trouble of waiting on them. The negroes of the Slave States, when sick, are (if they have kind masters and mistresses) as tenderly cared for as any member of the family, and are never without a home in health or in sickness. That lonely and wretched feeling of having no place to consider home, is not their experience. Connected with this subject, arises one to which we have never yet given much attention, but which forces itself on our mind as one calling for attention from the benevolent: it is the establishment of institutions for the afflicted portion of the colored population, both in Slave and Free States. We refer to the blind, the deaf and dumb, and the insane. We know of no separate institution for such, and no arrangement whatever, with the exception of limited arrangements for the insane, in connection with institutions for white people. Now and then we hear people advocate the old plan of binding orphans and destitute children. Whether that would be advantageous, would depend altogether on the kind of people to whom they were bound. Some servants soon fail, and and are not fit for service more than a few years. It arises mostly from their exposure to cold and dampness without being properly clothed and fed, and sometimes from a too free indulgence in the pleasures of the palate, particularly that of the consuming liquid which burns out life and sense. The hard work that most Irish women can perform, and the large number in this country, have made them the most numerous domestics in the Free States. They are generally employed as maids of all work. I think the number of American girls going into service is increasing. The majority of white female domestics in this country are single women, from sixteen to thirty-five years of age. In Providence, R. I., a census was taken in 1855, stating, among other particulars, the number of American families having servants, the number in foreign families, and the aggregate; but the number of white domestics has never been fully taken in the United States, even when collecting statistics for the census. A short time ago, we counted in the New York *Herald* eight columns of situations wanted, three fourths of which were by female domestics. It shows what a surplus there is of domestics in the cities, that no doubt could find situations through the country, and in the villages. The majority of female domestics would rather starve in New York than go to the country, or even little towns around for fair wages. I think it arises from the fear that they will not find associates. A social feeling is natural, but should be

controlled by circumstances. With many, the great drawback is
the fear that they may not be able to have the privileges of their
own particular church; and still another is that they may not find
the place to which they go, or are sent, exactly what it is represented to be, and the expense that would be incurred by a
return. Domestics are more respected in the country, and treated more as members of the family, than domestics in towns. The
preference is usually given, in towns and cities, to domestics from
the country, because of their superior strength and better health.
" For a person to be a good servant, there are three requisites:
first, she must have professional skill in her calling; secondly, she
must be a good woman; thirdly, she must have feelings of kindli-
ness and regard to her master and mistress." In 1853, domestics
were receiving wages in San Francisco proportioned to the prices
paid for everything else. Cooks got $100 a month, and board; house
servants, from $35 to $70, and board. Chambermaids $40 to
$70, and board. Prices have fallen since 1853 in California, but
good female domestics can now earn there from $25 to $30 a
month besides board. " In most towns through our country
domestics get from $1.25 to $2.50 a week, and board. We give
the rates of wages of domestics in New York (1857) at the intelligence offices. Maids of all work, very raw, $4 per month;
average, $5; good, $6 to $7. Chambermaids—good, $6. Cooks
—good, $7 to $8—extra $12 to $16. Laundresses $8 to $10.
The cooks who obtain the highest rates, sometimes reaching $20,
are employed mostly in hotels or private families, in New York.
Five or six years' education in a restaurant, during which period
the pupil is supporting herself, will thus often add seventy-five
per cent. to the market value." I have had numberless statements from different parts of Free States that it was almost impossible to obtain good domestics. I have just taken up a paper
in which I read: " Female domestics are scarce in Minnesota
and Wisconsin, and obtain employment readily at good prices
in almost all the river towns." More particularly are female
domestics scarce, where there are factories. Girls, especially
American girls, prefer to work in factories to being servants, as
they think it more honorable, and it secures to them more time—
in short, they are more their own mistresses.

449. Chambermaids. " Of the 200,000 female servants
in England, the largest in number, the shortest in life, and of
course the worst paid are the general housemaids, or unhappy
servants of all work." Chambermaids in the United States may
be classed under three heads: those in hotels, those in private
families, and those on steamboats. The business of a chambermaid in a hotel, or on a steamboat, is an occupation affording

variety in frequent change of faces. Of course, prices and conditions are stipulated for. Many get $20 a month, and do the washing of the boat, that is, the table and bed linen. Others get $25, $30, and $35 a month. On small boats, they are expected to do the washing of the boat, but in some cases have a woman hired while in port to assist them. On large boats, or small packet boats, there are generally two chambermaids. The first chambermaid attends to receiving lady passengers, seeing that they are furnished with berths, and giving them such attention as they need. She cleans the state rooms, and wakes any lady passengers that are to land in the night. The second chambermaid does the washing and ironing. In some cases, the washing is sent up from the boats, while in port, to laundries. But clothes are thought to be injured in that way, and the plan is not so popular as while the novelty lasted. Most of the rivers of the United States are either too low to be navigable, or are frozen over, part of the year; so, constant employment in that way cannot be found. The first chambermaid on the steamboat E. received $20 a month. Her business was to wait on the ladies She had several hours' time that she could devote to sewing for herself. The second chambermaid did the washing of the boat, and received $15 per month. A steamboat chambermaid told me she averages $20 a month (and board, of course); but, in addition to her services as chambermaid, is required to do the washing for the boat; that is, the sheets, table linen, and towels. In families, the prices for chambermaids are about the same as at hotels, and of course the duties are pretty much the same, except that in families all of a chambermaid's time is expected. In a hotel, a chambermaid is often through her work in the early part of the afternoon, and has several hours as her own. We think it advisable for a servant to keep a place with good people, even if her wages are less, rather than with more selfish and more remunerative people. The first mentioned would feel an interest in, and be more ready and willing to do for a servant in sickness or distress. Besides, they would be more apt to keep a watch over her welfare, should circumstances intervene to bring about a separation. It does not answer well for servants to move about much from place to place; it is likely to create suspicion of unfaithfulness or want of qualification. Yet, if they are not comfortable and satisfied, I would advise them to move, if confident they have a prospect of bettering their condition. The usual wages of chambermaids in cities are from $1.50 to $2.50 per week. In the Northern cities, white chambermaids are rather better paid than in Southern, as colored servants are preferred in the South. For doing housework by the day women receive in New York, fifty, seventy-five cents, and $1; for cleaning stores, they often receive $1.25 per day. Tidy, honest American girls will not find much difficulty in getting situations. If every family in New York city would take a girl, and either instruct her thoroughly or have her instructed in one branch of domestic service, there would not be such universal complaint of bad servants. In Paris, men are employed in some hotels as chambermaids. In a newspaper, we met with the following paragraph some time ago ; " Females áre so scarce in some of the interior towns of California, that men have to be employed to do the chamberwork."

450. Cooks. I know of several benevolent institutions in Philadelphia and New York where poor women are furnished with employment. From most of them sewing is given out; but, in a few, housework is given to those who cannot sew. A school of cookery is now in operation in London. The object is to give instruction, gratis, to the lower classes, in preparing the most common articles of food in general use. It was established by Miss Burdett Coutts. To acquire the higher branches of the art requires much time and practice. Much of the nutriment of food is lost in cooking. Health depends much on the kind of food eaten, and the way in which it is prepared. Simple diet is most healthy; yet what contributes to the nourishment of one person may not to another. Persons can better learn what is nutritious and beneficial to them in health than it were possible for an Æsculapius to prescribe. Eating too hastily and too hurriedly, when the mind is excited and agitated, is one cause of bad health. The modes of preparing food, in the most wholesome way, should be a matter of study and interest to all engaged in a matter where health is so much at stake. Articles of food that contribute to the nourishment of every part of the body should be used. Children should have not only wholesome food, but as much as nature craves, when the system is in a state of health. A morbid appetite, of course, should be regulated. Some cooks devote themselves exclusively to the making and baking of pastry. At hotels they command a good price. In New York and Philadelphia, cooks receive from $1.50 to $5 a week, but in the small towns adjoining do not get more than from $1 to $1.50. Much of the success of servants will depend upon themselves. They may rest assured they will be able to please most families if they are good-natured, honest, truthful, active, and willing to do what they can. They will need patience. They should consider there are many trials, cares, and griefs attendant on those occupying a more responsible station. Punctuality is a desirable item in a cook. A skilful cook, of taste and experience, can, at any time, for reasonable wages, obtain a situation in one of the

Northern cities. Hotel cooks are most frequently in demand, and receive from $12 to $25. A woman who cooks for a saloon frequented by gentlemen only, in a business part of New York, told me that she goes at 8 in the morning and remains, generally, until 2 o'clock next morning, when she goes home. She is paid $12 a month for her work, having her meals besides. A colored man, a public cook, told me he employs two or three women to assist him in getting up parties. He pays them from $6 to $7 a week. He loans plate for parties, charging for plated knives twenty-five cents a dozen, and the same price for forks, and thirty-seven or fifty cents for a basket. He keeps some articles, but hires most from another party. Sometimes he will receive three or four orders a day; then again he may not have one for two weeks. It is a very irregular business. He prepares lunches for bankers and political men, mostly; but finds it inconvenient, as these lunches are often given in their offices, and he prepares the dishes at home, and must have them warm when served up. In some offices, he can have an apartment for that purpose; in others, he cannot. A colored woman, who goes on a propeller in summer, and does the cooking for ten men, told me she receives $19 a month. The boats at New York seldom stop running longer than three months in the year. She thinks the trouble in New York is, you cannot have one kind of work regularly. In Germany, most of the women, in every class of society, learn to cook. In Stuttgart, a wealthy man died, leaving a certain sum, the interest of which goes to a given number of the best hotel cooks, to teach a limited number of young women the art. In some cities in Germany, ladies pay something to pastry cooks at hotels and restaurants for instruction in cooking.

451. Dining-Room Waiters. It would be well, had we such laws as England, for the protection and rights of servants. There, a servant cannot have her character scandalized, her good name maligned, or her faithfulness as a servant belied. Neither may a servant say aught that is false against her mistress. Scandalizing becomes, oftentimes, a curse in our Free States, and consequently self-respect, with servants, becomes, to a great extent, a defunct virtue. Nor is the fault confined to one party. Both are often culpable—mistress and servant. A good character is the best capital a servant can possess. Servants have an opportunity of improving themselves, and gaining much practical information from intercourse with their mistresses while in the discharge of their duties. If worthy American girls would get situations as domestics in respectable families, they would be likely to fare better than by working in shops; for they would lay by more money, secure the interests and good wishes of their employers, and be more certain of lasting employment. A servant should be active and quick in motion, to perform well the duties of a waiter. In 1854, from seventeen to twenty-four white girls were employed as dining-room waiters at the Delavan House, Albany, N. Y. Their wages were from $5 to $7, in one or two cases $8, a calendar month. The wages of men for similar service were from $14 to $20. The ages of the women were from seventeen to twenty-four. They dressed uniformly in calico, and were under a head waiter—a man. At that time, women had been employed at the establishment about two years and a half. The result was entirely satisfactory in every respect. A gentleman inquired of the proprietor, after he had employed them two years, if there was any inferiority to men's service, and was informed there was not any. They were more quiet than men, and less troublesome. In this time, only four had left the house of their own accord, and then to be married. When more hands were needed, there was no difficulty in getting them. It was apprehended that improprieties might occur, from the gallantries of the gentlemen. No difficulty of the kind had been experienced. It was suggested that it might be otherwise in a liquor house. In April, 1860, we had a few lines from the proprietor of the Delavan House, saying he found women would not answer for first-class hotels, where the crowd is very great, as the work is too severe. He changed the plan of having them in 1858.

452. Ladies' Maids. Some of the most wealthy or self-indulgent ladies have a female attendant to dress and wait on them, but it is not so common in the United States as in older and more wealthy countries. In Some States, a colored woman, graceful and good natured, is often set apart from the family servants for this purpose. The difficulty that attends the taking of a colored servant in travelling, sometimes calls for a white attendant to act in this capacity. The business is light, and brings good wages. A maid should endeavor to secure a place with a lady that is amiable and patient. She will find ability to perform the services of a lady's hair dresser a valuable acquisition.

453. Nurses for Children. None should enter this occupation unless they have a love for children. It requires affection and patience. Added to this, is needed a degree of mild firmness that children find it difficult to resist. It requires strength too, and a lady had better, if possible, furnish a grown nurse for her child. Nurses receive as wages from $1 to $1.25 per week. Wet nurses receive higher wages. Being able to speak the French and German languages correctly, is in some places a desirable qualification. Fashionable and educated people, who desire to have their children early instructed in the languages, are willing to pay a better price for such a nurse. The habit of nursing children is indicated, in both mothers and nursery maids, by the right shoulder being larger and more elevated than the left. C. thinks it would be well for young American girls to devote themselves to domestic service—thinks it a misplaced pride which prevents their doing so. Many would certainly be much better off in every respect than they now are, and, if their affairs were well conducted, would save money.

454. Saloon Attendants. "This class of labor is performed by young men and girls. Although the girls are preferred in some places, and do make most excellent waitresses, their remuneration is not as high as that paid to men. In some cases the men get as high as $14 a month; in most cases, however, they do not receive more than $12 a month. The girls get paid from $8 to $10 a month, varying according to experience. The hours employed do not exceed, in most cases, ten per day. These rates are exclusive of board and lodging. Where lodgings are not provided, an allowance is made for the purpose." The ladies that T. employs in his saloon, board in the International—a hotel connected with the saloon and confectionery. He pays them $6 a month, besides their board. M., Broadway, pays those that stay in his confectionery $12 a month, and their board. In the northern part of France, women are employed on some of the packet boats as table waiters. They are young and pretty, and misconduct among them is very rare.

455. Washers, Ironers, and Manglers. The plan of washing by steam is said to have been practised many years back in France. There were, some years ago, over 300 different models of washing machines at the Patent Office in Washington. Some families have their washing done by hand, some by machinery, and some at laundries. Where washing, ironing, and mangling are carried on extensively, it is mostly by men, but *women are employed to do the labor*. It is thought by some that clothes are injured when washed at laundries. We do not know whether it originates from the plan of washing, or the carelessness of those employed. In New York is a public washing house, where, for four cents an hour, steam, water, and troughs can be used for washing clothes. At the same price, the privileges of the wringing machine, the drying room, and the ironing room are granted. A mangler costs from $50 to $100. Those that are operated on by steam cost more, and are often used in laundries. A woman told me that she is paid fifteen cents a dozen for mangling sheets and table cloths. She can mangle eight or nine dozen pieces a day, and so earn from $1.20 to $1.25. It takes but a very short time to become expert. Strong arms and a strong back are more necessary than anything else. She could work her mangle all day, but it would be a hard day's work. She has much work in summer, before people go to the country. The prices given for family washing and ironing by the dozen, range from fifty cents to $1. Others make arrangements by the parcel, at so much a week or month. Those employed in ironing receive good wages. Where new shirts are done up for stores, the best prices are given. A woman employed in an establishment of the kind in Cincinnati, told me that she received for her work, which was ironing the bosoms of new shirts for stores, $7 a week. She ironed thirty or forty a day, averaging one, I think, every twelve minutes. I called on Mrs. S., who has a laundry. Women in that branch are well paid, both principals and employées. Some of the laundry keepers in New York go down to Castle Garden and get fresh emigrant girls. They give them their board until they can wash right well (for about four weeks), then pay them by the week or the piece. If by the week, $6 a month and their board, or allow them $1.50 a week to pay their board. They instruct some hands in ironing, if they need hands in that department. When qualified, they pay three cents a shirt for ironing; or, if by the week, $4.75. It is most satisfactory generally to both parties to pay by the piece. The best doers up of muslin and cotton goods are the French. New shirts are sent from Boston, Philadelphia, &c., to New York, to be done up. The openings for ironers are good, and the work pays well. A right active, skilful hand can iron fifty shirts a day, and so earn $1.50. When women are employed by the week, they are required to iron twenty-five shirts a day, and, if brisk, may get through by one or two o'clock. Mrs. S. charges $1.50 a dozen for store shirts, and $1 for others. Washers earn $12 a month; ironers, $21; and starchers, $14. The girls employed in laundries are mostly Irish, with strong muscular power. A shirt manufacturer told me that ironers of new shirts are much needed. He cannot obtain enough. Ironers can learn the business in three months. Ironers earn from $5 to $8 per week. I called on A. G., who charges from $1 to $1.50 a dozen for doing up new shirts, according to the quality and the work on them. She pays her ironers from $10 to $12 a month. I called at B.'s laundry. The proprietor and his family are Americans. They do only store shirts. They employ more than one hundred hands, who are boarded and paid by the month. Learners receive their board. Ironers are paid best. Those that work fast get through earliest in the day, each one having a certain number to do. I called at another laundry, where I was told all the girls receive $1.75 per week for board money. While learning, they are paid their board money, and more, if their services are worth it. The washers are paid $12 a month, and ironers from $10 to $25, boarding themselves. Some are fast, and some are slow; some smart, and some stupid. The ironers are paid $2\frac{1}{4}$ cents a piece for common shirts, $2\frac{1}{2}$ for fine ones. The proprietor says experienced ironers are so scarce, you never find a good one in an intelligence office. If a laundryman fails, a good ironer can go to another laundry and get a place at once. At another place, I was told their washers receive $5 a month and their board. Ironers are paid by the month, and required to do so many in that time. She corroborated the statement of the other that a good ironer need never want a place. I heard a washerwoman say that, as the system is very much relaxed by washing, the vapor from the suds and soiled clothes renders it unhealthy. H. pays ironers $10 a month and board; $1.75 a week. Some he boards in his own house. An ironer is expected to iron from twenty to thirty a day, according to the contract. It requires a long time to iron well. Almost all washers and ironers are Irish girls—they are stronger and quicker in their motions. He has washing done only for the New York stores, because the time and trouble of going to steamboats for those from other places and returning them, are more than he wishes.

MISCELLANEOUS OCCUPATIONS, AND WORKERS THEREIN.

456. Backgammon-Board Finishers. We called at L.'s backgammon-board manufactory, and saw a girl about thirteen years old, who has worked at the business for one year. She pastes the morocco on the back of the boards, and lays the gold leaf on, which is passed under a press, and receives, from a man who has charge of it, the ornamental gilding. They used to employ girls, and paid $4 a week, working from 7 to 6 o'clock—eleven hours. L. does not take learners—it is too much trouble. K. used to employ girls in finishing boards, but those he had were not steady and reliable.

457. Balloon Makers. Large balloons are stitched up by sewing machines. Prof. L.'s required several days' work. Prof. W.'s sister and niece make both cotton and silk balloons. They have the substance put on the silk by men with a brush. They think that part of the work would be rather hard on women, because of the stooping and bending.

19

458. Billiard-Table Finishers. I saw G., who employs one woman to make and put on the billiard bags at the corners and sides. He pays her such wages for her work that she can by industry earn $1.50 a day. He does not know of any woman that makes it a regular business, but thinks, if a woman could engage all that kind of work to be had at the billiard manufactories in New York city, it would be a good business, and probably pay about $3 a day. It is very easy work, and would require but a few weeks' practice. Besides, it would not require any capital, as the manufacturers furnish the materials. They pay twenty-five cents for making a cover of unbleached domestic, when two seams are sewed and it is hemmed at the ends. The cloth that is fastened on the table could not be put on by a woman, as it requires too much strength. Netting the bags is done by hand. I was told by a manufacturer that two women could do all the work for New York.

459. Bill Posters. This is a business confined to cities. W. heard of one woman that went through New York distributing circulars for some benevolent institution. I do not see why a woman might not be so employed. An immense quantity of waste paper is sold in London to grocers, butchers, fishmongers, poulterers, and others that need paper for wrapping up the articles they sell to purchasers.

460. Block Cutters. Block cutters prepare blocks of wood for the coloring of wall paper. A block about eighteen inches square and two inches thick is made perfectly smooth. The pattern is then traced on it with a lead pencil. It is then cut with chisels, which are of all sizes and many shapes. Each one, as required, is driven into the wood with a mallet. It requires considerable physical strength, but is remunerative when sufficient orders are given to keep one constantly employed. Each color, and even shade, in wall paper, requires a separate block. It is the same case where wooden blocks are used for printing calicoes. The wall-paper establishments in Philadelphia are the most extensive in the United States. A lady in Philadelphia, engaged in the business, told me that she got about $10 a week, working ten hours a day, but that she had not orders enough to keep her constantly employed. At N. & C.'s paper-hanging factory, New York, they employ six male block cutters, who earn from $2 to $2.25 a day. A boy, when apprenticed to a block cutter, receives $2.50 a week the first year, $3 the next, $4 the next, and $5 the last. There are probably from sixty to one hundred block cutters in New York city. Block letters, we were told, are made by machinery. A gentleman in Maine writes: " There are but very few females in this section who work at block cutting (blocks for printing oil carpets); but three or four in this State, I think. I have none with me excepting my wife. It is a branch of business that females cannot carry on alone, as the most of it requires considerable labor that women are not able to perform." In the census returns of Great Britain for 1850, we find four women under the head of block cutters.

461. Boatwomen. In the countries of Europe, it is not unusual to see women employed as rowers of boats, on the lakes and rivers. On the lakes of Scotland, made famous by the poetry and fiction of Sir Walter Scott, women are seen waiting in their little boats to take passengers out on the lakes. In the sealochs of Scotland, fisherwomen manage their own boats. In Germany, women also ply the oar. In the United States, it is seldom done; but I think Miss Murray, in her Travels, mentions being rowed upon a lake in New York State by a woman. Some of the Indian women, of the Arctic regions, are noted for their skill in the management of a boat; and some of the women of the Polynesian Islands are distinguished in the same way. In the census of Great Britain for 1850, in class eight, and third division (Carriers on Canals), are reported 1,708 bargewomen over twenty years of age, and 525 under that age.

462. Bone Collectors. Some collectors of bones sell them to people who make soup of them, and sell it to the poor at a penny a bowl. Some sell their bones to soap manufacturers, who boil them to obtain the marrow and oily substance, and then sell them to button makers, or makers of cane and whip handles. Some sell them to glue manufacturers, who boil them to obtain the gelatine for making glue. Some have establishments where they are ground and sold as a fertilizer for the soil. Some bone gatherers give toys to children for collecting bones. I saw a girl gathering some, who told me she sold them at fifteen cents a half bushel. She gathers sometimes half a bushel a day, and sometimes more. A boy told me he got thirty cents a bushel for bones; and another, that he got one cent a pound. The profit must be great of those who sell them again, judging from the price paid by the makers of cane handles. Yet it may be, so much is not paid by manufacturers for those taken from the street as for new ones.

463. Bottlers and Labellers. In large establishments where wine, porter, ale, or beer is corked, women could, and in some places do, have the job. When it is done from day to day, it affords a reliable resource. The payment is generally, I believe, by the dozen or hundred bottles. "In one house or more, in London, are seen from one hundred to one hundred and fifty women bottling pickles all day long, at the charge of sixpence a score of bottles, at which an industrious woman, without any extra exertion, will earn her two shillings a day." In establishments for the sale of patent medicines and other articles of a similar nature, women are employed. I saw a man bottling lager beer by hand. He is paid $15 a month, and full board. For labelling, another received $6 a month, and full board. In Europe, where women do such work, they wear wooden shoes to keep their feet dry. A woman could as well cork as a man, when it is done by hand, and, no doubt, could use the machines employed for corking. A large manufacturer of hair restorative employs two girls to put it up, and pays from $3 to $4 a week. A brewer writes that "women might be employed in the bottling department, cleaning, filling, corking, &c., but the proportion would be small in comparison with the number of men at work." A woman that buys and sells empty bottles says she and her husband made a comfortable living at it. If they make three cents profit on a dozen they do well. They send a wagon to hotels, groceries, and private houses, if the number is sufficient to justify it. They find a ready sale for their bottles. The bottles must be washed clean before they will buy them. I was told at the office of Mrs. W.'s S. Syrup, that girls are paid by the week, from $5 to $6. R., in putting up his Ready Relief, employs several girls to fill bottles, cork and label them. They earn from $3 to $6 a week. They are paid by the quantity, and the work is all done in daylight. Until the last few days they have had work all the year round. S. employs from five to ten girls, and pays from $4 to $5 a week for bottling medicines and putting up Seidlitz powders. He keeps his hands all the year. They can either sit or stand. He does not know of any women being so employed South or West. L. employs three, and pays $5 a week, ten hours a day. One is employed in putting up Seidlitz powders—the others in bottling. All three work at the store. K. employs three girls to put up Seidlitz powders, perfumery, &c. He pays from $3 to $3.50 a week. B. & M., stove-polish manufacturers, employ girls to put up the polish in papers. The paper is folded on a wooden block and pasted, then withdrawn, and the polish put in and sealed.

464. Broom Makers. C. employs a girl to paint the handles of brooms, paying $4 a week, of ten hours a day. After New Year is the most busy season. It requires but a short time to learn. A man can earn at broom making $1.25 to $1.75 a day. At some of the broom factories girls are employed to assort the broom by laying perfect pieces of a certain length in one pile, and those shorter in another, &c. Only strong, robust women could perform the entire process of broom making.

465. Bronzes. When a bronze appearance is desired for

some metals, bronze powders are used. I have been told that a patent has been granted for the making of them. Parties that we think competent to know tell us that "bronze powders are made in very few establishments in this country, and they think women and boys, much more than men, are both here and in Europe engaged in the making and working of bronze. They suggest that manufacturers, printers, japanners, and all who have operatives engaged in handling bronze powders should, in *all cases*, see that their people are protected, by gauze, sponge, or some sort of screen over the mouth and nostrils, from inhaling the fine particles that arise and impregnate the atmosphere where the powders are handled, and which are liable to cause serious injury to those who inhale them. The same might also be said of Dutch metal or gold leaf used in gilding house paper and other things." Magnetic masks are used by some grinders and polishers to prevent iron filings from passing down their throats. We suppose they would answer also for bronzers. Men oppose the introduction of women into the business. I saw three sisters bronzing in New York. They told me each receives $5 a week, and works about nine hours a day. It requires but a few months' practice to become perfect, and seemed to be an easy business. The young ladies employed at it looked genteel enough to grace any calling. Men get $10 a week. Women do it just as well, if not a little better, and accomplish just as much, yet receive only $5. I called in the store of the Ornamental Iron Works, New York. The young man says they employ about twenty-five German bronzers. It is a work easily done, and would require but a short time to learn. Women could just as well do it as men. If women were employed, it would be desirable to have a separate room for them to work in. Their men work ten hours a day, and receive from $1.50 to $2 a day.

466. Canvas and Cotton Bag Makers. The firm of B. E. C. & Co. employ about forty females during the whole year, and seventy during the summer. Men cut out the bags. The folding and turning is done by little girls, who receive, some $1.50 per week, and some more, while the sewing is done by machines, for which the operators receive $4.50 per week. I do not remember what the spoolers were paid. This business is confined exclusively to seaports or river cities, and is not very extensive. The usual time required is ten hours. For extra work, girls receive double wages. C. & Co. have certain regulations, requiring morality and order. The girls were more cheerful, neat, and genteel-looking than the general run of work girls. They have a dressing room, where each one has a peg for her bonnet and shawl, and a small box in which to lay her

dinner.   They have washbowls and all the conveniences needed.
Spring and fall are their most busy times, but they are able to
keep their hands all the year in prosperous times.   They are always busy just before the sailing of vessels, as they supply many
vessels with bags to carry grain.   They are well located for their
business, being immediately on the river.   The prospect for
learners C. thinks very good, as bags are considered almost as
essential as boats; and now they can be purchased so cheaply they
are used for purposes to which they were never applied before.
V. employs fifteen girls all the year, and sometimes extra help.
Some girls get $3.50, and some $4 a week, of ten hours a day.
Most of their machines are propelled by hot air.   They never
have any trouble in getting hands.   There are a few bag factories in the West.   W. & O. make cotton bags for flour, seed,
grain, &c.   We saw the girls sewing on machines moved by
steam.   They are paid $3 a week, ten hours a day.   Their girls
are not punctual, and are so often absent that they find it necessary to employ more hands than they want, that they may not
get out of a supply.   I met an old woman with bolts of heavy
unbleached cotton, who was going to make up bags, sewing them
with the needle.   She receives seventy-five cents for one hundred
bags.   A bag manufacturer in Boston writes: "We pay by the
week; girls, from $3 to $4—men, $7.25.   The men's branch re-
quires from six to twelve months to become proficient and reliable.
Women require about one week.   Perseverance and industry are
needed by workers.   Business in future is dubious.   Winter and
spring are the best seasons, but we are generally employed ten
months out of the year.   The hands work ten hours, unless driven
up by brisk trade, when extra wages are paid *pro rata.*   They
receive all the comforts which women of this class require, viz.,
sufficient to live upon, with a small surplus for the priest, and to
send to 'ould Ireland.'   The labor of the men and women are
entirely dissimilar.   The advantages have been entirely in favor
of the city of Boston; but from present indications, I fear that this
business, if done at all, will be done in the cities of Charleston,
Savannah, Mobile, and New Orleans.   The women can scarcely
read; none can write.   They can have free access to the city
library and free evening schools.   Board, $1.25—mostly whole
families in one room."

467. Carriage and Car Painters. At a very large car
establishment in New York, I was told that when they take boys
to learn ornamental painting, they pay $2.40 a week the first year.
After that, eight cents a day more, the next year; and so continue
until the apprenticeship expires.   Three or four years are usually
given.   We saw a foreman ornamenting the side of a car to be

sent to Liverpool, who was taken by the firm when a penniless boy. He now has $3,000 deposited with his employers, drawing a handsome interest. The painters are paid twenty-five cents an hour while ornamenting cars, and omnibuses. They do their work better than when paid by the piece. They prefer Germans, as they have more taste, and are more easily obtained. Miss H. knew a young lady that painted a cutter. Her father was a coach painter, and she painted in oils on canvas. A lady, if she would give time and attention, might become an ornamental painter of carriages, omnibuses, and cars. E. G. & Co., car builders, in Troy, write : " There are some portions of our ornamental painting women might be instructed to perform, that would be suitable for them, and, if proficient, they could make good wages at it."

468. Carriage Trimmers. I was told by G., a carriage maker, that women usually make the cushions and trimmings for carriages. At a railroad-car and omnibus factory, the trimmer told me the work was too hard for women. The sewing is all done by hand. Much wax must be used on the thread, and a machine will not draw the threads tight enough. A shield of leather is worn on the little finger. I have read that " landscape painters, upholsterers, and trimmers of cars and carriages receive from $1.50 to $2 per day, of ten hours, in New York and New Jersey. Women are not generally employed ; but they are occasionally serviceable in preparing the hair for seats, by which they could make, at steady employment, from $3 to $5 per week." B., at his carriage manufactory, said he intends employing two women to make curtains for his carriages. He now employs a girl to make covers for them. He thinks the curtains and much of the lining might be stitched by a machine. He thinks women might make fair wages at it—say, $4 or $5 a week. A carriage maker in Boston writes me : " I employ female labor only to the amount of about $50 a year. It is done by the piece, and a woman who is tolerably smart with her needle can in a very short time learn to do it, and can earn from eight to ten cents an hour. The work is irregular, a large portion of it coming in the months of April, May, and June, and sometimes requiring to be done at short notice." Car builders in Albany, N. Y., write : " Dear Madam—In reply to your inquiries, would say that, out of seventy-five to eighty hands employed by us, two only are women. One has charge of a sewing machine, the other picks curled hair. They have constant employment, at $5 a week." Carriage makers in Syracuse reply to a circular, saying : " We employ one lady to run the sewing machine in making leather and cloth tops for carriages. The work is healthy. We pay from $3 to $4 per week, of ten hours a day. Girls receive from one third to one half as much as men. It requires about two months to learn. Learners receive from $2 to $2.50 per week. The prospect for more such work to women is increasing. The employment is steady. There is a demand for women capable of good, heavy stitching." C—s, of New Haven, write: "We employ about twelve women in carriage trimming, running sewing machines, &c. Good wages are earned—from $5 to $9 per week, of ten hours a day. We pay mostly by the week. At the same kind of work our girls earn as much as men. The main part of their business being sewing, women are preferable at the same wages as men. In two days any ordinary person can learn to use a sewing machine; but to learn all parts of the business would require from two to three months' time. Girls receive a small compensation while learning. They are never out of employment, except in hard times, like the past winter. Two thirds are American girls. The girls employed by us are intelligent and happy; earning good wages, and always have work when we are doing anything. Board, $2.50."

469. Chair Seaters. The putting of seats in chairs, the material being of cane, hickory, flags, willow, and corn husks, is carried on very often in orphan asylums, institutions for the blind, or for the deaf and dumb, and in penitentiaries. There is a large establishment in Worcester, Mass., where women are employed. At the House of Refuge, on Randall's Island, I saw the boys seating chairs with rattan. It is learned in three months. It is very severe on the fingers at first. In a small second-hand furniture store, I saw a woman seating chairs with cane. I stepped in and inquired of the woman how long it required to learn the work. She said she learned it in one day, of a German who kept a furniture store next door, and who wished her to work for him. She could seat two chairs in a day, and earn by doing so a dollar. For such a chair as she would be paid sixty-two cents the cane would cost twelve cents, leaving her a profit of fifty cents a chair for her work. It cuts the fingers some. She has most family work in winter; but her husband can always get enough for her from the stores. Another German woman seating chairs said she could seat three in a day. She charged fifty cents apiece for ordinary chairs. At a chair-seating factory, I saw several girls caning chairs for the proprietor, who receives orders from stores. We were told that it is always piecework. Some girls earn from sixty to seventy-five cents a day. They have work all the year. The girls were very clean-looking. They stood while at work. A girl told us it would take but three weeks to learn. Work is most apt to be slack in January, February, August, and September. The work is mostly done by German women. At another factory, I was told the prospect for work is very good. The man said, three years ago he had more work for his women than they could do. They are not paid while learning, and have work the same all the year. His best hands can earn $4 or $5 a week. The work is always paid for by the piece. The superintendent of the Monroe County Penitentiary, N. Y., writes: "We employ our female convicts at the manufacture of both flag and cane chair seats. They are equally adapted to the employment of women; the flag seats, however, cannot be made except near a chair manufactory, because of the expense of transporting the frames upon which they are made. The cane-seat frames can be easily transported; but the market is overstocked, and has been for years. They are made in many Northern and more Eastern prisons, and are made by both sexes. At the Albany (N. Y.) Prison, the females are employed at cane-chair seating, and at some part of the manufacture of shoes. At the Erie County Penitentiary, Buffalo, N. Y., the female convicts are employed at cane chair seating and packing hardware, manufactured by the male convicts; and at the Onondago County Penitentiary, Syracuse, caning chair seats. New York, Massachusetts, Pennsylvania, and Michigan are the only States, probably, having county prisons, where the convicts are regularly employed. Cane seating is a business employing many females (free labor) in Massachusetts and New Hampshire, and is well adapted to girls and women of the lower grades of intelligence; and the same is applicable to flag seating. They can earn, on an average, about thirty cents per day. The business may be acquired in a few days—say, thirty." The proprietor of the Oswego chair factory writes: "I have in my employ about forty women and girls in the cane-seating department. An attentive worker, possessing ordinary skill, can earn about fifty cents per day, of ten hours. Young persons of either sex are much more sprightly at the work than older persons." By a chair manufacturer in Fitchburg, Mass., several hundreds of women, girls, and children are employed in seating chairs, which they do at home.

470. China Menders. All parts of this work are very suitable for women. Covering and repairing fans, mending china, wax dolls, works of virtu, &c., require care and taste. Connected with this might be the mending of jewelry, card cases, work boxes, and other ornaments of the toilet. A china mender told me he estimates his time at twenty-five cents an hour. His prices vary, according to the quality of the article, and the time and care required. He sells the composition for cementing at twenty-five cents a bottle. His work was beautifully done. I

talked with another china mender and glass driller. After the
fourth of July he goes to the country and mends ware. Some
learn his business in a short time. He charges $10 to teach
to make cement, drill, and mend articles. He thinks, in Boston,
Philadelphia, and Brooklyn, there are probably openings. He
says money can be made at the business by advertising, and having some one to go for the articles and collect the money. He
is recommended by one customer to another, and so has enough
to do; yet, from the want of capital, barely makes a living. If he
could get a place in a china store, ladies could get their china
mended there, and the store would give him some. He makes
between thirty and forty kinds of cement. Some of them stand
water. If a lady would learn, he would pay her $3 a week for her
services.

471. Cigar Makers. At F.'s, Philadelphia, we were
told that girls who make cigars are usually idle; but when we
afterward saw the rapid motion of their fingers, we felt disposed
to doubt the charge. Habits of order, temperance, industry, and
the *reverse*, are said to run in some trades. F. had heard some
employer lamenting that there is no such thing as a sober reed-
cutter. May not the flavor of tobacco, in making cigars, produce
an excitement that craves some artificial stimulus? We think it
would not be strange if it did; but have no means of ascertaining, and hope that it does not. Bending over was the only item
mentioned by F. as being uncomfortable or injurious in the work.
"In Philadelphia, the whole number of employés, journeymen
and girls, engaged in making cigars, is fully four thousand. The
average labor expended upon each thousand cigars costs $3.50,
and the average cost of each thousand cigars is $8." In Phila-
delphia, many Americans work at the business; but in New York,
almost all are Germans. In Germany, many women make cigars.
A cigar maker told me that some women find the odor too strong;
and even men with weak lungs are likely to have the consumption,
if they work at it long. He pays women the same price as men,
and he pays according to the quality and the workmanship—$2,
$3, $4, $5, and $6 per thousand. Quickness in the use of the
fingers is necessary. He has never known women to make the
finest cigars. At K.'s, New York, I saw some bright, pleasant-
looking girls at work. They are paid six cents a hundred. One
girl told me she generally made thirteen hundred a day—seventy-
eight cents. Women receive the same rates of wages as men.
The son of the proprietor told me he had thought the work not
altogether healthy; for the men you see working at the business
are pale and thin. His father's girls are kept busy all the year.
Girls generally make from $3 to $4 a week. There are enough

of girls at it in New York, though there are but few places where girls are employed. The atmosphere almost stifled me, the tobacco scent was so strong. I inquired of a girl if she thought it unhealthy. She said no—that when she first came there, her head ached all the time, and she had constant nausea of the stomach; but now she never notices the smell of the tobacco, and does not feel any bad effects. She said she had learned to make cigars in three weeks; another girl said she learned it in one week. In summer, when the days are long, a girl earns most. A bundler is paid the best price, as she receives six cents a hundred. It is very dirty work. A cigar dealer told me he pays from $2 up to $6 per thousand. A man can make two hundred per day, and so earn from 40 cents to $1.20. He thinks it not unhealthy, where there is a circulation of air. The rapidity in making cigars depends much on the quality of the tobacco. Some leaves are not so well dried, nor so fine and perfect, as others. Such, of course, require a longer time to make. D., New York, says women mostly make the quality called sixes; and he knows that, farther East, in making that kind they often earn $1 a day. They can make the common ones more rapidly than men. He attributes the inability of women to make fine cigars to the want of instruction. Men do not like to teach them, because they are afraid of the competition that may be created, causing them to lose work or have to do it at lower wages. Now and then a woman may be found who makes cigars equal to any man. It requires a knowledge of tobacco, to select the different kinds for the various grades. Some judgment and intelligence are needed to cut the leaf economically, and to select tobacco of proper strength for making various brands. It is usual for a boy to serve three years, who is paid about $30 a year, and boarded. He has boys fifteen years of age working for him as journeymen. He says cigar makers in New York earn from $6 to $15 per week. Good hands can usually find employment. It can easily be learned in one year. All seasons are favorable for the work. From five hundred to fifteen hundred cigars are made in a day, according to the expertness of the manipulator and the kind of tobacco. Machines have not as yet been found to work well. The machine cigars are finished at the end by hand. He remarked that machines never can succeed so well as men, until they have the brains of men. A very nice widow, who kept a cigar store in New York, told me that many more women are employed in making cigars in Philadelphia than in New York; but the cigars made and sold there are mostly of the cheap kind, selling for two or three cents apiece. Six months' practice is required by a learner, to become perfect. Careful and rapid movement of the fingers, and ability to use the left hand, are desirable. I would suggest that a few smart women learn of a competent workman to make the best quality, and instruct several of their own sex. I find the making of cigars is paid for, altogether, by the thousand, and cigar makers earn from $3 to $18 a week. The usual price paid for a thousand cigars is $5, and a fast worker can make fifteen hundred a day.

472. Cigar-End Finders. Mayhew says: "There are, strictly speaking, none who make a living by picking up the ends of cigars thrown away as useless by the smokers in the streets; but there are very many who employ themselves, from time to time, in collecting them. How they are disposed of, is unknown; but it is supposed that they are resold to some of the large manufacturers of cigars, and go to form a component part of a new stock of the best Havanas. There are five persons, residing in different parts of London, who are known to purchase cigar ends. In Naples, the sale of cigar ends is a regular street traffic. In Paris, the ends thus collected are sold as cheap tobacco to the poor. In the low lodging-houses of London, the ends, when dried, are cut up and sold to such of their fellow lodgers as are anxious to enjoy their pipe at the cheapest possible rate."

473. Cinder Gatherers. I saw some girls gathering cinders. They burn them at home, after washing them. One pailful lasts from one and a half to two days. The larger girls gather two pails a day, generally; the smaller girls each gather one.

474. Clear Starchers. The doing up of muslin, in large cities, has made for itself a separate calling. Where there is constant employment, it pays well. Mrs. N. charges from sixteen to twenty-five cents for doing up a set of muslin. She does most of the work herself, as she feels responsible for the way in which it is done, and would be afraid a stranger might tear or burn the muslin. When she has not enough to do, she fills up her time crocheting for the stores. I think the best locations must be in a part of the city where the best residences are.

475. Clock Makers. The amount and variety of wooden clocks manufactured in this country are very great. The low price at which they sell, puts it in the power of almost every one to purchase. Clock-case and clock-movement making are two distinct branches. Connecticut is the only State in which clock movements are made; but there are many shops all over the North in which the cases are manufactured. In 1845, there were twenty establishments in New York city, in which the cases were made. "Wages of clock makers are poor. Women are occasionally employed in painting the cases of clocks, painting the dials, and making part of the movements." The New Haven Clock Company employ women to paint the glass tablets, and in lettering, or putting the figures on the dial, at which work they can earn from 90 cents to $1 per day, of ten hours.   They also use quite a number in making trimmings, and the lighter part of the movements, at which they earn about seventy-five cents per day. All their work is done by the piece. The time necessary to learn depends much on the intelligence and aptness of the person. Manufacturers of clock dials in Farmington, Conn., write : "We employ twelve American women figuring clock dials. The spirit of turpentine used is unhealthy to some. They are paid by the piece, and average $2.50, with board. Men are not employed in the same department. It requires about four weeks to learn, and learners are furnished with board. The amount of employment in future is indefinite. Fall, winter, and spring are the best seasons for work ; but constant employment is given by us. Board, $2."

476. Clothes-Pin Makers. A clothes-pin manufacturer in Vermont writes : " Women are employed in packing clothes pins, and are paid from 25 to 50 cents per day, usually working ten hours. Our women are Americans. The clothes-pin business should be carried on in a sparsely settled community, where timber can be obtained at cheap rates."

477. Clothes Repairers. We have seen it suggested that shops for repairing, remodelling, and remaking ladies' clothes, would, in large cities, if conducted by competent persons, probably yield a support. The mending of ladies' shoes, and mending second-hand ones to sell again, could employ the time of a number.

478. Cork Assorters and Sole Stitchers. The principal use made of cork in this country is for bottle stoppers. It is also used in making cork soles for shoes. Cork is mostly imported from Spain, Portugal, and the south of France, in large blocks, and cut in the shapes wanted. A member of a large cork-cutting company at the East writes : " In France, Spain, and Portugal, women are employed to a limited extent in cutting the smaller description of corks, and a few are also employed in England, but not to any extent." He thinks the employment not suitable for women, and says none are employed in this country. But from the public reports of the city of his residence, I find women are employed as cork cutters in that city. At one establishment, we saw men at work cutting corks. There did not appear any objection to women employing themselves in this trade. A good deal of practice is required. S., of New York, cuts by machine, and employs six girls to assort. He pays 50 cents a day, of ten hours. At another cork store, I was told they employ boys and

girls to assort, who receive from $2 to $3 a week.   The coverings
of cork soles are put on by women with sewing machines.   A
good hand, we were told, can make eight dozen pairs a day, and is
paid eighteen cents a dozen.   I suppose it requires at least a day to
cut out and baste on the covering of that number; so the compensation is not as great as one might at first suppose.   Some can
baste five dozen a day, and could stitch from twelve to twenty
dozen a day.   Girls are paid 10 cents a dozen for basting, and
6 cents per dozen for stitching them on machines.   A cork-sole
manufacturer in the upper part of the city, pays for basting
covers on, 10 cents a dozen.   Some women baste five or six dozen
a day.   It requires care and a little skill.   If not properly done,
it is almost impossible to stitch them correctly.   He pays 6 cents
a dozen for stitching, and an operator can stitch from twelve to
twenty dozen a day.   He has often sold two hundred dozen in a
year.

479. Daguerreotype Apparatus.   In most large
cities, daguerreotype apparatus is manufactured.   A maker of
daguerreotype cases and materials told me that his girls earn
from 50 to 75 cents a day, the latter being the highest price ever
paid.   S., whose factory is in New Haven, employs about one hundred and fifty girls.   It is piecework.   The business is increasing,
but still is so limited that it cannot furnish employment for a
great many.   No difficulty is found in getting hands, as there are
a great many girls in New Haven.   No factory in the South or
West.   New York is the depot for everything made in a limited
quantity, and for everything new in style.   G. Brothers have
given work all the year until lately.   It is piecework.   Girls
earn from $4 to $6 a week.   It does not take a smart girl more
than eight days to learn.   The busy time commences in April.
It is an increasing business.   The foreman at A.'s factory said
a nice, steady, cleanly girl, that has sufficient dignity' to
command respect, can always get work.   One that is not very
sensitive to ridicule, and independent in the performance of duty,
will be sure to succeed in that establishment; for so many learners are taken in and need supervision, that such a one is sure to
be prized.   He has seventy-five girls.   It requires but a week to
learn, and the girl that instructs gets the profit of that week's
labor.   In some branches they stand, in some they sit.   They
are paid by the piece, and earn from $2 to $6 a week.   Some of
their girls learn bookbinding; so, when there is much to do in that
line, they find it difficult to get hands.   The manufacture of
daguerreotype apparatus is increasing; so the prospect for learners is good.   Most of his hands have work all the year.   He has
found many work girls very trifling.   (No wonder, with such train-

ing, and so little encouragement to do right.) They have all
their photograph pictures colored by ladies in New York, except
the glass ones. It pays well, and is done at home. I think some
lady would do well to learn to color the glass ones. No manufactories West or South. A firm in Waterbury write: " We
employ twelve women making daguerreotype mattings, &c. We
prefer them, because men work better with a few women to work
with them. We pay by the piece. They earn $3 per week, ten
hours a day. They are paid the same as male labor in the same
business. It requires one month to learn. Activity and
common sense are all that is necessary for a learner. The
majority are Americans, and pay for board $1.75 per week."

480. Feather Dressers. Those that purify the feathers
of beds, also renovate the hair and moss of mattresses. A gentleman told me he thought the business of a feather dresser too
hard for a woman. Carrying bags of feathers, weighing them,
assorting and filling other bags, he considered too heavy. Feathers are cleaned by steam. Some people, to renovate feathers,
place them in the sun for a few days in summer, and then bake
them. There is never any need of renovating feathers, if they
are properly cured at first.

481. Flag Makers. At A.'s, New York, the young
man said it requires about a year to learn the business thoroughly.
The hands employed in the house are paid by the week, and receive $4. They work from half-past seven to six o'clock, having
an hour at noon. Those working out of the house are paid by
the piece. They do not always have enough of good hands.
They do not require the girls to invent designs, but like to have
them quick to understand and execute any particular device or
new pattern. To sew well and rapidly are the principal qualifications. He thinks about two hundred women are employed in
this way in summer, but not more than fifty in winter. The
sewing and embroidering are confined exclusively to females. The
cutting is mostly done by those who carry on the business,
whether men or women. Learners receive a compensation of $2
per week while learning, after which they receive from $4 to $6
per week. Some employers require their hands to spend six
months at it as learners; but any one that can sew neatly, and has
taste, could as well make a flag, after it is cut out and basted, as
a bedquilt. The most busy seasons are spring, summer, and fall.
When employed by the week, the hours are ten. The business
is pretty well filled. Probably the most flags are made for vessels, and the next most for military and other processions. A
flag maker told me he employs some girls and women, paying from
thirty-seven to fifty cents a day, of ten hours, to those working in

his rooms. Those that work at home, often earn seventy-five cents, as they sew in the evening also, and are paid by the piece. He does all his cutting. He has most work to do in summer and in political campaigns. In winter, vessels are laid up, and consequently no flags are wanted for them. Most work is done in seaports. More is probably done in Boston than any other city. In Philadelphia, flag stitching is done by machines. He will not have it done so, because it will throw women out of employment, and their pay is small enough at best. He takes those that can sew, and pays from the first. He complains that most women are mere machines, and display no intelligence in their work. (Query: Whose fault is it?) Mrs. McF. pays her girls $3 a week, of nine and a half hours. She employs eight now (January, 1861), but sixteen in summer. In summer she makes flags for vessels, but in winter she has made national flags. When she wants any intricate pattern prepared, she employs a regular designer, but cuts the goods herself. Ability to draw well is a great assistance to a flag maker. She does all her own cutting, even to the letters that are placed on her flags. Her forewoman sometimes assists in cutting the figures. She works some for a house in Mobile that sells flags. It requires taste and ingenuity to succeed, but a good sewer can soon do the mechanical part. She has been in the business nineteen years. We suppose there are some openings in the South for this business.

482. Furniture Painters. F., who confines his business to the ornamenting of furniture, says it requires taste and a knowledge of colors. He thinks the Americans excel the Europeans in applying ornament to works of utility. He has a man of twenty-five that he employed when a boy in his store. He observed that he had such talents as would make him a good ornamental painter, so he gave him instruction. The first year he paid him $4 a week; the next, $6; and now he earns from $12 to $20. The young man invents when F. has given him an idea of the style he wishes. A manufacturer of enamelled furniture said no women are employed in enamelling, to his knowledge; that lifting and turning the furniture about would be too heavy for women. So it would; but they might have a man to do that. Another one told us he did not know of any women employed in enamelling furniture; but with a knowledge of painting, they might be. Men often earn $20 a week at it. A manufacturer of chairs told me that he pays ornamenters (men) from $9 to $18 a week, of ten hours a day. The men sit while painting them. A girl must have a natural taste for such work to succeed. The coloring requires experience. The French and Germans do most of it. It is piecework. A girl, no doubt, could get work, if she were competent. The Heywood Chair Company write : " We employ women to some extent in ornamenting chairs. The work is not considered especially unhealthy. We pay by the piece, and our women earn from $5 to $6 per week, averaging ten hours a day, the year round. There is no difference in the prices between the two sexes. Six months' apprenticeship is required, at $3 per week. Nimbleness, neatness, taste, and a true eye are needed in a worker. In ordinary times, there is no difference in the amount of work. We employ women, because they will do the same work better, faster, and cheaper than men. We would employ more, if they could perform other parts of the work. Women are inferior in strength to men, superior in manual dexterity, neatness, and taste. All are Americans. We can hardly speak with confidence of any considerable opening for female labor in our business. Most of our work requires skilled mechanics, or hard, rough bone and muscle. We have for five or six years employed all the females we could find room or work for, and can see no chance for any increase." According to the census of 1860, the number of hands employed in the New England, Middle, and Western States, in *making* furniture, were 21,953 males and 1,880 females.

483. Gilders of Mirror Frames. About the same arrangements are made with apprentices in this as in other trades. In the old country, women do as much of the work in all its branches as men; but in this country, the custom of women working in shops with men is not so common, and consequently some females that learned it in the old country will not engage in it, because of having to work with the men. I have been informed that in Dublin there are at least forty women employed in gilding —some in business for themselves. A good male worker earns $12 a week. Gilders calculate to make twenty cents an hour, the most usual price for good hands in all trades. In some trades men are paid twenty-five, some twenty, some eighteen, and in some but fifteen cents an hour. Gilders that manufacture frames for mirrors and artists, are most likely to have work all the year. In most shops there is a slack time just after New Year, and after the Fourth of July. It is a very close, confining business, in summer, while laying the gold leaf on, as it is so light it is apt to fly, and should be done in a close room. It is not at all unhealthy. Most of the work is done standing; but, I think, in gilding, women are permitted to sit. A German that sells ornamental furniture, thinks women might do the gilding on furniture. G. employs a number of girls in gilding oval frames. They earn, on an average, from $4 to $4.50. It requires but a short time to learn the business. B. used to employ some for the same purpose, paying $4, $5, and $6 a week. I think this work preferable for women to most mechanical employments, and, no doubt, in a few years many will be so occupied. I was told by a gilder that women are employed, because they can be had cheaper than men, seldom, if ever, receiving over $5 a week, of ten hours a day; and they have no knowledge of the business, except the one department in which they work. The frames are sold cheaply for photographs. There are no extensive gilders in the South or West, except one in Cincinnati, and one in Chicago. In the mirror and picture frame departments, there are now a great many stores that cut up the business of the large establishments, and the times are hard—so the business is dull. Not more than forty women in New York city are employed in gilding frames, and twenty of them are at G.'s. A gilder in New Hampshire writes: "It depends upon how much painted work there is in the same room whether the occupation is unhealthy. As far as my observation goes, women are as good workers at this business as men." One in Massachusetts writes: "My wife sometimes does my gilding, which is no harder than sewing. The carver's daughter in Essex, near here, did all his gilding for ten years." Gilders in Boston write: "We employ a girl to burnish, and pay from $3 to $5 per week, ten hours a day. Men get from $9 to $12. Fall and spring are the most busy seasons. Most of the cities northeast of Baltimore are good for this work. Board, $2 to $3."

484. Globe Makers. H., manufacturer of school apparatus in Connecticut, writes: "From four to six women are employed by us, in the construction of globes and other articles. Some are paid by the piece, and some by the week, and earn from $3 to $5 per week, ten hours a day. Women receive less than one half the wages of men. They do not perform the same kind of labor. Women are employed at the lighter work, requiring less strength, but an even amount of skill. The abundance of the supply of labor prevents the increase of wages. Learners are paid, and it requires but a few weeks to succeed. A nicety of eye and readiness of hand are necessary for a worker. The prospect of employment is good, but limited. The winter is best for the work, but hands are occupied at all seasons. The employment is pleasant, and as well paid as any in this vicinity. Women are employed in all parts of the work suitable for them. The work is best adapted to the Eastern States. All our employés are Americans, and live at home. Board here, $2 a week."

485. Hobby Horse Finishers. In summer time, Mr. —— has children's carriages trimmed by women. They are paid by the piece, and earn from $3 to $4 a week. At B.'s they are employed all the year. The horses and carriages could be painted by women, and the manes, tails, saddles and bridles could be put on by them. At C.'s, one lady is employed for trimming children's carriages—$5 a week—ten hours a day. She sews by machine. C.'s busy season for children's carriages, is from February to November, and he employs his hands the rest of the time at hobby horses. He says there is one factory in Columbus, two in Chicago. He thinks there are good openings (1860) in Richmond and Petersburg, Va., for they sell many there. He thinks wrong must succumb to right—that there is no justice in withholding from women their proper compensation for labor, and the time will come when the prejudice will be done away that now exists on that subject.

486. Horse Coverings. I was told, at a store in Philadelphia, they pay twenty-five cents a piece for ordinary blankets and linens, and a woman can make from three to four a day. One, on which was considerable chain stitching, the storekeeper paid $2 for making, and he thought a woman could make one in a day. A saddle and harness maker, New York, told me the prospect of getting such work is good. The wives of his workmen make his blankets, and can earn from $1 to $1.50 a day, as he pays thirty-seven cents a blanket. Another one told me his girls earn from $4 to $6 a week at such work; and another rated the payments still higher, from $1.25 to $1.50 a day. At a large store on Broadway, I was told all the work is given to one woman, who employs other women to help her. Her workers can earn $4 a week, if industrious. They make horse linens and blankets, and rosettes for head ornaments. Netting for horses is made by hand, in a large establishment near New York. L. L. & Co. pay for the coarsest blankets twenty cents apiece, and a woman can make two a day. For some they pay as high as from $4 to $5. A very swift sewer could make one such in little over two days —consequently her day's wages would be $2. So the prices vary according to style. The chain stitch, so much used for ornamenting, is done by hand, because in that way the edges of the cloth can be more neatly and securely turned under. L. L. & Co. employ ladies, who in their turn employ others. The coarse heavy blankets are generally lined, and the work is mostly done by Irish women. They are most busy on blankets from June to January, and on linen from February 1st to May 1st. Linen covers are used on horses in stables, as flies annoy horses much where they are standing quiet. Out of doors, nets answer, because they are kept in motion by the horse. When busy, L. & L. employ about one hundred girls. The business is growing. The blankets are

mostly used in the country. The manufacture of them is confined
principally to New York and Boston. Those in the cities are
different in style; indeed, each city has its own style. Many are
made in Chicago. The rosettes pay very well, but it requires a
long time to become expert. One lady they employ earns occasionally $50 a week. Tassels are paid for by the piece, and girls
can earn from $2 to $4. Tassel making requires some time to
learn perfectly. Cloth goods are confined to seasons, and consequently occupations in which they are involved are confined to
seasons. Styles of trimming are apt to change. A man who
makes blankets for a large wholesale house, employs from one
hundred to two hundred women. They earn from $3 to $7 a
week. The stitching is done by machine, but the ornamental
part by hand. Men do all the cutting. He has paid as high as
$100 for one pattern of blankets and ornaments. There are no
blankets made in the South or West, except here and there a sad-
dler's wife will make a few. In Williamsburg, I saw a number
of women in the basement of the employer's residence. They
looked sad, and the rooms were small, damp, and filthy. The employer told me most of his stitching is done by machine. Anybody that can sew tolerably well, and has strength, can do it.
Women seldom, if ever, cut them out; but I think they could.
A manufacturer in Brooklyn writes: "We employ women for
making horse clothing, who are paid by the piece, and earn from
seventy-five cents to $1 per day. Spring and fall are the best
seasons for work. We have no difficulty in procuring hands."

487. House Painters. The tools of a painter cost but
little. Women might be employed in glazing, and in painting the
inside work of houses. Their ingenuity and taste might be successfully exercised in embellishing walls and ornamenting doors.
The style for doors, called graining, would be particularly appropriate. The business could be best carried on by men and wom-
en in partnership, as the outdoor work is most suitable for men.
An apprenticeship should be served of two or three years. The
work would pay well. Most of it is done in spring. A woman
would need to make some change in her style of dress. The
Bloomer would probably be best—at any rate, hoops should be
laid aside. The vocation presents a very good opening to women,
who could best engage in it, at first, in towns and villages.

488. Japanners. Japanning is one of the few arts that
had its origin in a heathen country. It is now practised in all
civilized countries. Many metal articles are japanned—as tea
trays, candlesticks, &c. Wood is also japanned. In a late report of one of the schools of design in England, we observed on
the list of female students the names of two japanners. Care, and

ability to stand, are all that are required for success, to those doing the plain painting; but some taste is required for ornamental japanning. There is a good prospect for employment, as the tin trade has been increasing rapidly in the last two years, and is likely to, as our country grows older, and depends less on other countries for a supply. California has created quite a demand in the last few years, and it is supplied mostly from New York. M., in New York, told us he and his partner employ some women to japan. They pay from $3 to $4 a week. They have one woman to do the ornamental work, painting flowers and gilding. To ornamental painters they pay from $10 to $15 a week. They had a man to whom they often paid $15 a week. Most of the men that have been employed in ornamental japanning have gone to painting clocks, which pays better. They sometimes find it difficult to get hands—so if some women could take it up, they would be likely to find employment. The painters design as they paint, not using a pattern. Japanning of the heavy kind could not be done by women. The pieces are two heavy to lift. B., an ornamental japanner, used to employ women to put on the pearl scraps, but now employs boys, because he can get them cheaper and take them as apprentices. He can send them on errands and make use of them in that way. He pays an apprentice $1.50 a week for one year, then increases at the rate of fifty cents a week the next year, and so on. B. thinks no women are employed at it. Women are employed at such work in Paris. Japanning, he thinks, is not unhealthy, although the ovens into which japanners must pass are often heated to 260°. The spirits of tar used in japanning renders it healthy, and consumptives go frequently into japanning furnaces, feeling that they are benefited by it. At a firm of japanners, the boy told me they employ an artist to come and paint for them. They once had a lady that painted landscapes and flowers on piano boards in oils. They were not baked in a furnace afterward, but the oil permitted to dry, as with a painting on canvas. S. used to employ women in making pearl piecework, but it is not much used now. For painting clocks, not more than six cents a piece is paid for many. Men are so rapid that they can make money, but women could not earn more than $2.50 a week. Some men earn $25 a week, and formerly even $35, at painting the finer clocks; but there are now so many in the business that wages have fallen, though the business is increasing. At a tin manufactory in Williamsburg, I saw two girls employed in tying up goods, and seven girls employed in putting the first coat of paint on tin ware—grounding, it is called. They are paid from $1.25 up. One woman they have earns $6 a week. She is an English woman, and has been at the business nearly all her life.

She is quick and skilful. A boy who paints flowers on tin ware,
after the first coat is put on by the girls, gets $1 a day for his
work. Japanning is done in England by women. Many women
are employed through the country, in the Eastern States, in making tin canisters, &c., and some in japanning; but japanners carry
their work into ovens, which he thought would be too hard for
women. Yet he thinks doing so is not unhealthy. If the employment is unhealthy, it arises from the evaporation of the turpentine in the paint. The unhealthiness of the common painter's
business arises from the turpentine, in evaporating, carrying off
with it white lead, but no white lead is employed on the tin ware.
Girls are paid by the week. Men, for graining, a style resembling
the graining of wood, and in fact being the same except on a different material, received $2.50 per day. Male labor is twice or
three times as high in their establishment. Why women are not
better paid the man could not answer, but, like many other men
with whom I have talked, thought it unjust they were not paid
at the same rate as men. Their girls are employed all the year.
They work ten hours a day. They were mostly Americans, and
miserably dressed. The work soils their clothes greatly. They
wore old skirts over their dresses to work in. I think some men
and boys work in the same room with them. The fine work
could be well done by them, if they would take time to learn it
efficiently, for it requires taste, ingenuity, and delicacy of touch.
At an ornamental japanner's, I was told it requires three or four
years to learn the business well. A good workman earns from
$12 to $18 a week. It is piecework.

489. Knitters. The knitting done by machinery is not
so soft, so warm, or so durable as that done by hand. It is almost impossible to obtain ladies' hand-knit hose in cities. Gentlemen's are sometimes made by the Shakers, and bring a very high
price. We have no doubt but some old ladies might even now
find it profitable to knit to order, or supply some store where
their goods would be brought forward and disposed of to those
who can appreciate the difference between machine and hand knitting. The Germans are famous knitters. "The peasant women
of the Channel Islands, Jersey, Guernsey, &c., knit a great
deal. They are seldom, if ever, without the materials for this
occupation. On the way to and from market, and at other times,
knitting forms their almost constant employment." A knitting
machine has been invented in Seneca, N. Y., that is said to knit
a perfect stocking in less than five minutes. Aikens's knitting
machines are very popular. We have thought ladies would do
well to try them, and devote themselves to making up hosiery.
We doubt not but it would pay very well. The cloth is knit in

a straight piece, and another lady cuts it into shape and sews into the articles wanted. A machine has been invented by Mr. Aikens, also, for toeing and heeling socks. A manufacturer of knit goods writes : " We employ about twenty hands, one half of whom are girls. Their wages are from $3 to $5 per week, except when working by the piece. Those who run the knitting machines are paid by the piece, and earn from 75 cents to $1 per day. Males receive from $1 to $1.75 per day. The work done by them is generally harder, and such as females could not well do. To effectually superintend the knitting business would require at least five years. The part performed by females can be learned in six months. They are paid while learning, from $2.75 to $3 per week. The business is overdone at present; although there is always a demand in our section of country for girls. They work regularly throughout the year, twelve hours in summer, ten in winter. It would be better for all parties to run their mills only ten hours per day, and thus tend to keep down the production, and so keep up the prices to a fair profit. Those tending sewing machines are generally married, or widows with children, and in general support their families. Their machines are repaired by a foreman, but with a little practice they can learn to do it themselves. In other branches generally pursued by girls, they earn sufficient to dress well, but seldom accumulate. A location is preferred in some thickly settled place, on account of getting sewing done by hand, as all the goods are finished off by hand. After working twelve hours a day, they will be necessarily rather too much fatigued to go through any mental processes otherwise than reading a novel. If all the mills of all descriptions would work ten hours only, and establish evening schools, and request all to attend, it would greatly elevate them in the social scale. But selfishness rules, and where one manufacturer would agree to this arrangement, two would not. Board, $1.50 per week, including washing." A hose manufacturer in Holderness writes : " We employ about sixty females in the mill. Work is given out to three hundred. Almost all are American. Their wages are from $3 to $6 per week. The wages in the knitting department are not much less for women than men. Women learn the knitting so as to earn good pay in three months. Women are paid $2 per week for the first four weeks; after that, by the piece. A learner should be steady and quick with her fingers. The employment is healthy, as the knitters sit only about half the time. We run all the year eleven hours a day. There is not female help enough. We are trying women where men have been employed. I think women are in some respects superior workers to men." Manufacturers of seamless hosiery, in

Connecticut, write they "pay from $3 to $5 per week, eleven hours a day—that it requires from six to eight weeks to learn—that their hands have access to libraries; and board is for men $3, for women $2." At Cohoes, N Y., is a manufactory of shirts, drawers, &c. I have a letter from the company saying: "We employ two hundred and fifty women, and pay from 40 cents to $1 per day. Some are paid by the piece, and some by the week. Men receive from 75 cents to $2.50 per day, of twelve hours. The reason why they obtain better wages is that they do work which women cannot do. (Query: Do not the women perform work that men cannot do?) Men are continually learning. Women can learn to perform certain work in a few days. The best qualifications are soundness of mind and body, activity, steadiness, quick perception, and a desire to make money. The business is increasing yearly. Occasionally, in the winter, the mills stop for a month. There is at present (October, 1860) a surplus of labor. Board, $1.75 to $2." At L.'s knitting factory, in Brooklyn, the foreman told me there are six machines in operation, each of which cost between $5,000 and $6,000. The articles made by them are softer than any knitting done by machine I have seen; but it may be owing to the quality of the wool: I cannot say. Those working at machines stand, the others sit. The machine operators receive from $1.50 to $3.50: those in the finishing room are paid by the piece, and earn from $2 to $5. A foreman superintends the work and puts the machinery in order. A woman of good abilities can learn in three months, if the factory is in a position to put her forward. From May to December is the best time for work. Double price is paid the hands for night work in busy times. They prefer American girls, because they are neater. A manufacturer of factory supplies, in Massachusetts, writes: "We employ thirty women in knitting loom harnesses. The work is not more unhealthy than any employment that requires one to sit all the time. They are paid by the piece. The employment is sure so long as cotton manufacturing is good. The work is equally good all seasons. Board, $1.62 to $2.25 per week." The secretary of the Waterbury Knitting Company writes: "We employ one hundred hands, at from 50 cents to $1 per day, working twelve hours in summer, ten in winter. Women are paid as well or better than men of the same age; working by the piece, they are paid the same. The women are not thrown out of work at any season. Women are inferior in mechanical genius. We are obliged to keep a man to every fifteen women to overlook them. A woman will run a knitting machine for seven years, and never be able to straighten a needle, or knit the cloth slack or tight. A boy or man will learn to oversee a whole room in half that time. Women cannot be made to think or act for themselves in the least thing, or in any case to rely on their own judgment. This is equally true of the stupid Irish, German, and English, and of the more acute Yankee. Women are superior perhaps in good looks." S., of Enfield, N. H., has his daughter write : " I use three of Aikens's knitting machines, and other machinery for making yarn. The wool is first made into yarn and then knit into webbing, and marked for heeling and toeing. It is then divided into dozens, and distributed around the country to be heeled and toed, in which branch we employ usually five hundred American women. We pay $1 a dozen for heeling and toeing; for tending the machine, $2 per week, of eleven hours a day. Women are paid less, because they are not usually as strong as men, and therefore cannot do the same work, or, if the same kind, not so great an amount in a limited time. Men can be employed by paying them what they require, and as they are considered, or rather *seem to consider themselves* the ' lords of creation,' they demand higher wages than women. In four weeks the females can perform their part without trouble. Learners receive their board. The prospect is good for the same number employed as at present. The summer season is the best for work. If at any time there is a want of work, it is in January and February."

490. Lace Bleachers. Mrs. L. spent five years learning the business in Paris. A girl that spent two years learning with her, is now doing well in the business in St. Louis. She prefers to take learners a week on trial. She charges from $1 to $1.50 a pair for curtains. The French are the most successful in that line. She often has thirty or more pair from a hotel and other large houses. One can make a good living at it. L. says the work is unhealthy, particularly while the vapor of the chemicals is warm. The curtains are not wrung out, but the water pressed out with the hands. The dirt, of course, is first washed out. It requires strength to handle the goods. Curtains are put on frames to dry, and women, he says, are not strong enough. It requires strength to get the extra starch out, as it is done by squeezing. It is surprising how many objections, as regards health and physical strength required, can be presented by selfish men, who do not wish women to engage in their occupations. None but those who have had occasion to test the matter would believe it possible that the majority of men are so selfish and unjust in this respect. Another man told me he does all the washing and drying himself, because he is responsible for the goods, and is not willing to trust them to strangers. He charges $1 a pair, except for a very large size. Different kinds of laces require different methods of washing and ironing.

491. Lacquerers. Lacquering is warm work, and in summer is done in rooms the temperature of which is over 200°. M. thought women could be employed in burnishing, lacquering, polishing, and bronzing. Girls were at one time employed in lacquering gas fixtures on William street, New York; but they were dismissed, because they did not prove steady and efficient workers. The process previous to lacquering, called dipping, is dirty work. It requires but a short time to learn to lacquer. F. told me that in France women do all the fine lacquering, and they do it much better than men can. They take it home with them to do; and the same plan could be followed in this country, and probably will be before long. The finest lacquering, such as ormolu clocks, &c., is done with gold dust. The varnish must be put on evenly. It requires care and delicacy of touch. Most of the gas fixtures sold as brass are merely zinc gilded, and then lacquered—the bronzed part the same metal, bronzed. Zinc can be bought at six cents a pound—brass is thirty cents a pound. Mathematical instruments, daguerreotype cases, and gas fixtures are lacquered. A man earns from $8 to $10 a week, working ten hours a day. Lacquering, I was told, is not unhealthy, and a person can sit two or three feet from the fire while at work. A firm in New York, manufacturing gas fixtures, wrote to us as follows: " Lacquering is a suitable occupation for women; but we do not employ them, because men are considered more reliable as to regularity of hours, and are more easily managed. Women can be made equally good lacquerers with the men; but when employed by us, some years since, we found, with few exceptions, that they produced inferior work, owing, as we think, to want of application. Women are employed in similar establishments to ours in England and, we learn, in Boston. The employment is not unhealthy. They are paid by the week in England. It requires from three to five years to learn the business. Steady application and a good eye for colors will make a good lacquerer."

492. Life Preservers. R. employs two women to stitch his life preservers with a sewing machine, and pays the usual price of operatives. None are made South or West. (Would not New Orleans offer an opening?)

493. Lucifer Matches. This is a business that has been largely entered into in New York. The making and selling of matches have furnished employment for hundreds and thousands of boys and girls in all our large cities. The making of matches is a dangerous employment. Its unhealthy tendency (owing to the use of sulphur), and the long period of twelve, and even fourteen hours' confinement, no doubt serve to account for the sad and woe-begone faces of the poor little operators. At a match factory where I stopped, girls are paid three cents a gross for cutting matches and filling boxes. Some can do as many as forty gross a day; but very few can. It is best for girls to commence early in life, and most do so. Some girls earn as much as $5 to $6 per week, if we may believe the proprietor's statement. Girls are paid for filling the frames in which they are to be dipped, sixty-two cents 100 frames, each frame containing 1,500 double, or 3,000 single matches. The factory is open from seven in the morning to ten at night. The business for women and girls is not crowded. Most learners become discouraged and leave it, because it is so long before they can become expert enough to earn fair wages. It is not as healthy, he says, as some occupations. I should think not, judging from his sallow face, and the pale, spiritless faces of all I have seen in the match factories. He buys bundles of sticks, ready to cut for matches, of those who make it a business to prepare them. They are cut by hand. He pays twenty-five cents a bunch, and a man can cut a bunch in five minutes. They never stop work, except in December and January. A brisk hand can earn from $5 to $7 a week. They make from twenty to forty different kinds of matches, to suit all climates. At the store of this manufacturer, the bookkeeper told me that, if a person has a tooth extracted, the phosphorus will be absorbed by the jaw bone and cause it to decay, if the individual works in the factory before the gum is entirely well. A lady told me she knows a girl that earns $6 a week in a match factory. In H.'s factory, I saw small girls and boys putting matches in the frames to be dipped. They are paid sixty cents 100 frames, containing 1,500 double matches. They can seldom fill more than 85 frames a day. They commence work at $6\frac{1}{2}$ in winter, and work until 8; in summer, they commence at 6, and work until $7\frac{1}{2}$. They are not obliged to work all the time, as they are paid by the piece; but with the exception of an hour at noon, which all have the privilege of taking, they no doubt work the full time. They were poor, dirty-looking children. In the room where the boxes were filled, large girls worked. Most match makers are Germans and Irish. A manufacturer told me that he now employs boys only—that girls he found so wild he could not manage them. He says some of his girls used to earn $5 a week. He thinks none but strong, healthy persons should work at the business, as the fumes of sulphur are injurious. A manufacturer in Vermont writes: "Women are employed to pack matches. They are paid by the thousand, and their wages amount to fifty cents per day, of ten hours, after they get accustomed to it. Women's work in this department is lighter than men's—so will not yield as good wages. A learner will gain the trade in about six months. An increase of this business is not flattering. No difference in the seasons for work. Women are more nimble in the use of their fingers, and consequently succeed better in this kind of work."

494. Mat Makers. Door mats are made of sea grass, corn husks, worsted, manilla, hemp, and cocoa-nut fibre. At the largest manufactory in the United States, I saw the process of making several kinds. No girls or women were employed. The superintendent told us it was too heavy work for women. In one establishment in Philadelphia, girls are employed as tenders, which is merely picking the substance to be woven—jute, hemp, or wool—into bunches of the right thickness, and handing to the weaver. Some of their mat weavers earn $14 a week—boys, from $1.50 to $3. Mats are sometimes made by women of osier, rushes, and straw

495. Manufacturers of Musical Instruments. The manufacture of different musical instruments is engaged in as so many distinct branches of business. Musical instruments are usually classed as follows: 1. Wind instruments, of wood or metal. 2. Stringed instruments. 3. Keyed instruments. 4. Instruments of percussion. 5. Automatic instruments. 6. Miscellaneous articles in connection with musical instruments. On wind instruments made of wood and ornamented with metals, as flutes, clarionets, &c., women might be employed to polish the metal. Those that are all metal, as horns, trumpets, &c., are polished in making, and could not well be divided into a separate branch of work. Of stringed instruments, the ornamental part, as painting, inlaying of pearl, &c., would be very pretty work for women of taste. The smaller strings could be covered by women. Of keyed instruments, some of the smaller and finer work would be very suitable for women. In instruments of percussion, the drum and tambourine are probably the only instruments presenting a field for woman's work. Of automatic instruments, mechanical organs are the only ones, I think, at which women do work. I cannot learn that women are employed in making musical boxes, which are imported from Switzerland, Germany, and France. Women are employed to some extent, in other countries, in the manufacture of musical instruments. Z. thinks the reason women are not employed in the manufacture of musical instruments in this country is, that they do not understand the business.—1. *Wind Instruments.* Women might polish the metal on flutes, and even paint the woodwork. I was told by a manufacturer in New York, whose factory is in Connecticut, that he once employed women in that way, but they did not suc-

ceed, because they did not try.—2. *Stringed Instruments.* I called on L., engaged in the manufacture of harps. There are but two
harp manufacturers in the United States. Ladies might do the
gilding and ornamental painting on harps. Sizing is put on,
and then gold leaf laid on, and smoothed down with a small
brush. The varnishing could be very well done by women. The
same kind of work is executed on guitar frames, of which a
number are made in the United States. The painting is done
as on enamelled furniture. L. employs an Englishman to do the
gilding and ornamental painting. The other manufacturer, B.,
thinks there is no part of the work in making harps that could
be done by a lady. The ornamental part is done by the var-
nisher, and varnishing requires much strength. It requires a
regular apprenticeship, and some artistic taste. So few harps are
made in this country, that it would not pay a woman to learn. He
was evidently opposed to women having anything to do with
the business.—3. *Keyed Instruments. Accordions.* In making accordions women could put on the keys and kid, and do so in
Germany. Accordions are nearly all imported, because they can
be made more cheaply in Europe than in this country. L., Philadelphia, says he is in partnership with his brother in Germany,
who has musical instruments made there, and employs a number
of women and girls.—*Melodeons.* C., New York, manufacturer,
say he does not know of any women being employed in the making
of melodeons; but much of the work, I am sure, could be done
by women. Cutting the keys, polishing, gluing them on the
board, and fastening the hammers on, are done by hand, and the
work is as suitable for women as men. Men receive for such work,
$2 a day. Women properly trained, and with a good ear for
music could also tune the instruments. Men who do so, earn
about $3 a day. A manufacturer of melodeons writes : " We do
not employ women, but think larger firms might."—*Organs.* I
was told by a manufacturer that in Germany some women assist
their husbands in making the action, but there is lighter work
and more of it in piano actions. J., another organ builder, told
me that in England, in some organ factories, women are employed to gild the pipes. In making the organs turned by a crank,
used in some churches in England, women, he said, are employed
in putting the pins in the cylinders. They are made on the same
principle as the music box. J. seldom makes more than one of
these organs in a year, and I think he is the only one in the
United States that does make them. Mrs. Dall says " there
are women, who strain silk in fluting, across the old-fashioned
workbag, or parlor organ front."

Pianos. In England, the men engaged in making piano actions used to do much of the work at home, and their wives and daughters would assist them. In the United States, each branch in the making of pianos is now done separately, except in very large establishments, and consequently most of the work is done at home by the workmen. At a factory in New York, an apprentice, nearly out of his time, told me that an individual to learn the business is bound, and must remain until of age. Otherwise he could not get a certificate, and is not likely to find employment without one. An apprentice receives $3 a week the first year, $4 the second year, and more afterward if he is bright and quick to learn. A journeyman receives from $10 to $12 a week for his work. At W.'s piano manufactory, New York, we were kindly permitted to pass through and see the entire process of making. Among other parts that I thought could be done by women, were those of varnishing and polishing. This work forms a separate branch of itself, and requires an apprenticeship of three or four years. It looked to be very simple. The pianos are first rubbed with pumice stone, to render them smooth and susceptible of a polish, then with rotten stone. Rubbing with pumice stone all day might be too laborious, except for a very strong woman; but the other process is feasible for any woman of moderate health. Indeed, the finest polish could be better given by women than men, because it is done by the naked hand, and the softer the hand the better. The ornamenting of the sounding boards could be done by women that know anything of painting, and also the gilding on the inside top and outside front. I asked an old Frenchman, doing that kind of work, how long it would require to learn. He said he had been at it fifty years, and had not learned it perfectly yet. It is pretty work, and very suitable for a woman of taste. The delicacy of woman's touch, with some knowledge of drawing and painting, would enable her to succeed. Covering wire, and putting it in, is another branch that might be done by women. Bleaching ivory for the keys, cutting them, and gluing them on, are also within woman's range. Cutting leather and buckskin, and gluing it on the hammers, are very light and simple work. Another branch suitable for women is regulating the tone of pianos. Men, said W., would oppose women working at the piano business in large establishments, but a man would not be likely to suffer inconvenience from employing women in his own house to do the part he carries on. If he were independent of his business it would be better. At ——'s, New York, a manufacturer of pianoforte actions, I saw two girls at work. It is very nice, clean work. Part of the time they stand, and the remainder they sit.

One is paid $3 a week, and the other less. The young man who showed us through the factory, said much of the work in making pianoforte action that is now done by men could be done by women. D—'s girls looked to be Americans. They have work all the year. It mostly consists in covering hammers. A manufacturer of pianofortes writes: " Our men are paid both by the piece and by the week, according to the departments in which they are engaged. The time of learning is from five to seven years for men. Apprentices (boys) are paid from 25 cents to $1 per day, beginning with the first amount, and increasing from year to year. In some departments, physical strength is required, in others, aptness and ready tact—in others, a cultivated musical ear. The prospect for future employment is very fine in all branches for men—in some, equally good for women. The majority of workmen are below mediocrity, as compared with most all others in manufacturing." A manufacturer in Meredith, N. H., writes: " We once employed a lady in our key and action department. She was the wife of one of our workmen. She earned as much as her husband, and in every respect did her work as well. She learned her trade in half the time it took her husband to learn the same. Theirs was jobwork; the two earned about $3 per day. She did her housework besides. I think there might be many ladies employed in our business, to the advantage of all concerned. We expect to test the matter further by employing some in our varnish rooms soon."

Seraphines. A manufacturer writes: " I think women might be employed to advantage in some parts of the work, and in any part of it, if they could adopt a different style of dress, something like the Bloomer. The long dress with hoops, as now worn, must be an insurmountable barrier against their entering many employments. It is injurious to health, and prevents a proper development of form."

496. Musical String Makers. The manufacture of strings for musical instruments is carried on as a separate branch. A German violin maker told me that women are employed in Germany in winding wire for guitar strings. I find they are also in a factory in Connecticut, and the manufacturer said they could earn as high as $9 a week. It is rather severe on the fingers, but that can be avoided to some extent by wearing a glove finger. In New York, it is mostly done by Germans and French, who have taken the trade from Americans. The preparing of catgut from the intestines of sheep and goats, and making it into strings, is carried on mostly in Germany, and some women are employed at that. Most metal strings are of steel, and covered with fine wire of other metals. Mrs. Z., whose husband, when living, manufactured covered strings for musical instruments, told me, she and her daughters had often assisted in covering guitar strings and the lighter piano strings. She thinks a person of good abilities could learn it in from two to four weeks, with an attentive instructor. She usually rested against a bench while employed. A good worker will earn from $3 to $5 per week. She has never heard of any but English and German women being engaged in it. In some of the up town shops the machinery is moved by steam, but it does not answer so well, because it is not so easily slackened or checked. Harp strings and the larger piano strings cannot be made by women, because of the strength and firmness required.

497. Netters. Netting is now generally done by machinery. Seines are mostly made in that way. When by hand, it is done by old people, who receive a very inadequate compensation for their labor. The nets so much used for horses are mostly made in a large factory near the city of New York. In England, woollen netting is used by some gardeners for the protection of the bloom of fruit trees from frost. They are also used to prevent birds destroying currants, cherries, raspberries, and other small fruit. The making of purses of different kinds, and of hammocks, have employed a small number of people. Net and seine manufacturers in Gloucester write me: "We employ one hundred women who work at their homes, and are paid by the piece. It requires a year to learn. From October to June are the best seasons for our trade. A few that we employ to work by the week spend ten hours a day at it. The comfort of the occupation is good, but the pay poor. We think women better company than men. Health and strength are the best qualifications for our work. A net and twine company in Boston write: "We employ women for converting twine into netting. It is mostly job work, and they have cash for what they earn. The comparative prices of men and women are the same as those of factories in general. It requires about as long to learn as it takes a woman to learn to knit stockings. The business is good as long as the sea furnishes fish and mankind eat them. The employment of women in the work is a providential necessity. Nearly all ours are American. Women are quicker in their work—men stronger. Our women have the leisure that belongs to nearly all manual occupations."

498. Oakum Pickers. Perhaps some one reading this book may not know what oakum is. It is old rope, pulled to pieces until it is soft and pliable, like the original material, and used for the purpose of corking vessels. Ten years ago, the picking was done by hand, and many women employed. Now, this work is mostly done by machinery in this country, and very few women are employed. In some factories, women are employed in teazing, that is, untwisting the pieces of rope that are not pulled to pieces by passing through the machinery the first time. They are paid so much per hundred pounds, and do not earn more than $2 a week. It is dirty, disagreeable work. A firm in Maine write: "We have seen females, both young and old, at work in oakum mills in the State of New Jersey. In England (we believe) all oakum is made in their almshouses, consequently a part by females. The business is healthy. We use many boys that do work which might be done by females; but we prefer the boys."

499. Paper Hangers. An English lady, who has spent much time in various parts of Europe, told me she had known of women being engaged in paper hanging in small towns. I believe it is customary, when papering a room, to have one person put the paste on, and another put it up. We are confident women could do the first-mentioned part of the work.

500. Polishers. Women are employed in France in polishing furniture. They are mostly the wives of cabinet makers. It requires art to do it that some can never learn. A person must be able to put the gum shellac on evenly. A woman in London earned a very good living by applying French polish to the furniture of cabinet makers. A French woman that polished furniture in Paris, told me that the work is hard on the fingers, and one could not learn it in less than a year. A piano manufacturer told me that women could be profitably employed in polishing pianos. It is better learned by women than men, he thought. It is tedious, however, and requires patience. I have been told that the finest polish is imparted to furniture by the naked hand, and the softer and finer the hand the better. For that reason, women are employed in France to polish piano cases with the palms of their hands, and, when not employed, wear kid gloves to keep their hands soft and smooth.

501. Pure Finders. The finders of dog pure constitute a small class in this country; but Mr. Mayhew thinks in the city of London there are between two hundred and three hundred constantly employed. It is used for dressing leather and kid, and sold at from sixteen to twenty cents a bucketful. In our country, it is probably carried on with bone grubbing and rag gathering.

502. Rag Cutters. I find nearly all rag cutters are Irish, and they are mostly old women or young girls. The girls usually earn about 75 cents or $1 a week. I called at a rag dealer's, and was told by a woman that one cent a pound is paid

20*

for cutting the seams off, taking the linings out, and removing the buttons. A woman can earn, she says, from $2 to $2.50 a week. It is not unhealthy. They grow fat on it. Theirs are mostly old women, and all are Irish. For assorting they are paid by the week, and receive $2.75. They work from seven to five in winter; in summer, ten hours. The keeper of the wareroom sells his rags for making paper, and sends many to Europe. The women work all the year. No other kind of work could be done by women in that business, as the only other is packing in bales, and that, of course, must be done by men. The warerooms close at six; so the women have the evenings for themselves. P., a rag dealer, says he buys and sells according to the quality of the rags. It is customary to pay by the week for sorting rags. Some get $2, and some $2.50. Cutting the seams off is paid for by the pound. The odor was extremely offensive (it was a damp day); but the man said it was not unhealthy, unless the rags are worked with in a close room; then the dust is apt to affect the eyes. Occasionally the small pox is taken from rags. I called at a rag dealer's, and was told by a filthy, squalid, barefooted girl at work, that for cutting up rags a penny a pound is paid. She was assorting. For that work, hands are paid twenty-five cents a day, and their board. It is very dirty work. The dust and sand must affect the eyes and lungs. Some men can cut as many as thirty-five pounds a day. Men are paid twice as much as women for assorting. I inquired why. I was told by a young junk dealer, standing by, that they could pick twice as much in the same time, the truth of which the reader can decide as well as I. Some men earn at it, he said, $6 a week. A woman, who seemed to have some interest in the place, remarked the girls have work all the year. Called at the door of a large wareroom, where I saw men assorting waste paper to be sold for the purpose of being made into new paper.

503. Rag Gatherers. The chiffoniers or rag gatherers of Paris are said to number about 6,000; those of London about 800 or 1,000. The chiffonier in Paris can collect only from eight in the evening until early next morning, as the streets are all swept before six o'clock in the morning, as after that time until eight in the evening the citizens are passing. A few in Paris have realized fortunes; but we suspect the most, in all countries, barely gain a subsistence. They all lead a hard and gloomy life. In the United States, most of the rags collected are converted into paper. Some are sold at shoddy manufactories, and those unfit for either shoddy or paper are spread over corn land, or used as a fertilizer for hops. One of the most handsome buildings on Broadway is said to be owned by a man that commenced life in the petty business of a rag collector. So much for economy and industry! Most of the rag pickers in New York live in the Five Points, and near the Central Park. Scarcely any person that has seen the old women rag pickers of New York in rain and snow, cold and driving winds, partially clad, can ever deny that a woman is capable of very hard and degrading labor, when driven to it by want. Rag picking and rag assorting are distinct branches. Rag pickers make the most, and are chiefly Germans. The number of rag gatherers in New York is very great, and the majority of them are women. I never observe the face of an American or French woman. Rag gatherers have each their own province, and none of the rest dare intrude. The majority do not confine themselves to picking up rags only, but bones and bits of metal and glass. Some even carry a basket in which they gather waste vegetables or putrid meat, or the trimmings of uncooked meat, which they feed on themselves, or give to a pet pig, or trade with some neighbor better off that has a cow. When the rag collectors reach their homes, they assort the articles they have collected. They separate the rags into clean and dirty (the last they wash), into linen and woollen, and the paper into clean and dirty, white and colored. The life led by rag gatherers is very laborious, as they must spend all the hours of daylight on their feet, walking many miles. Their earnings are so scanty that they must be out in all kinds of weather. The enormous rent they pay for wretched accommodations is a disgrace to the landlords. Many of them sleep a dozen in a room, on the bare floor. By the most rigid economy and unremitting industry, a few are enabled to lay by a small sum for old age, or purchase a little cottage and a plot of ground, when they change their filthy occupation for a more healthy and agreeable one, that of raising vegetables for the market. If I had to make a living on the streets of New York, I would prefer carrying a wheel around to grind knives and scissors, or putting window-glass in, to collecting rags, for the work of neither is so filthy. The children of rag gatherers begin very early to follow the pursuit of their parents. I saw some children one day picking rags, that told me they received two cents a pound. They were at the dirt heaps where carts of dirt from town had been emptied. They sometimes gather forty pounds each a day. They cannot do so well in winter. I saw a rag collector who starts at five in the morning, and is gathering rags until eight in the evening. She eats nothing during the time. She was German. Her father and mother also gather rags. Her father sells them at two cents a pound. She did not know how many pounds she gathered, but said she got three large bags full every day in good weather. I saw other collectors, who told me they

gather each from ten to thirty pounds a day. Some families succeed in gathering from fifty cents' to $1.50 worth a day, in good
weather and good seasons. " The prices paid for the staple articles of their trade, purchased exclusively by middlemen, are :
bones, 36 cents per bushel ; rags, whether linen or woollen, $1
per cwt. ; paper, $1 per cwt. ; and these sell them again to the
down-town customers, the rags at $2.50 to $3.50 ; the paper at
$1.25 to $1.50 ; with a proportionate advance on bones, and all
the articles in the junk business."

504. Rope and Twine Makers. Ropes are made
of the fibres of various plants, and particular kinds of grasses,
and the fibres of the cocoanut cover. Hair from the manes and
tails of horses is also used. Hemp and flax are most common in
the United States. The simplest mode of making rope is under
long sheds. After the material is spun into yarn, it is doubled
or trebled, and twisted. Ropes for the rigging of vessels employ
a large number of men. The great variety and amount of cordage used make it an extensive trade. Ropes are now manufactured in some places by steam. A small number of women are
employed in rope making. S. & M., Philadelphia, employ about
fifty female hands. Some are engaged in spinning, and a dexterous woman will keep from forty to fifty spindles in constant
motion, some at carding, some at balling. The last-named operation is the only one in which the women can sit while at
work. They work ten hours, and earn from $1.50 (for young
girls), to $5 a week (for the experienced frame spinners). The
last mentioned are mostly English, Scotch, or Irish women,
who have followed the trade from childhood. It requires long
practice to command the highest wages. A good steady hand is
much valued, and is not liable to be thrown out of work. Water
power is used with the machinery. W., New York, employs
them in his manufactory for spooling only. A manufacturer on
Long Island writes : " I pay my hands $1 a week, for the first
four weeks ; then $1.50 a week, for the next four weeks ; and
for the four weeks following, $2 per week ; and so increase their
wages till I allow them $3.50 per week. I employ mostly boys
and girls. I pay them the same, regardless of sex. They work
from ten to twelve hours, and are employed all the year. Board,
$1.25 to $1.50 per week. At eighteen, my boys learn a trade.
I pay my hands well and use them well. I do not receive children
under twelve years of age. I encourage them in going to school
before and after they work in my factory." There are only two
factories of this kind in New York city that employ women. The
proprietor of the largest gave me the following items : " I employ thirteen girls and women (mostly Irish) in spooling, twist-

ing, &c. Most are paid by the week. Women receive $3.50; girls, from $1.15 to $3.50. The time of learning is one, two, or three weeks, according to the kind of work, and the ability of the girl. The prospect is poor for more learners. My girls work ten hours a day, and have employment the year round. There are enough of hands in New York. Some of the minor parts could be performed by women, that are not, but not enough to give many employment. Cities are the best for selling the article, country the best for making. Men do not perform the same kind of work women do. Women are best suited to their branches. Boys could be got to do the work of the girls for as low wages. Indeed, most boys work for less in New York than girls." We think the last assertion a mistake on the part of H. The agent of the Royal River Yarn and Twine Company writes: " We consider our employment healthy. It proves so. Take, for instance, a certain number, at random, of different ages, employed in cotton mills, and compare with the same number, taken in the same way, from farm neighborhoods, and you will find more sickness and death among farmers' daughters." (This is rather a startling statement, but we are not prepared to disprove it.) He adds : " The regularity in exercise, taking meals, and resting, accounts, I think, for the steady employment in cotton mills, and the like, being so conducive to health. I have been engaged as a machinist, &c., about a cotton mill, for thirty-five years ; and, according to my observation, more girls improve their health, taking ordinary care of themselves, than otherwise. Part of our hands are paid by the week, and part by the piece. They have from $2 to $4.50 per week, new hands having only $2. It takes from three months to two years to learn. Common sense and industrious habits are the only qualifications needed. Spring and summer are the best seasons, but work is furnished continuously the year round. Our girls go home now and then to spend a few weeks, visit, fix their clothing, &c. To shorten their time would be rather a disadvantage, as capital invested must pay, or no encouragement would be given to invest more. Demand for hands is steady ; and if a surplus, it is on the neatest and lightest kind of work. Women are neater, steadier, and more active than men. Our girls make the best of housewives. Overseers, agents, and business men marry them, and we may look around and see, in some that have worked in mills, the brightest and best mothers of the land. The faculties of the mind are quickened by the busy hum and movement of machinery. Board, $1.50, respectable and comfortable. Parties not regarding that, would not have respectable help."

505. Sail and Awning Makers. I think it would require considerable strength and long practice to make sails, but not more than some occupations in which women are engaged. L. sometimes employs women to run the binding on awnings, paying 2 and 2½ cents a yard. He thinks no women are employed in the United States in making sails. They worked at tents during the Mexican war, but now only men are employed. S. knows that, in France, women make the lightest kind of sails. In Russia, sails are made by women. A sail maker in a large maritime city writes : " Some women are employed in sail making in Massachusetts. It is a healthy trade, and men spend three years learning it. A sail maker needs a tough constitution and steady habits. Some parts of the work are suitable for women. The best locations are on the lakes or in seaport towns." An awning manufacturer told me he employs girls in summer, and pays from $4 to $5 a week, of ten hours a day. They work by hand, and bind and put on fringe. T. employs some girls for binding. They can earn from $3 to $4 a week when constantly employed. He usually pays by the week, and has it done in his shop. A sail maker in Connecticut writes : " Women are employed at sail making in France. A knowledge of arithmetic and draughting are essential. The work is done at all seasons. The occupation is filled. It is usual to spend four years as an apprentice. The best locations are in seaports or river towns. I think the occupation is too laborious for women."

506. Shoe-Peg Makers. A shoe-peg manufacturing association, in New Hampshire, furnish me a report of the work they have done by women, as follows : " Women are employed only to feed the machine with prepared blocks, and sorting pegs after they are split. The work is light, and well adapted to the physical capacity of girls and women. They can do the work just as well as young men and boys, and perhaps a little quicker. Wages are perhaps two thirds as much as that of men in the same branches. Two hundred women would do all the work, in their several departments, in the business, for the whole of North and South America. We employ sixteen in our mill, at $3.50 per week, including board, which is called about $1.75. Men are not employed in the same branches. A part could be learned in one month—nearly half of it would require from six to twelve months. Girls are paid $3 a week, while learning. Nothing needed but ready and quick application. They work eleven hours. Each hour less would be more than a private loss. All are Americans."

507. Shroud Makers. There is something repulsive in death—the shroud—the cap—the coffin—the sunken eyes—the still hands and ghastly face. Death is fearful, even in its mildest forms. And yet how we yearn for rest—how we long for quiet! How we pant for that glorious freedom from anxiety and care, that awaits the just in heaven! The change of the chrysalis to the butterfly, of the seed to the plant, of the earth beneath our feet, and the heavens above—the very consciousness within us, all proclaim unmistakably the truth that the spirit will not die—that it is immortal. There are duties connected with the house of mourning that afflicted friends and relatives have not the heart to perform. These, therefore, devolve upon persons interested in the dead, or hired attendants. Closing the eyes, washing the body, making the shroud and putting it on, are in some cases performed by the hired nurse, but generally making the shroud is done by the undertaker's wife. Some undertakers keep shrouds in their shops ready for sale. In large cities, an undertaker's wife is in many cases sent for by the nurse, to assist in laying out the dead, and receives, as a compensation, from $3 to $5. The wife of an undertaker told me that she lines the coffins for her husband. They buy their caps already made, of an old lady who brings them around. Mr.——, an undertaker, is always willing to dress the remains of any but those who have died of small pox. He charges $3 to wash and dress a corpse, $5 with shaving. An undertaker told me he knew women could be employed in plaiting the folds of silk in coffins, and making coffin pillows. The wholesale trade send away large quantities of shrouds and caps, and so have many made up. A man in Newark, who devotes himself exclusively to making shrouds, employs several women. In England, some undertakers employ women to make up mourning suits.

508. Sign Painters. Sign painting requires a long, steady, and regular apprenticeship. It requires also a correct eye and a steady hand. In large cities, sign and ornamental painting can be made a distinct branch of painting; but in a town or village it is combined with carriage or house painting, as one individual seldom has enough sign and ornamental painting to keep him constantly occupied. It is not more necessary for a painter to know how to mix the paints, and use judgment and taste in the selection of colors, than to form letters according to geometrical proportions. A painter must measure, more by the eye than a rule, the size and arrangement of letters in a given space. Good painters receive $3, $4, and $5 a day for their work, but generally are paid by the piece. When paid by the week, and they work regularly, they receive from $12 to $15 a week. Mrs. K., New York, says in Dublin there are many families that devote themselves to sign painting, but she knows of none in this country except her own. She employs a man to grind paints, put up signs, &c.,—also to paint out-of-door signs, that is, such as must be painted on the building. Her two daughters paint all the signs that are to be put up. Some of the large signs above stores in New York have been painted by them. They are paid as good prices as men. She thinks an individual should commence early to learn. Her daughters received their instruction and advice from their father. In that way they acquired maturity of judgment and nicety of hand. Judgment needs to be exercised in regard to size and space, and artistic taste in ornamenting. A sign painter told me that superior workers can earn from $3 to $15 a day, if they have sufficient employment. Many house and other painters, in cities, profess to paint signs, but in reality have it done. Germans do much of it in New York, because they do it cheaply, but many of them do not execute their work well. It is customary to have an apprentice three years, and pay the usual terms, $2.50 a week, the first year. A boy, during the first year, mostly grinds paints, goes errands, &c. Spring is the most busy season. Painting in oils is not neat work. A sign and carriage painter writes me: "The work is unhealthy on account of the poisonous vapors and dust. It requires two or three years to learn, and one must have a great deal of practice. A common education, natural taste, and a correct eye are the qualifications needed. Many parts of it are very easy and pleasant. Some parts might be done by women." The business pays best in large towns and cities. An ornamental painter writes me: "Women are employed in sign painting in England, France, Germany, and Belgium. The time required to learn would depend on the taste or genius of the individual. The qualifications requisite are those of an artist in a less degree." B., an emblematic sign painter, thinks the employment very suitable for females, but supposes there are better openings in other cities than New York. It requires two or three years to learn all the different branches well. During the first year a learner could not support herself, but after that could, if she had a taste for it, was industrious, and received enough orders to keep her busy.

509. Snuff Packers. At a snuff factory, I saw two women putting up snuff. The women color the bladders for holding snuff, in tobacco water, pack, cap, label, varnish, and wrap them. They are weighed after being packed, and women are paid at the rate of one cent a pound. Women always stand in packing. They can earn from $5 to $6 a week, and have work all the year. The woman with whom we conversed was a sensible American, who told us her health had failed greatly during the nine years she had worked in snuff. While working in the snuff, women wear caps, but are so covered with it that they might be mistaken for bags of snuff. Of course, a great deal is inhaled. Both the women I saw complained of difficulty in breathing, particularly when they lie down at night. One said, when suffering great oppression she would vomit, and throw up snuff as fresh in taste and smell as before it was inhaled. For packing snuff in jars, they are paid by the week, $4.50, and, for putting it in bottles still less. Men are mostly employed in packing snuff.

510. Stencil Makers. A stencil-plate maker told me that cutting the plates could be done by women, but it would require a strong, stout woman to hammer the plates after they are cool. In learning, a boy receives $2 a week. There are very few stencil cutters in the South and West. People send North for their plates, or get them cut by travelling peddlers, who are not allowed now in the South. The price of stencil plates has fallen very greatly. Such as would have sold for $5 a few years ago, can now be had for fifty cents. I saw a lady who cut stencil plates. She wanted an agent to sell her plates and ink.

511. Street Sweepers. The girls seen in New York sweeping the crossings in winter, are not paid by the city, but receive, now and then, from a passer by, a penny for their labor. If enough of strong men were employed by the city, and properly paid, it would serve to diminish the $13,000,000 annually spent in New York for preventable sickness, where thirty-one die every day more than in Philadelphia, while its natural advantages are greater. In Paris, women are employed as street sweepers.

512. Tip Gilders. Most hats and caps are made in New York city. There are six establishments in the city devoted to tip gilding, and morocco cutting and rolling, and four girls, on an average, in each. The girls put the sizing and gold leaf cn, and, when the impression is made, brush the loose gold leaf off. A man in the business told me he sometimes finds it difficult to get a good hand, and always prefers to teach a girl. He pays from $2 to $6 a week. The men cut the morocco for linings, and girls roll down the edge by running it through a small machine.

513. Tobacco Strippers. In tobacco factories, women are generally employed to strip the leaves from the stems. Smoking tobacco is cut in machines, and put in papers of different sizes. But little chewing tobacco is prepared in the Southern and Western States, though some factories have commenced it in the West during the last few years. Some leaf tobacco is put up in the South by slaves. In the West it is difficult to get hands, but in New York there is a surplus, though they are the very dregs of society. A. told me the women he employs are mostly

Irish, and of low origin. They are generally old women, not fit for much else, and they are quite as poorly paid as in any other branch of labor. The part done by women is not unhealthy, though some of the parts done by men in close rooms are thought to be unhealthy. H. pays by the pound for stripping, and the girls earn from $2 to $4 a week. They sit while at work. In packing they stand, because they can do more. He employs his hands all the year. For packing tobacco in papers and boxes the girls are paid by the paper, and earn about the same as the strippers. The work is dirty, and the hands change their clothes when they come and go. It requires some time to acquire expertness. H. considers tobacco very healthy, if not taken inwardly to excess. He says tobacco workers never have fevers. (?) I went through G.'s factory. I never saw females engaged in such degrading work, and so uncomfortably situated, in all my life. It is far worse than rag picking. A tier of bunks (two on a side), in dark, narrow rooms, the centre filled with hogsheads of tobacco, a hatchway, and machinery made up the furniture of the place. The air was so close and strong, that I was almost stifled during the short time I spent there. The floor was covered with filth and waste tobacco. In the lower bunks, in one room, it was with difficulty I could discover the features of the old women and neglected children, at work. A forewoman had the superintendence, who assisted the workers in weighing the tobacco, and keeping an account of the amount given each. They were mostly Irish. It is very filthy, disagreeable work. Their tobacco strippers are paid fifty cents one hundred pounds. They strip from twenty to fifty pounds a day, earning from $1 to $3 a week. The majority have no homes, but hire lodgings at thirty-seven cents a week, and buy something to eat. They work from seven to half past five or six, having half an hour at noon. At C.'s, the rooms were not so dark, cramped, and uncomfortable as at G.'s. They employ seventy-five women and children. The forewoman told me that a smart hand, working in good leaf, and having constant employment, can earn from $3 to $5 a week. They are paid two cents for three pounds. The packers, if active and skilful, can earn more. At a place on Greenwich street, they pay thirty-five cents per hundred pounds for stripping, and a woman may earn from $1 to $4 a week at it. At packing they can earn from $3 to $6. At L.'s, they employ one hundred and twenty-five girls and women. At packing their girls can earn from $4.25 to $9 a week, working only in daylight. Strippers can earn from $1.50 to $3.50, and are mostly old widow women with children. The foreman thinks it most healthy for packers to stand, as they are thereby saved from stooping. He tries to get the best class of girls he can, but he finds it impossible to secure the services of American girls. I am glad American girls object to working in the filthy weed. The girls at L.'s have employment all the year. M. pays forty cents per hundred pounds for stripping. His strippers earn from thirty to forty cents a day. Some packers are able to earn $1 a day. They have work all the year. Tobacconists in Albany write: "We employ women in papering tobacco, and pay by the dozen, the hands earning from $3 to $5 per week. They work ten hours a day, the year through." A tobacconist in Hartford "pays his women by the week, $3.50, for stripping tobacco. They work ten hours a day. It requires but a few weeks to learn the work done by women." B—'s, of Boston, write: "We always have employment for women, in stripping and papering tobacco, and other light work. They are employed, also, in making cigars. By some physicians the work is considered healthy. We pay by the week, from $3 to $5, working ten hours a day. The men who make cigars are mostly foreigners, thoroughly acquainted with their business, a kind of work which requires a regular apprenticeship to learn. The women never give their time to learn, and we cannot afford to teach them, on account of the low price of goods made in Germany, shipped here by millions. Hence, the men, in their part of the business, earn from $6 to $15 per week. Learners receive their board. It would be much better if a tariff, excluding cheap cigars, were passed. The comfort and remuneration are as good as any branch of female industry. Board, $2 to $3."

514. Toy Makers. The thousand and one inventions for amusing children have given exercise to a variety of talents. Any particular style of toy follows the fashion of the world—it passes away, and another takes its place. Pewter toys are made in New York, tin toys in Philadelphia and Connecticut. The reason more toys are not made in this country is the high price of labor and living. Children's drums are made both in the city and country. N. & Co., manufacturers of military and toy drums in Massachusetts, write: "We employ one woman only in our factory, who makes the straps for drums. She works by the piece, and earns $1 a day, boarding herself." A manufacturer of pewter toys, in New York, employs ten or twelve boys. He pays $1.75 per week, of ten hours a day. He could use girls just as well, but prefers boys. I called at a manufactory of tin ware. The proprietor makes tin toys, and employs some women to paint them. The work has to be done on the premises, as the articles have to be subjected to heat after they are painted. The girls work ten hours a day, and are paid $3 a week. H., New York, makes small boats and vessels. They range in price from 37

cents to $30. The highest priced are perfect in all their parts.
He pays a woman $80 a year for stitching by machine the edges
of the sails. B., manufacturer of mechanical toys, employs twenty
girls in soldering and painting. The painting is done by stencils.
It requires but a short time to learn. Good hands earn from
$2.50 to $4 per week. There are two departments in the manufacture of dolls—making and painting. D. employs women out of
the house to make bodies for dolls—muslin stuffed with wadding.
G., New York, pays his girls about $4 per week for dressing
dolls. At a large store in New York, I was told they employ a
number of girls for dressing dolls, paying from $3 to $4 per
week. They pay by the piece, according to the size, and style
of dress. In busy seasons, the girls are allowed to take some
dolls home and dress them in the evening. Doll dressing requires taste, expertness, ingenuity, and economy in cutting the
materials. Their room is superintended by a lady. At a store
for the sale of fancy goods, on inquiring about the canton-flannel
rabbits, mice, &c., I was told they give them to a school girl in
Brooklyn to make. She makes them out of school hours, and
earns $1.50 per week. They are sewed by a machine, because it
can be done faster. The treasurer of a firm manufacturing
Yankee notions, in Providence, writes they have six women
employed in labelling and packing light goods, who earn from
$3 to $6 per week, of ten hours a day. It requires about four
weeks to learn to do the work. There is no difference in seasons.
What work women do at all they do as well as men. Some
places are better than others for this style of manufacture.

515. Varnishers and Varnish Makers. In France,
women are employed as varnishers of furniture. At some varnish
factories, women are employed to separate the good from the imperfect gum, and I think are paid the usual price of woman's
work, 50 cents a day. Women might make spirit varnish.
Copal varnish has to be boiled, and is liable to take fire. As it
requires much strength to stir it, women could not very well
make it. The varnishing of pianos could be done by women.
A manufacturer of musical instruments told me a solution, one
constituent of which is pulverized marble, has been made for
varnishing, that is very substantial. A knife can be broken
against it, after it has become hardened on furniture. It will
probably be used very extensively.

516. Water Carriers. "Everywhere on the banks of
the Nile, the poorer sort of women may be seen bringing up
water from the river, in pitchers, on their heads or shoulders."
There are from one hundred to one hundred and fifty water carriers in London, but they are mostly or all men.

EMPLOYMENTS FOR THE AFFLICTED.

517. Blind Women. Many blind persons are employed as follows : Attendants in blind institutions, authors, basket makers, bead workers, broom makers, brush makers, carpet and rug weavers, chair seaters, flower and fruit venders, governesses, hair and moss pickers, hucksters, knitters, match sellers, mattress makers, milk sellers, music teachers, netters, newspaper and book agents, paper-box makers, seamstresses, stationers, straw braiders, teachers, umbrella sewers, washerwomen, willow workers. We think they usually engage in their work with pleasure and profit. Fortunately the tools employed in the occupations of the blind do not cost much. So if the blind have a thorough knowledge of some pursuit, and means to keep them until they are established and able to secure constant work, they may feel sure of a comfortable livelihood. Their occupations are of a kind to furnish them with most constant employment in a city. Though the compensation for each article is small, yet, when one's time is fully occupied, the aggregate is considerable.

518. Deaf Mutes. Deaf mutes can engage in most branches of book making, fancy work, sewing, shoe making, teach drawing, and teach those afflicted like themselves.

519. The Lame. The lame can braid straw, color photographs, copy, cut labels, edit papers, embroider, engrave, make mats, make pens, model, paint, sew—indeed, do almost anything. Lameness is no excuse for idleness. What do lame men do? None of them, that have any self-respect, beg or sit idle because they are lame.

UNUSUAL EMPLOYMENTS.

520. United States. Last summer, a lady ascended alone in a balloon, from Palace Garden, N. Y. She went up once in a balloon filled with hot air. She received part of the profits derived from the admittance fees, and the keeper of the garden the other portion, neither of which were very large. Several women have gone up with their husbands. We take the following items from the summary of the San Francisco *Alta California*, of December 5th : "At the recent election, two women were elected to fill office in Placer County—one as justice of the peace, and the other as constable. Each received one vote in the precinct, and there was no opposition." It is seldom that a lady's exertions are called forth as were those of Mrs. Patton, wife of the captain of the ship *Neptune's Car*. Yet, it goes to confirm what we have stated in some other place, that any valuable information acquired will always come in use. We will quote the extract as we saw it in a newspaper, copied from a San Francisco letter : " Fifty days ago, Captain Patton was attacked with the brain fever, and for the last twenty-five days has been blind. Previous to his illness, he had put the first mate off duty on account of his incompetency. After the captain's illness, the second mate took charge of the ship, but he did not understand navigation. The first mate wrote Mrs. Patton a letter, reminding her of the dangers of the coast, and of the great responsibility she had assumed, and offered to take charge of the ship; but she stood by the decision of her husband and declined the offer. She worked up the reckoning every day, and brought the ship safely into port. During all this time she acted as nurse to the captain. She studied medicine to learn how to treat his case, and shaved his head, and by competent care and watchfulness kept him alive. She said that for fifty nights she had not undressed herself. Few women could have done so much and done it so well. She was at once navigator, nurse, and physician, and protector of the property intrusted to her husband." The Geneva *Courier* notices the appearance in that village ' of a strong-armed, strong-backed, and, of course, strong-minded woman, in charge of a canal boat, of which she is owner and captain. She is of German origin, and manages her craft with great ability." In New York, I saw a woman driving a bread wagon, one rolling a wheelbarrow, and another drawing a similar wagon filled with ashes. A few women are employed in charcoal burning in New Jersey.

521. England. In looking over the census of Great Britain, for 1850, we are surprised to find that in some of those occupations most suitable for women, as physicians, music composers, teachers of mathematics, macaroni packers, mask makers, honey dealers, lecturers, reporters, and spice merchants, not one female is reported ; while, in occupations altogether unsuitable, many women are employed—in some, even hundreds. No doubt many of these women, perhaps a majority, and in some occupations it may be all, are the widows of men who have been engaged in the business, and who employ others to do the work. In some of the other occupations, the women probably do only the lighter work, under the direction of the masters or competent foremen. Circumstances, as regards occupation, certainly do much to influence the fate of every one. But in no respect is there a greater need of reform, than in the proper appreciation of employments by the sexes. Men have, in bygone times, seized upon the lightest and most lucrative occupations, and by custom still retain them. The most laborious and disagreeable work is left for women, and what is still worse, they are paid only from one third to one half as much as men, doing the same kind of work. Of the occupations that strike us as odd for women, in the census of Great Britain, are makers of agricultural implements, anchor smiths, barge women, barge boat builders, bell hangers, bedstead makers, bill stickers, blacksmiths, brass manufacturers, brick makers, bristle manufacturers, builders, carpenters, case (packing) makers, chimney sweepers, coke burners, commercial travellers, engine and machinery makers, ferriers, goldbeaters, grindstone cutters, gun makers, hawkers, hemp manufacturers, hinge makers, nail manufacturers, oil refiners, paper hangers, parasol and umbrella stick manufacturers, peat cutters, plasterers, potato merchants, railway-station attendants, razor makers, ring-chain makers, rivet makers, rope makers, saddle-tree makers, sail makers, scale makers, sawyers, scavengers, sextons, ship agents, ship builders, small steel-ware manufacturers, snuff and tobacco manufacturers, spade makers, spar cutters, spirit and wine merchants, stone breakers, stone quarriers, stove, grate, and range makers, sugar refiners, surgical-instrument makers, timber merchants, timber choppers and benders, tin manufacturers, trunk makers, turners, turpentine manufacturers, undertakers, vermin destroyers, well sinkers, wheelwrights, white-metal manufacturers, wine manufacturers, wood dealers, and zinc manufacturers. In the furniture trade of Great Britain, 5,763 women are employed, while 7,479 are engaged in conveyance. I would also add, that in Great Britain, women have been, and still are, to some extent, employed in coal, copper, iron, lead, manganese, salt, tin, and other mineral mines. Of those for men extremely inappropriate, are reported three hundred and sixty-six dress makers, and sixty-one embroiderers. " In the reign of George II. (says Mrs. Childs), the minister of Clerkenwell was chosen by a majority of women. The office of champion has frequently been held by a woman, and was so at the coronation of George I. The office of grand chamberlain, in 1822, was filled by two women ; and that of clerk of the crown, in the court of king's bench, has been granted to a female. The celebrated Anne, Countess of Pembroke, held the hereditary office of sheriff of Westmoreland, and exercised it in person, sitting on the bench of the judges. In ancient councils, mention is made of deaconesses; and in an edition of the New Testament printed in 1574, a woman is spoken of as minister of a church." Miss Betsy Miller has for years commanded the Scotch brig, Cleotus. Her father commanded a vessel plying between England and France. After his wife died, the daughter frequently accompanied him. On his death, being without a home on land, she took command of the vessel, and remained in the capacity of captain several years. An English correspondent of an American paper writes: "Walking, lately, near some white-lead works, about the hour of closing, we observed the sudden egress of about a hundred women from the establishment, all Irish, and all decently clad and well conducted. On inquiry, we found that they are employed continuously in the works, piling the lead for oxidation, and in various other processes, not by any means coming under the denomination of light labor." A few years ago, a singular death occurred in England. It was that of a woman, who, owing to harsh treatment from her parents when a child, left her home at the age of eight, dressed in boy's clothes, got work as a boy, learned the trade of a mason, and worked at it until about middle age, when the business was changed for that of a beer house, in which occupation the individual continued until her death, at the age of sixty. She always dressed as a man. When quite young, she was very industrious and hard-working. Many of the large houses and tall chimneys in Manchester and Salford were built by her. "The 7,000 women returned in the census under the head of miners, are, no doubt, for the most part, the dressers of the ores in the Cornish and Welsh mines. The work is dirty, but not too laborious; less laborious than the work which may perhaps be included under the same head—the supplying porcelain clay from the same regions of country. Travellers in Devonshire and Cornwall are familiar with the ugly scenery of hillsides where turf is taken up, and the series of clay pits is overflowing, and the plastered women are stirring the mess, or sifting and straining, or drying or moulding the refined clay. The mineral interest is, however, one of the smallest in the schedule of female industry; and it is likely to contract, rather than expand—except the labor of sorting the ores." In Great Britain, some women work in alabaster, and some in alum mines. In what is called the Black country, some women are employed on the pit banks, and some about the furnace yards. A London paper says: "Melton and its neighborhood can boast of three public characters, which, perhaps, no other can; namely, two independent ladies, who have taken out game certificates, and who enter the field, and can bring down the game equal to any sportsman, as well as those indulging in fishing, hunting over the country with hounds, &c. The third is a female blacksmith, a daughter of Mr. William Hinman, who is such an adept at shoeing a horse or working at the anvil, as to cause universal excitement. It was but the other day that she took off the old shoes of a horse, pared the feet, and fitted the shoes at the fire, and affixed them in the most scientific manner possible, and in considerably less time than her father could, who is called one of the quickest shoers in Melton." Some women are employed as kelp burners in Great Britain; and some, as bathers, manage the bathing machines used on the coast. In the census of Great Britain are reported some women as hack proprietors.

522. France. A Paris correspondent of the New York *Times* writes: " My washerwoman is a man. He lives in the Rue Blanc, and any one may see him up to his elbows in soap suds, or ironing frills on bosoms. His wife is a wood sawyer." It is not unusual, in the public gardens of Germany, and on the broad sidewalks of the Boulevards in Paris, for men and women to hire a chair for a sou to a passer by who wishes to rest. In France, some women are engaged in cutting and drying seaweeds, and some in making wooden shoes. " In the department of Sonne, France, women alone have the right to go into the fields and gather stones to repair the roads. In the cantons where peat is dug, the privilege of loading and unloading the boats which carry it is given them. At Cistal, in Provence, women alone have been authorized to sell the water which was brought from a fountain some distance from the city. No man could be a carrier of water. In other parts, to women is given the transport of trunks, valises, clothes bags, and effects for the use of travellers on packets. These resources are momentary. Accorded by one mayor, they can be withdrawn by another." " In Paris, women cry the rate of exchange, after Bourse hours." They also " undertake the moving of furniture, agree with you as to price, and you find them quite as responsible as men." The author of " Parisian Sights and French Principles " mentions a number of female employments rather novel to Americans : " I will say nothing of their laboring in the field, their driving huge carts through the streets of Paris, and other rude labors which soon rub out of them all feminine softness; but confine myself to the more agreeable duties which they have here usurped from men. Indeed, a man is but a secondary being in the scale of French civilization. The ' dames à comptoir' are as essential to the success of a Parisian *café* as the cook himself. More hats are donned at their shrines than before the most brilliant belles of the metropolis. My boot maker, or the head of the establishment, is a woman; my porter is of the same sex, older in years and worse in looks; my butcher, milkman, and the old-clothes man, newsboy, and rag gatherer beneath my window, ditto. They are waiters at the baths, door-

21

keepers at the theatres, ticket sellers, fiddlers, chair letters of the churches; they figure in every revolution, and have a tongue and arms in every fight; in short, they are at the bottom and top of everything in France." In the Hotel des Invalides, at Paris, is Lieutenant Madame Brulow, who entered in 1799, and has been there ever since. Her father, brothers, and husband were soldiers, and were all killed in battle; at the age of twenty she was a widow and a mother. She joined the French army at Corsica, where she behaved very bravely; but was disabled for service by the bursting of a bomb while in the discharge of her duties as sergeant. She is a woman of chaste manners and correct principles. She dresses in the uniform of the Invalides. Louis XVIII. conferred on her the rank of second lieutenant, and by the present Napoleon she was made a member of the society of the Legion of Honor. A female soldier, whose history is similar to Madame Brulow's, died near Paris, a short time since, at the age of eighty-seven. She was a dragoon, and served in Italy, Germany, and Spain, in all the campaigns of the French, from 1793 to 1812. When Bonaparte was first consul, he expressed a wish to see her, and she was kindly received by him at St. Cloud. She received many wounds in battle, and had four horses killed under her. We find the following article, taken from Galignani's *Messenger:* "In consequence of the success obtained by Madame Isabella in breaking horses for the Russian army, the French Minister of War authorized her to proceed, officially, before a commission of generals and superior officers of cavalry, to a practical demonstration of the method, on a certain number of young cavalry horses. After twenty days' training, the horses were so perfectly broken in, that the Minister no longer hesitated to enter into an arrangement with Madame Isabella to introduce her system into all the imperial schools of cavalry, beginning with that of Saumur."

523. Other Countries. Professor Ingraham, in his " Pillar of Fire," describing the Hebrews at work in Egypt, says: " The men that carried brick to the smoothly swept ground where they were to be dried, delivered them to women, who, many hundreds in number, placed them side by side on the earth in rows—a lighter task than that of the men. The borders of this busy plain, where it touched the fields of stubble wheat, were thronged with women and children gathering straw for the men who mixed the clay." " The Egyptian ladies," says the same writer, " employed much of their time with the needle, and either with their own hands, or by the agency of their maidens, they embroidered, wove, spun, and did needlework." Herodotus says: " It was expected of the virgins consecrated to the service of the

Egyptian temples to gather flowers for the altars, to feed the sacred birds, and daily to fill the vases with pure, fresh water from the Nile." During the middle ages, " women preached in public, supported controversies, published and defended theses, filled the chairs of philosophy and law, harangued the popes in Latin, wrote Greek, and read Hebrew. Nuns wrote poetry, women of rank became divines, and young girls publicly exhorted Christian princes to take up arms for the recovery of the Holy Sepulchre." " In the Greek island of Hinnin, the inhabitants gain a livelihood by obtaining sponges for the Turkish baths ; and no girl is allowed to marry till she has proved her dexterity by bringing up from the sea a certain quantity of this marketable article." The wife of the Burmese governor was observed, by some Englishmen, to superintend the building of her husband's ship. " In many of the South Sea islands, women assist in the construction of the buildings appropriated to common use. Sometimes a woman of distinction may be seen carrying a heavy stone for the foundation of a building, while a stout attendant carries the light feathered staff to denote her rank." " In Genoa there are marriage brokers, who have pocketbooks filled with the names of marriageable girls of different classes, with an account of their fortunes, personal attractions, &c. When they succeed in arranging connections, they have two or three per cent. commission on the portion. The contract is often drawn up before the parties have seen each other. If a man dislikes the appearance or manners of his future partner, he may break off the match, on condition of paying the brokerage and other expenses." In the " Art Student in Munich," we find this passage : " You know, in Germany, your neighbor's dresses by meeting the laundresses bearing them home through the streets upon tall poles, like gay pennons." " In Munich, a servant girl will be sent around with a number of advertisements and a paste pot, and pastes up the advertisements at the corners of the streets throughout the city." " At Homburg, Germany, four, six, or eight girls, according to the season, dip the water from the spring, by taking three tumblers by the handles in each hand, and filling them without stopping, and supplying those in waiting, so fast that there is no crowd and no jostling and impatience." Mrs. Nicolson says : " Many a poor widow have I seen in Ireland, with some little son or daughter, spreading manure, by moonlight, over her scanty patch of ground ; or, before the rising of the sun, going out, with her wisp about her forehead and basket to her back, to gather her turf or potatoes." " In the elevated, cold, dry regions of Thibet, the goats are furnished with a fine down or hair-like wool under the coarse, common outer wool. The long hairs are picked out, the remainder washed out in nice water, and then handspun by women." " In some African tribes, it is common for the women to unite with the men in hunting the lion and the leopard." During the reign of Anne of Austria, the French women often appeared at the head of political factions, wearing scarfs that designated the party to which they belonged. Swords and harps, violins and cuirasses, were seen together in the same saloon. There was a regiment created under the name of mademoiselle. " During the late war, Polish women assisted the men in erecting fortifications, and one of the outworks was called the ' lunette of the women,' because it was built entirely by their hands. The Countess Plater raised and equipped a regiment of five or six hundred Lithuanians at her own expense; and she was uniformly at their head, encouraging them by her brave example in every battle. The women proposed to form three companies of their own sex, to share the fatigues and perils of the army; but their countrymen, wishing to employ their energies in a manner less dangerous, distributed them among the hospitals to attend the wounded." " In the army of the King of Siam, one corps particularly attracts the attention of strangers, which is a battalion of the king's guard, composed of women. This battalion consists of four hundred women, chosen from among the handsomest and most robust girls in the country. They receive excellent pay, and their discipline is perfect. They are admitted to serve at the age of thirteen, and are placed in the army of reserve at twenty-five. From that period they no longer serve about the king's person, but are employed to guard the royal palaces and crown lands."

MINOR EMPLOYMENTS.

524. United States. A little boy told me he used to catch butterflies, and sell them in New York at a penny apiece for canary birds. Sometimes he would get one hundred a day; and at other times, not as many a week. Some women are seen on the streets of our large cities, selling baskets, brushes, sponges, and wash leather—and many with baskets containing tape, cord, pins, &c. Some women buy waste paper to sell to grocers, butchers, fishmongers, and such others as would use it for wrapping. A few resort to levees and warehouses to seek the scraps of waste cotton that are lost by the removal of bales. Some collect ashes, separate the cinders, wash and sell them ; while some collect wood scattered about lumber yards, and catch that drifting in rivers.

525. England. Some children on the streets of London are employed in the sale of fly-papers. Some sell paper cuttings to ornament ceilings. Sand is sold on the streets for scouring and for birds—also gravel for birds. Some women, in London, go around and buy the skins of rabbits and hares to sell again, and some keep little shops where they buy kitchen stuff, grease, and dripping. In England, women are hired to pick currants and gooseberries, put up fruit, weed gardens, bind grain, pick hops, and sometimes even to cut hay and dig potatoes. On the streets of London, some women sell conundrums and playbills, which are pinned to a large screen, and a number sell stationery. In old countries nothing is lost. Use is found for every article, even when no longer of value for its original purpose. For instance, old tin kettles and coal scuttles, we learn from Mr. Babbage, are cut up for the bottoms and bands of trunks, and by manufacturing chemists in preparing a black dye used by calico printers. In some cities of the old countries, every variety of second-hand miscellaneous articles are sold in shops, from a Jew's harp to a bedstead. In London, Mayhew says : " Among the mudlarks may be seen many old women, and it is indeed pitiable to behold them, especially during the winter, bent nearly double with age and infirmity, paddling and groping among the wet mud for small pieces of coal, chips of wood, copper nails that drop out of the sheathing of vessels, or any sort of refuse washed up by the tide. These women always have with them an old basket, or an old tin kettle, in which they put whatever they may chance to find. It usually takes them the whole tide to fill the receptacle, but, when filled, it is as much as the feeble old creatures are able to carry home." Little girls, too, eagerly press into the mud as the tide recedes, to secure what trifles they can, by which to gain bread.

526. France. In France, many women are employed in vineyards to pick grapes, tie up the vines, &c. L. told me he had seen women in France employed in preparing a kind of fuel made of clay mixed in water, cast in moulds, and dried. Females are employed by some of the merchants in Paris to carry goods home for purchasers. One of the most flourishing of the minor street trades of Paris is that in fried potatoes, invented some twenty-five years ago by a man that made his fortune at the business. A few years back might have been seen in the grounds of the Tuileries an old woman with a long stick, drawing off the surface of the water the feathers that loosened and fell from the swans that floated on the ponds.   That old woman sold the feathers to buy bread.

527. Occupations in which no Women are employed.   I have received information from persons saying women are never engaged in their branches of business, which are the following: Architectural Ornamentation, Bonedust, Buckets, Carriage painting, Copperas ("hard and unsuitable"), Currying, Drug Mills ("only fit for able-bodied men"), Edge Tools ("not adapted to the sex"), Emery Paper, Flour Mills, Glazier's Diamonds, Gunpowder ("dangerous"), India Rubber Belting, Magnesia, Melodeons, Mercantile Agencies, Metallic Furniture, Oil, Oil Cloth, Organ building, Paint Mills, Pattern making (of wood), Pearlash ("unsuitable"), Philosophical Instruments (except Globes), Pine Furniture, Pork packing, Reed making, Rivets, Roll covering, Seed crushing ("requires able bodied men"), Sellers of License, Ship Crackers, Shot and Lead ("dangerous and unhealthy"), Shovels, Slate, Spools, Starch ("too hard"), Steel-letter cutting, Stone quarrying, Street-lamp lighting, Sulphur ("unhealthy"), Superphosphate of Lime ("requires too much muscular strength"), Surveyors' and Engineers' Instruments, Tanning, Tinfoil, Trowels, Vinegar, Wholesale Fruit dealing, Wire drawing, Wool combing, and Zinc manufacture.

528. None in the United States.   There are no women employed in any capacity in connection with mining and shipping coal in our country.   Neither could any branch of the business be well placed under their supervision, for very nearly all the labor is performed by foreigners of the most low and illiterate class."   None are employed in Baggage transportation, Bleaching, Brokers' Offices, Chemical Works, Cutlery, Furniture moving, Glue drying, Gun making, Iron Works, Landscape gardening, Lead Pencils, Sail making, Savings Banks, Silvering Mirrors, Tending Sheep, and Wood carving.

529. Very few employed.   Attending in offices of ladies' physicians, Charcoal burning, China painting, Chiropody, Clock Work, Lacquering, Marble Work, Mirror Frames, Sign painting, Stencil cutting, and Stone Ware. "As a curious incident of the growing availability of female labor, Vermont returns four females engaged in ship building, and Virginia reports two so employed." Mrs. Swisshelm is an inspector of lumber, receiving a salary of $500 per annum. Mrs. N. Smith was recently elected mayoress in Oskaloosa, Iowa, the first time that office was ever filled by a lady.   We have been told of a Miss D., who furnishes houses, receiving a stipulated sum for the exercise of her taste and judgment, and the time and trouble of making purchases. In the Southern States, a few colored women are employed about sugar mills, and many in gathering cotton. I suppose that in some countries women may be, and probably are employed in the preparation of isinglass and gelatine; also, incollecting cochineal, and gathering rice and coffee.

530. The South. There will be openings in the South for business in the following branches:

Artificial Eyes, Limbs, and Teeth.
Artificial Flowers.
Bags (Cotton and Paper).
Baskets.
Belts (Ladies').
Bonnets.
Bonnet Ruches.
Bonnet Frames.
Books.
Braces and Trusses.
Brushes.
Buttons.
Candles (from the tallow tree of South Carolina and Georgia).
Candy.
Canes.
Caps.
Card Printing and Stencilling.
Carpets.
Carriage Trimmings.
Car and Carriage Ornamenting.
China.
Cigars.
Cloaks and Mantillas.
Clocks.
Clothing.
Cord.
Cordage and Twine.
Cutlery.
Daguerreotype Apparatus, &c.
Designs.
Drawings (Architectural, &c)
Dress Caps.

Dress Trimmings.
Embroideries.
Envelopes.
Factory Work.
Fancy Stores.
Feather Dressing.
Fishing Tackle.
Furniture.
Gilding.
Gold Chains.
Gold Pens.
Gold and Silver Leaf.
Grape Growing.
Gum-Elastic Goods.
Hair Dressing and Manufacturing.
Hardware.
Hats.
Hoop Skirts.
Horse Coverings.
Ink.
Jewelry.
Labels.
Lamps.
Lapidaries' Work.
Laundries.
Lead.
Leather.
Life Preservers.
Lithographing.
Maps.
Matches.
Military Goods.
Needle and Thread Stores.
Oils.
Paper Boxes.
Patterns (Ladies' and Children's).
Plated Ware.
Paints.

Painting and Staining of Glass.
Perfumery.
Photography.
Practising Medicine.
Picture Restoring.
Pipes.
Places of Summer Resort.
Porcelain.
Potash.
Pottery.
Printing.
Rag Collecting.
Sealed Provisions.
Sewing-Machine Labor.
Shoes.
Shot.
Soda and Saleratus.
Spectacles.
Stair Rods.
Steel Engraving.
Straw Working.
Surgical Instruments.
Suspenders.
Tailors' Work.
Tape.
Tobacco Stripping and Packing.
Toys.
Types.
Umbrellas and Parasols.
Under Wear.
Wall Paper.
Watches.
Willow Growing.
Window Shades.
Wood Engraving.

There will be openings in St. Louis and Chicago for fur sewers. There has been a demand for mill girls in Rhode Island.

There is a surplus now of workers in cotton mills, but not of operatives in woollen mills. A gentleman in Middletown, Conn., wrote me a boarding house for work girls is wanted there. Makers of ladies' dress caps and ironers of new shirts have been scarce in New York city.

531. Prices of Board for Workwomen, and Remarks of Employers. Aside from the prices of board for workwomen as mentioned in different parts of this work, I have intelligence from employers in one hundred and fifteen towns and cities of the Eastern States, New York, Pennsylvania, and New Jersey. These places number : Maine 4, New Hampshire 13, Vermont 4, Massachusetts 34, Rhode Island 5, Connecticut 29, New York 19, Pennsylvania 5, and New Jersey 2. Of the places in Maine, prices of board for women run from 1.33\frac{1}{3}$ to $1.50 a week. In New Hampshire, they make the same range. In Vermont, the price is given, of all places, at $1.50. In Rhode Island, from $1.50 to $3. In Connecticut, from $1.42. to $3. Massachusetts, from $1.25 to $4. New York, $1.50 to $3.50. Pennsylvania, $1.50 to $5. New Jersey, $1.25 to $1.75. The difference in board is something between a small town and a city in any State. The largest number of employers in cities give, as the most common prices, from $1.50 to $3 per week. Lights and washing are sometimes included in these prices, but washing very seldom— fuel in the rooms of the boarders, never. Employers write the boarding houses of their workwomen are comfortable and respectable. We hope they are so, and wish that as much could be said of all. But we must acknowledge that we feel disposed to question the comfort of the majority of those for which such prices are paid in cities as mentioned by the employers. In villages and towns, board could be had at such rates. But we are confident it would be impossible to furnish sufficient wholesome food and clean, well ventilated lodging rooms, at the rates mostly specified in cities, where rent and provisions are high, with any profit to the keepers of the houses. Some employers assert that women can live cheaper than men. They cannot, in most places, to have as good accommodations ; and when they can, the difference is slight. So a just proportion in wages is not observed, even with such a plea. Most men in industrial avocations receive $1.50 a day (many $2) ; women, from 50 cents to $1—most generally the former price. In France, a workman usually receives 60 cents a day ; a woman, over 30 cents. So women do not receive even as good wages, in proportion to men, in the United States, as in France. In Lyons, France, women have always been paid for work performed in the same proportion as men. Most hand seamstresses receive starvation prices in both countries. In most industrial employments in Dublin, Ireland, women receive six English shillings a week, for their work of ten hours a day. Yet on the dusty and disagreeable labor of sorting and picking rags, some are enabled to earn eight shillings a week, but they are paid by the piece. School children in Dublin, as well as the working classes, usually take Monday for a holiday. Nor is it confined to Dublin. In France and England, Monday is made a day of freedom from work, and of reckless dissipation, with a large portion of the working people. In most occupations open to women, the times for work are usually not more than six months in the year, while men's extend the year round. Some employers write their women have more time than inclination for mental improvement—that all their time is at their disposal, except those hours employed in the factory, workshop, or store, which run from ten to seventeen hours. A woman's wardrobe requires some hours' attention; and the more limited her means, the more time is needed to keep it in repair. We think employers could do much good by learning the condition of their work people— what their habits and home comforts are; and would recommend to those disposed to learn something of the results, to read a work called "The Successful Merchant." I have heard there is a great laxity of morals in some of the establishments of New York, where men and women are employed. Proprietors and foremen of correct principles could do much to prevent this. Much, too, might be avoided by a careful selection of work people. I learn from one employer that one of his workwomen reads aloud to the others while at work. It is an admirable plan, but, where machinery is employed, could not be adopted, because of the noise. The best policy for any government is a protection of home produce and manufactures—a policy that it is desirable to see carried out more fully in our country. It will be observed that the farther we go south, as a general thing, the better are the prices paid for labor. Living, however, is somewhat higher. So what is gained in one way is lost in another. A majority of workwomen in this country are foreigners. In New York, I have heard the opinion expressed that there are in that city fifteen foreign workwomen where there is one American. One source of trouble among workwomen is the indifferent way in which they execute their work, arising from the want of proper instruction, the want of application, or a careless habit they acquire. Another failing is stopping often when at work. A misfortune with many workwomen is that they have not the physical strength to do much work, to do it constantly, or to do it fast.

532. Number of Work Hours. In France, the number of work hours is 12; in England, 10; and in most of the United

States, 10.　In some of the United States there are no laws regulating the number of work hours; and in some States, where such laws do exist, they are evaded.

533. Extracts from the Census Report for 1860. In advance of publication, Mr. Kennedy, Superintendent of the United States Census Report, writes : " The whole number, approximately, of females employed in the various branches of manufacture, is 285,000.　The following are approximations to the average wages paid in New York and New England.　Monthly wages of females employed in making

" Boots and shoes,	. $11 25	Book folding,	. . $15 38
Clothing,	. . . . 12 00	Printing,	. . . . 13 65
Cotton goods,	. . . 13 30	Millinery,	. . . . 17 47
Woollen,	. . . . 16 00	Ladies' mantillas, &c.	16 00
Paper boxes,	. . . 14 30	Hoop skirts,	. . . 14 00 "
Umbrellas, &c.,	. 13 38		

APPENDIX.

INDUSTRIAL STATISTICS OF PARIS, IN 1848.

OCCUPATIONS.	Number of Men.	Number of Women.	Minimum of Men's Wages per Day. cents.	Maximum of Men's Wages per Day. $ cts.	Minimum of Women's Wages per Day. cents.	Maximum of Women's Wages per Day. cents.	Months when Work is slack.
Makers of Accordeons	217	51	40	1 00	15	35	Jan., Feb., Aug.
Sculptors in Alabaster Night Lamps, and Wicks	51	14	40	1 00	30	45	Jan., Feb., March.
Makers of Matches	184	357	25	1 00	12	60	May, June, July, Aug.
Manufacturers of Starch and Spongers of Cloths	88	4	45	0 80	30	:	June, July, Aug.
Dressers of Woven Goods, Silver and Copper	491	325	25	1 00	20	50	June, July, Jan.
Dressers and Drawers of Gold	81	8	50	1 20	20	60	Jan., Feb.
Gunsmiths	492	2	50	1 00	20	35	June, July, May, March.
Makers of Scales and Weights	205	8	60	1 10	..	..	Jan., Feb., Aug.
Whalebone Splitters	96	42	20	1 00	average 29	$2 00	Dec., Jan., Feb.
Bandage and Truss Makers	278	404	50	0 83	60	60	Jan., Feb., and part of Dec.
Beaters of Gold and Silver	195	377	50	1 20	20	60	Jan., Feb.
Polishers of Steel Jewelry	1,091	784	50	2 00	15	50	Jan., Feb., March.
Mourning Jewelry	170	54	40	1 20	20	50	Jan., Feb., July.
False Jewelry	1,507	456	25	1 60	20	80	Jan., Feb., March.
Fine Jewelry	2,942	637	20	2 40	16	48	July, Aug., Jan., Feb.
Garnishers of Jewels	83	4	50	1 10	..	40	Jan., Feb., and part of July.
Manufacturers of Implements for Billiards	216	9	40	2 00	20	60	July, Aug., Jan.
Toy Manufacturers	641	1,345	25	1 20	30	80	Jan., Feb., March, April.
Bleachers of Woven Goods	65	275	50	1 00	10	55	June, July, Aug., and part of Sept.
Washerwomen	86	7,491	40	0 70	20	60	Aug., July, Jan., Feb.
Wood Workers	43	20	40	1 00	15	60	July, Aug., Jan., Feb.
Cap Makers	1,068	1,565	18	1 00	8	50	Jan., Feb., July, and part of Aug.
Makers of Hooks and Eyes, and Buckles	127	75	60	1 00	20	35	Jan. and part of Feb.
Makers of Wax and Tallow Candles	186	113	40	1 00	15	60	June, July, Aug.
Bakers	1,996	643	25	0 60	30 and a loaf of bread every day.	60	June, July, Aug., Sept.
Embroiderers of Bags and Purses	7	876	60	0 80	15	60	Jan., Feb., July, and Aug.
Button Makers, Horn, Pearl, &c.	405	185	60	1 20	18	40	From Dec. to Feb., being most of 3 months.
Button Makers, Cloth and Metal	716	529	80	1 20	10	60	Jan., Feb., and part of July and Aug.

				$	¢			Commence in Nov. and end in March.
Bricks, Tiles, and Pipes for Chimneys	497	27	40	2	80	25	60	
Book Stitchers	188	678	70	1	20	20	65	June, July, Aug.
Tapestry Embroiderers	14	969	70	1	20	15	70	July, Aug., and part of Jan. and Feb.
Embroiderers	43	8,746	60	3	00	10	$1 00	Most active in Oct., Nov., and Dec.
Manufacturers of Bronze	2,515	27	45	1	25	25	70	" " "
Bronze Carvers	752	6	30	1	20	30	...	Oct., Nov., Dec.
Bronze Gilders	343	24	50	1	20	50	55	" " "
Bronze Founders	1,178	1	40	0	70	27	...	" " "
Bronze Mounters	82	11	40	1	20	25	70	Sept., Oct., and Nov.
Bronze Finishers	333	2	80	1	20	40	...	Oct., Nov., and Dec.
Bronze Turners	164	4	80	1	20	80	40	Sept., Oct.,and Nov.
Bronze Varnishers	168	283	80	1	20	25	$1 00	Oct., Nov., Dec.
Makers of Common Brushes	365	163	85	1	00	20	60	Jan., Feb., July, Aug.
Makers of Fine Brushes	371	421	80	1	00	15	60	" " " "
Coffee Toasters	37	22	80	0	80	30	40	June, July
Contractors for Washrooms and Public Washing Houses	193	45	40	1	00	25	55	Jan., Feb., March, April.
Manufacturers of Dials for Watches and Clocks	24	10	55	1	00	30	50	Jan., Feb., March.
Manufacturers of Mouldings for Gilt Frames	989	57	40	2	00	25	50	Jan., Feb., and part of July and Aug.
Manufacturers of Cotton Canvas	114	80	33	0	80	25	40	Jan., July.
Cane and Whip Makers	796	84	85	1	40	20	55	Jan., Feb. Dec., July.
Cane Chair Seaters	10	169	50	0	80	15	50	Jan., Feb., March.
Makers of Gum Elastic Works	259	310	50	1	20	20	60	Jan., Feb., June.
Coachmakers	3,685	2	80	1	60	$2 40		a month each and boarded. July, Aug., Sept.
Makers of Playing Cards	160	97	45	1	00	20	50	June, July, Aug.
Manufacturers of Pasteboard and Cards, Glazed Paper	210	121	80	1	80	20	45	Dec., Jan., Feb.
Manufacturers of Pasteboard Boxes	569	1,857	40	1	20	6	70	Jan., Feb., March, July.
Makers of Men's and Boy's Caps	81	8,929	80	1	20	10	60	Jan., Feb., July, Aug.
Manufacturers of Shawls	786	1,133	80	1	80	10	60	June, July, Aug.
Mounters and Trimmers of Straw Hats	173	1,974	50	2	00	15	$1 00	Work slack six months, from June to Nov.
Weavers of Braid for Straw Bonnets	12	108	50	0	70	20	60	" "
Bleachers and Pressers of Straw Hats	117	101	40	1	40	20	60	July to Jan.
Hat Makers	2,829	1,158	40	2	40	15	$1 00	July, Aug., Jan., Feb.
Meat Sellers	629	72	10	0	80	$30 to	$160	per year for female accountants. June, July, Aug.
Manufacturers of Articles for Hunting	162	82	80	1	00	20	85	Jan., Feb., March, Dec.
Embroiderers of Church Ornaments	9	174	60	1	00	25	80	Jan., Feb., and part of March.
Coppersmith ... wife of patron		1						
Makers of Woven and Knit Shoes	728	1,154	20	0	90	10	50	Dec. July, Aug., and part of March.
Hair Preparers, Dressers, Wig Makers, &c	678	280	80	1	40	15	60	June, July, Aug.
Washers and Assorters of Rags	27	44	50	0	70	12	40	Dec. and Jan.
Chocolate Makers	266	122	45	1	10	20	55	June, July, Aug., Sept.
Manufacturers of Blacking and Varnish	85	45	25	0	80	20	40	" " " "
Manufacturers of Wafers and Sealing Wax	57	23	40	0	80	30	40	July, Aug.

INDUSTRIAL STATISTICS OF PARIS, IN 1848—continued.

OCCUPATIONS.	Number of Men.	Number of Women.	Minimum of Men's Wages per Day. (cents.)	Maximum of Men's Wages per Day. ($ cts.)	Minimum of Women's Wages per Day. (cents.)	Maximum of Women's Wages per Day. (cents.)	Months when Work is slack.
Chasers and Engravers	830	21		$1 40	80	$1 20	July, Aug., Jan., Feb.
Makers of Bells and Clock Bells	40	2	50	1 20	80	25	Jan., Feb., and part of March.
Nailmakers	347	83	40	1 40	40	60	Jan., July, Aug.
Print Colorers	18	626	45	0 70	20	80	" " "
Makers of Women's Clothing	1	1,801		1 00	10	60	Jan., Feb., July, Aug.
Confectioners	867	284	40	1 20	20	60	June to Sept.
Makers of Nutritious Conserves	75	45	80	0 80	20	40	June, July, Aug., Sept.
Rope Makers	892	5	15	1 80	25	70	From Dec. to Feb.
Boot and Shoe Makers	18,553	6,718	15	0 80	8	70	Jan., Feb., July, Aug.
Makers of Shoes to Order	7,511	1,555	20	1 82	12	70	" " " "
Curriers	2,170	189	30	1 00	10	80	" " " "
Corset Makers	88	2,810	40	1 00	10	80	July, Aug., Sept., and part of Jan.
Costumers	87	47	60	1 10	20	50	June, July, Aug., Sept.
Makers of Colors and Varnish	510	12	40	1 10	80	50	Nov., Dec., Jan., Feb.
Knife Makers	503	39	25	1 60	25	50	July, Aug.
Mantua Makers		5,287			10	80	July, Aug., Jan., Feb.
Makers of Flannels and Blankets	404	215	80	0 70	$1 00	$1 80	Jan., Feb., March.
Makers of Crayons	65	21	85	0 90	20	40	" " "
Curd and Cheese Makers	53	30	40	0 60	20	40	Nov., Dec., Jan., Feb.
Makers of Horse-hair Goods	43	68	45	0 90	15	90	Dec., Jan., Feb.
Dressers and Liners of Horse Hair	145	72	40	0 80	25	50	Dec., Jan.
Manufacturers of Razor Leather	88	8	60	0 70	80		Jan., Feb., July.
Varnished Leather	175	9	60	1 00	80	40	June, July.
Daguerreotypists	84	8	45	1 00	40		Jan., Feb., March.
Pinkers of Shawls and Woven Goods	12	82		0 70	20	45	June, July.
Makers, Hookers, and Washers of Laces	1	817		0 70	12	70	June, July, Aug., Sept.
Makers of Artificial Teeth	68	20	50	2 00	85	40	July, Aug., Sept.
Designers for Manufacturers	579	48	50	4 00		40	July, Aug., Feb., March.
Designers for Embroidery	173	46	50	2 40	20	50	June, July, Aug.

							Busy Season
Manufacturers of Distilled Liquors and Sirups	294	13	30	0 90	30	45	July, Aug., Sept.
Gilders and Silverers of Ware and Jewelry	442	163	40	2 00	20	50	July, Jan., Feb.
Wood Gilders	773	257	40	1 20	20	60	Jan., Feb., July, Aug.
Gilders of Edges of Paper and Parchment	95	72	50	1 20	39	:	" " "
Mineral and other Gaseous Waters	177	12	40	1 20	30	40	Nov. to Feb. Women make powders for gaseous waters.
Furniture Makers	8,459	90	25	2 00	25	80	Jan., Feb.
Writers and Designers for Lithographs	54	11	70	1 60	20	80	June, July, Aug.
Publishers of Images and Engravings	856	464	50	2 40	20	60	Jan., Feb., July, Aug.
Manufacturers and Painters of Enamelled Ware	240	113	40	2 00	30	60	Jan., Feb., March.
Makers of False Stones and Enamels	19	14	50	2 50	30	50	" " "
Makers of Artificial Eyes, Porcelain Buttons, & Glass Links	93	408	55	2 50	30	40	" " "
Makers of Writing and Printing Ink	85	11	40	1 00	15	40	Jan., Aug.
Fancy Inkstands and Toilet Articles	150	12	50	0 55	12	40	
Grocers, Manufacturing	851	24	40	1 00	30	45	June, July, Aug., Sept.
Makers of Military Equipments	1,649	2,254	25	0 90	10	70	Jan., Feb., July.
Embossers	837	74	40	1 40	30	60	Jan., Feb., July.
Stampers and Engravers of Moulds for Goldware & Jewelry	220	9	40	1 60	30	40	Jan., Feb., July, and part of March.
Pewterers. . . . There are several branches.	102	17	50	1 00	30	40	Jan., Feb., July, Aug.
Fan Makers	252	264	40	1 20	12	$1 00	June, July, Aug.
Makers of Chairs and Arm Chairs	1,673	53	45	1 60	20	60	Jan., Feb., March.
Makers of Sheet Pewter	84	14	40	1 00	25	85	April, May, June, July.
Makers of Wax Figures	21	18	70	1 00	25	40	March, June, July, Aug.
Spinners, Dressers, and Twisters of Silk	47	113	30	1 00	18	40	Jan., June, Aug.
Spinners and Twisters of Cotton	578	1,334	35	1 00	14	45	Jan., July, Aug.
Spinners and Twisters of Wool	445	452	50	1 20	12	60	April, May, June.
Makers of Artificial Flowers	414	5,063	40	1 20	40	80	June, July, Aug., Jan.
Metal Melters	1,785	4	60	2 00	25	30	Jan., Feb.
Suet and Tallow Melters	80	3	50	1 40	50	80	From a month to six weeks in summer.
Melters and Engravers of Stamps and Metal Plates	624	183	50	2 00	25	50	Aug., Sept.
Fur Dealers and Dressers	180	21	50	0 90	25	50	July, Aug., Sept.
Block Makers	232	399	50	1 80	12	60	Mar., April, May, June, July, & part of Aug.
Old Clothes Women		50			12	60	Jan., Feb., March, Aug.
Sheath Makers	341	70	30	1 20	20	60	July, Aug., Jan.
Makers of Kid Gloves	1,045	873	40	1 20	15	50	June, July, Aug., Sept.
Makers of Cloth Gloves	19	203	40	1 00	8	50	June, July, Aug.
Stampers and Printers of Stuffs and Garments	136	89	40	2 00	20	60	June, July, Aug., Jan., Feb.
Gelatine and Glue Makers	78	85	35	0 60	20	85	Jan., Feb., Nov., Dec.
Makers of Cloth for Under Vests	751	869	20	0 20	20	60	April, Aug., Sept., Jan.
Carvers and Gem Engravers	165	17	60	1 60	35	60	Jan., Feb., and parts of July and Aug.
Mould Engravers	68	10	60	1 40	:	30	Jan., Feb.
Copper Plate Engravers	226	62	60	2 00	25	70	July, Aug.
Engravers on Wood and on Metal for Printing	160	6	60	2 00	60	$1 00	Jan., Feb.

INDUSTRIAL STATISTICS OF PARIS, IN 1848—continued.

OCCUPATIONS.	Number of Men.	Number of Women.	Minimum of Men's Wages per Day. cents.	Maximum of Men's Wages per Day. $ cts.	Minimum of Women's Wages per Day. cents.	Maximum of Women's Wages per Day. cents.	Months when Work is slack.
Engravers on Wood for Impressions on Stuff and Printed Papers	154	11	40	1 10	80	80	July, Aug., Sept.
Engravers on Metals for Seals and Clocks	205	7	30	1 60	70	70	June, July, Aug.
Legging Makers	73	206	40	1 00	20	$1 00	Aug., Sept.
Makers of Clocks and Clock Trimmings	1,826	155	85	2 50	12	60	June, July, Aug.
Lithographic and Copperplate Printers	1,909	186	80	3 00	20	60	June, July, Aug., Sept.
Cloth Printers	816	45	40	2 00	25	55	" " " "
Type Printers	4,053	804	60	8 00	10	80	Jan., Feb., Sept.
Makers of Surgical Instruments	247	14	40	1 40	40	70	Business most active in Oct., Nov.
Makers of Musical Wind Instruments	71	4	50	1 10	80	..	Slack in June, July, Aug., Sept.
Copper Musical Instruments	461	1	45	1 00	55	70	July, Jan., Feb.
Makers of False Jewels	192	26	50	2 00	80	80	June, July, Aug.
Makers of Fine Jewels	416	65	20	2 50	35	$1 00	May, June, July, Aug.
Makers of Lamps	1,856	24	40	1 60	25	60	July, Aug.
Makers of Coach Lamps	142	6	50	1 40	30	50	Jan., Feb., March, July,
Lapidaries	112	10	20	1 40	25	35	" " " " "
Box Makers and Packers	1,059	2	65	1 20	30	..	Dec., Jan.
Makers of Letters in Relief	95	7	50	1 00	30	40	Dec., Jan., Feb.
Cork Makers	159	58	60	1 00	26	40	Jan.
File Makers	418	10	45	2 10	25	60	July, Aug., Jan., Feb.
Contractors for Linen Drapery	80	3,974	..	1 10	8	80	Jan., Feb., July, Aug.
Manufacturers of Linen Drapery	80	2,312	50	..	12	80	June, July, Aug., Jan.
Design Readers	121	99	40	1 00	30	70	Dec., Jan., Feb., March.
Makers of Bed Clothing	257	410	40	1 20	16	80	Jan., Feb., July.
Makers of Spectacle Frames	836	44	40	1 20	12	60	Dec., Jan., Feb., March.
Trunk Makers	210	78	80	1 20	20	60	Jan., Feb., March.
Cutters of Marble for Furniture	574	45	50	1 20	20	60	Jan., Feb., March.
Cutters of Marble for Buildings	983	28	80	1 60	30	60	Jan., Feb., Dec.
Horse Farriers	846	2	30	1 30	80	..	June, July, Aug., Sept.

Veneerers and Carvers	306	84	40	1 00	80	50	Jan., Feb., July, Aug.
Alum Leather Dressers	164	1	40	0 80			
Looms for Weaving	176	21	50	1 20	25	30	July, Aug., Jan.
Trellis Makers ....Wives of patrons	50	3	40	1 40			
Looking-Glass Makers	515	96	40	0 90	20	55	Jan., Feb., March.
Milliners	24	2,854	50	1 00	20	$1 00	July, Aug., Sept., Jan., Feb.
Makers of Watch Cases	57	20	20	1 00	25	$1 60	June, July, Aug.
Makers of Mosaic Work	51	2	50	1 30	:	$1 00	June, July, and part of Aug.
Plaster and Composition Moulders	155	4	30	1 20	:	30	Jan., Feb., July, Aug.
Makers of Mouldings, Copper Pipes, and Show Cases	266	8	60	1 70	:	30	Jan., Feb.
Makers of Eyelet Holes, Percussion Caps, Pen Holders, &c.	223	85	35	1 20	15	40	Jan., Feb., July.
Makers of Instruments of Precision and Spectacles	1,684	101	40	3 00	30	40	Jan., Feb., July, Aug.
Makers of Silver-Plated Ware	544	59	40	2 00	25	60	July, Aug., Sept.
Makers of Silver Trinkets and Jewelry	828	81	40	1 60	30	70	Jan., Feb., July, Aug.
Manufacturers of Gold Plate	541	188	40	2 00	28	60	July, Aug., and part of Jan. and Feb.
Organ Manufacturers ....Wives of patrons	401	2	25	2 00	:	:	Commences in Feb., ends in July.
Wadding Makers	104	122	30	0 90	20	40	Commences in May, ends in Sept.
Mat Makers	57	91	30	0 90	8	35	Jan., July, Aug.
Makers of Paper Bags, &c.	40	120	50	1 20	10	45	Dec., Jan., Feb.
Makers of Fancy Papers	114	129	50	1 00	20	30	June, July, Aug., and part of Sept.
Makers of Wall Paper	1,855	93	40	2 00	20	60	July, Sept., Jan., Feb.
Makers of Parasols and Umbrellas	601	742	40	1 20	20	60	July, Aug., Sept.
Perfumers	349	866	30	2 00	15	80	July, Aug., July, Aug.
Makers of Lace Embroidery	2,545	6,046	20	1 20	5	80	"
Novelty Embroiderers	1,142	2,331	20	1 20	8	80	"
Embroiderers for Furniture	473	941	30	1 00	12	60	July, Aug., Jan., Feb.
Chenille Embroiderers	87	69	37	0 90	30	80	Jan., Feb., March.
Military Embroiderers	160	589	25	0 80	10	40	July, Aug., and part of Jan. and Feb.
Furniture and Coach Embroiderers	198	114	35	1 00	12	50	July, Aug., and Jan.
False and Fine Embroiderers	108	387	35	0 90	25	70	July, Aug., Jan., Feb.
Embroiderers of Braces and Garters	367	1,615	25	1 00	5	50	Jan., Feb., July.
Makers of Nutritious Pastry	92	59	45	1 40	25	60	June, July, Aug., Sept.
Pastry Cooks	973	60	20	1 10	30	45	"
Skinners and Morocco Dressers	644	15	40	1 20	25	30	July, Aug., Jan.
Makers of Articles for Fishing	40	25	30	1 00	25	50	Jan., Feb., Oct., Nov., Dec.
Comb Manufacturers	555	210	40	1 20	15	70	Jan., Feb., July.
Wool Combers	694	194	30	1 00	25	85	April, May.
House Painters	5,213	15	30	2 00	15	40	Jan., Feb., Nov., Dec.
Manufacturers of Plush	202	68	25	0 80	25	40	Jan., Feb.
Makers of False Pearls and Pearl Flowers	56	154	60	2 00	20	40	Jan., Feb., and part of Dec.
Stringers and Mounters of Pearls		52		1 20	15	40	Dec., Jan., Feb., and part of March.
Makers of Painters' Pencils and Brushes	114	129	50	1 40	20	30	Dec., Jan., Feb.
Polishers of Gold and Daguerreotypes	52	4	30		30	:	Jan., Feb., part of July and Aug.

INDUSTRIAL STATISTICS OF PARIS, IN 1848—continued.

OCCUPATIONS.	Number of Men.	Number of Women.	Minimum of Men's Wages per Day.	Maximum of Men's Wages per Day.	Minimum of Women's Wages per Day.	Maximum of Women's Wages per Day.	Months when Work is slack.
			cents.	$ cts.	cents.	cents.	
Plaiters and Winders of Cotton, Wool, and Cashmere....	170	492	30	0 60	10	85	Jan., Feb., July.
Plaiters and Winders of silk....	44	277	40	1 00	15	50	July, Aug., Jan.
Plumbers, Pump, & Fountain Makers....Wives of patrons	1,014	2	40	1 40			Dec., Jan., Feb.
Feather Dressers....	78	583	40	1 00	20	60	Jan., July.
Makers of Feather Brooms....	120	28	50	1 20	30	40	July, Jan., Feb.
Makers of Quill Pens....	55	44	50	1 40	15	50	June, July, Aug.
Cutters and Preparers of Hair for Hatters....	91	505	50	1 20	15	50	Dec., Jan., Feb.
Polishers and Burnishers of Gold and Jewelry....	23	284	40	0 90	15	65	Jan., Feb., July, Aug.
Decorators of Porcelain....	1,641	1,010	40	2 40	20	$4 00	Jan., Feb., part of March.
Makers, Moulders, Polishers, and Menders of Porcelain.	155	9	50	3 00	30	50	June, July, Aug.
Portfolios and Articles of Morocco....	506	807	25	1 80	20	55	Jan., Feb., July.
Makers of Articles of Earthenware, Stoneware, and China..	880	20	25	1 60	25	40	July, Aug., Jan., Feb.
Pewterers....	837	84	40	1 20	20	40	Jan., Feb.
Preparers of Animals....	15	20	60	1 20	12	60	June, July, Aug.
Makers of Chemical Products....	188	20	60	1 10	25	30	Dec., Jan., Feb.
Makers of Pharmaceutical Products.	108	75	35	1 00	20	55	July, Aug.
Makers of Ironware Articles....	226	5	30	1 00	25		Jan., Feb., July, Aug.
Refiners of Sugar....	425	5	30	1 20	30		About six weeks work is slack.
Makers of Registers....	43	123	60	1 00	20	50	June, July, Aug.
Makers of Rulers, Easels, &c....	89	12	60	1 00	85	60	Dec., Jan., Feb.
Paper Rulers....	85	143	80	0 70	30	50	June, July, Aug.
Bookbinders....	939	807	25	1 20	20	60	June, July, Aug., Sept.
Borers of Jewelry....		30			20	50	Jan., Feb., March, July.
Ribbon Makers....	19	80	60	0 70	85	45	Jan., Feb., and part of July.
Makers of Wooden Shoes....	60	84	50	1 00	15	40	March, May, June, July, Aug, Sept.
Ebony Sculptors (for Furniture)....	471	3	40	1 60	25	60	Jan., Feb., March
Modern Sculptors in Bronze....	448	15	40	2 00	30	40	Jan., Feb., some report. Others say, July, Aug.

							Busy Months
Wood Carvers	424	39	30	1 40	30	45	June, July, Aug.
Saddle and Harness Makers and Furnishers	1,347	142	30	1 20	12	40	Dec., Jan., July, Aug.
Saddle Belts and Girdles	124	80	40	1 00	15	50	Jan., Feb., Dec.
Saddle Spurs, Plates, and Ironware for Harnesses, &c.	447	28	40	1 60	20	50	Three months, part in winter and part in summer.
Mechanical Locksmiths	959	16	30	1 40	30	40	Jan., Feb.
Locks for Furniture	760	7	60	1 40	20	50	" "
Settings for Jewels .....Wives of patrons	46	2	50	1 20	:	:	July, Aug., Jan., Feb.
Makers of Spar Ornaments	10	63	50	0 60	8	40	Dec., Jan., Feb.
Makers of Coach Blinds	118	11	40	3 00	20	40	" "
Makers of Tinctures	184	11	40	1 40	25	80	Dec., Jan.
Toy Manufacturers	1,404	174	30	1 40	15	70	Jan., Feb., July.
Makers of Toy Umbrellas	264	6	40	1 20	15	25	June, July, Aug., Jan.
Edge Tool Makers	854	2	30	1 40	:	40	Jan., Feb., July, Aug.
Tailors	11,066	10,769	15	1 60	10	90	July, Aug., Jan., Feb.
Tailors who work by Measure	6,660	2,947	30	1 60	10	90	1st July to middle of Sept., and 1st Jan. to middle of March.
Carpet Clippers and Drawers	20	15	50	60	30	85	Feb., March.
Upholsterers	1,832	1,797	40	8 00	15	70	June, July, Aug., Sept.
Dyers of Thread and Woven Goods	149	20	40	1 10	30	60	July, Aug.
Dyers, Scourers	523	510	40	1 20	20	$1 00	Jan., Feb., July, Aug.
Dyers of Skins for Gloves	149	20	40	1 10	30	60	July, Aug.
Makers of Cloths for Robes, Buttons, Furniture	462	431	30	1 20	30	40	July, Jan.
Makers of Oil Paper and Cloth	144	30	30	1 40	7	40	Feb., and part of Jan.
Metal Varnishers, Painters, Gilders, and Silverers	300	111	40	2 00	25	40	Dec., Jan., Feb., March.
Constructors and Decorators of Tombs	357	86	35	1 40	20	40	Jan., Feb., Dec.
Metal Turners	646	12	40	1 20	15	30	Jan., Feb., March, and part of July.
Wood Turners	861	7	25	1 10	36	:	" "
Turners of Wood Furniture	316	11	30	1 00	30	60	Jan., Feb., March.
Chair Turners	665	284	30	1 20	15	50	" "
Makers of Metal Traps	411	43	60	1 20	25	60	Jan., Feb.
Seamless Bags of Hemp and Flax	20	29	80	0 70	20	85	Jan., Aug., Sept.
Basket Makers	281	27	18	1 00	20	40	Dec., Jan., Feb., and part of Aug.
Glass Blowers	76	6	30	1 00	30	40	Jan., Feb., March.
Painters and Gilders of Glass	103	85	30	2 00*	:	50	" "
Glass and Crystal Cutters, Engravers and Polishers	827	8	60	2 00	20	40	July, Aug., Jan.
Makers of Glass Beads	13	90	60	1 00	20	40	Jan., Feb., March.
Vinegar Makers	60	8	40	0 90	30	:	One has $80 per annum, board and lodging. June, July, Aug.
Makers of Morocco for Hats, &c.	296	856	40	1 40	10	50	July, Aug., Jan., Feb.

* Some, employed in painting church windows, get $2.

REMARKS ON PRECEDING TABLES.

Employed in the thirteen groups of *industriels*, 112,891 women; 7,851 girls, of whom 869 were under 12—rest from 12 to 16. To every two men employed, one woman. Women more numerous than men in the manufacture of garments and materials for them. None employed in the laborious occupations. Equal in fancy wares. Highest wages of women per day, 20 francs, least 15 centimes—average, 1 franc 63 centimes.

950 women's salaries		less than 60 centimes.
626	"	higher than 3 francs.
The bulk, or 100,050	"	range between the two extremes.

Extremely low salaries are exceptional. Thus only two were so low as 15 centimes, and one of these workers was aged sixty-eight, and the other seventy-one. Women's wages are rather over half what the wages of men are.*

---

* 5 centimes are equal to about one cent of our money, and a franc is equal to about 20 cents.

THE END.

CONTENTS.

American Labor: From Conspiracy to Collective Bargaining

AN ARNO PRESS/NEW YORK TIMES COLLECTION

SERIES I

Abbott, Edith.
Women in Industry. 1913.

Aveling, Edward B. and Eleanor M. Aveling.
Working Class Movement in America. 1891.

Beard, Mary.
The American Labor Movement. 1939.

Blankenhorn, Heber.
The Strike for Union. 1924.

Blum, Solomon.
Labor Economics. 1925.

Brandeis, Louis D. and Josephine Goldmark.
Women in Industry. 1907. New introduction by Leon Stein and
　　Philip Taft.

Brooks, John Graham.
American Syndicalism. 1913.

Butler, Elizabeth Beardsley.
Women and the Trades. 1909.

Byington, Margaret Frances.
Homestead: The Household of A Mill Town. 1910.

Carroll, Mollie Ray.
Labor and Politics. 1923.

Coleman, McAlister.
Men and Coal. 1943.

Coleman, J. Walter.
The Molly Maguire Riots: Industrial Conflict in the Pennsylvania Coal Region. 1936.

Commons, John R.
Industrial Goodwill. 1919.

Commons, John R.
Industrial Government. 1921.

Dacus, Joseph A.
Annals of the Great Strikes. 1877.

Dealtry, William.
The Laborer: A Remedy for his Wrongs. 1869.

Douglas, Paul H., Curtis N. Hitchcock and Willard E. Atkins, editors.
The Worker in Modern Economic Society. 1923.

Eastman, Crystal.
Work Accidents and the Law. 1910.

Ely, Richard T.
The Labor Movement in America. 1890. New Introduction by Leon Stein and Philip Taft.

Feldman, Herman.
Problems in Labor Relations. 1937.

Fitch, John Andrew.
The Steel Worker. 1910.

Furniss, Edgar S. and Laurence Guild.
Labor Problems. 1925.

Gladden, Washington.
Working People and Their Employers. 1885.

Gompers, Samuel.
Labor and the Common Welfare. 1919.

Hardman, J. B. S., editor.
American Labor Dynamics. 1928.

Higgins, George G.
Voluntarism in Organized Labor, 1930-40. 1944.

Hiller, Ernest T.
The Strike. 1928.

Hollander, Jacob S. and George E. Barnett.
Studies in American Trade Unionism. 1906. New Introduction by
    Leon Stein and Philip Taft.

Jelley, Symmes M.
The Voice of Labor. 1888.

Jones, Mary.
Autobiography of Mother Jones. 1925.

Kelley, Florence.
Some Ethical Gains Through Legislation. 1905.

LaFollette, Robert M., editor.
The Making of America: Labor. 1906.

Lane, Winthrop D.
Civil War in West Virginia. 1921.

Lauck, W. Jett and Edgar Sydenstricker.
Conditions of Labor in American Industries. 1917.

Leiserson, William M.
Adjusting Immigrant and Industry. 1924.

Lescohier, Don D.
Knights of St. Crispin. 1910.

Levinson, Edward.
I Break Strikes. The Technique of Pearl L. Bergoff. 1935.

Lloyd, Henry Demarest.
Men, The Workers. Compiled by Anne Whithington and
    Caroline Stallbohen. 1909. New Introduction by Leon Stein
    and Philip Taft.

Lorwin, Louis (Louis Levine).
The Women's Garment Workers. 1924.

Markham, Edwin, Ben B. Lindsay and George Creel.
Children in Bondage. 1914.

Marot, Helen.
American Labor Unions. 1914.

Mason, Alpheus T.
Organized Labor and the Law. 1925.

Newcomb, Simon.
A Plain Man's Talk on the Labor Question. 1886. New Introduction
  by Leon Stein and Philip Taft.

Price, George Moses.
The Modern Factory: Safety, Sanitation and Welfare. 1914.

Randall, John Herman Jr.
Problem of Group Responsibility to Society. 1922.

Rubinow, I. M.
Social Insurance. 1913.

Saposs, David, editor.
Readings in Trade Unionism. 1926.

Slichter, Sumner H.
Union Policies and Industrial Management. 1941.

Socialist Publishing Society.
The Accused and the Accusers. 1887.

Stein, Leon and Philip Taft, editors.
The Pullman Strike. 1894-1913. New Introduction by the editors.

Stein, Leon and Philip Taft, editors.
Religion, Reform, and Revolution: Labor Panaceas in the Nineteenth
  Century. 1969. New Introduction by the editors.

Stein, Leon and Philip Taft, editors.
Wages, Hours, and Strikes: Labor Panaceas in the Twentieth Century.
  1969. New introduction by the editors.

Swinton, John.
A Momentous Question: The Respective Attitudes of Labor and Capital. 1895. New Introduction by Leon Stein and Philip Taft.

Tannenbaum, Frank.
The Labor Movement. 1921.

Tead, Ordway.
Instincts in Industry. 1918.

Vorse, Mary Heaton.
Labor's New Millions. 1938.

Witte, Edwin Emil.
The Government in Labor Disputes. 1932.

Wright, Carroll D.
The Working Girls of Boston. 1889.

Wyckoff, Veitrees J.
Wage Policies of Labor Organizations in a Period of Industrial Depression. 1926.

Yellen, Samuel.
American Labor Struggles. 1936.

SERIES II

Allen, Henry J.
The Party of the Third Part: The Story of the Kansas Industrial Relations Court. 1921. *Including* **The Kansas Court of Industrial Relations Law** (1920) by Samuel Gompers.

Baker, Ray Stannard.
The New Industrial Unrest. 1920.

Barnett, George E. & David A. McCabe.
Mediation, Investigation and Arbitration in Industrial Disputes. 1916.

Barns, William E., editor.
The Labor Problem. 1886.

Bing, Alexander M.
War-Time Strikes and Their Adjustment. 1921.

Brooks, Robert R. R.
When Labor Organizes. 1937.

Calkins, Clinch.
Spy Overhead: The Story of Industrial Espionage. 1937.

Cooke, Morris Llewellyn & Philip Murray.
Organized Labor and Production. 1940.

Creamer, Daniel & Charles W. Coulter.
Labor and the Shut-Down of the Amoskeag Textile Mills. 1939.

Glocker, Theodore W.
The Government of American Trade Unions. 1913.

Gompers, Samuel.
Labor and the Employer. 1920.

Grant, Luke.
The National Erectors' Association and the International Association of Bridge and Structural Ironworkers. 1915.

Haber, William.
Industrial Relations in the Building Industry. 1930.

Henry, Alice.
Women and the Labor Movement. 1923.

Herbst, Alma.
The Negro in the Slaughtering and Meat-Packing Industry in Chicago. 1932.

[Hicks, Obediah.]
Life of Richard F. Trevellick. 1896.

Hillquit, Morris, Samuel Gompers & Max J. Hayes.
The Double Edge of Labor's Sword: Discussion and Testimony on Socialism and Trade-Unionism Before the Commission on Industrial Relations. 1914. New Introduction by Leon Stein and Philip Taft.

Jensen, Vernon H.
Lumber and Labor. 1945.

Kampelman, Max M.
The Communist Party vs. the C.I.O. 1957.

Kingsbury, Susan M., editor.
Labor Laws and Their Enforcement. By Charles E. Persons, Mabel Parton, Mabelle Moses & Three "Fellows." 1911.

McCabe, David A.
The Standard Rate in American Trade Unions. 1912.

Mangold, George Benjamin.
Labor Argument in the American Protective Tariff Discussion. 1908.

Millis, Harry A., editor.
How Collective Bargaining Works. 1942.

Montgomery, Royal E.
Industrial Relations in the Chicago Building Trades. 1927.

Oneal, James.
The Workers in American History. 3rd edition, 1912.

Palmer, Gladys L.
Union Tactics and Economic Change: A Case Study of Three Philadelphia Textile Unions. 1932.

Penny, Virginia.
How Women Can Make Money: Married or Single, In all Branches of the Arts and Sciences, Professions, Trades, Agricultural and Mechanical Pursuits. 1870. New Introduction by Leon Stein and Philip Taft.

Penny, Virginia.
Think and Act: A Series of Articles Pertaining to Men and Women, Work and Wages. 1869.

Pickering, John.
The Working Man's Political Economy. 1847.

Ryan, John A.
A Living Wage. 1906.

Savage, Marion Dutton.
Industrial Unionism in America. 1922.

Simkhovitch, Mary Kingsbury.
The City Worker's World in America. 1917.

Spero, Sterling Denhard.
The Labor Movement in a Government Industry: A Study of
Employee Organization in the Postal Service. 1927.

Stein, Leon and Philip Taft, editors.
Labor Politics: Collected Pamphlets. 2 vols. 1836-1932. New
Introduction by the editors.

Stein, Leon and Philip Taft, editors.
The Management of Workers: Selected Arguments. 1917-1956.
New Introduction by the editors.

Stein, Leon and Philip Taft, editors.
Massacre at Ludlow: Four Reports. 1914-1915. New Introduction
by the editors.

Stein, Leon and Philip Taft, editors.
Workers Speak: Self-Portraits. 1902-1906. New Introduction by
the editors.

Stolberg, Benjamin.
The Story of the CIO. 1938.

Taylor, Paul S.
The Sailors' Union of the Pacific. 1923.

U.S. Commission on Industrial Relations.
Efficiency Systems and Labor. 1916. New Introduction by
Leon Stein and Philip Taft.

Walker, Charles Rumford.
American City: A Rank-and-File History. 1937.

Walling, William English.
American Labor and American Democracy. 1926.

Williams, Whiting.
What's on the Worker's Mind: By One Who Put on Overalls to
Find Out. 1920.

Wolman, Leo.
The Boycott in American Trade Unions. 1916.

Ziskind, David.
One Thousand Strikes of Government Employees. 1940.